THE LETTERS OF WILLIAM AND DOROTHY WORDSWORTH

V. *THE LATER YEARS*

PART II

1829–1834

WORDSWORTH

from the chalk drawing by H. W. Pickersgill, R.A., 1832

THE LETTERS OF WILLIAM AND DOROTHY WORDSWORTH

SECOND EDITION

V

The Later Years

PART II

1829–1834

REVISED, ARRANGED
AND EDITED BY
ALAN G. HILL

FROM THE FIRST EDITION
EDITED BY THE LATE
ERNEST DE SELINCOURT

OXFORD
AT THE CLARENDON PRESS
1979

Oxford University Press, Walton Street, Oxford OX2 6DP

OXFORD LONDON GLASGOW
NEW YORK TORONTO MELBOURNE WELLINGTON
KUALA LUMPUR SINGAPORE HONG KONG TOKYO
DELHI BOMBAY CALCUTTA MADRAS KARACHI
NAIROBI DAR ES SALAAM CAPE TOWN

Published in the United States by
Oxford University Press, New York

© *Oxford University Press 1979*

British Library Cataloguing in Publication Data
Wordsworth, William
  The letters of William and Dorothy Wordsworth
  –2nd ed.
  3: The later years. Part 2: 1829–1834
  1. Wordsworth, William – Correspondence
  2. Poets, English – 19th century – Correspondence
  3. Wordsworth, Dorothy – Correspondence
  4. Authors, English – 19th century – Correspondence
  I. Wordsworth, Dorothy II. de Selincourt, Ernest
    III. Hill, Alan Geoffrey
  821'.7   PR5881   77–30691
  ISBN 0 19 812482 1

Printed in Great Britain
at the University Press, Oxford
by Eric Buckley
Printer to the University

CONTENTS

LIST OF ILLUSTRATIONS

ABBREVIATIONS

W. W., D. W., M. W., R. W., C. W.: William, Dorothy, Mary, Richard, and Christopher Wordsworth.

S. H.: Sara Hutchinson. E. Q.: Edward Quillinan. S. T. C.: Samuel Taylor Coleridge. C. C.: Catherine Clarkson. H. C. R.: Henry Crabb Robinson. I. F.: Isabella Fenwick.

SOURCES

Broughton	*Some Letters of the Wordsworth Family*, edited by L. N. Broughton, Cornell University Press, 1942.
Cornell	Department of Rare Books, Cornell University Library, Ithaca, N.Y.
Cottle	*Early Recollections, chiefly relating to the Life of S. T. Coleridge*, by Joseph Cottle, 2 vols., 1837.
Curry	*New Letters of Robert Southey*, edited by Kenneth Curry, 2 vols., Columbia University Press, 1965.
DWJ	*The Journals of Dorothy Wordsworth*, edited by Ernest de Selincourt, 2 vols., 1941.
EY	*The Letters of William and Dorothy Wordsworth*, edited by the late Ernest de Selincourt, second edition, I, *The Early Years*, 1787–1805, revised by Chester L. Shaver, Oxford, 1967.
Gillett	*Maria Jane Jewsbury: Occasional Papers, selected with a Memoir*, by Eric Gillett, 1932.
Griggs	*Collected Letters of Samuel Taylor Coleridge*, edited by Earl Leslie Griggs, 6 vols., Oxford, 1956–71.
Grosart	*The Prose Works of William Wordsworth*, edited by Alexander B. Grosart, 3 vols., 1876.
Hamilton	*The Life of Sir William Rowan Hamilton*, by R. P. Graves, 3 vols., 1882–9.
Haydon	*Correspondence and Table Talk of Benjamin Robert Haydon*, edited by his son, F. W. Haydon, 1876.
HCR	*Henry Crabb Robinson on Books and their Writers*, edited by Edith J. Morley, 3 vols., 1938.
Jordan	*De Quincey to Wordsworth, a Biography of a Relationship*, by J. E. Jordan, 1962.
K	*Letters of the Wordsworth Family*, edited by William Knight, 3 vols., 1907.

Abbreviations

Lamb	*The Letters of Charles and Mary Lamb*, edited by E. V. Lucas, 3 vols., 1935.
LY	*The Letters of William and Dorothy Wordsworth, The Later Years*, edited by Ernest de Selincourt, 3 vols., Oxford, 1939.
Mem.	*Memoirs of William Wordsworth*, by Christopher Wordsworth, 2 vols., 1851.
MLN	*Modern Language Notes.*
MLR	*Modern Language Review.*
Moorman i, ii	*William Wordsworth, A Biography*, i, *The Early Years*, ii, *The Later Years*, by Mary Moorman, Oxford, 1957 and 1965.
Morley	*Correspondence of Henry Crabb Robinson with the Wordsworth Circle*, edited by Edith J. Morley, 2 vols., Oxford, 1927.
MP	*Modern Philology.*
MW	*The Letters of Mary Wordsworth*, edited by Mary E. Burton, Oxford, 1958.
MY	*The Letters of William and Dorothy Wordsworth*, edited by the late Ernest de Selincourt, second edition, II: *The Middle Years*: Part I, 1806–11, revised by Mary Moorman, Part II, 1812–20, revised by Mary Moorman and Alan G. Hill, Oxford, 1969–70.
NQ	*Notes and Queries.*
Pearson	*Papers, Letters and Journals of William Pearson*, edited by his widow. Printed for private circulation, 1863.
PMLA	*Publications of the Modern Language Association of America.*
Prel.	*Wordsworth's Prelude* edited by Ernest de Selincourt: second edition, revised by Helen Darbishire, Oxford, 1959.
Prose Works	*The Prose Works of William Wordsworth*, edited by W. J. B. Owen and Jane Worthington Smyser, 3 vols., Oxford, 1974.
PW	*The Poetical Works of William Wordsworth*, edited by Ernest de Selincourt and Helen Darbishire, 5 vols., Oxford, 1940–9, and revised issues, 1952–9.
R.M. Cat.	*Catalogue of the Varied and Valuable Historical, Poetical, Theological, and Miscellaneous Library of the late venerated Poet-Laureate, William Wordsworth* . . . Preston, 1859; reprinted in *Transactions of the Wordsworth Society*, Edinburgh, [1882–7].
RMVB	*Rydal Mount Visitors Book*, Wordsworth Library, Grasmere.

Abbreviations

Rogers	*Rogers and his Contemporaries*, edited by P. W. Clayden, 2 vols., 1889.
Sadler	*Diary, Reminiscences and Correspondence of Henry Crabb Robinson*, edited by Thomas Sadler, 3 vols., 1869.
SH	*The Letters of Sara Hutchinson*, edited by Kathleen Coburn, 1954.
Southey	*Life and Correspondence of Robert Southey*, edited by C. C. Southey, 6 vols., 1849–50.
TLS	*Times Literary Supplement*.
Warter	*A Selection from the Letters of Robert Southey*, edited by John Wood Warter, 4 vols., 1856.
WL	The Wordsworth Library, Grasmere.

LIST OF LETTERS

PART II

1829

List of Letters

List of Letters

List of Letters

xiv

List of Letters

List of Letters

List of Letters

xxii

396. W. W. to CHARLES WILLIAM PASLEY[1]

MS. British Library. Hitherto unpublished.

Jan^{ry} 6th 1829.
Rydal Mount Kendal.

My dear Sir,

Immediately on the receipt of yours, not being willing to trust the Reports of provincial Newspapers, or vague intelligence, I applied to the Mayor of Kendal[2] for returns which he promised me and has not yet sent, to my great disappointment. I am going from home and leave the necessary intelligence to be added by my Daughter,—when it arrives. Ambleside is a small Town peculiarly circumstanced—a sort of monopoly—so that no return from this place would have been of value for your purposes.—Bread is not sold here by Assaye, or Quarter loaf.

After a weary length of time I received your most useful Book— for which you are entitled to the thanks of every friend to your Country, and I am happy on this occasion to [? add][3] my own.

I remain respectfully
Your much obliged
Wm Wordsworth

Turn over

The Mayor of Kendal is gone from home without sending me the promised return—but what you will find below is faithfully copied from a printed paper sent me from Kendal by his Agent.—

If I can be of any further service, it will give the greatest pleasure—

Burgh of Kendal Kirkby to wit

	lb	oz	dr
The Penny loaf wheaten, to weigh		5	8
do standard wheaten		5	12
Two Penny Do, wheaten		11	1
Do standard wheaten		11	9

---

[1] For Col. Pasley, see pt. i, L. 205. He was still investigating the most efficient and economical ways of supplying the forces with bread and meat. By 1831 his researches had extended into the feasibility of a general simplification of British weights and measures and money.

[2] Thomas Harrison, the surgeon (see *MY* ii. 427), now in his third term of office as Mayor.

[3] *Word dropped out.*

1

Six Penny Loaf, wheaten		2	1	5
do	standard Do.	2	2	12
Twelve penny Do wheaten		4	2	11
Do	standard wheaten	4	5	6
Eighteen penny Loaf, wheaten		6	4	1
Do	standard Do.	6	8	4

Assaye to Continue 7 days from the 6th of Jan^{ry} 1829

Beef in Kendal Market from 4^d to 6^d per lb.
In Ambleside Market we pay 7^d for choice pieces.

397. W. W. to ALEXANDER DYCE

Address: Alex^r Dyce Esqre, 72 Welbeck S^t, London.
Postmark: 13 Jan. 1829. *Stamp*: Kendal.
MS. Victoria and Albert Museum.
Mem. (—). *Grosart* (—). *K* (—). *LY i. 345.*

Rydal Mount,
Kendal,
Jan. 12th, 1829.

Dear Sir,

I regret to hear of the indisposition from which you have been suffering.

That you are convinced gives me great pleasure—as I hope that every other Editor of Collins will follow your example.[1]

You are at perfect liberty to declare that you have rejected Bell's Copy in consequence of my opinion of it—and I feel much satisfaction in being the Instrument of rescuing the memory of Collins from this disgrace. I have always felt some concern that Mr Home,[2] who lived several years after Bell's publication, did not testify more regard for his deceased friend's memory by protesting against this imposition. Mr Mackenzie is still living, and I shall shortly have his opinion upon the question—and if it be at all interesting I shall take the liberty of sending it to

---

[1] See pt. i, L. 367. On 9 Jan. Dyce had written to W. W., accepting his verdict on Bell's text of the *Ode on the Popular Superstitions of the Highlands of Scotland* (*Dyce MSS.*, *Victoria and Albert Museum*).

[2] John Home (1722–1808), author of *Douglas* (1757), to whom Collins had dedicated his poem.

you. Dyer[1] is another of our minor Poets—minor as to quantity—of whom one would wish to know more. Particulars about him might still be collected, I should think, in South Wales—his native Country, and where in early life he practised as a Painter. I have often heard Sir George Beaumont express a curiosity about his pictures—and a wish to see any specimen of his pencil that might survive. If you are a Rambler, perhaps you may, at some time or other, be led into Carmarthenshire, and might bear in mind what I have just said of this excellent Author.—

I had once a hope to have learned some unknown particulars of Thomson, about Jedburgh,[2] but I was disappointed—had I succeeded, I meant to publish a short life of him, prefixed to a Volume containing the Seasons, the Castle of Indolence, his minor pieces in rhyme, and a few Extracts from his plays,[3] and his Liberty;[4] and [I][5] feel still inclined to do something of the kind. These three Writers, Thomson, Collins, and Dyer, had more poetic Imagination than any of their Contemporaries, unless we reckon Chatterton[6] as of that age—I do not name Pope, for he stands alone—as a man most highly gifted—but unluckily he took the Plain, when the Heights were within his reach——

Excuse this long Letter, and believe me,

Sincerely yours,
Wm Wordsworth

[1] For John Dyer, see *MY* i. 521. He was born at Aberglasney, Carmarthenshire, and studied painting under Jonathan Richardson (1665–1745), and in Italy.
[2] James Thomson was born at Ednam, Roxburghshire, and went to school in Jedburgh. W. W. had visited the town during the Scottish tour of 1803.
[3] Thomson wrote five plays, of which *Tancred and Sigismunda* (1745) was the most successful. It was produced at Drury Lane with Garrick as Tancred.
[4] Thomson's poem *Liberty* appeared in 1735–6.
[5] *Word dropped out.*
[6] For W. W.'s estimate of Thomas Chatterton, see *MY* ii. 535.

398. W. W. to DIONYSIUS LARDNER[1]

Address: The Rev^d D^r. Lardner, etc. etc., 33 Percy S^t, London. [*In Dora W.'s hand*]
Postmark: 24 Jan. 1829. *Stamp*: Kendal Penny Post.
MS. Cornell.
LY ii. 913 (—).

Rydal Mount,
Kendal 12th Jany 182[9][2]

Sir,

I should have written to you immediately on my return from the Continent, but I was obliged to hurry through London, and since that time I have been without your address—

The subject which I had thought of is much more limited than you suppose—being nothing more than an Account of the Deceased Poetesses of Great Britain—with an Estimate of their Works—but upon more mature Reflection I cannot persuade myself that it is sufficiently interesting for a separate subject, were I able to do it justice. The Dramatic and other imaginative female Writers might be added—the interest would thereby be encreased, but unity of subject would be sacrificed.—It remains therefore for me to regret that I should have held out the least hope that I might undertake any thing of the Kind—for which I have no excuse but what you I hope will be satisfied with, that I was taken by surprize.[3]

I still am of opinion that something is wanted upon the subject —neither Dr Johnson, nor Dr Anderson, nor Chalmers,[4] nor the Editor I believe of any other Corpus of English Poetry takes the least notice of female Writers—this, to say nothing harsher, is very ungallant. The best way of giving a comprehensive interest to the subject would be to begin with Sappho and proceed downwards through Italy antient and Modern, Spain, Germany France and England—but, for myself, I could not venture to undertake the

---

[1] Dionysius Lardner, F.R.S. (1793–1859), scientific writer, of Trinity College, Dublin: from 1827 Professor of Natural Philosophy and Astronomy in the new University College, London. In 1829 he initiated *The Cabinet Cyclopaedia of Eminent Literary and Scientific Men*, which was completed in 1849 in 133 vols., and to which many of the eminent writers of the day, including Scott and Southey, contributed. He had recently approached W. W. as a possible contributor, but nothing came of the proposal discussed here. Two volumes on the *English Poets* by Robert Bell finally appeared in 1839.

[2] *Written* 1828. But the postmark is clearly 1829.

[3] W. W.'s continuing interest in the British poetesses is, however, reflected in later correspondence with Alexander Dyce. See L. 474 below.

[4] For Robert Anderson and Alexander Chalmers, see *MY* ii. 151–2.

employment, two requisites being wanting—Books (I mean access to Libraries)[1] and industry to use them.

Wishing you success in your [ver]y promising underta[king][2]

> I remain Sir—
> sincerely yours
> Wm Wordsworth

PS. The consequences of a severe fall have prevented me giving an earlier answer to your Letter—

[*M. W. adds*]

Mrs W, in Mr Wordsworth's absence (who has been from home for some days) has opened this letter, to say that it has been detained in the expectation of an opportunity of forwarding it by a frank. She has only to regret, that Dr Lardner has had the trouble of a 2^d application in consequence.

Jan^ry 22^d

399. W. W. to BARRON FIELD

MS. British Library transcript.[3]
K. LY i. 346.

Rydal Mount, 19th January, 1829.

My dear Sir,

Thank you for the extract from the *Quarterly*. It is a noble story.[4] I remembered having read it; but it is less fit for a separate poem than to make part of a philosophical work. I will thank you for any notices from India,[5] though I own I am afraid of an Oriental story. I know not that you will agree with me; but I have always thought that stories, where the scene is laid by our writers in distant climes,

---

[1] Phrase in brackets added in Dora W.'s hand.
[2] *MS. torn.*
[3] This letter is quoted in Barron Field's MS. Memoirs.
[4] In his letter of 24 Dec. 1828 (*WL MSS.*), Field had transcribed the story of the Hindu girl from Forbes's *Oriental Memoirs*, as requested by W. W. (see pt. i, L. 390), and he sent another anecdote from the same source. This was the story of the Brahmin who smashed a microscope he had recently acquired from a European, rather than have his religious preconceptions—and those of his race—shattered by the very different picture of Nature that it revealed. This story was quoted in the *Quarterly Review*, xii (Oct. 1814), 220–1.
[5] Barron Field was bound for Ceylon, not India, but he eventually accepted a post in Gibraltar instead. See L. 413 below.

are mostly hurt, and often have their interest quite destroyed, by being overlaid with foreign imagery; as if the tale had been chosen for the sake of the imagery only.

I remain,
Very faithfully yours,
W. Wordsworth

400. W. W. to UNKNOWN CORRESPONDENT

MS. untraced.
K (—). LT i. 347.

Rydal Mount, Kendal,
19ᵗʰ January, [1829]

My dear Sir,

. . . I was much pleased with a little drawing by Mr Edmund Field[1]—exceedingly so, and I wrote opposite it two stanzas which I hope he and Mrs Field will pardon, as I have taken a liberty with his name. The drawing is admirably done, and of just such a scene as I delight in, and my favourite rivers, the Duddon, Lowther, Derwent, etc., abound in. . . .

[*cetera desunt*]

401. W. W. to GEORGE HUNTLY GORDON

MS. Cornell.
Broughton, p. 11.

Rydal Mount
Jany 24ᵗʰ/29

My dear Sir

I employ Mrs Wˢ pen, being just arrived with starved fingers from Keswick, whither your letter was brought me yesterday. I am truly obliged to you for it, and for the copy from Mr Papendick's[2]— of which I take the same view as yourself, so far, as to be much

---

[1] Barron Field's brother. In his letter of 24 Dec. 1828 (*WL MSS.*), Barron Field had asked W. W. to write in Mrs. Field's Album, and this request produced the two stanzas (never printed by W. W.) quoted in *PW* iv. 387. On 26 Feb. Barron Field sent his thanks, '. . . my Brother is very proud of your praise'. As de Selincourt notes, he added another stanza beneath W. W.'s lines in the Album. See *PW* iv. 478.

[2] The tutor with whom Willy W. was to stay in Germany. See pt. i, L. 386.

pleased with the openness and gentlemanly candour of it. I read to Mr Southey both letters, and consulted him upon the prospects of my Son in connection with them; his view coincides with mine, and it is this. That Wᵐ with Mr P. would be boarded most advantageously with the prospect of being introduced into the best society of the place, and the advantage of Mr P's example and his superintendance, and protection from improper society—but as to tuition little or nothing can be *regularly* relied upon. The advantages are so great, that if my Son were the only Englishman in the house, Mr S. agrees with me in thinking he would be well placed there, as his acquirement of the German Language must follow of necessity—from not having a temptation or opportunity to speak his own tongue.

Thus by a speedy acquisition of German he would be enabled to profit either from the private Tutor or the School according to Mr P—s judgment. *But* should the Pupils in the house be English, I know too much of my Son's social dispositions not to dread the consequences of being with his fellow countrymen, and who being advanced in the language, would, out of kindness speak for him, when he ought to speak for himself etc., etc.—

As long as I expected that Mr P. could give classical Instruction himself I was reconciled to the probability of the Pupils spoken of, being English—because I thought, Mr P. being Master of English, that W. from the first would advance in Classics with his assistance —but now the speedy acquisition of German becomes of the *first* importance—and I could wish this consideration to be laid before Mr P. that I may know how far this objection which strikes Mr S. and myself so strongly can be obviated. If the Pupils are *not English* I should decide upon sending him back with Mr P. in April—at once.

I shall therefore be anxious to learn thro' you, as soon as may be from Mr P. his opinion and answer upon the point previously stated—and further than this I need not trouble you. As I have heard lately from a friend of a Dr Becker[1] residing at Offenbach—a man of letters who gives instructions in the languages to private Pupils. This prospect I prefer to Mr Lonsdales,[2] or any other I have heard of except Mr Papendick's.

[1] Karl Ferdinand Becker, M.D. (1775–1849), philologist. His *Deutsche Grammatik* (Frankfurt, 1829), drawing on the work of Grimm and Humbolt, was published by John Murray in an English translation in 1830 and long remained a standard work.

[2] For the Revd. William Lonsdale, see pt. i, L. 373.

The only reason for my not acknowledging your last kind letter was, that I was unwilling unnecessarily to encroach upon [your time, and waited till we had communications from Germany. I take the pen from Mrs. W's hand to thank you and bid you adieu. I have been nearly a week staying with Mr. Southey—who unfortunately was confined to the house by a severe cold—he is as usual very busy. Ever most faithfully

Your much obliged

G. Huntly Gordon Esq]¹   Wm Wordsworth

402. D. W. to GEORGE HUNTLY GORDON

MS. Cornell.
Broughton, p. 13.

Jan^ry 25 1829
Whitwick, near Ashby de la Zouche²

Sir,

Trusting that my Brother, Mr Wordsworth of Rydal Mount has prepared the way for me, I venture to take the liberty to request that you will be so kind as to forward the two enclosed letters to France. Some little time ago my Brother informed me that you had the means of forwarding letters to the Continent, and had kindly [of]-fered to do so for him, and knowing that I had occasion to write, he told me he would ask for your services to me in the present instance. I have not heard further from him; but hope I am not doing wrong in making this enclosure, and that you will, at all events pardon me. I am, Sir

Yours respectfully
Dorothy Wordsworth.

¹ As Broughton notes, the lines in brackets are copied in another hand, probably Gordon's, with the comment at the end, '(Original given away).'
² D. W. was spending the winter keeping house for John W. at his cnracy near Coleorton.

403. W. W. to JOHN MITCHINSON CALVERT[1]

MS. untraced.
LY i. 347.

Rydal Mount, Jan, 26th. 1829.

My dear Sir,

Having witnessed last summer the melancholy state of health and spirits in which your good father was I am less shocked than I should otherwise have been on learning that he is no more.[2] I take it very kindly that you should have thought of us so soon after his dissolution. I was among the earliest and without scruple I may say continued to be among the most attached of his friends. I shall ever respect his memory which is associated with many recollections of happy times long before you were born. Pray remember us (I mean Mrs W. and my daughter—no one else of the family is at home) most kindly to your mother and to your sister[3] and brothers.[4] Business may draw you into Cumberland. If so, fail not to give us a visit however short. The last week I spent with Mr. Southey at Keswick. He was suffering from a severe cold; in other respects I have not seen him so well for many years. Most of the family were also plagued with colds from which my daughter is not free. Her mother and myself are both well. I felt much indebted for your kindness to my son Wm. He cannot be made to work at medicine. I am about to send him into Germany with a view to his learning that language and going on with his classics at the same time, for an English university is a *pis aller*. John has been presented to a small living by Lord Lonsdale—Moresby near Whitehaven.[5] We expect him every day to read himself in.

I remain, my dear Sir,
Faithfully yours,
Wm Wordsworth

[1] John Mitchinson Calvert (see pt. i, L. 116), eldest son of W. W.'s old school-friend William Calvert, of Greta Bank (Raisley's brother). He had recently graduated in medicine from Oriel College, Oxford, and took his M.D. in 1831.

[2] William Calvert had died in London on 23 Jan.

[3] Dora W.'s school-friend Mary Calvert, now Mrs. Joshua Stanger (see pt. i, L. 166).

[4] For the Revd. Raisley Calvert and William Calvert jnr., see pt. i, L. 116.

[5] See pt. i, L. 383.

404. W. W. to JOSEPH COTTLE

Address: Joseph Cottle, Esqre, Bristol. [*In M. W.'s hand*]
Stamp: Kendal Penny Post.
Endorsed: Wm Wordsworth (18).
MS. The Rosenbach Foundation, Philadelphia.
K. LT i. 348.

27th Jan^{ry} 1829
Rydal Mount
near Kendal

My dear Sir,

It is an age since you addressed a very kind Letter to me[1]—
and though I did not receive it till long after its date, being then
upon the Continent, I should have replied to it much earlier, could
I have done so to my satisfaction.—But you will recollect, probably.
The Letter contained a Request that I would address to you some
verses. I wished to meet this desire of yours, but—I know not how
it is—I have ever striven in vain to write verses upon subjects
either proposed, or imposed. I hoped to prove more fortunate on
this occasion—but I have been disappointed. And therefore I beg
you to excuse me—not imputing my failure to any want of inclination, or even to the absence of poetic feeling connected with times
and places to which your Letter refers. You will not be hurt at this
inability, when I tell you that I was once a whole twelve-month
occasionally employed in vain endeavour to write an Inscription
upon a suggested subject—though it was to please one of my most
valued Friends.

I am glad to hear of your intended Publication. The Malvern
Hill from which you gave me a valuable extract I frequently
look at—it was always a favourite of mine—some passages—and
especially one, closing 'to him who slept at noon and wakes at
Eve,' I thought superexcellent.—

I was truly glad to have from Mrs W. and my Daughter so
agreeable an account of your family—and to have this account
confirmed by your own Letter. I often think with lively remembrance of the days I passed at Bristol—not setting the least value on
those passed under the roof of your good Father and Mother.—

Last week I spent at Keswick with Mr Southey himself—his
Family—Mrs Coleridge and Sarah, all well except for Colds—
scarcely to be avoided at this severe season. S. was busy as usual,
and in excellent spirits. His son[2] (about ten years of age) is a very

---

[1] See pt. i, L. 347.
[2] Charles Cuthbert, b. Feb. 1819, the future editor of his father's *Life and
Correspondence.*

fine youth—and though not robust enjoys excellent Health. Mrs Lovel[1] was but poorly—indeed her health seems quite ruined.— You probably have heard that Coleridge was on the Continent, along with my Daughter and self, last summer. The trip did him service—and though he was sometimes a good deal indisposed— his health upon the whole was, for him, not bad. Hartley lives in our neighbourhood—we see him but not very often. He writes a good deal, and is about (I understand) to publish a Vol: of Poems. You know that he is not quite so steady as his Friends would wish.—I must now conclude with the kindest regards in which my daughter joins with Mrs Wordsworth (my Sister is in Leicestershire) to yourself, and your sisters, and nieces. And believe me, my dear Friend, very faithfully yours,

Wm Wordsworth

405. W. W. to ROBERT JONES

Address: The Revd Robert Jones, *care of* Edward Jones Esqre,[2] Denbigh, N.W.
    To be forwarded.
Stamp: Kendal Penny Post.
MS. WL. Hitherto unpublished.

Rydal Mount
Jany 27th 1829

My dear Jones,

I am glad of an occasion to inquire after you and your Friends. Mrs Wordsworth has just stumbled upon a Letter, dated Denbigh 5th May.—28 addressed to me from R. P. Jones—M.D.[3] Sec^y of the Cymmrodorion Soc:—informing me that I am elected an Honorary member of the Soc: etc. I remember perfectly having written to your Brother Edward upon his mentioning to me that such an honor was either conferred upon me, or designed—and entreating him, as I was ignorant of the Forms upon these occasions, to make the proper acknowledgements on my part. But this Letter of the Sec^y arrived during a protracted absence from home, and if

---

[1] Southey's sister-in-law and a permanent member of his household.
[2] Robert Jones's elder brother (d. 1831).
[3] Richard Phillips Jones (d. 1867) graduated M.D. from the University of Glasgow in 1821. He later practised in Chester. The original Cymmrodorion Society, founded in London in 1751 for the study of the Welsh language and literature, had been wound up at the end of the eighteenth century, but it was revived in 1820 under the presidency of Sir Watkin Williams Wynn, Bt., Southey's friend.

my Sister ever mentioned it to me I have no recollection of the fact—so that I fear it has not been properly attended to on my part. As the Sec^y resides at Denbigh, your Brother I hope will be kind enough to give this explanation to him, with a becoming apology on my part for this apparent neglect of the communication. I should be sorry to be thought insensible to such a mark of attention. I have now done with the subject—only I observe that the Sec^y's Letter speaks of patronage and support—what is meant by this? At my years and residing at such a distance it is not probable that I shall be able to attend any meeting of this respectable society—which I doubt not they will excuse.

Pray give me a Letter and tell us how you all are—and if you are still in the Vale of Meditation[1]—thinking it doubtful I shall direct this to the care of your Brother, Denbigh.—I will now say a word about ourselves. We are at present a small family. My elder son is a Curate near Ashby de La Zouche, Leicestershire, and my Sister resides with him through the Winter. He has just been presented to a small living near Whitehaven, Cumberland, by Lord Lonsdale and will come to reside there about Trinity Sunday, as we hope. I have been more than 30 years under an engagement to show my Sister North Wales, and I hope that next summer I shall be able to fulfill that engagement, in which case we shall not fail to visit you. My daughter is at home, pretty well, except for a cold—and my younger son, I am sorry to say, is still with me. I cannot find [?a][2] situation for him. I went [?lately] to London with that hope but in vain. I am about to send him into Germany—to learn that language and French—and to go on with his Classics at the same time—in case he should be compelled to turn to an English University at last. I wish for an opening in some public office—having tried in vain among all my wealthy Friends to procure one for him in business—Mrs W. continues to enjoy good health as I do. Last winter she passed with her Daughter in Herefordshire for the benefit of a drier climate, and in Spring we three met at Cambridge and thence went to London. Dr Wordsworth was well and his Sons you know have distinguished themselves. In June, Mrs. W. left London to visit her Son in Leicestershire, and my Daughter and I went on to the Continent along with Mr Coleridge the Poet. We landed at Ostend—went to Bruges Ghent Brussels Waterloo—Namur, up and down the Meuse to Liege—thence to Spa—Aix la

[1] Jones had a curacy there in the village of Llanrwst, where the Wordsworths had visited him in 1824. See pt. i, L. 141.

[2] *MS. torn.*

Chapelle Cologne—up the Rhine as far as Bingen—on the banks of the Rhine we [?remained] a fortnight [?][1] through Holland, that is [?] Arnheim, Utrecht [?] Haarlem, Leyden, Rotterdam, Antwerp, and back to Ostend—being absent nearly 7 weeks. Dora was delighted —it was her first visit to the Continent. In Flanders, and on the Rhine—I was a hundred times reminded of our memorable trip.[2]— Now let me beg of you to come and see us this Spring—before the hurry of our summer visitors. We should be delighted to have you here—and I hope you would enjoy yourself more than the last time when our house was so crowded. Mrs W. and my daughter join in this wish, and unite with me in kindest remembrances to yourself, pray remember us also most kindly to your Brothers and Sisters—and believe me my dear Jones with the truest affection ever yours

Wm Wordsworth

406. W. W. to FREDERIC MANSEL REYNOLDS

Address: F. M. Reynolds Esqre, No. 48 Warren Street, Fitzroy Square, London.
 [*In Dora W.'s hand*]
Postmark: 28 Jan. 1829. *Stamp*: Kendal Penny Post.
MS. Harvard University Library.
LY i. 351.

[*c.* 27 Jan. 1829]

My dear Sir,

I have to thank you for the Keepsake,[3] (which arrived along with a Copy forwarded to Mr Southey) and also I have to thank you for granting my wish in behalf of Miss Jewsbury.[4]

I only alluded to my endeavours to induce Mr Rogers to write— as the most natural way of opening the subject. You desire my opinion on the merits of the Contents of your publication—at present I could not give it—for a severe accident shut me out from the use of Books for some time—a fall upon my head[5]—and since

---

[1] *Hole in MS.*
[2] i.e. their 'pedestrian tour' through France and Switzerland in the summer of 1790.
[3] For W. W.'s contributions to *The Keepsake* for 1829, see pt. i, L. 327.
[4] See L. 410 below.
[5] 'Wordsworth has had a most dangerous fall, headlong, from his own mount,' Southey wrote to George Ticknor on 17 Mar., 'but providentially received no serious injury. He is looking old, but vigorous as ever both in mind and body.' (Southey, vi. 40.)

my recovery I have been absent from home. I have the less regret in making this statement—because, supposing me to be a judge of the *absolute* merit of works of this kind, which really I am not, I deem such judgement of little Value. What you have to consider is the fitness of the Articles for the Market, everything else is comparatively insignificant; now this will depend as much upon the Manufacturer as the thing manufactured, more so—in all probability— therefore beat up among Lords and Members of Parliament and 'id genus omne'—and you may perhaps keep up your present Sale— but I think it clear there is not a market for more.—Allan Cunningham talked about making his Annual[1] reflect the Literature of the Age—and Southey told him in a friendly way, after all, dear C—, the best you can make of these things, is picture-books for grown Children.—I am something of his mind—but, Mr Heath[2] puts so much liberality into his work that I should be sorry if nothing better comes of it—and I do sincerely wish that by the joint Sales of the Book and of the Prints (sold separately) he may be remunerated. Tell me if this has been the case—I am sure he deserves the public patronage—I wrote my best for him.

I will conclude with giving you a proof of my sincerity—which I do not as a Critic but as a Friend—and on that account I am sure you will not be displeased when I say that your own Verses upon the Coquette are too coarse for so fine dress'd a publication—and your Invitation is not so happy as some light things I have seen from your Pen—I turned to these Pieces from the interest I take in you as a friend.

I must now come to a principle—which I cannot allow to govern the agreement between us. In your former Letter—you observed that my Contributions only filled eleven pages and a half—upon which assurance I readily agreed to make up the deficiency[3]—but I find that four Sonnets[4] of mine have not been inserted—which would have occupied at least two pages, making altogether 13— and a half pages. Now I care nothing about my Contributions being inserted—I mean on the score of personal vanity—but I certainly

---

[1] *The Anniversary.*

[2] For Charles Heath, proprietor of *The Keepsake*, see pt. i, L. 329.

[3] See pt. i, L. 388. This dispute with Reynolds developed into something like a quarrel as later letters show, and W. W. never again contributed to *The Keepsake*.

[4] *Roman Antiquities Discovered at Bishopstone, Herefordshire* (*PW* iii. 48), mentioned below, and probably the three other sonnets which seem to be associated with W. W.'s previous visit to Brinsop in Dec. 1827: *St. Catherine of Ledbury*, 'Four fiery steeds', and 'Wait, prithee, wait!' (*PW* iii. 34, 35, 45.)

don't expect that a claim for more should be grounded upon rejection, for you clearly see, if this principle be admitted—I might write on for ever, before my part of the Contract were fulfilled.[1] You rely upon my fair dealing not to send you anything I deem unworthy of myself—You have this confidence in me—and I shall take care not to abuse it——— Pray send me back the rejected Sonnets at your leisure—if you recollect we took a good deal of pains together about one line in the Sonnet upon Roman Antiquities—I corrected it—but I forget how—Tell me when you wish for my Contribution.

My Ladies have found much to entertain them in the Keepsake— ever faithfully yours

Wm Wordsworth

407. W. W. to H. C. R.

Address: H. C. Robinson Esqre, No. 3. Kings Bench Walk, Temple, London.
Postmark: [? 1829]. *Stamp*.: *Kendal Penny Post*.
Endorsed: 27 Jan. 1829. Wordsworth. Prof: Wilson, De Quincey, His other Critics.
MS. Dr. Williams's Library.
K (—). *Morley, i. 199.*

27th Jan^ry [1829]
Rydal Mount

My dear Friend

What an odd view do you take of the stability of human life! 'I accept your invitation'—these words set us all agog—we looked for you in ten days at most—then comes—'after my return from Germany—from Italy—and the Holy Land'—but that did not follow—as it well might have done.—Within the course of the last fortnight I have heard of the death of two among the most valued

---

[1] The principle which W. W. is contending for here had already been impressed on Hartley Coleridge, just before W. W. himself, contrary to his better judgement, became involved with *The Keepsake*. As Sara Coleridge wrote to Elizabeth Wardell about her brother on 2 Feb. 1828: 'I am sorry to say that he is a very bad bargain-maker, and Mr Wordsworth has read him some kind lectures on the subject: he says he must not write in Albums, and waste his powers in this manner, for that he cannot afford it. . . . Hood the Editor of the "Gem" has not I think used him well—he has inserted only one out of four sonnets, and that the worst; Hartley says he has doubtless done it for the best, but as Mr Wordsworth observes, Editors ought not to have this selecting and rejecting power; if they agree for a certain number of sheets or pages they ought to pay for the number they receive; otherwise they may pay only for what they insert and keep the rest for another year.' (*WL MSS.*)

15

of my Schoolfellows—Godfrey Sykes,[1] Sol: of the Stamp Off.—and Mr Calvert,[2] probably unknown to you by name—So we are thinned off—but you live in the light of Hope—and you are in the right as long as you can—but why not run down for a fortnight or three weeks—we should be so glad to see you!—and really the absence you talk of is a little formidable to a man so near 60 as I am.—

—About ten days ago I had a pop visit of ten minutes from Courtenay the Barrister,[3] who had been at Cockermouth Sessions—I recurred to the Law-life Insurance—which you will recollect we all talked about together, he continues to affirm that it is a most excellent Investment.—Now I am expecting every week a Legacy of 160 to Mrs Wordsworth. I dont wish to touch this money—but should like to make it up to 200—and invest it in this way for her benefit—in case of my demise. Mr C—says that no interest will be received for 4 or five years—and you will recollect that you offered to lend your name; as the Insurance must be in the name of some Barrister, whose honor may be depended upon. Will you be kind enough to call upon him, 23 Montagu street, Russel Square—and settle the affair with him—if you deem it an eligible thing, of which I suppose there is little doubt—the money shall be forthcoming at Masterman's Bank, as soon as required—Should you disapprove of the intended Insurance, pray let me know with your reasons—

I had a Letter the other day from Mr Richard Sharp[4] of the Corner of Park Lane Upper Grosvenor street, and of Mansion house place—about business—which I was obliged to reply to in so great a hurry—that I overlooked a notice of my Son's Station upon the list of Candidates for the Athenæum. I do not like to trouble him with another Letter till I have an opportunity of a Frank—which may not be shortly—therefore should you be passing either of these doors—but not else, will you be kind enough to step in—and leave upon a slip of paper—that my Son being beneficed in Cumberland—there is no probability of an Election to the Athenæum being of the least use to him—so that his name may be removed from the list of Candidates.—I shall have a Letter to Mr Sharp, to this effect ready for the first opportunity.

---

[1] See pt. i, L. 31.

[2] William Calvert. See L. 403 above.

[3] Philip Courtenay, W. W.'s financial adviser.

[4] Richard Sharp had written on 17 Jan. to say that he had put John W. up for election to the Athenaeum, and he raised the matter again in a letter of the 28th (*WL MSS.*). Early in 1827 W. W. had asked that his son's name be put forward (see pt. i, L. 279).

I have seen the Article in Blackwood alluded to in your last[1]—it is undoubtedly from the pen of Mr Wilson himself. He is a perverse Mortal,—not to say worse of him. Have you peeped into his Trials of Margaret Lyndsay[2]—you will there see to what an extent he has played the Plagiarist—with the very tale of Margaret in the Excursion, which he abuses—and you will also, with a glance learn, what passes with him for poetical Christianity—more mawkish stuff I never encountered.—I certainly should think it beneath me to notice that Article in any way—my Friends and admirers I hope will take the same view of it. Mr W's pen must be kept going at any rate—I am at a loss to know why—but so it is—he is well paid twice as much, I am told as any other Contributor—In the same number of Blackwood is an Article upon Rhetoric, undoubtedly from De Quincey.[3] Whatever he writes is worth reading—there are in it some things from my Conversation—which the Writer does not seem aware of.—Last week I passed with Southey—well (except for a Cold) and busy as usual. He is about to publish a book, two volumes of Dialogues—between the Ghost of Sir Thomas More—and Montesino—himself[4]—It is an interesting work—and I hope will attract some attention. But periodicals appear to have swallowed up so much money—that there is none left for more respectable Literature.—You advert to Critics that dont deal fairly with me[5]—I do not blame them—they

[1] In his letter of 31 Dec. (Morley, i. 197), H. C. R. had drawn attention to John Wilson's article on 'Sacred Poetry' in *Blackwood's Magazine*, xxiv (1828), 917–38 (repr. in revised form in *Recreations of Christopher North*, 3 vols., 1842): 'He argues that having so intense a love of nature and so devout a Sentiment towards the God of Nature, you cannot be a Christian because in your earlier works you were silent about Christianity—And because the little you have said in your later writings has been merely in praise of the Church of *England* and in fact worse than nothing.' In his article, which was ostensibly a review of James Montgomery's *Christian Psalmist* and *Christian Poet* and Keble's *Christian Year*, Wilson was particularly critical of the absence of revealed religion as a vital force in the tale of Margaret in *The Excursion*.

[2] Wilson's novel, *The Trials of Margaret Lyndsay*, appeared in 1823.

[3] 'Elements of Rhetoric by Dr Whateley', *Blackwood's Magazine*, xxiv (1828), 885–908; repr. in De Quincey's *Works* (ed. Masson), x. 81–133.

[4] *Sir Thomas More: or, Colloquies on the Progress and Prospects of Society*, a series of dialogues between himself and the ghost of More, was published by Southey in 2 vols. in 1829. The book is written in the first person (as Morley notes), but More on first appearing, addresses the author as *Montesinos*, and the name is used throughout the dialogue. For Montesinos see *Don Quixote*, II. xxii, xxiii. He was a legendary hero who retired in dudgeon to a cave in La Mancha, called the Cavern of Montesinos. There Don Quixote fell into a trance, in which he believed he saw Montesinos and others under the spell of Merlin.

[5] 'I will quarrel with no one who prefers the style of the Lyrical Ballads to that of your later poems', H. C. R. had written, 'but I have no patience with

write as they feel—and that their feelings are no better they cannot help. The older part of Critics like Gifford[1] had he been alive, have their classical prejudices and for the younger—I am not poetical enough, they require higher seasoning than I give.

Dont mind Franks in writing to me—that is never put off because you have not a Cover—I wish I had one for you—but here they are rarely to be had.

[*unsigned*]

408. W. W. to HUGH JAMES ROSE

MS. untraced.
Mem. Grosart. K. LY i. 328.

[late Jan. 1829]

My dear Sir,

I have taken a folio sheet to make certain minutes upon the subject of Education.[2]. . .

As a Christian preacher your business is with man as an immortal being. Let us imagine you to be addressing those, and those only, who would gladly co-operate with you in any course of education which is most likely to insure to men a happy immortality. Are you satisfied with that course which the most active of this class are bent upon? Clearly not, as I remember from your conversation, which is confirmed by your last letter. Great principles, you hold, are sacrificed to shifts and expedients. I agree with you. What more sacred law of nature, for instance, than that the mother should educate her child? Yet we felicitate ourselves upon the establish-

those who affecting to refuse the character of poetry to those works, now are quite silent at the appearance of the later poems—This is manifest unprincipled dishonesty.' (Morley, i. 197.)

[1] William Gifford (1756–1826), first editor of the *Quarterly Review*, 1809–24.
[2] See pt. i, L. 384. Rose had replied on 15 Jan.: 'Your praise of my last Sermons was indeed most gratifying. To receive commendation from one to whose works I owe so much, and to whom I look up with such implicit deference is the greatest pleasure I could receive in the way of human commendation.' As Christian Advocate at Cambridge, Rose had the opportunity of discussing the subject of education from the University pulpit, and in his letter he set out his own views and invited W. W.'s comments. 'We educate children . . . as *social*, not as immortal beings, and consider their progress in the world as the first thing needful, to say the least. Hence in the Lancastrian System, Religious Education is a blank, and in the Bell, only in fact an adjunct, whatever it may be

18

ment of infant schools[1] which is in direct opposition to it. Nay, we interfere with the maternal instinct before the child is born, by furnishing, in cases where there is no necessity, the mother with baby linen for her unborn child. Now, that in too many instances a lamentable necessity may exist for this, I allow; but why should such charity be obtruded? Why should so many excellent ladies form themselves into committees, and rush into an almost indiscriminate benevolence, which precludes the poor mother from the strongest motive human nature can be actuated by for industry, for fore-thought, and self-denial? When the stream has thus been poisoned at its fountain-head, we proceed, by separating, through infant schools, the mother from the child and from the rest of the family, disburthening them of all care of the little one for perhaps eight hours of the day. To those who think this an evil, but a necessary one, much might be said, in order to qualify unreasonable expectations. But there are thousands of stirring people now in England, who are so far misled as to deem these schools *good in themselves*, and to wish that, even in the smallest villages, the children of the poor should have what *they* call 'a good education' in this way. Now, these people (and no error is at present more common) confound *education* with *tuition*.

Education, I need not remark to you, is everything that *draws out* the human being, of which *tuition*, the teaching of schools especially, however important, is comparatively an insignificant part. Yet the present bent of the public mind is to sacrifice the greater power to the less—all that life and nature teach, to the little that can be learned from books and a master.[2] In the eyes of

in name.' (*WL MSS.*) W. W.'s long reply here develops many themes touched on in previous letters about education (see particularly *MY* i. 249–51), and anticipates the final statement of his position in his speech at the laying of the foundation stone of the new school at Bowness in 1836 (*Prose Works*, iii. 291–6).

   [1] The first infant school was set up by Robert Owen at New Lanark in 1816 (see *The Life of Robert Owen. Written by Himself*, 1857, pp. 138 ff.). This initiative was quickly followed by Brougham, Lord Lansdowne, and James Mill, who started the Brewers Green School in Westminster three years later. A group of Quakers, including William Allen (see *MY* ii. 589), began an infant school at Spitalfields about the same time, and the movement gradually spread to other parts of the country. The Quakers were now planning a school at Kendal on the same lines.

   [2] W. W.'s distrust of book learning compared with direct experience of the natural world was reflected in his approach to the education of young Basil Montagu at Racedown in 1797 (see *EY*, p. 180), and is the theme of *Expostulation and Reply* and *The Tables Turned* (*PW* iv. 56–7). It sprang from his reading in David Hartley (see *MY* i. 266) and eighteenth-century associationalist thinking, but probably owes something to earlier sources as well. See

an enlightened statesman this is absurd; in the eyes of a pure lowly-minded Christian it is monstrous.

The Spartan and other ancient communities might disregard domestic ties, because they had the substitution of country, which we cannot have. With us, country is a mere name compared with what it was to the Greeks: first, as contrasted with barbarians; and next, and above all, as that *passion* alone was strong enough then to preserve the individual, his family, and the whole State from ever-impending destruction. Our course is to supplement domestic attachments without the possibility of substituting others more capricious. What can grow out of it but selfishness?

Let it then be universally admitted that infant schools are an evil, only tolerated to qualify a greater, viz. the inability of mothers to attend to their children, and the like inability of the elder to take care of the younger, from their labour being wanted in factories, or elsewhere, for their common support. But surely this is a sad state of society; and if these expedients of tuition or education (if that word is not to be parted with) divert our attention from the fact that the remedy for so mighty an evil must be sought elsewhere, they are most pernicious things, and the sooner they are done away with the better.

But even as a course of tuition I have strong objections to infant schools, and in no small degree to the Madras system also. We must not be deceived by premature adroitness. The *intellect* must not be trained with a view to what the infant or child may perform, without constant reference to what that performance promises for the man. It is with the mind as with the body. I recollect seeing a German babe stuffed with beer and beef, who had the appearance of an infant Hercules. *He* might have enough in him of the old Teutonic blood to grow up to be a strong man; but tens of thousands would dwindle and perish after such unreasonable cramming. Now I cannot but think, that the like would happen with our modern pupils, if the views of the patrons of these schools were realised. The diet they offer is not the natural diet for infant and juvenile minds. The faculties are over-strained, and not exercised with that simultaneous operation which ought to be aimed at as far as is practicable. Natural history is taught in infant schools by pictures stuck up against walls, and such mummery. A moment's notice of a red-breast pecking by a winter's hearth is worth it all.

Alan G. Hill, 'Wordsworth, Comenius, and the Meaning of Education', *RES* xxvi (1975), 301–12.

These hints are for the negative side of the question; and for the positive,—what conceit, and presumption, and vanity, and envy, and mortification, and hypocrisy, etc. etc., are the unavoidable result of schemes where there is so much display and contention! All this is at enmity with Christianity; and if the practice of sincere churchmen in this matter be so, what have we not to fear when we cast our eyes upon other quarters where religious instruction is deliberately excluded? The wisest of us expect far too much from school teaching. One of the most innocent, contented, happy, and, in his sphere, most useful men whom I know can neither read nor write. Though learning and sharpness of wit must exist somewhere, to protect, and in some points to interpret, the Scriptures, yet we are told that the Founder of this religion rejoiced in spirit, that things were hidden from the wise and prudent, and revealed unto babes; and again, 'Out of the mouths of babes and sucklings Thou hast perfected praise'. Apparently, the infants here contemplated were under a very different course of discipline from that which many in our day are condemned to. In a town of Lancashire,[1] about nine in the morning, the streets resound with the crying of infants, wheeled off in carts and other vehicles (some ladies, I believe, lending their carriages for this purpose) to their school-prisons.

But to go back a little. Human learning, as far as it tends to breed pride and self-estimation (and that it requires constant vigilance to counteract this tendency we must all feel), is against the spirit of the Gospel. Much cause, then, is there to lament that inconsiderate zeal, wherever it is found, which whets the intellect by blunting the affections. Can it, in a *general* view, be good that an infant should learn much which its *parents do not know?* Will not the child arrogate a superiority unfavourable to love and obedience?

But suppose this to be an evil only for the present generation, and that a succeeding race of infants will have no such advantage over their parents; still it may be asked, should we not be making these infants too much the creatures of society when we cannot make them more so? Here would they be, for eight hours in the day, like plants in a conservatory.[2] What is to become of them for the other sixteen hours, when they are returned to all the influences, the dread of which first suggested this contrivance? Will they be better able to resist the mischief they may be exposed

---

[1] Perhaps Preston, where W. W. occasionally stayed with Samuel Horrocks, the cotton manufacturer.

[2] Cf. Doctor Blimber's establishment in Dickens's *Dombey and Son*, ch. xi.

to from the bad example of their parents, or brothers and sisters? It is to be feared not, because, though they must have heard many good precepts, their condition in school is artificial; they have been removed from the discipline and exercise of humanity, and they have, besides, been subject to many evil temptations within school and peculiar to it.

In the present generation I cannot see anything of an harmonious co-operation between these schools and home influences. If the family be thoroughly bad, and the child cannot be removed altogether, how feeble the barrier, how futile the expedient! If the family be of middle character, the children will lose more by separation from domestic cares and reciprocal duties than they can possibly gain from captivity, with such formal instruction as may be administered.

We are then brought round to the point, that it is to a physical and not a moral necessity that we must look, if we would justify this disregard, I had almost said violation, of a primary law of human nature. The link of eleemosynary tuition connects the infant school with the national schools upon the Madras system. Now I cannot but think that there is too much indiscriminate gratuitous instruction in this country; arising out of the misconception above adverted to, of the real power of school teaching, relative to the discipline of life; and out of an over-value of talent, however exerted, and of knowledge, prized for its own sake, and acquired in the shape of knowledge. The latter clauses of the last sentence glance rather at the London University and the Mechanics' Institutes[1] than at the Madras schools, yet they have some bearing upon these also. Emulation, as I observed in my last letter, is the master-spring of that system. It mingles too much with all teaching, and with all learning; but in the Madras mode it is the great wheel which puts every part of the machine into motion.

But I have been led a little too far from gratuitous instruction. If possible, instruction ought never to be altogether so. A child will soon learn to feel a stronger love and attachment to its parents, when it perceives that they are making sacrifices for its instruction. All that precept can teach is nothing compared with convictions of this kind. In short, unless book-attainments are carried on by the side of moral influences they are of no avail. Gratitude is one of the most benign of moral influences; can a child be grateful to a corpor-

---

[1] Brougham had put himself at the head of both these projects. See pt. i, Ls. 180 and 225.

ate body for its instruction? or grateful even to the Lady Bountiful of the neighbourhood, with all the splendour which he sees about her, as he would be grateful to his poor father and mother, who spare from their scanty provision a mite for the culture of his mind at school? If we look back upon the progress of things in this country since the Reformation, we shall find that instruction has never been severed from moral influences and purposes, and the natural action of circumstances, in the way that is now attempted. Our forefathers established, in abundance, free grammar schools;[1] but for a distinctly understood religious purpose. They were designed to provide against a relapse of the nation into Popery, by diffusing a knowledge of the languages in which the Scriptures are written, so that a sufficient number might be aware how small a portion of the popish belief had a foundation in Holy Writ.

It is undoubtedly to be desired that every one should be able to read, and perhaps (for that is far from being equally apparent) to write. But you will agree with me, I think, that these attainments are likely to turn to better account where they are not gratuitously lavished, and where either the parents and connections are possessed of certain property which enables them to procure the instruction for their children, or where, by their frugality and other serious and self-denying habits, they contribute, as far as they can, to benefit their offspring in this way. Surely, whether we look at the usefulness and happiness of the individual, or the prosperity and security of the state, this, which was the course of our ancestors, is the better course. Contrast it with that recommended by men in whose view knowledge and intellectual adroitness are to do everything of themselves.

We have no guarantee in the social condition of these *well* informed pupils for the use they may make of their power and their knowledge; the scheme points not to man as a religious being; its end is an unworthy one; and its means do not pay respect to the order of things. Try the Mechanics' Institutes, and the London University, etc. etc. by this test. The powers are not co-ordinate with those to which this nation owes its virtue and its prosperity. Here is, in one case, a sudden formal abstraction of a vital principle, and in both an unnatural and violent pushing on. Mechanics' Institutes make discontented spirits and insubordinate and pre-

---

[1] W. W. is thinking particularly of the educational programmes of Edward VI and Elizabeth, and of the foundation of his own Hawkshead Grammar School by Archbishop Sandys in 1585, an event celebrated many years before in his 'School Exercise' (*PW* i. 259–61).

sumptuous workmen. Such at least was the opinion of Watt,[1] one of the most experienced and intelligent of men. And instruction, where religion is expressly excluded, is little less to be dreaded than that by which it is trodden under foot. And, for my own part, I cannot look without shuddering on the array of surgical midwifery lectures, to which the youth of London were invited at the commencement of this season by the advertisements of the London University. Hogarth[2] understood human nature better than these professors; his picture I have not seen for many long years, but I think his last stage of cruelty is in the dissecting room.

But I must break off, or you will have double postage to pay for this letter. Pray excuse it; and pardon the style, which is, purposely, as meagre as I could make it, for the sake of brevity. I hope that you can gather the meaning, and that is enough. I find that I have a few moments to spare, and will, therefore, address a word to those who may be inclined to ask, what is the use of all these objections? The schoolmaster is, and will remain, abroad. The thirst of knowledge is spreading and will spread, whether virtue and duty go along with it or no. Grant it; but surely these observations may be of use if they tend to check unreasonable expectations. One of the most difficult tasks is to keep benevolence in alliance with beneficence. Of the former there is no want, but we do not see our way to the latter. Tenderness of heart is indispensable for a good man, but a certain sternness of heart is as needful for a wise one. We are as impatient under the evils of society as under our own, and more so; for in the latter case, necessity enforces submission. It is hard to look upon the condition in which so many of our fellow creatures are born, but they are not to be raised from it by partial and temporary expedients; it is not enough to rush headlong into any new scheme that may be proposed, be it Benefit Societies,

---

[1] James Watt (1736–1819), the Scottish engineer. W. W.'s high opinion of him is recorded by J. P. Muirhead, 'A Day with Wordsworth', *Blackwood's Magazine*, ccxxi (1927), 728–43: 'I look upon him, considering both the magnitude and the universality of his genius, as perhaps the most extraordinary man that this country ever produced.' The Mechanics' Institutes took their origin from the evening classes started in Glasgow in 1760 by John Anderson (1726–96), Professor of Natural Philosophy at the University, who left property at his death to found a college, Anderson's Institute, to carry on his work.

[2] William Hogarth (1697–1764), whose *Four Stages of Cruelty* depict the brutality and callousness of his age. The last stage, 'The Reward of Cruelty', is shown in the dissecting room. Dissections of criminals often took place in public after their execution as part of the sentence imposed on the prisoner. See Ronald Paulson, *Hogarth: His Life, Art, and Times*, 2 vols., 1971, ii. 103 ff.

Savings' Banks, Infant Schools, Mechanics' Institutes, or any other. Circumstances have forced this nation to do, by its manufacturers, an undue portion of the dirty and unwholesome work of the globe. The revolutions among which we have lived have unsettled the value of all kinds of property, and of labour, the most precious of all, to that degree that misery and privation are frightfully prevalent. We must bear the sight of this, and endure its pressure, till we have by reflection discovered the cause, and not till then can we hope even to palliate the evil. It is a thousand to one but that the means resorted to will aggravate it.

Farewell, ever affectionately yours,
W. Wordsworth

Query.—Is the education in the parish schools of Scotland gratuitous, or if not, in what degree is it so?

409. W. W. to GEORGE HUNTLY GORDON

MS. Cornell.
Broughton, p. 13.

Rydal Mount
Jan^y—29th—1829.

My dear Sir,

I cannot let a Post pass without thanking you for your most kind Letter, and begging you also to return my sincere acknowledge- ments to Mrs Oom[1] for her interesting communication. It is most satisfactory, and Mrs W. and I will be truly happy in placing our Son under so promising a superintendence.—and may I beg that this wish of ours may be made known to Mr Papendick, through such channel as you think most proper. My Son will be ready to return with Mr. P. in April—Mr P. wished to know what he had read in Classics—he is not a[t] present in the way—or I would take down from his own mouth the Account of what he has read. But alas!—as I told you before he is very backward—for upwards of two years of the most valuable part of his Youth he was kept from Books (except as an amusement) by medical prohibition—and he is also naturally much more disposed to active than studious life. But his health is now good—though I think him not capable of *severe*

---

[1] Mr. Papendick's sister.

application without injury—His wish to improve himself is, I think, ardent; and I trust that upon the whole Mr Papendick will not have reason to complain of him—But I believe I have already troubled you too much about his history—

Will you allow me to detain Mrs Oom's Letter? I am loth to part with it—I shall take care to let you know when my Sister and I go into Wales—as soon as the time is fixed which cannot be for some months.[1]

I have thought it best to introduce my Son to the German Grammar, which I should have done long ago, but from dislike of my vicious pronunciation. But upon the whole it seems best that he should be master of the Accidence—else a few weeks of his first residence in Germany could not turn to so good an account.

Excuse this brief scrawl—the main point is determined between us, and that will give value to the sheet—farewell—Mrs W. and my Daughter join in kindest regards, and my Son feels truly grateful for all the trouble you have taken on his account. Let me repeat my cordial thanks to Mrs Oom—

Ever most faithfully yours
Wm Wordsworth

I lately wrote a Tale (350)[2] verses the Scene of which is laid in Russia, though it is not even tinged with Russian imagery— It will give me great pleasure to shew it you— I think your Russian Friends would be pleased with it, in which number I include Mrs Oom and her Brother though Germans.

410. W. W. to MARIA JANE JEWSBURY

MS. untraced.
The Times, 6 Oct. 1931. Gillett, p. xlvi. LY i. 349. Letters of Dora Wordsworth,
ed. Howard P. Vincent, 1944, p. 51.

[late Jan. 1829]

My dear Miss Jewsbury,

When Mr Reynolds called upon me during his Editorial Tour early in the Spring of last year I was not unmindful of you, and mentioned your name to him in such terms as I am accustomed

---

[1] The proposed tour did not take place, owing to D. W.'s illness later on in the year.
[2] *The Russian Fugitive* (*PW* iv. 183), published in 1835. It eventually had 376 verses.

to use in speaking of you. He replied to my recommendation that their object was Authors of prime celebrity—and persons distinguished by rank or fashion, or station or anything else that might have as little to do with good writing. This stopped any further endeavour at that time—when I was in Town late in the Spring I frequently thought of you in connection with the *Keepsake* but Mr R. shewed me such an overflow of materials that I saw there was no room for any fresh Person—therefore I did not court a refusal. All this is mentioned that you may not be disappointed (I will not say mortified, for under such circumstances how is that possible?) if you hear, as I am afraid you will, that the application which I mean to make by the first opportunity proves fruitless. This apprehension is not agreeable to me, for at present the *Keepsake* can afford to pay better than any other of these Annuals— for so the plants are most characteristically entitled—if I may be allowed to judge from the little I have seen of them.

Mr A. Watts[1] must be an odd person—he has used you ill without any temptation—he had some from me but certainly not enough to justify him in saying, as he has done, that I not only extolled the *Keepsake* but spoke injuriously of every other publication of the class with the view I suppose of benefiting the one I myself wrote in. How he could think me capable of conduct so ungenerous and ungentlemanly I am at a loss to conceive. When I made my agreement with Mr R—and Mr Heath—I told them that Mr Watts had endeavoured to serve me in a bargain with certain Booksellers,[2] and now that I had been committed with these Periodicals (which was first done by the Winter's Wreath[3] being turned into one without my knowledge) I should much wish to send him a contribution—as I had given him cause to expect I might but for a general rule to the contrary. This permission they were unwilling to grant, as they said it was the exclusive possession of my name, which tempted them to offer me so considerable a sum for a few pages. I was therefore obliged to give way, which I did with much less scruple, as Mr Watts's endeavours to serve me had all had for their object a better bargain with Booksellers than I myself could make. All that I felt myself in honour bound to stipulate for—was that I should be at Liberty to contribute to any one who would pay me as well as they did. So stood the agreement last year and so it

---

[1] Alaric Watts, editor of *The Literary Souvenir*.

[2] For Watts's negotiations with Hurst and Robinson on W. W.'s behalf in 1825–6, see pt. i, Ls. 182, 189, 215–16.

[3] For W. W.'s contributions to *The Winter's Wreath* in 1828, see pt. i, L. 324.

stands this. I thought it derogatory to exclude myself altogether from other works—and should have deemed it unhandsome to let others have anything of mine at a cheaper rate than persons had who paid so liberally. Excuse this long story—these are the simple facts for which I have been unpleasantly treated. Messrs Longman have an interest in the Souvenir and if they believe Mr Watts's statements they have grounds to complain of me.

[. . .] I did recommend several [?per]sons so far as to say that if good writing could be had for high prices it would be found there—but I often added that this result was far from certain; though the Proprietors were not the less entitled to praise for their spirit. I think you do quite right in connecting yourself with these light things. An Author has not fair play who has no share in their Profits—for the money given for them leaves so much less to spare for separate volumes. Look at my own—Gagliani[1] has just published all my poems in one volume for 20 francs—here few will give £2 5/- for my five volumes when every body is going to and fro between London and Paris—as between town and country in their own Island. Therefore let the Annuals pay—and with whomsoever you deal make hard bargains.[2] Humility with these Gentry is downright simpleness. I am glad you like the Triad—it is a great favorite with all my friends who I have heard speak of it.

farewell affectionately
yours
W. Wordsworth

Pray come here in the Spring—second thoughts are not always best.

[1] i.e. Galignani.
[2] Miss Jewsbury failed to get a contribution accepted by *The Keepsake*, but she continued to contribute to other annuals.

411. W. W. to GEORGE WILKINSON[1]

MS. WL.
LY i. 353.

3ᵈ Febʳʸ 1829
Rydal Mount
Kendal

Sir,

My Son, I have reason to believe, will visit Moresby, for the purpose of being inducted, in the course of next week; in the meantime you may be assured that in respect to your vacating the Curacy he will do nothing irregular, abrupt, or unfeeling.

I am by no means insensible (nor will my Son be) to the feelings which a rightly constituted mind cannot but entertain upon a separation such as you are about to undergo.

Duly appreciating the kind manner in which you express yourself towards me, I am, Sir,

your obedient humble Serᵛⁿᵗ
Wm Wordsworth

412. W. W. to WILLIAM ROWAN HAMILTON

Address: Professor Hamilton, Observatory, Dublin [*In Dora W.'s hand*]
Postmark: 14 Feb. 1829. *Stamp*: Kendal Penny Post.
MS. Cornell.
Grosart (—). *Hamilton. K* (—). *LY i. 354.*

12ᵗʰ Febʳʸ 1829
Rydal Mount, Kendal

My dear Sir,

It gave me much pleasure to hear from you again[2]—and I should have replied instantly, but Mr Harrison[3] is at Hastings, and I knew not how to direct without troubling you with Postage, which I would willingly avoid, being aware that my Letter will scarcely be worth it.

Now for a few words upon your Enclosures. Your own verses[4]

---

[1] Curate of Moresby. See pt. i, L. 393.
[2] Hamilton had written to W. W. on 23 Jan., recalling their first meeting in the autumn of 1827 (see pt. i, L. 297): 'The pursuits indeed, to which I am devoted, are of an absorbing nature, and their tendency is somewhat unfavourable to the cultivation of poetical feelings; but they do not prevent me from sometimes enjoying such feelings, and still less can they hinder me from remembering your society, and prizing your friendship.' (*Hamilton*, i. 326.)
[3] George Harrison. See pt. i, L. 205.
[4] *The Enthusiast*. See *Hamilton*, i. 183.

are dated 1826.—I note this early date with pleasure—because, I think if they had been composed lately, the only objections I make to them would probably not have existed at least in an equal degree. It is an objection that relates to Style alone, and to versification. For example, the last line, 'And he was *the* Enthusiast no more', which is in meaning the weightiest of all is not sinewy enough in Sound—the syllable *the*, the metre requires should be long, but it is short, and imparts a languor to the Sense. The three lines, 'As if he were addressing' etc., are too prosaic in movement. After having directed your attention to these minutiae, I can say without scruple that the verses are highly spirited, and interesting—and poetical. The change of character they describe, is an object of instructive contemplation, and the whole executed with feeling.— I was also much gratified with your sister's[1] verses, which I have read several times over—they are well and vigorously expressed, and the feelings are such as one could wish should exist oftener than they appear to do in the bosoms of *male* astronomers.

The Specimens of your young Friend's[2] Genius are very promising. His poetical powers are there strikingly exhibited—nor have I any objections to make that are worthy of his notice, at least I fear not. I should say to him however as I did to you, that *style* is in Poetry of incalculable importance—he seems however aware of it, for his diction is obviously studied. Thus the great difficulty is to determine what constitutes a good style. In deciding this we are all subject to delusions; not improbably I am so, when it appears to me that the Metaphor in the first speech of his Dramatic Scene is too much drawn out—it does not pass off as rapidly as metaphors ought to, I think, in dramatic writing. I am well aware that our early dramatists abound with these continuities of imagery, but to me they appear laboured and unnatural—at least unsuited to that

[1] Eliza Mary Hamilton (1807–51), one of Hamilton's younger sisters. See also pt. i, L. 274.

[2] Francis Beaufort Edgeworth (1809–46), half-brother of Maria Edgeworth the novelist, had gained some reputation as a poet at Charterhouse. He went on to Trinity College, Cambridge, in 1826, but left without taking a degree, and after intermittent travels on the Continent (and marriage to a Spanish lady) he set up an unsuccessful tutoring establishment in London, before returning permanently to Ireland to manage his brother's estate at Edgeworthstown. Thomas Carlyle regarded him as one of the intellectual casualties of the age: 'A composed, dogmatic, speculative, exact and not melodious man. He was learned in Plato and likewise in Kant; well-read in philosophies and literatures; entertained not creeds, but the Platonic or Kantean *ghosts* of creeds; coldly sneering away from him, in the joyless twinkle of those eyes, in the inexorable jingle of that shrill voice, all manner of Toryisms, superstitions: for the rest, a man of perfect veracity, of great diligence, and other worth . . .' (*Life of John Sterling*, part ii, ch. iv). See also L. 444 below.

species of composition of which action and motion are the essentials. 'While with the ashes of a light that was', and the two following lines are in the best style of dramatic writing; to every opinion thus given, always add, I pray you, *in my judgment,* though I may not, to save trouble or to avoid a charge of false modesty, express it. 'This over-perfume of a heavy pleasure', etc is admirable—and indeed it would be tedious to praise all that pleases me.—

Shelley's Witch of Atlas[1] I never saw—therefore the Stanza referring to Narcissus and her was read by me to some disadvantage. One observation I am about to make will at least prove I am no flatterer, and will therefore give a qualified value to my praise:

> There was nought there
> But those three antient hills, *alone.*

Here the word 'alone,' being used instead of 'only,' makes an absurdity like that noticed in the *Spectator*—'Enter a king and three Fiddlers, *solus.*' The Sonnet I liked very much, with no drawback but what is, in a great measure, personal to myself. I am so accustomed, in my own practice, to pass *one* set of Rhymes at least through the first eight lines, that the want of that vein of sound takes from the music some thing of its consistency—to my mind and ear. Farewell—I shall at all times be glad to hear from you and still more to see you. With high respect I remain

sincerely yours,
W Wordsworth

413. W. W. to BARRON FIELD

Address: Barron Field Esqre, Southampton Row. [*In Dora W.'s hand*] [*re-addressed to*] 49 Charter House Square.
Postmark: (1) 1 Mar. 1829. (2) 4 Mar. 1829.
MS. Cornell.
K (—). *LY i. 382* (—). *Broughton, p. 66.*

26th Feb^ry—[1829]
Rydal Mount.

My dear Sir,

It gives me great pleasure that your destiny is changed:[2] Gibraltar is rather a confined situation, but I hope it may agree with

---

[1] Written 1820: first published by Mary Shelley in *Posthumous Poems,* 1824.
[2] See L. 399 above. Field wrote on 26 Feb. as he was setting out from

your health and Mrs Field's—It cannot but be greatly preferable to India—and is so much nearer home. There is not the slightest hope for my ever seeing you there—little indeed of my getting to Italy at all—Still it seems a good deal more probable that we may meet again than if your station had been the East—

I write this Note as an affectionate farewell—take with you our best wishes—and God bless you I remain yours

faithfully yours
Wm Wordsworth

414. W. W. to GEORGE HUNTLY GORDON

Endorsed: Mr. Wordsworth 26th Feby./29.
MS. Cornell.
Mem. (—). *Grosart* (—). *LY i. 356* (—). *Broughton, p. 14.*

Rydal Mount
Thursday Night
Feby 26th/29

My dear Sir,

W^m left us yesterday along with his Brother[1] for Leicestershire—Many thanks for your last, and the enclosed Card. Upon duly considering your proposal, I find the reasons against sending W. to Town outweigh the advantages and I have determined that he should remain with his Brother till Mr Papendick comes to London—Among those reasons the state of W^{ms} health is not the least important— He has had much anxiety in his mind—and I am persuaded hurt himself by wading among our swamps with his gun after snipes—and by over exertion in the novel pursuit of shooting. —I trust he will rally quickly under his Brother's quiet roof—as his general health with this exception has for some time been good.

You ask for my opinion on the Catholic Question—What I wrote this day to a Friend shall be transcribed.

London to Falmouth, to acquaint W. W. with his recent meeting with Murray, the publisher, and to let him know that Murray was now interested in taking over the publishing of his poems. 'He said that the reason there had never been any profits on your Poems was, that too few copies of an edition were printed to make any; and then you went to press again with a new edition, and all the profits fell to the printer. He said that no poetry paid well but Lord Byron's.' (*WL MSS.*)

[1] John W. had paid a brief visit to the north in order to be inducted into the living of Moresby (see L. 411 above), and he was now returning to finish his duty at Whitwick.

—This note is penned at a late hour of the night, to save to-morrow's post.—I had designed to write in the morning more at length—but I am summoned to a Funeral at a distance in the Country, and must attend early in the morning; so that I must beg of you to excuse so hasty a scrawl—Believe me ever faithfully your

Much obliged
W. Wordsworth

[*In Dora W.'s hand*]

Extract from a Letter to a Friend[1]

I dare scarcely trust my Pen to the notice of the Question which the Duke of Wellington tells us is about to be *settled*.[2] One thing no rational person will deny, that the experiment is hazardous. Equally obvious is it that the timidity, supineness and other unworthy qualities of the Government for many years past, have produced the danger the extent of which they now affirm imposes a necessity of granting all that the Romanists demand.

Now it is rather too much that the Country should be called upon to take the measure of this danger from the very Men who may almost be said to have created it. Danger is a relative thing—and the first requisite for judging of what we have to dread from the physical force of the Catholics is to be in sympathy with the Protestants. Had our Ministers been so, could they have suffered themselves to be bearded by the Catholic Association for so many years?

C——,[3] if I may take leave to say it, loses sight of *Things* in *Names*, when he says that they should not be admitted as Roman Catholics but simply as British Subjects. The Question before us is, Can Protestantism and Popery be coordinate Powers in the Constitution of a *free* Country—and at the same time *Christian belief* be in that Country a vital principle of action? I fear not—Heaven grant I may be deceived—WW.

---

[1] Another copy of this 'Extract' in Dora W.'s hand is preserved among the *WL MSS*. It varies in a few small details from the text printed here.

[2] In the King's Speech on 5 Feb. (the Duke of Wellington being Prime Minister), Parliament was asked for fresh powers to maintain order in Ireland and invited to review the laws which imposed disabilities on the Roman Catholics. On 17 Feb. a bill was passed suppressing the Catholic Association, and on 5 Mar. Peel (who had now come round to favouring concession) introduced a new Catholic Relief Bill, which passed both Houses by large majorities and received the royal assent on 13 Apr.

[3] Canning.

415. D. W. to H. C. R.

Endorsed: Apl 1829, Miss Wordsworth.
MS. Dr. Williams's Library.
K (—). *Morley, i. 208.*

[Cambridge]
[*c.* 1 Mar. 1829][1]
Again excuse bad penmanship

My dear Friend,

I cannot help slipping a note into a frank for London to thank you for your very kind letter which makes me not quite hopeless of having a sight of you before I quit the Midland part of England —yet perhaps I ought not to *hope* in this case as it seems if I *do* see you it will be at the expense of a long, perhaps tedious, and certainly to you melancholy journey into Scotland—At all events, however, I may lawfully be pleased that if you should have this journey to take you will remember me and the Curate of Whitwick, and turn aside to our lowly Vicarage.[2]

I must have expressed myself with strange obscurity (but I wrote in great haste) since you have understood me as asking for a sketch letter concerning your journey to the Pyranees. If I said any thing about a full account of that journey it was not as drawn up for my particular use and pleasure; but in connexion with your previous more detailed Tours, which—with that of the Pyranees also—I hope—now that you are aloof from the Cares of Courts of Justice—you will arrange and amplify—and at *some* time, publish— I do not recollect what I said; but the above is what I have often thought of—and in fact I had received your very interesting pyranean sketch and—in the ambiguous words of that hurried letter *meant* to thank you for it.—It is of no use to rake up in your memory the contents of my—(I fear too careless) letters—still less to hunt for them in your bureau—so my dear Friend, accept my thanks for this last and all former favours—The blunder gives me no uneasiness, being well satisfied that your friendship does

---

[1] In spite of H. C. R.'s endorsement, this letter was clearly written from Cambridge, where D. W. had been staying at Trinity Lodge since 6 Feb., and shortly before she left on 5 Mar. to return to Whitwick. Her MS. Journals (*WL MSS.*) describe her busy round of engagements with her nephews in College and University society and her meetings with Sedgwick, Whewell, Thirlwall, and many others.

[2] Dora W.'s attractive drawing of Whitwick parsonage (now in the possession of Mr. Jonathan Wordsworth) was reproduced by Ernest de Selincourt in his *Dorothy Wordsworth. A Biography*, 1933.

not hang on trifles of punctilio like these—so no more on this subject—

Probably before this reaches you you may have heard of the last honour bestowed upon my bright and amiable nephew, Christopher Wordsworth, the appointment to the Craven Scholarship. You may be sure that his good Father and all of us were made very happy last Monday morning when the unanimous Decision of the Examiners was pronounced. He had already received honours and prizes sufficient to satisfy youthful ambition but this is, besides the honour, an affair worthy of consideration,—£50 per annum for seven years. He does not intend to write for the Summer (the Brownonian) Medals—I believe not for any—not even for the Chancellor's Medal (for English Verse) This I am glad of, as it will leave him time, if he have the resolution, to apply sufficiently to the Mathematics, to obtain such a rank upon the mathematical Tripos as will enable him to strive for a place on the *classical*, which his Brother John has been excluded from by being utterly unable to do anything in mathematics. I said I am glad of Christopher's determination for the above reason; but also on other accounts—It is surely very discouraging to the competitors when *One* is sure to carry away all that he strives for, which in Chris$^{r's}$ case has hitherto always happened.

I assure you he is not in the least set up by the congratulations he receives—quite the contrary—He is very humble minded—and one of the happiest and cheerfullest of human Beings.—I have good accounts from Rydal. John W. is now on his road thence to Whitwick where I shall join him next Wednesday. William will accompany him on his road to London, whence he will depart in April for Bremen with a Mr Papendich, under whose care he is to remain for one year at Bremen, to learn the German and French Language; and, I hope, improve himself in other points—I have said William will be on his road to *London*; but in fact he will stay with us at Whitwick till summoned to London at the time that Mr Papendich is ready to sail for Germany.—I had intended leaving Cambridge as to-morrow; but have been tempted to stay where I am so happy and comfortable until Tuesday morning—when I shall take Coach to Leicester—sleep there, and the next morning proceed by the Ashby de la Zouche Coach to Huggleston (within two miles of Whitwick), whence I shall walk to W. leaving my luggage at H. I mention this as a guidance for you in case you should visit us in your way *from* London. Should you take us on your return, you must stop at *Loughborough* (seven miles from

Whitwick)—But when the time comes, of course you will apprise us, and I will again give you precise directions. . . . I have heard from dear Mrs Clarkson, and am sorry to tell you that for the last six weeks she has been prevented by illness from writing to me: but she is now. . .

[*cetera desunt*]

416. W. W. to CHARLES JAMES BLOMFIELD[1]

MS. WL.[2]
Mem. K (—). *LT i. 356.*

March 3, 1829.

My Lord,

I have been hesitating for the space of a week whether I should take the liberty of addressing you; but as the decision draws near,[3] my anxiety increases, and I cannot refrain from intruding upon you for a few minutes. I will try to be brief, throwing myself upon your indulgence if what I have to say prove of little moment.

The Question before us is, can Protestantism and Popery, or, somewhat narrowing the ground, can the Church of England (including that of Ireland) and the Church of Rome be co-ordinate powers in the constitution of a free country, and, at the same time, Christian belief be in that country a vital principle of action? The States of the Continent afford no proof whatever that the existence of Protestantism and Romanism under the specified conditions is practicable, nor can they be rationally referred to, as furnishing a guide for us. In France, the most conspicuous of these States, and the freest, the number of Protestants in comparison with Catholics

---

[1] Now Bishop of London (see pt. i, L. 353). He had written to W. W. on 21 Feb. about John W.'s appointment to Moresby: 'There is a troublesome nest of Sectaries at Moresby; but your Son will get the better of them by zeal and activity tempered with moderation.' And he added his view of the proposed Catholic Relief Bill: 'Such a measure, however expedient it may seem to be, as a means of present pacification, contains within itself the germ of future discord and political disturbances.' (*WL MSS.*)

[2] W. W. took care to keep copies of this letter by him, possibly with a view to eventual publication. It exists in three drafts: (1) Two almost illegible fragments of the opening paragraphs in W. W.'s hand, the first of which is quite different from the final version. It is now printed in the Appendix for the first time. (2) A complete version in M. W.'s hand, with a few minor textual variants from the final copy. (3) A fair copy in the hand of John Carter and M. W. This is the text followed below.

[3] The introduction of the new Catholic Relief Bill. See L. 414 above.

is insignificant, and unbelief and superstition almost divide the country between them. In Prussia there is no Legislative Assembly; the Government is essentially military; and, excepting the countries upon the Rhine, recently added to that power,[1] the proportion of Catholics is inconsiderable. In Hanover, Jacob[2] speaks of the Protestants as more than *ten* to *one*. Here, indeed, is a Legislative Assembly, but its powers are ill defined. Hanover had, and still may have, a Censorship of the Press,—an indulgent one: it can afford to be so, through the sedative virtue of the standing army of the country, and that of the Germanic League, to back the Executive in case of commotion. No sound-minded Englishman will build upon the shortlived experience of the Kingdom of the Netherlands. In Flanders, a benighted Papacy prevails, which defeated the attempts of the King to enlighten the People by education;[3] and I am well assured that the Protestant portion of Holland have small reason to be thankful for the footing upon which they have been there placed. If that Kingdom is to last, there is great cause for fear that its government will incline more and more to Romanism, as the religion of a great majority of its subjects, and as one, which by its slavish spirit, makes the people more manageable. If so, it is to be apprehended that Protestantism will gradually disappear before it; and the ruling classes, in a still greater degree than they now are, will become infidels as the easiest refuge in their own minds from the debasing doctrines of Papacy.

Three[4] great conflicts are before the progressive nations: between Christianity and Infidelity; between Papacy and Protestantism; and between the spirit of the old *Feudal and Monarchical governments*, and the Representative and Republican system as established in America. The Church of England, in addition to her Infidel and Roman Catholic assailants, and the Politicians of the

[1] The Rhineland and Westphalia had become Hohenzollern provinces as a result of the Congress of Vienna in 1815.

[2] William Jacob, F.R.S. (1762–1851), statistical writer. The reference is probably to *A View of the Agriculture, Manufacture, Statistics, and State of Society of Germany and parts of Holland and France, taken during a Journey through those Countries in 1819*, 1820.

[3] At the Congress of Vienna, Catholic Flanders had been surrendered by Austria and added to the new kingdom of Holland under the House of Orange. The restored monarchy of William I guaranteed the freedom of the Catholics in the south, but conflict arose in 1825 out of the King's measures to place education, hitherto the preserve of the Catholic Church, under state control. The revolution of 1830, which set up the independent state of Belgium, was brought about by the union two years before of the Catholics with the Liberals.

[4] 'In this classification I anticipate matter which Mr Southey has in the press, the substance of a conversation between us.' (Footnote added by W. W.)

Anti-Feudal Class, has to contend with a formidable body of Protestant Dissenters. Amid these several and often-combined attacks, how is she to maintain herself? from which of these enemies has she most to fear? Some are of opinion that Papacy is less formidable than Dissent, whose bias is Republican, which is averse to monarchy, to a hierarchy, and to the tything system; to all which Romanism is strongly attached. The abstract principles embodied in the creed of the Dissenters' catechism are without doubt full as politically dangerous as those of the Romanists, but fortunately their creed is not their practice. They are divided among themselves; they acknowledge no foreign jurisdiction; their organisation and discipline are comparatively feeble; and in times long past, however powerful they proved themselves to overthrow, they are not likely to be able to build up. Whatever the Presbyterian form, as in the Church of Scotland, may have to recommend it, we find that the Sons of the Nobility and Gentry of Scotland who chuse the sacred profession, almost invariably enter into the Church of England; and for the same reason, viz., the want of a hierarchy (you will excuse me for connecting views so humiliating with Divine Truth), the rich Dissenters in the course of a generation or two fall into the bosom of our Church. As holding out attractions to the upper orders, the Church of England has no advantages over that of Rome, but rather the contrary: Papacy will join with us in preserving the form, but for the purpose and in the hope of seizing the substance for itself. Its ambition is upon record. It is essentially at enmity with light and knowledge: its power to exclude these blessings is not so great as formerly, though its desire to do so is equally strong, and its determination to exert its power for its own exaltation, by means of that exclusion, is not in the least abated. The See of Rome justly regards England as the Head of Protestantism: it admires, it is jealous, it is envious of her power and greatness; it despairs of being able to destroy them: but it is ever on the watch to regain its lost influence over that Country, and it hopes to effect this through the means of Ireland. The words of this last sentence are not my own, but those of the head of one of the first Catholic Families of the County from which I write,[1] spoken without reserve several years ago. Surely the language of this Individual must be greatly emboldened, when he sees the prostrate condition in which our yet Protestant Government now

---

[1] Probably the Hon. Henry Howard (1802–75) of Greystoke Castle, nephew of the 12th Duke of Norfolk: M.P. for Steyning, 1824–6, and for Shoreham, 1826–32.

lies before the Popery of Ireland. 'The great Catholic interest', 'the old Catholic interest', I know to have been phrases of frequent occurrence in the mouth of a head of the first Roman Catholic family of England. And, to descend far lower,—'What would satisfy you?' said, not long ago, a person to a very clever Lady, a dependant upon another branch of that family. 'That church', replied she, pointing to the parish church of the large town where the conversation took place.[1] Monstrous expectation! yet not to be overlooked as an ingredient in the compound of Papacy. This 'great Catholic interest' we are about to embody in a legislative form. A Protestant Parliament is to turn itself into a canine monster with two heads, which, instead of keeping watch and ward, will be snarling at and bent on devouring each other.

Whatever enemies the Church of England may have to struggle with now and hereafter, it is clear, that at this juncture she is especially called to take the measure of her strength as opposed to the Church of Rome; that is her most pressing enemy. The Church of England as to the point of private judgment, standing between the two extremes of Popery and Dissent, is entitled to heartfelt reverence; and among thinking men, whose affections are not utterly vitiated, never fails to receive it. Papacy will tolerate no private judgment, and Dissent is impatient of any thing else. The blessing of providence has thus far preserved the Church of England between the shocks to which she has been exposed from those opposite errors; and, notwithstanding objections may lie against some few parts of her liturgy, particularly the Athanasian Creed,[2] and however some of her Articles may be disputed about, her doctrines are exclusively scriptural, and her practice is accommodated to the exigencies of our weak nature. If this be so, what has she to fear? Look at Ireland—might be a sufficient answer. Look at the disproportion between her Catholic and Protestant population. Look at the distempered heads of her Roman Catholic Church insisting upon terms, which in France, and even in Austria, dare not be proposed, and which the Pope himself would probably relinquish for a season. Look at the revenues of the Protestant Church, her

---

[1] W. W. had already told this story in a letter to Lord Lowther (see pt. i, L. 158). The reference is to Sheffield, where the Dukes of Norfolk owned large estates.

[2] The so-called 'damnatory clauses' were a source of disquiet to Dissenters in the seventeenth and eighteenth centuries and to Broad-Churchmen in the nineteenth. Both W. W. (see Grosart, iii. 473) and S. T. C. had serious misgivings about them. The Athanasian Creed was omitted from the American Prayer Book, and in more recent times its use in the Anglican communion has been considerably curtailed.

Cathedrals, her Churches that once belonged to the Romanists, and where *in imagination* their worship has never ceased to be celebrated. Can it be doubted that when the yet existing restrictions are removed, that the disproportion in the population and the wealth of the Protestant Church will become more conspicuous objects for discontent to point at; and that plans, however covert, will be instantly set on foot, with the aid of new powers, for effecting an overthrow and, if possible, a transfer?

But all this is too obvious. I would rather argue with those who think that by excluding the Romanists from political power we make them more attached to their religion, and cause them to unite more strongly in support of it. Were this true to the extent maintained, we should still have to balance between the unorganised power which they derive from a sense of injustice real or supposed, and the legitimate organised power which concession would confer upon surviving discontent; for no one, I imagine, is weak enough to suppose that discontent would disappear. But it is a deception, and a most dangerous one, to conclude that if a free passage were given to the torrent, it would lose, by diffusion, its ability to do injury. The checks, as your Lordship well knows, which are after a time necessary to provoke other sects to activity are not wanted here: the Roman Church stands independent of them through its constitution so exquisitely contrived, and through its doctrine and discipline, which give a peculiar and monstrous power to its priesthood. In proof of this, take the injunction of celibacy alone, separating the priesthood from the body of the community, and the practice of confession making them masters of the conscience, while the doctrines give them an absolute power over the will. To submit to such thraldom, men must be bigoted in its favour: and that we see is the case in Spain, in Portugal, in Austria, in Italy, in Flanders, in Ireland, and in all countries where you have Papacy in full blow. And does not history prove that, however other sects may have languished under the relaxing influence of good fortune, Papacy has ever been most fiery and rampant when most prosperous.

But many who do not expect that conciliation will be the result of concession have a further expedient on which they rely much. They propose to take the Romish Church in Ireland into pay,[1] and expect that afterwards its clergy will be as compliant to the Government as the Presbyterians in that country have proved.

---

[1] Wellington had proposed payment and licencing of the Irish priests, but the plan was dropped after objections from the English bishops.

This measure is, in the first place, too disingenuous not to be condemned by honest men; for the Government acting on this policy would degrade itself by offering bribes to men of a sacred calling to act contrary to their sense of duty. If they be sincere, as Priests, and truly spiritual-minded, they will find it impossible to accept of a stipend known to be granted with such expectation. If they be worldlings and false of heart, they will practise double dealing, and seem to support the Government while they are actually undermining it; for they know that if they be suspected of sacrificing the interests of the Church they will lose all authority over their flocks. Power and consideration are more valued than money. The Priests will not be induced to risk their sway over the people for any sums that our Government would venture to afford them out of the exhausted revenues of the Empire. Surely they would prefer to such a scanty hire the hope of carving for themselves from the property of the Protestant Church of their country, or even the gratification of stripping usurpation, for such they deem it, of its gains, though there may be no hope to win what others are deprived of. Many English favourers of this scheme are reconciled to what they call a modification of the Irish Protestant Establishment, in an application of a portion of the revenues to the support of the Romish Church. This they deem reasonable. Shortly it will be openly aimed at, and they will rejoice should they accomplish their purpose. But your Lordship will agree with me, that if that happen it would be one of the most calamitous events that ignorance has in our time given birth to. After all, could the *Secular* Clergy be paid out of this spoliation, or in any other way, the *Regulars* would rise in consequence of their degradation; and where would be the influence that could keep them from mischief? They would swarm over the country to prey upon the people still more than they now do. In all the reasonings of the friends to this bribing scheme the distinctive character of the Papal Church is overlooked.

But they who expect that tranquillity will be a permanent consequence of the Relief Bill, dwell much upon the mighty difference in opinion and feeling between the upper and lower ranks of the Romish Communion. They affirm that many keep within the pale of the Church as a point of honour; that others have notions greatly relaxed, and though not at present prepared to separate they will gradually fall off. But what avail the inward sentiments of men if they are convinced that by acting upon them they will forfeit their outward dignity and power? As long as the political influence which the Priests now exercise shall endure, or any thing like it, the great Proprietors will be obliged to dissemble and to conform in their actions to the demands of that power. Such will be the conduct of the great Roman Catholic proprietors; nay, further, I agree with those who deem it probable that through a natural and reasonable desire to have their property duly represented, many landholders who are now Protestants will be tempted to go over to Papacy. This may be thought a poor compliment to Protestantism, since religious scruples, it is said, are all that keep the Papists out: but is not the desire to be in, pushing them on almost to rebellion at this moment? We are taking, I own, a melancholy view of both sides; but *human* nature, be it what it may, must by legislators be looked at as it is.

In the treatment of this question we hear perpetually of wrong, but the wrong is all on one side. If the political power of Ireland is to be a transfer from those who are of the state-religion of the Country to those who are not, there is nothing gained on the score of justice. We hear also much of *stigma*; but this is not to be done away with unless all offices, the Privy Council, and the Chancellorship,[1] be open to them; that is, unless we allow a man to be eligible to keep the King's conscience who has not his own in his keeping, unless we open the Throne itself to men of this soul-degrading faith.

The condition of Ireland is indeed, and has long been, wretched. Lamentable is it to acknowledge that the mass of her people are so grossly uninformed, and from that cause subject to such delusions and passions, that they would destroy each other were it not for restraints put upon them by a power out of themselves. This power it is that protracts their existence in a state for which otherwise the course of Nature would provide a remedy by reducing their numbers through mutual destruction, so that English civilisation may fairly be said to have been the shield of Irish barbarism. And now these swarms of degraded people, which could not have existed but through the neglect and misdirected power of the sister island, are, by a withdrawing of that power, to have their own way, and to be allowed to dictate to us. A population vicious in character and unnatural in immediate origin (for it has been called into birth by short-sighted landlords set upon adding to the number of voters at their command, and by Priests, who for lucre's sake favor the increase of marriages) is held forth, as constituting a claim to

---

[1] The Lord Chancellorship was not opened to Roman Catholics until 1974.

political power, strong in proportion to its numbers; though, in a sane view, that claim is in an inverse ratio to them. Brute force, indeed, wherever lodged, as we are too feelingly taught at present, must be measured and met—measured with care, in order to be met with fortitude.

The chief proximate causes of Irish misery and ignorance[1] are Papacy, of which I have said so much, and the tenure and management of landed property; and both these have a common origin, viz. the imperfect conquest of the country. The countries subjected by the ancient Romans, and those that in the Middle Ages were subdued by the northern tribes, afford striking instances of the several ways in which nations may be improved by foreign conquests. The Romans, by their superiority in arts and arms, and, in the earlier period of their history, in virtues also, may seem to have established a moral right to force their institutions upon other nations, whether under a process of decline, or emerging from barbarism; and this they effected, we all know, not by over-running countries as eastern conquerors have done,—and Buonaparte, in our own days,—but by completing a regular subjugation, with military roads and garrisons, which became centres of civilisation for the surrounding district. Nor am I afraid to add, tho' the fact might be caught at, as bearing against the general scope of my argument, that *both* conquerors and conquered owed much to the participation of civil rights which the Romans liberally communicated. The other mode of conquest, that pursued by the northern nations, brought about its beneficial effects, by the settlement of a hardy and vigorous people among the distracted and effeminate nations against whom their incursions were made. The conquerors transplanted with them their independent and ferocious spirit, to reanimate exhausted communities; and in their turn received a salutary mitigation, till in process of time the conqueror and conquered, having a common interest, were lost in each other. To neither of these modes was unfortunate Ireland subject; and her insular territory, by physical obstacles, and still more by moral influences arising out of them, has aggravated the evil consequent upon independence, lost as hers was. The writers[2] of the time of Queen Eliz[abeth] have pointed out how unwise it was to transplant among a barbarous people, not half subjugated, the institutions

---

[1] W. W. is repeating here much of the argument of his letter to Sir Robert Inglis of 11 June 1825 (pt. i, L. 178).

[2] Particularly Spenser. See E. W. Marjarum, 'Wordsworth's View of the State of Ireland', *PMLA* lv (1940), 608–11.

that time had matured among those who too readily considered themselves as masters of that people. It would be presumptuous in me to advert in detail to the exacerbations and long-lived hatred that has perverted the moral sense in Ireland, obstructed religious knowledge, and denied to her a due share of English refinement and civility. It is enough to observe that the Reformation was ill supported in that country, and that her soil became, through frequent forfeitures, mainly possessed by men whose hearts were not in the land where their wealth lay.

But it is too late, we are told, for retrospection. We have no choice between giving way and a sanguinary war. Surely it is rather too much that the country should be required to take the measure of the threatened evil from a Cabinet which by its being divided against itself,[1] which by its remissness and fear of long and harassing debates in the two houses, has for many years past fostered the evil, and in no small part created the danger, the extent of which is now urged as imposing the necessity of granting the demands. Danger is a relative thing, and the first requisite for being in a condition to judge of what we have to dread from the physical force of the Romanists, is to be in sympathy with the Protestants. Had our ministers been truly so, could they have suffered themselves to be bearded by the Catholic Association for so many years as they have been?

I speak openly to you, my Lord, though a Member of his Majesty's Privy Council; and, begging your pardon for detaining you so long, I hasten to a conclusion.

The civil disabilities, for the removal of which Mr O'Connell[2] and his followers are braving the government, cannot but be indifferent to the great body of the Irish nation, except as means for gaining an end. Take away the intermediate power of the priests, and an insurrection in Brobdignag at the call of the K[ing] of Lilliput, might be as hopefully expected as that the Irish people would stir, as they now do, at the call of a political Demagogue. Now these civil disabilities do not directly affect the Priests; they therefore must have ulterior views: and though it must be flattering to their vanity to show that they have the Irish representa-

---

[1] The cabinet had been divided over the Catholic question the previous year, and Goulburn had voted with Peel against Burdett's motion in favour of concession in the May.

[2] In June 1828 O'Connell had been returned in the by-election for Co. Clare, but was ineligible to sit. Wellington and Peel feared that the Catholic Association would repeat their tactics elsewhere, and that an Irish rebellion might result.

tion in their own hands, and though their worldly interest and that of their connections will, they know, immediately profit by that dominion, what they look for principally is, the advancement of their religion at the cost of protestantism; that would bring every thing else in its train. While it is obvious that the political agitators could not rouse the people without the intervention of the Priests, it is true, also, that the Priests could not excite the people without a hope that from the exaltation of their Ch: their social condition would be improved. What in Irish interpretation these words would mean we may tremble to think of.

In whatever way we look, religion is so much mixed up in this matter, that the Guardians of the Episcopal Ch: of the Empire are imperiously called upon to shew themselves worthy of the high trust reposed in them. You, my Lord, are convinced that in spite of the best securities that can be given the admission of Roman Catholics into the legislature is a dangerous experiment. Oaths cannot be framed that will avail here; the only securities to be relied upon are what we have little hope to see—the R Ch: *reforming itself*, and a parliament and a ministry sufficiently sensible of the superiority of the one form of religion over the other, to be resolved, not only to preserve the present rights and immunities of the Protestant Church inviolate, but prepared, by all fair means, for the *extension* of its influence, with a hope that it may gradually prevail over Popery.

It is, we trust, the intention of Providence that the Ch: of Rome should in due time disappear; and come what may of the Ch: of E., we have the satisfaction of knowing, that in defending a Government resting upon a Protestant basis, which, say what they will, the other Party have abandoned, we are working for the welfare of human kind, and supporting whatever there is of dignity in our frail nature.

Here I might stop; but I am above measure anxious for the course which the Bench of Bishops may take at this crisis: they are appealed to, and even by the Heir presumptive to the Throne,[1] from his seat in Parliament. There will be an attempt to browbeat them on the score of humanity; but humanity is, if it deserves the name, a calculating and prospective quality; it will on this occasion balance an evil at hand with an infinitely greater one that

[1] Ernest Augustus, Duke of Cumberland, later King of Hanover (1771–1851), fifth son of George III, and a staunch opponent of Catholic emancipation. He was a strong influence on his irresolute brother the King, who was extremely reluctant to make any concessions.

is sure, or all but sure, to come. Humanity is not shewn the less by firmness than by tenderness of heart; it is neither deterred by clamour, nor enfeebled by its own sadness; but it estimates evil and good to the best of its power, acts by the dictates of conscience, and trusts the issue to the Ruler of all things.

If, my Lord, I have seemed to write with overconfidence in any opinion I have given above, impute it to a wish of avoiding cumbrous qualifying expressions.

Sincerely do I pray that God may give your Lordship and the rest of your Brethren light to guide you, and strength to walk in that light.

[I am, my Lord, etc.
W. Wordsworth]¹

417. W. W. to VISCOUNT LOWTHER

Address: The Lord Viscount Lowther, Spring Gardens, London.
Endorsed: Mr Wordsworth. Reduction of Distributors' allowance.
Postmark: 11 Mar. 1829. *Stamp*: Kendal Penny Post.
MS. Lonsdale MSS. Hitherto unpublished.

Rydal Mount
March 9ᵗʰ 1829—

Private
My dear Lord Lowther,

I am sorry to break in upon you at this busy time; but having received the Enclosed² this morning I hope you will excuse my begging your advice in what answer I ought to give it. Before you proceed with this, pray be so kind as to read the Letter.

If I rightly understand Mr Smith he means that Memorials should be presented individually unless a meeting of the Dist:ᵇʳˢ in London should be thought expedient.—May I ask if you think their interest would be promoted by such meeting, or that it would be better that each should separately memorialize, if so inclined?

The regulations within the last 18 months established, have increased the Distributor's trouble and anxiety incalculably, and if their profits are to undergo a further Reduction the proceeding would be obviously the reverse of the dictates of natural justice

---

¹ These last words are not in the MS. but are taken from the first printed text in *Mem.*, which presumably follows the text of the letter as sent.
² A letter from George Smith, Distributor for Nottinghamshire, informing W. W. that there might be a move by Ministers to reduce the rate of poundage allowed to Distributors.

unless the reduction be intended to apply only to Distributors hereafter to be appointed.

I remain my dear Lord L.
faithfully yours
Wm Wordsworth

418. W. W. to WILLIAM WHEWELL

Address: The Revd William Whewell etc etc, Trin: Coll: Cambridge ⌈*In Dora W.'s hand*⌉
Stamp: Kendal Penny Post.
MS. Trinity College, Cambridge. Hitherto unpublished.

Rydal Mount
March 12th, 1829—

My dear Sir,

I owe you thanks upon two accounts, for the detail of your underground labours;[1] and for your Commemoration Sermon.[2] It is worthy of the occasion, though I will take the Liberty of saying that it opens rather inauspiciously the first Sentence being unusually cumbrous for so few words.

But where the subject rises proud to view
With equal strength the Preacher rises to.

In the same parcel I received Orlandus,[3] a Present, I *suppose*, from the Author, for that no where appears; at all events if you or any one about you be in communication with him, pray let him be thanked heartily for the Pleasure I have had from the Company to which his Book has introduced me. Never did an Author's pages reflect the man so livelily as do these, and their precursors; and when the man is worthy of being reflected what a charm is that. Scarcely any thing in writing equal to it! In these delightful Volumes there is as much truth as there can be in Pictures where only one side is looked at—and foul befal the man who should with rival

[1] In Cornwall. See pt. i, L. 382.
[2] At the College Commemoration on 17 Dec. 1828. See Whewell's *Sermons Preached in the Chapel of Trinity College, Cambridge*, 1847, pp. 324 ff. The sermon begins: 'We are now met here to celebrate the return of a day, on which our ordinances call upon us annually to revive the feelings arising from our relation to the Institution within whose walls we live.'
[3] The fourth book of the enlarged version of *The Broad Stone of Honour* (see pt. i, L. 376), in which Kenelm Henry Digby explored the ethos of medieval chivalry.

zeal present the other as faithfully. The Catholic Religion to the Knightly Digby is a solemn glowing evening sky where the colours are fixed. In poetical moods, though I wish to see it under that aspect it is apt to appear to me as a piece of shot silk in which even the brightest part is subject to gloom, not cast upon it from without, but inherent in its nature and constitution. Yet I go willingly and thankfully with Digby's faith as far as I can—and as to Chivalry I would a thousand times rather take his delicate Extracts of it than face the good *and* the *bad* of its genuine annuals.[1]—

Preferring old lights to new, Oxford[2] is in greater favour with me at present than Cambridge. The latter has within my memory shown herself rather too often a time-serving Lady. She might have redeemed herself lately but lost the golden, some of her Sons would say the *leaden*, opportunity. *Leaden* then be it if we of another disposition, do indeed deserve the opprobrium.—Bear with us, and let us bear with each other. Yet believing, as sincerely as I do, that your University on the late momentous occasion was in no small degree above selfish considerations, and acted as she thought best for the general weal, I may be allowed to express a hope that you had more philosophy to guide you than appears in the House of Commons in behalf of concession.[3] If you have not, woe for the Country and its Institutions one of which[4] you have so feelingly panegyrized. Perhaps I am wrong, yet I cannot but think that there are orders of men, the hereditary Legislators and Bishops for instance and the leaders of learned Bodies, upon whom it is *especially* incumbent to resist and to check; and to be less afraid of error through reverence for, and confidence in, the past, than through dazzling hopes of the future.[5] The Relief-bill, notwithstanding all the pains that have been taken to prove the contrary, is in respect to things enacted and confirmed in 1688 a counter-

[1] i.e. annals.

[2] On 20 Feb. Peel had resigned his seat for Oxford University on changing his view of the Catholic question, and sought re-election. In the ensuing contest with Sir Robert Inglis (see pt. i, L. 178) he was defeated by 755 votes to 609, but was returned immediately afterwards for Westbury. Both the Oxford representatives voted against the Catholic Relief Bill. Inglis's fellow-member was Thomas Grimston Estcourt (1775–1853), a barrister: M.P. for Oxford University, 1827–47.

[3] Both of the Cambridge University members, Lord Palmerston (see pt. i, L. 212) and Sir Nicholas Tindal (see pt. i, L. 290), voted in favour of the Bill.

[4] The Established Church, which Whewell had upheld in his Commemoration Sermon.

[5] In a letter to W. W. of 20 Jan. about the Catholic question and Cambridge University politics, Whewell had written: 'I agree with you entirely that persons officially connected with our academic bodies as well as others who are

revolutionary measure and it has a like bearing upon a far more antient inheritance—the alliance of church and state. So much the better cry out the Liberals; but how do I make my point clear. By the very joy you are expressing, I should answer—and by the dissentions which are at hand in the Legislature between the Protestants (or rather Church of England men) and the Papist members, who while they are quarrelling about their temporals will give an opening to the Liberals for the destruction of Both. It is not the first time that popery and freethinking (take the word in its largest sense) have been united against our church. Do not style those who think in this way Bigots or feeble-minded alarmists, I pray you. Religion doing its own work in a vast empire is a beautiful Theory, and so is Republicanism; both streams flow from pure fountains in the Ideal, but let us beware of reckoning foul or distasteful the waters which this noble nation has so long drank of. Farewell.

W. W.

I *have* Sir Uvedale's[1] Letter.—

419. W. W. to C. W.

Address: The Revd Dr Wordsworth Trinity Coll: Cambridge. ⌈*In M.W.'s hand*⌉
Stamp: Kendal Penny Post.
MS. WL.
LY i. 368.

⌈13 Mar. 1829⌉

My dear Brother,
    You are sometimes in communication with your Friend the Chancellor of the Ex:[2]—could you convey to him the substance of

elevated by the civil and religious institutions of the country, should consider themselves as most particularly bound to resist the busy and impatient love of change and to keep steady and secure the maxims and institutions which have descended from other times and have grown with and formed the character of the people. But these persons, if they form themselves into a party which resists unrelentingly all interference and change, . . . cannot I think at present maintain their ground or benefit the country. And for my own part also I cannot conceive otherwise than human institutions must be, slowly no doubt and reverently, but still from time to time, modified . . . to accommodate themselves to the ever changing relations and forms of society which the tendency of ages brings into existence. I cannot therefore consider the immutability of the forms of our constituted legislative body essential to its excellence . . .' (*WL MSS.*)

[1] Sir Uvedale Price.

[2] Henry Goulburn (see pt. i, L. 212).

this Letter.—I have just been informed by a Brother Distributor,[1] that it is intended to make a further Reduction in our allowance— upon what scale I know not, nor how it is to be regulated. If, as most probable, it is to bear upon the present Distributors, to that part of them who undertook the office before the *last* Reduction it will be a great hardship, not to say more; among these I am, with the additional cause of Complaint, that my returns are small, on an average, 19,000 per ann:— When the former Reduction took place, part of the burthen was thrown by the Distributors on their Subs—but that Relief can be carried no farther. In my own case, I would observe, that I have been served during the whole time I have held the off:—nearly 16 years, by the same Clerk. In consideration of these services, his salary is now encreased to three times what it was at first—and till I heard of these intentions of the Treasury, I cherished a hope of being able to add still further to it upon some future occasion. If the Reduction bears upon men whose profits are as small as mine, I must abandon that hope; and for aught I know be forced on the verge of sixty to retire, and live abroad—till my younger Son is educated, and obtains some situation. The trouble of the office has been encreased since I entered upon it, incalculably; and more work and less pay, prolonged service and diminished salary is surely the Reverse of a dictate of natural justice. I have only to add that since I held the Stamps, 24 hours have not elapsed, save once, for a very few days, without myself, or one of my nearest connections being present. Excuse all this, of which indeed there is too much.—I have, however, omitted one important particular, that a Clerk is an indispensable part of a Distributor's establishment —his presence being frequently called for in different parts of his district, and the Board also requiring him to make inspections among those who act under him. Before the last Reduction took place the Treasury made a Minute, that it should not take effects upon the then existing Distributors—so convinced were they of the hardship of such a measure—but that considerate resolution was rescinded.

I turn to a more important subject, upon which nothing has passed between us. The part of the King's speech[2] which related to the Catholics gave me infinite concern. My apprehensions are in no degree abated by Mr Peele's speech,[3] nor can I be made to think by any thing I have yet heard that concession was expedient notwithstanding the remissness and errors of Government had to

[1] See L. 417 above.   [2] On 5 Feb. (see L. 414 above).
[3] On 5 Mar., introducing the new Catholic Relief Bill.

many made it seem necessary. Ireland was improving more rapidly perhaps than any Country in Europe, and nothing was wanting but a firm hand on the part of Great Britain to carry things forward in a still more promising way. The embarrassments of a divided Cabinet, and of an undecided parliament might have been got over, in Lord Liverpool's time, had he been a man of more political courage, and so might they have been by the Duke, if he would have thrown himself fairly upon the protestant feeling of the Country. I am no Friend of appeals to the people upon unnecessary occasions, but this was one that justified such a measure. Mr Peel does not treat the case with a sufficient sense of its magnitude, when he rejects every test of the people's judgement but the voice of parliament; nor, if his position could be admitted has he dealt with that test fairly. The result of the several elections afforded no proof that the people were reconciled to concession. As has been well observed in Parliament, they had confidence in Mr Percival[1] and Lord Liverpool, besides, as the cry of 'the Wolf is coming' had been so often heard that they almost ceased to regard it, the Returns of Members were naturally governed by ordinary party ties and interests. Nevertheless, where there were Contests, and this the only important part of the case seems to have been overlooked by Mr Peele, the Antipopery Candidate, I presume, had always the advantage. I am sure it was decisively so in Westmorland. Little as the people were alarmed, Mr Brougham lost several of his adherents on account of his attachment to the Catholic Cause; I mean at his last trial for the County,[2] and had that been the first, it would have affected his interests very much more—but people had chosen their sides, and honour bound them. The Catholic cause being now taken up by government, its opponents have lost much, but I am strongly persuaded, were Parliament dissolved and any man could be found of fortune sufficient to stand a Contest in Cumberland upon the Anticatholic principle, Sir James Graham[3] (who has been made the Instrument for uttering so many untruths in the House upon the Whitehaven Petition) would be thrown out, and *two* Anticatholics would sit for that County; though the cause would be under great disadvantages, there, from a political wish among many to be as far as they can in opposition to the powerful

[1] While Spencer Perceval (see pt. i, L. 354) was Prime Minister, the government had resisted all attempts to reconsider the Catholic question.
[2] In the election of 1826.
[3] Sir James Robert Graham (see *MT* ii. 536) had been elected for Cumberland on the death of J. C. Curwen (see pt. i, L. 391). The other member was Sir John Lowther, Bart. (see *MT* ii. 581).

family of Lowther. Nor would it be prudent in that House to attempt influencing a return for the other Cumberland members, even upon this constitutional call. But I have dwelt too long upon a local topic. Mr Peele's securities are not worth a rush. If by the swearing not to exercise the privilege for disturbing or weakening the Protestant religion, is meant (and what else can it mean after the provisions for the security of the Church Establishment and the right of property) that he who *takes* the oath will not promote any measure by speaking or voting, that may seem to be injurious to that Religion, the proposed oath[1] is *monstrous*, as it requires a man to abstain from what he is bound by a higher engagement to attempt; and it is *absurd* from its regard of the passions of human nature, and the subtleties of conscience, especially in a Romanist. And as to the disavowal of intention to subvert the P. Church, what should hinder but that the same power, called into action by Demagogues and Pries[ts] should be brought to demand the Repeal of this Oath as supporting an oppression intolerable to the Irish People, and palsying their Representatives in a vital quarter. This demand would undoubtedly be resisted on the ground that the Interests of the whole Empire are not to be sacrificed to those of a part. But such just views will not appease the Irish Priesthood, nor satisfy the People. The *Priests* will acquire no *direct benefit* by the Relief Bill, they who have done the work are to have no part of the pay—if they be men they must resent this, and they will point with shouting thousands at their heels, to the Disproportion between the number of the C—s and P—s, and the enormous wealth and invidious grandeur of a Church which they are taught is not of God; and which they know to be a Usurper, and if not a righteous one to be put down. But I am at the end of my paper. I am proud of your conduct and the Vicemaster's.[2] I had occasion yesterday to write to Mr Whewel[3]—the latter part of my Letter I should like you to see, as it touches upon the Conduct of Cambridge

> farewell most faithfully and affectionately
> yours W. W.

---

[1] It was proposed that a new oath be administered to Roman Catholics as a test of their civil worth, in place of the previous oaths and declarations by which they had been excluded. The declaration against transubstantiation was to be dropped, and a new Oath of Supremacy substituted in which Catholics were specifically required to abjure all intention of subverting the Church Establishment.

[2] The Revd. John Henry Renouard (1758–1830), Fellow of Trinity from 1783, and Vice-Master from 1806.

[3] See previous letter.

When I say that the securities are not worth a rush—I mean no reflection upon the Law officers who framed them. There can be no solid security, but the Catholic religion entering upon a Reform of itself; and a government in sympathy with the Protestants and sensible of the infinite superiority, if upon political consideration only, of one Religion to the other.

We were rejoiced at Chris's success,[1] and sit crosslegged for Charles[2]—Keswick John[3] is here with us on his way to Hawkshead, but happily the measles came out upon him, and are passed away.

When I was in Town, I undertook to thank you in the name of Mr Southey, then confined to his bed, for your Reply to the Gaudenists,[4] he thinks your tract triumphant, but I despair of his being able to review the subject in the Quarterly. I will mention it to him.

Pray do not destroy this letter.

[*Dora W. writes*]

My dear Uncle

I seize upon this little corner to offer my best thanks for your kind and highly prized Gift 'The Christian Year'[5] and would you say to Chris that I had intended writing to him this very day but when I found my Father was preparing a Letter for you I thought two Rydal Letters, in one day, was rather over-doing the thing so shall defer mine till another occasion—

Your very affectionate and grateful Niece

Dora Wordsworth

I dare say you do not know that you call me *Grand* Daughter in my little book.

---

[1] C. W. jnr. had just won the Craven Scholarship. See L. 415 above.
[2] Charles Wordsworth was an unsuccessful candidate for the Ireland Scholarship at Oxford.
[3] R. W.'s son, now at Hawkshead School.
[4] See pt. i, Ls. 151, 362.
[5] The celebrated volume of poems for the Sundays and holy days of the year by John Keble (see pt. i, L. 86), published in 1827.

420. W. W. to C. W.

Address: Revd Dr Wordsworth, Trinity Lodge, Cambridge [*In M.W.'s hand*]
Stamp: Kendal Penny Post.
MS. WL.
LY i. 372.

Mar 15th [1829]

My dear Brother,

I am obliged to write again. Lord Lowther thinks that any Reduction[1] which may take place will be confined to new Appointments—and advises me not to be hasty but to trust to the justice of the Treasury. I hope therefore this Letter may be in time to prevent you acting upon mine of Friday—unless you should hear that such Reduction is intended. I should nevertheless not be sorry, if an opportunity occurred (in Conversation particularly,) that Mr G—[2] should know how heavily such a Reduction would press upon me.

By the bye, when I was at Keswick not long since, Mrs Lightfoot[3] and her Husband alluded in a manner *very disagreeable* to me—to the Promissory Note, for which you were joint Security with her former Husband, and which was discharged out of his Estate:— I told her I could not remember the particulars, but I was certain that you were exonerated from that obligation. Pray let me know the particulars that I may put my foot upon such observations— I fear that they who survive to settle these affairs will be harassed by the Petyfogger with whom she has connected herself.—John[4] (I am glad to say) has got charmingly through the measles; he is an excellent Arithmetician for his years, and an admirable pen-man, seems too pretty fond of English Reading,—but of Latin he knows very little. I was truly glad that our dear and excellent Sister was with you,[5] and saw all her Nephews of whom she is so proud, and to whom she is so much attached.—I wish she could have stayed longer with you.—I was much pleased with the improvement of my Son John—he has a very sound understanding, great zeal, an admirable temper; and is now making steady advances in the practise of Composition, to which he had never been trained—I made many attempts to put him upon it, but always failed; his time was not come; which is another proof added, to the many I have

---

[1] In the allowance to Distributors.
[2] Henry Goulburn, Chancellor of the Exchequer.
[3] R. W.'s widow had now married John Lightfoot, attorney, of Keswick.
[4] R. W.'s son.
[5] See L. 415 above.

had that one should never despond—As a Preacher he has one gift of nature, a voice at once powerful and sweet, which when he is more perfect in the management of it, would fit him for a large Church and Congregation; which upon a proper occasion I should like the Archbishop of C—or Bp of London to know—for I am sure Churches in the Metropolis, especially if Gothic ones, require Readers and Preachers with a strong voice.—Many thanks for your invitation to Wm—before he goes abroad.—I hope he will make a good use of his time—he seems strongly inclined to do so— but for so clever a Lad he is the most unbookish I ever knew. One thing is remarkable, that his Letters are written in a most easy fluent, and sometimes elegant Style, though he has scarcely written half a dozen in his whole life—except now and then a note on some little business or trivial concern. I wish him by all [me]ans to visit you.—I wrote very reluctantly to the Bp of London on the C—Q— at considerable length,[1] and not at all to my own satisfaction.— I had not left myself time to do justice to any of the points. Pray remember me most kindly to Mr Rose. My Notes upon education[2] are not to be understood as if I were averse to the people being educated, quite the contrary. My wish was to guard against too high expectations—from that source, and to glance upon some grievous errors.—Lord Lowther tells me that neither the Friends nor opponents of concession were the least aware of what was intended till they were informed by the King's Speech.—Southey in a note I had from him yesterday, calls it Conspiracy. It certainly had, in this secrecy one feature of such action.—farewell, love again to you and yours—

W. W.

The Education most wanted is an improvement in the public Schools preparatory to one in the Universities.

I cannot help being anxious about Charles's success[3]—I wish it was over—

---

[1] L. 416 above on the Catholic question.
[2] i.e. L. 408 above to Hugh James Rose.
[3] In the competition for the Ireland Scholarship. See previous letter.

421. W. W. to GEORGE SMITH[1]

MS. *Harvard University Library.*
K (—). *LY i. 374.*

Rydal Mount
Near Ambleside
16th March 1829

Sir,

Accept my thanks for your Intelligence which was new to me. More work and less pay—prolonged service, and diminished Salary, are surely the Reverse of a dictate of natural justice; and this the Treasury know as well, and some of them perhaps as feelingly, as we do.—I have written to an experienced Friend[2] to advise with him what is best to be done, and when I receive his answer I shall trouble you with another Letter—I write this merely to thank you, and least you should deem me insensible of the wish you have expressed to be useful on this unpleasant occasion.

I remain Sir
Your obliged Servant
W[m] Wordsworth

422. W. W. to GEORGE HUNTLY GORDON

MS. *Cornell.*
Broughton, p. 16.

March 20th. [1829]

My dear Sir,

It seems an age since I heard from you. In my last hurried Letter, I left two points unnoticed as I expected to have had occasion before this to recur to them. I mean the intended Welsh Tour[3]— and the little Russian Poem.[4] You shall see it the first time I have the pleasure of seeing you; as to the Tour when will you be at liberty yourself[?] This is the main point—as my Sister and I are much more our own Masters than you are.—Any time not late in the Season, as far as I can now see would suit us.

---

[1] Distributor of Stamps for Nottinghamshire. See L. 417 above.
[2] Presumably Lord Lowther. See previous letter.
[3] The Welsh tour was cancelled owing to D. W.'s illness the following month. See next letter.
[4] *The Russian Fugitive.* See L. 409 above.

My son W^m's present address is *Whitwick* near Ashby de la Zouche; as soon as you learn any thing of the movements of Mr Pappendick and the probable length of his stay in England, I should be obliged if you would inform my Son—as it is his intention to visit his Uncle and Cousins at Trin Coll Camb. before he comes to Town—Meanwhile would you be so kind as to send him (if conveyable in a Frank) the Sheet-Gram[m]ar of the German language, mentioned in the Teacher's Card you sent me. I trouble you with this Commission supposing it to be a useful thing—You will judge if it be so—W^m will pay you for it, when he gets to London.—

I have not yet seen the Tuesday's Debates—Mr Peele's Speech[1] did not satisfy me.—I think the Favorers of Concession are influenced by principles too abstract for the present state of knowledge—Equality of civil rights without regard to Religious belief, and the sufficiency of the Church of England including Ireland to defend herself, as to her doctrines believing her to be a true Church I doubt not she is, but as to her immunities and property which are creatures of Law, I demur, farewell—

faithfully yours
Wm Wordsworth

423. W. W. to CATHERINE GRACE GODWIN[2]

MS. untraced.
The Poetical Works of the Late Catherine Grace Godwin, ed. A. Cleveland Wigan, *1854, p. v. K. LY i. 438.*

[Spring 1829]

Dear Madam,

I have long been in your debt—so long that I regret not having written my acknowledgment on the day I received your book. This

[1] Introducing the new Catholic Relief Bill on 5 Mar.
[2] Catherine Grace Godwin (1798–1845), second daughter of Dr. Thomas Garnett, Professor of Chemistry at the Royal Institution, had published in 1824 some rather crude verses which attracted the attention of W. W., Southey, and John Wilson. The same year she married Thomas Godwin (d. 1852) of the East India Company, and settled at Barbon, near Kirkby Lonsdale. Her next volume, *The Wanderer's Legacy; A Collection of Poems, On Various Subjects*, appeared in 1829 with a dedication to W. W. dated 'Burnside, November 1, 1828'. She was a prolific writer for the magazines and annuals.

would have been done, but I felt there would be little value in such a return for the mark of respect you have paid me; and I relied on your candid interpretation of any delay that might take place. I wished to read your volume carefully through before you heard from me. I have done so, and with much pleasure. Wherever it is read, such poetry cannot but do you honour. It is neither wanting in feeling, nor in that much rarer gift which is the soul of poetry, Imagination. There is a great command of language also, and occasionally fine versification; but here, and in some other points of workmanship, you are most defective, especially in the blank verse. Am I right in supposing that several of these pieces have been written at different periods of life? 'The Wanderer', for example, though full of varied interest, appears to me, in point of versification, and in some respects of style, much inferior to 'Destiny', a very striking poem. This, and the 'Monk of Camaldoli' are, in my judgment, the best *executed* pieces in the volume. Both evince extraordinary powers.

The fault of your blank verse is, that it is not sufficiently broken. You are aware that it is infinitely the most difficult metre to manage, as is clear from so few having succeeded in it. The Spenserian stanza is a fine structure of verse; but that is also almost insurmountably difficult. You have succeeded in the broken and more impassioned movement—of which Lord Byron has given good instances—but it is a form of verse ill adapted to conflicting passion; and it is not injustice to say that the stanza is spoiled in Lord Byron's hands; his own strong and ungovernable passions blinded him to its character. It is equally unfit for narrative. *Circumstances* are difficult to manage in any kind of verse, except the dramatic, where the warmth of the action makes the reader indifferent to those delicacies of phrase and sound upon which so much of the charm of other poetry depends. If you write more in this stanza, leave Lord Byron for Spenser. In him the stanza is seen in its perfection. It is exquisitely harmonious also in Thomson's hands[1] and fine in Beattie's 'Minstrel'; but these two latter poems are merely descriptive and sentimental; and you will observe that Spenser never gives way to violent and conflicting passion, and that his narrative is bare of circumstances, slow in movement, and (for modern relish) too much clogged with description. Excuse my dwelling so much on this dry subject; but as you have succeeded so well in the arrangement of this metre, perhaps you will not be

---

[1] In *The Castle of Indolence*, a favourite poem of W. W.'s.

sorry to hear my opinion of its character. One great objection to it (an insurmountable one, I think, for circumstantial narrative) is the poverty of our language in rhymes.

But to recur to your volume. I was everywhere more or less interested in it. Upon the whole I think I like best 'Destiny' and the 'Monk', but mainly for the reasons above given. The 'Wanderer's Legacy' being upon a large scale, and so true to your own feelings, has left a lively impression upon my mind, and a moral purpose is answered, by exhibiting youthful love under such illusion with regard to the real value of its object. The 'Seal Hunters' is an affecting poem, but I think you linger too long in the prelusive description. I could speak with pleasure of many other pieces, so that you have no grounds for the apprehensions you express—as far, at least, as I am concerned.

As, most likely, the beauties of this country will tempt you and Mr Godwin to return to it, I need not say that I should be happy to renew my acquaintance with you both; and I should with pleasure avail myself of that opportunity, to point out certain minutiae of phrase in your volume, where you have been misled by bad example, especially of the Scotch. The popularity of some of their writings has done no little harm to the English language, for the present at least.

Believe me, etc.
W. Wordsworth

424. W. W. to GEORGE HUNTLY GORDON

MS. Cornell.
Broughton, p. 16.

[*In Dora W.'s hand*]

Rydal Mount
April 9th 1829

My dear Sir

An inflammation in one of my eyes obliges me to employ an Amanuensis to thank you for your last letter and your attention in forwarding the Grammar to my Son who expresses himself as much pleased with it; but it grieves me to say that his studies of every kind have been almost set aside by a dangerous illness with which his Aunt has been visited.[1] He and his Brother are at present the only Relatives who are with her but Mrs Wordsworth who left us yesterday will we trust reach their Abode this night. The Disease was an internal inflammation and her medical attendants have pronounced her to be out of danger but she is reduced to such weakness that she cannot stand and can scarcely speak. I mention this to you not only on account of the concern which you will feel on the occasion for she is my only sister, and we have lived together for the last 35 years—but because this afflicting event has almost taken from me the hope that should she recover, she will be able to enter upon exertions so great as a Tour in North Wales this summer; at all events I think the possibility of her undertaking such a Tour ought not to stand in the way of your making any other engagement for your summer Holidays. Septe[r] would certainly be too late for us; the days are then too short for persons of our age.

I am much grieved to hear of Mr Papendick's indisposition—It is not likely that I shall come to Town this Spring which I have many reasons to regret and not the least the opportunity it would have given me of renewing my acquaintance with you and of seeing Mr Papendick and his Sister Mrs Oom. Mrs Wordsworth is gone to nurse her Sister which if I could have done as well I would have undertaken the office and she would have remained here with her daughter; and I being brought so much nearer to Cambridge and London would have certainly accompanied my Son William to both places in case of my dear Sister's recovery.

The necessity which reconciles you to the Relief bill does not produce the same effect upon my mind—nor do I think that it ought upon any ones, who is not prepared to give up the Protestant Establishment in Ireland without a struggle, if necessary of force against force.

I again take the liberty of troubling you with letters for the two-penny—one of which I do without scruple as it relates to the winding up of a Charity which has been twenty years in operation under the management of Mrs Wordsworth. So far back two Peasants (a Man and his Wife)[2] of the Vale of Grasmere were lost

[1] D. W. was taken ill at Whitwick a month after she returned there from Cambridge. Her MS. Journal for 3 Apr. reads: 'Very ill and so continued for several days. Mary W. arrived on the evening of Wednesday the 10th. I walked first in the Town on Monday: May 3rd.' (*WL MSS.*)

[2] For George and Sarah Green, see *MY* i. 201–2. The fund set up to care for their family (see *MY* i. 228 ff., 253) was now about to be wound up, and the balance of £480 distributed among the eight children. Their receipts for £60 each, dated 25 May 1829, and the account books of the charity are preserved among the *WL MSS.*

in the snow crossing the mountains and left an orphan family of nine Children the youngest of whom is just of age—and the residue of the subscription then made is about to be divided among them.

I remain my dear Sir

Very faithfully your much obliged
[*signed*] Wm Wordsworth

425. W. W. to EDWARD QUILLINAN

MS. Keswick Museum.
LT i. 375.

[9 Apr. 1829]

My dear Mr Quillinan,

Dora holds the pen for me my left eye being much distressed by an inflammation of the eye lid. You will be much concerned to hear that my dear and excellent Sister is now lying at Whitwick very ill tho' thank God pronounced out of danger except relapse should take place, of the disease internal inflammation, which Mr Carr[1] assures us we have not much reason to fear—

Mrs Wordsworth left us yesterday to proceed by Mail to Loughborough and we hope will reach the Invalid by ten o'clock tonight. My sister had been much weakened by an attack of Influenza which John also had had severely. The inflammation commenced last Tuesday but one, and for forty eight hours she was in excruciating torture—since, her suffering seems to have been entirely from weakness—so great that on Monday she told Willy 'She was alive—as her poor grandfather[2] used to say—and that was all.' Notwithstanding this Mr Carr does not appear to be alarmed for the issue—If she does not proceed towards recovery you will be sure to hear either from us or from Whitwick. Mr Papendick the Bremen gentleman whom William was to have joined in London during this month has been seriously ill so that his journey is put off. Wm will remain at Whitwick and at Cambridge till a few days before Mr P's return to Germany. You would do me a great kindness and render him an important service, if you would take him under your roof for the days, I hope only 3 or 4, that he will be obliged to stop in Town, as he will certainly not quit Cambridge till Mr P's departure from London is fixed. I congratulate you on your accident being no worse

---

[1] The Ambleside surgeon.   [2] William Cookson of Penrith.

—mine has left no traces of which I am conscious except a very very small lump on the ridge of the nose between the eyes—We condole with you on your business concerns being so unsatisfactory; it is too serious a matter to joke about or I should say that a counting house suits you less than would a Frier's Cell—and a ledger becomes you less as a thing to be wielded than w^d a vol: of the 'Acta Sanctorum'—We have not yet had a peep at the 'Bijou'[1]—and of My Mæcenas of the 'Keepsake'[2] I hear nothing tho' I told him more than two months ago that I was provided with my quota. We shall be truly glad to see you and still more so as the Conductor of our little Godchild;[3] were she here now we would go and gather bunches of Daffodils.

[*The next few lines have been cut away*]

. . . its being blotted out of the language. Many a time have I felt a wish tho' it would be making the innocent suffer for the guilty that the future Progeny of these offenders might come into the world with a Rat as a flesh mark upon their foreheads[4] (Oh wicked Father!) Now I surrender, as it is high time, the pen to my Daughter's guidance—farewell and God bless you, my heart is anxious for my poor dear Sister and my soul heavy. I should have gone to see her but that Dora would have been left alone in the house—be so kind as to send the account of my Sister's illness to H. C. Robinson. I would write myself but I cannot, the Insurance[5] I troubled him about I shall not proceed with at present

Ever most faithfully yours
[*signature cut away*]

[1] *The Bijou* for 1829 contained (p. 135) E. Q.'s verses 'To a Lady of Thanet'. He had written to Dora W. on 30 Mar. about his literary and business activities: 'As for Letters, I like the company of real literary men, because they are men of sense and information, but I aspire to no fame; I am profoundly sensible of my lowly stature, bodily and mental, and will not stretch my pigmy arm for fruit which is only within the reach of giants. My contribution to the Bijou was a stream of idle compliment to the Beauty of a lady whom I never saw, but of whom I have heard marvels. . . .—As the Man of business, if I could make money enough by it to pay for the trouble and disquiet, I would submit to the burden. I have no objection to wear a Hump by "buckling fortune on my back", but a mere slavish and unprofitable Business-Hump for the sole benefit of a sordid young trader who has already too much, I fling from me with as good will as your Friends Duke Wellington and Mr Peel have flung away their Anti-Catholic prejudices.' (*WL MSS.*)
[2] F. Mansel Reynolds. See L. 406 above.
[3] Rotha Quillinan.
[4] A puzzling passage which is unexplained.
[5] See L. 407 above.

426. W. W. to WILLIAM JACKSO

Address: The Revd William Jackson, Whitehaven.
Stamp: Kendal Penny Post.
MS. Cornell.
LY i. 376 (—).

[In Dora W.'s hand]

Rydal Mount
April 10th 1829

My dear Friend,

Many thanks for your letter and services of which John shall be duly informed. Mrs W. left us for Whitwick last Wednesday Evening you will be deeply concerned for the cause the severe illness of my dear and excellent Sister who that day week after a heavy influenza cold was attacked by internal inflammation and remained 48 hours in excruciating torture—the obstruction was then removed and she is pronounced out of danger but is so very weak that she cannot stand and can scarcely speak—but as relapses in this kind of disease we are told are rare—we are supported in our anxiety by strong hope which we have more reason to cherish as two days are elapsed without further news—which we were assured would be sent if any change took place for the worse. Mrs W. meant to proceed by mail and as we have not heard from her on the road we calculate pretty confidently on her reaching Whitwick last night before ten oclock and we shall receive tidings from her on Sunday at the latest—and if you do not hear from us again conclude that the poor Invalid is doing as well as can be expected for one so reduced.

We are grieved to hear that Miss Louisa Crumpe[1] is so unwell—and you will be concerned to hear that Mr Daniel Green[2] is considered to be far gone in Consumption—he is at his Father's. Mr de Quincey is returned but I have not seen him he has bought the Nab estate.[3] I now turn to the Catholic Question. I wish I could have seen you but except for our private gratification it is of no importance as through you your whole neighbourhood was stirred

---

[1] See pt. i, L. 85.

[2] The new curate of Langdale. See pt. i, L. 108.

[3] The residence of De Quincey's father-in-law John Simpson, beside Ryda Water. See Jordan, pp. 298 ff. On 12 Apr. Dora W. wrote to E. Q.: 'Mr de Q. has been in Edinburgh *two* years, Father says; coming home every month, and then every week. At last (about 3 months ago) his wife went to see after him and now I suppose somebody must go to bring the pair home.—Mr de Q is about buying the Nab Estate.' (*WL MSS.*)

to petition—I set on foot the one that was sent from here. I entirely concur in the views you take of the United Church of England and Ireland as an Establishment and also of her power as a spiritual Church to maintain herself independent of Kings and Ministers by the purity of her Doctrines—but that consideration cannot reconcile me to part with her temporalities, to which the measure, we have been contending against, points; because I regard those rights and immunities as an efficient means under Providence for supporting, regularly diffusing, and extending her spiritual influence, through these Islands and as the Head of the Protestant Community, throughout the whole world. Again, when narrowing my views I look at the property of the Church as essentially the Property of the people (not in a too common sense as being applicable by Parliament to public exigencies, but as paramount to any enactments of the Legislature except such as are regulatory of the mode of applying it to the maintenance of the Church), my desire to support the Church is greatly strengthened —The Church Property circulating from Individual to Individual and from family to family was the great power during the feudal ages for mitigating and qualifying that Iron despotism of inalienable inheritance among the barons. However great might be the occasion then given for deploring the abuse of spiritual agency, as a means of gratifying temporal ambition, it was a mode of substantiating under Providence the superiority of Mind to body— of argument to brute force. It also made palpable the Principle which can alone give a moral right to any species of property viz: that it is holden not for the good of the Possessor merely but for the benefit of the Community. Great reason have we to be thankful that so considerable a portion of this counterbalancing property has descended to our times holden under the express obligation that important public services are to be performed—transcending all others, as far as Eternity is of more concern to us than Time; but without going so high what Man can be so ignorant as not to perceive how by the circulation of this property families are refined, in the humble ranks of Society, and have their views exalted. You are able to pursue this train of thought full as feelingly as I can do and I am sure will join with me in opinion that there is no part of the Land, its proceeds, or of the wealth of the Country that the people at large would be so deeply interested in preserving inviolable, could they but see clearly, as that of the Church. Now when One considers that the direct representation of this Property in Parliament is wholly inadequate, Clergymen being inadmissable in the lower House, and the Bishops from the inequality of the Sees, being so much at the beck of Ministers as we have lately had deplorable proof, and when one considers that the Convocation[1] though reserved as a possible barrier for the Throne is never likely to be brought into action to support the legal rights of the Church can one be other than alarmed after what has just taken place. The first assault will be made upon the Irish Church: that that should stand seems to me next to impossible—the grounds of apprehension are probably as present to your mind as to mine yet when we meet they shall be discussed with all that concerns this momentous question which was constantly in my thoughts till the late distressful account of my Sister's illness.

As to your Bishop[2] I am quite of your mind that his conduct cannot, ought not, to pass unnoticed, by his Clergy as a body, but would it be decent to proceed hypothetically? I think not—ought it not to be known from himself what he did actually say; if he acknowledges that he used the words imputed to him it would be then proper to look out for precedents how an offended and injured Clergy have proceeded—under like circumstances; of this I am ignorant; but I know no one more likely to give information than my Brother and if you approve I will ask him.

My eyelid continues much inflamed—so that I neither read nor write farewell let us hear of you from time to time

Most faithfully Yours

[*signed*] Wm Wordsworth

[*Dora W. adds*]
Will you keep this letter as my Father may possibly have occasion at some time or other to address the public upon a question he has so much at heart. I am ashamed of this blotted untidy letter—pray put it all down to Father—I have so much to do owing to his poor eye that it is impossible for me to find time for transcribing it— —Dora W.

---

[1] See pt. i, L. 385.

[2] John Bird Sumner (1780–1862), an evangelical, had recently succeeded Blomfield as Bishop of Chester. While apparently opposed to concession to the Catholics, he had been among the nine bishops who had voted in favour of the Relief Bill, and then addressed a circular letter to his clergy vindicating his decision. An energetic diocesan, he was appointed Archbishop of Canterbury in succession to William Howley in 1848.

427. W. W. to EDMUND HENRY BARKER[1]

Address: E. H. Barker Esqre, Thetford
Stamp: Kendal Penny Post.
MS. Bodleian Library.
K (—). *LY i. 377.*

[*In Dora W.'s hand*]

Rydal Mount, April 23^d, 1829.

Sir,

In the 380th[2] page of the 2^d Vol. of the last Ed: of my Poems
(1827), you will find a notice of the Poetry printed by Macpherson under the name of Ossian, in which it is pronounced to be
in a great measure spurious, and in the 4th Vol: of the same Ed:
page 238, is a Poem[3] in which the same opinion is given. I am not
at present inclined, nor probably ever shall be, to enter into a detail
of the reasons which have led me to this conclusion; something is
said upon the subject in the first of the passages to which I have
taken the liberty of referring you. Notwithstanding the censure of
Mr Macpherson which is implied in this opinion you will see
proofs—both in the Piece[4] page 238, and in page 15 of the 3^d Vol:
of the same Ed: that I consider myself much indebted to Macpherson, as having made the English Public acquainted with the
Traditions concerning Ossian and his age. Nor would I withhold
from him the praise of having preserved many fragments of Gaelic
Poetry, which without his attention to the subject might perhaps
have perished. Most of these, however, are more or less cor-
rupted by the liberties he has taken in the mode of translating them.
I need scarcely say that it will give me pleasure to receive the Vol:[5]
in which you have given your reasons for an opinion on this subject
different from my own. If you take the trouble of sending it to

---

[1] Edmund Henry Barker (1788–1839), classical scholar, left Trinity College, Cambridge, without taking his degree owing to religious scruples, and
lived with Dr. Parr at his vicarage of Hatton, Warwickshire, 1810–15:
thereafter he settled at Thetford, and devoted himself to literary work. See
Memoir prefixed to his posthumous *Literary Anecdotes and Contemporary
Reminiscences of Professor Porson and Others*, 2 vols., 1852. Barker had recently
written to W. W. about the genuineness of the Ossianic poems (see Morley,
i. 204).

[2] In the *Essay, Supplementary to the Preface* (*PW* ii. 423; *Prose Works*, iii.
77).

[3] *Written in a Blank Leaf of Macpherson's Ossian* (*PW* iv. 38), composed
1824 and published in 1827.

[4] *Glen Almain* (*PW* iii. 75).

[5] The second volume of *Parriana; or Notices of the Rev. Samuel Parr, LL.D.,*
1828–9.

66

Messrs Longman he will forward it to me either in Mr Southey's first parcel or in some other way. Dr Parr[1] I never saw but once, and that in his latter days, for an hour or two at Mr Basil Montagu's. The only notice I possess of him is the following on a blank leaf of Ker's 'Selectarum de Lingua Latina'[2] from the Pen of Mr Headley,[3] Author of 'Select Beauties of Ancient English Poetry' 'Librum huncce studii et amoris erga me quodammodo Μνημόσυνον D.D. Vir ὁ πάνυ Samuelis Parr LLD. Pueritiae idem ille custos scilicet incorruptissimus, interque eos qui hujusce sunt aevi inque literis humanioribus feliciter operam navant, facile Princeps

> H. Headley
> Trin. Coll: Oxon
> June 4. 1783'
>
> I remain Sir faithfully yours
> [*signed*] Wm Wordsworth

428. W. W. to H. C. R.

Address: H. C. Robinson Esqre, King's Bench Walk, Temple, London.
Postmark: 28 Apr. 1829. *Stamp*: Kendal Penny Post.
Endorsed: 26 Apl 1829, Wordsworth, Investments, His Sister, Smith's Nollekens.
MS. Dr. Williams's Library.
K (—). *Morley, i. 205.*

> Rydal Mount Kendal
> April 26th 1829

My dear Friend,

Dora holds the Pen for me. A month ago the east wind gave me an inflammation in my left eye-lid which led, as it always does, to great distress of the eye, so that I have been unable either to read or write, which privations I bear patiently; and also a third, full as grievous, a necessary cessation from the amusement of composition,—and almost of thought—Truly were we grieved to hear of your illness first from Mr Quillinan, and this morning from your own account which makes the case much worse than we had

---

[1] The Revd. Samuel Parr (1747–1825), scholar and conversationalist: known as 'the whig Dr Johnson'. See also *MY* ii. 182.

[2] John Ker, M.D., *Selectarum de Lingua Latina observationum Libri duo . . .*, 1709

[3] Henry Headley (1765–88), one of Dr. Parr's pupils at Colchester and Norwich: author of *Select Beauties of Ancient English Poetry*, 2 vols., 1787.

apprehended—the mild weather, so slow to come, will I trust bring you about, but you must be very careful for the future, as I understand that these attacks leave a weakness and susceptibility, which dispose the frame to a recurrence of the disorder: I have at this moment an instance under my own eye: calling upon a friend the other day, whose health is in general most excellent, I found him nearly bound to the Sofa by Rheumatism in a part where several years ago he had been injured by a severe blow—I enter thoroughly into what you say of the manner in which this malady has affected your loco-motive habits, and propensities; and I grieve still more when I bear in mind how active you have ever been In going about to serve your friends, and to do good. Motion, so mischievous in most, was in you a beneficent power indeed!

You cannot consult a better travelling guide than Mr Sharp[1]— I would go no where, where he has been, without the benefit of his experience—Would that we could join you in Rome! but till my son William is provided for the hope cannot be encouraged—My Sister-in-law Miss *Joanna* Hutchinson, and her Brother Henry an ex-sailor are about to embark at the Isle of Man for Norway, to remain till July; were I not tied by the Stamp Off: I should certainly accompany them—As far as I look back I discern in my mind imaginative traces of Norway: the people are said to be simple, and worthy, the *Nature* is magnificent—I have heard Sir H. Davy[2] affirm that there is nothing equal to some of the Ocean Inlets of that region and lastly, the very small expense would suit my finances this last word brings me to money—Following the example of my kind Friend Mr Sharp—I have sold out of the French funds and in consequence have *2537 £* lying in the Kendal bank at $2\frac{1}{2}$ per cent. This money I am most anxious to lodge upon some unexceptionable security if possible at the rate of $4\frac{1}{2}$ per cent—If not I must descend in my expectations to 4. My wish is to renounce all speculation and to be secure from a fall in the Principal for the sake of those whom I may leave behind—Mr Sharp has kindly stated to me the supposed advantages and disadvantages of reinvestment in funds French, or English—The Interest in either case is something under

---

[1] Richard Sharp.

[2] Sir Humphry Davy (see *EY*, p. 289) did not apparently visit Norway until July 1824, so that W. W. must have seen him again after that date, almost certainly during his visit to the Lakes in Aug. 1825 (see John Davy, *Memoirs of the Life of Sir Humphry Davy, Bart.*, 2 vols., 1836, ii. 216–17). At the Congress of Vienna, Norway had been taken away from Denmark and allotted to Sweden, but the Norwegians contrived to keep their own Parliament and assert their claims to self-government.

4 p^r cent but with regard to the french *threes*, there is a possibility of a rise in the Principal. This however I w^d waive and am inclined to prefer the English 4 if I can do no better, but here I fear a decline in the principal which, our fortune being so small, would be mortifying after having gained from interest and principal upwards of 1000 £ on 1800 £ since 1820. You will most likely see Mr Sharp again. I am too much indebted to him to be justified in teasing him by letter about my money matters, would you be so kind as to state my wishes and consult with him and with any other Person whose experience and judgement you may rely upon—

It would have been a great joy to us to have seen you though upon a melancholy occasion—You talk of the *more* than chance of your being absent upwards of two years[1]—I am sorry for it on my own account the more so as I have entered my *60th* year—Strength must be failing and snappings off, as the danger my dear sister has just escaped, lamentably proves, ought not to be long out of sight.

What a shock that was to our poor hearts. Were She to depart the Phasis of my Moon would be robbed of light to a degree that I have not courage to think of—During her illness we often thought of your high esteem of her goodness, and of your kindness towards her upon all occasions—Our last account was of the 19th and that morning she had been out in the garden for ten minutes and we know that if she had not been going on well since we should certainly have heard—We look for a letter in course tomorrow—Mrs Wordsworth is still with her and I have entreated her to stay ten days more[2]—Dora is my house keeper, and did she not hold the Pen it would run wild in her Praises—Sara Coleridge, one of the loveliest and best of Creatures, is with me so that I am an enviable person notwithstanding our domestic impoverishment. Mrs Coleridge is here also—and if pity and compassion for others anxieties were a sweet sensation I might be envied on that account also for I have enough of it—I have nothing to say of books (Newspapers having employed all the voices I could command) except that the 1st Vol of Smith's 'Nollekens and his Times'[3]

---

[1] H. C. R. was abroad in Germany and Italy from June 1829 until Oct. 1831. See Sadler, ii. 420–513.

[2] M. W. actually left Whitwick on 11 May.

[3] John Thomas Smith (1766–1833), writer on the topography and antiquities of London, and Keeper of Prints and Drawings at the British Museum from 1816, had studied under Joseph Nollekens, R.A. (1737–1823), the sculptor, and published an unflattering biography, *Nollekens and his Times*, 2 vols., 1828.

has been read to me—and I am indignant at the treachery that pervades it—Smith was once very civil to me, offering to show me anything in the Museum at any and all times when he was disengaged—I suppose he would have made *a Prey* of me as he has done of all his acquaintance, of which I had at that time no suspicion having thought myself not a little obliged to him for his offer— There are however some good Anecdotes in the book, the one which made most impression on me was that of Reynolds who is reported to have taken from the print of a half-penny ballad in the Street an effect in one of his Pictures which pleased him more than anything he had produced—

If you were here I might be tempted to talk with you about the Duke's[1] [se]ttling' of the Catholic Question. Yet why? for you are going[2] [to Ro]me, the very Centre of Light and can have no occasion for my farthing Candle—Somebody has just sent me from Oxford the *4th* No: of a Literary Gazette[3] published there from which I learn that I am a prodigiously favorite Poet with one of its Contributors at least—My kindest regards to the Lambs tell them about my sister, And say that I have long wished to write to Charles and will certainly do so as soon as I recover the use of my eyes for a little reading which will be necessary for his Play[4] and for the books he sent me before I can make acknowledgements to my wish. Farewell I wish I could command a frank—Dora joins me in aff.te regards She is a staunch Anti-Papist, in a woman's way, and perceives something of the retributive hand of justice in your Rheumatism but nevertheless like a true Christian she prays for your speedy convalescence—

Ever most faithfully Yours
Wm Wordsworth

[1] i.e. Wellington.
[2] *MS. torn.*
[3] Untraced.
[4] *The Pawnbroker's Daughter* and *The Wife's Trial*, the only plays published after the collected edition of Lamb's works, in 1818, appeared respectively in *Blackwood's*, Jan. 1830 and Dec. 1828. The former was referred to by Lamb in a letter (July 1829) to Barton as 'an old rejected farce': the latter was written in 1827 and rejected by Kemble in 1828 (see *The Works of Charles and Mary Lamb*, ed. E. V. Lucas, 7 vols., 1903–5, v. 372–3). It is not possible therefore to be sure to which of the plays Wordsworth here alludes. (Morley's note.)

429. D. W. to H. C. R.[1]

Address: H. C. Robinson Esqre, 3 King's Bench Walk, Temple.
Postmark: 4 May 1829.
Endorsed: May 2nd 1829, Miss Wordsworth, Recovery.
MS. Dr. Williams's Library.
K (—). *Morley, i. 210, 212.*

Whitwick near Ashby de la Zouche
May 2nd [1829]

My dear Friend,

Your letter, which by some strange mistake was directed to me at Rydal instead of Whitwick, has just reached me with a few words written upon it by my Niece, telling me that her Father had written to you, From him you will have heard all particulars respecting where the dispersed of the Family are, what doing and what intending, and this I am glad of, not having time or room for a long letter.—It drew tears from my eyes to read of your affectionate anxiety concerning me. In fact it is the first time in my life of fifty six years in which I have had a serious illness, therefore I never before had an opportunity of knowing how much some distant Friends care about me—Friends abroad—Friends at home—all have been anxious—and more so, far more I am sure, than I deserve; but I attribute much of this to my having been so remarkably strong and healthy, it came like a shock to every one, to be told of a dangerous illness having attacked me.—I am now, through God's mercy, perfectly restored to health, and almost to strength; but quiet care—for a time at least, I am assured is necessary; and indeed my own frame admonishes me that it is. But for the sake of my kind friends I am bound to take care, and I promise them all—including you who will be far away from us, that I will be neither rash nor negligent—Indeed I never can forget what I suffered myself nor the anxiety of those around me.—My Nephew William was the tenderest nurse possible—It would have moved any body's heart to see him. But enough of this subject.—He is still at Whitwick, and we hear nothing of Mr Papendich's arrival in England; but I think we shall part from William finally in a week. His Uncle wishes to see him at Cambridge: There he will stay a short while and proceed to London, where he will take up his quarters with Mr Quillinan (to whom, if you see him, give my kind Love and tell him I am deeply sensible of the interest I know he has taken concerning me.) I am not hopeless of William's having the good

---

[1] Morley printed this letter as two separate items, but the two parts seem to belong together.

fortune to see you before your departure. Yours is dated the 27th and you say in about 10 days you shall go into Suffolk, pay the Clarksons a visit, and return to London—I wish this may catch you before your departure for Suffolk—indeed I *expect* it will, otherwise I should not have troubled you with the enclosure for Rydal. You must know we sent a letter thither yesterday, and today Dora's little note arrives (written in your's) and there is something in it which it is better to answer immediately, yet we cannot find it in our hearts to tax her with a second shilling, so, recollecting that you can almost command franks through your LOYAL Friends I take the chance; and shall be much obliged to you and the worthy Alderman if by your joint services it can be forwarded. The other letter is for the Twopenny post-office.—My dear Friend, I am truly concerned to hear of your lameness; for lameness it may still be called though removed from the leg to the arms; but have no doubt that the warm and *dry air* of the Continent will speedily remove it; however, even with that assurance, I am concerned; for the Rheumatism is a visitant that *will* return—again and yet again: however obstinately you may try to expel it: however this year a first visit is less discouraging than at other times. Those who are accustomed to it have it more severely than usual—and many who never felt its touch before have been visited.—Myself for instance— at the beginning of the cold weather . . . and now again during my illness, I felt rheumatic pains of which till this winter I had not in my whole life had the slightest feeling. I wish you would now and then write to us when you are abroad—How long do you mean to stay? God grant that we may all be alive and in good health at your return! And what a joyful welcome shall we give you at Rydal Mount!—If my Brother ever should be able to take us into Italy, we shall call on you to fulfil your promise of accompanying us—and what an accomplished guide you will be!

Did I not tell you I had had a letter from Mrs Clarkson while at Cambridge, that she had been very ill, and was going from home (though recovered) for the benefit of change of air? I conclude from your saying that you are going to see her that she is returned to Playford—and I hope in her best state of health, and that dear Mr Clarkson continues as well as[1] he was when she wrote to me. Tell her that I much regretted that her time of going to Bury was not a few days later. Had she been there while I was at Cambridge, I should have met her at her Sister's[2] which to all of us would have

---

[1] as *written twice.*   [2] Mrs. Corsbie.

been a great satisfaction. Mrs Clarkson will have been much concerned to hear of my illness, especially as I had so recently spoken to her of my extraordinary health and strength—(My dear Friend what a lesson for us! the old Women at my bedside talked of me to each other as if quite sure that I *must* die!).—

Tell dear Mrs Clarkson that it hurts me to turn northward without having seen her; but I hope if I live to travel southward again it will not be so. John gives up his Curacy after Trinity Sunday. Perhaps he may go to London for a week or ten days and rejoin me here to accompany me to Halifax, where I shall stay a few weeks, and then go to Rydal. John is not obliged to go to his living at Moresby until the end of July. I once had thoughts of visiting my Friends in Herefordshire[1] before my return to Rydal, but my illness has left a home-sickness behind it; and nothing but the claims of an aged Friend,[2] who took charge of me when a child at the request of my dying Mother could have induced me to linger on the road after *Whitwick* claims are satisfied.

I think you have heard me speak of Mrs Rawson of Halifax. Her Husband died last year. They were the oldest Couple in Halifax among the upper ranks. She is now eighty three and has all her faculties perfect, except that she is a little deaf.—

You have heard no doubt, of my poor Brother's eyes having been inflamed—Thank God they are better—and therefore my Sister has been the less wanted at home especially as Dora is unusually well. They have been very kind in sparing her to us so long.—All danger was over when she heard of my illness; but they could not be easy—and it is well she came; for without her I should not have myself perceived how weak I was, and how much care was needed, and I should certainly have had a relapse. In case of a similar attack, however I should know better, and could of myself avoid all risques—[3]

If this letter should not catch you before you go to Playford pray enclose this Scrap for Mrs Clarkson before you leave England,— and excuse the trouble I give you by close and bad penmanship— and do not forget us when you are gone—and believe me ever your faithful and affectionate Frend

D Wordsworth.

My sisters[4] most affectionate good wishes and John begs to be kindly remembered to you.

[1] i.e. the Hutchinsons at Brinsop.
[2] D. W.'s 'aunt', Elizabeth Rawson, née Threlkeld, with whom she had lived at Halifax 1778–87 (see *EY*, p. 1).
[3] Half a page cut away, presumably the note for Mrs. Clarkson.
[4] i.e. M. W., who was still at Whitwick.

I am very glad you have so good a Friend in your Chambers, and hope we shall be benefitted by him in hearing of you.

I have *not* seen the Review—but have seen enough of the cowardly manner in which people have relinquished their principles.

430. W. W. to FREDERIC MANSEL REYNOLDS

Address: F. M. Reynolds Esqre, 48 Warren S^t, Fitzroy Square, London
Postmark: 12 May 1829. *Stamp*: Kendal Penny Post.
MS. W.L.
LY i. 378.

[*In Dora W.'s hand*]

Rydal Mount
Saturday May 9th, '29

My dear Sir,

I have been so many months looking for a letter from you that I begin to fear you must have been seriously ill. I wrote to you[1] to acknowledge the receipt of the two 'Keepsakes' (mine and M^r S's) and added that my contributions for the next year were waiting your commands. I wrote as you might think in somewhat of a splenetic humor having had a serious accident and other causes of uneasiness which have since been aggravated by a dangerous illness of my Sister's, Miss Wordsworth, and a two months inflammation of my own eyes under which I am still suffering having tried your remedy[2] in vain; the season has here been very unhealthy, severe colds—rheumatisms and inflammatory attacks— and I cannot but hope that the persevering sharp east wind brought on the first inflammation in my lids and was also the cause of two succeeding ones, from which the eye itself has suffer'd much— three days ago I called in our medical attent and he tells me that there is a small speck on the Cornea, and he has order'd Poultices to hasten the bursting of the Abscess on the lid—if you have any thing to propose for the benefit of my case pray write without delay.

As you did not seem inclined to make use of 4 of my Sonnets I begged in my last that they might be returned to me; if they have been mislaid dont let that trouble you as it is of little or no consequence, except for *one line* in the 'Roman Antiquities'—of which I have lost the correction. I had two days ago a request for Con-

---

[1] L. 406 above.   [2] The 'blue stone'. See pt. i, L. 257.

tributions to the 'Offering',[1] a new Annual, but I consider myself
bound to you upon the same terms as last year, and I am certain
upon second thoughts you will acknowledge the reasonableness of
my objecting to the *Principle* of being called upon (as in your last)
to supply by new contributions the place of my own rejected articles
—a little in this way might be done by an arrangement *between
ourselves as friends,* but to admit the rule with you or anyone in the
abstract character of *Editor,* is what I cannot consent to on the
grounds before stated.

I still feel unable to give you any advice or opinion about the
Articles in the 'Keepsake'—pray let me hear from you as I am
really anxious to know how you and your family are; make my
kind regards to your Mother and Brother and my Comp^ts to
M^r and Mrs Heath. I should not exclude you Father[2] from the
expression of my good wishes if I could take the liberty. Your
good Friend my Sister is in Leicestershire where her dangerous
illness seized her and Mrs W. has been with her above a month,
and is expected home on Wednesday.

The weather for the last two or three days has been delightful
and I hope when the poulticing is over that my inflamed eye will
recover under its genial influence.

[*signature cut off*]

431. W. W. to WILLIAM JACKSON

Address: The Revd William Jackson, J. G. Crumpe's Esq^e, Queen Anne's St,
    Liverpool. [*readdressed to*] Post Office, Matlock, Derbyshire.
Postmark: 11 May 1829. *Stamp*: Liverpool.
MS. Amherst College Library.
LY i. 367.

[*In Dora W.'s hand*]

Rydal [May][3] 10th [1829]

My dear Friend,

Through the hand of Dora, my own eye being still *very* bad,
I congratulate you on the event which you so kindly announce as
being likely to take place; pray *present and accept our best* and kindest

---

[1] Presumably *Friendship's Offering*, edited until 1827 by T. K. Hervey
(see pt. i, L. 211), but now under a new editor.

[2] Frederic Reynolds (1764–1841). the dramatist, and author of nearly one
hundred plays that were ridiculed by Byron (see *English Bards and Scotch
Reviewers*, ll. 568–9). He published 2 vols. of autobiography, *The Life and
Times of Frederic Reynolds,* in 1826. His wife was a Miss Mansel, a Welsh
actress, whom he married in 1799.

[3] March *written in mistake for* May. The latter date is confirmed both by the
postmark and contents of the letter.

wishes for your joint happiness.[1] You w^d have been written to immediately upon the receipt of yours, but Dora was disabled by a severe cold from which she is recovered. We are much concerned to hear of Miss Louisa's continued indisposition and hope she may now be in a state to benefit by the mild weather which is come at last. My Sister continues to improve. Wm starts for Cambridge[2] this evening—thence to London and to Bremen. Mrs Wordsworth we expect on Wednesday. John and Miss Wordsworth mean to leave Whitwick about Whitsuntide. Thank you for your attention to John's business. You will not I trust be disappointed in your expectation of finding in him a zealous and not inefficient coadjutor in support of the good old Church—wh[ich] as you say has been most basely betrayed. What do you say to a Bishop of Winchester[3] presiding at a Bible Society—as four others of the Bench I am told have lately done? This would have been *foolish* at *any time*; to me *at present* it is *intolerable*. We have had enough of liberal Prelates in Abbot[4] and Williams[5] of old. I defer much that I have to say upon public affairs till I have the pleasure of seeing you and your Bride, could you not come round this way and pass a day or two with us before settling yourselves at your beautiful Rectory?[6] which I long to see in its improved state.

Poor Daniel Green[7] and Miles Huddleston[8] died and were buried on the same day. We know not who is to have Langdale but we are all in terror of the Sewels.[9]

[1] William Jackson was about to marry Julia Eliza Crump. For her and for her younger sister Louisa, mentioned below, see pt. i, L. 85.

[2] From Whitwick.

[3] Charles Richard Sumner (1790–1874), a younger brother of J. B. Sumner (see L. 426 above) and like him an evangelical. In 1826 he was consecrated Bishop of Llandaff, which he held in plurality with the deanery of St. Paul's, and the next year he was translated to Winchester by order of the King, and remained there till 1869. He was one of the bishops who had voted in favour of the Catholic Relief Bill. For W. W.'s (and C. W.'s) misgivings about the Bible Society, see *MY* i. 472–3.

[4] George Abbot (1562–1633), a churchman of Puritan sympathies: Archbishop of Canterbury from 1611.

[5] John Williams (1582–1650), Lord Keeper and Bishop of Lincoln, 1621, and Archbishop of York from 1642. He was noted for his underhand methods and accommodating disposition.

[6] i.e. Lowther, to which Jackson had been appointed in 1828 (see pt. i, L. 331).

[7] Curate of Langdale.   [8] One of the Huddlestons of Langdale.

[9] The Revd. William Sewell, master of the Free Grammar School in Ambleside, and incumbent of Troutbeck, had been a somewhat unsatisfactory curate at Wythburn. His sub-curate at Troutbeck (who was also the village schoolmaster) was his brother, the Revd. Jonathan Sewell. In the event, W. W.'s apprehensions about both were not put to the test, for Owen Lloyd (see pt. i, L. 152) succeeded Green at Langdale and proved an exemplary priest.

You must excuse this poor scrawled letter. We have had so much to do in letter writing our work having accumulated during Dora's sharp cold.

With kindest regards to all about you and a thousand good wishes

Believe me my dear Friend very faithfully yours

[*signed*] Wm Wordsworth

432. W. W. to GEORGE HUNTLY GORDON

Address: G: Huntly Gordon Esq.^e
MS. Cornell.
Mem. (—). *Grosart* (—). *LY i. 380* (—). *Broughton, p. 18.*

[*In Dora W.'s hand*]

Rydal Mount
May 14th 1829.

My dear Sir,

Your letter was very welcome, it gives me much pleasure to learn that Mr. Papendick is arrived. William, as he himself I understand has informed you, is now at Cambridge. I wont trouble you with any further particulars about him but enclose a note for Mr. Papendick which you will oblige me by reading if you think it worth while. Your kind letter reached me on Monday and would have been acknowledged by return of post had we not expected Mrs Wordsworth who arrived to our great joy yesterday in good health having passed at Macclesfield and Manchester thro' crowds of Men Women and Children silently and piteously filling the streets.[1] She left my dear Sister improving daily but after such a shock I could not trust her to such exertions as her spirit would put her upon among the mountains and wilds of W.W:[2] such was your own thought and its propriety is unquestionable. You will find many beautiful spots in Montgomeryshire. Five and thirty years ago I passed a few days in one of its most retired vallies at the house of a Mr Thomas[3] some time since dead. His ordinary

---

[1] There had been widespread rioting for several days among weavers in the manufacturing districts in protest against the lowering of wages.
[2] West Wales.
[3] William Thomas of Bryn Merlyn, near Holywell, Flintshire.

residence was upon an estate of his in Flintshire close to Mr Pennant's[1] of Downing with whom, I mean the Zoologist, then a handsome figure of a man in the freshness of green old age I passed several agreeable hours in his library; he was upwards of seventy, tall and erect and seemed to have fair pretensions for *15* years of healthful and useful life, but soon after he fell into a sudden languishment, caused mainly I believe by the death of a favorite Daughter, and died. With much becoming pride he shewed me several stout folios of his manuscripts entitled 'outlines of the Globe,' principally I believe Compilations which have never seen the light; all this has led me from his neighbour Mr Thomas' seat in Montgom: where an event took place so characteristic of the Cambro Britons that I will venture upon a recital of it. I was introduced to Mr Thomas by my old friend and fellow Pedestrian among the Alps, Robert Jones, fellow of St. John's Cambridge. One day we sat down une partie quarrée at the Squire's Table, himself at the head; the Parson of the Parish, a bulky broad-faced man between *50* and *60* at the foot and Jones and I opposite each other. I must observe that 'the Man of God' had not unprofessionally been employed most part of the morning in bottling the Squire's 'Cwrrw' anglisé strong Ale, this had redden'd his visage (we will suppose by the fumes) but I sat at table not apprehending mischief. The conversation proceeded with the cheerfulness good appetite, and good cheer, naturally inspire—the Topic—the powers of the Welsh Language. 'They are marvellous,' said the rev[d] Taffy. 'Your English is not to be compared especially in conciseness, we can often express in one word what you can scarcely do in a long sentence.' 'That,' said I, 'is indeed wonderful be so kind as to favor me with an instance?' 'That I will' he answered. 'You know perhaps the word Tad?' 'Yes.' 'What does it mean?' 'Father' I replied. 'Well,' stammer'd the Priest in triumph, 'Tad and Father there you have it'—on hearing this odd illustration of his confused notions I could not help smiling on my friend opposite; whereupon, the incensed Welshman rose from his chair and brandished over me a huge sharp pointed carving knife. I held up my arm in a defensive attitude; judge of the consternation of the Squire, the dismay of my friend, and my own astonishment not unmixed with fear whilst he stood threat[e]ning

---

[1] Thomas Pennant, F.R.S. (1726–98), of Downing, near Holywell, zoologist and traveller: author of *A Tour in Scotland, 1769,* 1771, *A Tour in Wales, 1770,* 1778–81, and a *History of Quadrupeds,* 1781. He planned *c.* 1793 a work in 14 vols. called 'Outlines of the Globe'; 2 vols. dealing with India and Ceylon were published, and vols. 3 and 4 on China and Japan appeared posthumously.

me in this manner and heaping on my poor English head every reproachful epithet which his scanty knowledge of our language could supply to lungs almost stifled with rage. 'You vile Saxon!' I recollect was one of his terms, 'To come here and insult me an ancient Briton on my own territory!' At last his wrath subsided 'et me servavit Apollo'. Not far from the little valley where this occurr'd is one of the most celebrated of the Welsh Waterfalls which probably you will visit 'Pistil-rhaidor'[1] (excuse the spelling which is probably wrong).

I do not like a summer to pass without making some excursion and being disappointed as to Wales I have turned by thoughts to as much of the West of Scotland particularly 'Staffa' and 'Iona' as is accessible by Steam Boat. These and the Sound of Mull upon which resides a friend of ours, Col. Campbell,[2] I have never seen,—the temptation is strong and would have been much more so could I have had the pleasure of your company.

You kindly inquire after my eyes which as you will judge from my not writing with my own hand are not well but I trust I have not at present much more to fear. I have had three successive inflammations of the left lid which last has distressed the orb of the eye greatly, but the ab[s]cess has burst and the eye tho' not yet *useable* for writing or reading is slowly recovering its tone. My Constitution must either have been in a delicate state or the season unusually severe for exposure to bracing air w^h after a time has hitherto always proved a specific, has on this last attack caused a renewal of the malady with aggravated symptoms. Mr Southey means to present me (as usual) his 'Colloquies' etc.—there is perhaps not a page of them that he did not read me in M:S: and several of the Dialogues are upon subjects which we have often discussed. I was greatly interested with much of the book but upon its effect as a whole I can yet form no opinion,[3] as it was read to me as it happened to be written; I need scarcely say that Mr Southey ranks very highly in my opinion as a Prose writer; his stile is eminently clear, lively, and unencumbered and his information unbounded and there is a moral ardor about his compositions

[1] Pistyll Rhaiadr, in the narrow valley of the Rhaiadr, on the boundary between Denbigh and Montgomery.
[2] Formerly a summer resident at Grasmere. See pt. i, L. 83.
[3] Southey's critique of contemporary society and the evils of the manufacturing system (which W. W. had also deplored in *The Excursion*) had some effect in progressive Tory circles and influenced the social thinking of the Young England Movement; but Macaulay in the *Edinburgh Review*, 1 (1830), 528–65, ridiculed both the argument and the form of the *Colloquies*.

which nobly distinguishes them from the trading and factious authorship of the present day. He may not improbably be our Companion in Wales next year. At the end of this month he goes with his family to the Isle of Man for sea air and said if I would accompany him and put off the Welsh Tour for another year he would join our party; notwithstanding the inducement I could not bring myself to consent but as things now are I shall remind him of the hope he held out.

Whoever could guarantee to me the integrity and safety of the united Protestant Ch: of England and Ireland would reconcile me at once to the late bill but my fears are not in the least abated.

Farewell and with best thanks for your attention to my Son.

Believe me very faithfully y^rs^
[*signed*] Wm Wordsworth

There is no probability of my being in Town this Season—I have a horror of smoking and nothing but a necessity for *health's* sake could reconcile me to it in William—Will you be kind enough to seal and direct the enclosure for Mr Papendeck.

433. W. W. to H. C. R.

Address: H. C. Robinson Esqre, 3 Kings Bench Walk, Temple. London. [*readdressed to*] Bury, Suffolk.
Postmark: 18 May 1829. *Stamp*: Kendal Penny Post.
Endorsed: 18th May 1829, Wordsworth, Investments and American Securities.
MS. Dr. Williams's Library.
K (—). *Morley, i. 214.*

[18 May 1829]

My dear Friend

Mrs W. holds the pen for me, having returned from Whitwick, where she left our dear Sister improving gradually last Monday.

I am almost ashamed to trouble you about my concerns, now that you must be so busy in settling your own. I have heard from Mr Courtenay to day, and he gives so flattering an account of the Law-Lives that notwithstanding the rise, I mean to avail myself of your kind offer—his words are, 'I firmly believe that Law-Live shares will pay you, if bought at any price under £11 per share, will pay excellent interest tho' nothing will be touched for the first 4 years—but the property will be encreasing, etc, etc.'

I have therefore placed £300 at your disposal in Masterman's Bank, and I beg that you will take the trouble of going thro' the forms necessary to effect for me this security—not omitting such considerations as will naturally suggest themselves to a Lawyer about to reside a couple of years in foreign parts. I am most sincere in the expression of my regret at imposing so much trouble upon you at this time, and am also truly thankful for your last interesting letter.[1] Will it tend in any way to repay you, if Mrs W transcribes the opinion of Mr Rathbone[2] the first American Mercht in Liverpool upon American Securities.

'I can only say, that my opinion is very favourable Their habits of legislature are oeconomical, they are not troubled with any refined feeling that should make them give any one of their public servants one farthing more than they think his services worth. In their public engagements they have been very punctual their rapid improvement in public wealth has left them without temptation to be otherwise—and their States to the Westward are growing with such accelerated encrease in population, that I consider the security either of the Stock of the States or of the federation as undoubted. The rate of Interest must depend upon the rate of Exchange at which the dividends are remitted, which varies from 8 to 12 pr Cent. My Sister has some money in Stocks of the United States by our advice. Some of the Stocks are more saleable than others, which is an object of consideration to those who may want their money, but where income is the Object, some of the heavy stocks pay the best Interest, The Ohio Stock is one of these latter. Of the Louisiana, I can only speak generally, not particularly. It is however a rapidly increasing State.'

Against the above opinion, which was asked for in consequence of your letter, I have nothing to say, but that Mr Rathbone being a Quaker may be somewhat biassed towards the Americans.[3] Mr Courtenay in conclusion says 'he should be sorry to risk the welfare of these dear to him by investment in French funds', and as his final opinion bids me look out for a good mortgage in

---

[1] H. C. R. had written in great detail on 4 May about investment prospects. He wrote again on 9 June to say that he had carried out W. W.'s commissions. (*Dr. Williams's Library MSS.*)

[2] Probably Richard Rathbone of Rathbone, Brothers, and Co., shipping agents and tobacco brokers, who was a neighbour of John Bolton's (see *MY* ii. 505) in Duke Street, Liverpool.

[3] W. W. had also, through H. C. R., consulted Richard Sharp, who wrote on 1 May: 'American United States Stock I think even safer than English, but they are very dear.' (*WL MSS.*)

England. 'I should prefer that says he to any other security.' This is what I, W. W. wish for—but where am I to find it?

Why did not you mention your Rheumatism—when you are abroad pray write to us and not unfrequently—Be assured I shall not grudge Postage; and do not trouble yourself about franks during your short stay in England.

If I excurtionize at all this summer, it will be by Steam to Staffa Iona etc. My eye that has plagued me so long is improving daily but I wish I had seen Rome, Florence, and the Bay of N[apl]es,[1] as the recurrence of these attacks throws a [?shade] over the future. Mrs W. wro[?te] this very [?bad]ly and says I am ungrateful to Providence and ought to take example by your cheerfulness.

Be it known however in my excuse that I have not opened a book for nine weeks!!—a fine holiday!! Have you seen Southeys coloquies,[2] if so how do you like them. Pray effect a meeting with my Son W[m],[3] who will be at Mr Quillinans in a few days—write him a note, and he will call upon you when, and wherever you may appoint.— Otherwise he will not seek you out, as he imagines you have left Town. I grieve that you are going without our seeing you at Rydal. Mrs W. travelled from Loughboro' to Kendal for less than two pounds—inside fare from Manchester to Kendal in a beautiful Coach, the 'Fair Trader' 2 horses in 9 hours 14/. outside 10/. Would this might tempt you to come down for a fortnight, and join Dora and myself in a Tour to the Duddon, and—which we meditate. Farewell—Mary and Dora join me in best wishes.

Wm Wordsworth

Mr Courtenay's letter rec[d] this morning is dated Manchester— but most likely he will soon return to town—can the shares be purchased without seeing him—when you see him read the E[xt][4] from Mr Rathbone.

---

[1] *MS. torn.*
[2] See also previous letter.
[3] In his letter of 9 June, H. C. R. described how he had missed seeing W. W. nr. while he was passing through London. (*Dr. Williams's Library MSS*).
[4] Extract.

434. W. W. to HENRY ROBINSON[1]

Address: Henry Robinson Esqre, Solicitor, St. Saviour's Gate, York.
MS. University of Colorado Library.
The Wordsworth Circle, Winter, 1974.

Rydal Mount 19 May 1829.

My dear Sir,

Pray excuse this letter following so close upon my last, but it is to rectify a statement therein.

Upon reviewing the matter it strikes me as indispensable that the Insurance of the House from fire should be in my own name and paid by me; so that there may be nobody between me and the fire office in case of an accident.—Furthermore that the property should be valued; so that we may know both its estimated worth and present rent, which you say is 100£.

A Friend of mine has just had a mortgage offered to him at Liverpool upon Houses, the Borrower being charged with the payment of the Policy; but he was to receive only 4½ PCent.

If it be intended that the Policy, in this case (if required) is to be at the expense of the lender, it is indispensable that the rate of insurance of such property be known, else I should be ignorant at what interest my money is to be lent; but I hope the Borrower is prepared to meet the expense of the Policy. This and all other particulars I should be glad to learn at your earliest convenience; with any further precautions which in your judgment may be necessary for my security.

The money is ready, if the thing meet with our united approbation.

I remain
Your affectionate Cousin
Wm Wordsworth

---

[1] Henry Robinson (see also pt. i, L. 37), seventh son of Mrs. Mary Robinson, the Admiral's widow (see Genealogical Table, pt. i, facing p. 704), who became a solicitor in 1826 and practised in York for twenty years. W. W. had recently consulted him about his investments, and the possibility of lending out some of his capital in the form of a mortgage on house property. See also L. 454 below.

435. W. W. to GEORGE HUNTLY GORDON

MS. Cornell.
Broughton, p. 21.

[*In Dora W.'s hand*]

Monday Evg.
½ past 7.
[late May 1829]

My dear Sir

The departure of the Post will not allow me time to reply to your kind letter as it deserves. It was received this m^g. and I am returned only half an hour ago from an excursion of 5 days. I have not the least objection to W's[1] going in the Steam Boat and it is fit that he should accommodate himself to Mr Papendick's convenience —I shall be most happy to receive Mr P's letter. Whatever money may be wanted by W for his voyage etc will be supplied by Mr Quillinan. I send the 'Retort'.[2] Keep it as long as you like, only take care not to lose it as it is curious in itself; is not to be had and was *extorted* from the Author by my Daughter—No attempt was made by Mr Q. to *suppress* it—but a 2^d Ed. being urgently called for he with[h]eld it in consequence of Mr Loc[k]hart having expressed his regret for the liberty that had been taken in the critique which he disclaimed having had anything to do with.

This morning I was for some hours on the banks of the Duddon and saw its fine features under the most beautiful morning lights and shadows. Farewell. my eyes are improving.

Mr Coleridge has not been well and seems to shut himself up even more than ever; so that I think you judged well in not accompanying W—— whose manners etc I am pleased you liked.

Most faithfully yours
[*signed*] Wm Wordsworth

----

[1] i.e. W. W. jnr.

[2] In 1814 E. Q. had published his first ambitious attempt at poetry, *Dunluce Castle*, which was ridiculed by Thomas Hamilton in *Blackwood's* in 1819 in a review entitled 'Poems by a Heavy Dragoon'. E. Q., erroneously supposing Wilson and Lockhart to be the authors of the criticism, attacked them in his *Retort Courteous* (1821), a satire consisting largely of passages from *Peter's Letters to his Kinsfolk* done into verse. The misunderstanding was finally dissipated through the mediation of R. P. Gillies (see *MY* ii. 167), and the parties were reconciled.

436. W. W. to GEORGE HUNTLY GORDON

Address: G. Huntly Gordon Esqᵉ.
MS. Cornell.
Broughton, p. 22.

[*In Dora W.'s hand*]

Rydal Mount
June 16ᵗʰ 1829.

My dear Sir,

Your packet was indeed welcome and we thank you cordially for it and your accompanying note. It gives us much pleasure that William was so well thought of by so excellent a judge as Mrs Oom[1] of whom *he* speaks quite in raptures. His voyage was rough and stormy. They reached Hamburgh on Monday and did not leave it till Wednesday—having dined with Mr and Mrs Canning[2] to whom Mr Papendick kindly introduced William—He is much pleased with Mr and Mrs Papendick and his home at Bremen so that we are full of hope he will benefit by his most promising opportunities—

I should have put off writing till tomorrow when perhaps we may hear from you had I not feared that as the Post (we understand) only goes twice a week, a delay of one day might occasion that of several—and William will at first naturally be anxious for tidings from Rydal.

We have at last had a night of rain after a parching drought of many many weeks; the streams of the mountains are again foaming and vocal and the verdure already of the mountain turf reanimated.

Professor Wilson whom I have not seen is at his Place[3] upon Winandermere six or seven miles from us. He has an Artist with him taking views—and a book from his pen upon the Lakes *is reported* as the probable result of this union.

Mr de Quincey the opium-eater is expected to resume his abode among us in a few days.[4] Mr Southey returns to Keswick next week not having quitted the coast of Cumberland.[5] His book of Dialogues[6] has not yet reached me. I am impatient for it.

---

[1] Mr. Papendick's sister.
[2] H. Canning was the British Consul in Hamburg.   [3] Elleray.
[4] At the Nab. See L. 426 above. W. W.'s first approaches to De Quincey were not encouraging. See *Letters of Dora Wordsworth*, p. 48 and Jordan, p. 332.
[5] Southey had planned a trip to the Isle of Man this May, but stayed instead for five weeks with his old friend Humphrey Senhouse of Netherhall (see pt. i, L. 38). See Southey, vi. 45–6; Curry, ii. 336.
[6] The *Colloquies*.

You would have enjoyed a walk I had this morning with Miss Coleridge now our visitor. With a spade, each a basket and an umbrella, for sunny showers were flying all about us—we went high up into a valley among the mountains behind this house to fetch the roots of a beautiful flower which she had seen for the first time a few days ago. We have planted it in the garden with many fears however that the soil is not moist enough for it to thrive in.

Thanks for your care in delivering yourself the M:S: to Mr Reynolds.[1] the enclosed to him are for the twopenny. Adieu

Believe me very faithfully

Your much obliged

[*signed*] Wm Wordsworth

William without putting Mr Quillinan to the trouble of going into the city c^d not get as much money for his journey etc as he was likely to want in consequence of which disappointment he will find himself nearly pennyless if he repay to Mr P. what he has disbursed for his travelling expences. I would send you a bill to this amount if through Mrs Oom or otherwise Mr P. could be repaid this sum. Mr P. wishes to be paid half yearly for Ws pension etc—but I should wish him not to be out of the money he has advanced.

437. W. W. to FRANCIS MEREWETHER[2]

Address: To The Rev^d. F. Merewether, Rectory, Coleorton, Ashby de la Zouche.
Stamp: Kendal Penny Post.
MS. Berg Collection, New York Public Library. Hitherto unpublished.

[*In M.W.'s hand*]

Rydal Mount June 22^d. [1829]

My dear Sir,

I cannot let my Son and Sister depart from Whitwick[3] without a word or two that may express, however imperfectly, the satisfaction I feel from one so dear to me having entered upon his Professional career in a situation that has proved so favourable;

---

[1] Presumably W. W.'s proposed contributions to *The Keepsake* for 1830, which were to include *The Egyptian Maid* (see pt. i, L. 373). In spite of the disagreement reflected in Ls. 406 and 430 above, W. W. was still at this stage ready to go ahead with his side of the bargain. But see L. 438 below.

[2] See pt. i, L. 153.

[3] According to D. W.'s MS. Journals (*WL MSS.*), John W. preached his farewell sermon at Whitwick on Sunday, 21 June. The following Tuesday D. W. left with him for Halifax.

and under your Auspices. During his residence in your neighbourhood, except for the dangerous illness of his Aunt, he appears to
have been as happy as his best friends could wish; and, if we are not
mistaken, making progress in almost every qualification that his
sacred duty requires. He has had to preach the Gospel to the Poor,[1]
and when I consider the vanity of so many human callings and
employments, I cannot but deem it an especial blessing that he has
entered upon active life almost exclusively with that engagement.
It is the best preparation both for heart and head, and I trust that
he will feel the benefit of this initiation as long as he is able to
exert himself, and to the last hour of his life.

I could have wished him to [spend] another year at least, at
Whitwick, had it not been for this opening[2] which, all things
considered, he was scarcely at liberty to turn away from—it will
introduce him into a new field of action and therefore I hope may
be useful in advancing his professional education. As to mere
temporals, there is cause to apprehend that his situation will not
be at all improved—but this little Preferment may, and probably
will, lead to something better. We are all much pleased to hear of
Drummond's Preferment.[3] Pray congratulate him in our names
upon it.

You are aware that I have been much inconvenienced by repeated attacks of inflammation in one of my eye-lids—the eyes are
still weak which is the cause of my employing Mrs W's pen on
which account I shall touch less on public affairs than I might
otherwise have been tempted to do. I cannot however conceal from
you, that during this Spring I have been in very bad Spirits for
what has been done, and still more [?is it inexcus]able[4] for the
manner in which it has been done—it has been utterly without
candour and dignity.

My fear for the Catholics is for the present pretty much confined
to the Irish Protestant Estb[mt]. Such inroads will be made upon that,
as must lead to little less than its utter destruction. There are many
points in which the Catholics agree more with us than the Dissenters, but my fear is, that they will concur with these, and with
the Infidels till they find it too late to stop, and both our Church
and theirs, *as establishments*, will be pronounced unnecessary, or
what I think far worse in a Country [? claiming] to be free, made

---

[1] The Methodists had been active among the coal miners of the district, and
the Church had lost ground.   [2] At Moresby.
[3] Robert Drummond, Mr. Merewether's curate (see pt. i, L. 336), had just
been appointed vicar of Feering, Essex.
[4] *MS. torn.*

stipendiary upon the Government. God grant that these forebodings may never be realized—but I cannot escape from them. Every day brings additional proof that the Institutions of the Country are losing ground in the favour of those who are the most ready to meddle with public business. And it seems to me next to impossible that the now existing order of Society can be preserved in Great Britain, unless our public Schools and Universities pursue a course of education more adopted to the exigencies of the times. We go on at full speed, teaching the Poor gr[ammar ?][1] as if there could be any Security for a State in that, while the Rich are no better taught —I mean not more wisely taught than they now are. In the North of E. thro' its great manufacturing and commercial towns, one cannot notice without alarm the great wealth and influence which has been acquired by the industry and activity of Scotchmen and other Foreigners, for such they are, with reference to the Institutions of our Country—the Ch: especially—At Manchester, in particular, the 2ᵈ Town in G.B. for wealth and power, a fierce opposition to the Constitution, or rather what we have left of it, exists, and is daily gathering strength. But why shᵈ I sadden you with these apprehensions? Impute it to my affectionate regard for you, and to my knowledge of your enlightened patriotism— farewell—with ten thousand thanks for your kind attention to us all, to which Mrs W. is also largely entitled, I remain very faithfully yours

[*signed*] Wᵐ Wordsworth

Mrs W. joins in affectionate remembrances to you and yours and to dear Lady B.

438. W. W. to GEORGE HUNTLY GORDON

MS. Cornell.
Broughton, p. 23.

[*In Dora W.'s hand*]

Rydal Mount
July 4ᵗʰ Saturday [1829]

My dear Sir,
    My letters to you have always to begin with thanks—You need not trouble yourself about the remittance. My Kendal Banker will

---

[1] *MS. torn.*

by this day's post be directed to provide thro' Messrs Masterman for the payment to Messrs Hebeler and Co. for my son or Mr Papendick.

The enclosure from William was most gratifying to us all in every particular except his mention of dizziness and headache, which we attribute to over application, but as we have given him a strong caution by the enclosed we hope we shall not hear of any further mischief.

I recur now to your former obliging letter. The botanical name of the flower is 'Primula favinosa' and I am rather surprized that Miss Coleridge who has been a great rambler among the hills had not met with it before as it is common in moist places. Here it is called, I believe improperly, the 'Mountain Auricula', in Withering[1] the vulgar names are 'Birds eye,' 'Birds-eyn', 'Bird's-eye Primrose.' Accompanied by my Daughter on horse-back, I went the other day to a high point of our mountains in search of a very rare and far more beautiful plant, which it would give me pleasure to describe to you had I the least hope of success—as possibly it might be found among the Mountains of Montgomeryshire; it flowers in the beginning of June and we could not find it—tho' sought where I had met with it many years ago.

I thought I had told you that Mr Southey had intended to pass a month at the Isle of Man and went to Whitehaven with that view but they could not proceed on account of an accident to the steam boat and remained on the Cumberland coast—Yesterday I received his 'Coloquies,' Poems and a letter from him in which he anticipates in the course of next session an attack on the Irish Prot Estat and apprehension on his part that many Irish Landholders will favour it, with the hope of thereby keeping from themselves the burthen of poor rates.

Professor Wilson I have not yet seen, nor am likely to have much of his company. Mr de Quincey I am sorry to say admits no one on account of illness which confines him in a great measure to his bed. This grieves me much, as he is a delightful Companion and for weightier reasons, he has a large family of young Children with but a slender provision for them.

I have taken the liberty of requesting Mr Reynolds to return through you the M.S.S. you were lately so kind as to put into his

---

[1] William Withering, F.R.S. (1741–99), physician and botanist. His *Botanical Arrangement of all the Vegetables naturally growing in Great Britain* . . . , 2 vols., 1776, became a standard work which reached its 8th edition by 1852. W. W. possessed the 3rd edition, 4 vols., 1796 (*R. M. Cat.*, no. 178).

hands¹—The Editor and the Proprietor of the 'Keepsake' have behaved to me as persons wanting either in *memory* or in *honour*. They have broken their contract and in consequence I have done with them—

Pray return my kind regards to your Father² and Mother when you write to them. My eyes are much better but it is not yet safe to resume my pen otherwise this letter would not perhaps have been so short. My amanuensis [has been employed for the *whole day*.

My eldest son is now with us on the way to his little rectory on the coast of Cumberland.

I wish you much enjoyment in Wales and remain faithfully your

much obliged
Wᵐ Wordsworth]³

439. W. W. to BASIL MONTAGU

MS. Professor Mark Reed. Hitherto unpublished.

Wednesday
Upon the banks of Ulleswater.
[July 1829]

My dear Montagu,

Having accidentally met with a Frank, I write merely to thank you for your last, and for the [? 10th]⁴ Vol:⁵ which I received some time since through the Cooksons,⁶ but no Book of Extracts⁷—This you had named in one of your former Letters—but it was not in the parcel only another Volume of Lord Bacon for the [Carrier].

---

¹ See L. 436 above. Since then, Reynolds had failed to give a satisfactory explanation of the point at issue between them (see *Letters of Dora Wordsworth*, pp. 53, 57), and W. W. was therefore breaking off the connection altogether.

² For Major Pryse Gordon, see pt. i, L. 351.

³ The last lines in brackets are in another hand, probably copied by Gordon so that he could give away W. W.'s autograph.

⁴ *MS. torn.*

⁵ Of Basil Montagu's edition of Bacon's *Works*.

⁶ The Cooksons of Kendal.

⁷ *Selections from the works of Taylor, Hooker, Hall, and Lord Bacon*, 3rd edition, 1829.

I shall be glad to see the other Vol: which you announce;—and remain

very faithfully yours
W Wordsworth

The Extracts, I suppose, must have been omitted in the Parcel by mistake. It would give me pleasure to have them.

440. W. W. to C. W.

Address: Dr Wordsworth, Trinity Lodge, Cambridge. To be read by the
   Housekeeper or Butler in case of D^r W's absence [*In M. W.'s hand*]
MS. Mrs. Edmond F. Wright.
Mark L. Reed, 'Wordsworth and the Americans: Two New Letters and Visits',
   Emerson Society Quarterly, no. 33 (1963).

[8 *or* 9 July, 1829]

My dear Brother

    I have only a moment to say that the Bearer of this is Mr Gould[1] an American Merchant, he is travelling with his Lady Sister of Mr Goddard, upon whose melancholy death there is an elegy in my Poems.[2] They are very interesting and amiable Persons. Their [stay][3] will be very short in Cambridge, but pray let them see the Lodge; and any little further attention you could shew them I should be grateful for

ever affectionately yours
W. W.—

[*M. W. adds*]

    Should Dr Wordsworth be from home Mr W. will be obliged to the Housekeeper or Butler to shew, the Gentleman and Lady who deliver this note, the Pictures in King Henry's room and the Dining room etc.

---

[1] Benjamin Apthorp Gould (1787–1859), until recently Principal of the Boston Public Latin School (where Emerson was his pupil), but now a merchant in Boston engaging in the Calcutta trade. He had married (1823) Lucretia Dana Goddard, whose brother Frederick Warren Goddard (see *MY* ii. 642) had drowned in the Lake of Zurich in Aug. 1820, and the couple had come to Europe principally to collect information about the tragedy. They arrived at Rydal Mount on 8 July with an introduction from Southey, dated 7 July (*WL MSS.*), and returned to breakfast the following morning. See *Letters of Dora Wordsworth*, p. 56, and (anon.), *Nathaniel Goddard, A Boston Merchant*, Boston (privately printed), 1906, pp. 191–213, 269–71. The Goulds later met H. C. R. in Rome.
  [2] *Elegiac Stanzas* (*PW* iii. 193).   [3] *Word dropped out.*

441. W. W. to SIR GEORGE BEAUMONT[1]

Address: Sir George H. W. Beaumont Bart, Grosvenor Square, London.
Postmark: 21 July 1829. *Stamp*: Kendal Penny Post.
MS. Pierpont Morgan Library.
K. LY i. 380.

[*In Dora W.'s hand*]

Rydal Mount,
Sunday, July 19th, 1829.

My dear Sir George,

Last night Mr Drummond arrived, and brought your very kind letter. The mournful event[2] which occasioned it, I was instantly informed of by the care—for which I was truly thankful—of Mr Knight,[3] and Mr Merewether.

The shock was very painful, and would have been still more so had we received it first thro' the public papers.

It is seven and twenty years since I first became acquainted with the lamented Pair whom we have lost. We soon became united in affectionate intercourse, which has known no abatement, but our friendship rather strengthened with time, and will survive in my heart till it ceases to beat. In the recently deceased we have lost one of the most disinterested and pureminded of human beings. Abundant proofs have I had, my dear Sir George, how strongly attached she was to you, and from the depths of my heart I condole with you and Lady Beaumont in this bereavement; but she was ripe for the change, blessed be God! and I trust is, or is destined to be, a glorified spirit.

We were sorry to learn from Mr Drummond that your own health had suffered under this trial. I should be glad to hear that nothing of the kind recurred from what you have yet to go through at Coleorton. The funeral will be to-morrow; may you be supported through it! Mr Drummond tells me that Mr Merewether has in his possession a paper, dated so far back as *1816*, signifying the wish of the departed upon this and some other points; which puts me upon naming that when Lady Beaumont conducted Mrs Wordsworth and myself to the monument of Sir George, she said, 'You observe there is just room for my name below'; but whether

---

[1] i.e. the 8th Bart. (see pt. i, L. 175), who had succeeded his cousin, W. W.'s patron, in 1827.
[2] The death of the dowager Lady Beaumont on 14 July. Sir George had written to W. W., 'one of her oldest and dearest friends', on the 16th (*WL MSS.*).
[3] A Coleorton acquaintance.

she meant on the same tablet, neither of us could venture to ask; but you may have more recent instructions.

We are most anxious to hear how my poor sister bears these afflicting tidings. She is at Halifax, in Yorkshire, where she was left by my son recovering from the effects of her late dangerous illness. Thankful at all events will she be that her dear friend's time of suffering was so short, and that she passed several days with her and Mrs Willes[1] so lately.

Along with my condolence, in which Mrs W and my Daughter join, to Lady Beaumont, present my sincere regards, and Believe me, my dear Sir George,

Faithfully, your much obliged

[*signed*] Wm Wordsworth

442. W. W. to FRANCIS MEREWETHER

MS. Cornell. Hitherto unpublished.

Thursday 22nd July [1829]

My dear Sir,

Having fallen in with a Frank I send you D. Wilson's Pamphlet[2] —It was very kind in you to add to the particulars to Mr Knight's Letter. Through Mr Drummond who begs his kind regards (he does not quit us till tomorrow) I received a very friendly Letter from Sir George, who as might be expected is much troubled by the loss of so affectionate [a] Friend.[3]

My Sister has been written to; and I am glad to find by her reply that the sudden shock did not disorder her as we apprehended it might.

Professor Wilson is still rambling some where or other with an Artist. I have not seen him, nor am very likely or very wishful for an interview, but your wishes shall be named to him.—The

---

[1] The late Lady Beaumont's sister.

[2] Either *A Letter to the Editor of the Christian Observer, on the Bill for the relief of Catholic Disabilities* [1829], or *Catholic Emancipation and Protestant Responsibility: A second Letter to the Editor of the Christian Observer* [1829]. Both were the work of the Revd. Daniel Wilson (1778–1858), a noted evangelical; vicar of St. Mary's, Islington, since 1824 and fifth Bishop of Calcutta from 1832. W. W. was to meet him many years later (*c.* 1845) at the Archbishop of York's (see J. Bateman, *The Life of Daniel Wilson, Bishop of Calcutta*, 2 vols., 1860, ii. 267–8).

[3] The dowager Lady Beaumont. See previous letter.

Magazine or that print[1] has been stained; but it is after all a disgusting Periodical.

With kind regards to Mrs M.
I remain my dear Sir
very faithfully yours
Wm Wordsworth

John left us on the morning of the day Mr Drummond arrived, for Moresby. Finding he had a . . .

[*cetera desunt*]

443. W. W. to EDMUND HENRY BARKER

Address: E. H. Barker Esq., Thetford, Norfolk.
Franked: Penrith August three 1829 W. Marshall.
Postmark: 3 Aug. 1829. *Stamp*: Penrith.
MS. Bodleian Library.
LT i. 382.

[*In Dora W.'s hand*]

Rydal Mount
July 24th 1829

Dear Sir,

Your little parcel was much longer in reaching me than I calculated upon. I have lately made a better arrangement and can have things once a month at the latest thro' Mr Longman with very slight expence of carriage.

Your books[2] for which I sincerely thank you have been in my possession only a few days; and my eyes are not yet recovered from a serious inflammation, so that I have scarcely been able to dip into them, and I fear I shall not be able to bestow upon the Junius the attention a subject so curious deserves and which I should have readily given at an earlier period of life. I will do my best to disperse the advert of your Classical Dictionary.[3] In future Editions of this work would the additions etc be printed separately? I ask

[1] The reference seems to be to *Blackwood's*, or some part of it, which Merewether had sent to W. W.
[2] *Parriana* (see L. 427 above) and one or more of Barker's pamphlets (1826–7) on *The Claims of Sir Philip Francis to the Authorship of Junius disproved* . . . W. W. probably received at this time Barker's edition of Cicero's *Orations*, 1829 (see *R. M. Cat.*, no. 579).
[3] Barker's new edition of Lemprière's *Classical Dictionary*, 1828.

this question as knowing that many private scholars of small fortune are deterred from purchasing by the mortification of finding the book they have bought superseded by a subsequent Edition.

I fear your transcriber from my Poems on the subject of Ossian may have put himself to much unnecessary trouble on your account. I referred to these passages almost exclusively to shew the interest which the poetic world must attach to the name of Ossian, for the knowledge of which we English are mainly indebted to Macpherson; it is therefore impossible for me not to feel towards him a degree of gratitude which makes me regret the more that he should have ever mixed up so much untruth with the subject.

You perhaps have seen the *second* series of Mr Landor's 'Imaginary Conversations'. In the preface to the first vol: he speaks of Dr Parr in terms which will much please you.[1]

Headley[2] was a most extraordinary young man—more remarkable for precocity of judgement than any one I ever read or heard of: in his Poems also are beautiful passages, especially in the 'Invocation to Melancholy',[3] that I think is the title, but I have not seen the Poems for thirty years. It would be well if you could obtain some account of so promising a genius which would appear with great propriety in an account of Dr Parr. He died if I recollect right at Norwich of a decline, and was married.

I remain dear Sir
faithfully your obliged servant
[*signed*] Wm Wordsworth

This letter may perhaps be detained a few days in the hope of a frank.

---

[1] In his Preface to the Second Series, i (1829), xxxii, Landor pays eloquent tribute to Dr. Parr. 'My first exercises . . . were under his eye and guidance, corrected by his admiration, and animated by his applause. His house, his library, his heart, were always open to me; and, among my few friendships I shall remember his to the last hour of my existence, with ardent gratitude.'

[2] For Henry Headley, see L. 427 above.

[3] *Poems and Other Pieces*, 1786, pp. 9–16.

444. W. W. to WILLIAM ROWAN HAMILTON

MS. Cornell.
Mem. (—). *Grosart. Hamilton. K* (—). *LY i. 383.*

[*In Dora W.'s hand*]

Rydal Mount
July 24ᵗʰ 1829

My dear Sir,

I have been very long in your debt. An inflammation in my eyes cut me off from writing and reading so that I deem it still prudent to employ an Amanuensis; but I had a more decisive reason for putting off payment, nothing less than the hope that I might discharge my debt in person: it seems better however to consult you before hand.[1] I wish to make a Tour in Ireland, and *perhaps* along with my Daughter, but I am ignorant of so many points, as where to begin, whether it be safe at this *rioting* period, what is best worth seeing, what mode of travelling will furnish the greatest advantages at the least expence. Dublin, of course, the Wicklow mountains, Killarney Lakes, and I think the ruins not far from Limerick would be among my objects, and return by the North— but I can form no conjecture as to the time requisite for this, and whether it would be best to take the Steam boat from Liverpool to Cork, beginning there, or to go from Whitehaven to Dublin. To start from Whitehaven by steam to Dublin would suit me as being nearer this place and a shorter voyage; besides my Son is settled near Whitehaven and I could conveniently embark from his abode.— I have read with great pleasure the 'Sketches in Ireland' which Mʳ Otway[2] was kind enough to present to me, but many interesting things he speaks of in the West, will be quite out of my reach— in short I am as unprepared with Tourists' information as any man can be, and sensible as I am of the very great value of your time I cannot refrain from begging you to take pity upon my ignorance and to give me some information, keeping in mind the possibility of my having a female companion.

It is time to thank you for the verses you so obligingly sent me. Your Sister's have abundance of Spirit and feeling. All that they want is what appears in itself of little moment, and yet is of incalculably great, that is, workmanship—the art by which the

---

[1] Hamilton's letter of 14 May (*Hamilton*, i. 331–2) had expressed the hope that W. W. would visit him in Dublin.

[2] For the Revd. Caesar Otway, see pt. i, L. 297. His *Sketches in Ireland* appeared in 1827.

thoughts are made to melt into each other and to fall into light and shadow regulated by distinct preconception of the best general effect they are capable of producing. This may seem very vague to you but by conversation I think I could make it appear otherwise— it is enough for the present to say that I was much gratified and beg you will thank your Sister for favoring me with the sight of compositions so distinctly marked with that quality which is the subject of them.[1] Your own verses are to me very interesting and affect me much as evidences of high and pure mindedness, from which humble mindedness is inseparable. I like to see and think of you among the Stars and between Death and immortality, where three of these Poems place you. The *Dream of Chivalry* is also interesting in another way—but it would be insincere not to say that something of a style more terse, and a harmony more accurately balanced must be acquired before the bodily form of your verses will be quite worthy of their living souls. You are probably aware of this tho' perhaps not in an equal degree with myself. Nor is it desirable you should for it might tempt you to labour which would divert you from subjects of infinitely greater importance.

Many thanks for your interesting account of Mr Edgeworth.[2] I heartily concur with you in the wish that neither Plato nor any other profane Author, may lead him from the truths of the Gospel without which our existence is an insupportable mystery to the thinking mind.[3]

Looking for a reply at your early convenience, I remain my dear Sir

Faithfully your obliged

[*signed*] Wm Wordsworth

[1] i.e. genius.

[2] For Francis Beaufort Edgeworth, see L. 412 above.

[3] In the course of his account of Edgeworth's intellectual difficulties, Hamilton had written: 'I trust that while he thus unspheres the spirit of Plato to unfold the discoveries that have been made by the light of ancient reason, he will not imitate some modern Platonists in despising that better light which has since risen on man, and which, though by the Greeks deemed foolishness, we know to be indeed the power and wisdom of God.' Edgeworth was converted back to Christianity at the end of his life by reading the works of Schleiermacher.

445. W. W. to GEORGE HUNTLY GORDON

MS. Cornell.
Mem. (—). *Grosart* (—). *K* (—). *LT i. 385* (—).
Broughton, p. 24.

Rydal Mount
July 29th [1829]

My dear Sir,

I hope you have enjoyed yourself in the Country, as we have been doing among our shady woods and green hills, and invigorated Streams. The summer is passing on and I have not left home—and perhaps shall not—for it is far more from duty than inclination that I quit my dear and beautiful home—and duty pulls two ways. On the one side my mind stands in need of being fed by new objects for meditation and reflection—the more so because diseased eyes have cut me off so much from reading—and on the other hand I am obliged to look at the expense of distant travelling, as I am not able to take so much out of my body by walking as heretofore—

I have not got my Mss back from the 'Keepsake,' whose managers have between them used me shamefully[1]—but my Complaint is principally of the Editor for with the Proprietor I have had little direct connection. If you think it worth while you shall at some future day, see such parts of the correspondence as I have preserved. Mr Southey is pretty much in the same predicament with them, though he has kept silence for the present. He apprehends that they purpose to extend such of his last years contributions as they did not publish, into this year,[2] which they have no right to do.—I am properly served for having had any connection with such things—My only excuse is that they offered me a very liberal sum, and that I have laboured hard through a long life without more pecuniary emolument, than a Lawyer gets for two special retainers, or a public performer sometimes for two or three songs—farewell. Pray let me hear from you at your early convenience

and believe me faithfully your
much obliged
Wm Wordsworth

[1] See L. 438 above.
[2] See Warter, iv. 124, 140. Southey had two poems in *The Keepsake* for 1829: *Lucy and her Bird*, p. 157, and *Stanzas Addressed to J. M. W. Turner, Esq. R.A. on his View of the Lago Maggiore from the Town of Arona*, p. 238.

446. W. W. to BASIL MONTAGU

MS. Cornell.
K (—). *LY ii. 595* (—).

Rydal Mount
29th July [1829]

My dear M—

The day after I wrote my last, arrived the Selections[1]—many of which I have read—they seem to me judicious.—How or where the Book had been detained I know not.

Hartley Coleridge has been staying some time with Professor Wilson on the Banks of Windermere, where he has been doing very well except for one disappearance, which lasted a few days. It is a thousand Pities that he should give way to these temptations, arising from a cause which is one [we][2] can guess at—[3]

What you Londoners may think of public affairs I know not; but I forebode the not very distant overthrow of the Institution under which this Country has so long prospered. The Liberals of our neighbourhood tell me that the mind of the Nation has outgrown its institutions; rather say, I reply, that it has shrunk and dwindled from them, as the body of a sick man does from his clothes.

We are on fire with zeal to educate the poor, which would all be very well if that zeal did not blind us to what we stand still more in need of, an improved education of the middle and upper classes; which ought to begin in our great public schools, thence ascend to the Universities (from which the first suggestion should come), and descend to the very nursery.

If the Books from which your Selections are made were the favorite reading of men of rank and influence, I should dread little from the discontented in any class. But what hope is there of such a rally in our debilitated intellects? The soundest Heads I meet with are, with few exceptions, Americans. They seem to have a truer sense of the benefits of our government than we ourselves have. Farewell,

with many thanks
yours faithfully
W. W.

[1] See L. 439 above.
[2] *MS. torn.*
[3] Hartley Coleridge's irregularities continued to worry all those who had his welfare at heart, especially his mother (see *Letters of Hartley Coleridge,* ed. Griggs, pp. 102–4).

447. W. W. to JOSEPH COTTLE

Address: Joseph Cottle Esq, Bristol [*readdressed to*] Mr Kilministers, Shire-hampton.
Franked: Penrith August three 1829 J Marshall.
Postmark: (1) 3 Aug. 1829 (2) 6 Aug.
Stamp: (1) Penrith (2) Bristol.
MS. WL.
Cottle (—). *LY i. 386* (—).

Patterdale 2ⁿᵈ August 1829.

My dear Sir,

I received yesterday, through the hands of Mr Southey, a very agreeable mark of your regard, in a present of two Volumes of your miscellaneous works,[1] for which accept my sincere thanks.

The state of my eyes which have been much troubled with inflammation has not left me at liberty to read much but I have nevertheless looked over a good deal of your Volumes with much pleasure, and, in particular, the 'Malvern Hills', which I find greatly improved. I also have read the poem upon Henderson,[2] both old favourites of mine; and have renewed my acquaintance with your observations upon Chatterton, which I always thought very highly of, as being conclusive on the subject of the forgery.[3] I promise myself much gratification from the remainder of the Contents which I shall read at my earliest leisure, but having today an opportunity of [a][4] Frank I avail myself of it. Mrs Wordsworth and my Daughter join in kind regards to yourself and Sister; so would my Sister have done but she is at present in Yorkshire. Early in Spring she had, you will be sorry to hear, a very dangerous illness of the inflammatory kind from which, through God's mercy, she is at present perfectly recovered. About ten days ago I saw Mr Southey and his family all well.

> With many thanks, I remain
> My dear Mr Cottle
> Your old and affectionate friend
> Wᵐ Wordsworth

[1] The 4th edition of *Malvern Hills, with minor poems and essays.*

[2] *Monody on John Henderson, A.B., late of Pembroke College, Oxford.* (*Malvern Hills*, ii. 339). In the same volume (pp. 349 ff.) is Cottle's essay 'On the genius and character of John Henderson', a tribute to the Bristol scholar who had died in 1788 at the age of thirty-one.

[3] 'On Chatterton, and the Rowleian Controversy', *Malvern Hills*, ii. 382 ff. Cottle and Southey had edited *The Works of Thomas Chatterton* in 3 vols. in 1803, and fully investigated the controversy surrounding the authorship of the 'Rowley Poems'.

[4] *Word dropped out.*

448. W. W. to WILLIAM ROWAN HAMILTON

MS. Cornell.
Hamilton. K (—). *LY i.* 387 (—).

Patterdale
August 4ᵗʰ 1829.

My dear Sir,

I am truly obliged by your prompt reply to my Letter,[1] and your kind invitation, which certainly strengthens in no small degree my wish to put my plan of visiting Ireland into Execution. If I do, depend upon it my first object in reaching Dublin will be to find out your hospitable abode.—At present I am at Patterdale on my way to Lord Lonsdale's, where I shall stay towards the conclusion of the week, when I purpose to meet my Wife and Daughter in their way to my Son's at Whitehaven—and if I can muster courage to cross the Channel, and the weather be tolerable, I am not without hope of embarking, Friday after next. This is Monday—August 4ᵗʰ.[2] I believe every Friday the Steam Boat leaves Whitehaven for the Isle of Man; whether it proceeds directly to Dublin or not, I do not know, but probably it does.—I do not think it very probable that my Daughter will accompany me, yet she may do so, and I sincerely thank you, in her name and my own, for the offer of your hospitalities, which as we are utter Strangers in Dublin could not be still more prized by us. I say no more at present than [that][3] if I do not start at the time mentioned above, the season will be too far advanced; and I must defer the pleasure to another year. May I beg to be remembered to your Sister—and believe [me][2] my dear Mr Hamilton, most sincerely your much obliged

Wᵐ Wordsworth

---

[1] L. 444 above.   [2] Monday was the 3rd.   [3] *Word dropped out.*

449. W. W. to ROBERT JONES

Address: Rev. R. Jones, Plas yn Llan, Ruthyn, North Wales.
Franked: Penrith August three 1829 W. Marshall.
Postmark: 3 Aug. 1829. *Stamp*: Penrith.
MS. WL. Hitherto unpublished.

Patterdale
August 4th 1829[1]

My dear Jones,

We had looked for you with a good deal of confidence, and were not a little disappointed in not seeing you. I am now on my way to Lowther, and should have written you from thence to inquire after you. It gives us much concern to hear of your Brother's illness, the more so as you speak of its having been a dangerous one; and I know well that under the most favorable circumstances the irritation causes great uneasiness.—

As you do not mention your own health, I hope it is pretty good. My excellent Sister you will be sorry to learn had in Spring a most dangerous sickness, an internal inflammation, which subsided after keeping her 48 hours in acute pain, I might use a much stronger expression, and this is the cause why we cannot visit Wales this summer; for though she is recovered almost from the extreme weakness the malady left, still a year's tranquillity at least must be tried, before she can safely be trusted to any extraordinary exertion or excitement. Pray thank your Brother Edward for his kind attentions, and express our regrets that this agreeable Excursion must be given up for this year.—

My Son John has been presented to a small Living by the Earl of Lonsdale. It is near Whitehaven—he is gone to take possession, and Mrs. W. will follow in a few days to see that he is comfortably established. There is no parsonage—so that he must lodge somewhere. My Daughter and I intend to follow in a few days; her Mother thinking that sea-air and perhaps Bathing may strengthen her against the Winter. She is, thank God, in pretty good general health; but far from being so strong as might be wished—in particular she has a weakness in the throat which is very liable to be affected either by damp, or very hot weather.

Moresby is the name of my Son's living, and it is very agreeably situated on the Coast, and as a Coach passes from Ambleside thither every other day, and the Mail Coach every day it is in very easy

---

[1] It is clear from the postmarks of this and the next letter that W. W. has mistaken the date in both cases.

and expeditious communication with Rydal. This is very agreeable
to both parties. My younger Son I have sent into Germany to pass
there or in Switzerland where French is spoken, a couple of Years.
He promises to be a very interesting young man, and is a favorite
with everyone—but the dreadful illness he brought with him from
the Charterhouse many years ago, so impaired his Constitution,
that I fear it will be very difficult to find a situation for him in these
times where he can get his bread: and I have sent him abroad to
get information in German and French, etc., etc., seeing that he
cannot bear confinement for severe study of any kind. Now my
dear Jones, let us hope that another year we may have the pleasure
of seeing you at Rydal; and that our brewing of Ale for you, will
not be fruitless as it was this Spring—With kindest regards to
you and all about you in which Mrs W. and my Daughter would
unite were they here

I remain ever faithfully your old Friend
W Wordsworth

450. W. W. to EDWARD QUILLINAN

Address: Edward Quillinan Esq, Bryanston St, Portman Sq^e, London. [*re-
addressed to*] Col. Barrett's, Lee Priory, Wingham, Kent.
Franked: Penrith August three 1829. J Marshall.
Postmark: (1) 3 Aug. 1829 (2) 5 Aug. 1829. *Stamp*: Penrith.
MS. WL.
LY i. 386.

Patterdale
Monday August 4th [1829]
I believe

My dear Sir,

Dora forgot to beg you would let us know whether you had
received the Mss which unfortunately I entrusted to the Editor of
the Keepsake.[1] Those *Gentlemen* have used me between them most
scurvily, and I am rightly served for having degraded the Muses,
by having any thing [to][2] do with the venal. If you have not

---

[1] See L. 438 above. According to Dora W.'s letter to E.Q. of 25 July,
W. W. had told Reynolds to send the parcel of MSS. to E. Q.: '. . . we were
anxious to get it out of Reynolds' hands as soon as possible. He is a pretty
one—claims a right to spread a *one* year's contribution over *two* or *twenty*
if he pleases; Father will have nothing more to do with them . . .' (*WL MSS.*)
[2] *Word dropped out.*

received the Pacquet pray let me know by return of Post, under cover to the Earl of Lonsdale, Penrith. I must then have recourse to some measures for recovering the Papers. At all events write me a short note.

I am thinking of starting for Dublin, by the Whitehaven Steam boat Friday after next, this is Monday—How I wish I could have your Company—if I go I will see Killarney if possible. My Host at Dublin, will be Professor Hamilton of the Observatory. After all I fear I shall not have courage to go. I wish it however much. Ever faithfully

Yours,
Wm Wordsworth

450a. W. W. to D. W.

Address: Miss Wordsworth, Saltmarsh, Howden.[1]
Franked: Penrith fifth August 1829 Lonsdale.
MS. WL Hitherto unpublished.

Lowther Castle Wednesday.
⌈5 Aug. 1829⌉

My dearest Sister,

I send you three little copies of verses,[2] which may perhaps amuse you at a distance; if read at home with your heart so full as it will be then I hope of pleasant things, they would scarcely have told.

On Sunday I left Rydal on Sara's pony, James on Dora's, meaning to go to Hallsteads that day and to Lowther next—but I found Mr and Mrs W. M.[3] at Patterdale and they laid an Embargo upon me. Mrs W. looks delicate, but she has got a fine intelligent Baby. On Monday I rose at six meaning to go to Hallsteads to Breakfast —but it rained torrents; I did not get off till 12 and then in pretty heavy rain. I found Mr and Mrs John[4] at Hallsteads, and as my

---

[1] See L. 456 below.

[2] The poem which follows below was later entitled *Rural Illusions* and published in revised form in 1835. See *PW* ii. 168, 496. It was assigned to the year 1832 by de Selincourt on the strength of the I.F. note, but it is now clear that the original version of the poem was composed three years earlier.

[3] John Marshall's eldest son William (1796–1872), of Patterdale Hall, was M.P. for Petersfield (1826–30), Beverley (1831–2), Carlisle (1835–47), and East Cumberland (1847–68). In 1828 he married Georgiana Hibbert (1801–66), of Munden, Herts. He had purchased the Patterdale estate from Mounsey, 'King of Patterdale', a few years before this (see pt. i, L. 208).

[4] For John Marshall jnr. and his wife, see pt. i, L. 70.

visit [would]¹ otherwise have been so very short I stopped the night; and Mr and Mrs John Mar[shall] brought [me] hither in the Carriage yesterday. Every body was well at Hallsteads. Here I found only Lord and Lady L., Lady Frederic,² Miss Thompson³ and Mr O'Callan,⁴ an old acquaintance Brother of Lord Lismore, all [?except] Lord Lonsdale looking remarkably [   ]⁵

. . . and imprudently as it proved one day exposed herself too much and too long to the heat in working with her Rake to clear the terrace. The weather has been very bad and cold and this morning's Letter tells me that her cough continues—her throat too was much relaxed; but I hope, so does her Mother, that change of air and improvement of weather will take the cough away and brace the throat. Mary is only waiting for a summons from John to Moresby. Dora will follow and I expect to meet her at Keswick, and will proceed with her to Moresby. Chris. W.⁶ is now at the Isle of Man. I am quite uncertain about Ireland even as to my self. I dread the risks as to health, the fatigue, and the expenses of taking Dora and the long sea sickness. So that Idea I think must be given up, though very reluctantly on my part. I have had an urgent invitation from Professor Hamilton of the Observatory Dublin, including one for Dora—but still I am afraid she is so delicate, and we are so poor. Wmˢ expenses are heavy, and our money is [?turning] much of it to no account—and Reynolds⁷ has tricked me out of the 200 guineas which would have been a great help.

Mr Marshall has talked of going with me by Holyhead—but this seems very uncertain—so that all that is fixed is the Moresby trip.

1

Sylph was it? or a Bird more bright
    Than those of fabulous stock?
A second darted by—and lo!
    Another of the flock,
Through sunshine flitting from the bough,
    To nestle in the rock.
Soon was the pride of Fancy tam'd,
    Conjecture set at ease,

¹ *Hole in MS.*
² Lady Frederick Bentinck (see pt. i, L. 43).
³ See pt. i, L. 372.
⁴ i.e. George O'Callaghan (see pt. i, L. 115).
⁵ *MS. cut away.* The surviving text resumes with news of Dora W.
⁶ C. W. jnr.
⁷ F. Mansel Reynolds, editor of *The Keepsake.*

The brilliant Strangers hailed with joy
   Among the budding trees,
Prov'd last year's leaves, push'd from the spray
   To frolic on the breeze.

2

Maternal Flora! shew they face
   And let that hand be seen,
Here sprinkling softly full grown flowers,
   That, as they touch the green,
Take root, so seems it, and look up
   In honor of their Queen.
Yet, sooth, those little starry specks
   That not in vain expir'd
To be confounded with live growths
   Most dainty, most admired,
Were only blossoms dropp'd from twigs
   Of their own offspring tir'd.

3^d

Thus gentle Nature plays her part
   With ever-varying wiles,
And transient feignings with plain truth
   So well she reconciles,
That those fond Idlers most are pleas'd
   Whom oftenest she beguiles.
Not such the *World's* illusive Shows,
   Her wingless flutterings,
Her blossoms which though shed outbrave
   The Floweret as it springs,
For the undeceived, smile as they may,
   Are melancholy things.

If we live to another year, with health, you and I will make the
Tour of North Wales. It rejoices me to learn you are so well and
strong, but we none of us can bear this Idea of [?exertion] or
fatigue for you, till you have had [?][1] of a year.—If I go to Ireland
from Whitehaven it will certainly not be later than friday after
next. If I go with Mr Marshall not later than the first of next
month. So that you would be at Rydal, so that I may see you before

[1] *MS. illegible.*

my departure if it takes place at the beginning of Sept^r.—I have had a melancholy time with my eyes. They are at present so well as to allow me to read and write; but I have apprehensions that as I grow older they will fail me terribly, so little disorders them, fatigue, change of weather . . .

[*cetera desunt*]

451. W. W. to C. W. JNR.

Address: Christopher Wordsworth, Esq., Isle of Man.
MS. British Library. Hitherto unpublished.

Lowther Castle
5th August [1829]

My dear Chris:

An opportunity of sending this by frank, tempts [me]¹ to congratulate you, on your arrival in Mona² (Caesar's, I believe). I have a further object which is to entreat that you would take Rydal Mount in your return. We all wish this much, Dora in particular will never forgive you; if you disappoint her. I have no news—and little to say—but that I should like to know something about the last Cambridge election, and what motives determined your father to support Cavendish.³ We are all going to Moresby, John's Curacy, and shall be quite your neighbours. How came Charles to think of selling his Classics.—

We have good news of W^m in everything but his health; he had applied six hours a day to his Books, dizziness, headaches, etc., the consequence—the latter still continue—farewell do not reckon

¹ *Word dropped out.*
² C. W. jnr. was on holiday in the Isle of Man with his college friend Frere.
³ The appointment of Sir Nicholas Tindal (see pt. i, L. 290) as Lord Chief Justice on 9 June had created a vacancy in the Cambridge University representation. William Cavendish (1808–91), later 2nd Earl of Burlington (1834), and 7th Duke of Devonshire (1858), who had just graduated at Trinity as Second Wrangler, came forward as Whig candidate, and on 18 June he was elected to the vacancy, the first Whig to represent the University for many years. Two years later, he was rejected on account of his support for parliamentary reform. He was Chancellor of the University, 1861–91. D. W. had met him during her visit to Cambridge the previous February.

this scrawl any thing but a note, sent as it were by a guess; tell me something about France,[1] when you can find time to write—

> Your very affectionate
> Uncle
> Wm Wordsworth—

452. W. W. to [? ROBERT DRUMMOND][2]

Address: Joseph Cottle Esqre., Bristol.
Franked: Penrith Aug. ten 1829. J. Marshall.
MS. Cornell.
Broughton, p. 66.

> Lowther Castle Friday
> August 7th 1829

My dear Mr [   ][3]

I deferred acknowledging the receipt of your kind Letter, till I came to this place; where though I have been three or four days I have not had an opportunity of speaking to the Master of the House upon public affairs, nor heard any mention of them. My own apprehensions are however not the less strong—if I open a Review or a magazine, or take up a newspaper, I am almost sure of meeting with some thing hostile to the Institutions of the Country, some thing tending to bring the government into contempt, or to alienate the affections of the people from it. The most marked object of dislike at present seems to be the Tythes,[4] and through them the first attack will be made upon the Church. But too much of this —sufficient for the day etc—

I regret our mistake about the fare of the Mail—yet after all that was perhaps as good a way as you could have taken.

---

[1] For C. W. jnr.'s tour in France the previous summer, see pt. i, Ls. 362, 376.

[2] There seems to have been some confusion over the addressing of this letter by the franker, who appears to have sent it to Cottle by mistake. The note of the addressee which W. W. put on one of the outside folds was Mr. D[   ], much of the name being illegible, but the contents of the letter strongly suggest that it was addressed to Robert Drummond, Mr. Merewether's curate, who had recently visited Rydal Mount (see L. 442 above).

[3] *Name crossed out.*

[4] The agricultural depression following the Napoleonic Wars had made tithes very unpopular with the farmers. Some attempt was made to regulate them by the Act of 1836.

John I am sure will be happy to attend you upon an Excursion through that part of our Lakes and Mountains which you have not seen.

On Monday next I proceed to Moresby to join Mrs W. and my Daughter, whose health we hope may be benefited by sea air. I am still uncertain about Ireland.

Excuse this hasty scrawl and believe my dear Mr D——

very sincerely yours
Wm Wordsworth

Pray thank your father[1] for his kind invitation

Sat:

P.S. Since I wrote the above I have had a long conversation with Lord L. upon public affairs—he shewed me some interesting private Documents; he is dispirited, and quite at a loss to know how things are to be carried on.—John is at Moresby, after a trip to the Isle of Man.—[2]

453. W. W. to WILLIAM ROWAN HAMILTON

MS. Cornell.
Hamilton (—). *K* (—). *LY i. 388* (—).

Whitehaven
Augst 15th 1829—[3]

My dear Mr Hamilton,

The Steam-boat has been driven ashore here; so that I could not have gone in her to Dublin. But my plans had been previously changed. My present intention is to start with Mr Marshall[4] M.P. for Yorkshire, who gives me a seat in his Carriage, for Holyhead, on the 24th Instant, so that by the 27th or 8th we reckon upon being in Dublin; when I shall make my way to the Observatory, leaving him and his Son[5] to amuse themselves in the City,

---

[1] Admiral Sir Adam Drummond (1770–1849), of Megginch, Perthshire, who married Charlotte, eldest daughter of John, 4th Duke of Atholl.

[2] To see his cousin C. W. jnr. See previous letter.

[3] Address and date in Dora W.'s hand.

[4] John Marshall of Hallsteads.

[5] James Garth Marshall (1802–73) of Headingley and Monk Coniston, John Marshall's third son: M.P. for Leeds, 1847–52.

where he purposes to stop three days, which time if convenient I should be happy to be your guest. We then proceed upon a tour of the Island by Cork, Bantry, Killarney, Limerick, etc etc up to the Giant's Causeway, and return by Port Patrick. This arrangement will prevent my profiting by Mrs,[1] Mr and Miss Edgeworth's obliging invitation,[2] for which mark of their esteem, pray return them my cordial thanks.—Some other season I may be so fortunate as to avail myself of their offer, when I shall hope to be favored with your Company also.—Though I speak of designing at present a Tour of the Island—it must be a rapid one, and I doubt not it will leave such recollections behind it, as will tempt me to revisit the Land with my Daughter or Sister, if circumstances permit.—

Hoping to see you so soon, I shall only add that I remain my dear Sir

very faithfully yours
Wm Wordsworth

454. W. W. to HENRY ROBINSON[3]

MS. untraced.
K. LY i. 388.

Sea View, Whitehaven,
Saturday, August 15th, [1829]

My dear Sir,

I have no objection whatever to advance £2,000 upon un-objectionable security, and therefore will thank you to let me know the particulars, with your judgment thereupon, as speedily as you can. I remain here till this day week, so that, if you can address me here, pray do. On Saturday I return to Rydal, and remain there till Sunday evening, when I depart upon a tour which might make it more difficult to communicate with me. About the 27th or 28th inst. I shall be in Dublin, where a letter addressed Post Office, under

[1] Frances (d. 1865), daughter of the Revd. Daniel Augustus Beaufort (1739–1821), the Irish geographer, had married (1798), as his fourth wife, Richard Lovell Edgeworth (1744–1817), the writer on education and inventions. She was Francis Beaufort Edgeworth's mother, and stepmother to Maria Edgeworth (1767–1849), author of *The Absentee, Castle Rackrent*, etc.
[2] See *Hamilton*, i. 337–8, 341. The invitation was accepted after all (see L. 466 below).
[3] W. W.'s cousin, the solicitor at York. See L. 434 above.

cover to John Marshall, Esq., M.P., will find me; but I hope it will
be convenient for you to write me to this place.

I remain, dear sir, faithfully yours,
Wm Wordsworth

455. W. W. to MRS. JOHN BOLTON[1]

MS. Mrs. Greenwood. Hitherto unpublished.

Rydal Mount
Wednesday 2 o'Clock
[26 Aug. 1829]

Dear Mrs Bolton

Yesterday on my arrival here from Whitehaven I found your
obliging Note of the 19th to which I should have been glad to reply
in person. But I have been detained in Whitehaven longer than I
expected, and must be at Kendal tomorrow morning by eleven to
meet Mr Marshall—If the day had been tolerable I should have
tried my chance of a bed at Storrs and proceeded to Kendal in the
morning—but though it is past 2 I have not been out yet; and I
have Mr Clarkson to see who is with Mrs Luff,[2] and his Son's
Bride—[3] and also my Cousin Mrs Smith,[4] of whom I had a glimpse
at Whitehaven on Monday where she has been with her sister
Mrs Harrison[5] to see their Relations.—Mrs W—returns to Rydal
next Tuesday, leaving her daughter to attend as Bride's Maid at
Miss Coleridge's wedding[6] at Keswick. We had wretched weather
at Whitehaven. I saw your brother[7] the Collector twice, and we
exchanged calls but missed each other. He is well.—

Your absence, and the cause of it were much regretted by all
at Lowther—one of the most melancholy circumstances attending
attacks of illness is the uncertainty it causes in one's little schemes of
pleasure—I regret much that I have not a day more to spare which

---

[1] Mrs. John Bolton (see also *EY*, p. 515), wife of John Bolton of Storrs.
She was Elizabeth, daughter of Henry Littledale, banker, of Whitehaven.
[2] At Fox Ghyll.
[3] Tom Clarkson had just married his cousin Mary, daughter of Thomas
Clarkson's brother John (see pt. i, L. 197).
[4] W. W.'s cousin Mary (1780–1867), formerly wife of Capt. William
Peake (see *MY* ii. 96, 112) who had died in 1813, was now married to William
Proctor Smith (d. 1853), purser R.N.
[5] Mary Smith's sister Dorothy, now Mrs. Benson Harrison (see pt. i,
L. 313).   [6] On 3 Sept. See L. 462 below.
[7] John Littledale, Collector of Customs at Whitehaven.

111

I would have gladly given to Storrs. If Mr and Mrs Stanniforth[1] be with you pray offer them my kind regards, with the expression of my regret in not seeing them.

My Son likes Moresby much, and bids fair to be liked in turn.

I heard the Bp's charge[2]—there was nothing said about clergymen's calling in the aid of Deaconesses, as reported in the C. Pacquet of yesterday, but something was recommended too much in the style of Methodist classification of Lay Assistants of the minister, for the Church of England taste. The Bp appears however to be [   ][3] and excellent man; he has offered to subscribe £50 towards building a church at Whitehaven for the poor exclusively, that is entirely of free sittings, if Lord Lonsdale and the Town are disposed to encourage the plan.[4] This and an Evening Sunday Service seem much wanted, particularly the latter, which probably would be a check to the very unbecoming appearance of the streets on a Sunday afternoon—where young men and women are floating about in all directions. As to the utility of the new church it would depend entirely on the Zeal and abilities of its Ministers.

> With kind regards to Mr Bolton I remain dear Madam
> faithfully yours W. Wordsworth

PS

Be so good as mention to the family at Calgarth[5] my disappointment in not being able to call before my departure.

456. D. W. to C. W. JNR.

MS. WL. Hitherto unpublished.

Halifax. 28th August [1829][6]

My dear Christopher,

The bearer of this is Mr Christopher Saltmarsh, who is returning to the Isle of Man to rejoin his Wife[7] and three little Girls. They

[1] Mrs. Bolton's sister Mary had married Samuel Staniforth, Stamp Distributor, of Liverpool. Their son, the Revd. Thomas Staniforth, inherited Storrs on Mrs. Bolton's death.

[2] A Charge to the Clergy on the spiritual duties of the ministry, delivered by the new Bishop of Chester (see L. 426 above) during his primary visitation at Whitehaven on 24 Aug. He suggested that in larger parishes the clergy might avail themselves of the assistance of the laity, 'instancing those who were employed in the apostolic ages, particularly the deaconesses, an instance, perhaps, which from the vast enlargement of the Church, and the still greater difference in the customs and manners of the present generation . . . had better not be *too* closely imitated'. (See *Cumberland Pacquet* for 25 Aug. 1829.)

[3] *MS. torn.* [4] The proposal came to nothing at this time.

[5] Mrs. Watson, widow of the Bishop of Llandaff, and her daughters.

[6] Since she left Whitwick on 23 June, D. W. had been staying with Mrs. Rawson in Halifax. [7] Formerly Elizabeth Rawson, Mrs. Rawson's niece.

have taken a house for a few weeks in, or near, the village of Concham, and I wish if not very inconvenient to you that you would call upon them, as it would give them great pleasure to see you and your Friend, Mr Frere also, if agreeable to him. Mr and Mrs Saltmarsh are very aimiable People—further they are nephew and niece of Mr Wᵐ Rawson, our deceased Friend, and therefore have some little claim upon you. Perhaps Mr Saltmarsh himself may find you out in your lodgings. When you go [to] see them pray ask for the children. You will be pleased with them.

What dreadful weather! The two last windy nights have much disturbed my sleep, for your uncle was to leave Kendal on Monday with Mr Marshall on their way to Holyhead and thence to Ireland; and I have a hundred fears of their crossing the Sea in one of these storms. You will wonder to find that I am still at Halifax and shall remain here until the beginning of the week after next i.e. about the 10ᵗʰ Septʳ.[1] My sister and Dora are at Whitehaven, and neither of them will be at home till the 3ʳᵈ. I am just returned from a visit with our aged Relative to her Husband's Sister—Mrs Saltmarsh of Saltmarsh,[2] mother of the gentleman with whom I wish you to become acquainted. In spite of bad weather we had a most agreeable visit of a fornight, for she is a charming woman, and lives in a very interesting and beautiful place, though in the midst of an ugly dead flat. The River Ouse a magnificent navigable stream passes the door, and its appearance is constantly changing with sloops, boats, ships etc etc.

From Mrs Hoare I have heard of your Father. Heartily do I wish he may get rid of his Rheumatism and all maladies before his return to Cambridge labours. I am very glad to hear that we are to have the pleasure of seeing you and Mr Frere at Rydal, and hope you will stay as long as you can.

Believe me, dear Chris.
Your affectionate Aunt
D Wordsworth

Mrs Rawson begs to be remembered to you. She talks of all of you with great interest, and would be very glad to see you again.

---

[1] D. W. actually left Halifax on 7 Sept.

[2] A village on the Ouse near Goole. D. W. stayed there 11–24 Aug., according to her MS. Journals (*WL MSS*).

457. W. W. to M. W. and DORA W.

Address: Mrs Wordsworth, Robt Southey's Esqre, Keswick, Cumberland.
Franked: Holyhead Aug. twenty nine 1829. J. Marshall.
Postmark: 30 Aug. 1829. *Stamp*: Holyhead.
MS. WL.
LY i. 389 (—).

Holyhead, Saturday nine p.m.
⌈29 Aug. 1829⌉

My dearest M. and D.

Here we are after a pleasant journey, to embark at 11—sail at
1—and be in Dublin Bay, God willing, at 7. There is little wind—
—a side breeze from the North—so we have as fair a prospect as
we could wish.—We slept on Thursday a mile beyond Chorley—
then Wigan, Warrington, Frodsham, whither I rode to meet Sara[1]
—Chester—Wrexham where we saw the interior of the fine
Church, and the celebrated monument by Roubillac,[2] thence to
Llangollen including a round of 4 miles to see Wynnestay,[3] Sir
Watkin's Park, and the aquaduct over the Dee[4]—slept at Llangollen—too late to go to Valle crucis—Left L. this morning
at half past six—the first three miles exquisite—and the whole
pleasant to Corwen—then to Cervige[5]—you will remember the
bridge over the chasm and the waterfall, on our left to-day.
Thought of dear Jones at Cervige[6]—and before we had looked up
the vista of the river Alwyn noticed the Inn on our right
where we, M. and D., slept—soon came the descent along the
⌈   ⌉.[7] Admired the falls of the Conway—went down
to them—you cannot believe how interesting I found everything
we had seen together, crossed the Conway by the Iron bridge and
to Bettws—thought of our dinner—the Bridge and fall of water
under it are very romantic, seen from the other side—up the
River towards Capel Kurig[8] and came to the water fall on our right,
which you and I missed through my stupidity—it is a fine scene.

[1] Sara Coleridge, who had perhaps been staying with her friend Elizabeth
Wardell (see pt. i, L. 85).
[2] The monument (1750) in the north aisle to Mary Myddleton (d. 1747)
by Louis Francois Roubiliac (? 1705–62), the sculptor. W. W. was familiar
with his work at Trinity College, Cambridge—the famous statue of Newton in
the antechapel (cf. *Prel.*, pp. 74–5), and the series of busts of famous scholars in
the Library.
[3] Residence of Sir Watkin Williams Wynn, 5th Bart. (1772–1840), M.P.
for Denbigh, Southey's friend.
[4] For Pont-y-Cysylltau see pt. i, L. 141.   [5] Cerrig?
[6] W. W. is recalling the route of the Welsh tour of 1824. See pt. i, Ls.
140–1.
[7] *Word dropped out.*   [8] i.e. Curig.

From the garden of Capel Kurig we could not see the top of Snowdon or any of its outline—only the Lake and its drear sides—but there were gleams of sunshine—a pleasant drive to Bangor, but the mountain tops shrouded with mist—the tarn or lake looked wild as you will remember—the Inn where Jones and we dined—very dreary—as we approached Bangor the afternoon brightened more and on the whole the day had been very pleasant—had a cold dinner at the Castle—Bangor, looked into the Cathedral, which has been repaired—took 4 horses and on to Menai Bridge, nothing could be finer than the approaching—a dazzling sun behind it, the light of which turning the Bridge[1] and its chains etc. into brilliance the metal gave to it an aerial or celestial appearance that was quite enchanting—such was the effect of all the ironwork which contrasted strikingly with the aquaduct arches or arch, which you will distinctly remember. Nothing can be more dreary than the Interior of Anglesea: the first two or three miles gave us fine views of the Strait and Lord Anglesea's grounds,[2] and of the Mountains of the Mainland though the summits of most, particularly Snowdon, were concealed. It was dark an hour before we reached this place—so that I can say nothing about it, except that 20 Lamps or more at equal distances made a bright semicircle half enclosing a segment of the sea.

I looked with great interest at the Slate Quarries which we had seen together, and at many objects and scenes which we will talk about—I hope dearest Dora's cold is better. God grant it may—and that you Mary and all at home and Keswick are well, and in as good spirits as the thoughts of parting will allow. Present my affectionate farewell to dear Sara C. and her Mother, and remember me kindly to the Bridegroom[3]—with my best wishes for their happiness. Tomorrow I shall to Professor Hamilton's. You shall hear again from Dublin.

The complaints of the Subs.[4] rather vexed me, for I think them unhandsome, as Mr Garsall who was probably loudest, took the stamps again, having complained and none of the rest ever complained to me. Dearest Mary, ask Mr Carter to shew the copy of his letter to the Board, and tell me how you like it. I did not see the Cooksons[5]—nor had time to write. I wish you could say what I

---

[1] Telford's famous suspension bridge, built 1819–26.
[2] Plâs Newydd, seat of Henry William Paget, 1st Marquess of Anglesea (1768–1854), the distinguished cavalry commander in the Peninsula and at Waterloo: Lord Lieutenant of Ireland, 1828–9 and 1830–3.
[3] Henry Nelson Coleridge. See L. 462 below.
[4] i.e. the sub-distributors, of whom Mr. Garsall was one.
[5] At Kendal.

meant to have said, that either I wish the money to be paid or to have collateral security—this from the alarming state of the times. Pray do this.

Farewell W. W.

Love to my dearest Sister, when she reaches Rydal, and a thousand welcomes.

If you can read this you are conjurors—it is a stupid Letter, but the names of the places will recall the Images to your minds. Mr Marshall was much pleased with Llangollen etc. etc. and the line of road which was new to him. Lord de Tabley[1] put me on [?][2] this Route. Again farewell. Best regards to all the Southeys etc. etc.

My trunk was [?][2] injured the first day by the heavy rain—but I bought a painted cloth which protects it. The night is perfectly calm—though the air is cold.

458. W. W. to HIS FAMILY AT RYDAL

Address: Miss Wordsworth, Mrs W. Rawson's, Saville Green, Halifax.
[*In M. W.'s hand*][3]
Stamp: Kendal Penny Post.
MS. WL.
LY i. 391 (—).

Dublin Sunday noon [30 Aug. 1829]

My dearest Friends—

Here we are after a most pleasant passage—I am going to find out the Professor[4]—I can say nothing of Dublin yet—I was not in the least sick, the water was so smooth, nor was one of our party—This note is merely to set you at ease as to our voyage—We are all well—Most affectionately yours—I long to hear from home. We shall leave Dublin on Wednesday morning unless something peculiar hinder—again farewell

W. W.

Welcome to Rydal dearest D—
Direct to Cork and under cover to Mr M.[5]

---

[1] For Lord de Tabley, see pt. i, L. 358.
[2] *MS. obscure.*
[3] This letter was sent on to D. W. (who was still at Halifax) by M. W., who added a short note.
[4] W. R. Hamilton.
[5] Mr. Marshall.

459. W. W. to HIS FAMILY AT RYDAL

Address: Mrs Wordsworth, Rydal Mount, Kendal.
Franked: Wexford Sept. five 1829. J. Marshall.
Postmark: 6 Sept. 1829.
MS. WL.
LY i. 391.

Wexford Friday Night.
[4 Sept. 1829]

My dearest Friends,

We left Dublin on Wednesday as I said we should—I was so busy when there—that I had scarcely a moment at command—and having sate up late every night, and being over stimulated with talking, my left eye gave way, and I could neither read nor write without injury—Today it is a good deal strengthened and I sit down to write a few lines before going to bed. On Sunday at Noon I took a Car and proceeded to the observatory 4 or five miles but the Carman lost his way and it proved nearer 7. I found the Pr.[1] at home and received from him a hearty welcome—his Sisters were not returned from Church—The observatory stands on a moderate eminence commanding a pleasing view of the vale of Liffey and opposite are the Dublin mountains on the left Phoenix Park the City and still further the bay of Dublin. After rambling about 2 hours we called on a neighbouring gentleman a master in Chancery formerly a member of Parliament for the City of Dublin. His name is Ellis[2] he invited us to dine next day and my Fellow Travellers also—on my return I found the Professor's four Sisters,[3] the Poetess included, and one a Girl. They are all plain, and somewhat old-fashioned in manner; but nothing could be more hospitable or kind—The next morning the Prof. and I went in a car to Dublin, called on the M's[4] and saw many of the Lions, Trinity College, the Lord Lieutenant's Palace etc.—etc.—The public buildings are many of them splendid—but there is little or nothing antient in the City except St Patrick's Cathedral built by our King John; we called on Mr Otway,[5] who engaged to breakfast with the Pro: next day. Dined as invited with Mr Ellis—and met there a Mr and

---

[1] Professor Hamilton. For an account of W. W. at the Dunsink Observatory by Eliza Hamilton, see *Hamilton*, i. 311–14.

[2] Thomas Ellis (1774–1832), of Glenasrone, Co. Limerick.

[3] Eliza the poetess, Grace (1802–46), Sydney Margaret (*c.* 1810–*c.* 1882), and Archianna Priscilla (1815–60).

[4] Marshalls.

[5] The Revd. Caesar Otway.

117

Mrs Napier.[1] Mrs N. had lodged some time with the Flemings[2] a[t] Rydal the year we were on the Continent—next morning came to breakfast Mr Otway and the Great O—[3] Tell Edith[4] at your leisure I found him a very clever and agreeable Man. Mr. Otway brought me a map of Ireland in two parts on Silk—deares[t] Dora like yours of the Netherlands, and I will give it you—He is a most obliging person; he had traced on the Map the Route we ought to take through Ireland and gave us notes of instruction besides.— We returned, the Pro. he and I, to Dublin to complete the tour of the City and they brought a friend to breakfast with M. the next day at his Hotel.—We then visited St. Patrick's Cathedral etc about these things I will tell you; the Pro. and I returned to the Obser: and we dined at Lord Francis Gower's,[5] the secretary for Ireland—Lady Francis very pretty, almost beautiful, and engaging. The day before the Pro. and I had called on Lord Fr. at his office in the Palace—I will tell you about all when we meet: next morning left the Hospitable Ladies of the Obser. along with Mr Hamilton, and reached Dublin at nine—and left it at 11—the Pro. and Mr Otway having engaged to meet us at the 7 Churches next day. This was very acceptable—We left Dublin, crossed the Dublin mountains by the pass of the Scalp to Iniskerry—then explored the beautiful valley of the Dargle—and spent an hour with Mr Grattan,[6] member for the county of Wicklow who lives on the banks of the stream, saw Powerscourt[7] and the celebrated waterfall, and proceeded through the Glen of the Downs, above which live the Latouches[8] where we could not call and slept at Newtown Mount

[1] Richard Napier (1788–1868), barrister, Fellow of All Souls College, Oxford, 1811–18: brother of Sir William Napier, historian of the Peninsular War. His wife was author of *Woman's Rights and Duties considered with relation to their Influence on Society and on her own Condition*, 2 vols., 1840. They were members of the Edgeworthstown circle.

[2] At Spring Cottage.

[3] An obscure reference, which is unexplained.   [4] Edith Southey.

[5] i.e. Francis Egerton, 1st Earl of Ellesmere (1800–57), man of letters and Canningite of liberal leanings: chief secretary (1828–30) to the Marquess of Anglesea, Lord Lieutenant of Ireland. His wife was Harriet Catherine (1800–66), granddaughter of the 3rd Duke of Portland, and author of a number of religious works.

[6] James Grattan (1783–1854), elder son of Henry Grattan, the Irish statesman, served in the Peninsula, and was M.P. for Co. Wicklow, 1821–41. Tinnehinch House, on the banks of the Dargle, was presented to his father by the Irish Parliament in 1782.

[7] One of the great country houses of Ireland, noted for the grand saloon where George IV banqueted in 1821: seat of Richard Wingfield, 6th Viscount Powerscourt (1815–44).

[8] The La Touches of Bellevue, Co. Wicklow, were a family of Huguenot descent who had settled in Ireland after the Revocation of the Edict of Nantes.

Kennedy. I rose at six—and took a walk of about six miles to see a place called Dunran—and a little after eight we set off to meet our friends but we were delayed by restiff Horses—At last however we joined them and found they had been punctual, we breakfasted together at a place called Roundwood and proceeded to the 7 Churches. We were highly delighted—I defer particulars—We saw all the antiquities and the scenery and parted about four o'clock with much regret. We went down the Avonmore to Rathdrum where we slept—this morning off at six—a charming drive down the Avon— saw Col. Howard's place[1]—at the celebrated meeting of the waters—and proceeded along the famous Ovoka River to Arklow— and here I will say on taking leave of the county of Wicklow that we saw its most celebrated features—with the exception of the Devil's Glen which would have thrown us too much out of our way. The best things of this morning's ride on the Avon and Ovoka, particularly about the meeting of the waters, reminded me of Wharfdale and of Fascally in Scotland, superior to the former but inferior to the latter—the junction of the two Avons does not by any means equal that of the Garry and Tummel. From Arklow to this place—Wexford by Enniskorthy our walk of this afternoon infinitely less interesting—Tomorrow we go to Waterford and up the Suir to Clonmel—here I shall see the beauties of Blackwater— and so on to Cork. I received a short letter from you at Dublin with one from John C[2]—thank him—and say nothing further need be done about the Subs.[3] till I return which I expect will be in five weeks. Mr Marshall thinks it better not to write to any of this or even to speak of it but to keep our ground.—Has dearest Dorothy arrived and well, and how is dearest Dora—How unlucky about Mr Gordon[4]—Had my eyes allowed I should have written to her —I long to hear of you—Direct to Killarney. I shall write again from Cork. The weather has been delightful—but this evening it rains hard—nobody has the least notion of Charges for Travellers— the thing if mentioned would be laughed at. I saw nothing at Dublin that pleased me so much as the Manner in which the Irish

The present representative of the family was Peter La Touche (1777–1830), who was related to W. R. Hamilton. Alexander Knox, the theologian (see L. 740 below) was an honoured guest at Bellevue for many years.

[1] Castle Howard, Co. Wicklow, which W. W. seems mistakenly to have thought belonged to Col. Howard of Levens (see pt. i, L. 203), was actually the seat of Col. Robert Howard, a relative of the Earls of Wicklow.

[2] John Carter, W. W.'s clerk.

[3] The sub-distributors, who were pressing for a higher rate of remuneration

[4] George Huntly Gordon.

Ladies *sit* their jaunting Cars, of which you see vast numbers—
Mr Hamilton is a most interesting person quite a man of Genius
and always very lively—but I was over stimulated; and could not
have stood it long—Today I asked at Enniskorthy the prices of the
Articles of our Dinner in the hotel—salmon 5^d—capital beef
stake 4$^{d\frac{1}{2}}$ and mark,—cheese—Shropshire or perhaps Cheshire
scarcely better than our Lancashire 13^d a pound. Why should not
our English Farmer make his fortune in Ireland. Mr Ellis gave
nine thousand five hundred pounds for an Estate—a few years ago
for which he has received for some time a clear thousand a year—
but too much of this. Farewell. God bless you all—Our Tour is
likely to prove a very agreeable one—it is now half-past ten and
I shall be up by five again farewell.

[*unsigned*]

460. W. W. to C. W.

MS. British Library.
K (—). *LY i, 394* (—).

Saturday
Wexford Ireland Sept^{br} 5th [1829]

My dear Brother,

If you have not heard from others of my movements you will be
surprized at the date of this. But before I speak of myself let me
thank you for your 2 Letters; the former is ready if I should ever
hear another word on the subject from that quarter or any other—
the latter I received at Whitehaven whither Dora and I had accompan[ied][1] Mary to see John settled in his new situation; and for
the benefit of sea air for a slight cough of Dora's which has lasted
rather too long. The change removed it—but she is very subject to
colds—and she caught another before I left her there last Tuesday
week——On Thursday Morning I took my seat in Mr Marshall's
carriage with Mr James his third son—and we bowled away
through a most stormy day to Chorley, where we slept; next
night at Llangollen, and next on board the Holyhead Pacquet;
and disembarked at Howth 9 miles from Dublin at 8 in the morning,

---

[1] *MS. torn.* The reference is to C. W.'s letter of 17 Aug. from Brighton, in
which he complimented W. W. on the latest edition of his poems which C. W.
had been reading 'with great delight'. 'The Excursion I think you have improved very much by the revision—in compression etc. I should rejoice to hear
that the Recluse was making way.' (*WL MSS.*)

after a quiet passage without sickness to any one. For this we were indeed thankful for only a day or two before three vessels had been wrecked on the Coast of Anglesey, all perishing except one of the crew. The weather has proved favorable to us, both through Wales, and what we have yet seen in Ireland. My Quarters were at the Observatory four or five miles from Dublin, with Professor Hamilton—a young man of extraordinary genius, the successor of Dr Brinkley.[1] In the course of two days I saw as much of Dublin as I wished: all the public buildings inside and out; Trinity College its Hall, Library Various MSS—etc., including the Fagel collection 20,000 Volumes for which during the French Revolution the College gave between 8 and ten thousand pounds—the Bank formerly the Parliament House[2] etc., etc. We left Dublin Wednesday noon, and have since seen all the crack places of the Wicklow Mountains and Country—the Devils glen excepted. The scenery is certainly charming, and either for residence, or occasional Touring from Dublin, must be delightful. But I have yet seen nothing in Ireland comparable to what we have in Wales, Scotland and among our Lakes. The celebrated Vale of Ovoca and the Glen of the Dargle are both rich in beauty, the latter in character something between Wharfdale and Fascally in the Highlands where the Garry and Tummel meet below the pass of Killiecrankie; superior to Wharfdale, but yet in a greater degree inferior to the Scotch Scenes. You have heard probably of the 7 Churches. The ground so famous for the Miracles of St Kevin we visited; and were highly interested—a deep valley with two Lochs or Pools, the one of the Serpent unholy, in which no one will bathe, and the other sacred. Near three of the Churches of which alone considerable Remains are left stands a very lofty round Pillar, very much like a light House, but as are the churches, of extreme antiquity. While we were look[ing][3] round upon this sad solemn and romantic scene with a train of poor hangers-on, and our guide—a woman about 30 years of age passed bearing a sickly child in her arms. Mr Otway a Protestant clergyman who along with Professor Hamilton had kindly come from Dublin to meet us here, knowing what she must be about, put to her some questions; from which we learned that she was going to dip the Child in a part of the stream, called St Kevin's pool—to cure its lameness; she had already come

[1] The Revd. John Brinkley, D.D. (1763–1835), Professor of Astronomy at Trinity College, Dublin, from 1792, and Bishop of Cloyne from 1826.
[2] Begun in 1729 by Sir Edward Pearce to house the Irish Parliament, it was bought (1801) after the Act of Union by the Bank of Ireland Company.
[3] *MS. torn.*

four long miles to do this—a trouble she had taken three times already, and said her prayers nine times kneeling on 4 corner[s] of the rocks in the bed of the River, in succession. Afterwards I went to see this Pool. Near it stands a sacred thorn which I found hung with innumerable little rags of linen cloth—small slips, hung there to wear away in the weather; from a belief that as the rags consume—the disease will abate also—It would have affected you very much to see this poor confiding creature—and to hear the manner in which she expressed her faith in the goodness of God and St Kevin. What would one not give to see among protestants such devout reliance on the mercy of their Creator, so much resignation, so much piety—so much simplicity and singleness of mind, purged of the accompanying Superstitions: The tenderness with which she spoke of the Child and its sufferings and the sad pleasure with which she detailed the progress it had made towards recovery would have moved the most insensible—but after all her resignation to the event be it what it might was uppermost. After nine of these visits had been performed, and all the rites gone through the sufferer assumed that God and St Kevin would either *mend* or *end* the Child—What the result will be I fear, that if she continue as poor as she is, after this is done, the Child will perish through neglect when care, it is concluded, can be of no use. Now the question is Do the Priests encourage these superstitions, or do they only tolerate them: I cannot tell—but it is lamentable that near the 7 Churches Protestants were once numerous, but Popery has gained ground fast upon them by neglect, etc. As Mr Otway was relating to us, among the tombs and ruins, several of the wildest Legends— an odd half-mad half-drunk protestant, a fully well dressed Man, and of good property—exclaimed—Aye gentleman that's all regular sense, and not a babble of nonsense. But whether he meant that it was the true tradition, or that the things had actually happened, I cannot tell. But I must quit this endless subject. At Dublin I dined one day with Lord Francis Gower[1] and another with Mr Ellis, formerly Member for Dublin, and now [?Master][2] in chancery—a staunch Brunswicker. Everybody laughs at the notion of any danger for *Travellers*; though the Report must have told you that ugly things have happened in the County of Tipperary. But it is all among themselves—They never trouble Strangers.

I am afraid you would be disappointed in the Country between Havre and Rouen. I speak from *Report*—but Lady Frederic

---

[1] See previous letter.   [2] *MS. illegible.*

Bentinck[1] told me lately it was not interesting. I long to hear some thing of your Normandy Ramble and also all which you have observed of the French people—whether they appear to [be][2] advancing in civilization or not. Give my kind regards to Mr Rose.[3] To day we meant to proceed to Waterford but Mr Marshall has had a slight attack of the Bowels and possibly we may stop here—an uninteresting place—round which I have walked this morning in the rain. Near Enniskorthy yesterday we saw Vinegar Hill memorable for the defeat of the Rebels in '98[4] and the massacre of the Protestants. We passed Ferns where is a new Cathedral—which we did not stop to look at. My dear Brother, the above I scrawled at Wexford last Saturday—it is now Friday and we are at Killarney, balked by a wet day. We have seen Waterford—The Banks of the Suir, and the Black Water, from 4 or 5 miles below Lismore Castle to Fermoy thence to Cork—of which the harbour is most beautifully gay and rich. With the Scenery of Ireland excepting what could be seen of Killarney from one point of view yesterday, and what we have caught a glimpse of this morning, I am upon the whole disappointed—not with the County of Wicklow but all the rest—except this truly *enchanting* neighbourhood, for such it seems. But how mortifying this vile weather. I must content myself with saying that this region appears deserving of all the praise that has been lavished upon it. You shall hear of it at large and of the rest when we meet; at present I shall confine myself to the people. The condition of the lower orders is indeed abject as you well know. But there are everywhere, more or less scattered, symptoms of improvement, and in some places great advances have been made. Of this too I can say much when we meet. As to the results of the Relief bill, and the dispositions of the people respecting it they are various. I have seen however nothing materially to affect my own previous views; though I am inclined to think less unfavourably of the dispositions of the Upper ranks of the Catholics to exalt their Church; however much they may wish ours to be depressed. They have been mortified by the power of the priests; but still they have sufficient motives of a temporal nature for hostility to our Church.

Whenever I have asked any of the lower not the lowest ranks what they expect to gain by the eligibility of Catholics to Parlia-

[1] See L. 450a above. [2] *Word dropped out.*
[3] C. W. had been in France with Hugh James Rose and his wife and brother.
[4] Vinegar Hill was the final position occupied by Irish confederate forces after the capture and sack of Enniscorthy in 1798. On 21 June they were routed by General Lake.

ment, the answer is that in time they hope to be relieved of Church rates—and the Tythes which many of them are reconciled to upon religious grounds they wish should in just proportion (that is according to members of either Religion) be divided between them. But this is their more rational view of the Case—for there is undoubtedly great aversion to the protestant religion in the minds of numbers. Yesterday we walked with a respectable looking man at Macroom to see a large Catholic Chapel erecting there. The town is considerable, but this Building which would hold 2,000 people is not large enough for the Congregation. From our deportment and manner this Man took us for Catholics, and also from the interest we appeared to take in the new Edifice. He appeared to be a serious and thoughtful person, and when I offered him a shilling on our quitting the Chapel he would not take it, but it was obvious that his feelings towards the protestant Church were very hostile— and in general there appears a notion prevalent among the Catholics that the Protestants have no well principled attachment to their Religion, but are mainly swayed by interest. They speak well of their Priests according to the little I have seen; now this was not so in Italy where the commonalty treated them with derision. I have to apologize for sending you a Letter so dull—but I trust that my talk will make amends when we meet. Notwithstanding all that has been said about conversion I entertain faint hopes of good being done in that way for a length of time. Romanism is overspreading I much fear almost the whole south of Ireland; Chapels rising up everywhere, though the large one I spoke of at Macroom has been eight years in building. At New Ross on Sunday I entered a large Chapel during mass, it was overflowing with people—the Gallery Stairs crammed with poor people kneeling on them—but I must break off. Farewell my dear Brother and God bless you. I have heard particulars of your future plans, which have awakened in me a strong desire to see you at Cambridge in the Spring—love to John and Charles; I am afraid Chris: will have passed through Rydal before my return, we shall [?][1] heard be he at home before a month is over.

Yours most affectionately
W. W.

[1] *MS. illegible.*

461. W. W. to M. W.

MS. WL.
LY i. 396.

Cork Wednesday 9ᵗʰ [Sept. 1829]

My dearest Mary,

We arrived here this day at eleven a.m. where I found your Letter. Tomorrow if we are not detained on the road for want of horses or other accident, we shall be at Killarney—and in something less than a month I expect to be at Rydal Mount, for in 3 weeks and 3 days we hope to have finished Ireland and in three more will be home I trust—I am truly sorry to learn that Wm's health continues so indifferent I would gladly write to him from Ireland but I am afraid I shall scarcely find opportunity, my eyes are so often in the the state that makes writing or reading hurtful; though at present they are pretty well. My dear Sister, I hope, is by this time safe at home and well, and Dora continues well—I cannot say how anxious I am to hear of and still more to see you all.—I dispatched a letter for you just as I left Dublin this day week, hoping for an answer here but the allowance of time was too small, it will follow us—the day you receive this by all means write directing to Iniskilling where we hope to be in 10 days. You will naturally look for some account of what we have seen—but I must beg leave to be brief and dull hoping to make amends when we meet.—Upon the whole, but don't say so, I was rather disappointed with the scenery of Ireland—though by no means so with the general effect of the Tour, as far as concerns both country and people. On the day we left Dublin (last Wednesday) we slept, look at the great Map, at New Town Mount Kennedy, have crossed the Dublin Mountains through an over-celebrated pass called the Scalp and seen the beautiful valley of the Dargle and the too-famous waterfall of Powerscourt. In the morning I rose early and walked 3 miles out and as many back to see Dunran a wild glen, but we left unseen a spot still more famous the Devil's Glen, and proceeded from New Town M.K.—six miles where our Friends the Professor[1] and Mr Otway from Dublin met us and we breakfasted, thence to the 7 Churches with which and the wild romantic situation of three that I saw together with a huge Pillar near them we were highly gratified. About 4 o'clock we parted with our friends and slept at Rathdrum. Next day Friday down the Avon to the celebrated meeting of the waters and

---

[1] Professor Hamilton.

125

down the Ovoka to Arklow, all this through a charming country but by no means equal to Fascally and the Tummel and Garry and Tay. On Saturday night we reached Wexford, having passed through Enniskorthy and under Vinegar Hill where the Rebels were defeated in 98—At Wexford—a dull Town we stopped all Saturday, a day of heavy rain—On Sunday we went to Waterford—with which we were much pleased, and slept at Carrick-on-Suir, on Monday at Shanbally Castle (near Clogheen) the seat of Mr O-Callan's Brother.[1] We found the latter at Home—the next [day][2] to Lismore upon the Blackwater and up it to Fermoy where we slept last night and here we are—but I will not trouble you with these dull particulars in future—I have only a quarter of an hour to say that I have laid in much observation to muse upon and think of—and as to our future Tour I expect the same—But for splendor and beauty of scenery, what I have yet seen of Ireland is not to be compared to Scotland, the North of England or Wales.—The Wicklow Mountains make a charming tour for the people of Dublin and are well worth a stranger's holiday, but no Englishman, still more would I say no Englishwoman, should trouble herself to visit them till she has seen the best part of our own island; I therefore do [not][2] much regret that neither of the Dorothys have yet taken the trouble and put themselves to the expense of the voyage and journey—I will describe everything as well as I can when we meet—the people are just what we supposed—I mean the poorest of them, nothing can be more wretched than their appearance and habitations; but the Country shows thus far great signs of improvement, in roads, in habitations, bridges etc—All these you shall hear of—Today we have had a charming drive along the justly celebrated waters of Cork down to a place called the Cove—ridges of land on both sides richly covered with groves and gentlemen's houses, etc.—but I must conclude—the post goes out—farewel Love and welcome to the 2 Dorothys, say how they like the house improvements[3] I hope to write you shortly.

ever faithfully yours—

W.

---

[1] i.e. Cornelius O'Callaghan, 1st Viscount Lismore, eldest brother of Lord Lonsdale's friend George O'Callaghan (see pt. i, L. 115).
[2] *Word dropped out.*   [3] See next letter and L. 464 below.

462. DORA W. and D. W. to MARIA JANE JEWSBURY

Address: Miss Jewsbury, Grosvenor Street, Oxford Road, Manchester.
Stamp: Kendal Penny Post.
MS. Historical Society of Pennsylvania.
LY i. 398. Letters of Dora Wordsworth, p. 61.

[*Dora W. writes*]

Sept. 11th 1829.

My dearest Friend,

I have been so long in your debt and have so much to tell I know not where to begin—Oh yes—I will tell you last news first—the fish are arrived safe and well, eight of them, beautiful silent creatures when my idle tongue is noisily disposed I shall go and learn of them—my Mother and Aunt delight to watch their graceful movements as much as myself, and I am sure when Father becomes acquainted with them he too will be delighted—and I shall be much disappointed if some time or other he do not throw off a few lines,[1] a fellow to the Dove Poem[2] and elegant as that. Many many thanks—I am ashamed to think how far my thanks have to go back—even to the little packet which brought the pretty dandy shoe horn for my Father a long letter for me and the Poems (transcribed by your sister[3]) with which we were much pleased— then for a second letter and the 'Bridal Band' which found me at Keswick two days after the wedding[4]—the pleasure and admiration these verses excited caused them to be left behind—I was asked for a transcript and feeling sure you would not object gave several, when the Poney chair was ready at the door to bring me home I had not quite finished one to send to Sara's Brother Derwent in Cornwall—so at last in my bustle I left my letter on the desk.—[*D. W. writes*] Dora has this moment departed on her pony attendant on the Bride and Bridegroom to Coniston with a parting charge to me—'Do finish this letter'—begun as you will see on the 11th and

---

¹ He did: see *PW* iv. 151.

² *The Poet and the Caged Turtle Dove* (*PW* ii. 163), one of the poems W. W. had submitted for the next issue of *The Keepsake* (see *Letters of Dora Wordsworth*, p. 57): composed apparently in Dec. 1828, and not (as the I. F. note states) in 1830.

³ Geraldine Jewsbury.

⁴ After a protracted engagement and much last-minute uncertainty, Sara Coleridge was married to her cousin Henry Nelson Coleridge at Crosthwaite Church, Keswick, on 3 Sept. The ceremony was performed by John W., and Dora W. and Southey's three daughters were among the eight bridesmaids. See Stephen Potter, *Minnow Among Tritons. Mrs S. T. Coleridge's Letters to Thomas Poole 1799–1834*, 1934, p. 153.

this is the 15th—'tell her how I have been busied from morning
till night; and attest for me that I have not had one moment to sit
down apart from friends'——True is all this and I will now give
you an account as short as I can (having a host of letters to write
this morning) of what has happened among us. I left Halifax on
Monday, the 8^{th1} and reached home on Tuesday afternoon—
James[2] met me at K.[3] I breakfasted at Staveley and was detained
there by rain till after dinner—called on Mrs. Elliott[4] whom I found
pacing dolefully before the door of her quiet home with a Mrs. Reid,
the Sister of Miss Waller, who came to the Wood on a visit, and
was at that moment in the stupor of Death, and did actually
die two days after. At home I found my dear Sister alone, and
how happy we were to meet I need not try to tell you. The improvements in house and garden delighted me—Change is not what I
like and still less *seek* for in familiar scenes—but every thing pleased
me. Next day (Wednesday) arrived our sweet Dora—and looking
so much better than I expected that I was doubly delighted to hear
and see her once again. On Thursday to dinner arrived the bridal
Pair—very interesting—and the most pleasing company I ever had
to do with at a time so engrossingly interesting to themselves.
Sara always was interesting; but she is now much more so—She is
so quietly *happy* and chearful—and not abstracted as she often
used to be. Friday was a very showery day which kept them at
home—and on Saturday the like, and we had the Harrisons[5] and
Mr. and Mrs Smith[6] to dinner. You know of Mrs Smith—She
is Cousin Dorothy's Sister, and like Dorothy in sweetness of temper
etc., but has had the advantage of being much in good company,
and has a stronger understanding. On Sunday the Bride *appeared* at
Chapel, and dear Mr. Fleming[7] gave us one of his very goody
sermons; with so much heartfeeling that it was impossible not
to sympathize with him—yet at the end of it you could not say
what his object had been. On Monday the sun shone and Dora
and her Friends visited the Langdales, came home delighted, and
had only one shower to encounter. This day (Tuesday) is still
more promising, and all gladness they left us. Dear little Sara who

[1] Monday was the 7th.
[2] The Wordsworths' gardener and handyman.   [3] Kendal.
[4] Mr. and Mrs. Elliot, formerly tenants of Ivy Cottage, Rydal, were now
tenants of The Wood, Bowness (see also L. 484 below). Miss Waller was a
friend of theirs.
[5] Mr. and Mrs. Benson Harrison.
[6] For William and Mary Proctor Smith, see L. 455 above.
[7] The Revd. Fletcher Fleming, curate of Rydal.

seats herself with such dawdling efforts in the poney chaise with her helpful Husband to pack her up in her wrappings—and Dora all independence on the poney. Owen Lloyd[1] breakfasted with us, and D. was well pleased when he consented to be *her* attendant; for to be solitary in that capacity with a Honey-moon pair is not quite the most satisfactory thing in the world, though I must say they behave so prettily as never to remind any one that he or she is in the way. My Brother writes in good spirits from Ireland. Their Tour has been a very pleasant one; yet on the whole I think he esteems the scenery as over-rated: but observe he had not then been at Killarney or the Giant's Causeway. His eyes are certainly much better, though I am grieved to say, not invariably well. Mrs. Luff, among the rest, has been greatly delighted to see [me][2] again at home, and I am in high favour as approving of all her improvements—as such considered—but say I to her 'Where is your motive?—I see none for all this trouble and expense'—She replies 'The trouble is my pleasure etc., etc.' Even the Garden-wall does not absolutely horrify me—if she would but make it the supporter of trailing ornamental plants, and have a flowery grove on the Bank below—but no—it is to bear loads of fruit in spite of me—and that it never *can* do—and what so ugly as a range of blossomless fruitless fruit-trees!

It is time to thank you for your kind letter received at Halifax on my return from Saltmarsh. I very much regretted not seeing your Father, and was truly sorry to hear from Miss Simpson[3] that your health had suffered from your return to Manchester. She told me your Father thought the place disagreed with you, and that he feared you must go away again. Is this so? and whither shall you turn?—My dear Friend, I wish I had been at home when you were here.[4] How beautiful is the place. The flower border on the front is even yet gay with potentilla climbing up every green Bush—Asters Dalias etc., etc.,—and not forgetting the humble pansy—purple and yellow which no doubt you looked on in summer. But I must have done—tho' lots of visitors have come in [   ][5] Mrs Wordsworth's absence at Fox Ghyll, and I shall not get half my work done,—so God bless you! I say nothing of the fish which are a private pleasure for each pair of eyes—and the most useful

---

[1] Charles Lloyd's son, the new curate of Langdale.
[2] *Word dropped out.*   [3] A friend of Maria Jewsbury.
[4] Miss Jewsbury had spent nearly a month at Rydal Mount in late May and June 1829, while D. W. was away at Whitwick.
[5] *Edge of MS. worn away.*

drawing-room companions in the world. Whenever there is a pause turn to the crystal Globe, and ever-moving creatures. But cannot you tell us how they are to be fed? Is there no food that will not discolour the water? Mrs Wordsworth returns. Her kind Love

Yours ever truly
D. W.

I have omitted to notice your very pretty verses on the 'Bridal Band'. The Bride and Bridegroom are very much pleased with them, and so are we old Folks. Tuesday Morning.

463. D. W. to JANE MARSHALL

Address: Mrs Marshall, Hallsteads, Penrith.
Stamp: Kendal Penny Post.
Endorsed: 1830?—Sara Coleridge's marriage. Irish Tour of Mr W. Wordsworth and J. G. M.
MS. WL.
K (—). *LY i. 401.*

Tuesday 15th September [1829]

My dear Friend,

I did not intend to be a whole week at home without writing to you or to your Sister[1] (for it was to *her* I intended to write); but, after all, the letter must be addressed to you as I have not time for a thoughtful retrospect, or for minute details, which could alone justify my selecting her, who is but my occasional correspondent; and she I know will be glad to hear of me through you.

I parted from our dear Friend[2] at Saville Green on Monday, the 7th. Miss Ferguson[3] kindly accompanied me to Bradford upon a beautiful sunny morning; but, as usual, the rain came on, and I had a dull journey to Kendal; but a pleasant day for my *last* journey in the pony-chaise from K. to Rydal Mount—where I found my dear Sister alone—delighted to see me, and I equally so to see her looking well, in excellent spirits, and as active in Body as ever I saw her. On Wednesday Dora arrived from Keswick where she had been officiating with seven more young Ladies as Bridesmaid to her Friend Sara Coleridge.[4] I was most

---

[1] Ellen, Mrs. Marshall's elder sister (see *EY*, p. 5).
[2] Mrs. Rawson.
[3] Anne Ferguson, Mrs. Rawson's niece (see *EY*, p. 42).
[4] See previous letter.

agreeably surprized with her comparatively healthy looks—for notwithstanding the bad weather for the Seaside, she had received great benefit from her visit to the neighbourhood of Whitehaven, and is now really, *for her*, strong and well. I see no symptom of ailment except now and then a slight grumbling among her teeth. This, it is true, would be bad enough should it increase; but I hope it will not. She is as lively as a Lark, and is now gone to Coniston with the Bride and Bridegroom, who have been staying with us since Thursday—a very interesting pair. I saw him in 1820 at Cambridge, and then thought him rather affected; but that is worn off. He is clever and agreeable; and seems likely to make a very kind Husband. If his health do not fail I doubt not he will prosper in his profession.

They are to leave us tomorrow—and on Thursday Mrs Coleridge (the Mother) will come to us to stay till Monday Morning, when she is to depart for Helston in Cornwall on a visit to her Son Derwent, who is settled there, as Curate and schoolmaster. Mrs Coleridge will be brought hither by a Miss Trevenan,[1] a parishioner of Derwent—a very wealthy Lady (travelling in her own carriage) who will take Mrs C. into Cornwall after spending a day with us. I am glad to tell you of any good-fortune attending S. T. Coleridge's Sons therefore will add that this Lady is ever quite the patroness of Derwent, stood God-mother for his Child—and is very much attached to D. and to his Wife.

You may be sure, my dear Friend, that I am thankful and happy to find myself at home again, and it is very pleasing to me to observe the joy in every face at sight of me—looking, as they say, healthy and well. So indeed I am; but I find I must not yet try my strength at all. Ever since the attack of Cholera Morbus which I had at Halifax, it is true that I have walked a couple of miles without fatigue; but I am not to be depended upon; for yesterday I did the like, with a long rest at the end of the mile, yet came home much fatigued—and worn. This perhaps was accidental—but the air damp, the state of my bowels not quite settled, it proves that for a while I should be very careful, and so I shall be. I took an hour's rest upon my Bed, and was quite well in the evening, and am so today.

[1] Emily Trevenen, only child of the Revd. Thomas Trevenen (1758–1816), rector of St. Mawgan-in-Meneage, Cornwall, and niece of Admiral Sir Charles Penrose (1759–1830), of Ethy, near Lostwithiel. Her first cousin, Mary Penrose, married Thomas Arnold. For her visit to Keswick, see Anne Treneer, 'Emily Trevenen's Album', *The West Country Magazine*, ii (Autumn 1947), 172–8; and G. H. Healey, *The Cornell Wordsworth Collection*, 1957, no. 3186.

It is always an affecting parting from our dear old Aunt—At her age it is not possible that *she* should not feel each parting as likely to prove the last—and that I should not apprehend that it *may be so*—yet she is so absolutely healthy, so tranquil yet so chearful that I see strong reasons for *hoping* that we may yet have many meetings in this World. To all appearance, if no sudden disease attack her, she may yet live many years. I left her surrounded by her Nieces. Poor Martha[1] is very feeble—has far less muscular strength than her Aunt; and is altogether shattered. Yet at times, when sitting still, she looks in the face as pretty, and as healthy too, as twenty years ago. Her spirits were always good when I was in her company; and many very happy days—I may say *weeks*—did we spend together at Saville Green. Anne Ferguson looks remarkably well; and if it were not for her voice, I should say is younger in appearance and in constitution than ten years ago. Edward[2] is hardly changed. Like his Sisters, he is made up of kindness and good-will. The improvements he has made at [Bullan] Trees[3] are really surprizing. I consider them quite as a work of genius; for who but himself could have contrived a comfortable family house; and given to every thing an air of elegance, out of such a shabby, ugly inconvenient cottage as *his* was when he began with it? The young Fergusons[4] were to leave Saville Green on the 19th to join their Uncle and Aunt[5] at Liverpool. They are very pleasing sensible, good Girls, and Georgina is remarkably pretty, and has a delightful temper. Poor things they set out on their long voyage all hope and gladness without one misgiving.

And now, my dear Jane, it is time to turn to our own travellers. Our last letter was from Cork. One or two bad days were mentioned but no general complaint of weather, and my Brother seems to have been much more than satisfied with the tour—highly delighted. More, perhaps, with the society, the opportunities of observation etc., etc., than with the scenery—yet the Seven Churches and other particular objects had struck him very much. He speaks with the greatest pleasure of his companions.[6] In short I think the scheme must have answered for all the three; otherwise it could not have

[1] Martha Ferguson (see *EY*, p. 42).
[2] Mrs. Rawson's nephew, Edward Ferguson.   [3] *MS. obscure.*
[4] Georgina, Sarah, and Elizabeth, the daughters of Samuel Ferguson (d. 1816), younger brother of Martha, Edward, and Anne. He had married Elizabeth Day in 1802 (see *EY*, p. 375), and she died in 1823. See also L. 554 below.
[5] John Day and his wife. He had emigrated to New York and became Samuel Ferguson's partner.
[6] John Marshall and his son James.

answered so well for him, as satisfaction, or the contrary, is always mutual upon such occasions, where people share the same fortune for so many weeks together. You will begin soon, as we shall soon do, to long for their return; but we are very desirous that they should do and see all they wished for, and not cut the matter short.

I conclude my Friend Jane Dorothea[1] and her Husband are still with you—I long to see *her*—and to know *him*, and hope I shall have that great pleasure before they leave the country, here or at Hallsteads.

In the mean time, my dear Jane, let me hear from you and know what you are doing, what intending, and when you should most wish to see me, provided health and strength allow of my crossing the mountains. Perhaps you may prefer our all visiting you together after our Friends' return, for my Sister tells me she has promised *you* a second visit, and promises *herself* much pleasure from it—or perhaps you may wish to see me alone *before* the Irish party return —or perhaps my Sister, Dora, and I should come together. In my present state of uncertainty I mention all these possible things— leaving it to you to suggest whatever suits you, in the hope that our engagements may not jar with it. But when your Sister wrote to Mrs Rawson your house was full of company—mor[e ex]pected —and when you were likely to be left to y[ourselves][2] I know not. By yourselves I mean [your] own Family.

I know your good Sist[ers] are likely to have a Bed for me at any time, so that if *your* House should be full, and we Rydal mounters should all visit you together *I* might house with *them*. Pray give my kindest Love to them, and tell them how I am contriving—though after all, being at the mercy of the weather, I have a hundred fears that your numerous engagements and bad weather which has so faithfully attended upon us during the summer, and hitherto during the autumn, may put a stop to whatever plans we may form. *This*, however, is a fine day and Dora, on her pony, is gone to Coniston with the Bride and Bride-groom in the pony chaise, and I do really expect that they will reach home without having encountered a single shower. I speak lightly; but truly this untoward season is a serious affliction—yet never did so much rain fall with so little apparent damage to the corn. This reminds me of Saltmarsh, where I saw immense fields of Wheat ready for the sickle and then

---

[1] Jane Dorothea (1804–51), Mrs. Marshall's fourth daughter, had married in 1828 John Temple (1801–71), second son of Sir Grenville Temple, 9th Bart.
[2] *MS. torn.*

mostly in fine condition; but how it has been gathered in, or whether at all, or not, I know not. By the by, we had a most agreeable visit at Saltmarsh. I was delighted with Mrs S.[1]

And now, my dear Friend let me beg you to remember me particularly to your Sister Ellen whom I have not seen since the year 1822, with poor Harriot[2] at Edinburgh. I shall be truly glad to meet her again at Old Church,[3] and I doubt not she will have a melancholy satisfaction in recounting to me the particulars of her departed Sister's latter days, as I shall have in listening to them.

I trust you continue to receive good accounts from Brighton, and that the Patterdale Family, and the Headingley Family are going on prosperously. Remember me most kindly to those at Patterdale and tell your Son William that I shall have great pleasure in seeing his little Boy.[4] The Askews[5] are coming to an Ambleside Ball to which we doubt not you and your young people have been invited, but we conjecture you are not coming, as we have not heard from you; for we conclude that if any of the young Ladies had been coming you would have had the kindness to quarter them at Rydal Mount, where we could well have accommodated them. Pray tell Captain and Mrs Temple that if they tour this way we shall much rejoice to see them. Adieu my dear Friend   ever yours

D. W.

My sister and Dora send their love.

[1] For D. W.'s visit to Mrs. Saltmarsh, see L. 456 above.
[2] Mrs. Marshall's younger sister who had died recently.
[3] A converted church on the Hallsteads estate, used as an annexe and residence for Mrs. Marshall's sisters.
[4] John William (1829–81), heir to Mrs. Marshall's eldest son William Marshall (see L. 450a above).
[5] The Revd. Henry Askew (d. 1852), rector of Greystoke, 1798–1850, a remote relation of the Wordsworths, married Anne, third daughter of Col. Thomas Sunderland (1744–1823), of Ulverston, and had by her a son and two daughters. His grandfather Adam Askew (d. 1773) of Newcastle, who married Anne, daughter and co-heir of Richard Crackanthorpe of Newbiggin, had purchased the patronage of the living of Greystoke from the Howards, and it remained in the family; but Mr. Askew also had a house at Glenridding overlooking the lake. See also *MY* ii. 395–6.

464. W. W. to HIS FAMILY AT RYDAL

Address: Mrs Wordsworth, Rydal Mount, Kendal, Westmoreland.
Franked: Nenagh Sept. eighteen 1829. J. Marshall.
Postmark: 19 Sept. 1829. *Stamp*: Nenagh.
MS. WL.
LY i. 406.

Limerick Septr 17th [1829]

My dearest Friends,

I received your letter (Mary's and Dorothy's) at Killarney. I thought that in a letter sent from Dublin the day we left it, I had directed you to write to Cork; but as I have had no such Letter, I suppose I have been mistaken. I am truly thankful dearest Sister that you are so well; and glad to hear such a good account of Dora; but poor dear Willie I am almost alarmed about him—how is he [to]¹ stand the winter yonder, I fear the climate does not agree with him. Does he speak of a cough; and have you charged him again on no account to injure himself in the least degree by application. I long to hear more of him and wish I had directed you to write to this place where we are just arrived—Mr Marshall and his Son are gone out; and here are six Letters on the table for him at his return, but not a line written for me—alas—alas. I wish I could have heard from you at least twice a week: But our movements and rate of travelling are so uncertain—hindrances from weather and want of post-horses so often occurring—We are now travelling northward direct having left Killarney yesterday slept at Askeaton and reached this place, after visiting the ruins of Adair²—where are three Abbeys, and a Castle within less than a quarter of a mile of each other—Of the manner in which Mr James Marshall and I exerted ourselves in the County of Kerry (look at the map) I will give you a specimen—We left Kenmare each on a vile Irish Hack horse at five in the morning, rode 3 hours, breakfasted and sailed on the bay of Glengariff upwards of two hours and called on Mr White,³ Brother to Lord Bantry, at his beautiful cottage or Castle upon Glengariff bay, walked about his charming grounds, lunched with Mrs White and her two interesting daughters of whom and his glen and bay you shall hear when we meet—returned to Kenmare on the Hacks in three hours over vile roads; reached

---

¹ *Word dropped out.*   ² i.e. Adare.
³ Simon White (d. 1838), who married Sarah, daughter of John Newenham of Maryborough: brother of Richard White (1767–1851), who was raised to the peerage of Ireland for his exertions in repelling the threatened French invasion at Bantry Bay in 1797, and created 1st Earl of Bantry in 1816.

the place by eight—were up next morning between 4 and five—off
on our hacks after a poor breakfast about half past six, rode 11
Irish miles (about 15 English) took to our feet, clomb and clomb
till we reached the summit of a ridge, descended something less
than 1,500 feet, mounted another ridge as high, descended and
then took the mountain of Carranthouel[1] the highest in Ireland,
3–4000 feet above the level of the sea—descended walked two
hours—then two hours more—mounted our horses which we had
sent round the mountain, and rode 4 Irish miles to Killarney which
we reached at ten—having taken nothing all day but a bad breakfast—one crust of bread, and two basins of milk, and glass of
whiskey. When we reached Killarney we found Mr Marshall,[2]
Mr Dawes' Pupil, sitting with our Mr M—they had dined together
and were astonished at the performance especially for one in his
60th year. And to say the truth I was neither stiff nor fatigued,
though my horse had the vilest paces that ever plagued a Rider.
We left Killarney at six next morning, not so—I am mistaken, we
rose at half past five but did not get off for an hour—Carranthouel
as a mountain is a much sublimer object than any we have; and
Killarney's three lakes with the navigable passage between the
upper and lower lake, take the lead I think of any one of our lakes,
perhaps of any *one* of our vales, but that may be questioned—but
of all this you shall hear when we meet. Suffice it at present to say
that we spared no pains in seeing everything; though one day was
almost useless; it rained all day.—But upon the whole I reckon the
weather has favoured us though it is raining hard now, and has done
so all day. Mr Marshall has just come in—and has opened his
Letters,—none for me how could there be [? a sorry][3] blockhead
as I am. I beg therefore that you will not fail to write by return of
post, directing to Coleraine and 4 days after to Lurgan—Lurgan I
have written the word twice, the first letter is an L. Tomorrow
we go to Nenagh, next day we hope to reach Edgeworth Town
where we shall meet the Professor,[4] thence to Londonderry, and
so forth. I shall despatch this from Limerick though it tells you
so little. Limerick is a large uninteresting town—and I wish we
were out of it; but this morning we were much pleased with the
ruins at Adair, and also though in a less degree with those of

[1] Carrantual.
[2] A former pupil at Mr. Dawes's school in Ambleside: probably John
Markham Marshall (1804–32), of Callinafercy House, Miltown, Co. Kerry,
who entered Magdalen College, Oxford, in 1821: son of Ralph Marshall,
High Sheriff of Co. Kerry, 1799, who was killed in the Peninsular War.
[3] *MS. obscure.*   [4] Professor Hamilton.

Askeaton. On our way we met a characteristic sight today—a [hearse]¹ bedizened with white plumes; the Driver with a white hat-band—and by his side sat on the box a beggarly looking² Woman, her elderly cheeks streaming with tears and her countenance looking the genuine Irish howl or ululation. At the back of the hearse sat aloft, precisely as people do with us behind a coach, two ragged people with countenance nearly as ludicrously woeful. I should scarcely have mentioned this but that similar contrasts are so common every where in Ireland. Yesterday we met on the high road a Lady upon a Donkey, the Rider most flauntingly overdressed—by her side walked a Gentleman carrying on his arm a huge lap Dog, as Frenchmen do—he too was wondrous fine and with them walked three or four young ladies all in full feather—it was quite a continental exhibiton with something in it nevertheless peculiar to this strange Country.—We do not in future expect interesting scenery; so that we must depend mainly on what we can collect concerning the people. Marshall was quite mortified that he saw so little of us. He is much respected about Killarney but he lives ten miles off—and quite out of our road. The Douglasses³ had left their names in the Book of our hotel dated the 6ᵗʰ. We reached Killarney four days after—I am glad we missed them.—Pray remember me to all Friends—Harrisons⁴—Robinsons⁵—Mrs Luff—The Carrs—Mr Barber⁶ etc etc and give my kind regards to John Carter, and the servants. You do not tell me how you liked the improvements, and what Dorothy thought of our new room.⁷ I hope you all continue well—I have worked so hard in sight-seeing—never having been in bed later than six and staring about all day that I have written to no-one except a Letter of 2 sheets and a half to Dr Wordsworth. I wish I could find the eyesight and spirits to write a long letter to dear Wm whom I think of

---

¹ *Word dropped out.*   ² *Written* looked.
³ Harriet Douglas's brothers, George (1792–1860) and William (1795–1861): Harriet herself kept away from Ireland this summer to avoid meeting an importunate suitor. She had narrowly missed W. W. in Wales, and earlier this month stayed a night with M. W. at Rydal Mount on the way to Southey's (Angus Davidson, *Miss Douglas of New York*, 1952, pp. 148–150).
⁴ The Benson Harrisons.
⁵ Mrs. Mary Robinson, widow of the Admiral, and her numerous children; but particularly perhaps Capt. Charles Robinson's family, now settled in Ambleside (see pt. i, L. 23).
⁶ Samuel Barber of Gell's Cottage, Silver Howe.
⁷ Internal alterations had been carried out at Rydal Mount this summer, including, probably, the addition of the attic room on the second floor. In her letter to C. W. jnr. from Whitehaven on 27 Aug., Dora W. had referred to 'our end of the house down'. (*WL MSS.*) See also L. 468 below.

anxiously and perpetually. Pray tell him so and give my love to John whom Marshall would be glad to see—he talks of coming to West[nd] this winter. Sir Aubrey de Vere[1] another of Mr Dawes' pupils was not at home—Yesterday we came in sight of the Shannon (see the map) at Tarbert—the shores are low and naked and the River wide—it was our Companion a long way—but not a very interesting one—and the Suir and Blackwater had disappointed us before as had the Slaney so that we have little to say in favour of the rivers of Ireland. Tomorrow we shall see more of the Shannon. Our Tour has been most agreeable without mishap of any kind—and no drawbacks but the weather and our missing some persons we wished to see—For example, today Mr Spring Rice[2] member for Dublin and our host Mr Ellis, both of whom we expected to meet here and who could have given us desirable information. —Is dear Sarah[3] come—give my hearty welcome to her, with best love—Say how you like the Bridegroom,[4] and how the Bride carried herself; and give my love to the Southeys.—The Counties of Wicklow and Kerry are well worth seeing indeed for their beauty particularly the latter, there are some pretty spots elsewhere and Cork harbour is splendid—but nothing save those two counties is worth coming to see except for the sake of the people; who present a perpetual subject for thought and reflection—how often have I wished for you all and for your journalizing pens—unfavourable as our mode of travelling is to conversing with people, you would find much to set down and describe, particularly you, dearest Dorothy. In Kerry I was frequently reminded of your Scotch journal, and old as we are I should well like to pass a month with any of you not excepting dearest Dora, in that singular region. As to Tarns, West[nd], Cumberland and the whole country are poor

---

[1] Sir Aubrey de Vere, 2nd Bart. (1788–1846), formerly Sir Aubrey Hunt, of Curragh Chase, Co. Limerick, had been one of Mr. Dawes's pupils at Ambleside before going on to Harrow (see *Recollections of Aubrey de Vere*, 1897, p. 36). He married Mary Spring Rice, sister of the 1st Lord Monteagle (see below), and Aubrey de Vere, the poet and friend of W. W., was his third son. Sir Aubrey de Vere was himself a minor poet, author of *Julian the Apostate* (1822) and *A Song of Faith, Devout Exercises and Sonnets* (1842), dedicated to W. W. who thought highly of his sonnets. He visited Rydal Mount with his wife and daughters in 1833 (*RMVB*).

[2] Thomas Spring Rice, 1st Baron Monteagle (1790–1866), of Brandon, Co. Kerry: Whig M.P. for Limerick (*not* Dublin, as W. W. writes) 1820–32, and thereafter for the town of Cambridge: an expert on Irish affairs; Secretary to the Treasury in Lord Grey's administration, 1830–4, and Chancellor of the Exchequer in Melbourne's second administration, 1835–9. His second wife was Mary Anne, daughter of John Marshall of Hallsteads (see pt. i, L. 208).

[3] S. H., who had been away for some months at Brinsop.

[4] Henry Nelson Coleridge, married this month to Sara Coleridge.

in comparison with it, one Hill alone is said to show 300 of these, and from the top of Caranthouel are seen heaven knows how many, and one (tell Southey) at vast depth to which the fine one on Saddleback is a meer pool. The Sun I think never shines upon it or its volcanic crater. I have brought Mrs Robinson a small stone from its summit where grows the mountain or sea-pink (thrift) and all up the sides as does London pride both so common in our garden— on the Cushions of the pink I trod everywhere for softness sake— The Irishwomen one meets, but do not repeat this, are never lovely, and scarcely ever handsome—but I must stop for tea and bed, how I long to hear of you all—Farewell my dearest Friends

[unsigned]

465. W. W. to C. W.

Address: The Master of Trinity, Cambridge *[readdressed to]* Mrs Hoares, Hampstead, London.
Franked: Nenagh Sept. eighteen 1829. J. Marshall.
Postmark: (1) 19 Sept. 1829 (2) 21 Sept. 1829 (3) 23 Sept. 1829.
Stamp: (1) Nenagh (2) Cambridge.
MS. British Library.
K. LY. i. 410.

Limerick, 17th [Sept. 1829.]

My dear Brother,

Read this first. This letter, begun on the 5th, I could not think worthy of being sent off, and I never have found time to write a better, for I really have worked hard. Day before yesterday Mr James M.[1] and I breakfasted at 5, set off from Kenmare at half past, rode 10 Irish miles, took to our feet, ascended nearly 15,00 feet, descended as much, ascended another ridge as high, descended as much, and then went to the top of Carrantuohill,[2] 3,000 feet, the mountain being the highest in Ireland, 3,410 feet above the level of the sea. We then descended, walked nearly two hours, and rode on bad horses an hour and a half or more, and reached Killarney at ten at night, having eaten nothing but a poor breakfast of spongy bread without eggs and one crust of the same quality, and drank milk during the whole day. I reached Killarney neither tired nor exhausted after all this. We were richly recompensed by a fine day, and most sublime views. We saw every thing at and about Kil- larney, the bay and the glen of Glengariff (a celebrated scene not

---

[1] James Marshall.   [2] i.e. Carrantual.

far from Bantry) included. With the county of Kerry I have been much pleased, and by some parts almost astonished.

As to the Irish people, our mode of travelling is not favorable to conversing much with them; but I make the most of my opportunities. Poor laws cannot, I think, be introduced into Ireland. There is no class to look to their administration, and the numbers who would have a claim for Relief are so vast that any allowance which would tell for their benefit could not be raised without oppression to those who are already possessed of some property. I have no more room, and the subjects before me are inexhaustible. Farewell. God bless you, my dear brother. We shall push on as fast as we can from this place.

Affectionately yours,
W. W.

466. W. W. to HIS FAMILY AT RYDAL

Address: Mrs Wordsworth, Rydal Mount, Kendal, Westmoreland.
Franked: Sligo Sept. twenty three 1829. J. Marshall.
Postmark: 24 Sept. 1829.
MS. WL.
LY i. 411.

Birr, recently named Parson's Town
Friday 18th [Sept. 1829]

My dearest Friends

Today I posted for you at Nenagh a Letter written at Limerick, which uninteresting place we left this morning in the rain (which has persecuted us all day) and breakfasted at Castle-connel a very agreeably situated village on the banks of the Shannon. It is a place of resort for drinking waters like the German Spa, and the Shores of the River are sprinkled with Villas and gay pleasure-boxes. On a bold limestone rock stand and lie the remains of an old Castle overgrown or richly hung with ivy—the whole landscape exceedingly pleasing. Here we took boat perhaps a little incautiously, and soon found ourselves in the noisy bed of the Shannon among water breaks and wears for the catching of salmon. We were hurried down the foaming bed of the river among waves that leapt against the stream and on one side was an eddy which would have swallowed us up had the Boatmen been wanting in skill to avoid it. But they understood their business. Imagine to yourself a River a good deal broader to the best of my remembrance than the Neckar at

Heidelberg, and foaming along over rocks and shelves much more furiously—on each side were groves and Country houses—but what were we going to see—the *falls* of Doonas—falls they scarcely are—but tremendous rapids which as we saw them today would have swallowed up any vessel that should venture among them.—We disembarked and walked along the margin of the magnificent stream to a limestone Rock that rises abruptly from the bed of the river, and makes part of a pleasure garden. Here we stood and saw a curve of the agitated stream of at least 500 yards —it remind[ed] me as I have said of the Neckar, of the Rhine, dearest Dora, which we saw below Bingen last summer and above St. Goar—but the trouble of the water was many degrees more formidable than in any of those places. Our Boatmen told us that when the River is swoln to its utmost by the water-floods—there are here Billows like those of the Atlantic and the River drove against the elbowing lime-stone rock as if it would sweep the barrier away in the excess of its violence. I can easily conceive this —for today the sight was very impressive—from the sides of the rock grows a large Ewe tree which extends its branches some yards over the stream, and in hot weather the Salmon are accustomed to take shelter in numbers from the beams of the Sun. Distant Hills terminate the landscape but we could not see them for mist and rain. We left this truly interesting spot after drying and changing our wet clothes and proceeded up the Shannon to Killaloo—a Bishop's See with its Cathedral and some very antient ecclesiastical Ruins. It is a poor place but well situated below the outlet of Lough Derg. Had the day been fine we should have taken a boat and sailed on the water—the banks of which here are pretty high hills of rather heavy forms but pleasantly ornamented with wood— a good way up the lake is the holy island—with the ruins of seven Churches, and a tall column[1] among them as we saw at Glendalough in the county of Wicklow. These Churches of Lough Derg have probably disappeared in a great measure as several of those in Wicklow have done—but today we distinctly saw at some distance the Pillar rising from the holy island—which the Postboy told us was the most fertile piece of ground in Ireland; and certainly it looked green as Emerald—had the day been favorable I should have liked to visit this spot—nearly opposite to it the road left the lake altogether—but not till we had a view of this immense sheet of water to its head—The Shores of the upper part are so flat that we left it without regret—and have seen nothing

[1] The round tower.

worthy of remark since except the small Town or Village of Borusakene[1] where about two months ago 20 people or so were killed in a disturbance. These fatal events arise out of unwillingness in the people to submit to the Police—so they quarrel and lives are lost—but it does not seem that religion has anything to do with these disputes.—A little time before we came to Nenagh the Postboys alighted and in the highway redressed themselves in full view of their Lords and Masters in the Carriage. What are you about we exclaimed—only making ourselves dacent plase your honor before we enter the Town. Accordingly off they took their coarse great coats and upper waistcoats—like jockies before a race —made many adjustments and appearing before us in smart drab jackets with gold Buttons, mounted their jaded and restive horses to their own infinite satisfaction—and not a little to our amusement. Tomorrow we proceed to Edgeworth Town I believe by Athlone, which if you look in the Map stands exactly as you will see in the centre of the Island at the outlet of Lough Rea—and here I will stop for the present—

Sligo 22nd

My dearest Friends here we are, having come from Edgeworth Town where we passed two days this morning. At Athlone, the streets of which are very narrow, the Postboys ran the carriage against a cart laden with hay which caused an injury to it that detained us three hours and a half. So that we were obliged to sleep at a place called Bally-mahon and did not reach the Edge-worths till breakfast time Sunday morning. Here we found Mr Edgeworth,[2] proprietor of the Estate, Mrs Edgeworth[3] a lady sixty years of age, Widow of old Edgeworth, an antient Sister of Honora Sneyds,[4] Miss Edgeworth the authoress, two daughters[5] of that Mrs Edgeworth who was Honora Sneyd, and Francis Edgeworth, a young man of Genius, the youngest Son of the whole

---

[1] i.e. Borrisokane.

[2] Lovell Edgeworth (1776–1841), only child of Richard Lovell Edgeworth by his second wife, Honora, daughter of Major Edward Sneyd of Lichfield.

[3] Richard Lovell Edgeworth's fourth wife (see L. 453 above).

[4] i.e. of the second wife. Another sister, Elizabeth Sneyd (d. 1797), became Richard Lovell Edgeworth's third wife. The sisters were noted members of Miss Seward's circle at Lichfield.

[5] W. W. is, hardly surprisingly, a little confused here. Honora, the second Mrs. Edgeworth, had only one daughter, who died in 1790. The reference here is probably to Emmeline, a younger daughter of the first marriage (sister of Maria Edgeworth, the novelist), who had married John King of Bristol in 1802; and Honora (d. 1858), surviving daughter of the third, who in 1831 married Admiral Sir Francis Beaumont.

medley. Professor H—[1] was here also and we passed two agreeable days, though it rained all Sunday. Five miles on this side of Athlone, as I ought to have observed, we passed through Auburn, Goldsmith's famous village, where are the Ruins of a Hawthorn said to be planted by him, and a roofless House in which his father or brother once resided as a parish priest passing rich with forty pounds a year.[2] Goldsmith was born at Elphin and educated at Edgeworth Town. At Athlone during our detention I made the best use of my time in conversing with the people. Today we have had an agreeable drive, but nothing striking except Lord Lorton's[3] house and grounds upon Loch Key, and Boyle Abbey, a fine old ruin at Boyle; the last hour and a half we were in the dark, having been detained by General King,[4] Lord Lorton's Brother in looking about the place. We saw Lord Lorton himself, but he was going out, and committed us to the care of his Brother and a Clergyman. They both described the state of the country as more unquiet than ever, and forbode the very worst from Catholic bigotry and intolerance in alliance with political Demagogues. But remember Lord Lorton and his family are Brunswickers of the first water; Mr Edgeworth whom we had left in the morning sees things in quite a different point of view.—For my own part my apprehensions are little abated—but I will not now enter into particulars, it is late and I bid you all goodnight as I purpose to be up before six to look about me. The Country around Sligo is hilly I believe, and almost mountainous; and said to be beautiful—in the morning I shall be able to judge. I expect a Letter at Inniskilling which we shall reach tomorrow. In eight days we calculate upon reaching Belfast; so write by return of Post to that address. Do not fail.—God bless you all most affectionately yours. We liked the Edgeworths much— the authoress is very lively—again and again Farewell

W. W.

---

[1] Professor Hamilton. For his visit to Edgeworthstown, see *Hamilton*, i. 342.

[2] See *The Deserted Village*, l. 142. Goldsmith was born at Pallas, near Ballymahon, Co. Longford, in 1728. His father was curate, and then rector, of Kilkenny West. He was sent to the village school there, and thereafter to Elphin and Edgeworthstown.

[3] The Hon. Robert Edward King (1773–1854), second son of the 2nd Earl of Kingston, was created 1st Viscount Lorton in 1806. His seat, Rockingham House, Co. Roscommon, was noted for its scenic beauty.

[4] General Sir Henry King, K.C.B. (d. 1839).

467. D. W. to GEORGE HUNTLY GORDON

Address: To Mr Gordon
Endorsed: *Miss* Wordsworth. 21 Sept^r/29.
MS. Cornell.
Broughton, p. 25.

Rydal Mount Septr 21st [1829]

My dear Sir,

Along with the usual dispatches to my nephew William, I take the liberty of enclosing a letter for Boulogne, which I shall also be much obliged to you if you will forward as you have before done in one or two instances. In recollection of the frankness and kindness with which you offered to repeat this service for me, I will make no apology for the trouble I am giving.

Our last letter from William, as usual, brought reports of his happiness and contentment; but he did not speak so favorably of his state of health as might be wished; we are, however, not so uneasy concerning him as we should have been under other circumstances; for it could scarcely be expected that a youth whose constitution had been so much shaken by illness, should enter at once upon a course of study (with change of climate also) without in some degree suffering from it. I hope he will learn to manage himself prudently, and then, I trust, all will be well.

My Brother writes in excellent spirits from Ireland. His Tour has hitherto been most interesting. We do not expect him at Rydal Mount until the middle of next month. You will, I am sure, be happy to hear that his eyes have of late given him but little uneasiness.

Mrs Wordsworth and my Niece beg to offer their best regards. I am, dear Sir very respectfully,

Your much obliged
Dorothy Wordsworth Senr.

We should be glad to hear of the Manuscripts[1] being in your possession. They were not sent to Bryanston Street.[2]

---

[1] The poems which W. W. had submitted to Reynolds, and now wished to be returned to him.
[2] i.e. to E. Q.

Address: Miss Wordsworth, Rydal Mount, Kendal, Westmorland.
Franked: Enniskillen Sept. twenty four 1829. J. Marshall.
Postmark: 26 Sept. 1829.
MS. WL.
LY i. 414.

Thursday Evening
Inniskilling 24th [Sept. 1829]

My dearest Sister,

We did not reach this place till today at 2—having been agreeably detained at Sligo in the neighbourhood, so that we were obliged to sleep at a place called Manor Hamilton, and could not proceed farther today, the only sleeping place in our direction is so far distant.—

Your Letter[1] my dearest Dorothy was very welcome though dated far back—I am glad to hear you are all well—and I now write merely to acknowledge the receipt of yours and to tell you how we go on; and to say that as soon as we can be tolerably sure as to the time of our reaching Halsteads; within a day or two, I will write to you with a view to your meeting us on our arrival if that does not interfere with the Penrith races, because in that case there would not be beds for us at Halsteads.—Mr Marshall's present calculation is that he will reach home towards the latter end of Penrith race week. We have no object before us except the Giant's Causeway and the promontory of Fair Head that are at all dependent upon weather—but still there are so many impediments from want of Horses and Sleeping places where it would suit us to find them and from other causes that it is impossible to calculate with exactness our movements.

I cannot find time to write to Wm and Mr Gordon and Mr Pappendike also, and therefore I do earnestly beg that you would instantly write in my name and your own, and enjoin Wm not to fatigue himself by application and beg that Mr Pappendike would insist upon it. Pray do this for me. You cannot guess how hard I work to see and hear all I can. I am never in bed later than half after five, and often rise at five—so that I am obliged to go early to bed, and my eyes do not serve me for much writing by Candlelight—I could not bear to write to dear Wm unless I wrote him an entertaining Letter, which would cost me a great deal—I spoke to Professor Hamilton about John's wish for a pupil, and he mentioned it to Mr Otway, who wished to know John's terms,

---

[1] This letter has not apparently survived.

which if I recollect right were £100 for tuition alone—I should fear there is little prospect of succeeding in Ireland. I forgot to mention it to his Uncle W— to whom I wrote a Letter of 2 sheets and ½ since I came to Ireland. I have not written to the Howards.[1]

How do you think of getting to Halsteads, I fear the fatigue of your crossing Kirkstone—for heaven's sake let no dread of expense tempt you to any exertion or exposure—take a chaise to Paterdale and the M.s would meet you there, if you go before the Race week, for you cannot be there then—We must indeed economise but I cannot reconcile myself to your proposal as to the 20 pounds.

Yesterday was a very productive day—we had the company of Mr Avenbury,[2] a protestant clergyman, who showed us every-thing interesting in the neighbourhood—the scenery is beautiful, and his conversation was highly interesting. When I place the map of Ireland before you my dearest friends I shall tire you with what I have to say as to the face of the Country—and as to the people though I have learned little I have learned something. The Romanists are entirely (that is the lower orders) under the command of their priests, ready to stir in any commotion their spiritual leaders may be inclined to incite them to—and besides this the lower Irish of all persuasions are ever ready for a broil—so that the country may be pronounced to be in a most unwholesome if not alarming state—it becomes then a question whether the priests and populace will be seconded by the Catholic gentry now that the Relief bill is passed—not certainly by so many of them as before—but still there are the political Agitators and through them and the priests and the bigotry and ignorance of the lower orders who are so prodigiously numerous, I dread the worst for the Established Church of Ireland—after all tranquillity might be established and the country preserved if the English Parliament and Government could see their interest and would do their duty— The fact is they know not how formidable popery is, how deeply rooted it is, how that it is impossible that Ireland can prosper or be at peace, unless the protestant Religion be properly valued by the Government. But no more of this—This morning I walked out before six at Manor Hamilton—it is seated among hills and Rocks of Limestone—The Sun though not above the horizon had filled the East with purple and gold—One mountain opposite of Majestic size and varied outline was steeped in deep purple, so were the

[1] Col. and Mrs. Howard of Levens (but see L. 459 above).
[2] Unidentified.

battlements and towers of a Ruined castle at one end of the small town—the Ruin is one of the finest we have seen in Ireland—the stream was visible in the valley, blue smoke ascending from the thatched cottages, and in different parts of the valley forming itself into horizontal lines resembling vapour, and on the sides of the hills also, all was quiet and beautiful, glowing light and deep shadow—yet not two months ago two persons were killed here and 15 wounded in a fray, between the Protestants and Catholics, because an old Woman sang in the streets a Ballad which one of the Parties did not like.—About the same time six people were killed in another quarrel in a village not far from which we passed—so that it is truly deplorable to reflect upon the hatred which exists between the two parties—Of this I will tell you much when we meet.—At present my eyes hint that I must conclude—but upon the whole I have suffered little from them—though I cannot read at all by Candlelight having left my spectacles at Rydal. Dearest Mary and Dora why did not you write to me—You cannot imagine how I long to see you all, and how deeply I regret having so miscalculated our movements. I directed you before to write to Lurgan—if you write by return of Post I think another Letter might reach us at Lurgan—but if you do not, write again to Belfast—for I think I have already directed you to write to that place. Pray tell me as many facts as you can—I am delighted you are so well pleased with the improvements.—Our Tour has answered our expectations to the utmost. My Companions are very interesting; and we have been fortunate upon the whole in weather, having mostly had it good where we most wanted it. Today has been beautiful—but the Country not half as interesting as yesterday. Tomorrow we coast the western side of Lough Erne to Ballyshannon, and thence we go to Donegal and if possible a stage further thence to Strabane, Londonderry and after that to the Causeway and Fair Head—when our Tour as to objects of Nature will be finished—Love to you all—Sarah I hope is arrived—

most affectionately yours
W. W.

Give my love to John when you write.

This day we have visited Florence Court, seat of Lord Iniskilling,[1] Lord Belmour's[2] also, said to be the finest House in Ireland, and a

[1] John Willoughby Cole, 2nd Earl of Enniskillen (1768–1840).
[2] Somerset Lowry-Corry, 2nd Earl Belmore (1774–1841), of Castlecoole, Co. Fermanagh, the great Grecian mansion designed by the elder Wyatt.

place called Bellisle upon the upper lake of Lough Erne, formerly Lord Ross's[1]—

469. W. W. to HIS FAMILY AT RYDAL

MS. WL.
LY i. 418.

Donegal Friday 25th [Sept. 1829]

My dearest Friends,

I posted a Letter for you this morning at Enniskillen, and here we are this evening—having expected to get a stage further but could not for want of horses at Ballyshannon, so that we had to wait there upwards of two hours. This day our journey has been on the Western side of Lough Erne, that is the lower of the two lakes of that name. This morning I rose at five, and dressed in the dark, and 20 minutes before six went out and ascended a Hill near Enniskillen from which I had a view of the town below me, which stands upon a ridgy island, with waters visibly sleeping or creeping about it almost on all sides—It is rather a pleasant situation and the Town neat though almost every other house is thatched; as is the Hotel (the best in the Town) in which we slept— There is one conspicuous Church with a Tower, and a Roman Catholic chapel.—

Our journey has not today been very interesting, though some of the views of Lough Erne as we came along are striking—one in particular where we looked down upon it from our Eminence, and saw a number of Islands chiefly wooded and what looked like a shoal of huge whales that had been stopped in their course up the channel of Waters and fixed in their present position. The lower part of the Lake is about eight Irish miles wide and without Islands. The River that flows out of it falls furiously over rocks, at a place called Belleek; and also at Ballyshannon—in strange and striking contrast to the lazy diffusion in the two lakes among swamps and Islands. At Belleek I fell into conversation with a person who no doubt was a Protestant—his report was that the Country was inwardly more discontented than ever and that it was unsafe for Protestants to live in it. Such seems pretty generally the opinion of the lower class of this persuasion; my own is that all will depend

---

[1] Lawrence Parsons, 2nd Earl of Rosse (1758–1841), of Birr Castle (which W. W. had seen the previous week).

upon the firmness of the united Parliament, and of the Government; if the former is to continue to be deceived as in my opinion it has been as to the degree in which the Catholic Religion is pernicious and formidable, and the latter to oscillate and crouch as it has been doing hitherto—my decided opinion is that the whole country will be in confusion—if a contrary course be pursued by the Government, then a convulsion may be avoided.—— There is nothing interesting between Ballyshannon and this place, Donegal, a small Town scarcely so large as Ambleside, lying in a hollow between Limestone Hills and rocks with a rocky river small also, and in the Town upon the banks of the stream are the roofless walls of a large old Edifice something between a Castle and a Mansion—Beside it stands a newly erected Church—and a little below is a small quay where two Sloops were lying at Anchor. One of the hills above commands a striking view of the upper part of the Bay of Donegal besprinkled with Islands, and almost bisected with promontories.—

Though there is great want of employment all these little towns are increasing and improving. We see also few beggars, a convincing proof of protestant influence—but alas—the Romanists appear gaining ground in these more protestant parts as well as elsewhere—and this will continue to be so unless the standard of civilization be raised generally throughout the Country, and information and knowledge spread both in conjunction with such improvement in the condition of men and for the sake of truth as truth.—

Tomorrow we hope to reach London Derry, where perhaps I may add something to this Scrawl—At present good night. I hope you have written about Dear Willy who is seldom out of my thought—but I begged earnestly that you would do so in my letter from Killarney—Thank you again Dearest Sister for being so particular about your health, I cannot say how anxious and fearful I am about you all—Goodnight once more—

Strabane 2 o'clock

We left Donegal a little after six—a gloomy wet morning—which deprived us in a great measure of the sight of a mountain pass called Barnesmoor which is thought much of in Ireland—After we had left it we entered on a moorish Country without grandeur or beauty or the least sign of cultivation. We breakfasted at [   ]1 reached this place at noon—it is a thriving Town situated in a spatious [   ]1 upon a fine stream which

<hr>

1 *Blank spaces in MS.*

a little below joins another and they pass on their way to London Derry. Mr Marshall has called on some person upon business which detains us here longer than we expected—I find nothing to interest me, and therefore have sate down to scribble this, having in vain tried the Booksellers shops—nor have I had an opportunity of entering into Converse with any one, which rarely happens. We are now in a Protestant Country the appearance of things generally improved—it is pleasing to observe in this spatious vale how high cultivation is carried up the hills—here are few or no beggars, and the tillage is improved and everything looks well; though trade is languid as I suppose here as elsewhere—having reach[ed] the bottom of the sheet I bid you adieu.

470. W. W. to HIS FAMILY AT RYDAL

Address: Mrs Wordsworth, Rydal Mount, Kendal, Westmorland.
Franked: Coleraine Sept. twenty seven 1829. J. Marshall.
Postmark: 29 Sept. 1829. *Stamp*: Coleraine.
MS. WL.
LY i. 420.

London Derry 7 in the Evening
Sat. 26th [Sept. 1829]

My dearest Friends,

According to our best calculation we shall reach Penrith the middle of week after next—that is the race week; and we are of opinion that if you are not gone to Halsteads you must put off your journey till after my return, as the House at Halsteads will be full. I therefore shall make the best of my way to you, either through Patterdale, or by Keswick as conveyances may serve—If John has not come to see his Aunts could he not wait till my return—I should be so glad to see him—

—I expect a Letter from you tomorrow at Coleraine and another if not two at Lurgan—write to me again also at Port-Patrick as soon as you receive this—And a note at Halsteads to let me know how you are, in case I pass that way.—Londonderry is one of the pleasantest Irish towns I have seen, it stands upon a hill with a broad stream below it, over which is a wooden bridge of a vast number of arches, the walls of the Town, which are perfect, make an excellent walk and at the top of the Town stands a very handsome Church with a commanding spire.—

Mr Marshall having seen the Giant's Causeway,[1] does not mean to incur the fatigue again—he goes with us no farther than Coleraine—and Mr James[2] and I will proceed in a Car to Bush Mills and then take to our feet—we shall see Dunluce Castle, the subject of a poem by Mr Quillinan,[3] and also Fairhead, a Promontory which you will find on the map—and rejoin Mr Marshall on his way to Antrim, so that in a couple of days, as far as sights go, I consider our Tour to be over; and I cannot tell you how anxious I shall be to see you all again.

—Give my kind regards to John Carter, remember me also to Mr Barber, the Harrisons, Robinsons, Mrs Luff etc etc and to the Servants Anne and James and Mr Bell's scholar.[4]

Dearest Sister I am delighted you were so much pleased with the improvements; I hope Sara will be so too—As to our bedroom no words can express the comfort it has been to me—

Have you found the drab cloth for the waistcoat. I bought it at Harrogate, which Anne and I had such a rummage for; Anne would tell you. I took something of yours for a Letter-case, I might as well have left it behind me for I have used Mr Marshall's pen and ink etc., etc.

You will observe that we shall not take the direct way to Belfast from the Causeway—our Route thence is to Antrim and parallel to the vast lake of Loch Neagh to Lurgan at its head—from Lurgan to Banbridge Lisburne Belfast Donaghadee.—I shall call at Carlisle to see if the Dentist cannot supply [me] with a tooth for the under one I have lost, but this I fear cannot be done without putting me to a good deal of pain as the stump remains in—God bless you all and take care of yourselves. Doro—keep clear of cold—You did well as Bridesmaids not to risk your fame by a 2nd exhibition—I see that you will all make good women if prudence be sufficient, what are the young men about

Ever yours
W. W.

Coleraine, Sunday 3 oclock

My dearest M.

Your letter just received—and Mr James and I start almost immediately for Bush Mills 2 miles from Giants Causeway—and

---

[1] First popularized by William Hamilton (1755–97), the Irish naturalist and antiquary, in his *Letters Concerning the Northern Coast of Antrim* . . . , 1786.

[2] James Marshall.   [3] See L. 435 above.

[4] i.e. Hartley Coleridge, boon companion of Jonathan Bell, landlord of the Red Lion, Grasmere.

will join Mr Marshall at Ballimena on this side of Antrim—on Tuesday.—I received your letter enclosing Heaths[1]—at Killarney— but the one for Cork never reached Mr Marshall—I am pleased with the news from Longman, wholly expected. Londonderry is most pleasantly situated—we walked round the Ramparts this morning—today we passed a great thriving Town, and Coleraine is the same but the drive was in other respects uninteresting.

The Scotch Presbyterians are numerous in this neighbourhood, and industrious and well-behaved People. Farewell. Love to all

W. W.

I never read these Letters again so you must supply all gaps and guess well.

471. D. W. to DERWENT COLERIDGE

Address: To The Rev[d] Derwent Coleridge [*delivered by hand*]
MS. Victoria University Library, Toronto. Hitherto unpublished.

Rydal Mount, Sunday 27th Sep[br] 1829

My dear Godson,

I thank you heartily for your kind letter, and still more for the great pleasure for which we are indebted to you—the acquaintance with—I hope I may add the *friendship* of—Miss Emily Trevenan.[2] We, at Rydal Mount, much regret that so little of her time in the North has fallen to our share; but we have seen enough to feel that at first sight all kindly hearts must lean to her; and that the more she is known the more she must be beloved—In short, I never met with any one in my life for whom I have felt the same degree of interest upon so very brief an acquaintance—and this because she seems to be composed of loving-kindness and self-forgetfulness—and is, withal, so sensible, and so agreeable in her manners—but I must have done, least you should suspect me of seeking to flatter you through my praises of your Friend.

Your poor Mother will leave us tomorrow morning—Happy as she has cause to be in your and her Daughter's happiness, I truly sympathise in her present melancholy feelings at parting from a country where she has spent so many of the best years of her life— and where two of her three Children were born—Above all, it is

---

[1] Charles Heath, proprietor of *The Keepsake*.   [2] See L. 463 above.

distressing to her to leave Hartley *unseen*, which we fear will be the case; as he has not been at Grasmere since her arrival here; I trust, however, that when you have her quietly settled with you for the winter, she will cast off her *anxious* thoughts concerning him;[1] and will enjoy better health at a distance. He drank tea with us last Wednesday but one, just after Sara and Henry had left us: and was then in good spirits and looked very well. In fact his health is excellent—Nothing is wanted but the ability to emply himself steadily, —and I would fain hope that when he finds himself *alone*—without one stay—except that of Friendship (and I will say he has never been deserted by a single Friend) he may be able to write, read, and study with more regularity.—We much regret that my Brother has had no opportunity of seeing Miss Trevenan: Could she have stayed ten days longer they might have met; for we expect him at home at the beginning of next week. He has had a delightful and profitable Tour in Ireland, and his eyes have been in their better way.

Surely when you can leave your Mother to take care of affairs at home you might snatch your summer's holiday to bring your Wife, to let us see her, and to shew *her* our Lakes and Mountains, and the store of Friends, old and young, that you left behind you so many years ago. I can assure her she would be heartily welcomed amongst us, and pray [tell][2] her so with my *Love*. I will not repeat any of the fine things I hear concerning your *extraordinary* Baby;[3] but I do assure [you][2] that, if ever it be my lot to travel into Cornwall it will be one of my very great pleasures to see, and become acquainted with this child of yours—You can hardly imagine with what delight good Miss Trevenan talks about him—and indeed about all the Inmates of the Parsonage.

John spent last week with us, and rode back to Moresby yesterday, to do his Sunday's duty. He is very happy, and takes to his duties with steadiness.

Poor Willy has not been quite well since he went to Bremen; but the last accounts of him were good, and we hope he is becoming accustomed to the change of diet, habits etc—He always writes in

[1] Mrs. Coleridge's letters to Thomas Poole at this period are full of anxiety and perplexity about Hartley, which cannot have been allayed by the kind of letters he wrote to her. 'My Brother gets a wife—well—my Sister is to have a Husband—well—I remain alone, bare and barren and blasted, ill-omen'd and unsightly as Wordsworth's melancholy thorn on the bleak hilltop.' See *Letters of Hartley Coleridge* (ed. Griggs), pp. 98–104.

[2] *Word dropped out.*

[3] Derwent's son Derwent Moultrie Coleridge (1828–80), known as 'Dervy'.

excellent spirits, and is much attached to the amiable Family with whom he resides, and it appears they are equally so to him—All news I leave for the fire-side with your Mother—and you, dear Derwent will I know excuse this hurried scrawl—Our Friends are so soon to leave us that I do not like to cheat away the time in letter-writing—only I could not help telling you with my own hand that we all rejoice in your present happiness, and bright prospects for the future—and that I sincerely and truly, am your and your Wife's affectionate Friend

Dorothy Wordsworth Senr.

Mrs Wordsworth, Miss Hutchinson and Dora send their kind love—We old ones are well; though we begin to look a little aged —Dora's health has lately been much improved.

472. DORA W. and W. W. to EDWARD QUILLINAN

Address: Edward Quillinan Esqre, Post Office, Leeds.
Stamp: Kendal Penny Post.
Endorsed: 1829. Dora Wordsworth Rydal Mount Octr 13.
MS. WL. Hitherto unpublished.

[11 Oct. 1829]

Father, Mother, Aunts, and Child beg to inform the ex-Dragoon that it will give them real pleasure to welcome him and his Girls to Idle Mount whenever they think proper to make their appearance.

N.B. The Hutton[1] has a tremendous rod in pickle for the Dragoon who must make a Dragon of himself or he will be absolutely devoured, the Hutton's fury is so great.—And why? because the rambler did not take Brinsop in his way to Birmingham, or rather when he was in those parts.

[*W. W. writes*]

Rydal Mount
Monday[2] Oct^br 11th 1829

Just returned from Ireland—will be most happy to see his friend.

W. W.

[1] i.e. S. H.
[2] The 11th was a Sunday.

As also will M. W.—So would D. W. say were she astir, but I grieve to add she is very unwell at present, but will be restored by the sight of the aforesaid Dragoon.

[*S. H. writes*]

I perhaps may forgive when I see you here—So come.—S. H.

473. W. W. to GEORGE HUNTLY GORDON

Endorsed: Mr Wordsworth.
MS. Cornell.
Broughton, p. 26.

[12 *or* 13 Oct. 1829]

My dear Sir,

Yesterday I reached home from Ireland where we roamed about for 5 weeks with better luck than you upon your late excursion in Wales, as we preserved our health, and had no ill accidents—I hope that you are well, and feel no remains of your indisposition.

You will naturally expect that I should say something of my late Tour; but I should be at a loss where to begin, and still more where to end. We went by Holyhead to Dublin, where we remained 3 days, we then explored the Wicklow Mountains, and traced the courses of the Slaney, the Suir and Blackwater, where most interesting, visiting Wexford, Waterford and afterwards Cork, and so on to Killarney, which is worthy of its high reputation—We took pains with the County of Kerry, far the most beautiful in Ireland, saw the best parts of the Shannon, turned aside to Sligo, and by Enniskillen and the bank of the Erne etc etc etc and through Londonderry, and Coleraine we went to the Giants Causeway and along the coast, concluding by Belfast, and embarking at Donaghadee for Portpatrick.

Of the people I know not what to say, but that I trust they are improving and in many parts rapidly. But the materials of discontent exist to a most formidable degree; and the advance of the Country in well-doing, will depend upon the wisdom of the Imperial Parliament, infinitely more than is generally supposed—But I cannot pursue the subject: it is far too important for me to venture upon.—

Enclosed is a note for Mr Heath calling upon him to deliver my Mss[1] to you; I cannot say how much I am obliged to you for coming

---

[1] W. W.'s contributions to the next issue of *The Keepsake*, which he now wished to be returned to him.

into contact with these people, upon such an unpleasant business. Mr Southey—and, as I am told by his Nephew and Son in law, Mr Coleridge[1] have been subject to the same sort of ill treatment as myself. It has fallen to my share, while I was insisting upon my own rights, to fight Mr Southey's Battle, and in consequence he is free of them; which I shall not consider myself to be till, like him, I have my Mss returned. The Sum of the affair is this: I was going to tell you what, but my Daughter says never mind—I told you enough of it before—

With a hundred thanks I remain my dear Sir

faithfully your obliged
Wm Wordsworth

[*Across the back of the letter M. W. writes*]

Mr Wordsworth will thank Mr Gordon to fill up the address to Mr Heath's note

474. W. W. to ALEXANDER DYCE

Address: The Revd Alex^{r} Dyce, 9 Gray's Inn Square, London.
Postmark: 19 Oct. 1829. *Stamp*: Kendal Penny Post.
MS. Victoria and Albert Museum.
Mem. (—). *Grosart* (—). *K* (—). *LY i.* 422.

Rydal M^{t}, Kendal, Oct. 16th, [1829]

My dear Sir,

On my return from Ireland, where I have been travelling a few weeks, I found your present of George Peele's Works,[2] and the obliging letter accompanying it; for both of which I offer my cordial thanks.

English Literature is greatly indebted to your Labours; and I have much pleasure on this occasion of testifying my respect for the sound judgement, and conscientious diligence, with which you discharge your duty as an Editor. Peele's works are well deserving of the care you have bestowed upon them, and as I did not previously possess a copy of any part of them, the beautiful book which you have sent me was very acceptable.

[1] Coleridge's dealings with Reynolds and Heath were as unsatisfactory as W. W.'s and Southey's. See Griggs, vi. 777–8, 800–8.

[2] Dyce had sent his new edition of George Peele (1558–96) on 27 Sept.: '—Without the works of Peele a poetical library is incomplete . . .' (*Dyce MSS., Victoria and Albert Museum*).

By accident, I learned lately that you had made a Book of Extracts, which I had long wished for opportunity and industry to
execute myself. I am happy it has fallen into so much better hands.
I allude to your *Selections from the Poetry of English Ladies.*[1]
I had but a glance at your work; but I will take this opportunity
of saying, that should a second Edition be called for, I should be
pleased with the honor of being consulted by you about it. There is
one Poetess to whose writings I am especially partial, the Countess
of Winchelsea.[2] I have perused her Poems frequently, and should
be happy to name such passages as I think most characteristic of
her Genius, and most fit to be selected.

I know not what to say about my intended Edition[3] of a portion
of Thomson. There appears to be some indelicacy in one poet
treating another in that way. The Example is not good, though
I think there are few to whom the Process might be more advantageously applied than to Thomson; but so sensible am I of
the objection, that I should not have entertained the thought,
but for the Expectation held out to me by an Acquaintance, that
valuable materials for a new Life of Thomson might be procured.
In this I was disappointed.

Mr Longman can forward Books to me at little or no expense,
through a Country Bookseller, once a month and sometimes I
believe oftener. I mention this from being unwilling that you
should have to pay for carr[iage] of any mark of your attention
of this sort with which you may honor me.

With much respect, I remain, dear Sir,

Sincerely yours,

Wm Wordsworth

P.S. Excuse my observing that the expression, in your Edition
of Collins, of *shamefully* incorrect as applied to a Transcript made
by Sir Egerton Brydges in the Sylvan Wanderer,[4] is too harsh,
or rather not sufficiently [?][5] to so distinguished a person who is at

[1] i.e. *Specimens of British Poetesses*, 1825. For W. W.'s interest in a volume
of this kind, see L. 398 above.

[2] For Anne Finch, 5th Countess of Winchelsea, see *MT* ii. 154.

[3] See L. 397 above.

[4] *The Sylvan Wanderer; Consisting of a Series of Moral, Sentimental, and
Critical Essays* appeared from the Lee Priory Press in 4 vols., 1813–21. In his
edition of Collins (see pt. i, L. 367), Dyce accused Sir Egerton Brydges of
'shameful incorrectness' (p. 24) in his discussion of the poet in *The Sylvan
Wanderer*, i. 74–8, in copying a letter of John Ragsdale containing an account
of Collins. Brydges produced his own edition of Collins's *Poetical Works* in
1830.   [5] *MS. obscure.*

the same time so ardent an Admirer of Collins, though I think it the duty of an Editor to point out all faults of this kind if considerable.

475. W. W. to MESSRS. LONGMAN AND CO.

MS. Mr. W. Hugh Peal. Hitherto unpublished.

Rydal Mount
October 17th
1829

Dear Sirs,

Be so kind as to send in your first Parcel of Books for Mr Wm Curry and Co,[1] Dublin, A copy of my Book on the Lakes,[2] adding to it one of my Letters to Mr Gray upon Burns,[3] if you have any— for the Revd C. Otway, Dublin. Also—two Copies of each, by the same conveyance, to Professor Hamilton of Dunsink near Dublin—

I am Gentlemen yours sincerely
Wm Wordsworth

476. D. W. to CATHERINE CLARKSON

Address: Mrs Clarkson, Playford Hall, Ipswich, Suffolk.
Stamp: Kendal Penny Post.
MS. British Library.
LY i. 423.

Begun Monday 18th [4] October [1829]

My dear Friend,

It is with inexpressible delight that I take pen in hand and my blotting paper book on my knee to write to you—for in whatever state the letter may find you and your dear Husband I am sure that the very sight of my irregular hand-writing will impart pleasure, and still more when you learn from myself that I am not only improved in health and strength almost to a miracle, but that I advance so regularly—(though day by day *imperceptibly*) that it seems hardly presumption to speak of hopes that the Spring may

---

[1] The Dublin publishers.
[2] *A Description of the Scenery of the Lakes in the North of England*, 4th edn., 1823.
[3] *A Letter to a Friend of Burns*, 1816.
[4] The figure is illegible; it may be the 18th, but the 18th was a Sunday. (de Selincourt's note.)

find me no longer on the invalid list or at the very bottom of it—I will say nothing of what is past, for it is no chearful subject for *your* consideration, and *I* am completely tired of it. Only so far I will go—as to tell you that pain and weakness long continued have prepared me for actual enjoyment in my present state; and with sincerity do I answer 'very well' to the question 'and how are *you*, Miss Wordsworth?' There *were* times when I could neither read nor listen to reading—much less employ my hands in sewing or any thing else—and I could not stand for a minute together even leaning upon another. Sickness and violent perspirations— hot and cold—with pains in my Bowels were my daily, and often almost constant, companions—This leads me to the point where I began, my present state, I go up and down stairs without help and walk about in the house a quarter of an hour at a time, which gives me but little pain—only there is a sense of weakness with unconquerable stiffness—I say unconquerable because it goes away so slowly, but have no reason to conclude that it will con- tinue so, for, only looking back to the time when Henry Robinson[1] was here to lend a helping arm, the change surprizes me. If autumnal cold dampness had not come on, I think I should now be able to walk far enough to have a Look at the prospect from the old Terrace, but cold is my horror; for it flies instantly to my bowels so I must not execute this large scheme till we have Spring Breezes and sunshine. Whenever the weather allows I continue to go out daily either in the Family phaeton which is dragged by one of the steadiest and best of horses guided by a very skilful Driver (my dear Niece)—or the Manservant takes me round and round the garden and upon the lower new-made green terrace in a Bath- chair formerly used by old Mrs Curwen[2] of the Island; but that little carriage cannot be drawn up the steps leading to the old Terrace and I have not been there for several months. By way of special Treat James and his Master bore me thither on a Chair, which indeed was my first mode of taking exercise out of doors.— A whole page all about myself! I should be ashamed were it not for my reliance on your tender friendship which makes me confident of imparting pleasure to you.

Do not suppose, my dearest Friend, during all this long period

---

[1] H. C. R.

[2] Isabella Curwen (b. 1765), of The Island, Windermere, only daughter and heir of Henry Curwen (1728–78), of Workington, M.P. for Carlisle (1762) and for Cumberland (1768): 2nd wife of John Christian (later John Christian Curwen) of Workington Hall (see *MY* i. 311–12), who had died the previous December (see pt. i, L. 391).

of my confinement to bed or chair, that I have been forgetful of absent Friends. Never was my mind more busy and active. And my thoughts have been very much with you. When your long and interesting letter came to me detailing your past sufferings and present weakness I was too ill to read the letter with my own eyes—much less to answer it, and dear Sarah promised me she would do it, but I think she did not, and I do not wonder, she was so fully occupied by anxiety on my account. After that time better tidings reached us;—and a few weeks ago Sarah transmitted your letter to her, from Brinsop, which spoke chearfully of your improved state, though you were then labouring under peculiar anxiety for Mr Clarkson, as you expected him to go to London to have the operation performed in two or three weeks.—He seemed to be waiting only for the cure of a slight wound on his leg; and I have been in constant expectation of hearing of the journey, and very anxious for the result; but now I fear there is some cause for further delay. Pray let me have a letter (I care not how short it is; for, like me, to write a long one you require many beginnings) I am too anxious to hear of poor dear Mr Clarkson to wait patiently for additions to the facts connected with the condition of his eyes and general health, and of yours on the latter point—we have all in this house, within a few weeks past, had more than ordinary cause for turning our thoughts to you. William has been suffering from his eyes far more than ever before.[1] The right eye was first seized with inflammation, and was bad indeed when he applied to the Surgeon (Mr Fell, Mr Carr's partner, Mr Carr being (with his Wife) then on a Tour on the Continent.) Mr F, tho' a very thoughtful, is a young, man and could therefore have had little experience, and we regretted bitterly that Mr C was from home; but by God's good providence it happened that a skilful physician who has given up practice, and has himself endured much from inflammation of the eyes, was lodging at Ambleside; and Mr Fell, seeing at once how alarming was my poor Brother's state, instantly laid the matter open to *Dr Vose*,[2] who attended daily (with Mr F) prescribing with the utmost skill and tenderness. Mr Carr being absent, we should certainly have thought it right for my Br and Sister to go to London without delay, though it was very satisfactory to find that Mr Fell's judgment of the case previous to

---

[1] For the genesis of W. W.'s eye trouble, which intermittently inhibited him from reading and composition for long periods during the later years, see *MY* i. 461.

[2] Dr. James Vose of Liverpool.

consulting with Dr V. exactly coincided with his—You will perceive, however, that Mr F's inexperience of such disorders of the eye would have been sufficient ground for our not trusting to him alone—nor do I think he would have consented we *should* do so. I will not detail the melancholy progress of a disease which long threatened total blindness in the *left* eye, the *right* being relieved in a comparatively short time. The Ball of the eye was opaque for a long time; but in the course of last week Dr V. left his patient with the power of distinguishing a dull light from darkness; and the inflammation was nearly subdued. The means used have been tedious and distressing,—frequent bleeding with leeches, blisters, and a course of powerful medicines, of which calomel was I believe the foundation; and the effect upon his bodily feelings is oppressive, besides the irritability occasioned by such medicines—and the weakness by low diet. Mr Fell, though Mr Carr is returned, continues his daily visits, and each day reports more and more favorably of the progress made. The eye is almost clear (they *tell* me, for I have not yet ventured to look upon it, being unable to be of the least use) and he can distinguish objects in the room; for instance, the pictures—and can now say which is a print, which a painting. The progress has been much more rapid than Mr Fell expected, and I have no doubt of his reports since Dr Vose's departure giving the most lively satisfaction to Dr V—, who warned us that the recovery would be *very slow.* My dear Friend, I should not have ventured upon this minute detail to any one but you—you who are so much interested in my sufferings—and in *his* so peculiarly as centring in the eyes—though I suppose Mr Clarkson's malady is of a very different kind, and not attended with so much pain—Let us turn to something else; but not till I have again entreated you to write as soon as you can. I hope you will see Henry Robinson ere long[1]—perhaps at Xmas for he will then probably visit his Friends at Bury, and he was not only very anxious concerning Mr Clarkson's eyes and your health but actually promised to send me a report of your domestic condition—What a wonderful Creature he is both as to activity of body and mind! That gift which he has of dropping asleep at will, and waking up like the Lark most likely I think repairs nature in an extraordinary way; for after fatigue, so refreshed, he will go on talking with unabated and unabating vigour as long as there are ears to hear. I did not observe one symptom in him of derangement either bodily

---

[1] H. C. R. in fact remained abroad for two years.

or mental except that thrice, when he was in bed at night, and I awake on my pillow, I heard the most dreadful screams proceeding from his room. Once (lame as [I]¹ was) I was on the point of getting up to make a loud knocking at his door, when silence relieved me: I cannot tell you how much I value Mr Robinson's friendship. He is a rock on which I could lean in all difficulties assured of support—and how kind he is to every one!

Tuesday 27th October. It was a week on Monday since this letter was begun, and thus far advanced at 3 Sittings: Alas! this is the first morning I have had since Thursday when I have had the power of finishing, which I must do as briefly as possible, allowing myself time to assure you there is no cause for alarm my malady being subdued, I have had a diarrh[*del.*]oea* and have not sate up half an hour: I now write on the Bed, and am easy and comfortable as possible. Dora in her lively way has just been telling me I look charmingly—and indeed she observed seriously that I had n[ever] had an attack which had told so little on my looks. One thing it has done—entirely reduced the swelling of my eyes.

      * I cannot get that word rightly spelt. D. W.

There has been no tendency to inflammation in the Bowels— I have only had bilious sickness—headaches, and sharp pains of the Bowels. Conclude if you hear nothing that we go on well. I *must* not be a letter-writer but promise you shall know if we are suffering from sickness or distress of any kind.—Remember 'No news is good' if we be silent.

Farewell and may God preserve your dear Husband through his trial—and both of you be allowed some years longer of peace and content.—William's eyes have gone on as well as possible all the week—He can now discern all objects that are near him—and walks with his daughter every day.

I must be done—What a little matter is too much for me to perform!—All send love and best of wishes! dearest Friend ever your affecte D. W. I can not ask any thing I wish to know—

¹ *Word dropped out.*

477. W. W. to D. W.

Address: Miss Wordsworth, Rydal Mount, Ambleside.
Stamp: Kendal.
MS. WL.
K (—). *LY i. 428* (—).

[Lowther]
[25 Oct. 1829]

My dear Sister,

At Patterdale I took to my feet having the mortification of seeing Mr Dobson's[1] Boat pull before me on its way to the Stag Hunt at Lyulph's Tower.[2] At Patterdale Hall all gone to the Stag hunt. I was in luck however for just as I came opposite Lyulph's Tower lo—Lady Lonsdale's Carriage and I got a seat to Lowther on the Box.—Your Letter gives a sad account of poor Peggy's[3] fate—I have not mentioned the matter here and I am very shy about these things but I will try—Today, Sunday, I shall write about it to Hallsteads. This Morning I had a Letter from Miss Marshall accompanying my Carpet bag left there when I returned from Ireland.—I wish to see Mr Marshall particularly for my money concerns; but unluckily he does not return till Sunday next which will force me very late if I wait for him either here or at Hallsteads. Sunday is the 1st Novbr—on Wednesday at the latest I must be at Levens. Lady Frederic luckily will be there at the same time; and I understand from her that Southey had received an invitation and only waited to hear from me about the time. As S. has not written I fear Mr H. Col:[4] may have forgotten my Letters. Had it not been for this puzzle about Mr Marshall I intended to leave this place on Tuesday and return to Rydal on Wednesday, at present I am quite at a loss.—The Bp of Durham[5] was so deaf the day he was here there was no conversing with him. Tomorrow we shall have the Bp of Carlisle.[6] There is no company here but Henry Lowther,[7] his sister, Miss Grisedale[8] and Mrs O'Callan.[9]

---

[1] Lancelot Dobson, of the King's Arms.

[2] The Gothic hunting-box above Ullswater, built by the Duke of Norfolk in 1780.

[3] Probably Margaret Wilkinson, formerly servant at Rydal Mount and latterly housekeeper at Ivy Cottage, who was now seriously ill. See L. 511 below.

[4] Hartley Coleridge.   [5] For William Van Mildert see pt. i, L. 371.

[6] The Revd. Hugh Percy, D.D. (1784–1856), Bishop of Carlisle from 1827: Dean of Canterbury, 1825, and Bishop of Rochester, 1827, but translated to Carlisle after a few months on the death of Samuel Goodenough (see pt. i, L. 203).

[7] For the Revd. Henry Lowther, rector of Distington, see pt. i, L. 230.

[8] A friend of Lady Lonsdale's.

[9] i.e. Mrs. George O'Callaghan (see L. 461 above).

My dearest Sister you must not walk not even in the garden to *fatigue* yourself—everything of the kind is to be avoided like the grave. Lady Lonsdale had a dreadful Illness a few years back, she is now strong and stout and capable of any fatigue; but premature exertion would have destroyed her. Henry Lowther says the same of his own case—he has just recovered from dangerous Cholera and is confident that he must have died, had he persisted in the White-haven Doctor's mode of Treatment, but he wrote to Dr Ainslie,[1] who prescribed for him as stated above. Dr Ainslie is at Kellet near Burton and continues there till the first week of November and I have a strong desire to consult him on your case, if you would write down briefly the history of your three illnesses, and how you have been treated: Mr Carr, I trust, would not be offended at my consulting Dr A. for our future guidance if unfortunately any of these complaints should recur, as all would be done subject to Mr Carr's approval. I will bring a frank along with me, come when I may. How unlucky Mr Marshall should not return earlier. Give my kindest regards to Mr Quillinan with my regrets that I am so little likely to see him.—Mr H. Lowther will call at Rydal between the Thursday and Saturday next and will explain whatever is needful.

I have sent the enclosed not without being fully aware that no two cases in medicine are exactly alike—and to shew you how a case may be mismanaged. Dr Ainslie after Mr H. Lowther had taken the blue pill a few days, though[t] the purging ceased, yet after eating meat there was a degree of fullness and nausea—pretty generally.—That nausea proceeded mainly from debility, which was much relieved by a tea cup full of cold camomile tea with a tea spoonful of Cordial wine, or a little brandy—and it was finally removed by a little tincture of Quinine.

Cold meat disagrees with Mr Lowther; boiled chicken is good. Port wine put into a hot pan and burnt with cinnamon and cloves, with the spirit gone, excellent.

Dr Ainslie himself was suffering under the same complaint which he treated as he did Mr Lowther's with perfect success, but [? only] when he adopted that mode.

[*Enclosed is an account of Dr A's treatment, 'kindly written down by Mr H. Lowther'.*]

[*unsigned*]

[1] For Dr. Henry Ainslie, see pt. i, L. 326.

478. M. W. to GEORGE HUNTLY GORDON

MS. Cornell.
Broughton, p. 27.

Rydal M^t. Octr 28th [1829]

Dear Sir

In Mr Wordsworth's absence I think it right to acknowledge, in his name, the receipt of all the Mss belonging to him which were in the hands of Mr Reynolds—except two Sonnets which you speak of as being mislaid—and at the same time beg to express his best thanks for the trouble you have taken in this unpleasant business—as well as for all your other services—especially in your great kindness in affording us such frequent opportunities of communicating with William who, as well as his friends at home, is truly grateful to you.

May I, on the present occasion, request you to forward the enclosed to France at your *perfect convenience.* I do not now trouble you with aught to Bremen—Mr Quillinan, who is here, is about to take a Parcel for him to Town—(which is to be forwarded thro Mr Hebeler) [and] renders my doing so unnecessary. I cannot however omit telling you that W's last letter gives us an excellent report of his health—and he never fails to speak with entire satisfaction of his situation with, and the great kindness of Mr Papendicks Family towards him.

My daughter joins me in best regards and believe me

Dr Sir to be your ob^{ld}
M. Wordsworth

Mr W. will not fail to send you a separate acknowledgment by the next communication

479. W. W. to [?] GEORGE HUNTLY GORDON

MS. Cornell.
Broughton, p. 29.

Rydal Mount
Nov^{br} 14th 1829.

My dear Sir,

I have received through your hands all the Mss of mine which were in the possession of Mr Reynolds, with the exception of two

Sonnets, which Mr R, I hope, will succeed in finding, as I have not a perfect Copy of them. This acknowledgement with my best thanks you would have received earlier had I been at home.

I remain My dear Sir
Your much obliged
Wm Wordsworth

480. W. W. to GEORGE HUNTLY GORDON

Address: G. Huntly Gordon Esqre
Endorsed: Mr Wordsworth. 14th Nov^r/29.
MS. Cornell.
Broughton, p. 28.

14th Novr 1829.

My dear Sir,

I am quite at a loss what to say about Ireland. Its political condition is not a little alarming as is obvious to every one from the late trials. In my own mind I have no doubt that the same disposition to conspire against Landlords, Magistrates, and the supporters of Protestantism are spread through much the greatest part of Ireland. Will the leading people who have been propitiated by the Relief-Bill prove a compensation for that loss of strength which is unavoidable where intimidation is known to have been the cause of success? I fear not.—But my pen might for you be more agreeably employed in giving you some account of the impression which the scenery of Ireland and the face of the Country made upon my mind. This, except for the wretched state of swarms of the inhabitants was very favorable. We were five weeks travelling about and saw almost every thing. The County of Kerry far exceeds the rest; so much so it well deserves that a leading artist, and a man of taste and general information should unite their powers to illustrate it. With the Coast of Antrim also, including the Giants Causeway, which is however far from being the most interesting object it presents, I was highly delighted.—

I could not resist the temptation to ascend the highest mountain in Ireland, higher than any of our's—Carran-thuil its name[1]— 3,410 feet above the level of the sea. The mountain is itself a magnificent object from many points of view—and the prospect from it very splendid; gulphs of awful depth below and sea and

---

[1] Carrantual in Co. Kerry, the loftiest of Macgillicuddy's Reeks.

land, and inland waters, and bays spread around within a vast horizon. I was not disappointed with Killarney—and that is saying a great deal. In the County of Wicklow objects are upon a smaller scale—but very attractive, especially as scenes of recreation for the neighbouring Inhabitants of Dublin—Of the Rivers the Shannon struck me most—The Slaney, the Suir and the Blackwater have their several attractions—but upon the whole they disappointed me—even the celebrated meeting of the waters the two Avons is far inferior to that of the Garry and Tummel near Fascally; and in general the Irish Rivers fall short in interest of those in Scotland and Wales—I ought to add that we were much pleased with the neighbourhood of Sligo, which is mountainous though upon a much smaller scale than the County of Kerry.

We are all pretty well—W^m included, his last letter being very satisfactory in all respects. With kind regards from my family

I remain dear Sir
Your most obliged W^m W.

[*M. W. writes*]

Mr W. in his usual haste when letter-writing, has turned over two sheets but which, I doubt not, you will excuse. Thanking you for all your kindness believe me very sincerely yours M. W.

481. W. W. to FRANCIS MEREWETHER

Address: The Revd Francis Merewether, Trinity Lodge, Cambridge. [*In M. W.'s hand*]
Stamp: Kendal Penny Post.
MS. Cornell. Hitherto unpublished.

Rydal Mount Monday
[mid-Nov. 1829]

My dear Sir,

Long absence from home has occasioned such a press of engagements that I must be very brief in answer to your kind letter— Professor Wilson whom I saw but once has left this Country some time, and I am told is at Edinburgh. A Letter addressed to Professor Wilson Edinburgh could not, I think, fail to reach him.—

Your account of dear Lady Beaumont's feelings is very interesting—in answer to your request I have only to say that to make any promise of the kind would be the surest way of defeating the object altogether—You may be assured however generally that if I live

167

and have health and spirits to write verses, a tribute will not be wanting, some where or other, among my works to the Memory of so dear a friend and so excellent a person—[1]

I have no means of removing your doubts as to the point respecting Ireland—Mr Southey will be here to day, and I have not answered your Letter by return of Post, from a hope that he may be enabled to speak somewhat decisively on the subject.—

We were sorry you made no mention of Whitwick.

My dear Sister's health, I grieve to say, yet occasions us a good deal of anxiety—she does not throw off the effects of her Whitwick illness—

Excuse this extreme haste and believe me my dear Sir with affectionate remembrances to my brother and Nephews in which all here join,

Most sincerely Yours
Wm Wordsworth

Mr Southey is come—he says the only way of doing is to refer to the laws—which we have not at hand, but which you might have access to probably at Cambridge.—

These severe laws, I would remind you, were not as you seem to suppose the consequence of the rebellion, but were passed after the revolution,[2] and began to be repealed in the beginning, I believe, of George the Third's reign.—One was this, I believe, that the near Relative of a Catholic who turned papist might claim his Estate.—But it is indispensible to be accurate in these matters, if mentioned at all—

482. D. W. to JOHN WORDSWORTH and C. W. JNR.

Address: John Wordsworth Esq, Trin. Col., Cambridge.
Franked: Penrith Nov. twenty 1829 J. Marshall.
Postmark: 20 Nov. 1829. *Stamp*: Penrith.
MS. WL. Hitherto unpublished.

Wednesday 18th Nov^r [1829]

I heartily thank you both, my dear Nephews, for your chearful pleasant letter, not the less welcome because late, nor yet for all

---

[1] See *Elegiac Musings* (*PW* iv. 270), composed in Nov. 1830.

[2] The Toleration Act of 1689 granted freedom of worship to dissenters on certain conditions, but Roman Catholics were expressly excluded from its benefits. A measure of relief for Catholics was subsequently afforded by the acts of 1778, 1791, and 1793, but the major civil disabilities were not removed until 1829.

Cousin Dora's grumblings 'Out of sight out of mind!—they think no more of *us*' etc etc in which, of course, I was obliged to join, and perhaps with not less eager determination to be out of humour than *she* felt. With both, however, your peace is made, and she bids me say that if you, John, will keep your word and spend Christmas with us, or even come during any part of the winter she will return with you to Cambridge—but I must tell you that after this free resolve, most sincerely made, she went on thus, 'but perhaps *that* will keep him away—he will not like the trouble of me.' Your Uncle would have been very glad, as would all at Rydal Mount, had you come after the musical Festival; but better late than never; and be assured that at all times and whenever it suits you, he will rejoice to see you, and will join with us all in the wish to keep you as long as we can. The above is addressed to John, but it applies equally to Chris, though we do not look for *his* coming again so soon—and if Charles is at Cambridge, *to him also*. What Charles's plans, after Degree-time, are, I know not—only pray tell him that we can always find a corner for him at Rydal.—

You have heard of your aged Uncle's pedestrian feats (I am still addressing John) in Ireland; and now that he has been many weeks at home I am truly happy in being able to tell you that I never saw him more active or in better health. This morning, under a clear frosty sky, with brilliant sunshine he is walking to Langdale to look after the Constellation Farm,[1] with Dora by his side on her poney. He has paid all his visits (to Lowther, to Hallsteads, Levens Park and Storrs Hall) and is vigorously disposed to commence his winter's labours—and if the eyes keep tolerably well, I trust something important may be done. He does intend to fall to the 'Recluse' being seriously impressed with the faith that very soon it must be too late (His next Birth day will be his 60th)—but, in the mean time he has been busy with other less important matters, polishing the small poems he wrote last year, and actually he has written another *Sonnet*![2] This we were not glad of, fearing it might be but the beginning as heretofore, of a *Batch*: he has, however, promised that he will write no more. Now I should have little faith in this promise, if it were not plain that his mind is set upon doing its best at the great Work. Before I take leave of you, dear John, let me repeat that we hope you will come to Rydal Mount at your first leisure and stay as long as you can; and further: that Dora would gladly

---

[1] For the Ivy How property, see *MY* ii. 509.
[2] This cannot be identified with certainty, but see *PW* iii. 52 for two sonnets which may belong to this period.

return with you to Cambridge if it suit her uncle—in which case, no doubt her Father, *at least*, would fetch her home again.

And now, dear Chris, do you accept my best wishes for a glorious passage through the Trials of the Senate House—and the same I send to my young Friend Mr Frere, who, as you know, is a great favorite with me, and with all under this roof.[1] We hope that you and he together will find your way to us again, especially as you were both so well contented while amongst us. Thank you for your good tidings concerning your dear Father's health! Surely his next summer's excursion will be northward!—and what if we were all to go together to visit Iona, Staffa and the Highlands!—This is a pleasant passing thought.—I have long laid aside the habit of planning for *this* summer *or the next*, yet if God grant us life and health such a thing *might* be.

I wish, when you wrote, you had heard what were the effects of the Tennis Court upon Charles's lame leg; for it would be a serious grief if he were laid up again at this time—not to speak of the folly of trifling away the strength of his Constitution. I shall be anxious to see his name among the 'Firsts', and pray desire him, whatever be his station, to send me an Oxford paper when his work is done,—and mind you must do the same with the Cambridge, when *yours* is done.—I hope you will join me in persuading John to come to Rydal as soon as he can. He will have Dora's Room for his bed-chamber and study, with a constant fire. She has moved to the front of the house for the winter, because her own room is too cold for her without a *fire*, which though to me and to many others a great comfort, is to her an annoyance—perhaps chiefly because she was during a whole winter confined night and day to one room and one fire-side. You will be glad to hear that she has of late been tolerably free from the tooth-ache (from which indeed she suffered grievously after you left us) and is in other respects very well. Her appetite is improved; and I think she looks better. Miss Hutchinson is gone to spend a few weeks with her Sister Joanna at

---

[1] C. W. jnr. had recently stayed with his friend John Frere at Rydal Mount on their way home from the Isle of Man. In a letter to his mother written from Rydal on 13 Oct., Frere gives an enthusiastic account of the Wordsworth household: 'There is so much to be learnt from Mr Wordsworth's conversation about those subjects which are dearest to me that I never could have enough of staying here, and cannot help thinking that all time when I do not have him is thrown away; besides this he is never like Coleridge in the clouds, and will talk on any subject and hear what you have to say, and what is to me a great thing, in tone of voice and manner of delivery he so much resembles my uncle Frere that I have an additional claim from remembrance in hearing his talk.' (*WL MSS.*)

Whitehaven, where she will have an opportunity of profiting by her nephew's preaching, of whom, by the by, very favorable reports reach us from various quarters; and he himself seems to be contented in his situation, and like a good parish priest has made himself acquainted with his whole Flock (or nearly so), rich and poor. Owen[1] too, is very happy and most zealous in the discharge of his duties and, in short, seems to have attained the summit of his earthly ambition, in the Curacy of Langdale. Have you heard that he has a pupil?—one of the Sons of Mr Curwen[2] of the Isle. He lives with him at the post-office. They drank tea with us the other day. He is a good natured healthy-looking, fat-faced youth. I should think without any troublesome habits; for the Tutor seems to be very sociable and comfortable with him.—You wish to hear of my health therefore I must just turn to a subject of which I am heartily tired.—After you left us I continued neither ill nor well, but good for nothing a week or more; but, by degrees, am become my former Self; and hope to keep so, through extreme care, which indeed I find absolutely necessary: being now convinced by experience, that exercise of any kind that amounts even to a slight degree of fatigue is injurious.—I know not what the world may say of Mr Barber and your old Aunt—for he dutifully comes to drive me in his poney-chaise every fine day that he is disengaged.—Mr Quillinan's intended Stay of three days, to our great satisfaction, was stretched out to three *weeks*. The Coleridges[3] left us, as intended, on the Monday after you. They had but a doleful journey as poor Sara's face continued to enlarge without diminution of pain; and when she reached London she was obliged to take to her Bed. A Surgeon was sent for, who perceived that an abscess was forming within her cheek, to prevent the bursting of which *outwardly* (which would have scarred that pretty cheek for life) he lanced the abscess and ordered a very spare diet, which brought her to a state of great weakness, from which she was recovering when she wrote to her Cousin Edith[4] a week ago,—and the pain was gone. They have taken lodgings in Barnard Street; but are at present at *Lawyer* Pattison's[5] (Henry's Brother-in-law). Miss Southey (Edith) has

[1] Owen Lloyd.
[2] John W.'s future father-in-law, Henry Curwen (see *MY* ii. 432). The reference here is to one of his younger sons, probably Henry (1812–94), who had just left Shrewsbury and was preparing for Trinity College, Cambridge. He was rector of Workington, 1837–94.
[3] Sara and Henry Nelson Coleridge.   [4] Edith Southey.
[5] Sir John Patteson (1790–1861), barrister on the northern circuit, and judge, married in 1824 as his second wife, Frances (1796–1842), daughter of Col. James Coleridge of Ottery St. Mary.

been with us above a fortnight, and we hope to keep her at least
a fortnight longer. Dora and she are very happy in each other's
company. They are now off in the poney-chaise, and when Edith
has had her drive Dora will take me out, my Lover, as they call
Mr Barber, being engaged today gallanting the Misses Edmunds[1]
to the Fairy Chapel and all his other curiosities. The Father and
Daughter, being rather too late in setting off yesterday, did not
get so far as Little Langdale, and today your Uncle and Aunt are
gone on foot to the Constellation Farm—a walk of at least ten
miles. Fortunately, now that the Sister is set aside on the Shelf,
the wife has gained renewed strength, and really walks with less
fatigue than in the days of her youth. Believe me, I stay at home
very contentedly; for after two or three trials *in a little way*, I find I
must act the Invalid however well I feel myself to be, and however
strong.—We know nothing of the 'Union Society'[2] or of its effects,
more than may be gathered from the enclosed paragraphs taken
from our Rival Newspapers. We have not seen Mr Fleming since
your inquiries; and as I cannot 'trot away' to call upon him I will
not wait for such information as may be obtained from him; but
will get all I can when we *do* see him; and, if it be worth the postage,
will write again. From Carlisle Mr Wm Jackson writes (He has
been visiting the Bishop[3] at Rose Castle) that the Manufacturing
Poor are in a sad state, and that there are three combination
Societies among them, they having sent to Birmingham for an
Organizer of the same. A travelling Packman from Carlisle a few
days ago told Mr Barber that hundreds and hundreds of people in
that town never taste bread now-a-days. They live upon two meals
of potatoes. The average wages of an able weaver are 2/10½ per
week.—Do not be cross with my bad penmanship. I would not
have written so small but am afraid of over-weight, having another
letter to put under the Cover to Mr Marshall; but it is not fair,
Chris! to task you with the labour of decyphering and guessing—
you whose head is now so busy with more important matters—
and for the same reason I ought to apologise for writing so long a
letter about nothing.—We have heard twice from Willy. He seems

---

[1] Of Ambleside.

[2] There were several local 'union societies' at this period, and the one referred to here cannot be identified with any certainty. Mr. Fleming, whom
D. W. goes on to mention, is either Thomas Fleming, owner of Spring Cottage,
or the Revd. Fletcher Fleming. The reference is perhaps to the Kendal Union
Cricket Club, the activities of which were discussed in the *Kendal Chronicle* and
the *Westmorland Gazette* on 19 Sept.

[3] Dr. Hugh Percy (see L. 477 above). Rose Castle was his official residence.

to have fitted himself to his way of living, and with horse exercise, and not over-hard study he goes on very satisfactorily, and has been free from head-aches and all other maladies. The manner in which he speaks of Mr and Mrs Papendick and their Children is very pleasing. He seems to be quite one of the Family: and he is, besides, satisfied with his progress in the German language. We told him of your scheme of travelling in that country next summer, and of seeing him at Bremen, which he says would be for him so great a happiness that he will not venture to believe that it *is to be.* If you *should* go thither, I am sure it will be impossible for him to resist the temptation to accompany you to some place or other, though but for a week or ten days of your Company.—Dora has just shewn me your first effort with the pencil, the Ruin on the Rhine.—Why, you are already quite an artist, a natural Genius in that line!—and I can venture to say will very soon equal your instructress, who, however, will be very happy either at Cambridge or Rydal to impart to you all she knows.

I am glad to find that good Mrs Merewether has been at Cambridge. She promises me a letter, which I hope will contain many particulars passed over by her Husband both respecting Cambridge and Whitwick. It appears that Mr Pricket[1] gives satisfaction to the Vicar and his poor parishioners, which it is most pleasing to us to hear.—I have not yet written to Mrs Hoare—not that she has not been often in my thoughts, and the cause of my delay is one which her kindness will make her allow is a more than sufficient excuse. Even letter writing has fatigued me, and I have shrunk from any work that was not absolutely necessary, till within the last ten days. I am now, however, equal to any thing in a quiet way, and hope to write to her ere long. I was truly rejoiced to hear of Miss Hoare's recovery, and I beg that whoever first writes to Mrs H. will tell her so with my kind love to both.—How is Sophy?[2]—when you see her do not fail to give her my kind remembrances.

With kind love to my dear Brother, and to you all there, my dear Nephews, believe me ever your affec^te Aunt

Dorothy Wordsworth

[1] The Revd. Marmaduke Prickett (1804–39), of Bridlington, Yorks., had graduated from Trinity in 1826. He published antiquarian works and was Chaplain of Trinity, 1836–8.

[2] One of the servants at Trinity Lodge, now Mrs. Carter.

Thursday 19th Nov^r

My kind regards to Mr Frere.

If Mr Rose[1] be at Cambridge pray offer to him my respectful regards. Has Dr Mill[2] left England? What do you know concerning his health and prospects in India?

You will be frightened at the sight of this long prosy letter—indeed I am ashamed of it.

483. D. W. to MARY ANNE MARSHALL[3]

Address: To Miss Marshall [*delivered by hand*]
MS. WL.
LY i. 429.   Thursday Novr. 19th [1829]

I thank you heartily, my dear Mary Anne, for your very kind letter, which, as it does not speak at all of your Mother's cold (I was going to say Mama but the word Mother dropped from my pen to myself unconsciously)—and tells me that your poor dear Sister Ellen's[4] sufferings are diminished, brings as good tidings as I could have expected. All hope of seeing any one, two, or three of you on this side Kirkstone had long left us—yet it was most mortifying that this capricious unrelenting season should have checked your friendly purposes when Papa and you were so very near to us—with a fair road before you—as at Keswick. It is, however, a pleasure to us to find that such were your friendly intentions—an earnest for the future—for if we all live and enjoy health and spirits, you may, in the course of next summer, execute a like scheme; for you will both want to look after the Scale Hill[5] Trees which you have so heroically planted in cold and wet. By the bye the scheme of improving the precincts of that Inn pleases me much, as not only a local, but even a patriotic service—for to whom, in these travelling days are not the names of the Low Wood Inn, the Grasmere Red Lion the Wytheburn Nag's head the Buttermere Inn, and the Scale Hill familiar Names?

---

[1] Hugh James Rose, whom D. W. had met in Cambridge the previous March.

[2] The Revd. William Hodge Mill, D.D. (1792–1853), Fellow of Trinity, 1814, and first Principal of Bishop's College, Calcutta, 1820–38. He was well known as a Sanskrit and Arabic scholar, and was Professor of Hebrew at Cambridge, 1845–53.   [3] Later Lady Monteagle (see L. 464 above).

[4] The Marshalls' fifth daughter.

[5] In the township of Brackenthwaite, near Buttermere, of which John Marshall was lord of the manor.

My Brother and Sister join with me in thanks to Mr Marshall for his kind offer of a supply of apples, which we gladly accept as of *much more* value than the carriage. They will send a cart for them early in next week (perhaps on Tuesday or Wednesday unless we should hear from you that the apples will not then be ready.) Our Man, James, will accompany the Cart—a great privilege for him—as he wishes to see your Place—Gardens, hot-houses, Green house etc. If you should happen to be at home you will not be displeased to hold a little discourse with James—nor would your Aunts[1]—there is about him so much old bachelor like (yet he is not *old*) simplicity and innocence. In the first place, he never in the course of his whole life drank a drop of spirituous or fermented liquors. Of course he has no *wish* for them, and I believe the taste would be disgusting to him; but his entire estrangement to the very taste of liquor arose from a promise made to his Mother at ten years old on her death-bed—never to indulge in drinking—a vice which to his Father had caused disgrace and poverty—and to *her* wretchedness. This promise he considered in the light of a vow, and he solemnly, at that early age, resolved never to suffer any intoxicating liquor of any kind to enter within his lips.

He knew nothing of gardening when he came to us—but took kindly to the work; and is now even passionately attached to the garden—especially the ornamental part. As my Sister says, 'he *worships* his flowers.' Every morning from her bed-room window does she see him going his Rounds and standing over every particular Plant that pleases his fancy.

Observe, with all James's simplicity he is the very man for *us*. His health is delicate and he could not stand hard exercise; and the business of our garden, the two ponies, and the poney-chaise exactly suits him. What a long round-about story I have unconsciously slipped into, little thinking that to you it may be very tiresome—and I have deferred to the last, the second part of my business, namely to ask Mr Marshall if he has any of the same kind of potatoes with which he once supplied us, and which to this day we talk of as the best potatoes in the world—(the long black-skinned kidneys I believe). The stock still survives, planted by a neighbour of ours; but he is able to let us have but a very small quantity. Now if you have any of these same potatoes my Brother would be greatly obliged to Mr Marshall if he would order a few to be added to the apples which he kindly intends for us. We should be thankful even

---

[1] Mrs. Marshall's sisters.

for the smallest possible quantity—and if very small would preserve the whole for seed for next year.

Dora's teeth, I am happy to tell you, are now at ease, and her health and looks much improved since I wrote to Mrs Pollard[1]— She has been much disappointed at seeing none of you this year— and especially her name-sake, to whom, if still at Hallsteads she sends her kind love. You do not mention her. Give my most affectionate regards to all your Aunts, with wishes for a prosperous journey and a happy meeting with their old Friend, to whom I beg my respectful regards.—Pray tell Mrs Pollard that I find daily comfort (or rather *fair* day comfort) in her muff and tippet as well as Mrs Catherine's[2] Merino Gown—which by the way, is trimmed with Mrs P's fur, and keeps me so warm and comfortable in the poney chaise. I have continued quite well since my last writing, but this I am now convinced comes only from acting the Invalid, however strong and well I feel myself to be: for I find that exercise amounting to the slightest degree of fatigue invariably disorders me. Your dear Mama and other Friends told me this long before I found myself strong enough to make the trial; but no conviction is so strong as that which is produced by experience. I suppose you have now no female companion at home except Susan[3]—unless Mrs Temple[4] be still with you.—To Julia[5] give my best Love, and tell her that I tried out some Christmas verses for her; but could not make a finish of them.—

And now, my dear Mary Anne, let me beg your excuses for this rambling, long dark-hued letter. I hope for a few lines from you by James, if not gone when he arrives; and at all events do let me hear from Headingley as soon as possible after Mama's return: How is Mrs William Marshall?[6] How long will they remain at Paterdale? How is your Brother? Remember me to both and believe me, dear Mary Anne, your much obliged and very affectionate Friend

Dorothy Wordsworth

My Brother and Mrs Wordsworth are walking to Langdale— ten miles at least!—He bade me say to Mr M that he was very sorry not to see him again.

---

[1] Mrs. Marshall's eldest sister. Dora's 'namesake', whom D. W. goes on to refer to, is Jane Dorothea, the Marshalls' fourth daughter (see L. 463 above).

[2] Mrs. Marshall's elder sister.

[3] Susan Harriet, the Marshalls' seventh daughter. In 1842 she married the Revd. Frederick Myers of Keswick.   [4] i.e. Jane Dorothea, mentioned above.

[5] The Marshalls' sixth daughter (see pt. i, L. 70).

[6] Mrs. William Marshall (see L. 450a above) had recently given birth to a son (see L. 463 above).

484. D. W. to MARY ANNE MARSHALL

Address: To Miss Marshall. [*delivered by hand*]
MS. WL.
LY ii. 765.

Wednesday 25th Nov. [1829]

Many thanks, my dear Mary Anne, to yourself and your kind Father for your bountiful presents, all of which, in their several ways will be very useful, and the more prized as coming from you. Dora is much pleased with the green-house plants, and with James's assistance, hopes to nurse them well during the winter. I was delighted to see your Mama's hand-writing on opening the cover of your letter; and though the first page of its contents was distressing, as reporting of poor Ellen's severe sufferings after her Comforters arrived, the conclusion was consolatory—the worst for the present having passed away—and even the worst, as my dear Friend says, less distressing actually to behold than to image to oneself at a distance, the calmness and patience of the Sufferer being such, as it appears, as almost to amount to happiness—nay happiness it is—and what at one period or other of our lives each one of us may, and probably will, have cause to envy if such a word may be used in connection with our needs and our desires for what is heavenly.

But dear Mary Anne, I did not intend to moralise, and hardly know how my feelings have led me into this strain. You will forgive, and now let us turn to the *business* of my present letter.

In the first place Mrs Luff returns her best thanks for your kind remembrance of your promise to her Green-house; and in the second I must tell you that she is the Friend who wishes to dispose of some of her treasures, and that by this day's Mail she will send the Chess-men and chess-board—directed for you *to the care of Mrs Jackson at the King's Arms*, Kendal.[1] The price of them is ten guineas. Now Mrs Luff desires me to entreat that you will consider yourself, in this matter, as treating with a perfect stranger, and in deciding whether you shall keep them or not she earnestly entreats you will entirely set aside her wish to sell them—and if the purchase does not please you (and there may be many reasons why it should not—the Chess-men may not be handsome enough—or their shapes may not take your fancy) she begs that you will leave the parcel to Mrs Jackson's care, to be returned to her; and be assured that, so far from being hurt at your rejection of her offer, it would grieve

---

[1] The posting house in Stricklandgate. The landlord was John Jackson.

her very much that you should accept it unless more agreeable to yourself than not. Mrs Luff adds to the parcel a black mantle inwoven with silver, which was worn by a Madagascar Princess, and was very costly in that country. The only use that can be made of it, as we think, is for a Table cover—and, *for that*, it is remarkably handsome. The price fixed upon for it by Mrs Luff is ten guineas (as for the Chess-men and board). Should you entirely reject this latter article, leave it to Mrs Jackson's care—but unless *that* be the case, as the carriage of it will be no inconvenience you might take it to Headingley for your Mama's inspection; and if she does not chuse to have it keep it to be sent by the first arrival from Headingley next spring or summer. With regard to the Chessmen it would be better *not* to take them to Leeds, *unless* you determine to keep them.

Mr and Mrs Elliott,[1] whom we are about to lose as neighbours; are just come to spend the day with us, through driving snowshowers. They had engaged to come if weather favoured and it is truly so bad that we had no hope of seeing them. This being the case you must excuse a hasty conclusion. I fancied I had much more to say to you, but this arrival has driven it out of my head, and indeed I have no right to go on scribbling while our good friends are chattering around us. I believe *you* know something of the Elliotts (your Mama and Aunts I know do). They are excellent people and we are heartily sorry to lose them. Their House, the Wood, was rented by Mrs John Barlow,[2] who let it to *them*, and is now coming to live there herself.

My Brother's very kind regards to Mr Marshall, whom he begs to assure that he shall rejoice to see again next summer, and to talk with him and your Brother James over their adventures in the Sister Isle.

I shall shortly write to Mrs Marshall. In the meantime I thank her, through you, for her welcome letter.

God bless you all! and grant you a happy meeting—and pray let me hear of it ere long. My Sister and Dora beg their kind Love. Remember my message to Julia. Ever your affectionate Friend

D. Wordsworth.

James was delighted with his visit. He was never so well treated in his life before; and it was so kind in Mr Marshall to

---

[1] Formerly tenants of Ivy Cottage: more recently of The Wood, Bowness.
[2] A local friend, frequently mentioned in D. W.'s MS. Journals.

send for him to speak to him in his own room; and he was 'such a nice quiet spoken Gentleman. I never saw such a pleasing nice Gentleman'; and you were a very 'kind Lady'. I did not desire you to mark James's Bow. I wish I *had*, for you might not notice it. James's Bow is the most exquisite sample of respectful Simplicity I ever saw.

Sad penmanship!—I hope you are a good Reader and have not weak eyes.

485. W. W. to ROBERT SPENCE[1]

Address: Mr Robt Spence, North Shields.
Stamp: Kendal Penny Post.
MS. Mrs. Spence Clepham. Hitherto unpublished.

Rydal Mount
26th Nov^br 1829—

Dear Sir,

Though not particularly fond of sending samples of penmanship so vile as mine, I have pleasure in complying with *your* request, and am grateful for the account you have given me of the Family of your late excellent Father in Law—whom I was always so glad to see on his periodical visits to my neighbours.

I have not forgotten my own visit to Hebblethwaite, though I cannot call to mind the walk which I took with you—so long ago.

I am sorry that I cannot send a specimen either of Mr Southey or Mr Coleridge, but I have had so many applications of the same kind, that they go as fast as they come—but I will think of you and will reserve some to be sent in a Frank.

Believe me faithfully yours
Wm Wordsworth

Dum vivimus, vivamus
Live while you live, the Epicure will say,
And give to Pleasure every fleeting day;

---

[1] Robert Spence (1784–1845), woollen draper and banker at North Shields, and a Quaker, was born at Whaite Mill House, near Darley, Yorks., and married in 1810 Mary (1790–1846), daughter of Robert Foster (1754–1827), of Hebblethwaite Hall, near Sedbergh (see *MT* ii. 84). He seems to have known W. W. from around 1807. See *Robert and Mary Spence of North Shields, containing Robert Spence's journal*, ed. Philip Spence, Newcastle upon Tyne (privately printed), 1939.

Live while you live, the pious Preacher cries
And give to God each moment as it flies;
Lord! in my views let both united be,
I live in pleasure while I live to Thee!
Dr Doddridge's paraphrase of the Motto to his
Family Arms. Dum vivimus vivamus.[1]

Wm Wordsworth

486. W. W. to EDWARD QUILLINAN

Address: Edward Quillinan Esq., Bryanston Street, Portman Sq. [*In M. W.'s
hand*]
MS. Miriam Lutcher Stark Library, University of Texas.
LY i. 432.

[late Nov. 1829]

My dear Q.

Thanks for your Letter. I should have replied to Mr Gleig's[2]
Letter—but I have been from home. I have neither industry nor
talent for the kind of labour in which he would engage me.

Thank you also for the trouble you have taken in my pecuniary
matters.[3] I trust the affair will be satisfactory to all concerned. I
have the highest opinion of Col^{nl} Barrett, and my peace of mind is so
dependent upon this sum being in security for my family, that I am
sure Col^{nl} B— would not deal with me were he not convinced it
would be for my benefit. This is Saturday—on Thursday a little
before eleven I left Rydal Mount with two Gentlemen in a Car—we
proceeded to Keswick, took a fresh horse, went up into Borrowdale
as far as Stonethwaite, a mile beyond Miss Barker's,[4] returned to

---

[1] This piece by the nonconformist divine Philip Doddridge (see *EY*, p. 31)
was considered by Dr. Johnson to be 'one of the finest epigrams in the English
language'.

[2] The Revd. George Robert Gleig (1796–1888), the popular historian and
novelist, served in the Peninsula, published *The Subaltern* (1825), became
Chaplain of Chelsea Hospital (1834), and Chaplain-general to the forces
(1844). He was now about to launch *The National Library*, which ran to fourteen numbers between 1830 and 1832, and had apparently asked W. W. to be
a contributor.

[3] E. Q., who had recently spent three weeks at Rydal Mount, wrote to
Dora W. from Coventry on 19 Nov.: 'Tell Mr Wordsworth that Barrett
thinks he will be able to find him a mortgage which shall give him 5 per cent,
but he shall hear on his return from Geneva. He has no land left which he can
sell that will produce that interest.' (*WL MSS.*)

[4] i.e. the house formerly occupied by Miss Barker, who now lived in
Boulogne. See *MY* ii. 42, 644.

Keswick by the opposite side of the Lake, and I passed the Evening at Southey's; where Dora is; she does not complain—but certainly she has not recovered her good looks, since she suffered so much from the late attack of the teeth. The Southeys are all pretty well. Yesterday we returned to Ambleside by Lyulph's tower, and Patterdale—over Kirkstone in a fierce storm, which astonished my Companions who were both Londoners—farewell. Mrs W. begs me to say that it appears from Wm's Londo[n] accounts, that he paid for a hat and strong box to take it to Bremen—1. 10—and his Mother has asked him today to whom he paid this money, and as in his last he speaks of writing to you, [you][1] will have his answer——

W. W.

487. W. W. to GEORGE HUNTLY GORDON

MS. Cornell.
Grosart (—). LY i. 433 (—). Broughton, p. 29.

Rydal Mount
Decr 1st 1829.

My dear Sir,

You must not go to Ireland without applying to me as the Guide Books for the most part are sorry things, and mislead by their exaggerations. If I were a younger man and could prevail upon an able Artist to accompany me, there are few things I should like better than giving a month or six weeks to explore the County of Kerry only. A judicious topographical work on that district would be really useful both for the Lovers of Nature and the Observers of manners. As to the Giants Causeway and the Coast of Antrim you cannot get wrong; there the interests obtrude themselves on every ones notice.

The subject of the Poor Laws was never out of my sight whilst I was in Ireland. It seems to me next to impossible to introduce a general system of such laws principally for two reasons—the vast numbers that would have equal claims for relief, and the non-existence of a class capable of looking with effect to their administration—much is done at present in many places; (Derry for example, by voluntary contributions) but the narrow minded escape from the burthen which falls unreasonably upon the charitable so that

---

[1] *Word dropped out.*

assessments in the best disposed places are to be wished-for, could they be effected without producing a greater evil.

The great difficulty that is complained of in the well managed places is the floating poor who cannot be excluded, I am told, by any existing law from quartering themselves where they like. Open begging is not practised in many places, but there is no law by which the Poor can be prevented from returning to a place which they may have quitted voluntarily or from which they have been expelled, (as I was told).

Were it not for this obstacle compulsory local regulations might I think be applied in many districts with good effect.

It would be unfair to myself to quit this momentous subject without adding that I am a zealous friend to the great Principle of the Poor Laws as tending, if judiciously applied, much more to elevate than to depress the character of the Laboring Classes. I have never seen this Truth developed as it ought to be in Parliament.

The day I dined with Lord F: L: Gower at his Official Residence in the Phoenix Park I met there with an intelligent Gentleman Mr Page[1] who was travelling in Ireland expressly to collect information upon this subject which no doubt he means to publish. If you should hear of this Pamphlet when it comes out procure it for I am persuaded it will prove well worth reading.

The account you give us of William was very gratifying and he tells us himself that he is now in excellent health.

Farewell faithfully yours
Wm Wordsworth

488. W. W. to WILLIAM ROWAN HAMILTON

MS. WL transcript (—).[2]
Grosart (—). *Hamilton. K* (—). *LY i. 434.*

Rydal Mount,
December 23, 1829.

My dear Mr Hamilton,

Your letter would have received an immediate answer but for the same reasons which prevented my writing before its arrival,

---

[1] Frederick Page (1769–1834), of Newbury, Berks., barrister. In 1830 he published *Observations on the state of the Indigent Poor in Ireland, and the existing institutions for their relief: being a sequel to 'The principle of the English Poor Laws illustrated and defended'* (a work that had appeared in Bath in 1822).
[2] By Susan Wordsworth.

viz. numerous engagements, and a recurrence of inflammation in my eyes, which compels me to employ an amanuensis.

The pamphlets[1] were intended for yourself and Mr Edgeworth,[2] as you conjectured; the poem you were so kind as to enclose[3] gave me much pleasure, nor was it the less interesting for being composed upon a subject you had touched before. The style in this latter is more correct, and the versification more musical. Where there is so much of sincerity of feeling, in a matter so dignified as the renunciation of Poetry for Science, one feels that an apology is necessary for verbal criticism. I will therefore content myself with observing that *joying* for *joy*, or *joyance*, is not to my taste—indeed, I object to such liberties upon principle. We should soon have no language at all if the unscrupulous coinage of the present day were allowed to pass, and become a precedent for the future. One of the first duties of a writer is to ask himself whether his thought, feeling, or image cannot be expressed by existing words or phrases, before he goes about creating new terms, even when they are justified by the analogies of the language. 'The cataract's steep flow' is both harsh and inaccurate—'Thou hast seen me bend over the cataract' would express one idea in simplicity, and all that was required; had it been necessary to be more particular, *steep flow* are not the words that ought to have been used. I remember Campbell says in a composition that is overrun with faulty language,

> And dark as winter was the *flow*
> Of Iser rolling rapidly—[4]

that is, flowing rapidly. The expression ought to have been *stream* or *current*.

Pray, thank your excellent sister for the verses which she so kindly entrusted to me. I have read them all three times over with great care, and some of them oftener. They abound with genuine sensibility, and do her much honour; but, as I told you before, your sister must practise her mind in severer logic than a person so young can be expected to have cultivated; for example, the first words of the first poem, 'Thou *most companionless*.' In strict logic, 'being companionless' is a positive condition not admitting of more or less, though in poetic feeling it is true that the sense of it is deeper as to one object than to another; and the *day* moon is an object eminently calculated for impressing certain minds with that

[1] See L. 475 above.　　　　[2] Francis Beaufort Edgeworth.
[3] *To Poetry*. See *Hamilton*, i. 316.　　　[4] *Hohenlinden*, stanza i.

feeling; therefore the expression is not faulty in itself absolutely, but faulty in its position—coming without preparation, and therefore causing a shock between the common-sense of the words, and the impassioned imagination of the speaker. This may appear to you frigid criticism, but, depend upon it, no writings will live in which these rules are disregarded. In the next line,

Walking the blue but foreign fields of day,

the meaning here is walking blue fields which, though common to see in our observation by night, are not so by day, even to accurate observers. Here, too, the thought is just; but again there is an abruptness; the distinction is too nice, or refined, for the second line of a poem.

'Weariness of that *gold* sphere.' *Silver* is frequently used as an adjective by our poets; *gold*, as I should suppose, very rarely, unless it may be in dramatic poetry, where the same delicacies are not indispensable. 'Gold watch,' 'gold bracelet,' etc., are shop language. 'Gold sphere' is harsh in sound, particularly at the close of a line. 'Faint, as if weary of my golden sphere,' would please me better. '*Greets thy rays.*' You do not greet the *ray* by *daylight*; you greet the *moon*; there is no *ray*. 'Daring *'flight'* is wrong; the moon, under no mythology that I am acquainted with, is represented with wings; and though on a stormy night, when clouds are driving rapidly along, the word might be applied to her apparent motion, it is not so here; therefore 'flight' is here used for unusual or unexpected ascent, a sense, in my judgment, that cannot be admitted. The slow motion by which this ascent is gained is at variance with the word. The rest of this stanza is *very* pleasing, with the exception of one word—'thy nature's *breast*'—say 'profane thy nature'; how much simpler and better! 'Breast' is a sacrifice to rhyme, and is harsh in expression. We have had the *brow* and the *eye* of the moon before, both allowable; but what have we reserved for human beings, if their features and organs etc., are to be *lavished* on objects without feeling and intelligence? You will, perhaps, think this observation comes with an ill grace from one who is aware that he has tempted many of his admirers into *abuses* of this kind; yet, I assure you, I have never given way to my own feelings in personifying natural objects, or investing them with sensation, without bringing all that I have said to a rigorous after-test of good sense, as far as I was able to determine what good sense is. Your sister will judge, from my being so minute, that

I have been much interested in her poetical character; this very poem highly delighted me; the sentiment meets with my entire approbation, and it is feelingly and poetically treated. Female Authorship is to be shunned as bringing in its train more and heavier evils than have presented themselves to you sister's ingenuous mind. No true friend, I am sure, will endeavour to shake her resolution to remain in her own quiet and healthful obscurity. This is not said with a view to discourage her from writing, nor have the remarks made above any aim of the kind; they are rather intended to assist her in writing with more permanent satisfaction to herself. She will probably write less in proportion as she subjects her feelings to logical forms, but the range of her sensibilities, so far from being narrowed, will extend as she improves in the habit of looking at things through the steady light of words; and, to speak a little metaphysically, words are not a mere *vehicle*, but they are *powers* either to kill or to animate.

I shall be truly happy to receive at your leisure the prose MSS. which you promised me. I shall write to Mr. F. Edgeworth in a few days. I cannot conclude without reminding you of your promise to bring your sister to see us next summer; we will then talk over the poems at leisure, when I trust I shall be able to explain myself to our mutual satisfaction. With kind regards to all your family, your cousin[1] included,

I remain my dear Mr Hamilton
Yours most sincerely,
Wm Wordsworth

My sister Miss Wordsworth and Miss Hutchinson beg to be kindly remembered to you.

[1] Arthur Hamilton, LL.D. (1776–1840), barrister, a frequent visitor at the Dunsink Observatory.

489. W. W. to FRANCIS BEAUFORT EDGEWORTH[1]

MS. untraced.
K (—). *LY i. 437.*

[late Dec. 1829]

. . . As you were so much struck with the yew-tree at Mucross,[2] do not fail, if ever you come near Askeaton, to visit the ruins of its abbey, where you will find a much finer cloister, with a tree standing exactly in the centre as at Mucross. The tree is infinitely inferior to that of Mucross in gloomy grandeur, but the whole effect being of the same kind, the impression on my mind at Mucross was not so deep as it would have been if I had not seen Askeaton before.

The faults I found with Killarney were, the bog between the town and the lake, the long tame ridge which you complain of, the want of groves and timber trees, though there is a prodigality of wood, the heavy shape of the highest hill, Mangerton, and the unluckiness of Carrantuohill[3] being so placed as only to combine with the lake from its tamest parts. Your objection to the rocky knolls in the upper lake, as savouring of conceits in Nature, is a sensation of your own, which it would be absurd to reason against. I did not feel it when on the spot, nor can I admit it now. . . .

[*cetera desunt*]

490. W. W. to SARA COLERIDGE

MS. Victoria University Library, Toronto. Hitherto unpublished.

[? late 1829][4]

My dear Sara,

I wish you were back again in Cumberland—and take care that you keep your health, and the good looks of which I hear so much— farewell my very dear Friend—

Wm Wordsworth

[1] After his meeting with W. W. at Edgeworthstown (see L. 466 above), Edgeworth had visited Killarney, and he had written to W. W. on 9 Dec. (*WL MSS.*) describing his disappointment with it. He wrote again the following January acknowledging receipt of the *Letter to a Friend of Robert Burns* and the *Description of the Scenery of the Lakes in the North of England*, and praising the harmonious qualities of the latter. 'There is nothing that disturbs in the least the calmness of enjoyment.' (*WL MSS.*)

[2] Muckross Abbey, founded in 1440, situated on the peninsula which separates the Lower and Middle Lakes at Killarney.   [3] Carrantual.

[4] Possibly, but not necessarily, written shortly after Sara Coleridge's marriage. The letter is marked 'For Sara in London'.

491. W. W. to W. W. JNR.[1]

MS. Amherst College Library. Hitherto unpublished.

[late 1829 or early 1830]

. . . especially. I assure you I never was so puzzled in my life; nor can at all understand how the Powers of Europe could permit Russia to advance to Constantinople.[2] Every body seems to be equally ignorant—You perhaps are aware that after the Relief bill[3] was past last Session of parliament the ministry were so weak that they could not make up a House for ordinary business. So that some not inconsiderable changes are expected upon the opening of *next* Session, but no one knows who will be [   ][4]

—Your very affectionate Father, W W—

492. D. W. to WILLIAM PEARSON[5]

MS. untraced.
Pearson. LY i. 440.

Rydal Mount,
Jan. 5th 1830.

My dear Sir,

My niece desires me to request that you will be so good as to procure for her a supply of straw, which I believe you kindly promised to do in case she should want it. I suppose she and you settled about the quantity, as she has left me without directions on that point—however, for your guidance, in case nothing was said on that score, I will remind you, that we have two ponies; and I suppose she wants enough for the winter.

---

[1] This letter was written to W. W. jnr. at Bremen some time after Parliament was prorogued on 24 June 1829, but before it reassembled on 4 Feb. 1830. It was almost certainly written after W. W.'s return from Ireland.

[2] During the recent war between Russia and the Ottoman Empire, the Turks had suffered serious defeat and Russia had expanded westwards towards Constantinople. The Turks refused the terms offered by Great Britain and France (who were negotiating the settlement of Greece) as the price of their intervention, and by the treaty of 14 Sept. 1829 Russia remained in possession of large areas of Turkish territory pending the payment of a considerable indemnity.

[3] The Catholic Relief Bill.

[4] *Rest of letter obliterated.*

[5] The Wordsworths' farmer friend from Crosthwaite.

You have been so much interested concerning my health, that I must not close this note, without telling you that I am now perfectly well; but, in order to keep myself so, I avoid exposure to cold, which in one or two instances, has been injurious. I therefore do not go out in the frosty weather, at all; and this confinement agrees with me as well as air and exercise used to do; and I trust that in Spring, I shall be able in degree, to resume my old habits.

You will be glad to hear that my Brother and Sister, and the rest of the family are well. Two Miss Hutchinsons[1] are with us, and my nephew John also, who after spending a week at Rydal, is going to Oxford to take his Master of Arts Degree. He is much pleased with his situation at Moresby.

I hope it will not be long, before we have the pleasure of seeing you at Rydal Mount.

Of one thing you may be secure, that you will never now, find the house emptied of its inhabitants; for I am always at home, except, indeed, for an hour or two in the mornings, when the air is mild. I then always go out in the pony chaise.

My Brother and Sister join with me in sincere wishes, that you may spend the coming year happily.

Believe me, dear Sir,
Your obliged and sincere Friend,
D. Wordsworth, Sen[r].

493. W. W. to GEORGE HUNTLY GORDON

Address: G. Huntly Gordon Esq[e].
MS. Princeton University Library. Hitherto unpublished.

[*In Dora W.'s hand*]

Rydal Mount
Jan[y] 6th 1830

My dear Sir,

My Daughter holds the pen for me, which the state of my eyes does not allow me to do without injury, tho' my object in writing only is not to wish you a Merry Xmas for that closes today but the good old fashioned Comp[t] of "a happy New Year". The season here has been very pleasant and I have had some delightful skating

---

[1] S. H. and Joanna H.

on the Lake which would have been renewed today but for the thaw. It is nearly six weeks since we heard from William and to pacify his mother's anxiety I have suggested what is not improbable a letter may be lying in your Chambers waiting your return from some holiday excursion. We have thought it best however to dispatch the present packet which I will thank you to forward with the other letters.

Excuse this short note and Believe me dear Sir

> Faithfully your much obliged
> [*signed*] Wᵐ Wordsworth

494. D. W. to MARY LAMB

Address: To Charles Lamb Esqʳᵉ, Enfield Common, Enfield. *For Miss Lamb.*
   D. W.
MS. Henry E. Huntington Library.
LY i. 441 (—).

Rydal Mount 9ᵗʰ Janʳʸ, 1830

My dear Friend,

My nephew John will set off to-morrow evening to Oxford, to take his Master of Arts degree, and thence proceed to London, where his time will be so short that there is no chance of his being able to go to see you; but there is a *possibility* that your brother may happen to be in town at the same time, in which case it would grieve *him* and *us* at home not less, that he should not see him. Therefore, if it should happen that your Brother is in Town at any time from the 17ᵗʰ to the 26ᵗʰ of this month, pray desire him to inquire for the Revᵈ. J. Wordsworth at Mr Cookson's,[1] No. 6 Lincoln's Inn. There he will be sure to learn where John may be found, of which at present he knows no more than that he will not *lodge* at Mr Cookson's though he will certainly call there, and leave his address immediately after he reaches Town.

I do not write *merely* for the sake of giving John a chance of seeing your Brother (and you also if you happen to be in London) but to inquire after you both, for now that our good friend Henry Robinson is absent *you* might as well be also living in Rome for any thing we hear concerning you; and believe me we are often

---

[1] W. Strickland Cookson, son of the Kendal Cooksons, and W. W.'s solicitor.

uneasy in the thought that all communication seems cut off between us; and sincerely and earnestly do we all desire that your Brother will let us have a *post* Letter (no waiting for Franks or private conveyances) telling us minutely, how you live, what you both are doing, and whom you see—of old Friends or new—as visitors by your fireside. I do not ask *you*, Miss Lamb, to write, for I know you dislike the office; but dear Charles L., you whom I have known almost five and thirty years, I trust I do not in vain entreat *you* to let me have the eagerly desired letter at your earliest opportunity, which letter will, we hope, bring us tidings of H. C. Robinson. We have not heard any thing concerning him since his departure from England, though he promised absolutely to write on his arrival at Rome, and if his intentions were fulfilled, he must have been a resident there for many weeks.[1] Do you see Talfourd?[2] Does he prosper in his profession? What Family has he? etc etc. But I will not particularize persons, but include all in one general inquiry (Miss Kelly[3] amongst the rest). Tell us of all whom you know, in whose well-doing you know us also to be interested; but above all, be very minute in what regards your own dear selves, for there are no persons in the world, exclusive of members of our own Family, of whom we think and talk so frequently, or with such delightful remembrances.—Your removal from London (though to my thought London is hardly London without you) shall not prevent my seeing you both in your own cottage,[4] if I live to go there again, but at present I have no distinct plans leading me thither. Now that Mr. Monkhouse[5] is gone, we females have no absolute home there, and should we go it will probably be on our own way to the Continent, or to the southern Shores of England.

[1] H. C. R. had spent the summer and autumn of the previous year in Germany. The highlight of his visit was the renewal of his acquaintance with Goethe (see Sadler, ii. 420 ff. and *HCR* i. 366 ff.). He arrived in Rome on 17 Nov. 1829.

[2] Thomas Noon Talfourd, lawyer and author (see pt. i, L. 4), had married (1822) Rachel, eldest daughter of John Towill Rutt (1760–1841), the politician and writer. Their son, Charles Lamb Talfourd, was born in 1828 (see *Lamb*, iii. 184–5). In his reply to W. W. later this month (*Lamb*, iii. 245) Lamb wrote: 'Miss Kelly we never see; Talfourd not this half-year; the latter flourishes, but the exact number of his children, God forgive me, I have utterly forgotten, we single people are often out in our count there. Shall I say two? One darling I know they have lost within a twelvemonth, but scarce known to me by sight, and that was a second child lost.'

[3] For Fanny Kelly, the actress, see *MY* ii. 613.

[4] Charles and Mary Lamb had been living in their cottage on the Chase at Enfield since Sept. 1827.

[5] Thomas Monkhouse, M. W.'s cousin, a close friend of Lamb's, who had died in 1825 (see pt. i, L. 163).

HENRY CRABB ROBINSON
from the crayon drawing by J. Schmeller, 1829

Wishes I do now and then indulge of at least *re*visiting Switzerland, and again crossing the Alps, and even stretching on to Rome; but there is a great change in my feelings, respecting plans for the future. If we make any, I entertain them as an amusement perhaps for a short while, but never set my heart upon any thing which is to be accomplished three months hence, and have no satisfaction whatever in *schemes*. When one has lived almost sixty years, one is satisfied with present enjoyment, and thankful for it, without daring to count on what is to be done six months hence. But, forgive me, I am prosing and do not say a word to satisfy your desire to know how we all are and what doing. To begin then with the heads of the house. My Brother and Sister are both in excellent health. In *him* there is no failure except the tendency to inflammation in his eyes, which disables him from reading much, or at all by candle-light; and the use of the pen is irksome to him: However, he has a most competent and willing amanuensis in his Daughter, who takes all labour from Mother's and Aunt's aged hands. His muscular powers are in no degree diminished; indeed, I think that he walks *regularly* more than ever, finding fresh air the best bracer of his weak eyes. He is still the crack skater on Rydal Lake, and, as to climbing of mountains, the hardiest and the youngest are yet hardly a match for him. In composition I can perceive no failure, and his imagination seems as vigorous as in youth; yet he shrinks from his great work, and both during the last and present winter has been employed in writing small poems. Do not suppose, my dear Friends, that I write the above boastingly. Far from it. It is in thankfulness for present blessings, yet always with a sense of the probability that all will have a sudden check; and if not so, the certainty that in the course of man's life, but a few years of vigorous health and strength can be allotted to him. For this reason, my sister and I take every opportunity of pressing upon him the necessity of applying to his great work, and this he feels, resolves to do it, and again resolution fails. And now I almost fear habitually, that it will be ever so. I have told you she is well, and indeed I think her much stronger than a few years ago, and (now that I am for the whole of this winter set aside as a Walker) she takes my place, and will return from an eight miles' walk with my Brother unfatigued. Miss Hutchinson and her sister Joanna are both with us. Miss H. is perfectly well, and Joanna very happy, though she may be always considered as an invalid. Her home is in the Isle of Man, and, with the first mild breezes of Spring, she intends returning thither, with her Sailor Brother Henry; they two 'toddling down the hill' together. She is an example for us all. With the better half of her property she purchased Columbian Bonds, at above 70, gets no interest, and will not sell. Consequently the cheapness of the little Isle tempted her thither on a visit, and she finds the air so suitable to her health, and every thing else so much to her mind that she *will*, in spite of our unwillingness to part with her make it her home. As to her lost property, she never regrets it. She has so reduced her wants that she declares herself to be now richer than she ever was in her life, and so she *is*; for she has always a little to spare at the end of the year—and in her little way can always assist the distressed. I believe you never saw Joanna, and it is a pity; for you would have loved her very much. She possesses all the good qualities of the Hutchinsons. My niece Dora, who remembers you alw[ay]s with the greatest affection, has lately been in much better health than within the last few years, she is very active and a most useful personage at home—her Father's helper at all times; and in domestic concerns she takes all the trouble from her mother and me. I trust that in course of a year or two she may become strong; but now she is no walker—cannot climb a mountain. It is not improbable that her Father may take her to Cambridge in the spring, and if so to London—and in that case they would see you: but no plans are laid, though now and then Dora amuses herself with talking about it. As for myself you will be glad to hear that I am perfectly well; but after this pleasant assurance I must tell you that my health had a sad shaking last April, when I was with John in Leicestershire. The disorder was inflammation of the Bowels. In June I left that country—and from want of care have had two or three attacks, but neither so severe, nor of the same kind; however, enough to convince me of the necessity of great care; and therefore *now* though perfectly well I am acting the invalid, never walk except in the garden and am driven out whenever weather permits by my Niece in the pony chaise. By this means I hope to resume my former habits next summer, during the present winter laying in a stock of strength. My dear Friend your eyes are weak, and you will find this a sad troublesome prosy letter, and vexed I am, for (using proper discretion) I might have told you all I *have* told in one half the number of lines—pray forgive me and entreat your kind Brother to send me a written assurance that you do so and with that to send us a minute account of all that concerns yourselves and as much about mutual Friends as he has leisure for and inclination. My Brother, Sister, Miss H., and Dora unite with me in sincerest good wishes for the coming year, and

every succeeding one of your lives, and that they may be many.—
God bless you both, and my dear Miss Lamb,
Believe me your affec^te Friend

D Wordsworth

Strange that I should have written this long letter without a
word of our absent William to whom you were so kind when a
London Schoolboy.[1] He has been at Bremen since last June. When
he left Rydal Mount his health was but indifferent—but in Leicestershire he recruited and left *England* in good health but at first the
change of climate, habits etc etc disagreed with him and he was
very unwell, yet always wrote in good spirits and I am happy to
tell you that his late letters have onl[y] spoken of 'excellent
health'. But it [is now][2] nearly two months since his last and we
are anxiously expecting letters. He is much attached to the excellent Family with whom he lives; and we have reason to believe
that his time passes profitably.

Do you ever see Mr and Mrs Thomas Clarkson? Mr Clarkson's
health is improved, but his wife is less equal to exertion than
formerly.

John makes an excellent parish priest, other particulars, if you
meet, he will tell you himself.

495. W. W. to CHARLES LAMB[3]

Address: Charles Lamb Esqre, Enfield Common, Enfield.
Postmark: 16 Jan. [18]30. *Stamp*: [illegible].
MS. Henry E. Huntington Library.
LY i. 446.

Sunday Jany 10th 1830

My dear Lamb,
    A whole twelve month have I been a Letter in your debt—for
which fault I have been sufficiently punished by self-reproach.

---

[1] See *Lamb*, ii. 265. Willy W. was then (Nov. 1819) at the Central School
in Baldwin's Gardens, preparing for Charterhouse.
[2] *Words dropped out.*
[3] Enclosed with previous letter, and posted by John W. in London. For
Lamb's reply see *Lamb*, iii. 241 ff. 'The last long time I heard from you, you had
knock'd your head against something. Do not do so. For your head (I do not
flatter) is not a nob, or the top of a brass rail, or the end of a nine pin—unless a
Vulcanian hammer could fairly batter a Recluse out of it, then would I bid the
smirch'd god knock and knock lustily . . .'

I liked your play[1] marvellously, having no objection to it but one, which strikes me as applicable to a large majority of plays, those of Shakespear himself not entirely excepted, I mean a little degradation of character, for a more dramatic turn of Plot. Your present of Hone's Book[2] was very acceptable, and so much so, that your part of the Book is the cause why I did not write long ago.—I wished to enter a little minutely into notice of the Dramatic Extracts, and on account of the smallness of the print deferred doing so till longer days would allow me to read without candle light, which I have long since given up. But alas! when the days lengthened my eyesight departed, and for many months I could not read three minutes at a time. You will be sorry to hear that this infirmity still hangs about me and almost cuts me off from reading altogether. —But how are you? And how is your dear Sister? I long much, as we all do, to know.—For ourselves this last year, owing to my Sister's dangerous illness, the effects of which are not yet got over, has been an anxious one, and melancholy. But no more of this—My Sister has probably told everything about this family, so that I may conclude with less scruple, by assuring you of my sincere and faithful affection for you, and your dear Sister.—

Wm Wordsworth

My son takes this to London.—

[*D. W. adds*]

Sunday 10th

My Brother has given me this to enclose [with][3] my own—His account of me is far too doleful—I am, I assure you, perfectly well—and it is only in order to become *strong*, as heretofore, that I confine myself mainly to the house.—And yet, were I to trust my *feelings* merely, I should say that I am strong already—His eyes, alas! are very weak—and so will, I fear remain through life; but with proper care, he does not suffer much.

DW.

[1] See L. 428 above.

[2] *The Table Book*, 1827, by William Hone (see also *MT* ii. 410), contained Lamb's extracts, 'after-gleanings', supplementary to his *Specimens of English Dramatic Poets, who lived about the Time Shakespeare*, 1808, culled from the collections bequeathed to the British Museum by Garrick. See *Lamb*, iii. 61–2.

[3] *Word dropped out.*

496. D. W. to MARIA JANE JEWSBURY

Address: Mr Thomas Jewsbury, 48 Grosvenor St, Oxford Road, Manchester.
By favour of Mr John Wordsworth.
MS. Historical Society of Pennsylvania.
Letters of Dora Wordsworth, p. 64 (—).

Rydal Mount
Sunday 10th Janry.
[1830]

My dear Friend,

Dora is so busy collecting her Brother's cloaths etc etc.—that she cannot write a line of introduction for him—therefore I undertake to do it—not but that you have seen his face before—and he yours—and you will at once recognise the Wordsworth countenance. John has spent one short week with us—is now on his way to Oxford—has promise of service at his Church for three Sundays and must be back at Moresby—reckoning from last Monday—at the end of the Parson's three weeks. He will tell you that Dora is *for her*—very well—yet she has had a terrible barking cough—the barking, however, was the worst of it—for her chest was but little affected, and her throat not at all—and strange to say! a Drive with her Father to near his Oak at Bowness—on one of the coldest days we have had (a bitter frost and boisterous north-wind)—almost wrought a cure. She is all life and activity—as housekeeper takes all care from her Mother and me—and as Amanuensis to her Father—and Reader—spares our aged hands, eyes, and voices. All this is very good and it is plain she cannot feel herself ill—yet we are not quite satisfied—for she is very thin and her complexion is yellow and bilious. Mr Carr is convinced (and so are we) that the liver does not exactly perform its functions, and he wishes to administer the Blue Pill in small doses—but neither he nor we can prevail. She says—"if I were *ill* I would take *that* or any thing; but being well I *will not*". I can only say that I hope Nature by aid of her own energies will do the work; but, if not, ere long I doubt not she will feel herself ill. My dear Brother— what a [? bounder][1] he is!—Still the Crack Skater upon Rydal Lake—and though companionless now on his moonlight walks— as heretofore he walks hour after hour—and sits down by the fireside amongst us unfatigued and gay as a Lark. God grant that this may continue! But when I look upon him thus at sixty years of age—often does my heart sink within me. The suddenness of change

---

[1] *MS. obscure.*

195

in such constitutions is often painful—and I tremble for what may be *his* fate. His Wife is wonderful also. She takes my place as a brother—and her strength is certainly much beyond what it was a few years ago. Miss H. is well—and dear Joanna (now with us from the Isle of Man) is comfortable and happy—as good and sweet a creature as ever the sun shone upon. In nature resembling Mrs Wordsworth—though much her inferior in talents and acquirements.—You will, I know, rejoice [with]¹ her that I am quite well, though submitting chearfully to enact the Invalid during the whole of this winter. Dora faithfully drives her two Aunts (Joanna and me) by turns whenever weather permits; but lately I have been out but little—as cold is what I shrink from—and in fact, every ailment I have lately had has been the effect of cold. I have found the best remedy against uncomfortable feelings has been the shutting out of cold. Hence I have a fire in my Bedroom—morning and night—and during the day this pretty little Room of mine serves for a retiring-place for all the family. In regard to your Father tell him I am much obliged for the pains he and you took in selecting the black silk; which is both good and cheap. Remember me kindly to Brother Harry² and Geraldine. My dear Friend, take care of yourself—I am afraid when I hear of so many hours' mental labour—

One of the silver fishes³ has thrown us into alarm by a *black* appearance near the head. We are told this is the first change preparatory to death: however the fish lives and thrives among the rest and its silvery scales are becoming golden. We anxiously look for the result.

The Doves are happy and thriving as ever—It is very pleasant to see Anne do her morning service to these Birds—She loves them almost as if they were children that understood her kindness— God bless you dear Friend—in haste with [every good] wish yours ever

DW

My kind remembrances to Miss Kelsall and Miss [?]⁴—and to young Barbara. How are the Howits⁵ going on? My regards to them.

---

¹ *Word dropped out.*   ² Henry Richard Jewsbury (b. 1803).
³ Following her visit in May and June 1829, Miss Jewsbury had presented the poet with a bowl of fish, commemorated in *Gold and Silver Fishes in a Vase* (*PW* iv. 151).
⁴ *MS. illegible.*
⁵ For William and Mary Howitt, see pt. i, L. 293

497. W. W. to GEORGE HUNTLY GORDON

Endorsed: Wordsworth. Jany 16/30.
MS. Cornell.
Broughton, p. 30.

Rydal Mount
Jany 16th/30

My dear Sir,

The account of W^m was satisfactory—there was also an agreeable Letter from Mr. Pappendick.

The Miss Jewsbury you speak [of]¹ is a friend of ours—and lives at Manchester. She means to be in town for a short time in May, and it will give us pleasure to furnish you with a Letter of introduction—which at least would give you an opportunity of seeing her—should nothing more come of it from her short stay, and the pressure of both your engagements.

I am not acquainted with the duties of the Sheriffs of Scotland, and therefore cannot form a judgement how far such an institution would suit the case of Ireland. The state of moral sentiment is so perverted in Ireland, and the passions so mounted, that it is in vain to look for an impartial and efficient administration of justice whatever be the form of the Institution. Witnesses cannot be procured, and jury men will not look at the truth. A *steady* hand of Power can alone put the Country in the way of improving itself—Time and gradual knowledge must do the rest—

I should have waited a few days before I thanked you for your yesterdays communication, and for your kindly forwarding my Letters but for the sake of the enclosed to [*Here Dora W. takes the pen*] Messrs Hebeler which relates to a mischance that has befallen thro neglect of Coach Prop^rs a box containing two beautiful specimens of Moor game (stuffed) and intended as a present from William to the Museum of natural history at Bremen. Our English Moor game is unknown on the Continent and the collection at Bremen only contained the Ptarmigan and Black Game—and William to gratify the keeper of the Museum promised to procure him a specimen. To save further expense we have taken the liberty of requesting Messrs Hebeler to answer thro' you. The enclosed which explains the accident is left open for your perusal if you think it worth while to look at it.

Thank you for the Pacquet Paper and Believe me duly sensible of you kind attentions and with sincere respect Faithfully yours

Wm Wordsworth

Word dropped out.

197

498. W. W. to ROBERT SOUTHEY

MS. WL transcript. Hitherto unpublished.

[late Jan. 1830]

My dear S,

Mr Townsend,[1] your present neighbour, is, I believe, the author of the late series of Blackwood's Articles upon me and my writings. From what I have seen and heard of this work I infer Mr T. may find it less disagreeable to give verbal answer *through you* to the question whether it is his or not than a written one to myself, and you perhaps will have no objection to ask him. If you are the least unwilling to do so pray content yourself with enclosing this note to him.[2] Had Mr T. been a stranger to me, I should not have condescended to make the Enquiry, nor thought I had a right to make it; but as we have been upon terms of friendly tho' not frequent intercourse for many years, and it is not unlikely we may meet again, I wish to have the best possible assurance upon the point, for my particular and general guidance as to whom I may converse with in future and under what limitations.

Ever faithfully yours
Wm Wordsworth

[1] Chauncy Hare Townshend (see pt. i, L. 4) had recently published 'An Essay on the theory and the writings of Wordsworth' in *Blackwood's Magazine*, xxvi (Sept.–Dec. 1829), 453–63, 593–609, 774–88, 894–910. His aim was to show 'that Wordsworth's genius is overrated by his partisans', and 'that it is underrated by his detractors', and he was particularly critical of the excessive adulation offered to the poet by his disciples. 'A praying Quaker, a preaching Whitfieldian, is nothing to a spouting Wordsworthian.' In the course of a lengthy examination of Wordsworth's theory and practice as a poet, Townshend singled out the *Ode: Intimations of Immortality* and *The Excursion* for condemnation, and while acknowledging Wordsworth's grandeur and descriptive power, he concluded that he was not one of our greatest writers, though one of 'the band of true poets'. See next letter, L. 503 below, and *SH*, p. 367.

[2] Southey replied on 7 Feb. enclosing a copy of the covering letter he sent with W. W.'s to Townshend: 'When you read the enclosed note from Mr W. to me, and know also that he considers the papers in Blackwood as containing much scoffing, much literary misrepresentation, and personal disparagement,— you will readily believe that few circumstances in which I am not directly implicated could have given me so much uneasiness.' (*WL MSS.*)

499. W. W. to EDWARD QUILLINAN

Address: Edward Quillinan Esq., No 12, Bryanstone Street, Portman Square, London.
Postmark: 6 Feb. 1820.
MS. British Library.
'*Some Unpublished Letters of William Wordsworth*', *Cornhill Magazine*, *xx* (1893), 257–76 (—). *LY* i. 447.

Rydal Mount, 4th Febry 1830.
Private and confidential.

My dear Sir,

I write this in consequence of the P.S. to Miss H.'s just received—I am still in want of a Mortgage—for between 2 and 3000. My Soltr is Mr Strickland Cookson, No 6 Lincoln's Inn. But I have first to speak with you on this matter as a Friend. In Mortgages every one says avoid distressed Borrowers, you are neither sure of principal or interest. Now if this money be wanted for the Lee Family there is not a member of it but C. B.[1] on whom I could rely. Sir E. B.[2] is too distressed a Man and too little of a man of business.

Therefore do consider well of this for me, and let me know if it be at all advisable to have dealings in that quarter. Verbum sat. Perhaps the money may be wanted for some one else.

Poor Dora has suffered dreadfully for some days from a swoln face, with Rheumatic cold—aggravated if not caught by last Sunday's Church. She is in bed—the rest of the family are well.— It is to be regretted that Jemima[3] has missed the measles. John was unlucky in not seeing you, he reached Rydal looking anything but well—he travelled from London on the top of the Coach, and his humanity induced him to lend his cloak to a poor Female who was perishing with cold—a violent diarrhoea was the consequence —and he arrived much exhausted.—Miss W. is doing very well— Your message will be delivered to Barber probably to-day—as he intends to call. Your theatrical performances amused us much. I should have liked to be a spectator—particularly when the author made his appearance. The Revd Chauncey Hare Townsend[4] is as pretty a rascal as ever put on a Surplice. He is one of Southey's most intimate Friends and has been so for about a dozen or 14 years—during a good part of that period I have occasionally seen him upon very friendly terms, both at Cambridge, where I had dined with him, at Keswick and at my own House where he has

---

[1] Colonel Barrett, E. Q.'s brother-in-law. [2] Sir Egerton Brydges.
[3] E. Q.'s younger daughter. [4] See previous letter.

slept—and where he was cordially received twice while this attack upon my person and writings was in process. The Thing as an intellectual production is safe in its own vileness. Who that ever felt a line of my poetry would trouble himself to crush a miserable maggot crawled out of the dead carcass of the Edinburgh review. But too much of this.

Below is a note for Mr S. Cookson.

Dear Strickland, I think you know Mr Quillinan, he is the Bearer—and calls to name a matter of business to you, to which as my professional adviser I beg you to give your attention.

> ever faithfully yours
> W. Wordsworth

Love from every one to the Little ones. Kind regards to Col. Barrett. I like Dora's watch and trust that it keep the promise of its good looks. I am afraid of hurting the sale of the present Edition[1] if I publish before it is nearly out. On this consult with the Longmans.[2]

500. W. W. to UNKNOWN CORRESPONDENT[3]

MS. Cornell. Hitherto unpublished.

> Rydal Mount
> Febr 8th. 1830

Dear Sir,

It would have given me pleasure to meet your wish in sending you an Engraved Portrait of me, but no such thing exists. A promising artist[4] did indeed many years ago make a portrait of me—from which an Engraving was procured for some Magazine or other; but the Picture was a Juvenile work and though I think

[1] i.e. the *Poetical Works*, 5 vols., 1827.

[2] See L. 502 below.

[3] The addressee of this letter cannot be identified with any certainty, as D. W. met so many people in the course of her last visit to Halifax. But W. W.'s correspondent was possibly one of the Rawsons, whom D. W. saw frequently: perhaps Mr. J. Rawson the mill-owner.

[4] For Richard Carruthers and his portrait of Wordsworth (1819), see pt. i, L. 45, and Frances Blanchard, *Portraits of Wordsworth*, 1959, pp. 57–9, 146–7. The portrait was engraved by Henry Meyer (1782–1847) for the *New Monthly Magazine* in Feb. 1819, and later by John Taylor Wedgwood (*c.* 1783–1856) for the 'pirated' edition of W. W.'s poems published by Galignani in Paris in 1828.

highly of the talents of the Painter, he was not successful in this attempt—and the Engraving does no justice even to his imperfect attempt. It is in fact a wretched Thing—A medallion from Chantry's Bust[1] was in progress a year and half ago, by an Artist in London whose name I forget, I have never heard of his performance since. It promised to be a good thing.

My Sister who had the pleasure of seeing you at Halifax, is here and begs to be remembered to you—as does Mrs Wordsworth and her Sister

I remain dear Sir
faithfully yours
W[m] Wordsworth

501. W. W. to C. W. JNR.

Address: Chris Wordsworth, Esq[re], Trin: Coll:, Cambridge.
MS. British Library. Hitherto unpublished.

Rydal Mount
Feb[ry] 8th 1830

My dear Chris:

I have owed you a letter of congratulations for some time upon your place in the Tripos[2] with which I, as your Uncle, and all here, are more than satisfied. I am urged to write at present by a Letter I have just received, signed L. Raymond,[3] Willow Walk, Cambridge. Its purport is to solicit my Subscription for an Edition of two plays of Molière with Notes etc,—The application is somewhat in forma pauperis, and I do not like to put the Writer to the expence of a post Letter, nor to subscribe unless he be a respectable person. If You think it reasonable I should subscribe pray put my name down, and I will contrive to pay you—and be so kind as to call upon the Man or let him know by Note that I have received his Letter—and that you will pay him for the book—if you disapprove no notice must be taken of his Letter or the subscription.

---

[1] See Blanchard, *Portraits of Wordsworth*, p. 151, and *MY* ii. 615. The bust was completed in the summer of 1820. It was subsequently engraved by Achille Collas (1795–1859) as a medallic portrait from a relief by Henry Weekes, R.A. (1807–77), and published in his *Authors of England*, 1838—and again by William Finden (1787–1852) for the 1845 edition of W. W.'s poems.

[2] C. W. jnr. had been declared Senior Classic in the Classical Tripos and 14th Senior Optime in the Mathematical Tripos.

[3] Unidentified: his edition of Molière does not appear to have been published.

I will now tell you how we all are—first and foremost your Aunt D. by great care and self denial is at present quite well. She rides out in the pony-chaise as often as the weather will permit—but we do not trust her to any walking whatever—and her diet is strictly regulated. Dora is just recovered from a severe attack of swelled face, caught by going to church sunday before last. She is in good spirits—but of course rather weak. Mrs W. is at Moresby with John, who has been obliged to go into new lodgings, and her business is to put things into order about him, and into a good train. John has just been at Oxford to take his Master's degree, and he was in London—but had not time to return by Cambridge. He is now I trust well—but he came home looking shockingly—he had caught a severe cold on the roof of the Coach. Miss Hutchinson is here well—so is Miss Joanna—and in her better way. Miss Cookson[1] of Kendal or rather Staveley is also a Visitor with us and for myself I am as well as usual—and my eyes at present in such a state that I can read and write—a comfort I have had little of for the last 12 months.

This long Bulletin presumes a good deal upon the interest you take in us all. I hope your dear Father is well—and that yourself John and Charles are so also. Give our best love to them all—We have had a strange and by no means a disagreeable season of frost since the last week in Nov[br] little skating however on account of the snow. We have no news from this quarter. Owen[2] is unusually well and in high spirits—quite delighted with his humble curacy. He is a man to all the country dear—and passing rich with sixty pounds (I fear not more) a year.

Do you know? (yes you do the outside of him at least) the Rev[d] Chauncy Hare Townsend[3]—he is Author of the series of Articles that have lately appeared in *Blackwood* upon me and my writings. I was simple enough to take him for a Friend—and treated him in a certain degree as such—and he has repaid me like a Scoundrel. When do you sit for the Medal[4]—and who are likely to be your Competitors—

I wish this Letter had been better worth posting and the trouble it will take in the decyphering—ever your affectionate Uncle

W. Wordsworth

---

[1] Elizabeth Cookson.
[2] Owen Lloyd, C. W. jnr.'s cousin.
[3] See L. 498 above.
[4] The Chancellor's Medal for Classics, which C. W. jnr. won.

502. W. W. to EDWARD QUILLINAN

Address: Edward Quillinan Esqre, 12 Bryanston S^t, Portman Sq^re, London.
Postmark: 13 Feb. 1830.
MS. WL.
LY i. 449 (—).

[In Dora W.'s hand]

Rydal Mount
Feb^ry 11th 1830

My dear Friend,

My first words must be an expression of regret and shame for having omitted in my last to thank you for the elegant Copy of the 'Lay of the Papist',[1] in fact business upon which I wrote and the unpleasant affair of Parson Townshend[2] (who has confessed) put it out of my head and I was greatly mortified at so unbecoming an act of forgetfulness when it was too late to repair it.

I write with reluctance not having command of a frank, but it seems that I ought to write to say that there is no man living in whose honor I have higher confidence than Col. Barrett,[3] so that as far as that goes I am perfectly satisfied; the rest must be taken care of by my Solicitor to whom I will write upon the subject as soon as I am informed that it is likely to go forward.

Dora you will perceive is my Amanuensis. She is now without pain but as yellow as a gipsy and as thin as a Lath (Is it not too bad to *insist* upon *my* writing this) she has not yet been out of doors. Miss Wordsworth is going on very well. Thanks for your kind notice of your little Ones, so no more at present from your's faithfully

[signature cut away]

[Dora W. writes][4]

It was only a little after dinner laziness in my Father to make me hold the Pen for him, his eyes are very tolerable indeed—he reads an hour or two every evening by Candle light. I hope you may be able to come to some terms with Longman[5] now that his eyes are so much better. I long for the Poems to be going thro' the Press

---

[1] Unidentified: perhaps one of E. Q.'s own poems.
[2] Chauncy Hare Townshend.　　　　　　[3] See L. 499 above
[4] Below her own letter to E. Q.
[5] W. W. was contemplating collecting all his recent compositions into a new volume supplementary to the *Poetical Works* of 1827, and E. Q. was acting as his intermediary with Longman; but the plan came to nothing at this time. See also L. 515 below.

—I am to have the honor of being his sole Amanuensis, whilst this little vol: is printing. Mother and Aunts are to have *nought* to do with it.

503. W. W. to ROBERT SOUTHEY

MS. WL transcript. Hitherto unpublished.

[mid-Feb. 1830]

My dear S,

Before you proceed, read the enclosed. Though I have no doubt, still the confitentem reum (and silence I should consider as such) is the most Solid ground to build upon.—You will excuse me speaking of a Friend of yours[1] as I am about to do—but the sincerity of *our* Friendship requires it—

> Some have for wits at first then Poets past
> Turned Critics next and proved plain fools.[2]

I wish that Mr C. H. Townsend who has undergone these several transmigrations had proved nothing *worse*. He is a Gentleman by rank—a Xtian minister by profession—we have exchanged hospitalities—a few weeks ago I received him cordially, while this farrago of insolent scoffing profligate literary misrepresentation and personal disparagement, not to say calumny, was covertly in course of publication, in a Periodical with innumerable channels prepared to carry it into all parts of the world where English Literature enters. Had a *hint* been given me that Mr T. was so engaged I should have revolted from the *suspicion* as a slander upon human nature. Farewell.

Aff[ly] yours
Wm Wordsworth

---

[1] Chauncy Hare Townshend, author of the anonymous articles on W. W. in *Blackwood's*. See L. 498 above.
[2] See Pope, *Essay on Criticism*, ll. 36–7.

504. W. W. to GEORGE HUNTLY GORDON

Endorsed: Mr Wordsworth 18th Feby/30.
MS. Professor Paul Betz.
The Wordsworth Circle, Spring, 1970.

[*In Dora W.'s hand*]

Rydal Mount
Feby 18th 1830

My dear Sir

Having a double letter to send to Mr Quillinan, and as it concerns my own affairs I feel unwilling to tax him with the postage. You will not therefore, I trust, think me encroaching upon the privilege you have granted me, if I enclose it to you and request you to send it to the twopenny.

[*W. W. writes*]

My dear Sir, I am suddenly called off to Keswick upon business of my office—I am likely to be a sufferer there, by the free Trade in Bankruptcy now going on in our unhappy neighbourhood.

ever faithfully yours W. W.

505. W. W. to EDWARD QUILLINAN

Endorsed: 1830 Mr Wordsworth.
MS. British Library.
LY i. 450.

Rydal Mount
18th Febry, [1830]

My dear Friend,

I have just written to Strickland Cookson, 6 Lincoln's Inn, my Solr. The sum I have named is £3500 or £2500 as may best suit the Borrower, if the security is found undeniable. Colnl Barrett will therefore be so kind as to communicate with Mr Cookson at his earliest convenience.—

This Letter might have been sent you yesterday—through a Frank—Dora tells me that it shall—I am glad of it, being ashamed to put you to the expense of mere letters of business—which I cannot make interesting by any sort of embroidery. Our life here is utterly unvaried, even in the Valentine season, when Miss H. complained of being forgotten by you.—Dora says you are a pretty Man of your Word, having sent Rotha to Langholm place—those *daft* vanity fair people of Derbyshire,[1] she thinks, have turned your head, they have had more weight and influence than our Philosopher and *all* his Ladies.—As to Longman's people I, for my own part, am very glad they have not written; being decidedly of opinion that the publication[2] would not be prudent unless the present Edition were nearly exhausted, which it is not.

Enclosed you will find an Education advertisement, words surely to my taste—I really am serious, but promise and performance are very different things. Dont suppose by this, that I presume to recommend the School to you, but I am told that without such open profession, the Hendon School[3] did aim at and succeed in something of the kind.

I have called upon and seen Mr De Quincey—looking very well, and busy (he says) in writing a series of Canterbury Tales,[4] for money—which he is in great need of, and his wife, of something still more pretious,—health. She has been suffering long in the jaundice. He named your call, and said that he should have been happy to return it—but it would have looked so ill, to appear at my House, upon a call not meant for me; and he had resolved not to be seen among his neighbours, till the foresaid Tales were concluded.

Did I name poor Hartley C. to you? he is wandering about like a vagabond, sleeping in Barns, without the dignity of Gipsy-life, and picking up a meal where he can—in and about Ambleside. Barber is in a very low key, both as to health and spirits—and poor Man the latter evil and his treacherous friends are in a great measure accountable for. They keep him low in pocket—he names no one—but we suspect that Mr S.[5] of Field head near Hawkshead has taken him in. B. said to me lately with a look at once wild and sour, that he was eating his own heart and very bad diet he found it. Duplicity and treachery are damnable things in life; and the image of a Man who has been guilty of this is odious in one's memory. As an author, I have been, I hope, singularly unfortunate, in falling in with persons of that stamp, but the last case[6] is far far the worst, inasmuch as it was utterly unprovoked. I wish I could

---

[1] Apparently a reference to E. Q.'s friends among the Sitwell circle (see pt. i, L. 364)—but the drift of W. W.'s remarks is not clear. Langholm Place is presumably Langham Place, near Cavendish Square in London.

[2] See L. 502 above.　　　　　　　　　　　　[3] The school kept by Mrs. Gee.

[4] This project apparently came to nothing, but De Quincey's interest in fiction is reflected in *Klosterheim*, 1832.

[5] William Henry Smith of Fieldhead House, who was later believed to have swindled Barber and contributed to his unhappy end (see L. 686 below).

[6] i.e. the case of Chauncy Hare Townshend.

see Dora looking well.[1] Make my kind remembrances to your Brother and say to Col. Barrett that he is one of the few whom I always think of with entire pleasure.

most faithfully yours
W. Wordsworth

506. W. W. to JOHN WILSON CROKER

MS. Rush Rhees Library, Rochester University.
Robert F. Metzdorf, 'A Wordsworth Letter', MLN lix (1944), 168–70

Rydal Mount
near Ambleside
Febr*y* 24th 1830

Dear Sir,

Having learned with pleasure that you are about to edit a new Edition of Boswell's Life of Johnson,[2] I think the following Transcript from a blank page of my Copy of that Work may not be uninteresting to you. The words were dictated by the late Sir George Beaumont, and signed by him, in my presence.

I remain
dear Sir
very sincerely yours
Wm Wordsworth

[? *In John Carter's hand*]

Sir Joshua Reynolds told me at his Table, immediately after the publication of this Book, that every word in it might be depended upon as if given upon oath. Boswell was in the habit of bringing the proof sheets to his house previously to their being struck off; and if any of the company happened to have been present at the

---

[1] *Dora W. erases a passage and adds*: Nonsense which Father had written about me and my looks, which I have taken the liberty of putting out.

[2] Croker had been at work on his edition since Jan. 1829. It was published by John Murray in 5 vols. in 1831. See Croker's *Correspondence and Diaries*, ed. L. J. Jennings, 3 vols., 1884, ii. 24 ff. He acknowledged W. W.'s contribution on 26 Feb. and expressed his intention of using it: 'Boswell's *accuracy* seems above suspicion, not so his candour and fidelity. He was never guilty of *suggestio falsi,* but he now and then indulged in a little of the *suppressio veri,* and he certainly published or suppressed Johnson's Sarcasms . . . according to *his own* feeling towards the object.' (*WL MSS.*) Sir George Beaumont's note was duly printed in the Preface to the new edition (I. x), and the material credited to W. W.

conversation recorded he requested him or them to correct any error—and not satisfied with this he would run over all London for the sake of verifying any single word that might be disputed.

G. H. Beaumont

Rydal Mount
Sepr 12. 1826

507. D. W. to MRS. S. T. COLERIDGE

Address: To Mrs S. T. Coleridge, at the Revd D. Coleridge's, Helleston, Cornwall. *Single Sheet.*
Stamp: Kendal Penny Post.
MS. Victoria University Library, Toronto.
LY i. 451 (—).

Friday March 5th 1830.

My dear Friend,

I have at length the satisfaction of being able to say something decisive concerning your poor Hartley, and more satisfactory for you than till the present time has been in my power. From time to time, since my writing to you, we heard of him—calling at this house or that—where he was supplied with a meal—and housing at night in Barns etc. One evening he came, faint and hungry, to Mr Fell's[1] lodgings—was supplied with refreshment, and Mr F. took him to one of the Inns, and paid for his bed and breakfast next morning. We commissioned every one likely to see him with a message requesting him to come to R. M^t, and last Friday evening the message was delivered to him by Mr Fell. He replied that he was actually coming hither: however, he did not arrive; but on Monday we heard that he was at Jonathan Bell's.[2] He (Jonathan) had come over from Cockermouth to arrange his last business, remove beds etc. No debt was incurred by H., for of course J. could make no charge for those few days and when we paid him (a fortnight ago) we had desired him to inform the people who were to succeed him that Mr C. was not intending to remain at any publick house, and that if they received him neither his mother nor any other person would be answerable for payment. We had during the long time of H.'s wanderings been turning over in our minds all places likely for board and lodging; but till he 'cast up' we could

---

[1] William Fell, the Ambleside surgeon.
[2] i.e. at the Red Lion, Grasmere.

take no steps whatever: however as soon as we knew him to be safe at the Red Lion we applied at that very place which of all others we thought the best; and I am happy to tell you that the people are willing to make a trial; and he is now most comfortably and respectably lodged and boarded with old Mr and Mrs James Fleming[1] in a small cottage (which I hope you recollect) lately built by them close by. The Garden looks towards Thomas Ashburner's old Barn at the Town End, and the front of the house, (with a little court before it towards the new Road and the Lake. Mrs Fleming came over to speak to us—but as neither she nor we had seen Hartley we could make no final arrangement respecting Terms—only she undertook to mend his stockings and linen, and to wash for him. We told her that *more* than £40 per ann. could not be given, that you had mentioned between 30 and 40; and to this she replied that till she had seen him and knew what he required she could not say what she could do it for—only this was settled, that *at present* she was to take him in. Her bed was well aired, and there was no bed left for him at the Red Lion. As soon as Mrs F. had left us my Brother went to Grasmere, saw H. (I need not repeat their conversation) and invited him to dinner the next day. Accordingly he came (on Wednesday) looked as well as usual, and ate *more* heartily than formerly. His conversation and spirits in no respect changed. But when my Brother and I were left alone with him and began to talk of his past and the future, he was much agitated and poured out thanks and promises. He was quite satisfied with his lodgings in all respects—had agreed with Mrs F. that he must dine alone at his own hour, and have a room to sit in alone, with a fire when necessary, to do his work. They had not fixed their terms, but he thought she would do all for £40, and we think she will not be willing to take less, or that we ought to require it—in consideration of the extra accomodations of separate dinner and private sitting-room. We have had the whole of Jonathan Bell's account from June 1827 up to the time of H's last running off. At the beginning, especially, of the account (which you know had never been completely settled) there is often so much set down for liquor (wine, spirits, etc.) that we were inclined to take off for all extra liquor—but on hearing what Jonathan had to plead we could not stand to that mode of settling the account. He told us that though when you had seen the Bills you had frequently complained and remonstrated, you were well aware of the

---

[1] For James and Mary Fleming and the Ashburners of Town End, see *MY* ii. 109.

nature of them and that he had told you, his house being a *publick house*, he could not do otherwise—that Guests came—invited him to drink—he could never refuse—and would himself call for liquor—that you had observed you could possibly get him cheaper boarded and lodged in a private house, and that it might be better—but [? then] you observed he would go off to the publick houses and on the whole perhaps was better where he was—and therefore you wished him to remain there. This being the case we must deduct on another principle. You had seen the accounts (up to the time of your departure I believe) and beginning from that time J. took off 6d per day. Observe that the extra liquor was not nearly so much in the last account. J's bill amounts to 49£. 13ˢ. 1—we paid him in full of all demands 46£—10ˢ—. Observe on the last account he has not charged anything for H's bed on those nights when he was absent, and took off 6ᵈ per day since the 29ᵗʰ of September. I have paid the washerwoman to the present time 14/-. A bill has come in to me from Preston[1] of Ambleside for two hats (Janʳʸ 1825—Do—1826—) I told Hartley you had given him money to pay for a Hat for him, expecting that he would want a new one, I supposed not knowing of this: therefore I should pay Preston. He thanked me and said he now *does* want a hat; but can pay for it when he receives the money from Liverpool. He has cloth for a new suit unmade which he got at Elleray. This he has not paid for—but said he would pay as soon as he got money for the Edinburgh articles 'now ready to be sent off'. He owes something also to the shoe maker and said he would take that debt on himself, to which I replied that if the Man were pressing and his money not ready I would pay it in order that he might work with a more easy mind. We told him that we had mentioned to Mrs Fleming that he should have a pint of good table beer to dinner, and do. to supper and his answer was that he should not take it. He would drink nothing but water. This, I fear, he will never hold to, and aware of the danger of a vow being a snare to him, William told him that, however glad he might be that he should lay such a resolution, he would have him consider it only as a trial, and if he found it necessary—take the Beer, for after arrangement could be made with his hostess. How thankful shall I be if after the end of the year we find that he has really worked, so as to be able to pay off his debts of honour (of which no doubt he has several at the publick houses) to provide himself with cloaths and to repay you a part at least of what you

[1] John Preston, the Ambleside tailor.

have made such sacrifices to advance for him. At all events you will have (by being answerable for board and Lodging) the satisfaction of knowing that you at least have done all you can to guard him from perishing of cold and hunger. You say you can always help him out with cloaths; but my dear Friend, let me warn you against holding out to him this expectation. He ought to be thrown upon his own exertions for this—and for whatever he may chuse to spend in extras, and this I am sure of, it will be the more likely means to assist in enabling him to earn much more and to foster in him an ambition to release you from the very incumbrance which you voluntarily and openly take upon yourself. I have just written a letter to H. saying over again some things that I expressed in conversation and adding others that I omitted, but there is no need of troubling you with the details. It is enough that I have spoken with the utmost freedom, though kindly. Mrs Southey has sent me on your account 3£—16— (I think that is the sum; but I have all written down)—you will perceive that enough remains with me for small tradesman's bills should I be called upon. Sara H. is going to Keswick in a fortnight or three weeks, she will then write to you. In the meantime, if you do not hear from me you may conclude that we have settled to our satisfaction with Mrs Fleming, and that all goes on smoothly. I trust that my dear God-son[1] is now perfectly recovered. I do not venture to hope that he is yet strong enough to resume his labours, and trust he will not do so till his strength is entirely restored. Give my kind love to him. What a good creature his Wife is! My affectionate regards to her and to Miss Trevenan.[2] My dear Friend, what a load of misery you have lately had to bear about with you! I trust you will now be composed and easy. As to Derwent's charging himself with obligations for H. that cannot be. There would be no justice in this, and I am sure Henry and Sara have nothing to spare. We are all well except Dora, who says always that she is so, but she looks wretchedly—and is often worried with tooth ache. She is now staying with Mrs B. Harrison[3]—Joanna still here; God bless you ever your affectionate

                                                    D W

4 o'clock Friday afternoon. I have broken the seal of my letter to tell you that, though the place where we have fixed Hartley is that which above all others we most wished for, we were so

[1] Derwent Coleridge.   [2] For Emily Trevenen, see L. 463 above.
[3] Mrs. Benson Harrison.

fearful that Mrs Fleming would not take him that my Brother
applied to Mr Fell to inquire at and near Ambleside, but this
morning he tells us that nobody would take him—his habits being
such that they could not have any body else, and in fact they dare
not venture and that less than 40 £ would not do, in fact John pays
for lodging and fire alone 25 pounds, and near Whitehaven is very
cheap. John finds his own candles and every thing, washing etc etc.
It is most satisfactory that there is no place so good or so respectable
as that we have got—but we are [   ].[1]

508. W. W. to EDWARD QUILLINAN

Address: Edward Quillinan Esqʳ, Bryanston Street, Portman Square. [*In
Dora W.'s hand*]
Postmark: 10 Mar. 1830.
MS. British Library. Hitherto unpublished.

Rydal Mount
8ᵗʰ March. [1830]

My dear Q,

As you can receive this through the Twopenny, I write to
merely to [*sic*] say, (perhaps I have said it before) that I have
opened the business of the proposed mortgage to Mr Strickland
Cookson, Scott and Claytons, 6 Lincoln's Inn, and as I have heard
from him twice since, and he does not name his being in communication with Colⁿᵉˡ Barrett or his Agent, I am anxious to know
(time being precious and the money at a Bankers) whether Colⁿᵉˡ
Barrett is likely to want the money.—Therefore be so good as
write to me as soon as you know any thing certain.

—Miss [? Lockier][2] neglected to deliver a message from Mrs
Luff to thank you for remembering so kindly her commission.

Miss Dowling[3] is buried today—

The Landlord[4] of the royal Oak Ambleside hung himself lately;
and two days ago poor Jonathan Bell of the Red lion Grasmere
drowned himself in the Lake. He was Hartley Coleridge's host—

Dora is staying with Mr and Mrs Harrison, near Ambleside,
in a day or two she goes to Keswick. She has not recovered her
looks.

Every body's love.
W. W—

1 *MS. illegible.* 2 For the Misses Lockier, see *MY* ii. 612.
3 Mary Dowling had died on 1 Mar. 4 John Walker.

509. W. W. to UNKNOWN CORRESPONDENT[1]

MS. Mr. J. D. McClatchy. Hitherto unpublished.

Rydal
Thursday Evening.
[? mid-Mar. 1830]

My dear Sir,
    At twelve o clock on Tuesday it will suit me to meet you at Ambleside, either at the Salutation or Commercial Inn. I will make a point of being there, of course you need not write again unless something should occur to prevent your coming.

ever truly yours
Wm Wordsworth

[*In John W.'s hand*]

If the weather be favorable on Wednesday I am going into Cumberland for a few days—

510. W. W. to C. W., JOHN WORDSWORTH, and C. W. JNR.

Address: The Revd Dr Wordsworth, Trinity Lodge, Cambridge. *Single.*
MS. British Library.
K (—). *LY* ii. 581 (—).

[mid–late Mar. 1830]

My dear Brother,
    We all heartily congratulate you upon the academical success of your Son Christ: which gave us very great pleasure[2]—A fellowship it is to be hoped will come almost of course—
    My Nephew John[3] will have been a year at Hawkshead when Easter comes. I have written to Mr Sleigh[4] the agent at Penrith for a Statement of the Accounts. When it is made out I shall be able to let you know what surplus there is, if any, to meet the

---

[1] Perhaps addressed to the Solicitor of Stamps, successor to Godfrey Sykes (who had died in Dec. 1828), and referring to W. W.'s business expedition to Ulverston and the Duddon Valley mentioned in the next letter and L. 514 below.
[2] For C. W. jnr.'s academic successes, see L. 501 above. He was elected a Fellow of Trinity later this year. John Wordsworth wrote to his aunt D. W. from Trinity this month about his brother's success: 'If mitres are to be had twenty years hence, Chris I think in all human probability has as fair a chance of wearing one as anybody.' (*British Library MSS.*)
[3] R. W.'s son, 'Keswick John', at present at Hawkshead School.
[4] For Isaac Slee, see *MY* ii. 383.

expenses of his Education. I have paid his Bills up to Christmas, advancing the money. The £25 you were so kind as to offer may be remitted to Messrs Masterman and Co to be placed in my account with Wakefield's Kendal bank. John is but a poor learner, and what line of life will be best for him I cannot determine.—I have had a good deal of trouble lately with my Sub-dis^r at Keswick—a Bankrupt—but I hope I shall lose nothing. Our Friends, the Cooksons of Kendal, have had the bailiffs in their house; and their affairs are sadly disordered. There is more distress in this neighbourhood than has ever been known—but it is nothing compared with what is spreading elsewhere. The rest of this, that shall be for your Sons, only let me tell you that our excellent Sister is to appearance well—but certainly continues altogether unable to endure the exposure, and support the exertions she has been used to--so that she must long be managed as an Invalid. Dora is now at Keswick, on her way to Moresby. She writes that she is well—but says nothing of improved looks or better appetite, or gaining flesh, all of which she stood in need of when she left us a fortnight ago—The rest of us are well—

I have myself been moving about a good deal twice on business—it is lucky for me that my engagements of that kind must of necessity lead me through a beautiful country. Last Friday I was called to Ulverstone; I went down Coniston Water side, and returned by Broughton up the Duddon, and over Wrynose. The Vale of Duddon I had never seen at this season, and was much charmed with it. Most of the Cottages are embowered in fir trees mixed with sycamore, and in laurel, which thrives luxuriantly in this sheltered vale, and at this season is most pleasant to look upon. John was my companion,—we parted 5 miles up the Duddon, he turning up over Birker Moor for Whitehaven. John takes cordially to his profession, is much respected, and having a good voice he is highly thought of as a Preacher. He does not appear to trust himself to the entire composition of Sermons; but he is very successful in curtailing, remodelling, and adapting to his Congregation the works of others, especially the old Divines. He has a logical head; a good judgement; and certainly was much benefited by his Oxford Education. Owen is happy as the day is long—an excellent Minister, and beloved by every one; so that we have great satisfaction in these two young men. Another of my excursions was of two days with the Sec^y and Sol^r of Stamps, whom their official duties had brought to Lancaster; they came on to the Lakes, and pleased to shew them a kindness, I went with [them] to Keswick, up Borrowdale, as far as Stonethwaite, and round by Lyulph's

Tower, Patterdale, etc, You see how strangely I have dealt with my intention of giving the remainder of this Sheet to John and Chris: I might as well go on and let it be a joint Letter to you all. Dear Father and Sons! but to begin with Chris:—Your printed Quarto showed Us most agreeably your place in the Classical Tripos and your Cambridge Paper, your acquisition of the first medal. I should detest your honours if I thought they would cause you to love classical Literature less for its own sake when the stimulus of reading for distinction is withdrawn. But I have no apprehension of this fatal and too common result, in your case. You entertained me by your extract from Mr Le Bas's[1] Letter. The Paper, on [   ][2] he alluded to I never read, but I know it to be the last of a series written by that wretched Fribble Chauncey Hare Townsend, in all of which, except this concluding one, I was abused by Bell book and Candle; at a time that the Author was presenting himself at my Door as a Friend and cordially received as such. He hoped to remain concealed, but that was impossible—But too much of this—You are all far better employed than reading such trash; I will only add that if any one had hinted to me, while the publication of these Papers was going on that the Rev[d] C[y] H.T. was their author, I should have revolted from the suspicion as a slander upon human nature—

Dear John, what you tell us of Mr Rose's success as a Preacher is highly gratifying.[3] He is a sincere devout Man, and, I suppose, very industrious. How honourable is it to your University that such crowds go to hear him! He is out, as you are out about Laodamia.[4] No stanza is omitted. The last but one is however substantially altered. Hare[5] disliked the alteration; but I cannot bring my mind to reject it. As first written the Heroine was dismissed to happiness in Elysium. To what purpose then the mission of Pro-

---

[1] The Revd. Charles Webb le Bas (1779–1861), Fellow of Trinity (1802), rector of St. Paul's, Shadwell (1812–43), mathematical professor and Dean in the East India College, Haileybury (1813–37), and Principal (1837–43): a High-Churchman of the old school, who frequently contributed to the *British Critic*, and wrote for H. J. Rose's 'Theological Library'.

[2] *MS. illegible*—but the reference is clearly to C. H. Townshend's 'Essay on the theory and the writings of Wordsworth', in *Blackwood's* (see L. 498 above).

[3] In his letter to D. W., John Wordsworth had described the success of H. J. Rose's sermons: 'He borrows largely from my uncle, I think I recognised today more than a dozen passages from the Excursion and the Sonnets. His admiration for my uncle's Poems is absolutely without bounds.' Rose, like Barron Field (see pt. i, L. 334) was compiling his own critical edition.

[4] See *PW* ii. 267 ff. and app. crit. for the alterations in the 1827 edition to the last stanza but one, which W. W. goes on to justify. For W. W.'s debt to Virgil in the poem, see *PW* ii. 519.

[5] For Julius Charles Hare see pt. i, L. 123.

tesilaus—He exhorts her to moderate her passion—the exhortation is fruitless—and no punishment follows. So it stood; at present she is placed among unhappy Ghosts, for disregard of the exhortation. Virgil also places her there—but compare the two passages and give *me* your opinion. Hare said, any punishment stopping short of the future world would have been reasonable—but not the melancholy one I have imposed as she was not a voluntary suicide. Who shall decide when Doctors disagree? Do not let your etymological researches[1] interfere with your fellowship Studies. I rejoice, however, to hear that fellows of Colleges are so engaged. Were I a younger Man or had better eyes, I should be happy in being admitted as a Cooperator. Thus and thus only—can a tolerable Dictionary be produced. I am not surprized at your account of the Bᵖ of London.[2] I offended him with the freedom of my Letter upon [the] R. C. [Question][3] at least I infer so, as he did not answer it. It certainly was done in too great a hurry, and not sprinkled with complimentary expressions to himself, which he really deserved— I will shew you, my dear Brother, a copy of it. I find in it one clerical error of importance—the word *papacy* is often inconsiderately used for *popes*—this was owing to haste.—Dear Chris: put down Mr Southey's name as a Subʳ to the Moliere[4]—and charge me with the sum, let both be deducted from what your Father will have to remit for me to Mastermans. Willy has suffered from the severity of the winter at Bremen by heavy colds. Poor Fellow what am I to do with him when he returns—My paper is exhausted—Kindest love to all from all—

ever faithfully yours
W. W.

[*D. W. writes*]

I thank you heartily, my dear Nephew John, for your very cheerful and kind letter—I only wish in addition to the pleasant facts you communicate you had added that your Father and others had thoughts of visiting the North in summer. I often wish that your Uncle would resolve on a Trip to Cambridge this spring with

---

[1] According to John Wordsworth's letter, a new Etymological Society had been founded in Cambridge, 'for the illustration of the history of the English Language, and to fix the dates and trace the origin of its words'.

[2] John Wordsworth was very critical of Blomfield, the Bishop of London, for his innovations and 'the overweening confidence which he has in his own udgment'.

[3] *MS. torn*. The reference is to L. 416 above.

[4] The proposed new edition mentioned in L. 501 above.

Dora before the dispersion of Master and students—Kind love to all and congratulations to Chris.

Yours ever

D. W.

I have just been reading Milman's His. of Jews[1]—Such books are likely to do more harm than good: He makes wry faces at the Mosaic Miracles; and is anxious to explain as many as he can into natural phenomena. Better give up the whole at once—the whole character of Moses is damaged.

511. D. W. to MARIA JANE JEWSBURY

Address: Mr Thomas Jewsbury, Grosvenor St, Oxford Road, Manchester.
For Miss J.
MS. Historical Society of Pennsylvania.
Letters of Dora Wordsworth, p. 66 (—).

Rydal Mount—March 22nd

[1830]

To Mr Jewsbury

If this letter be opened by Mr Jewsbury I must beg him to take the trouble to read the first paragraph and should Miss J. not be at Manchester the letter itself may be kept for some private opportunity of forwarding it to her as it will not be worth the postage. My reason for requesting Mr J's attention in the first instance is this, that we are in immediate want of another piece of black silk, which we shall be much obliged if he will purchase, and forward it by Canal, directed to Mr Wordsworth, Rydal Mount, near Kendal. The last purchase Mr J. took the trouble to make for us gave entire satisfaction, therefore I have only to say, that if he can do for us as before we shall be greatly obliged. Mr J. will order the Bill to be enclosed—and Money to discharge it will be remitted *immediately*, therefore the dealers must allow discount or charge a ready-money price. Be so good as to send also a dozen pieces of fine Tape in sizes—and—a Dozⁿ D° of *Bobbin* in sizes—

---

[1] Henry Hart Milman (1791–1868), clergyman and poet, was rector of St. Mary's, Reading, from 1818 and Keble's immediate predecessor as Professor of Poetry at Oxford (1821–31). In 1835 he became rector of St. Margaret's, Westminster, and in 1849 Dean of St. Paul's. His *History of the Jews* (anon., 1829) caused something of a stir because it treated the Jews as an oriental tribe and played down the miraculous elements in sacred history. He went on to produce his *History of Latin Christianity* in 1855. W. W. got to know him later, and he visited Rydal Mount in 1843 and 1846 (*RMVB*).

To Miss Jewsbury

And now my dear Friend, after dinner in a stupid mood with only half an hour before me, (though I have had three weeks notice to prepare a packet for Miss Bailey's departure) I begin to write to you. Daily have I expected a promised letter from Mrs Barlow to apprise me of her Niece's having fixed her time for departure, and I now begin to suspect some mistake, and that the young Lady is actually gone; therefore to secure your getting the letter at all should this be the case, I have in my enclosure of it to Mrs Barlow desired her to forward it by the Post. Should you have left home I hope your Father will not put you to further expense by sending it on to London; but wait, as I have desired him, for a private opportunity. And now to be as brief as I can with facts; for I am far too stupid to expatiate.

It will be three weeks on Thursday since Dora left Rydal Mount to visit 'Cousin Dorothy'[1] at Green Bank. When there she received a pressing letter from Edith S. urging her to go to Keswick, which accordingly she did on the Wednesday following, and she is still there: but if next Thursday be fine John will ride over to Keswick from Moresby and conduct her back with him to stay a month at M:. Judge what a loss we are suffering at home: however, we are well reconciled to it; for even the slight change to Green Bank was of service to her health—(at best her looks and complexion were improved) and she now not only says she is 'quite well'—but writes in such a strain of gaiety that we are assured she actually *is* so—and do hope and almost expect that the yellow tinge will have passed from her face; and more flesh have crept upon her Bones before she returns to us. I still enact the Invalid; but am in truth perhaps in better health than any one in the house. Those who take no care of themselves have head-aches, twinges of rheumatism etc etc. All these I escape, and indeed feel myself, besides, equal to almost my former ordinary exertion. However by way of security, I am willing to submit, though looking forward with pleasure to something like emancipation when the Spring brings us settled weather. When Dora left us she intended writing to you and forwarding her letter to me to be forwarded to Miss Bailey: but she has found no leisure for writing, having been general Nurse and cheerer of bad spirits at Greta Hall. Every one of her young friends has been suffering from a most oppressive influenza. What a sad thing it would be were *she* also to fall ill! We have had a great

[1] Mrs. Benson Harrison.

shock in the sudden death of Sir Robert Farquhar;[1] and Mrs Luff, as you may suppose, has been much affected by it. If you live to our Age how fast will your Friends drop off from around you! Our losses in this kind within the few last years have been very great and many of them sudden also. Miss Dowling is dead; but this was an event long prayed for by herself and those who loved her best—for her sufferings (borne with true Christian patience) were very great. You must recollect Mr Tillbroke's housekeeper? She used to sit at Chapel in the Pew next to Mrs Luff's—Poor thing! She had a long illness and last Friday was bourne to her Grave at Ambleside from the Ivy Cottage. Our Servant Anne, was Margaret Wilkinson's faithful Friend, and often sat up with, and attended to her wants during her slow decline. This and other circumstances kept us up in daily intercourse with her to the last—and as she was our Servant at the very commencement of her course of life—a sweet-tempered innocent Girl and perfectly beautiful—we have always been interested for her—therefore her Sickness and Death have been like a domestic sorrow. She came to us when John was a Babe in arms. But why should I get into this melancholy strain? Our little goings-on at home are chearful enough—we have had better news of Willy's health—John has spent a week with us—an example of goodness—and con[?][2] also,—with an Income of £120 per an[num]. My sister is active and chearful (being spared rheumatic pains)—and my dear Brother—who last week was called to Ulverston upon Business which looked frightfully at him—at once hitting upon a scheme to convert the job into a pleasure takes his son John with him. They jog on together on horseback—and the Father comes home with all the raptures of youth. They tracked the Duddon almost to its source and never did he speak with more animation of the charms of his own romantic country. Well then, as another proof of the Poet's vigour and cheerfulness, I must tell you that he is making *another* new terrace—at the head of his own little field—the same terrace that was to have been at the point of his house—and he is delighted with it. So will *you* be whenever you come to Rydal Mount as I already am—I who now confine my walks to our own [? parapet]. There will be a little gate opening upon this new terrace from the Garden—and thus with the three terraces together we have a very great length of walk with constant variety of slope and level, and prospect. [?][3] after you and yours but no room for them—nor time. Tell us all. Poor Mr Cookson of

[1] See pt. i, L. 131.   [2] *MS. damaged.*
[3] A line of script in the fold of the sheet is illegible.

219

Kendal has had a cruel press of creditors. They are however now satisfied and will allow him time. We were for a while very anxious. Elizabeth and Harriet intend to begin a day-school[1] at Ambleside in June—a school now kept by a lady who gives it up. God bless you—ever your affecte—D. Wordsworth

I have mentioned Tape and Bobbin understanding it is to be got cheap at the manufacturers, but do not give yourself any trouble about it.

512. D. W. to WILLIAM PEARSON

MS. untraced.
Pearson, K (—). LY i. 456.

25th March, [1830]
Rydal Mount.

My dear Sir,
Though I have been so slow in acknowledging your kindness, I assure you it has not been because I was insensible of it. My Brother happened to be from home when your letter arrived, which prevented my answering it (according to my usual custom) immediately, and thus from day to day, I have delayed.

My brother was much interested by the information you had gathered from your vagrant neighbours, the Gipsies;[2] so was I, and every member of this family, and we sincerely thank you for it, and for the readiness with which you complied with my Brother's wishes. He intends, if you have no objection, to send the account to be inserted in the 'Naturalists' Magazine', if the matter be thought new or sufficiently important. To us, as I have said, it was very interesting.

You will be glad, I know, to hear that we are all well. My niece has been with Miss Southey a fortnight at Keswick, and, if weather permit, her brother purposes riding over to K. from Moresby to-morrow, to conduct her back with him: and he hopes for her company during a whole month—a great loss to the Father at home!

As you were so kind as to interest yourself concerning Mr—,[3] I must tell you that he dined with us last Sunday, was in good spirits,

[1] See *SH*, p. 372.
[2] In his letter of 15 Feb. Pearson had written: 'Pray inform your Brother that I have been endeavouring to learn something more of the habits and character of that poor persecuted animal the Hedge-hog from our neighbours the Gipsies and have been twice at their camp for that purpose . . .' (*WL MSS.*)
[3] Hartley Coleridge: Pearson had sent news of his whereabouts.

and very agreeable; and is now settled in most respectable lodgings at Grasmere.

I hope when fine weather tempts you again to Rydal, that my Brother may be so fortunate as to be at home.[1] This happened the last time; but how often it has been otherwise!

My Brother and Sister unite with me in kind regards

> Believe me, dear Sir
> Yours sincerely
> Dorothy Wordsworth.

513. W. W. to WILLIAM JACKSON

Address: To the Revd Wm Jackson, Whitehaven.
MS. Cornell. Hitherto unpublished.

[early Apr. 1830]

My dear Friend,

We congratulate you both, heartily, upon the *acquisition* of which your kind Letter informed us, which would have been immediately acknowledged but for the near opportunity of Joanna's departure— We hope that Mrs Jackson and the Infant are doing well—May this Little-one grow up to be a comfort and blessing to you both!

If you have seen John and Dora you may perhaps have heard of my business-trip to Ulverston. I returned up the Duddon— a charming ride, at all seasons! We have no news from this place; I would willingly supply the deficiency by some account of a Letter we have had from our Nephew John at Cambridge, but I fear Dora who has seen the Letter may have anticipated me, in which case what I am about to write will be weary, stale, flat and unprofitable, indeed! Dr Wordsworth, it appears, has been in active correspondence lately with the Bp of London upon ecclesiastical affairs; and has spent a day with him at Fulham. The wiser Heads of Cambridge, among whom be assured I reckon my own B^r, are afraid of Blomfield's meddling propensities. His attachment to the Church is not doubted, but his respect for the Church as *by law established* is not sufficient to abate his overweening confidence in his own judgement.[2] His rash and *illegal* dealing with the Whitehall

---

[1] Pearson had recently called at Rydal Mount. 'I got well home the other night—without much rain.—Indeed, whenever I have been at Rydal Mount, let it be dark or late when I return, I always find my mind in that state that my journey neither seems long nor lonely.'

[2] See L. 510 above.

Preachers[1] gave great offence at Cambridge. The Master of Trinity's object no doubt would be to temper and restrain his impetuosity—You would be pleased to hear that Mr Rose has been delivering a course of Sermons at St Marys which have made a great impression.[2] John says upwards of two hundred Gownsmen were unable to gain admission on the last day of the course, the Church was so crowded. This is surely to the honor of the rising generation, and in no small degree to the Preacher. If you have heard all this from Dora or from John pray excuse my bad luck; if I could have sent you any news from this quarter, I should have preferred doing so. I regret much that John is not oftener at your house[3]—but I hope that his leisure time is not thrown away. With kindest regards to Mrs Jackson and yourself from all believe me faithfully yours

W Wordsworth

Has Mr Coleridge's book on Church and State[4] reached you—we learn from his Daughter that a 2nd Edition is called for. Neither Southey nor I have seen it; nor Hartley.

514. W. W. to DORA W.

MS. WL.
LY i. 466.

[early Apr. 1830]

My dearest D—

I cannot let your Uncle and Aunt[5] depart without a word from me. News I leave to them and shall confine myself to requests

---

[1] The Whitehall Preachers were instituted in 1723 by Edmund Gibson (1669–1748), Bishop of London, to serve the royal Chapel in Whitehall. They were chosen from the fellows of the colleges in Oxford and Cambridge. Blomfield had recently made minor alterations in the system which caused offence: the numbers were drastically reduced in 1837, and after 1890 the office lapsed altogether.

[2] Hugh James Rose's sermons as Christian Advocate at Cambridge, in which he discussed the prevailing literary and cultural climate in relation to Christianity, were published later this year as *Brief Remarks on the disposition towards Christianity generated by prevailing Opinions and Pursuits*. See also L. 510 above.

[3] i.e. in Whitehaven. William Jackson, rector of Lowther, was still incumbent of St. James's, Whitehaven, as well.

[4] *On the Constitution of The Church and State, according to the Idea of Each: with Aids towards a Right Judgment on the late Catholic Bill*, 1830. See Griggs, vi. 787–8.

[5] Joanna and Henry Hutchinson, who were calling on John W. at Moresby (where Dora W. was staying) on their way home to the Isle of Man. They left Rydal Mount at the end of March or in early April (*SH*, p. 369).

and exhortations. Never *walk* to church but always go on your Poney—and avoid fatiguing yourself by walks in any direction.— Eat some animal food however small a quantity at luncheon, and ride every day if possible. Have I sent you the proper German Grammar? We have no Letters from Willy and I fear none by this morning's Post for any one. Your Mother and I called at Nicholson's[1] last night and he promised to send them with your Aunt's clothes. He has not appeared. Attend particularly to John's pronunciation at Church.—his un*a*ty, his char*a*ty, his inexpress*a*ble, and the northernisms that must unavoidably be creeping upon him. I congratulate you dearest D. on this enchanting weather— tell me where I can sleep when I come to see you Both which I [am][2] most wishful to do by and bye.—Let John pay a little more attention to Mr Jackson,[3] it is fitting that he should, and if I may allude to anything of that kind, *politic* also.—I now begin to fear that the *heat* will be too much for you—if so you will do well to ride in the afternoon, but your dinner hour seems awkward. All your Doves were out in the sunshine of yesterday. To-day we have Hayes[4] digging among the Gooseberries, and Tom Jackson[5] and his boy preparing for the Gate of Entrance to the new Terrace. This walk charms everyone that has seen it. Mrs Barlow[6] and Miss Bailey[7] saw it yesterday—the former with great pleasure. Miss Bayley passed John at Calder Bridge the day we parted, she did not venture to speak to him. Had John any rain that day? I had none till one o'clock, and should have reached home without a drop if I had not called upon David Huddlestone,[8] whom I found quite chearful even gay, under stone and gout and with the prospect of a speedy operation. The Spring is here, Mrs Luff says, a month forwarder than last year. Tell John that our Ulverstone journey[9] was not fruitless. Mr Church the other Ex[r] will take the trouble and send the Leg: Forms down to me—and the duty be paid at Ulverstone—One of the Testator's daughters has but a few days to live, Mr Church says; how this will affect the Duties he does not

[1] Joseph Nicholson, the Ambleside postmaster.   [2] *Word dropped out.*
[3] William Jackson.   [4] Richard Hayes, a gardener from Ambleside.
[5] Probably Thomas Jackson, a baker in Ambleside.
[6] Owner of The Wood, Bowness (see L. 484 above).
[7] Mrs. Barlow's niece.
[8] David Huddlestone (1765–1832) of Elterwater Hall: one-time partner in the Maude, Wilson, Crewdson Bank in Kendal, but latterly gunpower manufacturer in Langdale and owner of the slate quarries in Troutbeck Park.
[9] The journey on Stamp Office business, mentioned in L. 510 above. The details which W. W. goes on to give here resemble the case outlined in W. W.'s letter to John Spedding, printed in *MY* ii. 525, and that letter should therefore perhaps be dated to 1830, and not 1819.

say further than that it will make the payment simpler. James gave but a poor account of Aunt Sara's pony on his return from Keswick, he says it is growing weak in its forequarter and very numb in its feet. I wish we could sell it—but it is no time to think of *new* expenses for the interest of money is falling to nothing. Now dearest Dora take pains to enjoy yourself; move about according to your strength—Mr Adam's[1] pretty Garden will be a temptation and not beyond your strength, and if you can, let us hear that your appetite is improved. Do not hang over any sort of Books—above all beware of novels—and do not take too much of German! farewell, let us hear from you often. Best love to John—Your ever affectionate and *dutiful* Father

Wm Wordsworth.

I have returned thanks for the Descent into Hell[2]—a forbidding kind of journey, worse than a descent into one of your coal pits—and for the Pilgrim of the Hebrides.[3]

515. W. W. to JOHN GARDNER[4]

Address: John Gardner Esqre, 16 Foley Place, Portland Place. [*In D. W.'s hand*]
MS. Library of Congress.
K (—). *LY i.* 458 (—). *Mark Reed, 'Wordsworth's Letter to John Gardner, 5 Apr. 1830', NQ ccx (Nov. 1965), 409–11.*

Rydal Mount
Kendal 5th April 1830

Dear Sir

For so I venture to reply to a Stranger sympathizing with me as you must do, from the manner in which you speak of my writings.

---

[1] W. W. means Anthony Adamson of Mill Grove, Moresby, where John W. had his lodgings.

[2] The poem by John Abraham Heraud (see L. 581 below).

[3] *The Pilgrim of the Hebrides, a lay of the North Countrie. By the author of 'Three Days at Killarney'*, 1830 (see *R.M. Cat.*, no. 621). The author was the Revd. Charles Hoyle (1773–1848), Seatonian Prizeman at Cambridge in 1804 and 1806, Librarian of Trinity, 1803–9, and vicar of Overton, Wilts., from 1813.

[4] John Gardner (1804–80), medical writer and practitioner, founder of the Royal College of Chemistry: author of *The Great Physician: the Connexion of Diseases and Remedies with the Truths of Revelation*, 1843. In 1832 W. W. placed his nephew John (R. W.'s son) under his care to be trained as a surgeon. See Ls. 663, 665, and 674 below.

I was aware of the existence of Gagligniani's Edit:[1] and have been assured from 2 credible quarters that the Sale of it has been very extensive. I know also that many Copies have found their way into England; but how it can be publickly sold here I cannot understand. For any Bookseller to import it, or for *any* one to do so with that view, would, I imagine, be a breach of the Law. If you look further into the state of the fact, I apprehend you will find that you have been led into a mistake.

I admire the delicacy with which you decline purchasing this Work to my injury; These Piracies do no credit to the Parisian Publisher. As far as relates to the *Continent,* I am rather glad of this practice, but surely it is unfair upon Authors to be deprived of such benefit as they might draw from the Sale of their works among their own Countrymen, and in their native Land; the more so when the short duration of copy-right, as allowed by our Law, is considered.[2] That Law at present acts as a premium upon mediocrity, by tempting authors to aim only at immediate effect.

Some years ago I named to my Publishers my wish to try a cheaper Edition such as you recommend—but I was assured by them that the return of Profit to myself would be little or nothing. Readers, I am aware, have since encreased much, and are daily encreasing; Perhaps also my own Poems are gaining ground upon the Public; but you cannot have failed to observe what pains are taken in many quarters to obstruct their circulation and to lower their character. Be it so, you would probably say, and that is a still stronger Reason for their Author putting them in the way of being more generally known. The misrepresentations whether arising from incapacity, presumption, envy or personal malice would be best refuted by the books becoming as accessible as may be. I trust that it would be so; but still, having neither inherited a fortune, nor having been a maker of money; and being now advanced in Life, with a family to survive me, I cannot be indifferent to the otherwise base consideration of some pecuniary gain. The Edit: you possess of 1827 is getting low; and a new one will probably be called for erelong. My intention at present is, to reprint the whole pretty much in the same form; only I shall print *two* Sonnets in a page, a greater number of *lines* also; and exclude all blank paper (called I believe by the Printers, *fat*) and by this care I hope

---

[1] Galignani's edition, Paris, 1828 (see pt. i, L. 370). W. W. had received a presentation copy from the publisher.

[2] W. W.'s energetic support for the cause of Copyright reform later on (1838–42) sprang from his long-standing convictions about the injustice of the existing laws which, increasingly, he criticizes. See also L. 556 below.

to reduce the price of the Work; and perhaps to compress it into four Volumes, though there will be a good deal of additional matter. This, however, will be printed separately also,—to accomodate the Purchasers of the former Editions.—Now having written at this length all that I can do further, is to request that, if you think it worth while, you would call upon Messrs Longman (this Letter would be your introduction), state your wishes, and your reasons and hear what they have to say. If your proposal could be reconciled with a reasonable emolument to myself it would gratify me to adopt it.[1]—Should you wait upon these Gentlemen, pray let me know the Result. Is it not your proposal that there should be two Editions—of different sizes?—I remain with sincerest thanks for the Letter with which you have honored me,

truly your obliged Ser^vt
Wm Wordsworth

[*D. W. writes*]

Pray do not trouble yourself to pay the postage of your next.

516. W. W. to BASIL MONTAGU

MS. Harvard University Library.
K (—). LY i. 457.

Rydal Mount, Kendal,
5th April, 1830

My dear Montagu,

I ought to have thanked you long ago for the 12th Vol: of Lord Bacon,[2] which I received through John; and also for your little treatise on Laughter[3] which has amused me much. You have rendered good service to the Public, by this Edition of the Works of one of the greatest Men the world has produced—I wish I had been younger to make a more worthy use of so valuable a Present. —Let me ask whether it would not have been better, to print the Letters of which the last Vol: consists not as you have done but in chronological order, only taking care to note from what Collection the several Letters were taken. I should certainly have

---

[1] Gardner's proposal for a cheaper edition came to nothing at this time, but it encouraged W. W. to explore the possibility (see L. 530 below), and led eventually to the *Poetical Works*, 4 vols., 1832.

[2] The sixteen-volume edition was completed in 1836.

[3] *Thoughts on Laughter. By a Chancery Barrister*, 1830.

much preferred that Arrangement, so would Southey; but perhaps you have reasons for this plan, which do not strike me.

With many thanks, I remain, dear M.

faithfully yours
Wm Wordsworth

John was gratified by the attentions you paid [him][1] for which we all return our thanks.—

517. W. W. to GEORGE HUNTLY GORDON

MS. Cornell.
Mem. (—). Grosart (—). K (—). LY i. 459 (—). Broughton, p. 31.

Rydal Mount
April 6th 1830

My dear Mr Gordon

You are kind in noticing with thanks my rambling notes—Wms Letter brought a most agreeable account of the Family of Mr P.[2] (Ws own case included) throwing off their severe winter-colds.

We have had here a few days of delicious summer weather—it appeared with the suddenness of a Pantomime trick—stayed longer than one had a right to expect—and was as rapidly succeeded by high wind, bitter cold, and Winter snow over hill and dale—

I am not surprized that you are so well pleased with Mr Quillinan—The more you see of him the better you will like him. You ask what are my employments—According to Dr Johnson[3] they are such as entitle me to high commendation; for I am not only making two blades of grass grow where only one grew before, but a dozen. In plain language I am draining a bit of spungy ground. —But do not set me down for an Agricultural Patriot; my grasses are in my little Policy and grown more for beauty than profit. If the ground is to be depastured I must be Nebuchadnezzarized[4] and e'en take to grazing myself, for I dare not trust to Cows nor Horses—they would trample and defile my Walks, nor to sheep— they would devour my Plantations, which are upon too[5] small a

---

[1] *Word dropped out.* John W. had met Montagu while he was down taking his M.A. degree at Oxford.
[2] Papendick.   [3] Or rather Swift: see *Gulliver's Travels*, ii. 7.
[4] See Daniel 4.   [5] too *written* two.

scale to be worth being severally enclosed—In the field where this goes on I am making a green Terrace, that commands a beautiful view over our two Lakes Rydal and Windermere, and more than two miles of intervening vale with the stream visible by glimpses, flowing through it. I shall have great pleasure in shewing you this, among the other returns which I hope one day to make for your kindness.

Adieu Yours W W

518. D. W. to C. W. JNR.

Address: Chris^r Wordsworth Esqre, Trinity College, Cambridge [*readdressed to*] c.o. Archdeacon Bayley,[1] West Meon, near Alton.
Postmark: (1) 20 Apr. 1830. (2) 21 Apr. 1830. *Stamp*: (1) Kendal Penny Post. (2) Cambridge.
MS. WL. Hitherto unpublished.

13th April [1830]

My dear Christopher,

I write to *you* rather than to John (though it is to *him* that I am indebted for a kind and most acceptable letter) for the same reason which induced me in a former instance to write to *him* rather than *you*, that you are now the man of leisure and he still plodding up the Hill of labour. Well! I trust he will ere long reach the top and meet with the reward he so well deserves. There are few things that would give me more pleasure than to hear of his being elected a Fellow of Trinity, and thus made free to chuse his further calling, after taking such feeding Rest as may best suit his turn of mind. As for you, dear Chris, surely your already-acquired honours will insure you an easy admission to the good Society of Fellows, without further tasks. Could you but know the satisfaction you have given at Rydal Mount by shewing us your name at the top of the Tripos, and by adding this last medal[2] to your stock, your own satisfaction would be more than doubled. Dora was at Keswick when the latter tidings arrived, and I am sure we must have had a great loss at home in not witnessing her joy. No doubt family pride had some little share in it; but I assure you she is a most affectionate cousin, and it is impossible for me to tell you how deep an interest she takes in the well-doing and success of every one of

---

[1] The Revd. Henry Vincent Bayley, D.D. (1777–1844), a close associate of C. W.: Fellow of Trinity College, Cambridge (1802), Sub-Dean of Lincoln (1805–28), Archdeacon of Stow from 1823, and rector of West Meon, Hants. from 1826. [2] The Chancellor's Classical Medal.

you. She is enlivening John at Moresby and writes us frequent and very pleasant letters, in her gay style recounting their goings-on. Both seem to be very happy. Their lodgings are comfortable, and much preferable in Situation to those occupied by John when you were at Moresby. He lives very frugally; and in so doing is quite contented; but there is one luxury in which for various reasons he is obliged to indulge—that of keeping a horse—and though this is done at very little expense (compared with that of horses in general) I think it will appear at the end of a year, that the proceeds of his Living will hardly suffice for all his needs, though he thinks otherwise. On the whole I am truly glad of his removal from Whitwick and establishment at Moresby. He seems likely to be very useful where he is, and is very much respected; and though his income does not much exceed that of his Curacy, the demands upon it are not half so numerous or pressing, for there is comparatively little of poverty and distress.

Your uncle passed his 60th Birthday on the 7th of this month, and thankful am I to say that his activity and strength are hardly perceptibly diminished during the last ten years (I date from 1820 recalling the exertions he made on the Alps at that time) but he has of late complained of headaches after exertion, which used much to trouble him in his youth but left him in middle life. I hope this return is only accidental. He has lately laid aside poetical labours and has been much out of doors, presiding over workmen who are making us a *third* Terrace in the field purchased for the house,[1] which, to my great satisfaction, was you know, only built in the air. This new Terrace is a beautiful thing, but I will not describe it, you must all come and walk upon it.

A new edition of the Poems will soon be called for. We females wish him to publish the numerous poems now in store immediately, in one small volume, that they may have a Boom, and the Edition get sold off before the 5 vols. are again printed, when the new little volume might be incorporated with them, which would be very fair, as the purchasers of the former would have the opportunity of adding the new little volume. Now in his heart, he approves of our plan; but his aversion to publication at all, is so great that he *will not* resolve to do it, and would much rather smuggle the new ones in among the rest, as he did before, and thus get nothing for them. A much better plan than this would be to publish nothing new, and let the whole remain for the benefit of his Family after death.

[1] The Rash, or Dora's Field, which W. W. had planned to build on in 1826, if the Wordsworths were required to leave Rydal Mount. See pt. i. L. 206.

Now that you are at leisure from College duties, may I ask you dear Chris to fag through the 4 numbers of the Blackwood criticism,[1] and to give me your opinion. I withhold my own, as I would not bias you if even I had the power, only I will state that different persons, when the two first parts came out, told us that Envy and Detraction had been very busy etc etc etc. The opinion given by Mr Le Bas[2] was from the last number. His notions agreed no doubt with those of the critic in those points which impressed him, but I should suspect that Mr Le Bas had not read to the end. Very few people have leisure so to do, or to give an undivided and steady attention to any article in a magizine. I do not ask John to trouble himself with the task I impose on you. He has far too much of his own work to do.

Pray desire Charles to send us an Oxford paper when the examinations are over. I hope to see his name in the first Class notwithstanding his own croakings: however, if that pleasure be denied me I shall console myself in my full persuasion of his various merits, and shall have no doubt but that untoward circumstances have been the cause of failure. When you write to him pray give my love and best wishes, and tell him that we shall rejoice to see him again at Rydal Mount.—John gives us no notion of the summer plans of any of the Family, therefore I much fear there is little chance of our seeing the Master of Trinity here, but surely some one or more of you may turn northwards. No doubt you will see Owen at Cambridge at Degree time. He is now very healthy, and invariably chearful, at home with every individual of his rustic parish,[3] and far happier than if he were Bishop of Chester. As I told you Dora is at Moresby, and we know not when she will return; for John will be loth to part with her; but their Father talks of paying them a visit shortly and may probably bring her home; for he has a sad want of her. You know he is not easily moved to planning any thing to be done at any particular time; but very casily, to avail himself of opportunities and motives when they arise. Now, I know that he has a great desire to see his Brother and all of you at Cambridge and to take Dora along with him; and you may be sure *she* would be a most willing companion; but he says nothing of the when and the how. Now should any present motive for an excursion of Father and Daughter arise before the end of May I should like to be prepared with some knowledge of where my good Brother, the Master, is likely to be—where you his three Sons—and whether

---

[1] Chauncy Hare Townshend's articles.   [2] See L. 510 above.
[3] Owen Lloyd was now curate of Langdale.

(about the end of May, and say the month of June) it is likely that it would suit him to receive his Brother and Niece. Do not in your answer let it appear as if I had put the Question, only tell me, as far as you can, the facts of your plans, intentions and wishes, for if it suits your uncle to give to himself and his Daughter the treat of a visit to Cambridge, I should be very sorry it should be prevented by any fanciful conjectures respecting your Father's arrangements.

We heartily sympathise with all belonging to Trinity Lodge in their cares and apprehensions for our poor Church, and privately and inwardly does it grieve me to observe that my dear good Brother is overlooked always in every promotion and change. I know it will not please him to hear this from me, but I hope he will forgive me for I do indeed *wish* that I could look upon that matter with as much calmness as he does.

I find by a letter from Mr Merewether that he has lately been at Cambridge, and there [through][1] a sleepless night, planned a series of letters to the Master of Trinity, hereafter (*with his approval*) [to] be published. Now I have no doubt of the soundness of [Mr Merewether's] notions and opinions, but was sorry to hear [that he intended to] publish them; and was fearful of your Father being called upon to perform an unpleasant office, that of giving advice on an occasion in which pious zeal, and many honorable and noble feelings and sentiments are the first movers, and these powerfully supported by the Love of Authorship. Poor Mrs Merewether has always a thousand cares and apprehensions whenever a Tract or a pamphlet is meditated.—John's account of Sophy's[2] prosperity and happiness gives me great pleasure. But you have never told us how her place is supplied at the Lodge. I am afraid my Brother must have found a great change when she was gone. When you next see *Mrs Carter* pray give her my remembrances.— I hope Mrs and Miss Hoare continue well. Give my love to them. What does she (Mrs Hoare) think of Moore's attacks upon her Friend Lady Byron and her Family?[3] We much approve of Lady B's

---

[1] *Hole in MS.*   [2] Sophy Carter, formerly servant at Trinity Lodge.
[3] Lady Byron, formerly Anne Isabella Milbanke (1792–1860), a friend of Joanna Baillie and the Hoares of Hampstead, had recently published her *Remarks occasioned by Mr. Moore's Notices of Lord Byron's Life*, in which she took exception to Thomas Moore's *Letters and Journals of Lord Byron, with Notices of his Life*, the first vol. of which had appeared this February. Her highly critical stance was defended by Thomas Campbell in a notice of the two publications in the *New Monthly Magazine*, xxviii (Apr. 1830), 377–82, in which he violently attacked both Byron and Moore: 'As her friend, I could not keep my mind quiet about her feelings under this ill-starred resuscitation of the question concerning her.'

letter, but not so of that of her Defender Campbell. Save us all from the promises of our *Friends*!

Pray give my best thanks to John for his interesting letter. He must take as much of this as he has patience to read, as an answer to it, and do you, my dear Chris, remember that I ask for, and expect an answer from you. Do not, however, *wait* for the reading of the Blackwood articles—I can be very patient on that score—only reply to my other inquiries. Has Frere[1] left Cambridge? If not give our regards to him. We always remember him with pleasure, and shall be glad of his prospering.

My Sister and I are both well. Your cousin John[2] is here for the Easter Holidays. We think him improved. Our last letters from William brought better accounts of his health. He had witnessed woeful devastation on the Weser after the Storm—houses undermined and washed away, and many lives lost at Bremen. A dreadful cold winter, [   ][3] general sickness consequent on it [   ] away.

We all join in love to you [all] Believe me, dear Chris

your affectionate [Aunt]
D Wordsworth[4]

519. W. W. to DORA W.

Address: Miss Wordsworth. [*delivered by hand*]
MS. WL. Hitherto unpublished.

[mid-Apr. 1830]

. . . Nab Scar and the opposite part of Loughrigg fell are white with sleet down to the Enclosures—in front of the Mount Loughrigg has a faint sprinkling only upon the summit. I was indeed glad to hear that you had been able to ride three hours upon the Heights,[5] because I am sure you would not have remained so long had you either been chilled or fatigued. Have you ever been at

---

[1] John Frere, C. W. jnr.'s college friend.
[2] R. W.'s son.
[3] *Hole in MS.*
[4] C. W., when forwarding this letter, added a brief note:
Dearest Chris, I hope you will answer this nice letter immediately. The part about the visit to Cambridge, I will undertake, in a day or two. Kindest regards to your Meonian Friends. John goes to Hampstead on Saturday. Ask the Archdeacon to give you Bishop Wilkins. . . . Ever yours most effect[ly] C. W.
[5] Above Whitehaven. Dora W. had gone to stay with John W. at Moresby.

Harrington—would not that be an agreeable ride.[1] Though you be in the land of spinsters, and at a formidable age yourself, I still have hopes of you. But if it be your destiny to be laid upon that dusty shelf I will then say, proudly say (a poor consolation this for you!) that there is no discernment in the age.

Poor Hartley—have you been told that he is off again, and has been lying intoxicated in the roads and unwell.

You talked of new Books finding their way to Rydal. This moment I have received a parcel containing Webster's Dramatic Works[2] 4 Vols, and Specimens of British Poetesses,[3] both beautifully printed Books, from a very kind Correspondent the Revd A. Dyce—a letter also in which he speaks of the effect of my Poems upon his own mind in terms that would delight you,—but I must send it you, though unwilling to part with it till I have answered it.

[*cetera desunt*]

520. W. W. to SIR GEORGE BEAUMONT

Address: To Sir Geo Beaumont Bart, Coleorton Hall, Ashby de la Zouche.
[*In M. W.'s hand*]
Stamp: Kendal Penny Post.
MS. Pierpont Morgan Library.
K. LY i. 460.

Rydal Mount, Kendal
April 15th [1830][4]

My dear Sir George,

The Papers inform me that a second Son[5] has made his appearance at Coleorton Hall. We all congratulate you and Lady Beaumont sincerely upon this happy event. May the newly-arrived, and his Brother, live to be a blessing to their Parents.

---

[1] Harrington was a coal port between Whitehaven and Workington, which had recently been developed by the Curwens. W. W. seems to go on to imply that there was a possible suitor there for Dora's hand, perhaps the Revd. John Curwen, the rector.

[2] Alexander Dyce's edition of Webster had just appeared. See L. 521 below.

[3] See L. 474 above and Ls. 521 and 529 below.

[4] This letter seems to belong to 1830 rather than 1831 (where Knight places it), when W. W. was away in London in April.

[5] Apparently the baby mentioned in L. 533, who did not long survive, and not Sir George Beaumont's second surviving son, William Beresford, b. 13 Mar. 1831.

I congratulate you also upon having got through your trouble-some office of Sheriff;[1] as it is so much more agreeable to look back upon such an employment, however honorable, than to have it in prospect.

My dear Sister, though obliged to keep to the habits and re-straints of an Invalid for prudence-sake, is, I am happy to say, in good health. She and Mrs Wordsworth join with me in best wishes and regards to yourself and Lady Beaumont, as would my Son and Daughter have done; but they are now together in his abode, I cannot say his Parsonage (for the Living has none), at Moresby near Whitehaven.

I remain, my dear Sir George,
Faithfully yours
Wm Wordsworth

521. W. W. to ALEXANDER DYCE

Address: [*deleted and readdressed to*] the Revd Alexander Dyce, Rosebank, Aberdeen, Scotland.
Postmark: 20 Apr. 1830. *Stamp*: Kendal Penny Post.
MS. Victoria and Albert Museum.
Mem. (—). *Grosart* (—). *K* (—). *LY i. 471* (—).

Rydal Mount
[*c.* 19 Apr. 1830]

I am truly obliged, my dear sir, by your valuable Present of Webster's D. Works[2] and the Specimens.[3] Your Publisher was right in insisting upon the whole of Webster, otherwise the book might have been superseded, either by an entire Edition separately given to the world, or in some Corpus of the Dramatic Writers. The Poetic Genius of England with the exception of Chaucer, Spenser, Milton, Dryden, Pope, and a very few more, is to be sought in her Drama. How it grieves one that there is so little probability of those valuable authors being read except by the

---

[1] Sir George Beaumont was Sheriff of Leicestershire for this year, and was therefore only at the start of his period of office, which Lady Beaumont de-scribed in her letter to D. W. on 18 July. (*WL MSS.*)

[2] Dyce's edition of Webster appeared this year in four volumes.

[3] *Specimens of British Poetesses.* The volume included (p. 426) D. W.'s *Address to a Child* (*PW* i. 229). Dyce had written to W. W. on 10 Apr.: 'I trust Miss Wordsworth will not be displeased at finding that I have taken the liberty of inserting a copy of verses which are universally attributed to her.' (*Dyce MSS., Victoria and Albert Museum.*)

curious. I questioned my Friend Charles Lamb whether it would answer for some person of real taste to undertake abridging the plays that are not likely to be read as wholes, and telling such parts of the story in brief abstract as were ill managed in the Drama. He thought it would not—I, however, am inclined to think it would.—

The account you gave of your Indisposition gives me much concern. It pleases me, however, to see that, though you may suffer, your industry does not relax, and I hope that your pursuits are rather friendly than injurious to your Health.

You are quite correct in your notice of my obligation to Dr Darwin. In the first edition of the Poem it was acknowledged in a note,[1] which slipped out of its place in the last, along with some others. In putting together that edition, I was obliged to cut up several copies, and as several of the Poems also changed their places, some confusion and omission also, and in one instance a repetition was the consequence. Nothing, however, so bad as in the Edition of 1820, where a long poem, The Lament of Mary Queen of Scots,[2] was by mistake altogether omitted. Another unpleasantness arose from the same cause; for, in some instances, notwithstanding repeated charges to the Printer, you have only two Spenserian Stanzas in a page (I speak now of the last edition) instead of three; and there is the same irregularity in printing other forms of Stanza.

You must indeed have been fond of that pondrous Quarto, the Exc: to lug it about as you did.[3] In the edition of 27 it was diligently revized; and the sense in several instances got into less room, yet still it is a long Poem for these feeble and fastidious

---

[1] See *To Enterprise* (*PW* ii. 280), ll. 114–16:

> and now a living hill
> That a brief while heaves with convulsive throes—
> Then all is still;

To these lines W. W. had appended in 1822 the note:

> Awhile the living hill
> Heaved with convulsive throes, and all was still.

—Dr. Darwin describing the destruction of the army of Cambyses.

[2] *PW* ii. 37. The poem was, however, restored in proof, as it appeared for the first time in the 1820 volume.

[3] In his letter of 10 Apr. Dyce had noted: 'Some years ago, I had a curacy in a remote part of Cornwall: *The Excursion* was one of very few books I took with me to the small farmhouse where I resided; and never can I forget the delight I used to feel in stealing away to the sea shore in the fine evenings of summer, with that huge 4to under my arm, to read it among the rocks in utter solitude.'

times. You would honor me much by accepting a Copy of my poetical Works; but I think it better to defer offering it to you till a new Edition is called for, which will be ere long, as I understand the present is getting low.

A word or two about Collins—you know what importance I attach to following strictly the last Copy of the text of an Author; and I do not blame you for printing in the Ode to Evening 'brawling' springs; but surely the epithet is most unsuitable to the time, the very worst, I think, almost that could have been chosen. I have not been able to find my Copy of Martin's St Kilda,[1] but I am certain that the Bee not being known there is mentioned by him—and it is well that a negative which is so poetical, should rest upon the authority of fact.

I now come to Lady Winchelsea; first however let me say a few words upon one or two other Authoresses of your Specimens. British Poetesses make but a poor figure in the 'Poems by Eminent Ladies'.[2] But observing how injudicious that Selection is in the case of Lady Winchelsea, and in Mrs Aphra Behn,[3] from whose attempts they are miserably copious, I have thought something better might have been chosen by more competent Persons, who had access to the Volumes of the several writers. In selecting from Mrs Pilkington,[4] I regret that you omitted (Look at page 255)[5] 'Sorrow', or at least that you did not abridge it. The first and third Paragraph are very affecting. See also 'Expostulation', 258; it reminds me strongly of one of the Penitential Hymns of Burns.[6] The few lines upon St. John the Baptist, by Mrs Killigrew[7] (Vol. 2. page 6), are pleasing. A beautiful elegy of Miss Warton[8] (sister to the Poets of that name), upon the death of her father has escaped you notice; nor can I refer you to it. Has the

[1] See pt. i, L. 367.
[2] 2 vols., 1755.
[3] Mrs. Aphra Behn (1640–89), poetess, dramatist, novelist, and translator.
[4] Laetitia Pilkington (1712–50), friend of Swift: her poems were interspersed in her autobiographical *Memoirs*, 3 vols., 1748–54. As de Selincourt notes, lines from *Sorrow* were included in W. W.'s MS. volume *Poems and Extracts chosen by William Wordsworth* [from the works of Anne, Countess of Winchelsea and others] *for an album presented to Lady Mary Lowther* in 1819 (published, ed. H. Littledale, 1905).
[5] i.e. *Poems by Eminent Ladies*, ii. 255.
[6] Burns's early poems in the metres of the Scottish metrical psalms.
[7] Anne Killigrew (1660–85), maid of honour to the Duchess of York, and celebrated in Dryden's famous Ode. The poems were published in 1686. W. W. gives the 'St. John the Baptist' in the *Poems and Extracts*.
[8] Jane Warton (d. 1809), sister of Joseph and Thomas. Her Elegy is included in *Poems and Extracts*.

Duchess of Newcastle[1] written much verse? her Life of her Lord, and the extracts in your Book, and the 'Eminent Ladies', are all that I have seen of hers. The Mirth and Melancholy has so many fine strokes of Imagination that I cannot but think there must be merit in many parts of her writings. How beautiful those lines, from 'I dwell in groves', towards the conclusion, 'Yet better loved the more that I am known', excepting the 4 verses after 'Walk up the hills'. And surely the latter verse of the couplet,

> The tolling bell which for the dead rings out,
> A mill where rushing waters run about,

is very noticeable; no person could have hit upon that union of images without being possessed of true poetic feeling.—Could you tell me anything of Lady Mary Wortley Mont:[2] more than is to be learned from Pope's Letters and her own? She seems to have been destined for something much higher and better than she became. A parallel between her genius and character and that of Lady Winchelsea her Contemporary (though somewhat prior to her) would be well worth drawing.

And now at last for the poems of Lady W.[3] I will transcribe a

---

[1] Margaret Cavendish, Duchess of Newcastle (1624–74), maid of honour to Queen Henrietta Maria and voluminous writer, published *Poems and Fancies*, 1653, *Plays*, 1662, *Life of the Duke of Newcastle*, 1667, etc.

[2] Lady Mary Wortley Montagu (1689–1762). Her poems were published by Dodsley in 1747.

[3] Anne, Countess of Winchelsea. Dyce had included four of her poems in his *Specimens*, and in his letter of 10 Apr. he sought further advice about her best work: '. . . I attach a greater importance to your opinions on poetry than to those of any man alive; and . . . I think all the verses which have been written in the present age are poor indeed compared to yours.' W. W. possessed the edition of 1713. De Selincourt supplies the following particulars by which the poems W. W. speaks of can be identified in other editions.

Fragment, i.e. poem beginning 'So here confin'd'.

Page 42.   So the sad Ardelia lay
             Blasted by a Storm of Fate
             Felt, thro' all the British State
                           (*Petition for an Absolute Retreat*)

263. i.e. *Moral Song* Would we attain, etc.
280. 'So here confin'd'.
Page 3. From *Mercury and the Elephant*.
Page 163. The *Critick and the Writer of Fables*.
148. In the *Tale of the Miser and the Poet*.
Page 36: from the *Petition for an Absolute Retreat*, revives on p. 47: Let me then, indulgent Fate!
82. *The Poor Man's Lamb*—towards the end.
92. *The Spleen*.
113. *The Shepherd and the Calm*.

note from a blank leaf of my own Edition, written by me before
I saw the scanty notice of her in Walpole.[1] (By the bye, that
book has always disappointed me, when I have consulted it upon
any particular occasion.) The note runs thus: 'The Fragment,
page 280, seems to prove that she was attached to James 2nd, as
does page 42, and that she suffered by the Revolution. The most celebrated of these poems, but far from the best, is the 'Spleen'. The
Petition for an Absolute Retreat and A Nocturnal Reverie are of
much superior merit. See also for favorable Specimens, page 156,
on the Death of Mr Thynne, 263; and 280, Fragment. The fable
of Love, Death, and Reputation, page 29, is ingeniously told.'
Thus far my own note. I will now be more particular. Page 3,
'Our vanity', etc., and page 163 are noticeable as giving some account from herself of her Authorship. See also 148 where she alludes
to the Spleen. She was unlucky in her models—Pindaric odes and
French Fables. But see page 70, The Blindness of Elymas, for
proof that she could write with powers of a high order when her own
individual character and personal feelings were not concerned. For
less striking proofs of this power, see page 4, 'All is Vanity',
omitting verses 5 and 6, and reading 'clouds that are lost and gone',
etc. There is merit in the 2 next Stanzas, and the last Stanza towards
the close contains a fine reproof for the ostentation of Louis 14,
and one magnificent verse, 'Spent the astonished hours, forgetful
to adore'. But my paper is nearly out. As far as 'For my garments',
page 36, the poem is charming—it then falls off—revives at 39,
'give me there' page 41, etc., reminds me of Dyer's Grongar Hill;
it revives on page 47, towards the bottom, and concludes with sentiments worthy of the writer, though not quite so happily expressed
as in other parts of the Poem. See pages 82, 92. 'Whilst in the
Muses' paths I stray.' 113. The 'Cautious Lovers', page 118, has
little poetic merit, but is worth reading as characteristic of the
author. 143, 'Deep lines of honour', etc., to 'maturer age'. 151, if

143. From *Poem for the birthday of Lady Catharine Tufton*.
151. *The Change, init.*
154. *Enquiry after Peace.*
159. *On the Death of the Hon. Mr James Thynne.*
217. *To a Friend, in praise of the Invention of Writing Letters.*
259. *that* you have: i.e. Dyce had included it in his *Specimens*. The poem is
Life's Progress.
262, 263, 280. *Hope, Moral Song, Fragment* (So here confin'd).
290. *The Tree.*
291. *A Nocturnal Reverie.*

[1] Horace Walpole, *A Catalogue of the Royal and Noble Authors of England,
with Lists of their Works*, 2 vols., 1758 (enlarged in subsequent editions).

shortened, would be striking; 154 characteristic; 159, from 'Meanwhile ye living parents', to the close, omitting 'Nor could we hope', and the five following verses, 217, last paragraph, 259, *that* you have. 262, 263, 280. Was Lady Winchelsea a Catholic? 290, 'And to the clouds proclaim thy fall': 291, omit 'When scattered glow-worms', and the next couplet—I have no more room. Pray excuse this vile scrawl.

Ever faithfully yours,
W. W.

I have inconsiderately sent your letter to my Daughter (now absent) without copying the address. I knew the letter would interest her. I shall direct to your publisher.

Thanks for your apology to Sir E. Brydges.[1] Your notion of his character is just. How sadly Auld Robin Grey[2] is spoilt by the Authoress' 'last' improvements! The music of the song might require the Ohs! but they ruin the poem.

I have through Longman and the Ambleside Bookseller a monthly communication with London—pray bear this in mind. I cannot allow you to incur the expense of Carriage.

522. D. W. to H. C. R.

Address: à Monsieur, Monsieur H. C. Robinson, la Poste restante, à *Rome*.
Postmark: 30 Apr. 1830.
Endorsed: April 22ᵈ 1830. Reced May 20. Ansᵈ. Miss Wordsworth.
MS. Dr. Williams's Library.
K (—). *Morley, i. 216.*

Rydal Mount—April 22nd 1830

My dear Friend

Your scrap of a letter gave us more satisfaction than I can express; and it allayed anxieties which had often troubled us on the score of your health; but I assure you we had much rather you had not been so sparing of our money and had given us a real letter bearing the Post mark of the *'eternal City'*. I ought I will confess, however, in gratitude for the very great pleasure your few lines

[1] Dyce had apologized to Sir Egerton Brydges for his remark about him in his edition of Collins (see L. 474 above), and had received a friendly reply. 'He appears to be somewhat super-sensitive as an author; but his enthusiastic love of literature, damped neither by age nor sickness, undoubtedly renders him a very interesting person.'

[2] By Lady Anne Lindsay (1750–1825), first published anonymously in David Herd's *Ancient and Modern Scottish Songs*, 1776.

gave, to have complied with your request, and written immediately: but as that feeling did not serve to spur me on, it is *strange* that the selfish one of insuring a return—a real letter—one of your own animating and cheering kind—and bearing the glorious Stamp of *Rome* did not impel me instantly to take the pen—Well! I shall not take up your time or my own with explanations—still less with EXCUSES—for I have none to offer that satisfy myself—though no doubt, while all this long time has been passing away, I have found a hundred— —[1] such as a stupid head—or having nothing to tell that was worthy of being sent so far—or having some other occupation which *must* be ended—etc etc—and, besides, I have wished my *Brother* to write, as thinking a letter from him would be more worthy of the honour of travelling so far, and being read on classic ground—and he *did* promise me that he *would* write.— A message which, at third hand, has reached me from Mr Owen Lloyd determines me to wait no longer for my Brother, though I should have wished first to see Mr L to learn further particulars. The message was simply this, that you 'expected to hear from us'. We conclude you were well—or he would have added something about your health—for I doubt not, we shall find that you are further spoken of in the letter—either directly or *in*directly—so that we may gather some information respecting your goings-on— and perhaps your *plans* for the future.—My dear Friend, now that I am actually beginning my letter—I know not what I have to say— I seem to have nothing to *tell*: whereas if you had been all the winter at home and I writing to you once a month, I should have found a thousand things—I will, however, begin with a sober review of the Autumn and Winter, as they have passed away with us in our quiet home—leaving all public and general matters to the newspapers, which, no doubt, you read more regularly than *we do*.—I think you left England about the time of John's exchanging his Leicestershire Curacy for the small Rectory of Moresby in Cumberland. We left Whitwick with regret; but have now many reasons for rejoicing in the change—; and but three weeks after parting with our kind Friend Lady Beaumont, her sudden death[2] tended to reconcile us—for without *her* Coleorton and Whitwick would not have been the same places they used to be. An unusually severe winter, and low wages and want of work in the stocking factory on which Whitwick depends, in a few months *completely* reconciled us to our removal from a place where poverty and distress

---

[1] These dashes are D. W.'s, concealing an obliteration.
[2] See L. 441 above.

that we could not effectually relieve would have daily met our eyes. John is very happy at Moresby, in a small parish—yet sufficiently peopled both by poor and rich to require and call forth constant moderate exertion, without that depressing accompanying conviction that all we can do is of no avail for permanent relief. John's income is not much larger than Whitwick; but he is a richer man; and is comfortably situated in lodgings where he can at any time receive one or two of us—His Mother spent three weeks with him in the Winter—and Dora is now his Companion, and will remain till fetched home by her Father—who finds a sad want of her; but he willingly submits, the young people being so very happy, and her health improving with sea-air—and horse-exercise with her Brother. They have each a poney. Her winter's cough has dealt more gently with her than usual; yet she has been very far from well, though with an inexhausible stock of lively spirits— and of activity within doors though utterly unable to follow the example of her Mother's youth and mine in *walking*. The Family *summer plans* are not yet fixed; but I think the Father and Daughter will be tripping off to Cambridge before the Commencement— and *perhaps* my Sister may visit her own Relations in the County of Durham at the same time. As for me, it seems to be decreed that I must stay at home—and surely it is no punishment to be confined to this beautiful spot—I have been enacting the Invalid ever since the month of November, though, in truth I have had no one ailment since the beginning of January. Whenever the weather has been tolerable I have gone out in the poney-chaise—or walked; but not farther than the Terrace. Since the trees began to bud I have extended my walks a little further; and do indeed feel myself equal to much more than I venture to attempt. In compliance with the judgment and advice of those who I suppose are much better judges of what is safe than I am myself, I shall continue to use similar caution during the whole of next summer—and the following winter, if I live so long,—and after that time I hope I may be safely trusted to my own feelings as a Guide in ascertaining the measure of my strength. In the mean time it is certainly my duty to submit to be guided by those who have already suffered so much anxiety on my account, and there is no hardship in it—for this different mode of life has no effect whatever upon my spirits—and certainly it has agreed with my health; for, as I have told you, I am, and have been since January, perfectly well. It was a sad illness I had at Whitwick—and again I was very ill at Halifax—whence I came to Rydal the first week of September, and since have not slept one night from home. My Brother has enjoyed his accustomed good health—and though he passed his sixtieth Birth-day on the 7th of this month—is really as active—in as good walking plight as when we crossed the Alps in 1820. My Sister too retains *her* strength and activity wonderfully, though with some drawbacks from rheumatism, and a weak arm that was sprained above twenty years ago. Dora longs to go to Rome—the Father would dearly like it—the Mother would fall into any plans that could reasonably be formed for such a purpose—and, as for me—I think I should lack none of the Zeal which would have accompanied me thither twenty years ago. But we say not much about it—We are past the scheming age (except Dora) and there seem to be so many obstacles, that I cannot think we shall ever accomplish a journey of such magnitude,—and, indeed—whenever I venture upon a *wish* it carries me no further than dear Switzerland—but who knows what *circumstances* may do for us! When you come home you will so rouze and inspire my Brother's aged heart by his own fire-side that strange schemes may arise—and all be realized with as much ease as our journey of 1820!—This leads my thoughts to the woful state of money and the 'Money Market' Every year we grow poorer—interest so low—Rents not paid etc. etc. etc.! But in this happy remote corner little do we see of what is endured among the lower orders, though we see and know that all who are of our own condition sensibly experience a change. Mr Owen[1] is instructing the Londoners in 'the Science of Society'—and *he* is to point out a remedy.—The Parliament Folks seem to be quite easy in the discovery that *they* can do nothing—It seems that emigrations are numerous both from the manufacturing and farming Districts—The latter are in a wretched state—Mrs Hutchinson writes that prices are so low and poor rates so heavy she knows not what will become of them in a few years. They have long had to pay Rent from their stock property.—We have had one most delightful letter from Charles and Mary Lamb[2] since you left England. *She* writes as if very happy and contented in being released from house-keeping cares—and gives on the whole a good account of her Brother, though from his own letter (written with great spirit and humour) we could hardly know whether he was oppressed by being turned out of his usual course or not—S. T. Coleridge

[1] Robert Owen was now propagating his social ideas through Sunday lectures in London, 'co-operative congresses', and magazines. In 1830 he launched *The British Co-operator*, and later the *Co-operative Miscellany*.
[2] See L. 495 above.

continues to live at Highgate, as usual—attacked by occasional fits of sharp illness; but always, to a certain point, recovering from them—and I believe, he is publishing some new Work[1]—upon the old abstruse subjects. His Daughter is happily settled near him in London,[2] but they cannot see much of each other. To *walk* is impossible—and to be otherwise [co]nveyed far too expensive for a young Lawy[er's][3] wife who has his [? fortune] to make. Mrs Coleridge is with her son D[erwent] and does well in his Curacy and school in [? Cornwall. Hartley is] at Grasmere writing now and then for Blackwood and the Annuals[4]—and when he has money in his pocket wandering off nobody knows whither. Miss Hutchinson is with the Southeys. They have all had a bad Influenza. Southey was off his work; but is better, and as busy as ever. What he does is wonderful. He was much affected by the Death of his Brother's Wife, Mrs Dr Southey.[5] My Brother has laid his poetry aside for two or three months. He has enough of new matter for a small volume, which we wish him to publish; but I think he *will not*, he so dislikes publishing. A new Edition of his poems will soon be called for. He has lately been busied day after day out of doors among workmen who are making us another new and most delightful Terrace. I hope you will soon come and walk on it, so I shall not describe. We have good news of William from Bremen; but his health (in common with that of all of Mr Papendich's Family) suffered much from the severity of the winter. William was an eye witness of the loss of lives and houses from inundations when the ice broke. He seems to be much beloved in Mr P's family, and is exceedingly attached to them. I had lately a long; but melancholy letter from Dear Mrs Clarkson. She had been very unwell all winter—never leaving her own bed-room and an ad-joining sitting-room; but was then hoping to get out among her flowers, which she could see from her window ready to welcome her again to the fresh air. Mr Clarkson was well—but her Daughter-in-law very delicate. No doubt you have seen our nephew Chris's name at the top of his Classical Tripos. The first Classical Medal has since been adjudged to him. The Master of

---

[1] On the Constitution of The Church and State, according to the Idea of Each: with Aids towards a Right Judgment on the late Catholic Bill, 1830.

[2] After a few months in a London lodging near Russell Square, Sara and her husband had settled in a cottage on Downshire Hill, Hampstead.

[3] MS. torn.

[4] See Letters of Hartley Coleridge (ed. Griggs), p. 100.

[5] Louisa Gonne, daughter of a Lisbon merchant, was second wife of Southey's younger brother, Henry Herbert Southey (1783–1865), the successful Harley Street physician. See Warter, iv. 169. He married for the third time in 1831.

Trinity enjoys better health than a year or two ago. I hope, my dear Friend, that you receive comfortable letters from your Brother. I was much concerned to hear of the death of your Nephew's[1] Son—both for his sake, and his Father's and yours. This is a poor dull letter to travel so far; but I know you will be glad to hear of us and to receive our assurances of affectionate remembrances—in which we three—(the only ones at home) do heartily join. Pray give our kind regards to Mr and Miss Harden[2] and their Family and write immediately—Tell us all about yourself and mention the Hardens with what news of them you can send. Adieu, my dear Friend, Believe me ever

Yours affectionately
Dorothy Wordsworth.

We have a very wet and mostly *cold* spring after an unrelenting winter. How is it with you? Our Shrubs are budding—larches green but the trees very backward and the soil is so soddened with wet that even the flowers look comfortless.

23rd April. I have just asked my Brother what message for our Friend H. C. R. 'Nothing' he replies but remembrances and good wishes; and tell him I have better hopes, that with life and health I may see Rome.—I can, I find, get leave from [the] Stamp Office.

523. D. W. to CATHERINE CLARKSON

Address: Mrs Clarkson, Playford Hall, Ipswich, Suffolk. *Single Sheet.*
Stamp: Kendal Penny Post.
MS. British Library.
K (—). *LY i. 461.*

[1830]

Begun many days ago—ended 27th April. Indeed it is a shame to write so illegibly and not to have the patience to correct

My dear Friend

I delayed answering your long and interesting, though to me rather melancholy letter, in order to save you from the burthen of it lying beside you unanswered, for what you might deem an

---

[1] Thomas Robinson jnr., who had married a Miss Hutchinson in 1822.
[2] The Hardens of Brathay (see pt. i, L. 50) were in Rome.

unreasonable length of time. But this, between you and me, is foolish; and I will wait no longer. You must cast off the burthen —not thinking ever that you have a letter to *answer*; but only that you have a Friend who at any and all times rejoices to hear from you, and that there is only one imperative reason for your writing at this time or that but to do away uneasy conjectures which *will* force themselves upon us during long fits of silence. In the last instance I had imagined nothing worse than the truth— but *that* was bad enough—an indisposition to writing from being unwell and uncomfortable—and lacking strength to help you through any labour that *might* be put off. God grant that your return to the fresh air and your spring flowers may have invigorated you!—Yet *with us* it is a far more chearless season than the winter. The flowers blow—and the rain beats them down and they look absolutely comfortless in their sodden beds. *I enjoyed* the winter; for when, in other quarters snow choked up the roads— our way was always clear before us—and we had much more than our share of sunshine. The cold, it is true, was very severe; but except in furious winds—or snow-falls, one may always fence it off—by warm cloathing abroad—and good fires within doors. It is a fact, that I suffered less from *cold* weather last winter than I ever remember to have done since my youthful days. Early in November the Frost began—I shivered and shook—and was wretched at rising in the mornings—I took to a fire in my Bed-room—and ever since have had it lighted before getting up and really do think that to this comfort I am indebted for the excellent health I now enjoy. I have been perfectly well since the first week in January—but go on in the invalidish style—enjoying the pony-chaise—and *walks* whenever weather allows. As to my strength I hardly know its measure, for my Friends having had so much anxiety concerning me, I think it my duty not to *try* it. My longest walks have been to Fox Ghyll and back again, and such moderation I shall continue for another year—the time fixed by better judges than I am, that is needful to ascertain a perfect restoration of strength in the Bowels after such an attack as I had at Whitwick last April. But too much on this dull subject, which I promise not to renew in my next, if I continue as I now am and have been since the year—30 began. My spirits are not at all affected by sitting so much more than formerly within doors—and with such a prospect from the windows—and such terraces to walk upon there is no cause to lament this comparative imprisonment. My health is now *equable*, not exposing myself to headaches or to any other symptoms of over fatigue—and every one tells me I *look* well. Now my dear Sister is a wonder—but *she* is sometimes overdone with her exertions—and looks wearied—but spirits never fail her—she lies on the sofa for ½ an hour's rest and rising restored, never shrinks from any fresh call of duty. Yet she is rheumatic and her weak arm—sprained a few months before the Birth of her daughter Catherine, feels more of the rheumatic pain than any other part—She always holds that exercise is the best cure for rheumatism—and so I doubt not it is—but there are few who could have the resolution to use such a remedy! *She does*, however, and I believe is indebted to that elasticity of mind which enables her to do so for being preserved from anything that can be called a *fit of rheumatism*. Long may it be before it forsakes her! My Brother, though he passed his 60th Birthday on the 7th of this month, is as good a walker as most of the best young ones of 20, and is not much inferior to what he was himself at that age. His eyes are pretty well—with the application of a stimulating ointment when inflammation threatens; but never more can they be serviceable to him in reading or writing the day through. We are however very thankful for what has been gained since this last twelve months. He had a very severe attack of inflammation—Mary was attending at Whitwick—poor Dora, his sole companion at home—had a sore throat—cough and fever—and when these passed away she was left voiceless—so that the blind Father, and his then helpless Daughter were pitied by the whole neighbourhood. John Carter, the clerk was employed as a Reader and kind neighbours would come in and lend their voices (among them was good Mrs Elliot[1] formerly Miss Maltby of Norwich. By the bye she and her Husband have lived in various houses in this neighbourhood—but are now residing elsewhere. They are, however, so fond of this country that I think they will yet return to it as heretofore after an absence of a year or two. This was a digression to which I was led by fancying you must know something of Mrs Elliot. She is a very clever woman—at first not attractive—from having a sort of commanding—decisive—*regulated* style of conversation and manner; but the more she is known the more beloved and esteemed. Indeed she is an excellent creature and a valuable Friend.) To return to William's eyes—Mary left me—convalescent[2]—and found the invalids at home—also fast mending—and William has never since had a bad inflammation; but is obliged to be constantly

---

[1] Lately tenant of The Wood, Bowness.   [2] i.e. at Whitwick.

watchful not to expose his eyes to sudden transitions or anything that may irritate—and he cannot continue reading for more than an hour or two without injury—Dora has been seven weeks from home—One week with our cousin Dorothy—a good soul as ever lived—who has married a goodly man and a rich[1]—and is our neighbour at Green Bank—the late Miss Knott's residence. Thence D went to Keswick where she found all the Family except Mrs Southey and Mrs Lovel in a bad Influenza—and she was the chearer of their spirits, their comforter and nurse—Southey called her 'the young Béguine.'[2] This reminds me to tell you that S is very fond of Dora and very kind to her, and she is much attached to all his Daughters—especially Edith—and D is Edith's first Friend after Sara Coleridge. After a fortnight at Keswick John rode over from Moresby to fetch her, and she has been a month with him. They ride daily on their ponies when weather permits, and are very happy together—and we at home, are well reconciled to our present loss as D's health has greatly improved while she has been with John. She has recovered her appetite, and is very much stronger, as appears by the *long* rides she is able to take—The last letters from William brought a good account of his health; but the winter's cold sadly disagreed with him. He is very happy, and I doubt not full as industrious as his strength will allow him to be. Mr. Papendich speaks very favourably of him in all respects, but seems well aware of his peculiar delicacy of constitution, and therefore of the absolute necessity of not overclose application and of regular exercise out of doors, especially on horseback—You know how affectionate are William's dispositions—he seems to love every member of Mr Papendich's Family and it appears they are not less attached to him. Sarah H is at Keswick, has been there a fortnight. We *had* some hope of the Southeys becoming our neighbours; but they have renewed the lease of their present house, and really I am disinterested enough to be glad, as, though wishing to be near us, they dreaded a removal. S. was *very ill* with Influenza, but he and all are recovered. Poor Mrs Coleridge! we miss her very much out of the country, though we saw little of her. She regrets what she has lost bitterly,[3] yet is well pleased with her daughter-in-law, and has great comfort in Derwent; but, at her age, it is a

---

[1] Benson Harrison.

[2] In his *Colloquies* Southey had advocated the foundation of religious orders for women on the model of the Belgian *béguinages* as a means of alleviating the social distress of the age.

[3] i.e. her daughter Sara, now married to Henry Nelson Coleridge. Mrs. S. T. C. was at present living with Derwent Coleridge at Helston.

great change—to a boarding school with ten boys in the house—and a little Baby to boot and another expected ere very long—but in September (and this I think is no cause for joy) Sara is to be confined—and, of course her Mother goes to nurse her—and I almost fancy that after that time Sara will not be able to go on without her help—S. T. C. himself has been very ill—is recovering —but alas! thought [to be] breaking up—What, however, is worst of all is Hartley's hopeless state. We had provided good lodgings for him.[1] He had no one want, was liked by the people of the house, and for seven weeks was steady and industrious. Money came to repay him for his work, and what does he do? Instead of discharging just debts, he pays a score off at a public house, and with eight sovereigns in his pocket takes off—is now wandering somewhere, and will go on wandering till some charitable person leads the vagrant home. We have only heard of his lodging at first at different inns—this no doubt while the money lasted—and since of his having been seen on the roads, and having lodged in this Barn or that. It has been my sad office to report to his poor mother of his doings, but my *late* reports have been of a chearing kind. I now dread the task that is before me. I shall not, however, write till he is again housed with the charitable Matron who is willing again to receive him. You will perhaps say, my dear friend, 'Why do you not rouse the country, and send after him? or at least yourselves seek him out?' Alas we have done this so often without any good coming we are determined not to stir— but it is impossible not to be very much distressed and uneasy in mind, and especially for his Mother's sake. Of course you will not speak of what I have told you—though it is notorious enough in these parts. I have no room left for inquiries—or sympathy in your distresses—but believe me I have not been thoughtless concerning any of them—and most of all am I grieved to hear of your dear Mary's[2] very delicate health. I know we should all take heartily to her were we known to each other—and how unlucky our not meeting, and Rydal Mount being left to itself, a thing that never before happened—I was at Halifax—Sara H in Herefordshire —Dora at Whitehaven for sea-air—and her Father and Mother there also, because driven from home by Workmen pulling down all the chimneys—Well! I hope Tom will bring her again—and that we shall have better luck. Mrs Luff is out of spirits and un- settled in mind by Lady Farquhar's not knowing yet what her

---

[1] With the Flemings. See L. 507 above.
[2] Tom Clarkson's wife.

plans will be[1]—whether to go abroad or to come to Fox Ghyll. Poor Mrs Luff's health suffers with her spirits—We drank tea with her on Saturday. Her House is very nice, but really better for a large family than for a single Lady. Now if Lady F. does not live here a good deal—what a pity she should have buried so much money in that garden and house—and even if she *does* two thirds of the money might as well have been spared. Farewell may God Bless you my dearest Friend

yours ever
D. W.

My love to your Sister.[2] I am very glad her son is so hopeful a Boy.

Dear Mr Clarkson! I have not even named *him* give my very best love to him—and William and Mary send love to you both.

I cannot read over this scrawl—Understand as much as you can make out.

524. W. W. to EDWARD QUILLINAN

Address: Edward Quillinan Esq[re], 12 Bryanstone Street, Portman Square, London. [*In M. W.'s hand*]
Postmark: 28 Apr. 1830. *Stamp*: Kendal Penny Post.
MS. British Library.
LT i. 469 (—).

[*c.* 27 Apr. 1830]

My dear Mr Q.

Your Letter has given me concern, as I was in hope that this money which has plagued me so long was at last about to find a satisfactory resting place. I have this morning sent to Mr S. Cookson[3] an extract of what you have written; and I added as follows. 'Col. B.[4] may not be aware that 2500 was the sum *first* mentioned to Mr Q:, through whom the transaction commenced. An additional £1000 was afterwards named as forth-coming; but that was withdrawn (by Miss J. Hutchinson to whom it belonged) and disposed of elsewhere, upon the proposed Estate being declared by you not sufficient security for 5 per ct. This is repeated least the fact being unknown perhaps to Col. Barrett he might impute

---

[1] Her husband had died recently (see L. 511 above).
[2] Mrs. Corsbie (see pt. i, L. 4).
[3] Strickland Cookson, W. W.'s solicitor.   [4] Barrett.

unsteadiness to me. I now wish it to be understood, that alarmed as I have been by the depreciation of landed property in Kent, that, if your Principals (to whom I refer as having more experience than yourself) be satisfied that the Estate first mentioned is an adequate security at the rate of 4 per cent. for 3000, that sum, which is all I can command, is ready. I beg this may be explained to Col Barrett.'

Thus far to Strickland Cookson—to you I will say that I shall be a good deal disappointed if this matter falls to the ground. I am of a most anxious temper when the interest of others as in this case constitutes the very essence of the business, and I do heartily wish that this money were well disposed of—I therefore still hope that Col. B. and I may come to an arrangement through our Lawyers.

How shall I make this Letter worth postage? We are glad to hear of Rotha's recovery from the measles, and should rejoice also that Jemima had got well through the same complaint. My sister is well, but we think it necessary for her to keep to the Invalid regimen and restrictions as to exposure and exercise. Miss Hutchinson is staying with the Southeys, Dora still with her Brother at Moresby: she writes in high spirits, but we cannot learn that her looks and complexion are improved—I shall be going over to see her in a little while. We have had an irruption of all the Douglases,[1] another sister included. The two Sisters lodged with us one night, and the whole party proceeded to Liverpool next day. Hic, Haec, and Hoc, had been called from Rome by the death of their excellent Mother,[2] who along with her Daughter, an Invalid also, had come to Europe for the benefit of her health, but she, the Mother, expired at Liverpool three weeks after her arrival there. I see more merit in the whole of the family than you seem inclined to do. For the sake of the Invalid Sister they are going to Bristol or its neighbourhood. Miss Douglas is executrix to her Mother's will, and means to return to America in about 12 months; but women's intentions are liable to change, especially by certain events that are never wholly out of hope.—

Mr Dyce has just sent me his edition of Webster, fresh from the Press. He tells me that he has with great sincerity apologized

[1] i.e. Harriet Douglas, her younger brothers George and William, and elder sister Margaret (1787–1830), an invalid.
[2] She was Margaret, daughter of Capt. Peter Corné of Hull, and married George Douglas (d. 1799), a New York businessman of Scottish descent, in 1784.

to Sir E. B.[1] who is quite satisfied, and who has written to him a couple of interesting Letters. He seems justly to estimate Sir E's great merits.—Miss Jewsbury is in Town, Charlotte Street Fitzroy Square, but Dora has the Letter and I have forgotten the number. If you have any wish to call upon her Sara Coleridge knows her address.

I am far more idle than you or any one can be in London. My time is past chiefly among catchpenny Publications, of our Ambleside Book society, and in overlooking two Labourers whom I employ in draining part of the field behind Mr Tillbrooke's Cottage where we have just made a beautiful green Terrace. Excuse this vile scrawl. Love from Mrs W. and my Sister ever yours

W. W.

[M. W. writes]

My dear Friend, Be very cautious not to expose dear Rotha to cold winds—The chest is for a long time susceptible after that sickening disease, which I am thankful she has gotten so well thro'—wish sweet Mima had also taken it—but she *may* yet, and a favourable season is coming on. God bless them both and you, my d[r] Friend—M. W.

525. D. W. and W. W. to C. W.

Address: The Rev[d] D[r] Wordsworth, Trinity Coll: Cambridge. *Single Sheet.*
Stamp: Kendal Penny Post.
MS. British Library.
Mem. (—). *K* (—) *LY i. 460* (—).

Rydal Mount—April 27th [1830]

My Dear Brother,

I make haste to thank you for your kind letter which would have given us unmingled pleasure had you not reported rather less favorably of your health than we wished—or indeed *expected*; for latterly we have had pretty good accounts of you; however it is not worse than we *might* have reckoned upon; for, excepting your rheumatic pains, you seem to have no ailments that Rest and Relaxation will not speedily cure—but of these, before the end of June, you will surely stand in need. Now my reason for not letting a day pass over without acknowledging your letter is this—that I would be beforehand in our proposal in order that Rydal Mount

[1] See L. 521 above.

may have its fair chance when you make your decision as to whither you shall turn your solitary steps—(for it does not seem that any one of the *young* Men will be with you)—You can here have constant possession and command of a quiet sitting-room above stairs, and as pleasant a bed room as heart could desire—for any part, or the whole of the next summer; and it is not possible for me to say what pleasure it would give to William and Mary myself and every other member of the Family if you would take possession of them for as many weeks of your holiday-time as you can afford. William says, after such a severe winter and such a deluge of spring-rains that we may expect a dry summer, and he hopes you would not have the same cause for complaints of our moist climate as when you were at Ivy Cottage[1]—and—even at the worst—this situation being so elevated, we have, comparatively, a bracing air; in the hot and damp season always very different from that of the Valley below us. You need not dread the idleness of the 'Idle Mount' for you may always shut yourself up from it in your own apartments; and, further: I can assure you that we have less and less every year of that sort of bustle; you would have no want of Books ancient or modern—Lady Fleming allows W^m free access to her old library, and would really be proud of your making use of it. There is also the Hawkshead School Collection[2] of Divinity and other Books —and Southey's large library—not to speak of the miscellaneous assemblage on our own Shelves. All other motives for directing your steps hitherwards I leave to your own suggestion—only my dear Brother I pray you never to lose sight of that strong one the pleasure you would give to William, Mary and me and your God-child Dora, who would be half wild with joy to ride about with you among her and your native Hills—Remember, too, how many summers are gone by and how few yet remain for *us* who are fast travelling towards our final home. Though I have been so speedy in urging my plea do not suppose we look for an equally speedy reply—we only wish to have the start of other claimants; and shall require but very short notice if you at length determine to come to us.

William, of course, now gives up all thought of visiting you next month, or in June with Dora, which he would have been inclined to, had the time better suited. The young Men's important occupations quite put it out of the question; he hopes, however,

---

[1] In the summer of 1822. See pt. i, L. 74.

[2] For some account of this Library, which had been considerably augmented by gifts from former pupils, see T. W. Thompson, *Wordsworth's Hawkshead*, ed. Robert Woof, 1970, pp. 345 ff.

that at the time you mention there may be no obstacles—and, if so, he would be very glad to turn his steps towards Cambridge, accompanied by his Wife and Daughter. I say *at least*—for though they are fearful in prospect of a long journey for *me*—I cannot at once say it would be absolutely impossible for me to accompany them. However: being all three past the planning age, we will for the present let the matter rest under this assurance; that William, Mary and Dora will gladly accept your kind invitation if time and circumstances allow of it—and if I cannot be of the party I shall remain very contented at home with one kind companion.

My first wish is that your dear Son John may be elected Fellow of Trinity—without much further anxiety: labour I suppose he *must* have to the very last. My next that Chris. may also be elected, and thus spared the going through so much as has fallen to his Brother's lot. You do not mention Charles's prospects—John told me he was not very hopeful of reaching the First Class; but I do expect to see his name there; and shall be anxious for the Oxford paper (which pray desire him to send me whether he be first, second,—or *un*named). Whatever be his place I shall have no misgivings—no doubts about his well-doing.

We have been anxious about the King's health—but the papers tell us he is recovering[1]—which could hardly be expected if what they first told us were true. I do not recollect any thing having happened among us since I last wrote, therefore will leave the rest of my paper, hoping our dear Brother will fill it up—Give my kind love to John and Chris—with a thousand good wishes for a happy end of their Labours—and the like to Charles when he is written to—and believe me, my dear Brother,

Your ever affectionate Sister
D. Wordsworth.

Dora is still at Moresby.

[W. W. writes]

My dear Bro: with Mr Burke's Colleague at Bristol[2] I say ditto to all that she has so ably expressed upon your coming hither.

[1] George IV's health had been failing for some time: on 12 Apr. he drove out for the last time: on 15 Apr. he was reported ill in the *Courier*: he died on 25 June.

[2] Henry Cruger (1739–1827), member of a leading mercantile family connecting New York with Bristol and the West Indies, and Burke's colleague in the Bristol election of 1774. His declaration that he was willing to carry out all the instructions of his constituents prompted Burke's very different definition of an M.P.'s duty—that he should act always according to the dictates of his own conscience and best judgement.

Mary says ditto also. Is it politic for the two Brothers to contend at the same time? but you know best. Owen means to take his Master's degree next commencement; I told him you would all be absent—he replied he could run down to [? Cambridge] to see his cousins and consoled himself with the hope of meeting some Contemporaries brought to Cambridge upon the same occasion as himself. I have had notice of the £25 being paid to Masterman. I wrote to you all at length, you have forgot to say if that my Letter was received. This morning we heard from Willy—he has been suffering somewhat in his bowels, which probably keeps him weak—Was Mr Rose's Course of Sermons[1] upon Education? The more I reflect upon the subject the more I am convinced that positive Instruction even of a Religious character is much overrated. The education of Man, and above all of a Christian is the education of duty, which is most forcible taught by the business and concerns of life; of which, even for children, especially the children of the poor, book-learning is but a small part. There is an officious disposition on the part of the upper and middle classes, to precipitate the tendency of the people towards intellectual culture in a manner subservise[2] of their own happiness, and dangerous to the peace of Society. It is mournful to observe of how little avail are lessons of Piety taught at school, if household attentions and obligations be neglected in consequence of the time taken up in School tuition; and the head be stuffed with vanity, from the gentlemanliness of the employment of reading.

farewell W. W.

526. D. W. to GEORGE HUNTLY GORDON

Address: G. H. Gordon Esqre.
MS. Cornell.
Broughton, p. 32.

[late Apr. 1830][3]

My dear Sir,

After my Brother had prepared the enclosed Budget of letters, to which he intended adding one addressed to yourself, he was called suddenly away, and requested me to beg of you to excuse him, and to transmit his promise not to use you so ill the next time he should have a favour to beg of you.

---

[1] The sermons referred to in L. 510 above.   [2] i.e. subversive to.
[3] This letter was written soon after 21 Apr. when D. W. recorded in her MS. Journal: 'Wrote letters for abroad (5).' (*WL MSS.*)

You will see what large advantage my Brother has taken of your kindness—and indeed I am ashamed of adding to *his* packet an enclosure of my own, the French letter[1]—but as you have with such hearty good will served me in former instances, with the assurance also that it was without difficulty, I venture again to trouble you—trusting in your sincerity. Still, however, I must again beg you to tell me if the foreign letters put you to *inconvenience*; and must beg also that if you are not able to send them FREE, you will call upon Mr Quillinan at your next meeting to discharge my debts.

Poor Mrs Wordsworth is suffering from a second attack of lumbago, though now in the way of recovery; I am happy to add that my Brother is quite well, and wonderfully active for his years —I mean active in Body—for, as you know, he does not give much rest to his *Mind*.

At present he is particularly busy out of doors, in improving his pleasure-ground. Do you ever talk of keeping holiday in the North? This is charming weather for such employment, and no doubt you do snatch a holiday somewhere each summer. I hope I need not add that it would give my Brother and all of us much pleasure to see you among the Lakes.—I am, dear Sir

faithfully your much obliged
D Wordsworth, Senr.

I ought to have said that my Brother will be much obliged if you will send the rest of the letters to the Twopenny P. office.

527. W. W. to DORA W.

MS. WL.
LY i. 468.

Tuesday Morn, [late Apr. *or* early May 1830]

My dearest Dora,

It gives me great pleasure to learn that I can be accommodated with a bed under Mr A's[2] roof, pray give him my thanks for meeting your wishes so readily. We are all delighted that you write in such good spirits—could you but add to what you say of your improved appetite that your looks (or rather complexion) were mended and that you had gathered some flesh we should be quite content and

---

[1] Probably a letter to the Baudouins.
[2] Probably Mr. Adamson of Moresby (see L. 514 above).

happy. What a pity that you had not reserved the Letter you sent to Mrs Hodgeson[1]—Mr [? S. Til:][2] could have brought it so nicely; but perhaps you thought that like certain sorts of wine, it would mellow and improve by keeping.

My improvements, owing to interruption from weather, and loss of one of my workmen, proceed slowly, but all I trust will be complete some time before you return. My visit must depend upon your stay; I should like to be with you about ten days, three of them with Mr Jackson,[3] and seven with John and you; and that you and I should return together; so in your next let us know what time will suit you best. Mr Barber calls not unfrequently—he told us yesterday that Chauncey Hare[4] who has been prowling about this neighbourhood for some time had at last succeeded in forcing himself for three hours upon the Opium Eater—he had called on Owen Lloyd also, as he himself informed us. Upon the whole notwithstanding our loss I am pleased that the Southeys are to stay at Greata Hall.[5] There was great hazard that the change might not suit all; and the trouble and expenses of removing would have been very great. My ride the other day to Mr Greives'[6] upon Billy was very pleasant; the morning being soft though sunless, still waters and an indigo tint upon the Fells, that was brought into harmony by the grey atmosphere with the lively hues of the budding trees seen to great advantage along the tract of the Calgarth Woods.—I called both on Mr Fleming[7] and Mrs Barlow—both at home.—But I assume that Billy is not safe for me, perhaps for anyone to ride; he took fright at a rush or spout of water near the road, and made a most ugly stumble; but I kept him from his knees. My fear is of being entangled in the stirrup, as I certainly should be were he to come down —then, you know, he is so timid that he would fly off in desperate fright, dragging anyone along with him and perhaps dashing their brains out—but for this apprehension I should care little about his coming down with me.

Your Aunt is I think doing very well, notwithstanding she has so little exercise out of doors, the pony chaise not being returned yet. Your Mother is well except sometimes for headaches and

---

[1] Mrs. Frances Hodgson, W. W.'s sub-distributor at Whitehaven.
[2] Apparently Samuel Tillbrooke, owner of Ivy Cottage, who was on a visit to the Lakes.
[3] William Jackson.   [4] Chauncy Hare Townshend.
[5] See L. 523 above. Southey was about to renew his lease (see Southey, vi. 97).
[6] Probably Capt. Robert Greaves of Ferney Green, Bowness, a local magistrate.
[7] The Revd. John Fleming of Rayrigg, W. W.'s old school-friend.

always for her lame arm, and a general senile queerness about her joints, as if they were determined to slip out of their place.

Thanks to Almighty God, though she is not many months short of the close of her 60th year and I have completed mine, we neither of us have yet felt, like the melancholy Cowper, that

'Threescore winters make a wintry breast.'[1]

Our affections are young and healthful. You rally me upon Hypochondriasis—but erringly—for I do gravely assure you that I have suffered much from headaches upon comparatively slight exertion. 'Non sum qualis eram' and who ought to expect it? Your Aunt reads incessantly, if she be not writing but too much as we all do in a desultory way. Your Mother is at this moment sermonizing—and I have been trying my skill upon one of Dr Donne's, which I hope to make something of. I prefer this Writer because he is so little likely to be explored by others; and is full of excellent matter, though difficult to manage for a modern audience. I have given over writing verses till my head becomes stronger or my fancy livelier— you have there mightily the advantage of me, as a comparison between our Letters abundantly shows. Farewell, love and love and love for ever,

W. W.

Best regards to the Jacksons and love to John.

528. D. W. to WILLIAM PEARSON

MS. untraced.
Pearson. K. LY i. 476.

Rydal Mount,
May 5th, 1830.

My dear Sir,

My Brother would have had great pleasure in lending you Mr Coleridge's new work,[2] had he possessed it—I am sorry to say he does not; nor has Mr Hartley Coleridge yet received it. I hope the book may find its way hither in course of time, and then you will have an opportunity of reading it; so pray do not put yourself to the expense of buying—much as I wish for the prosperity and sale of my friend's writings, I should be very sorry to hear that you were a purchaser.

---

[1] Cf. *Yardley Oak*, 1. 3.
[2] *On the Constitution of The Church and State, according to the Idea of Each.*

My brother intends sending the 'Hedgehog'[1] to the Naturalists' Magazine, and probably, I should think, with a few words from himself. After it has appeared there, it might be extracted for the Kendal papers, but better not insert there, first. This reminds me, that when I wrote to you, and also when I saw you, I forgot to ask (as I had intended doing) for a sight of the little poem, which you said you had written, on behalf of that poor, injured creature, many years ago. I hope you will not refuse to let us see it, however much you may be dissatisfied with your performance.[2]

My Brother intends joining his Son and Daughter at Moresby before the end of this week; and as he purposes to remain with them a fortnight, you had better defer your visit a little while. Indeed, I think you would hardly be certain of finding him at home, even within three weeks from this time, as he talks of making a little tour with his Daughter on their way to Rydal. Indeed, the time of my Brother's return is so uncertain, I will, on second thoughts, write you a line to say when he arrives, and when you are likely to find him disengaged; for I should be sorry that you should again be disappointed.

The new Terrace[3] will be finished to-morrow—much to our satisfaction. It is a beautiful walk, and we hope the draining will be found complete. We have much enjoyed the late fine weather, living almost the day through in the open air.

You will be glad to hear that my Niece's health is, we hope, improved. She is in good spirits. I am quite well.

I am, dear sir,
Yours truly,
D. Wordsworth.

[1] For Pearson's article on the hedgehog see L. 512 above.

[2] In his reply of 23 May, Pearson sent a copy of his verses, 'written before I had heard your Brother expressing his regret at the cruelty practised towards the poor animal in question'. (*WL MSS.*)

[3] D. W.'s MS. Journal for 1 May reads: 'On new Terrace—Sun bursts out before setting, unearthly and brilliant—calls to mind the change to another world—Every leaf a golden lamp—every twig bedropped with a diamond. The Splendour departs as rapidly.' (*WL MSS.*)

529. W. W. to ALEXANDER DYCE

Address: A. Dyce Esqre, 9 Grey's Inn Square.
Postmark: 12 May 1830. *Stamp*: Charing Cross.
MS. Victoria and Albert Museum.
Mem. Grosart. K. LY i. 477.

Rydal Mount, Kendal, May 10th, [1830]

My dear Sir,

My last was, for want of room, concluded so abruptly that I avail myself of an opportunity of sending you a few additional words free of Postage, upon the same subject.

I observed that Lady W.[1] was unfortunate in her models— *Pindarics* and *Fables*; nor does it appear from her Aristomenes[2] that she would have been more successful than her contemporaries if she had cultivated Tragedy. She had sensibility sufficient for the tender parts of dramatic writing, but in the stormy and tumultuous she would probably have failed altogether. She seems to have made it a moral and religious duty to controul her feelings, lest they should mislead her. Of Love as a passion she is afraid, no doubt from a conscious inability to soften it down into friendship. I have often applied two lines of her Drama (page 318)[3] to her affections

Love's soft Bands,
His gentle cords of Hyacinths and roses,
Wove in the dewy spring when storms are silent.

By the bye, in the next page are two impassioned lines spoken to a person fainting—

Thus let me hug and press thee into life,
And lend thee motion from my beating heart.

From the style and versification of this so much her longest work I conjecture that Lady W. had but a slender acquaintance with the drama of the earlier part of the preceding Century. Yet her style in rhyme is often admirable, chaste, tender, and vigorous; and entirely free from sparkle, antithesis, and that over-culture which reminds one by its broad glare, its stiffness, and heaviness of the double daisies of the garden, compared with their modest and sensitive kindred of the fields. Perhaps I am mistaken but I think there is a good deal of resemblance in her style and versification to that of

[1] Lady Winchelsea. See L. 521 above.
[2] *Aristomenes, or the Royal Shepherd*, a tragedy which was never performed
[3] In the 1713 edition. The lines occur in Act ii, Sc. i.

Tickell,[1] to whom Dr Johnson justly assigns a high place among the minor Poets, and of whom Goldsmith rightly observes, that there is a strain of ballad-thinking through all his Poetry, and it is very attractive. Pope, in that production of his Boyhood, the ode to Solitude, and in his Essay on Criticism, has furnished proofs that at one period of his life he felt the charm of a sober and subdued style, which he afterwards abandoned for one that is to my taste at least too pointed and ambitious, and for a versification too timidly balanced.

If a 2nd edition of your Specimens should be called for, you might add from H. M. Williams the Sonnet to the Moon, and that to Twilight;[2] and a few more from Charlotte Smith, particularly 'I love thee, mournful, sober-suited night'.[3] At the close of a sonnet of Miss Seward's are two fine verses—'Come, that I may not hear the winds of night, Nor count the heavy eave-drops as they fall.'[4] You have well characterised the Poetic powers of this Lady[5]—but, after all, her verses please me with all their faults better than those of Mrs Barbauld, who with much higher powers of mind was spoiled as a Poetess by being a Dissenter, and concerned with a dissenting Academy. One of the most pleasing passages in her Poetry is the close of the lines upon life, written, I believe, when she was not less than 80 years of age: 'Life, we have been long together', etc.[6] You have given a specimen of that ever-to-be-pitied Victim of Swift, Vanessa.[7] I have somewhere a short piece of hers upon her passion for Swift, which well deserves to be added. But I am becoming tedious, which you will ascribe to a well-meant endeavour to make you some return for your obliging attentions.

I remain, dear Sir, faithfully yours,
Wm Wordsworth

[1] For Thomas Tickell, see pt. i, L. 201.
[2] Helen Maria Williams, *Poems on Various Subjects*, 1823, pp. 206, 204. This was the edition W. W. had in his library (*R.M. Cat.*, no. 685).
[3] *To Night*, Sonnet xxxix in the 5th edn. (1789) of Charlotte Smith's *Elegiac Sonnets*, p. 39. The sonnet was not included in the first edn. of 1784.
[4] *Invitation to a Friend*, Sonnet xli in Anna Seward's *Sonnets*, 1799.
[5] Dyce writes in *Specimens of British Poetesses* (p. 285), 'She was endowed with considerable genius, and with an ample portion of that fine enthusiasm, which sometimes may be mistaken for it; but her taste was far from good, and her numerous productions (a few excepted) are disfigured by florid ornament and elaborate magnificence.'
[6] *The Works of Anna Laetitia Barbauld, with a Memoir by Lucy Aikin*, 2 vols., 1825, i. 261–2.
[7] Esther Vanhomrigh. Dyce included her *Ode to Spring* in the *Specimens*, p. 147. For her lines *To Love*, see *Poems of Jonathan Swift*, ed. Harold Williams, 3 vols., 1937, ii. 717.

530 W. W. to GEORGE HUNTLY GORDON

MS. Cornell.
Broughton, p. 33.

May 10th [1830]

My dear Sir,

Pray get the Books, and as cheap as you can. Send them to Whitakers, Ave Mary Lane, to go with Mr Troughton's[1] first parcel to Ambleside, under cover to me.

A Gentleman of the name of Gardiner,[2] unknown to me, has written to beg that a cheap Edition of my Poems might be published. He resides [at][3] No. 16 Foley place, Portland place. He tells me that the French printed Edition is sold in England to a great Extent. I cannot but doubt this, as such a sale would be contrary to Law. He has made enquiries of Booksellers and tells me that their opinion is decidedly in favor of cheap editions, and adds that in my particular case he was told by a Retail Bookseller who had during the last year sold about 12 of my last Edition, 5 vol. £2–5 that if the Contents could have been sold something under a pound, he believes he could have sold ten times as many.

Now will you be so kind as to trouble yourself in your rambles to make enquiries occasionally among the Retail Booksellers whether they are of opinion that a cheap Edit. of my Poems would answer for me; I mean make amends by encrease of sale for diminution of price. If you could settle my mind on this subject I should be inclined to try the experiment as the last Edition is I believe getting low. Excuse great haste and believe me my dear Mr Gordon

sincerely your much obliged
Wm Wordsworth

531. D. W. to JOHN WORDSWORTH

Address: To John Wordsworth Esqre, Trinity College, *Cambridge.*
MS. WL. Hitherto unpublished.

Rydal Mount 11th May[4] [1830]

My dear John,

I believe it would be rather more correct were I to send my congratulations to Chris. himself than through you to him, but I have two reasons for adopting the latter plan. First, that probably

---

[1] Thomas Troughton, bookseller, and W. W.'s sub-distributor in Ambleside.
[2] For John Gardner, see L. 515 above.   [3] *Word dropped out.*
[4] D. W. writes 'May', but the contents of the letter suggest March.

261

he is so busy with preparations for future honours that at this time *no* letter would interest him very much and as little as any a *stupid* one (which this will be) from his old Aunt. The second reason for addressing you in preference to Chris is a selfish one: I think my chance of a speedy answer is better, as, undoubtedly, you must at this particular time have more leisure than he. Besides, you already owe me a letter, which letter *was to have given* me a report of the Tripos etc etc etc. You must not, however, wait for the medals, for I understand they are not given till June. I shall be well satisfied with tidings of good health, good spirits, and your every-day goings-on. I wish you could have witnessed the triumphant joy of Dora's countenance when she ran up stairs to me with Chris's letter in her hand, open but unread, her eyes resting on his name at the Top of the Tripos which name, by the bye, in a cooler moment of reflexion, she pronounced to be the prettiest name of the Set. I should have liked to see Frere[1] in the first Class, but perhaps he did not expect it, and if so there can be no disappointment, and I suppose a place in the second is very honorable. We expect Owen and his good-natured fat pupil[2] to Tea: and I have but a quarter of an hour for writing before their arrival. Owen is to forward this tomorrow in a frank along with an advertisement of a *Lady's* neat cottage to let in summer. We think it would very nicely accommodate three Cantabs, having three Bedrooms and two sitting-rooms, a Servant in the house.—Rent two guineas per week. I mention these particulars, not knowing whether the advertisement is to be sent to you or to some other Friend of Owen's. He called on Tuesday, and was then suffering from a severe cold caught by attending the marriage of your pretty cousin Mary Braithwaite.[3] The meeting-house was heated by Stoves and full to overflowing, so that poor Owen was in a state of dissolution, and it was well he brought home no worse malady than a blinding cold in the head. A female voice spake, which he supposed was that of Aunt Anna;[4] but so disguised by whining and squeaking that he could not recognise it and did not see her face. Mr Crewdson the

---

[1] John Frere, C. W. jnr.'s college friend.

[2] Henry Curwen jnr. (see L. 482 above).

[3] Mary (1807–33), eldest child of George Braithwaite (1777–1853) the Kendal Quaker, and Mary Lloyd (1784–1822) of Birmingham, John Wordsworth's aunt. Mary Braithwaite married Dr. Charles Hingston (1805–72) of Devon on 8 Mar.

[4] Another of Priscilla Lloyd's sisters, Anna (1788–1859), who married Isaac Braithwaite (1781–1861) of Kendal (see also pt. i, L. 159), younger brother of George Braithwaite. She was prominent in the Society of Friends and made long journeys on its behalf in America in the 1820s.

Banker[1] preached a desultory sermon, of great length on the doctrines of the Christian Religion impelled thereto, as Owen supposes, by seeing such crowds gathered together, of all persuasions. Dora is at Keswick: otherwise she would, no doubt, have slipped a little letter for Chris. into the frank. I can assure him I should not have checked *her* effusions, however little I might be disposed to break in upon his studies with my own. She has ere this had an agreeable sur-prize today, a visit from her Father. At Breakfast-time this morning two Lawyers (I have forgotten their names as I did not see them) called on your uncle. Tired out with waiting for their Causes coming on at Lancaster, they had come for two day's pleasure among the Lakes, and he at Sixty, with the ardour of sixteen, said 'I will go *with* you.' The offer was gladly and gratefully accepted by an old Friend, and in a quarter of an hour the party were off to Keswick.

It will be six weeks before we see Dora again. John is coming on Monday to Rydal. He will stay here till Thursday, and on his way home will call for Dora at Greta Hall, and take her on to Moresby. He has changed his lodgings since Chris. was at Whitehaven, and has now very comfortable accommodations, both for himself and a visitor. John is very happy and contented, and much liked by his parishoners, but I do wish his Living were a little more lucrative. It is but 120 pounds per ann. independent of Surplice fees and they are small. The last accounts of Willy were better, but he has not regained his strength. We are satisfied with Mr Papendick's report of his progress, and he seems to be much beloved by the family. What news of Mrs and Miss Hoare? I wrote to Mrs H about Christmas. Give my Kindest Love to your dear Father. Does he think of coming to see us next summer. How happy it would make me if he *would* come, with at least one of you!—How is Charles? I hope well and able to prepare for a good degree, God bless him, and all of you.

Your affectionate Aunt
D Wordsworth

Remember me to Mrs Carter (Sophy).

As my Brother is not at home I send no answer respecting the money for John Wordsworth.[2] He grows tall and strong—Was with us at Shrove-tide.

---

[1] William Dillworth Crewdson (1774–1851), the Kendal banker, had married Deborah Braithwaite (1775–1844), sister of George and Isaac, mentioned above. The Braithwaites and Crewdsons were frequent callers at Rydal Mount in the later years (*RMVB*). [2] R. W.'s son, 'Keswick John'.

532. W. W. to JOHN GARDNER

Address: John Gardner Esqre, Foley Place, Portland Place, London.
MS. untraced.
K (—). *LY i. 479.*

May 19th 1830
Whitehaven
(I return home in a few days.)

My dear Sir,

I feel that I ought to thank you for your judicious Letter, and for the pains you have taken towards settling the question of the eligibility of low-priced Publications.[1] Messrs Longman talk strangely when they say that my annual Account will shew what is advisable. How can that shew anything but what number of Purchases I have had? it cannot tell me how many I have missed by the heavy price. Again, Messrs L. affirm that my Buyers are of that class who do not regard prices—but that class, never perhaps very large, is every day going smaller with the reduced incomes of the time—and besides, in this opinion I believe these Gentlemen to be altogether mis-taken. My Poetry, less than any other of the day, is adapted to the taste of the Luxurious, and of those who value themselves upon the priviledge of wealth and station. And though it be true that several passages are too abstruse for the ordinary Reader, yet the main body of it is as well fitted (if my aim be not altogether missed) to the bulk of the people both in sentiment and language, as that of any of my contemporaries.—I agree with you, (and for the same reason) that nothing can be inferred from the failure of cheap publication in Kirke White's[2] case. To the above considerations I would add the existence of the pirated editions, and above all an apprehension that there is a growing prejudice against high-priced books. Indeed I am inclined to think with my Friend Mr Southey that shortly few books will be published except low-priced ones, or those that are highly ornamented, for persons who delight in such luxuries. These considerations all seem in favor of the experiment which you recommend. Yet I am far from sure that it would answer. It is not to be questioned that the perpetually supplied stimulus of Novels stands much in the way of the purer interest which used to attach to Poetry. And although these poorer Narratives do but in very few instances retain more than the hold of part of a season upon public attention, yet a fresh crop springs up every hour. But to bring these tedious *pros* and *cons* to a close, I will

[1] See L. 515 above.
[2] The *Remains* of Henry Kirke White (1785–1806), with a 'Life' by Southey, were published in 1807.

say at once that if I could persuade myself that the Retail Book-seller you speak of is not mistaken in his notion that he could sell *ten* copies, (or less than half of that number,) when he now sells *one*, were the price something under a pound, I would venture upon such an edition. I ought to say to you, however, that I have changed my intention of making additions at present, and should confine myself to inter-mixing the few poems that were published in the Keep-sake of year before last.[1] I have already stated to you my notions as to the extreme injustice of the law of copy-right; if it has not been mis-represented to me, for I never saw the Act of Parliament. But I am told that, when an Author dies, such of his Works as have been twice fourteen years before the Public are public property, and that his heirs have no pecuniary interest in anything that he may leave behind, beyond the same period. My days are in course of nature drawing towards a close, and I think it would be best, in order to secure some especial value to any collection of my Works that might be printed after my decease, to reserve a certain number of new pieces to be inter-mixed with that collection. I am acquainted with a distinguished Author who means to hold back during his life-time all the Corrections and additions in his several works for the express purpose of benefiting his heirs by the superiority which those improvements will give to the pieces which may have become the property of the public. I do sincerely hope and trust that the Law in this point will one day or other be brought nearer to justice and reason.[2] Take only my own comparatively insignificant case. Many of my Poems have been upwards of 30 years subject to criticism, and are disputed about as keenly as ever, and appear to be read much more. In fact thirty years are no adequate test for works of Imagination, even from second or third-rate writers, much less from those of the first order, as we see in the instances of Shakespeare and Milton. I am sorry that want of room prevented me from being favored with your account of the effect my attempts in verse had produced upon your mind. It would, I doubt not, have pleased me much and might have been of service to my future labours if I should write any more. With sincere thanks for the trouble you have taken, I remain dear Sir

faithfully yours
W. Wordsworth

[1] See pt. i, L. 327.
[2] W. W.'s growing convictions about the injustice of the existing law on Copyright finally prompted his vigorous campaign for reform, 1838–42. See also L. 515 above and L. 556 below.

533. D. W. to DORA W.[1]

Address: W. Wordsworth Esq[re], Rydal Mount, Kendal, England. Steam Boat
via Hamburg. Single Sheet. [*In W. W. jnr.'s hand*]
Postmark: (1) 14 May 1830 (2) 18 May 1830 (3) 19 May 1830.
Stamp: (1) Bremen (2) Ship Letter London.
MS. WL. Hitherto unpublished.

Friday morn[g].
[21 May 1830]

Dear Dora,

I forgot to say we sent no more cloth; thinking you w[d] not have
time to write now, and had better bring home the Shirts to mend.
What a relief for William[2] when he gets his Father's letter. My
opinion is, that the best thing he can do is to turn his face to the
Rhine, or some other chearful pleasant part in the South of Germany,
and board himself in a respectable family—(which surely there
can be no difficulty *to him* in hearing of—) where nothing but
German is spoken—and if with access to acquaintances who speak
French, so much the better; but by no means go to France till he
has had opportunity of German daily, hourly Talk. On any other
plan, the [?][3] would be wasted, as I think.

I met Owen Lloyd on the hill this morning, on my road to visit
John Backhouse's[4] dying Child. He will probably *walk* to Scale
Hill[5]—but at all events, intends to meet you at S. Hill on Tuesday
evening, if he does not hear to the contrary. I went on to Rose's,[6]
as we want to employ him for a day. He, poor Fellow! was working
in his garden and more chearful than one could expect with such a
family and no work, and very thankful for a day's employ—
Deplorable the Spectacle at [? Vickars's]![7] At best she is a poor
complaining creature—and *he* also was sitting by the fireside, as if
life were a burthen—'Work! work! work every where!' his cry.—
I met M[r] Fell and sent him up to Mary—[8] walked very leisurely,
and am not tired—The whole house still as busy as possible and
topsy turvey—

I *hope* we shall have done before you come home. The labour of
papering is really tremendous. I wonder at Mary's and Sarah's

---

[1] Written very illegibly at the end of a letter from W. W. jnr. to his father,
and sent on to W. W. and Dora W., who were still with John W. at Moresby.
[2] W. W. jnr.   [3] *MS. illegible.*   [4] A Rydal farmer.
[5] Near Buttermere.   [6] A local handyman.   [7] *MS. obscure.*
[8] M. W.

strength in going thro' it. Mr Carter is very good natured, and a superlative workman.

The letter from this pack was from Sir G. Beaumont to tell you [he] had given orders for payment of the annuity[1]—and that press of business, and recent affliction had caused the delay. Their younger Babe is dead.[2] This we are very sorry for—

God bless you all! and ever yours D W.

[*M. W. adds*]

I have seen Mr Fell—he says that the boil is nothing more than those that the coutry folk say are healthy—but they are something of a carbuncle—very painful and tedious till the core is discharged when they heal—that, no doubt it is the consequence of being weakened by the succession of colds; and he certainly advises a change of Situation.

It is pleasant to find the dear fellow's[3] letter so perfectly in sympathy with his Father that I hope he will soon receive [?][4] will be such a comfort to him!—

Owen's horse took a shivering fit as soon as it got into the Stable from Workington, and could not stand on Sunday morn^g— so I fear, unless he walks he can not meet you at Scale hill, but I have not seen him since. M. W.

534. W. W. to GEORGE HUNTLY GORDON

Address: G. H. Gordon Esqre.
MS. Cornell.
Broughton, p. 34.

30th May [1830]
Rydal Mount
Kendal

My dear Mr Gordon,

I am glad you approve of my determination. We have had a further Letter from W^m expressing a decided opinion that it does not answer either mine or his own views that he should remain at Bremen. At the same time he speaks in the highest terms of Mr P. and his family to whom he is strongly attached.

The enclosed to Mr Aders[5] is to inquire for some situation in a

---

[1] The allowance paid to W. W. by the late Sir George Beaumont.
[2] The second child referred to in L. 520 above.   [3] i.e. W. W. jnr.'s.
[4] *MS. illegible.*   [5] For Charles Aders, see pt. i, L. 342.

mild climate, somewhere upon the Rhine, and in a family where German and French only, or German alone are spoken—

You will be concerned to hear that my Daughter is unwell—She has been staying with her Brother 9 weeks. I went to conduct her home. We had projected a pleasant tour through the mountains, I walking by her side—but an imprudent exertion of walking in the Town of Whitehaven, followed by dining out, brought on a bilious fever; and I was truly glad to get her home as speedily as possible— She is recovering I trust but slowly.—

Thanks for your enquiries among the Booksellers,[1] and your purchase of the Books etc. We have generally a small running account with Mr. Quillinan, and to avoid multiplying these little things will you have the kindness to procure the money of him. The subject shall be named to him in our first Letter—

As to the Portrait to be prefixed according to the suggestion of the Booksellers—the notion to me is intolerable. These Vanities should be avoided by living Authors—when a man is departed the world may do with him what it likes—but while he lives let him take some little care of himself.

You did well in calling my attention to the word Piracy, as applied to Gaglianianis[2] proceedings. But I must say that I only meant it in a moral not a legal sense. He neither violates the law of France nor of England—but surely he breaks through the good old Christian Law of doing as he would be done by. As he is well aware he injures others not his rivals in trade for that might be fair, for his own benefit; but authors who perhaps in some cases have not a tenth part of his income.—

My residence near the sea would have been charming had it not closed with my Daughters illness. The seacoast is bold near Whitehaven, and the Scotch Hills on the opposite side of the Solway frith, and the Isle of Man are fine objects. I was favored also with two or three glorious spectacles of the sun setting upon the sea; and the little *ghylls*, Cleaves, or Dingles, running down into the sea, and also along the cliffs and shore were gay with innumerable spring flowers, and the upper lands resounding with skylarks and the cry of the Corn-craik or Land-rail neither of which Birds, are found in our deep mountain vallies.

> farewell and believe me
> your sincere friend
> W Wordsworth

---

[1] See L. 530 above.   [2] Galignani.

Mrs Hemans[1] will be with us in the course of next month,—to stay a short time—she speaks of her health as much deranged.

You will perhaps be troubled with another Letter in a very few days, as we are looking for Mr Papendicks answer, to which I shall have occasion to reply.—Can we continue to profit by your power to forward Letters, after W. leaves Bremen. If you were at any expense in sending the letters to Bremen, pray add it to the account with Mr. Quillinan.

[*M. W. writes*]

Mr Wordsworth had intended mentioning to Mr Gordon the subject of the enclosed unsealed letter to Mr P.—but being called off on business he takes the liberty thro' Mrs W to request Mr G. to read the letter and be kind enough to put a seal upon it, and forward it with his Son's packet to Bremen at his convenience.— If Mr. G. was not able to forward the letter to Rome, sent by the last despatch free Mrs W. will thank him to charge the Postage to the Book account.

535. W. W. to GEORGE HUNTLY GORDON

MS. Cornell.
Broughton, p. 36.

[31 May 1830]

My dear Sir

Writing in haste yesterday immediately after reading William's letter I forgot something that required notice, and hope that the letter I now send may be in time to add to the Pacquet without giving you further trouble than what is occasioned by this letter following so close on the other. If our packets are too large, or too frequent pray be so kind and candid as to say so. Mrs W. holds the pen for me—this sudden change in the air from hot summer to almost winter—and exposure to the strong easterly wind of yesterday during a walk of 12 or 13 miles has caused a slight inflammation or blight in one of my eyes.

You will excuse my calling upon you to read so long and ill-penned a letter as that to Mr Papendick, yesterday—but I felt that I owed to your kindness by which W. was placed where he enjoys so many advantages, an account of my dissatisfaction in that one but most important particular upon which the letter dwells.

---

[1] For Mrs. Hemans, see pt. i, 246.

To remain abroad mainly for the purpose of acquiring the German language in a house where English is spoken by the Principals of the family, as the ordinary tongue, would not answer for any one—and for W^m who has been confined so much to the house by inclemency of weather and who is not strong enough to support hard study, it is peculiarly disadvantageous; and cannot but defeat in a great measure the end I had in view by sending him abroad.

If you could point out any place for next winter where the climate is milder than at Bremen and where he could have the benefits which you know I require, I should be very grateful to you.

I am glad to find that the King's health seems to be improving.[1]

Ever faithfully yours
Wm Wordsworth

536. D. W. to JOHN WORDSWORTH

Address: To John Wordsworth Esqre, Trinity Lodge, *Cambridge*, or Dr Wordsworth or Mr C. W.
Stamp: Kendal Penny Post.
MS. WL. Hitherto unpublished.

Rydal Mount—June 1st [1830]

My dear John,

This letter will be a sort of family concern; but I address you as the last of the three to whom I am indebted for a reply to mine.

We begin to be anxious to know that we actually are to have the pleasure of your dear Father's company at Rydal Mount, and if he can say positively that he will come (with the usual promise that if nothing unforseen happens to prevent it) we shall be much more happy than I can tell you. I cannot but believe that during all this long time he has been unable to decide or he would have indulged us with the enjoyment of an agreeable certainty, or not have suffered us to indulge false hopes. However the matter stands I must beg of him, or you, or Chris. to inform us as soon as possible—only this I must add, that provided my Brother cannot yet positively say that he will come, he must not say *may* as long as there is the smallest chance of affairs so turning out that he *can* come: we only wish to learn what his present views are: and if they fix him upon a visit to Rydal Mount, we wish as soon as may be to *know* that the pleasure is in store for us. Your Aunt desires me to repeat

---

[1] The final decline set in soon after this. See L. 525 above.

(what I believe I before said very distinctly) that a sitting-room up stairs as well as that pleasant Bed-room which he occupied when last here, will be allotted to his private and entire use—and this without the slightest inconvenience to the rest of the family. I hope that poor Dora, if her uncle *does* come, may be able to enjoy the satisfaction which she has anticipated with so much delight of accompanying him on his rides; but alas! she is again in a very weak state. Three weeks ago her Father went to Moresby, and found her wonderfully improved in health and strength, and he hoped to bring her home as gay as a lark: unfortunately, however, last Friday but one, she had a most severe bilious attack attended with fever, prostration of strength, and followed by loss of appetite. Yet the disorder was subdued sooner than usual, and thank God! she and her Father reached home in safety last Thursday. She was not so much fatigued by the journey as might have been expected; has regained, *for her*, a good appetite, and is perceptibly, though slowly, gathering strength so that I trust she may in the course of two or three weeks arrive again at the state in which her Father found her at Moresby—but what a grievous thing that she should be so often cast down! I think I never saw her so thin as she is at present; but her spirits, even at the worst, when she was but in a lodging-house, and had no one to nurse her but her Father and Brother, never failed her, and she is now so happy in being at home again; and so lively and cheerful, that if it were not for sickly looks, and evident want of strength, nobody might suspect that anything had ailed her.—It is curious enough that Miss Dixon,[1] the very same lady who had the good fortune, which she never fails to speak of when we see her, of having you for her companion in the Coach on her way to Storrs, should have had what she will no doubt call similar good fortune on Thursday with Dora and her Father. This morning she has addressed a note of kind inquiries to D. and I see, poor Girl! she would gladly have dispensed with this Kindness (I will not call it ceremony) for it is a heavy task to her to make a proper reply, not having yet taken again to pen, book, or needle. I trust, however, that in a few days we shall see her able to employ herself as usual.

Our last accounts from Bremen were not very favorable. No sooner had William[2] begun to recruit after the various illnesses of the severe winter than he was confined to the house by a boil upon one of his legs—and this is really disturbing as the Doctor pronounced horse-exercise as necessary for the restoring and preserving

[1] One of the Storrs circle.　　[2] W. W. nr.

his health. It had long been decided that he was not to pass another winter at Bremen, the climate being unsuitable to his Constitution, and the country wet and unpleasant: and the present state of his health (with other circumstances) has determined his Father that he shall go elsewhere as soon as possible. We are waiting for a second letter, in order to fix plans, but at present your uncle thinks it adviseable that he should journey towards the Rhine on horseback, and perhaps fix himself for a few weeks or months at or near Godesberg (not far from Bonne). He must look out for a respectable Family where only German—or German and French—is spoken. In all other respects his present situation at Bremen is as favorable as possible. Mr and Mrs Papendick are excellent people—affectionately attached to William—and he to them, and it will grieve him much to leave them; but English is far too much spoken in the house, and it was absolutely necessary in order to attain the chief end for which he went abroad, that he should place himself in a Family where the English Tongue is never heard.

John was with us last week. He brought home Dora's poney, she being unable to ride it herself, and remained till [   ][1] dull enough at the thought of his Solitary fireside. Yet he is contented with his lodgings; and, on the whole, very well Satisfied with his Parish, its situation etc etc. His Father and Dora were charmed with the walks, rides, and prospects. Did you see Mr Merewether in London? And was the message delivered to him respecting the six pounds which he wanted to pay to John? I was afterwards vexed that I had yielded to Mrs Wordsworth's suggestions and imposed that trouble upon Mrs Hoare and your Father, or you; but was led to it by my unwillingness to tax Mrs Merewether with postage merely in reply to that one unimportant part of her letter.—Mrs Luff is anxious to let her house[2] for the summer; and my sister and I thought that if Mrs and Miss Hoare could be prevailed upon to come to the Lakes they would find it a most comfortable and pleasant residence. Therefore I mentioned it to Mrs. Hoare, though with little hope of prevailing on her to resolve on so long a journey; and not having heard, I conclude she has no thoughts of it. I urged as an inducement, that your Father might probably be their neighbour at Rydal Mount. Dear John, we are all very sorry that neither you nor Chris. can come, and that Charles gives us no reason to expect him. I hope however that the Autumn will set you all at liberty.—Two more Trinity Fellowships vacant—surely

[1] *Hole in MS.*   [2] Fox Ghyll.

Chris. has an excellent chance of being elected in September!---
Notwithstanding this, I was very sorry for the last vacancy, by the
death of Frederick Malkins.[1] His poor mother, after all her afflictions will, I think, be heart-broken at last! Will Frere[2] be a candidate along with you in September?

I am hurried to close my letter by the arrival of our Cousin
Julia Myers,[3] who will take it to the post—so cannot look it over,
and you must excuse all mistakes—and [?][4] is you write soon

With love to all, ever your affect. Aunt
D Wordsworth.

We expect Bertha Southey this afternoon, to stay a while.—
The poor King how he suffers and lingers!

537. W. W. to EDWARD MOXON

Address: Edward Moxon Esqre, 64 New Bond St. [*In M. W.'s hand*]
Postmark: 7 June 1830. *Stamp*: Mount St.
MS. Henry E. Huntington Library.
K (—). *LY i. 481.*

Rydal Mount Kendal
June 2^d 1830—

My dear Sir

It gives me pleasure to learn from yours, received this morning,
that you have commenced business on your own account.[5] You
have my cordial wishes for your success both for your own sake,
and as patronized by my excellent friend, Mr Rogers.—I shall
perhaps know better if it be in my power to serve you, and how,
when I receive the cards which you mean to send, and which I shall
take care to distribute as judiciously; as I have several Friends in
the University of Cambridge in particular who are fond of Books,
and as I propose visiting that place in the Autumn, I trust I may
be of some use to you there.—As to publishing any thing new,
myself, I am not prepared for it; but I believe the Edition of my
poems of —27 is now low, and in consequence of an urgent application I have entertained some thoughts of republishing when this

---

[1] Frederick Malkin (1800–30), Fellow of Trinity from 1825, had died on
22 May. His *History of Greece* was published this year by the Society for the
Diffusion of Useful Knowledge.
[2] John Frere.   [3] For Julia Myers, see pt. i, L. 2.   [4] *MS. obscure.*
[5] Moxon had recently left Longman to launch out on his own. See pt. i,
L. 265 and *Lamb*, iii. 282.

Edition is all sold, in a cheap Form;[1] something under a pound, instead of 45 shillings the present price.—I should like to know from experienced persons whether such a mode of publication would be likely to repay me—Perhaps you may be able to throw some light upon the subject.

It will give me much pleasure to receive the Vol: of Mr Lamb,[2] through you. It may be sent to Whitakers Ave Mary Lane to be forwarded to Mr Troughton Bookseller of Ambleside—in this case I shall be sure to receive it punctually, and at a trifling expense. Believe me dear Sir

very sincerely yours
Wm Wordsworth—

538. W. W. to SAMUEL ROGERS

Address: Samuel Rogers Esqre, St James's Place, London.
Postmark: 7 June 1830. *Stamp*: Kendal Penny Post.
Endorsed: not to be Published S. R.
MS. Sharpe Collection, University College, London.
Rogers. LY i. 482.

Rydal Mount
Kendal: June 5th [1830]

My dear Rogers,

I have this morning heard from Moxon who in communicating his new project,[3] speaks in grateful terms of your kindness. Having written to him, I cannot forbear inquiring of you, how you are and what is become of your Italy.[4] My Daughter (who, alas, is very poorly, recovering from a bilious fever which seized her a fortnight ago) tells me that she is longing to see the work— and that it would do more for her recovery than half the medicines she is obliged to take.

It is long since we exchanged Letters. I am in your debt—for I had a short note from you enclosing Lamb's pleasing verses upon

---

[1] See L. 515 above to John Gardner.
[2] *Album Verses, With a Few Others*, by Charles Lamb. London: Edward Moxon, 64 New Bond Street, 1830.
[3] Of setting up as publisher on his own account. See previous letter.
[4] The illustrated *Italy* (with plates after J. M. W. Turner and Thomas Stothard) was going through the press. See *Rogers*, ii. 2–4. It was published in quarto by Moxon jointly with T. Cadell later this year, and brought considerable prestige to his new publishing house (see H. G. Merriam, *Edward Moxon, Publisher of Poets*, New York, 1939, pp. 27–9).

your lamented Brother[1] just before you set off for the Continent. If I am not mistaken I heard, and I think from Lady Frederick Bentinck, that some untoward circumstance interrupted that Tour—Was it so?

My dear Sister you will be glad to hear is at present quite well, but in prudence we do not permit her to take the long walks she used to do, nor to depart from the invalid regimen. The remainder of us are well. My daughter's illness was the consequence of over-fatigue while she was on a visit to her Brother at Moresby, near Whitehaven. I passed with her there a fortnight, which would have flown most agreeably but for that attack. An odd thought struck me there which I did not act upon, but will mention now—it was to bespeak your friendly offices among your great and powerful acquaintances in behalf of my son, who enjoys the dignity of a *Rector* with an income of £100 per ann. This Benefice he owes to the kind patronage of Lord Lonsdale, who must be his main-stay, and who, we venture to hope, will not forget him upon some future occasion. But you know how much the patronage of that family has been pressed upon, and it would on this account please me much could something be done for him in another quarter. I hope it is not visionary to mention my wishes to you, not altogether without a hope that an opportunity may occur for your serving him. Testimonials from a Father are naturally liable to suspicion, but I have no reason for doubting the sincerity of his late Rector, Mr Merewether of Coleorton, who wrote in the highest terms of the manner in which he had discharged his duty as a Curate. I will only add that he has from nature an excellent voice, and manages it with feeling and judgement.

How is Sharp[2] in health? When he wrote to me last he was suffering from a winter cough. He told me, what did not at all surprize me to hear, that the *Sale* of your Pleasures of Memory, which had commanded public attention for 36 years, had greatly fallen off within the last two years. The Edinburgh Review tells another story, that you and Campbell (I am sorry to couple the names) are the only Bards of our day whose laurels are unwithered. Fools! I believe that yours have suffered in the common blight (if the flourishing of a Poet's Bays can fairly be measured by the sale of his Books or the buzz that attends his name at any given time), and that the ornamented annuals, those greedy receptacles

[1] Daniel Rogers, the poet's eldest brother, who had died the previous year. For Lamb's sonnet, see *Rogers*, ii. 27 and *The Works of Charles and Mary Lamb* (ed. Lucas), v. 56.
[2] Richard Sharp.

of trash, those Bladders upon which the Boys of Poetry try to swim, are the cause. Farewell! I know you hate writing Letters, but let me know from inquiries made at your leisure, whether you think an edition of my Poems, in 3 vols to be sold for about 18 shillings, would repay. The last of —27 is, I believe, nearly sold. The french Piracy (for in a moral sense a Piracy it is) I have reason to think is against me a good deal; but unless I could sell 4 copies of a cheaper edition than my own where I now sell one it would scarcely [pay];[1] again adieu, faithfully yours

W Wordsworth

What is likely to become of the Michael Angelo marble[2] of Sir George—is it to be sold? Alas! alas! That Picture of the picture gallery, is that to go also? I hope you will rescue some of these things from vulgar hands, both for their own sakes and the memory of our departed Friend.

539. W. W. to SIR WALTER SCOTT

Address: Sir Walter Scott, Abbotsford, Melross, N.B. [*In M. W.'s hand*]
Stamp: Kendal Penny Post.
Endorsed: William Wordsworth 7 June 1830.
MS. National Library of Scotland.
K (—). *LY i. 484.*

Rydal Mount Kendal, June 7th [1830]

My dear Sir Walter,

Being upon a visit lately to Workington Hall, I there met with the elder brother by the Father's side of Mr Curwen of that place, Mr Christian[3] of Unerigg in Cumberland, and Deemster of the Isle of Man. He asked if I was acquainted with you. I replied that I had for thirty years, nearly, had that honor, and spoke of you with that warmth I am accustomed to feel upon such an occasion. He then told me that Professor Wilson, at his request, had some time ago undertaken to write to you upon a point in which, innocently, you had been the cause of a good deal of uneasiness to him. You

---

[1] *Word dropped out.*

[2] For the Michelangelo bas-relief bequeathed to the Royal Academy by the late Sir George Beaumont, see pt. i, L. 281.

[3] John Christian (see also *MY* ii. 564) of Milntown, Isle of Man, and Unerigg (or Ewanrigg), near Maryport, Deemster of the Isle of Man, 1823–47. He was half-brother of Henry Curwen of Workington Hall, being the only son of John Christian Curwen by his first wife Margaret (d. 1778), daughter of John Taubman, Speaker of the House of Keys.

will guess, perhaps, that he alluded to the Novel of Peveril of the Peak.[1] So it was. The conduct and character of his ancestor, Christian,[2] had there been represented, he said, in colours which were utterly at variance with the truth, and threw unmerited discredit upon his Family. He said that the great Historic Families of the Country were open to the Fictions of men of genius, the *facts* being known to all persons of education; but in the case of a private Family like his, it was very different; a false impression was easily made: and could not be obviated or corrected in the present instance, except by an acknowledgment from the Author himself. He added that had the Novel of P. not appeared before he, by the death of his Father, had become the head of the Family, he should have written to the Author himself; but so much time had elapsed since it was published that he preferred addressing you through some Friend of yours, or acquaintance. He thought that Professor W. might not have written, or that, in the multiplicity of your important engagements, the affair had slipped from your memory. He then asked if I could take the liberty of naming it to you; and added that he was anxious this should be done before the Edition of the Novels, now in course of Publication, came to the Peveril. He was prepared, he said, to furnish you, if you wished it, with documents unquestionably proving that Christian was entitled to, and possessed, the gratitude of the *Isle-of-Manners* of his own and subsequent times, and that he was idolized in the Country; as a Martyr, I suppose in a good cause.[3] I replied that no one, I was sure, had a greater respect for Ancestry than yourself, and that I could not think you would regard me as an unwarrantable intruder if I reported his wish that some notice should be found in the

[1] Published 1822.

[2] William Christian (1608–63), 'Black William', commonly regarded as a champion of Manx liberties. As Receiver-General of Man, 1648–58, he was appointed commander of the Manx Forces by the 7th Earl of Derby, hereditary Lord of Man, but surrendered the island to the Parliamentarians in 1651. He later escaped to England, and after the Restoration contrived to return, trusting in the Act of Indemnity; but he was arrested by the 8th Earl of Derby, found guilty of treason by the Manx authorities, and executed in 1663 to the indignation of Charles II—since his treason was against his feudal superiors, and not the English Crown. Soon afterwards, the family of Christian moved from Milntown to Unerigg in Cumberland, and its fortunes were consolidated by coal-mining, and marriage into the Senhouses and the Curwens. Their mansion at Unerigg was considerably enlarged towards the end of the eighteenth century, but has since been largely demolished. See Edward Hughes, *North Country Life in the Eighteenth Century*, ii. 110–32.

[3] Scott's reply of 2 July, promising to set the record straight, is given in *The Letters of Sir Walter Scott* (ed. Grierson), xi. 370. In the next edition of the novel (1831) he published a long Appendix provided for him by John Christian, and made full acknowledgements of his historical inaccuracies.

forth-coming edition, by which the reader might be set right as to the real character of the Person who came to so melancholy an end.—Mr Curwen (the Brother as I said above of the Deemster), and Head, by the Mother's side, of that antient House, a genealogy with which you are probably acquainted, was present at the conversation. He is a very intelligent and amiable Man, and seemed in no small degree to share the Complainant's feelings upon the occasion.

The Countess of Derby[1] was not a Catholic, according to the Deemster. There were also several small mistakes respecting the Island, with corrections of which he would be happy to furnish you if you thought it worth while.—Pray excuse the length of this— I have not left myself room for much of a private nature that I wished to say. I should have visited you in the course of last summer but I could not resist a tempting call to Ireland which to my shame I had never seen. In Autumn I must pass some time with my Brother at Cambridge, or I would strain a point to see you, yours, and your plantations. Farewell. Kindest regards from my wife, Sister, and daughter.

[unsigned]

540. W. W. and DORA W. to C. W. JNR.

Address: Chris. Wordsworth Esqre, Trin: Coll: Cambridge. *[In Dora W.'s hand]*
Stamp: Kendal Penny Post.
MS. WL. Hitherto unpublished.

[c. 7 June 1830]

My Dear Chris,

By return of the Post that brought me yours I wrote to Mr Marshall with an Extract from your letter. I regret that not having the pleasure of Mr H's[2] acquaintance I was not able to support the application by personal knowledge of my own. However I did all I could to assist Mr H in that quarter.

[1] i.e. Charlotte, 7th Countess of Derby (d. 1663), daughter of Claude de la Trémouille, Duke of Thouars. She became William Christian's feudal superior after her husband was captured after the battle of Worcester and put to death.
[2] Unidentified. According to D. W.'s MS. Journals (*WL MSS.*), C. W. jnr.'s letter arrived on 5 June, and W. W.'s reply must have been written soon after.

On another part of this sheet you will find a note which I beg you would cut off and forward to Professor Sedgewick[1] of whose present address I am ignorant.

It grieves me to say that Dora has been very poorly—this day she feels herself much better.

In the family Council about to be held pray do not forget your Cousin W^m, nor the head of the family now at Hawkshead School[2] —what is to be done with these 2 forlorns I know not.

Your Letter, we [are][3] glad to see, leaves us hopes that we may see your dear Father at this delightful place. Your aunt is marvellously well, but we still keep her to Invalid regimen and restrictions. I ought to have told you that I am about to remove W^m from Bremen—he has many advantages there and is much attached to the Family, but unfortunately English is so much spoken in the family that German is not to be learned by means of familiar conversation. I am very anxious for Charles[4] at Oxford—farewell.

your affectionate uncle
W Wordsworth

[*Dora W. writes*] Pray forward the enclosed directly as time is very precious—the election[5] takes place on the 16th. And pray do use your influence with dear Uncle and persuade him to come and see our new terrace—this spot is looking more beautiful than ever. With kind love to John and to Charles, for whom I w^d trot off to the Wishing Gate 'To speed the current of his fate,'[6] if my strength w^d serve me for so long a journey

Ever dear Chris
Your very affect^te
Dora Wordsworth

Father bids me request you [to] read his note to the Professor and if you have any interest with any of the members of the Athenaeum you will use it in Mr Quillinan's behalf.

---

[1] For Adam Sedgwick, the Cambridge geologist, see pt. i, L. 382. W. W. had written asking him to support E. Q.'s candidature for the Athenaeum (see next letter).

[2] R. W.'s son.

[3] *Word dropped out.*

[4] Charles Wordsworth was now approaching his Finals. See also L. 547 below.

[5] The election for the Athenaeum.

[6] See *PW* ii. 299.

541. W. W. to EDWARD QUILLINAN

Address: Edward Quillinan Esq, 12 Bryanston S^t, Portman Square. [*In M. W.'s hand*]
Postmark: 13 June 1830.
MS. WL.
LY i. 486 (—).

Patterdale Hall
Wednesday. [9 June 1830]

My dear Mr Quillinan,

Miss Hutchinson promised to write to you some days ago, whether she has or not I am ignorant—but having an opportunity of sending this Note Postage free to London, I take up the pen to thank you for your obliging letter respecting the mortgage received some time ago.—I am sorry it could not be arranged, my money is still in the Kendal Bank.

I wrote to Dr Holland[1] from whom I have received an answer promising his support on the general election,[2] but expressing a fear that your application is too late for success in first Selection by the Committee.

I wrote also to Chantrey, to Moore, to Sedgewick,[3] and to Davies Gilbert,[4] perhaps to some others, but I cannot affirm positively not having the list at present before me—in short to almost every member of the Com: whom I know except Lord Farnborough[5] whom I knew too well to expect the least favor from him except where I could make a return.

Some of these letters may not have reached their destination. I addressed to Rogers the Letter for Moore, that for Sedgewick to one of my nephews at Cambridge, and Davies Gilbert's to London.

From no one except Dr Holland have I yet received an answer. Now I recollect I wrote to Croker[6] also. Dr Holland surprizes me

---

[1] For Dr. (later Sir Henry) Holland, see pt. i, L. 42.

[2] For the Athenaeum. See also previous letter.

[3] Professor Adam Sedgwick.

[4] Davies Gilbert (1767–1839), scientist and antiquarian, who wrote much about the history of his native county of Cornwall: friend of Sir Humphry Davy: M.P. for Helston, 1804, and for Bodmin, 1806–32: President of the Royal Society, 1827–30.

[5] Charles Long, 1st Baron Farnborough (1760–1838), of Bromley, Kent: M.P. for Rye (1789–96), Midhurst (1796–1802), Wendover (1802–6), and Haslemere (1806–26): a Lord of the Treasury, 1804–6, Joint Paymaster General, 1807–17, and Paymaster General, 1817–26. He was a director of Greenwich Hospital, 1799–1829, and one of the original trustees of the National Gallery from 1824.

[6] John Wilson Croker of the Admiralty: one of the founder-members of the Athenaeum.

by the request which he says admissions are in. Members of Par:
have solicited his support referring to their speeches on such and
such occasions in support of their claim. I fear that in my letters I
did not treat the matter so formally as I ought to have done.

When I apply again I will set forth all your accomplishments
and prove your fitness to be a member of his Club and 5000 others
worth 50 of it.—

I will tell you a bit of news if you have not heard it from Miss H.
John is going to be married, you shall hear to whom by and by.
Do not think about my [? fortune][1]

Ever faithfully yours W W.

[*M. W. adds*]

Dora recovers very slowly—love to the Darlings.

Sincerely y^{rs} M.W.

542. W. W. to GEORGE HUNTLY GORDON

MS. Cornell.
Broughton, p. 36.

10th [June 1830]

My dear Mr Gordon,

I am up to the ears in company and engagements. My Daughter
after whom you so kindly inquire is convalescent, and with our
care will I trust do well. I did not like to lose a Post in reply to
Mr P's[2] Letter. This morning by very good luck a Gentleman has
called upon me from London (and is still here) who was a year upon
the Rhine, to learn the G—— Language. from him I have collected
much that will be useful to W^m. Pray excuse my writing more at
present.

Ever faithfully yours
W. Wordsworth

There is a young Person of the name of *Moxon* who has just set
up as a Bookseller in New Bond Street[3] (He is a very respectable
Poet also). He is Patronized by Mr Rogers, and I believe him to be
a truly liberal and worthy Man. Be so kind as to look in upon him
at your leisure, mentioning my name. Mr Southey is interested in

---

[1] *MS. obscure.*   [2] Papendick's.   [3] See L. 537 above.

his well doing and will assist him to the best of his power—
Adieu—

Did I ask whether you could assist us in communicating with
W^m upon the Rhine, by Post?

543. W. W. to C. W.

Address: The Revd Dr Wordsworth, Trinity Coll: Cambridge.
Stamp: Kendal Penny Post.
MS. British Library. Hitherto unpublished.

[12 June 1830]

Private

My dear Brother,

You will be surprized at what I am going to mention. Your
Nephew John, of Moresby, has engaged himself and is to be married in Sept^br or Oct^br. A bold step you will apprehend, of a
Rector of 100—per Ann. But the object of his choice is Miss
Curwen[1] eldest daughter of Mr Curwen of The Island, Winder-
mere, and of Workington Hall. The Father's allowance to his
Daughter is so liberal as to remove every objection upon prudential
grounds. The young Lady is in her 23^d year, bears the highest
character for feminine virtues, and in her demeanour and appearance
is truly engaging, but her health is, I grieve to say, delicate.
This affair came upon us with as much surprize as it will upon you.
Dora, who has known Miss Curwen, for some time suspected
John's attachment—but we knew nothing of it, till he had declared
himself to the young Lady, and was accepted by her. The Union
has the entire approbation of Mr and Mrs Curwen, and nothing can
be more generous and disinterested than the behaviour of both;
that of the father, as appears from a Letter of his (addressed to me
in the *first* instance) which I will shew you, is above all praise, in
candor and frankness, and every feeling becoming the occasion.

May I hope that this event will strengthen your motives for
coming down to us this summer?—Pray do so if you can—John is
very anxious that the Ceremony should be performed by you, as he
will tell you himself [by][2] Letter, but I fear the time may not suit
with your engagements; as the wedding is not to be earlier than

---

[1] Isabella Curwen (1808–49), eldest daughter of Henry Curwen (see L.
482 above) and his wife Jane (d. 1853), daughter of Edward Stanley of Whitehaven. According to D. W.'s MS. Journals (*WL MSS.*), W. W. dined with
the Curwens at Belle Isle on 11 June, and this establishes the date of this letter.
[2] *Word dropped out.*

September, nor later than October. I will not now enter further into particulars—before I knew of their attachment, I dined and slept at Workington Hall; and yesterday I dined at the Island,—the affair having been previously settled by Letter, between Mr Curwen and myself. These Interviews have given me an opportunity of seeing something of Mr Curwen beyond what concerns this weighty affair, and I can say with much pleasure that he is a man of extensive reading, accurate memory, and very intelligent: His habits are those of a retired Man, and I like him the better on that account. [He][1] mentioned to me that communications [of the] most cordial nature had passed [between] Lord Lonsdale and himself some time [ago]—this you will be glad to hear as I was.[2]—Say nothing of the contents of this Letter except under charge of secrecy, to your Sons—Of course these things cannot be kept long concealed, but it will not be named by me beyond our own family except to Lord Lonsdale and Southey.

Dora gains no flesh, and but little strength but we are full of hope notwithstanding—

ever your affectionate B.
W.W.

Your Sister is quite well, as we all are. Owen[3] will be with you to take his degree; unless the engagement be mentioned by her and publicly known, I would rather that his Cousins did not speak of it to him.

544. D. W. and W. W. to HARRIET DOUGLAS

MS. untraced.
Davidson, Miss Douglas of New York, p. 272.

June 12th, 1830.

My dear Miss Douglas,

I will give you a brief detail of what has happened among us since the receipt of your letter of the 11th and 13th of May, from which you will draw out an explanation of the cause why it has remained so long unanswered. We forwarded the letter to Moresby, where my Brother then was; but so busily (and at first so happily) was he employed that he could not find time to reply to it as the letter

[1] *MS. damaged.*
[2] The Curwens were political rivals of the Lowthers in Cumberland, but Henry did not follow his father John Christian Curwen in playing a vigorous part in local politics (apart from a brief intervention in West Cumberland in 1832). [3] C. W.'s nephew, Owen Lloyd.

deserved; and when he came home he brought a load of care and anxiety to be shared by all—so that we were little disposed to letter-writing besides being unwilling to make you uneasy. My Brother was delighted with his son's place of residence; and almost as happy as Father could be in finding his Daughter's strength restored and her health very much invigorated. You may judge in what spirits he wrote to us, and how hopeful we were; but alas! a few days before that fixed for their return to Rydal, poor Dora was seized with a bilious fever, which brought her to a state of extreme weakness, and detained her at Moresby several days beyond the stated time. Happily the disorder did not continue long in its utmost violence—otherwise I know not what would have been the consequence—and she had no relapse: consequently her Mother did not (as she at first resolved to do) go to nurse her; and as soon as the journey could be undertaken the Father and Daughter came home; for when she became convalescent, being but in lodgings, she began to pine after home comforts; and you will not wonder at their joint anxiety to come to us: but, poor Creature, when she *did* arrive it was not possible to repress fears that they had hazarded too much, she looked so dismally and was so very weak. Happily our fears were not realized; and she has been recovering (I hope daily) though it is so very slowly that one is obliged to look back a few days to satisfy oneself that she really *is* in the straightforward course. It is very extraordinary that as soon as the violent pains in her head—and that weakness which made her disposed to fainting whenever she moved—were gone, her good spirits returned, and she has continued to be, and is now, as lively as a lark. *So* she is in our own domestic circle; but has not yet strength enough to bear her up the day through; and she does not rise till between eleven and twelve o'clock—and when any company comes to the house does not appear among them—the excitement and exertion are too much for her, as we once found when, having three or four Friends to tea, she was induced to remain with us. No sooner were they gone than she appeared to be completely exhausted, and it was several days before she regained what she had lost. However, we trust in God that she has nothing now to struggle with but weakness; and, with due care, that a little time will restore her.

I have exhausted too much of my paper with this one subject; but it is very near my heart, and you will therefore excuse it: besides, it is not through selfishness that I have done it; but in reliance that you take so much interest in this dear young woman that you would hardly have been satisfied had I not entered into particulars concerning her. She begs her very kind love to you, and often repeats how much she regrets that she had not the good fortune to be at home when you were here, but hopes that you may yet again visit Scotland—and if so the North of England, and our country of the Lakes.

My Brother returned to us in perfect health; and his eyes, I think (thanks to the American Ointment sent by Mr. Goddard[1]) have continued in their better way. My sister is quite well. So are we all, though I am not yet allowed to erase my name from the invalid list—which I might almost be judged entitled to do, having gone through all the changes of this hitherto changeable summer without cold-taking or any other mischief. The weather is wet, and ungenial; so that the fruit is checked and even the grass in the fields seems to stand *still*; but the short season of warmth which we had at the end of April, and in the first week of May, did so much for vegetation that in spite of all after-checks the country is most rich, and beautiful to the eye. This cold air is very much against poor Dora's restoration to activity and health—as long as it continues she cannot have the benefit of exercise out of doors—but when a favourable change comes I trust we shall daily see the effect of it upon her.

It is time that I should thank you for your very interesting letter, which I do most heartily; and believe me you have our entire sympathy in all your distresses, cares, and anxieties. Among the first of these is your dear Sister's[2] state of health, which gives us great concern both for her own sake and yours; and we much wish to know what was the result of those letters which you were writing to dissuade her from a hasty removal from the Physician with whom you were all so well satisfied.

I feel an uncomfortable uncertainty while now addressing you— not knowing even that you are upon this Island, for it seems to be just as likely that you may have joined your Sister in Ireland as that she may have met you at Torquay; but I will hope that the latter is the fact; and that you and she together with your good Brothers are enjoying the gentle sea Breezes on the soft warm hills of Devonshire; and that the cough and all other distressing symptoms are removed. But, my dear Miss Douglas, pray satisfy us on this point—and as speedily as you can—and any other details concerning the past, or your plans for the future, will interest us. Do not fail

---

[1] D. W. probably means Mr. *Gould*, brother-in-law of F. W. Goddard (see L. 440 above).

[2] Margaret Douglas (see L. 524 above), an invalid, was now seriously ill.

to mention your Brother George's health—which I hope has gone on improving—and say whether he has yet been able to persuade your Sister into the belief that our overgrown and full-ripe country is better than your improving one—or she still looks (with you) across the Atlantic for an abiding home.

We feel for you deeply in all that you tell us concerning your departed Mother. The loss is indeed a heavy one—and can never be thought of by you but with solemn sadness—yet what a blessing to have had such a Mother, and to go to your own grave bearing with you such recollections as you have of her! You speak of "reminiscences" written by Dr. Ralph[1] concerning your departed Mother—are those reminiscences published? If so, cannot you procure a copy for us? But if not, should we again have the happiness of meeting, you will, I know, suffer us to read some parts of the records that remain of her which you so justly prize.

My Brother promises to add a few lines, therefore I must hasten to conclude—but first let me tell you that the Mrs. Coleridges (Mother and Daughter) are well. Mrs. Henry C. expects to be confined in September. Her Husband has taken a small furnished house at Hampstead, and the Mother will join them there previous to her Daughter's confinement. Mrs. C. is still at Hellstone in Cornwall with her son Derwent, who is quite recovered from the dangerous illness he had had a short time before you were here. Mr. and Mrs. Southey and their Family are well and chearful. Miss Bertha Southey has been with us a fortnight and I hope we shall yet keep her for some time. She is a sweet-tempered, amiable creature; and a delightful companion for our poor Invalid. Mrs. Hemans is coming to see the Lakes, and we expect her company at Rydal Mount for a few days. I am not one of those who are always onging to see famous people: therefore I do not anticipate her coming with unmingled pleasure—or rather I should say that sort of pleasure with which I anticipate the coming of old and known Friends is wanting. I have not yet even seen Mrs. Hemans, and she is personally a stranger to the whole Family.

But I must have done—or you will be angry with me for stealing from my Brother. So with kind love to your Sister and sincerest wishes for her perfect recovery and for your happiness and hers withersoever you turn. Believe me ever, dear Miss Douglas, your affectionate Friend D. Wordsworth Senr.

[1] The Revd. Hugh Ralph, D.D., minister of the Scotch Kirk in Oldham Street, Liverpool, where the late Mrs. Douglas had been a member of the congregation.

Many thanks for your care concerning my little Store of money! Remember me kindly to your Brothers.

[*W. W. writes*]

My Dear Miss Douglas,
I wished to have had a little more paper but now I have scarcely time to employ the little left; for I am under a most pressing engagement to go this day to Patterdale with Mrs. Wordsworth, and the weather has suddenly cleared up so that we must be gone or not at all. Be assured of my friendship, and that I sympathize with the trials[1] you have to undergo. God bless you, and give you as much earthly happiness as He thinks good for you. Ever yours W. W.

545. W. W. to WILLIAM ROWAN HAMILTON

Address: Professor Hamilton, Observatory, Dublin [*In M. W.'s hand*]
Postmark: 15 June 1830. *Stamp*: Kendal Penny Post.
MS. Cornell.
Hamilton (—). *K* (—). *LY i. 487* (—).

[*c. 14 June 1830*]
My dear Sir,
I will not waste time in apologies for no adequate ones can be offered for deferring so long to thank you for your interesting communications which I have repeatedly perused with much pleasure. Summer is at hand, and I look forward with much pleasure to the time when you are to fulfil your promise of bringing your Sister[2] to this beautiful place.—I am likely to be at liberty, which I was not sure of till lately, for the whole of July and August, and remainder of the present month; with the exception of one visit of a week or so. Therefore do not fail to come, and I will shew you a thousand beauties, and we will talk over a hundred interesting things. During some part of September also I shall probably be disengaged; but if possible let me see you earlier.
Is Mr. Edgeworth[3] gone to Italy? About the same time that brought your papers, I had a letter, a book and a MS from him. There are now lying in my Desk a couple of pages of two several Letters which I have begun to him, and in both of which I was

---

[1] Miss Douglas was still finding it difficult to make up her mind about her various suitors, and aired her problems and uncertainties in her letters.
[2] Eliza Hamilton, the poetess.
[3] Francis Beaufort Edgeworth (see also L. 489 above).

unfortunately interrupted, and so they never came to a conclusion: if you are in correspondence with him pray in mercy to me tell him so, and if you come soon I will write to him with a hope that you will add something to my Letter, to make it acceptable. I know not whether you can sympathize with me when I say, that it is a most painful effort of resolution, to return to an unfinished Letter, which may have been commenced with warmth and spirit; there seems a strange and disheartening gap between the two periods; and if the handwriting be bad as mine always is, how ugly does the sheet look!

I hope yourself and family have been in good health since I last heard of you. In my own, I have had much anxiety and uneasiness. My Daughter is slowly recovering from an attack of bilious fever, and my younger Son who has been in Germany during the winter has suffered much from the severity of the Climate; he was at Bremen, and is now moving towards the Rhine. Farewell; pray accept the kind regards of this family, and present them to your Sisters—and believe me, my dear Mr Hamilton, with high admiration, sincerely yours

Wm Wordsworth

546. W. W. to SAMUEL ROGERS

Address: To S. Rogers Esqre, St. James's Place, London.
Endorsed: not to be published S. R.
MS. Sharpe Collection, University College, London.
Rogers. LY i. 488.

Wednesday, 16th June [1830]
Rydal Mount

Being sure, my dear Rogers, that you take a cordial interest in anything important to me or my family, I cannot forbear letting you know that my eldest Son is soon to quit that state of single blessedness to which you have so faithfully adhered. This event has come upon us all by surprize; when I wrote a short time ago I had not the least suspicion of an engagement, or even an attachment in any quarter. I expressed to you some years since my regret at my Son's being disappointed of a Fellowship,[1] to which he had very good pretensions until we discovered that his place of Birth excluded him from being a candidate, and you then said, I remember, it is lucky for him, he will have less temptation to build upon the life of a Batchelor, and will be far happier. May your prophecy be

---

[1] At Merton College, Oxford, in 1825. See pt. i, Ls. 203–4 and 207.

fulfilled! I trust it will, for I have seen the young Lady,[1] am highly pleased with her appearance and deportment, and in a pecuniary point of view the alliance is unexceptionable. Their income, through the liberality of the Father, who highly approves of the match, is, for the present, quite sufficient, for I trust their good sense will prevent them from giving an instance of the truth of the french phrase, C'est un vrai gouffre que le ménage.

In somewhat of a casual way I recommended in my last, my Son to your thoughts, if any opportunity should occur in the wide sphere of your acquaintance of speaking a good word in his behalf. Had I known this delicate affair was pending, I should at that time have probably been silent upon the subject of his professional interests. It cannot, however, be amiss for any one to have as many friends as possible, and I need not conceal from you that my satisfaction would, upon this occasion, have been more unmingled had my Son had more to offer on his part. I shall merely add that if through his future life you could serve him upon any occasion I should be thankful. I regret that I am not at liberty at present to mention the name of the Lady to more than one Individual[2] out of my own family.

Do you know Mrs Hemans?[3] She is to be here to-day if winds and waves, though Steam boats care little for them, did not yesterday retard her passage from Liverpool. I wish you were here (perhaps *you* may not) to assist us in entertaining her, for my Daughter's indisposition and other matters occupy our thoughts, and literary Ladies are apt to require a good deal of attention. Pray give our kind regards to your Brother and Sister.[4] We hope that you all continue to have good health. Do let me hear from you however briefly and believe me,

my dear Rogers
faithfully yours,
Wm Wordsworth

[1] Isabella Curwen.   [2] W. W. had told Lord Lonsdale.
[3] Felicia Hemans probably owed her visit to Rydal Mount to her friendship with Miss Jewsbury. On 31 July S. H. wrote to E. Q.: 'For one *long* fortnight we had Mrs Hemans and one of her boys—he was a sweet interesting creature —but she tho' a good natured person is so spoilt by the adulation of "*the world*" that her affection is perfectly unendurable. Don't say this to Miss Jewsbury who idolizes her. Mr W. *pretends* to like her very much—but I believe it is only because we do not; for she is the very opposite, her good-nature excepted, of anything he ever admired before either in *theory or practice*.' (*SH* p. 370.) See also H. F. Chorley, *Memorials of Mrs. Hemans*, 2 vols., 1836, ii. 106 ff; *Memoir of the Life and Writings of Mrs Hemans by her Sister*, 1844, pp. 206 ff. After leaving Rydal Mrs. Hemans spent some weeks in the neighbourhood at Dove Nest, Ambleside, and then (after another visit to Scotland) settled in Dublin.   [4] Henry and Sarah Rogers.

547. W. W. to CHARLES WORDSWORTH

Address: Charles Wordsworth Esq., Christ Church, Oxford [*readdressed by Dora W. to*] Trinity Lodge, Cambridge.
MS. Mr. Jonathan Wordsworth.
Charles Wordsworth, Annals of My Early Life, 1891, p. 65 (—).

Rydal Mount: Thursday
[? 17 June 1830]

My dear Nephew,

The pleasant news of your station in the first class reached Rydal Mount yesterday—but I was from home and did not learn it till this morning, when I entered the house from Patterdale, and Dora who is always the first to report well of her Cousins, called out to me from the top of the Stairs, "Charles is in the first class". We all congratulate you most heartily; and I hope, notwithstanding some disappointments heretofore,[1] that you feel yourself recompensed, as far as honour goes, for your Labours. But I trust that you value the honor infinitely less than the habits of industry and the knowledge which have enabled you to acquire it. You have hitherto been in study a busy Bee; let the "amor florum" and the "generandi *gloria* mellis",[2] continue to animate you, and be persuaded, my dear Charles, that you will be both the better and happier.

Your Aunts are both well; your aunt Dorothy has had no relapse for a long time, though She complies with our earnest request in retaining her invalid precautions. Dora, alas! had a severe attack of bilious fever three weeks ago—she is convalescent, but regains her strength slowly.—I have a piece of domestic news for you, which I will thank you not to repeat. Your Cousin John is to be married in September or October.[3] To whom, as a young man, you perhaps will little care, provided he is likely to be happy—I trust he is so, for the object of his choice is truly amiable, and her fortune such, as enables them to marry without imprudence. [*Dora W. writes in*: This is a twice told Tale, but my Father forgot when writing that you must now be in Cambridge.]

The other day I had the pleasure of being greeted in the road by your Bowness Tutor and Friend—Martin.[4] He was in excellent

---

[1] Charles Wordsworth added in the margin: 'I had twice been a Candidate for the Ireland Scholarship (1828–9) without success; tho' on the former occasion I came in second.'
[2] Virgil, *Georgics*, iv. 205.   [3] To Isabella Curwen. See L. 543 above.
[4] Francis Martin (1802–68), Fellow of Trinity College, Cambridge, 1825–68, and Vice-Master, 1862–8. Charles Wordsworth, in company with his two

Spirits, and looked well: One of his Companions was a young Man, Fellow of Trinity, whose name, though they drank tea with us, I did not learn. He was guiding them through the country.

The weather has been with us very cold—but sometimes such as to make walking truly delightful. I found it so this morning, when with Mrs W. I crossed Kirkstone. She rode to the top of the mountain; but down hill we tripped it away side by side[1] charmingly. Think of that, my dear Charles, for a Derby and Joan of sixty each!! Farewell; where are you going this summer—to Cambridge first no doubt, but whither afterwards? Could not you come hither with your father? I fear we could not *lodge* you both in the house, but at the foot of the hill we can procure a bed, with due notice beforehand. Ever your affectionate uncle,

W.W.

548. W. W. to ALEXANDER DYCE

Address: Revd Alexander Dyce, 9 Gray's Inn Square, London.
MS. Victoria and Albert Museum.
LΥ i. 490.

[mid-June[2] 1830]

My dear Sir,

I have at last lighted upon Martin's Pamphlet entitled a Voyage to St Kilda[3]—4th Edition, London 1753—The passage I alluded to some time ago stands thus page 19—'no sort of trees, not even the least shrub grows here; nor has a Bee ever been seen here.

> *Hard* is their *shallow* soil and bleak and bare,
> Nor ever rural Bee was heard to murmur there.

In the preceding Paragraph Martin gives an account of the soil which scarcely agrees with the words of the Poet. Hard is the shallow soil etc, saying—the soil is very grateful to the Labourer producing ordinarily 16 or 18 or 20 fold—they use no plough but a kind of inverted spade—their harrows are of wood, as are the teeth in front also, etc etc. I have transcribed these notices hoping for an op[p]ortunity to send you this note Postage paid.

I remain dear Sir
faithfully yours
Wm Wordsworth

---

brothers, and other Cambridge undergraduates, had joined him in a reading-party at Bowness in the long vacation of 1827 (see pt. i, L. 290).

¹ by side *added in Dora W.'s hand*.   ² Date fixed by next letter.
³ See pt. i, L. 367.

549. W. W. to ALEXANDER DYCE

Address: Revd Alexander Dyce, 9 Gray's Inn Square, London.
Postmark: 23 June 1830. *Stamp*: Charles St.
MS. Victoria and Albert Museum.
LY i. 491.

Rydal Mount Kendal
22nd June [1830]

My dear Sir,

A few days ago I prepared the enclosed note to be sent by the first opportunity; and this morning has furnished me with one and brought your obliging Letter—

Many thanks for your information about Lady Mary Wortley M—.[1] I shall look after that edition of her Works. The Duchess of Newcastle's Life of her Lord is very interesting, as I have been told by Charles Lamb.—

I am not surprized with what you tell me of E. B.[2] There is some cause for fear, least he should prove rather a troublesome correspondent. Of some of these Poets whom he would include in a new Corpus I am utterly ignorant; but one of them has produced an exceedingly pleasing poem with a very original air. It begins 'There was a time my dear Cornwallis, when'[3] I first met with it in Dr [? Enfullser's][4] Exercises of Elocution or Speaker, I forget which. It is by Davies, and well merits preservation.

Without flattery I may say that your editorial diligence and judgement entitle you to the highest praise—and I hope that you

---

[1] Lady Mary Wortley Montagu. See L. 521 above.

[2] Sir Egerton Brydges. In his letter of 17 June Dyce had written: 'He beguiles his tedious nights of illness by literary correspondence . . . It is strange how his mind dwells on the "minora sidera" of literature:—not those of the Elizabethan age, (who are almost all more or less interesting,) but little twinklers of the last century, who were scarcely visible even in their own dark times: he writes me whole pages about the excellencies of Sneyd Davies, Bagshaw Stevens, and Capel Loft etc etc, and thinks they should enjoy places in the next Edition of the British Poets.' (*Dyce MSS., Victoria and Albert Museum.*)

[3] 'To the Hon. and Rev. F. C.' [i.e. Frederick Cornwallis, Archbishop of Canterbury] by Sneyd Davies (1709–69), Archdeacon of Derby and Canon of Lichfield. The lines begin:

> In Frolick's hour, ere serious thoughts had birth,
> There *was* a time, my dear C——s, when
> The Muse would take me on her airy wing . . .

See George Hardinge, *Biographical Memoirs of the Rev. Sneyd Davies*, D.D. . . ., [1817], p. 70.

[4] *MS. obscure.* The work has not been identified.

will be able to proceed with these Labours, which one day or other must be duly appreciated.

I wish you had thought of returning from Aberdeen through the Lake Country, I should have been truly glad to see you at this beautiful place.

> Believe me my dear Sir in haste
> very sincerely yours
> Wm Wordsworth

550. D. W. to WILLIAM PEARSON

MS. untraced.
Pearson. K (—). LY i. 492.

> Rydal Mount,
> June 22nd, [1830]

My dear Sir,

I promised to write to you on my Brother's return from Moresby; but alas! he brought his Daughter home in such a weak state, that I could not possibly say when we could look forward with pleasure to seeing you at Rydal.

She was seized with a bilious fever a few days before the time fixed for her return, detained by it at Moresby, and at length, returned to us sadly shattered; and we were long very anxious; though all disorder, except from weakness, had left her, and she has had no return. The weather has been very unfavourable for an invalid—so extremely cold—yet she has gone on gaining strength, though very slowly; and I trust that she may, now, make more rapid progress, if the air becomes in the least summer-like. Her spirits are excellent and her looks are begining to improve.

As far as Dora is concerned, we should be glad to see you at any time; but I cannot say when we shall have no company. At present our house is quite full—one of the Miss Southeys and her Brother,[1] and a nephew of Mrs Wordsworth's[2] are here, and others expected when they are gone. But this fact ought not to prevent your directing your pony's head this way; when you are disposed to take a day's holiday if you can make up your mind to the disappointment of finding my Brother not at home, or engaged.

[1] Bertha and Cuthbert Southey.
[2] Young Tom Hutchinson (1815–1903) from Brinsop.

We are much obliged for the copy of your verses on the Hedgehog.[1] They are interesting, if but as a record of an incident connected with that harmless, oppressed creature.

I can only further say, that you are always welcome at Rydal Mount, but that it is impossible, during 'the height of the season', to fix a time when the family will be left to itself, or other engagements are not pressing upon us.

My Brother begs his best regards.
I remain, dear Sir,
Your sincere Friend,
D. Wordsworth.

Pray excuse this very hasty and incoherent scrawl.

Since writing the above my Brother has met you at Fell Foot, and I find he has promised to inform you when we are without company. I am sorry to hear from him that your looks were not of the best; and that you had been poorly. I have broken open my letter to add these few words, having neglected to forward it under the idea that you only get letters on Saturdays.

551. W. W. to WILLIAM ROWAN HAMILTON

MS. Cornell.
Hamilton (—).

[*In Dora W.'s hand*]

Friday [late June 1830]

My dear Mr Hamilton

Yesterday I sent you a message of thanks by Mr Johnstone[2] for your very acceptable letter, and now I write to say, that it is exactly the term you name—the last week of July and the first of August—that would [suit] us to have you with us. In the 2nd week of the latter month we expect my brother, the Master of Trin. Coll. Cambridge, and an event important to our family which will involve us in many engagements is speedily to follow. I allude to the marriage of my elder Son, the Clergyman. If the weather prove favorable I hope to be able to shew you and your Sister[3] the

---

[1] See L. 528 above.
[2] The Revd. Edward Johnston, a Dublin friend of Hamilton's, whom W. W. had met the previous year. He was formerly tutor in the family of Sir Aubrey de Vere, Bart. (see L. 464 above). The Journal, which he was proposing to launch, is unidentified. [3] Eliza Hamilton.

beauties of our neighbourhood so as to recompense you for the voyage—Most likely you will come by steam to Liverpool. If you could so contrive as to cross the Lancaster Sands to Ulverstone, you could approach the lakes to the best advantage up Conistone Water and so to Rydal. A Car might be hired at Ulverstone, and there is I think a daily coach from Lancaster to Ulverstone—but in this point you would do well to be governed by time and convenience.

The Lady whose death you deplore in your elegant verses,[1] I recollect most distinctly, and do sincerely condole with her parents in their affliction. My only Daughter I am sorry to say still continues weak, and unable to bear excitement, so that I fear she will be unable to see much of any of our visitors during the Summer. At present M[rs] Hemans[2] is with us, but she departs today after a fortnight's residence under our roof—not however to quit the country as she purposes to take lodgings in this neighbourhood for a few weeks. I therefore cherish the hope of having an opportunity to introduce yourself and sister, to one in whom you cannot fail to be much interested.

It would give me much pleasure should M[r] Johnstone succeed in his journal. I am too old to meddle with periodicals, having kept clear of them so long—otherwise I should have willingly complied with his wish to send him a small contribution—

Ever with kind regards to your Sister
faithfully
W[m] Wordsworth[3]

552. W. W. to GEORGE HUNTLY GORDON

MS. Cornell.
Broughton, p. 37.

[*c.* 1 July 1830]

My dear Mr Gordon,

W[ms] Letter, I grieve to say, gives *no* account of his health but from this cause we fear he had not any good tidings to send. On the 24th Ult he was to start for Dusseldorf in a hired carriage

---

[1] *Easter Morning* (*Hamilton*, i. 379) on the death of the daughter of Thomas Ellis (see L. 459 above), at whose house, Abbotstown, W. W. had dined during his visit to Dublin the previous year.
[2] See L. 546 above.　　　　　　　　　　　[3] Not signed by W. W.

with his saddle horse running at the side; and was to proceed from
Dusseldorf to Godesburg on Horse back. Godesburg is a league or
two above Bonne, and his Physician recommends the waters. Poor
fellow! we are anxious for another Letter—You have forgotten to
say whether we can send and receive Letters through you, while he
is on the banks of the Rhine. Pray let us know. in the meanwhile the
enclosed are sent at a venture; in perfect confidence that if either
receiving or sending them puts you to a farthing expense, you will
be so kind as to keep an account that we may repay the debt,
either through Mr Quillinan or otherwise.—

Many thanks for your visit to my young Bookseller Friend,[1]
who expresses himself as pleased with the attention—the like had
been paid him by Mr Quillinan—

Mrs Hemmans[2] has been staying with us a fortnight, and one of
her Sons also, a very interesting boy, 11 years of age. She has
taken lodgings upon the Banks of Windermere, and we expect her
this afternoon to tea with two other of her Sons. We should have
enjoyed Mrs Hemans company more had it not been for the deranged health both of my Sister and Daughter; which made us
anxious and cast a cloud over our spirits. She is a great Enthusiast
both in Poetry and music, and enjoys this beautiful Country as
much as any one can do who is new to such scenery.

Ever faithfully yours
W Wordsworth

553. W. W. to WILLIAM ROWAN HAMILTON

Address: Professor Hamilton, Dunsink Observatory, Dublin.
Postmark: (1) 11 July 1830 (2) 12 July 1830.
Stamp: Kendal Penny Post.
MS. Cornell. Hitherto unpublished.

Friday morn. 9th July [1830]

My dear Mr Hamilton,

I lose not a moment in replying to your Letter, the delicacy of
which I thoroughly feel. But I can honestly assure you that we shall
all be grieviously disappointed if your Sister and you do not come
as was proposed and urged in my last.[3]—My Daughter's health
has within these two or three days improved decidedly, you need

---

[1] Edward Moxon. See L. 542 above.
[2] For Mrs. Hemans's visit, see L. 546 above.   [3] L. 551 above.

not therefore be under apprehension; but above all, you need not doubt but that even if she should have a relapse, care will be taken that she does not suffer from the presence of our Friends, and we will deal so openly and sincerely with you that you may be confident, if any sacrifices on her account or any other are called for while you are here, you will be told so.

Therefore if we hear nothing from you to the contrary we shall expect [you]¹ in the last week of this month.

Ever with kind remembrances to all around you,
sincerely yours
Wm Wordsworth

554. D. W. to JOHN and JANE MARSHALL

Address: John Marshall Esqre M.P., Hill Street, London.
Postmark: 15 July 1830. *Stamp*: Kendal Penny Post.
Endorsed: 13 July 1830— the Marriage of J. Wordsworth. Congratulations on my Father's retiring from Parliament.
MS. WL.
LY i. 493.

Rydal Mount July 13th [1830]

My dear Mr Marshall,

As it is possible that parliament may be dissolved before this reaches its destination, I will not run the risque of your having to pay double postage, but my letter will be addressed to your Wife, therefore be so good as to give it to her without having the trouble of reading it yourself.

To Mrs Marshall.

My dear Friend

Your letter of the 27th of last month would not have remained so long unanswered (for we felt ourselves greatly obliged by your early communication of Mr Marshall's important resolve)² had not I wished at the same time to tell you of an event likely very soon to take place in our family, which until now I have not been at liberty to do *in full*—and half intelligence is often worse than none at all. Know then that my eldest Nephew, John Wordsworth of Rydal, is engaged to be married to Miss Curwen, the eldest Daughter of

¹ *Word dropped out.*
² To resign his seat in Parliament. John Marshall had represented Yorkshire since 1826.

Mr Curwen of Workington and Belle Isle. The acquaintance began some months ago in consequence of John's being, at Moresby, a neighbour of the Curwen Family, but the engagement has not been of very long standing; and the marriage will most likely be before the end of October. During Dora's stay with her Brother she saw a good deal of Miss Curwen, visited several times at Workington Hall, and spent a few days there at one time, and very much did Miss C. and she take to each other. John was then a hearty admirer; but it was not till after his Sister had left him that he ventured to offer himself to the young Lady. She immediately accepted his addresses on condition of parents' approval. This was immediately granted on the side of *her* parents i.e., as soon as it was made known to them; but before that time John's Father and Mother had discouraged him most decidedly; they disapproving very much of long protracted engagements; and John's present preferment being so small as to render marriage—without first waiting for a better Living—a very imprudent step, unless matters were made easy in another way. On this account, my Brother and Sister (and we all joined in giving such counsel) advised John not to follow up the proposal already made to Miss C. by laying it before her Father. In the meantime, however, she herself had opened out her mind; and both her Father and Mother willingly, nay *joyfully*, gave their consent—and not only so, Mr Curwen proposed to do every thing in his power to render the accomplishment of the young People's wishes easy to them. About that time Mr Curwen's Family was removing from Workington to Belle Isle; and as soon as possible they came to spend a day with us. Mr Curwen, during his Father's life-time resided at Belle Isle;[1] but, strange as it may appear we had never been in his company; for, until the old man's death, he lived quite retired. My Brother had visited him when at Moresby in the Spring; but even *he* had never had any other intercourse with Mr Curwen; but our *Family-meeting* at Rydal Mount was really like a meeting of old Friends.

Nothing could be kinder or more affectionate than the manners of both Father and Mother—and, as to their Daughter, we were all charmed with the sweetness of *her* manners and deportment. A few days after this meeting, Miss Curwen went to London with her Mother; and returned home last Wednesday—and on Friday, her Father and Mother again accompanied her hither, and left her

---

[1] Belle Isle on Windermere had been acquired by the Curwens during the lifetime of Henry Curwen's father, John Christian Curwen, who had laid out the grounds. The highly unusual mansion, cylindrical in shape, with a dome and lantern, was designed by John Plaw in 1774.

with us; and we expect she will remain at Rydal Mount till next week. John arrived yesterday, and has procured a substitute for his next Sunday's duty, so we shall probably have his company for about ten days.

Never was there so happy a Creature as he appears to be at this moment. Sincerely do I hope and pray that he may prove worthy of the treasure he has obtained in the affections of as pure minded and amiable a woman as I ever had an opportunity of knowing. Miss Curwen is *interesting* in appearance rather than *pretty* or handsome; her manners and address are Lady-like, though perhaps at first even *painfully* shy; but that shyness soon wears off, though her modesty is always remarkable. She gains daily and hourly on our affections; for she has great good sense, an excellent judgment, and, in every thing she does or says, you can trace the best of dispositions. My Brother and Sister both desired me to write to you today, as being the first day on which I was at liberty to name the Lady destined to be their daughter. They beg that you and Mr Marshall will accept their affectionate regards; and they add that they are assured of your sympathy on this occasion. I ought to add that Mr Curwen's conduct through the whole affair has been the most disinterested (I may say the most *generous*) that could be imagined. He is quite delighted with the connexion.

Poor Dora is very happy in the prospect of having a Sister, who is disposed to share in all her feelings; and they now are in a state of perfect enjoyment in each other's society. We trust that she will have quite regained her strength before October; for she has lately made rapid advances; but till *very lately* we have been kept exceedingly anxious and uneasy. She is now able to take short rides on horseback or in the pony-chaise; her looks are improving, and her appetite is not bad, and she has, in fact, now no actual malady to struggle with—unless her still-lingering weakness may be called so.

To turn to the subject of your letter—My dear Friend, I do from the bottom of my heart congratulate you upon Mr Marshall's withdrawing from the very arduous office which he has so honorably and usefully held, though I foresee some present loss to himself in the want of occupation sufficiently interesting during the period of your residence in London. But dear Jane, another parliament would have been too much to look forward to!—health and strength for the fatigues anxieties and late hours of another six or seven years! Besides, while in the country his quietly active mind always finds sufficient employment, and of that kind best suited both to his early and later habits—and, *even in London*, when I consider the variety of his tastes, and the multiplicity of his affairs and of his connections, it seems to me that he will have more than enough of salutary employment to satisfy the craving of any mind however active, that has borne the Brunt sixty years. We hear of parliament being dissolved on the 19th. This will set you all at liberty; and I can fancy Mr Marshall the gladdest of the glad on returning to his beautiful home among the mountains, without being subject to a Call of Committees but free to stay in the quiet retirement that you all love so much, till winter storms drive you away; or you are drawn to other quarters by other domestic ties or by private concerns of business or friendship. Heartily shall I rejoice to hear of your safe arrival, with good tidings of the Daughters you will leave behind; and of the Travellers abroad, who I hope are now in complete enjoyment in the romantic country of Switzerland. You have not mentioned that Party in your two last letters; but I conclude all was well when you heard of them. Your account of dear Ellen[1] and her Sister Dora was most satisfactory. God grant that they may spend a happy summer together, and free from extreme pain!

We had a note from Patterdale Hall this morning—written in pretty good spirits; but as you may suppose, with longings for the arrival of Husband and Friends. The weather has lately been so bad as to make home the only desireable place; otherwise we should have grieved much at not seeing Mrs W. M.[2] during her time of solitude. The two last days have been fine, and will I hope set her to thinking of crossing Kirkstone, and if the Rain keeps off and the cold abates, we venture yet to hope that we may see her. It is long since I heard from Halifax except indirectly, through the Friend of a Lady passing through Ambleside, that Mrs W. Rawson was quite well. On Sunday evening a Mr and Mrs McVicar[3] and their two daughters (introduced to my Brother by Bishop Hobart[4] of New York) informed us that Mr and Mrs Day[5] and Georgina Ferguson

[1] Jane Marshall's fifth daughter. 'Dora', Ellen's sister, is Jane Dorothea, now Mrs. Temple (see L. 463 above).

[2] For Mrs. William Marshall, see L. 483 above.

[3] The Revd. John MacVickar (1787–1868), Professor of Moral Philosophy at Columbia College, New York, and one of the earliest teachers of political economy in the United States. He had visited Coleridge the previous month, and after spending two days at Rydal Mount (10–11 July), went on to see Southey and Scott. He wrote an influential tract *Hints on Banking* (1827), and a two-part biography of Bishop Hobart (1834–6), and in 1839 wrote the introduction to the New York edition of Coleridge's *Aids to Reflection*.

[4] For Bishop Hobart see pt. i, L. 141.

[5] For John Day and his wife, see L. 463 above.

had been their Fellow-passengers to Liverpool and that Sarah and Elizabeth Ferguson[1] had remained at New York to visit the Falls of Niagara, and would return to England in the Autumn. This American Family interested us exceedingly—Father, Mother, and Daughters—all as agreeable and as well-informed and well-mannered people as ever I saw. You cannot think how much I was pleased on discovering their intimacy with the Days and the Fergusons. They spoke of Mr Day with the highest respect as a man of ten thousand. This Family party had crossed the Atlantic on account of Mr McVicar's health. He is a professor in the College at New York. They are going to Scotland and mean to travel on the Continent as far as Switzerland. They have left six Children at home.

I must not cross any more of my paper or you will not be able to read. Adieu. Believe me ever your affectionate Friend

D. Wordsworth

What a loss shall I have of Mr Marshall's franks! My love to your Sisters.

555. D. W. to ELIZABETH HUTCHINSON[2]

Address: To Miss Elizabeth Hutchinson, Brinsop Court, Herefordshire.
MS. WL.
LY i. 497.

Rydal Mount, 16th July 1830

My dear God-daughter

As the time approaches when we are to lose the pleasant company of your Brother[3] I will prepare a letter, being perfectly at leisure; and, were I to delay till the last day, some engagement or employment might arise to prevent my writing at all;

I must first thank you for your pretty letter, and very acceptable present. I assure you I was in want of just such a pincushion as you have sent me, therefore I prize it on that account; but still more as a mark of your attention to an old Friend and as a proof of your skill in the use of the needle. I am, indeed very glad to find that you are so neat a workwoman. Now, having expressed

[1] Georgina, Sarah, and Elizabeth were the daughters of Samuel Ferguson and had accompanied their uncle and aunt to America. See L. 463 above.
[2] Daughter of Thomas and Mary Hutchinson of Brinsop: known in the family as 'Ebba'.
[3] Young Tom Hutchinson, who had been staying at Rydal Mount

my satisfaction in the progress you have made in one needful accomplishment, I must tell you that the penmanship and expression of your letter gave me much pleasure. You will write an excellent plain hand; for your letters are well-shaped. I advise you, for a long time, to continue to write a large hand, which will fix the character of your penmanship and prevent careless habits of scrawling, which young people are apt to fall into. I give you the warning from personal experience of a contrary course. When I was a little girl, like you, I wrote very neatly and also what was called *a very good hand*; but with making French exercises and scribbling long letters to one of my Companions I fell into a careless way of making crooked lines and irregular words, and have never been able to get the better of it. There is one fault in *grammar* in your letter which I take a Godmother's privilege to tell you of. You say your 'Father took Mary and *I* on our ponies'. Now you ought to have written it 'took Mary and *me*'. This is a very common mistake, but when you are once told of it, I think you will not again fall into it. *I* is the *nominative* case (to speak in school language) and you have used it instead of the *accusative*. You will see my meaning—(or your Mother or Miss Urwick[1] will explain it to you) when I reverse your words—Father took *I* and Mary etc'—You could not possibly have written thus had you put yourself *first*. You would have said '*me* and Mary'.

Your Brother went to Keswick yesterday, where I doubt not he will be very happy with Cuthbert Southey and his sisters. He has yet another visit to pay of which I doubt not, he will give you a pleasant report; for it will be to a delightful place, namely the great Island on Windermere, and he will have one nice companion of his own age, the youngest son[2] of Mr Curwen. Tom will tell you what a pleasing young Lady Miss Curwen is, and I have now much pleasure in imparting a secret to you, that Miss Curwen is likely soon to be numbered among your Cousins. She is engaged to be married to your Cousin John; and I think the marriage will take place before Christmas.

Your Cousin Dora has been very ill; and she long remained extremely weak; but she is now fast recovering, and will, I hope be quite well long before she is called upon to act as Bridesmaid.

Dora joins with me in love to Mrs Lough[3] and in best thanks for her kind wish to see us again and for her anxious inquiries after

---

[1] Governess to the Hutchinson children (see also *MW*, p. 132).
[2] William Blamire Curwen (1816–99).
[3] Mrs. Letitia Luff, or Lough, of Fox Ghyll, who had visited Brinsop.

our health. She will, I know, rejoice to hear that Dora is so much better, and that I am quite well.

It happened that when your Aunt Sarah wrote I was very poorly; but I assure my kind Friends at Brinsop that it was only an accidental illness which passed off in a day or two; and since the month of January I have been as well as most people—indeed, I may say, in perfect health, though I have never tired myself with taking long walks or encountering any sort of fatigue.

Your Uncle and Aunt Wordsworth, and John are quite well; and we have today had a chearful letter from William, who also says that *he* is quite well. This good account of William has made his Mother very happy for she had been made anxious by the former reports of his state of health. The winter was even much colder at Bremen (in Germany) than with us, and the cold did not agree with William; and when the ice broke up the great River Weser made such large and extensive floods as to render the air very damp and unwholesome, so I doubt not your cousin often wished himself at home again among our dry mountains and clear lakes and chearful fast-flowing rivulets. He is now residing at Neu[w]ied, a pretty town on the right Bank of the Rhine where the country is very pleasant with hill and dale-vineyards, gardens, castles and villages.

I have been trying to recollect some news for you; but as you know nobody who lives here-abouts I cannot hit upon anything worthy of being related. This morning a letter reached us from your Mother to your Aunt Sarah. I am sorry to find that the weather in Herefordshire has been no better than with us; and in some respects you have suffered more than we; for very little of the hay has yet been mown, and we still hope for a favourable change, in which case we should have the advantage over your richer country. At present, however, there is no sign of amendment—it is only between heavy showers that our young Ladies can venture out; and we are very sorry for this, as nothing is so beneficial to your cousin Dora's health as fresh air with gentle exercise. I hope it will not be very long before your Sister Mary,[1] after the example of Tom, becomes acquainted with this lake and mountain country; and after Mary *your* turn will come and I doubt not you will both be as much pleased as he has been. We hear rumours of a Contest at the next Election; but no candidate except the Lowthers, has yet offered, so we are in *hopes* that the Election may pass over quietly. Though in one respect we shall be great losers, for in case of a

---

[1] Mary Monkhouse Hutchinson (1817–37).

contest, we should certainly have the happiness of seeing your Father and your Uncle Monkhouse at Rydal.[1]

You must give my best love to Mary and George;[2] and tell Sarah[3] something about your Godmother in Westmorland that when I come to Brinsop she may not look on me as a perfect stranger. I should like very much to see her and to renew my acquaintance with Brinsop Court and its pleasant neighbourhood.

Give my love to your Father and Mother and Uncle Monkhouse. Tell them we are very sorry that Tom's holiday-time is so short. I think he has spent his days very happily, and am sure of this, that he has been an exceedingly good Boy, and has won the regard of all who know him, and we shall part from him with regret. I wish I could have sent you a more entertaining letter; but hope that Tom will make amends for it by a narrative of all his adventures; and he will tell you about the Miss Southeys, the Master Hemans's[4] and all the young people with whom he has become acquainted. I hope you will write to me again when you have an opportunity, and believe me to be, my dear Elizabeth

your affectionate Friend and Godmother
Dorothy Wordsworth

The Miss Cooksons[5] are comfortably settled in a very pretty Cottage at Ambleside, and your Godmother, Miss Cookson, is in perfect health. She often walks between Ambleside and Rydal.

---

[1] The election was in the event uncontested (see L. 562 below), so that Thomas Hutchinson and John Monkhouse of Stow did not need to come to Westmorland to exercise their voting rights as freeholders in the Ivy How estate in Langdale (see *MY* ii. 509).

[2] George, the Hutchinsons' younger son.

[3] Ebba's younger sister.

[4] Mrs. Hemans's three boys, who were staying with her in Ambleside (see L. 546 above).

[5] Thomas Cookson of Kendal had fallen on hard times, and Elizabeth and her sister had opened a day school in Ambleside to relieve their father of expense (see *SH*, p. 372).

556. W. W. to SIR WALTER SCOTT

Address: Sir Walter Scott Bart, Abbotsford, Melrose. [*In Dora W.'s hand*]
Stamp: Kendal Penny Post.
Endorsed: W. Wordsworth.
MS. National Library of Scotland.
K (—). *LY i. 500.*

Rydal Mount—sometimes called Idle-Mount, and in the
address of your last misnamed Mount-Rydal—
20th July [1830]

I feel truly obliged, dear Sir Walter, by your attention to Mr
Christian's wishes.[1] He is perfectly satisfied. When I mentioned the
matter to you I had not the least suspicion of an event being in
progress, which has already connected me with the family of Christian by a tie much stronger than that of common acquaintance. My
eldest Son has been accepted by Miss Curwen, with the entire
approbation of her Parents, as her future husband, and they are soon
to be married. She is now upon a visit to us, and we are quite
charmed with her amiable disposition, her gentleness, her delicacy,
her modesty, her sound sense, and right notions—so that my son
has a prospect before him as bright as Man can wish for.

It would gratify me much, very much to visit you, and soon—
but I fear that it cannot be effected. In the last week of this month,
I expect Mr Hamilton, Professor of Astronomy in Trin. Coll.
Dublin to stay with me a fortnight—then comes my Brother the
Master of Trin: Coll. from Cambridge—and a greater obstacle
than any of these is the delicate state of my Daughter's health.—
She was attacked with bilious fever two months ago, left very
weak, and makes little progress towards recovery of her strength.
Gladly would I have brought her to see you and yours—but she
has been and is too weak to bear the excitement of company even
in our own House; and though the medical Attendant recommends
travel, it is rather to avoid company than to seek it. If the weather
would take up, we would venture upon a Tour along the sea coast
under the protection of one of her Aunts, and a trusty Servnt, and
this is the utmost she is equal to. So that all that remains for me is
a hope of getting on the top of a Coach, and visiting you alone
during the winter, or under favorable auspices next summer with
some part of my family, wife, daughter or Sister. This last had
also a severe and dangerous illness about 18 months ago which has

[1] Concerning *Peveril of the Peak*. See L. 539 above.

made havoc with her Constitution that will, I fear long be felt, if not to the end of her days.—Excuse this melancholy account which you would have been spared did I not know that you are seriously interested in what touches me so nearly.—

I hear frequently of Southey who is well and very industrious. Coleridge has also rallied from an Illness with which he was seized in Spring. From Rogers I heard the other day—I believe he is quite in force—and seems though a Bachelor likely to make a happy old Man. Mrs Hemans lately stayed a fortnight with us and is now lodged upon the banks of Windermere along with three of her Sons—all fine Boys.

Among the points many and various which I should like to discuss with you, is one in which surely your family is interested far above that of any other; I mean the short duration of Author's copyright according to the now existing Law. Am I right in supposing that 28 years would put an end to the pecuniary interest of a family in a posthumous work—and that all Works become publick property immediately after an Author's death provided they have been published that period of years? If so the law is exceedingly unjust, and ought to be altered—but perhaps I am mistaken as to the fact.—

Pray remember us kindly to Mr and Mrs Lockhart and to Miss Scott—and accept for them and yourself our best wishes, and believe me my dear Sir Walter very faithfully yours

Wm Wordsworth

557. M. W. to WILLIAM ROWAN HAMILTON

Address: Mr Professor Hamilton, Post Off., Kendal.
Stamp: Kendal Penny Post.
MS. Cornell. Hitherto unpublished.

Sat: morn^g [24 July 1830][1]

My dear Sir,

I write a line from Ambleside to welcome you and your Sister on this side the Channel—and to thank you for your thoughtfulness in not coming upon us unawares, which under other circumstances

[1] W. R. Hamilton and his sister Eliza left Dublin on 21 July for their promised visit to the Lakes and Rydal Mount (see Ls. 545 and 551 above). They stayed with the Wordsworths about three weeks, visiting Belle Isle and Lowther Castle, and meeting Mrs Hemans; and on their return journey to Whitehaven they called on Southey. See *Hamilton*, i. 368–9, 384–8.

would have been of no consequence—but tonight and tomorrow night our beds are really all engaged. On Monday morning 3 of our present Household leave us, and on that day we shall be most happy to receive you. I the less regret this delay as Mr Wordsworth is at present at Lowther Castle—he will certainly be at home tomorrow evening or early on Monday, and will rejoice that he is so soon to have the pleasure of meeting his Irish friends.

> With much esteem believe me to be very truly y^{rs}
> M. Wordsworth.

558. D. W. to GEORGE HUNTLY GORDON

Address: G. Huntley Gordon Esqre.
Endorsed: Miss Wordsworth. 25th July/30.
MS. Cornell.
Broughton, p. 38.

Rydal Mount 25th July [1830]

My dear Sir,

You are so kindly disposed to serve us that I know you will find it more easy to pardon the liberty I am taking than I do to excuse myself; for I am really very unwilling to trouble you with another enclosure so soon after our last, especially as I am conscious that with a little more fore-thought I might have spared you this second trouble. My letter for Boulogne *might* have been ready; and sent at the same time with Mrs Wordsworth's last to William at Neuwyd. Having confessed this much, I trust your good-will for forgiveness, only must stipulate that you deal frankly with me—and that if it be inconvenient to you to forward so many letters to so many different quarters as I have ventured to charge you with—you will tell me so.

You will be glad to hear that my letter for *Rome* was duly received, and has brought us a most interesting reply from an excellent Friend, who intends to spend another winter in Italy. He was our companion on the Continent in our Tour of 1820, recorded by my Brother in his 'Memorials' and promises speedily, after his return to England next year to make his way to Rydal Mount and retrace by our fire-side the wanderings of this, his much longer journey. Mr Henry Crabbe Robinson (*that* is our Friend's name) makes London his home—and I am sure you will be glad to become acquainted with him, and my Brother to be the means of making you so when he returns.

I am sorry to send this, unaccompanied by a line from my Brother. He is gone from home for a few days.

I kept back my letters—and now my Brother is at home again; and as he himself intends writing I will trouble you no further; and pray dear Sir, believe me to be, with much respect

Your much obliged
(though unknown) Friend
Dorothy Wordsworth

I am happy to tell you that my Niece's health has, of late, been much improved; and we trust that a little time will restore her strength.

27th July

559. W. W. to SAMUEL ROGERS

Address: S. Rogers Esqre, St James's Place.
Postmark: 30 [July] 1830.
Endorsed: not to be published S. R.
MS. Sharpe Collection, University College, London.
Rogers. LY i. 502.

Rydal Mount
Friday [30 July 1830]

I cannot sufficiently thank you, my dear Rogers, for your kind and long Letter,[1] knowing as I do how much you dislike writing. Yet I should not have written now but to say I was not aware that you had any such near connections in the Church; I had presumed that your Relatives by both sides were Dissenters,[2] or I should have been silent on the subject; being well assured that I and mine would always have your good word as long as we continued to deserve it.

Lord Lonsdale, to whom I mentioned my son's intended Marriage, naming (as I was at liberty to do in *that* case) the Lady, has written to me in answer with that feeling and delicacy which mark the movements of his mind and the actions of his life. He is one of the best and most amiable of men; and I should detest myself if I could fail in gratitude for his goodness to me upon all occasions.

---

[1] Rogers's (undated) reply to W. W.'s letter of 16 June (L. 546 above) is among the *WL MSS*.

[2] For Samuel Rogers's Non-conformist background, see P. W. Clayden, *The Early Life of Samuel Rogers*, 1887, ch. i. In his letter, Rogers described the predicament of his nephew, 'as learned and as honest a man as any in England', who could not get preferment in the Church.

I wish Lady Frederick's mind were at ease on the subject of the Epitaph.¹ Upon her own ideas, and using mainly her own language, I worked at it—but the production I sent was too long and somewhat too historical—yet assuredly it wanted neither discrimination nor feeling. Would Lady F. be content to lay it aside till she comes into the North this summer, as I hope she will do. We might then lay our judgements together in conversation, and with the benefit of your suggestions and those of other friends with which she is no doubt furnished, we might be satisfied at last. Pray name this to her, if you have an opportunity.—

Your Italy² can no where, out of your own family, be more eagerly expected than in this House. The Poetry is excellent we know, and the Embellishments, as they are under the guidance of your own taste, must do honor to the Arts. My Daughter, alas, does not recover her strength; she has been thrown back several times by the exercise, whether of walking in the Garden or of riding, which she has with our approbation been tempted to take, from a hope of assisting nature.

We like Mrs Hemans much—her conversation is what might be expected from her Poetry, full of sensibility—and she enjoys the Country greatly.

The Somnambulist³ is one of several Pieces, written at a heat, which I should have much pleasure in submitting to your judgement were the fates so favorable as that we might meet ere long. How shall I dare to tell you that the Muses and I have parted company— at least I fear so, for I have not written a verse these twelve months past, except a few stanzas⁴ upon my return from Ireland, last autumn.

---

¹ Lord Lonsdale's daughter, Lady Frederick Bentinck (see pt. i, L. 43), had sought W. W.'s advice about an epitaph for the memorial to her late husband which was about to be set up in the south aisle of Lowther parish church. In his letter to W. W., Rogers wrote: 'Lady Fredᵏ, as you know, is very anxious about the Epitaph, and I wish you were here to assist, for I am utterly incapable.'

² The illustrated *Italy* (see L. 538 above).

³ *PW* iv. 49, 410–11. The idea for the poem arose out of an expedition with Rogers and Sir George Beaumont to Ullswater and Lyulph's Tower in the summer of 1826.

⁴ In Nov. 1829 W. W. had considerably expanded the original version of *On the Power of Sound* (see pt. i, L. 386 and *PW* ii. 323, 525). In the I. F. note, W. W. later recalled the addition of the lines about the eagle in stanza xiii, which were suggested by his experience near the Giant's Causeway during the Irish tour; but Dora W.'s letter to E. Q. of 21 Nov. 1829 describes a more fundamental revision of the whole poem, including the moving of the original opening stanza to another place, and the composition of another stanza to make a better introduction. 'We all think there is a grandeur in this Poem but it

Dear Sir Walter! I love that Man, though I can scarcely be said to have lived with him at all; but I have known him for nearly 30 years. Your account of his seizure grieved us all much.[1] Coleridge[2] had a dangerous attack a few weeks ago; Davy[3] is gone. Surely these are men of power, not to be replaced should they disappear, as one has done.

Pray repeat our cordial remembrances to your Brother and Sister, and be assured, my dear Rogers, that you are thought of in this house, both by the well and the sick, with affectionate interest—ever faithfully yours

Wm Wordsworth

560. W. W. to JOHN MITCHINSON CALVERT[4]

Address: Dr Calvert, Ryde, Isle of Wight.
MS. untraced.
LY i. 512.

[Summer 1830][5]

My dear Dr Calvert, or as I would still rather say for the sake of old times, dear John Calvert, my wife and sister and I cannot sufficiently thank you for your kind and considerate letter to John, which does equal honour to your head and heart. We have suffered so much in the case of the deranged health of our own daughter that Mrs W. and I could not but be anxious lest Miss Curwen's constitution had been seriously injured by her long and dangerous illness. Nothing, therefore, could be more welcome than an assurance to the contrary from such a quarter.

ought to have been in the "Recluse" and Mother on that account but half enjoys it.' (*WL MSS.*) W. W. seems to have forgotten that he composed two other poems in the autumn of the previous year, *Liberty* and *Humanity* (*PW* iv. 153, 102).

[1] 'Scott was coming, when an illness alarmed him and the Lockharts are gone to him. It is his habit to sleep after dinner—and, not awakening at the normal time, his daughter roused him—when he was unable to speak; nor did his speech return to him for some minutes—a violent affection of the nerves, no doubt and a warning that will not, I hope, be lost upon him.' Scott's *Journal* breaks off on 18 July and was not resumed until 5 Sept.

[2] See Griggs, vi. 841.

[3] Sir Humphry Davy had died at Geneva on 28 May.

[4] For Dr. John Calvert, see L. 403 above.

[5] According to de Selincourt, who saw the MS., this letter is undated; but it must have been written some time between John W.'s engagement in June and his marriage in October.

561. W. W. to GEORGE HUNTLY GORDON

Address: G: Huntley Gordon Esqre. [*In Dora W.'s hand*]
MS. Cornell.
Broughton, p. 39.

[early Aug. 1830]

My dear Mr Gordon,

Accept my sincere thanks for so long a Letter written under such pressure of business—which I hope has not continued into the season of severe heat which has prevailed here for some days.— W^m has reached Neuwied upon the Rhine a couple of leagues below Coblentz where in all probability he will remain a month or two. His health is considerably improved but he speaks of himself as being very weak yet, compared with what he was 18 or 20 months ago.—You will oblige me by putting my name down as a Subscriber to Mr Klauer's Manual;[1] W^m, with his best thanks to you, declines it, as he is in the Country—and does not wish at present to encrease his number of Books—Professor Hamilton, Trin. Coll. Dublin is now with me and begs to have his name put down as a Subscriber. His Book may be sent to Hodges and Smith Booksellers, College Green, Dublin. As they are Booksellers in pretty extensive business Mr Klauer's Publisher will have no difficulty in finding out their London Correspondent. My Copy might be sent as usual to Whitakers, Ave Mary Lane, to be forwarded in Mr Troughtons first Parcel to Ambleside; and paid for through your kindness—

I know not whether the name of Mr Hamilton may have reached you. He is a young man of great Genius—especially for Mathematics—and was called to the chair of Prof^r of Astro^y as Successor to Dr Brinkley now Bp of Cloyne.—Mr H's Sister is also staying with us. Her poetical genius is highly promising, and her modest and unassuming manners have recommended her much to the Ladies of this family. Yester afternoon we had Mrs Hemans who favored us with music. She is restricted from singing by her medical advisers, but she plays upon the Piano with great feeling and taste. We meet her tomorrow also.—I could say much very much in praise of Mrs Hemans—but certainly, though I beg it may not be repeated from me—as she has been our Inmate, there is a draw-back. Her conversation, like that of many literary Ladies, is too elaborate and studied—and perhaps the simplicity of her character is impaired by the homage which has been paid her—both for her accomplishments and her Genius.

[1] Wilhelm Klauer-Klattowsky, *Deutsches Handbuch, The German Manual or Self-Tuition*, 2 vols., London, 1831.

We have had here a more than tropical heat for a few days, two of which we employed in Excursions upon the water, and in the recesses of the mountains, where we dined one day in a chasm fanned by the breath of a waterfall and which not a sunbeam could penetrate. The shade and coolness were delicious—The heather was blooming luxuriantly on the rocky shelves of the chasm, and the honey suckle hung from the rocks in full flower—not at all impoverished by its sequestration from the sun but of more delicate hue.

If you happen to see Miss Jewsbury pray give our kind regards and caution her from me not to fatigue herself, and to avoid being over stimulated by London Society.—Have you heard of Mrs Heber's[1] marriage to a Greek Count—Frailty thy name is woman —She is gone with her Bridegroom to Paris, on her way to Corfu his place of abode—

We have not received the copy of South[2] yet—think no more about the unfortunate shilling—We cannot come at the truth without hunting back among Letters which are probably mislaid— for I grieve to say ours is a house of confusion in this point from our having so many correspondents in common.—

Farewell and believe with kind regards from all my family most sincerely

Your friend
Wm Wordsworth

You never mention Major and Mrs. Gordon.[3] How are they?[4]
We enclose a Letter to Wm and are thankful for our Letters being forwarded as far as they can.

---

[1] See also *SH*, p. 372. She was Amelia, daughter of Dr. Shipley, Dean of St. Asaph, and had married Reginald Heber in 1809. He had died in Trichinopoly in 1826, and her *Life of Reginald Heber, D.D., Lord Bishop of Calcutta* appeared in 2 vols. in 1830, the year when, to the consternation of her late husband's family, she married Sir Demetrie Valsamachi, an Ionian count. See *The Heber Letters*, ed. R. H. Cholmondeley, 1950, pp. 336–7.

[2] Perhaps as Broughton suggests, Robert South (1634–1716), the celebrated preacher and divine, whose *Sermons Preached upon Several Occasions*, 6 vols., 1727, are listed in the *R.M. Cat.*, no. 295.

[3] Huntly Gordon's parents, resident in Brussels (see pt. i, L. 351).

[4] The last part of this letter, including the signature, has been cut away, presumably for the autograph, and the missing words copied in (probably by Huntly Gordon). The missing portion of the original letter has recently come to light and is among the Cornell MSS.

562. D. W. to C. W.

Address: The Revd Dr Wordsworth, Great Hotel, Buxton, Derbyshire.
Stamp: Kendal Penny Post.
MS. British Library. Hitherto unpublished.

Green Bank, Ambleside[1]
Friday 6th August [1830]

My dear Brother,

Your letter has just reached me, and I answer it by return of post, as you will be anxious to know how we are going on, and to arrange your own plans accordingly; but first I must say it has been daily a disappointment that we did not hear of your being actually fixed at Buxton some time ago—then came the newspaper report of your appearance at Court,[2]—which left us quite in the dark, except thus far—that we were afraid something further had delayed you, and that you remained uncertain as to the time, of your coming—which caused your silence. This morning's letter has cleared away all doubts; and we may now I hope reckon upon seeing you in little more than a fortnight. I cannot but grieve that your time with us has been shortened; but am very thankful for what is left—and would by no means wish you to shorten your stay at Buxton; but give the Waters a fair and thorough trial; therefore I shall not even *think* of your moving in *less* than three weeks from your arrival there. The end of that time I shall fix upon in my own mind for expecting you to set off; but let us hear again when your departure is fixed on: remember, however, that the curing your rheumatism is the first object, and do not, for the sake of a few days or a week more or less to be spent with us, cut your trial of the Waters short. I press this the more, because, from what I have heard at Halifax concerning rheumatic patients cured at Buxton, I have always wished *you* to go thither.

Our last letters from William brought much better accounts of his health. According to his Father's instructions, he quitted his kind Friends at Bremen, travelled by Land to Dusseldorf on the Rhine and thence to Cologne—and so on, by steam up the River—as far as Neuwyd on the right Bank (about 2 leagues from Coblentz) where he is now comfortably settled, and his strength, we hope, is returning. He says he is now quite well, excepting weakness.

---

[1] Home of Mrs. Benson Harrison, with whom D. W. was staying at the time of this letter.

[2] The Duke of Clarence (1765–1837) had been proclaimed King as William IV on 26 June, and on 19 July C. W. formed part of a deputation from the University of Cambridge to present a loyal address at St. James's Palace.

Your Cambridge Men are found in every pleasant place. Only think of W^m being in the same town with Hymers[1] and his Flock! Hymers and he drink tea together once in the week, and he gives him a little instruction in German. This, if continued, will be a great advantage to William—and he promises to avoid the Company of the rest of the English. He is now in a much better situation for learning to talk German than at Bremen, for there is only one inhabitant of Neuwyd who can speak English.

John very much regrets, as we all do, that the marriage ceremony cannot be performed by you. Mrs Curwen had asked her Brother (Mr Stanley,[2] Rector, I believe, of Plumblands) to do this office even at the very time we had thought of you. However, it is the less to be regretted that the appointment is not in our hands, as the marriage-day will not suit your time. It is not to be till the 11th of October—the day fixed by Mrs Curwen, it being that of her own marriage. Isabella Curwen is very much pleased with the thought of being so soon acquainted with you, and promises to come and stay with us while you are at Rydal. I am sure you will be as fond of her as she will be of you—for she is just such a person as you would most love and admire—but I will not enter into particulars—but leave you to feel and judge for yourself.

My dear Brother you inquire anxiously after my health—and glad, I know, you will be to hear that I am really quite well, though not yet so strong as formerly, but hope, through caretaking for a certain time, to become so.

Poor Dora has had a serious illness; and was very long in regaining strength: but within the last three weeks, the change has been wonderful; and I think she now looks better even than before she was called an invalid. At that time her complexion seemed clearly to indicate that something was amiss; but she thought herself well, until a violent bilious attack reduced her to extremity. She is now staying with her destined Sister at the Windermere Island—as happy and gay as possible. She is to be conveyed home on Monday by *Miss Curwen* and on the same day her Father and Mother will return. He went to Lowther on Wednesday to accompany Lord L. to the Election[3] at Appleby—and Mary crossed

---

[1] The Revd. John Hymers (1803–87), mathematician: Fellow of St. John's College, Cambridge, 1827–53, President, 1848–52, and thereafter rector of Brandesburton, Yorks.: a distant connection of W. W.'s.

[2] The Revd. Edward Stanley (1776–1834), son of Edward Stanley of Whitehaven and his wife Julia, daughter of John Christian of Ewanrigg: rector of Plumbland, near Maryport, 1802–34, rector of Workington, 1831–4.

[3] The proclamation of William IV was soon followed by the dissolution of Parliament (24 July) and a general election. Wellington's ministry could no

the Mountains with her Husband and will remain at Patterdale
till he rejoins her there. Professor Hamilton is with him—a very
interesting Man whom we wished that you should meet at Rydal
Mount; but he will be gone before your arrival.

I have been with our Cousin (late Dorothy Wordsworth of
Branthwaite) Mrs Harrison,—who lives near Ambleside, since
W^m and M. and D. left home, and shall remain here till Monday.
Mrs Harrison was, I believe, unborn when you were last at
Branthwaite.[1] She wishes very much to become acquainted with you.

Respecting your journey hither, the only advice I can give you
is, to take the Coach from Buxton to Manchester; and thence
proceed to Kendal either by the Mail or another of the two daily
Coaches. I do not think there is any Manchester Mail that goes
through Buxton; but, if there be, *that* probably would be the quick-
est conveyance: but I *know* that there is an excellent daily Coach,
(for I travelled in it myself when I went to Whitwick) which takes
four inside passengers—and I know also that your nearest and
best road is by Manchester.

I am very sorry to find Owen Lloyd's report of my Nephew
John's[2] present delicate state of health confirmed by yourself;
but hope with you that relaxation from study, and change of air
and scene will speedily restore him; and I only regret that he did
not choose the North for his holiday abode. Poor Owen has been
very low and anxious concerning his Mother, and Sisters;[3] but
the late reports of a restoration of present tranquillity at Paris[4]

longer count on Whig support, many Tories were disaffected, and the Duke,
who was committed to the existing system of representation, only lasted in
power until 15 Nov. In Westmorland the election proceeded quietly and on 6
Aug. Lord Lowther and Col. H. C. Lowther were returned unopposed; for
Henry Brougham stood and was returned as one of the members for Yorkshire,
and thus, as the *Westmorland Gazette* for 7 Aug. put it, 'political animosity'
was laid aside for the first time in many years. (See also *Carlisle Patriot* for
31 July and *Cumberland Pacquet* for 10 Aug.)

[1] Mrs. Benson Harrison, formerly Dorothy Wordsworth, was born at
Branthwaite, a small village near Workington, in 1801.

[2] John Wordsworth's weak health continued to give cause for alarm. Later
this year he was elected Fellow of Trinity.

[3] Charles Lloyd had moved his family to France some years before this. His
wife Sophia died later this month (see L. 574 below).

[4] Failing to make headway against the liberal opposition, Charles X and
his reactionary Polignac ministry issued ordinances abolishing the liberty of the
press, dissolving the newly-elected Chamber of Deputies, and summoning a
new Chamber under a system of election which violated the constitution. The
result was a popular uprising in Paris in the last days of July, which ended all
attempts to re-establish the tyranny of the old regime. The deputies assumed the
government, Charles and his descendants were excluded from the throne, and
Louis-Philippe, Duc d'Orléans (1773–1850), was proclaimed King on 7 Aug.

have allayed his anxiety; and he hopes they will not find much difficulty in returning to England. James Lloyd[1] is gone to France hoping to be useful as a protector.

I must now conclude, my dear Brother, with hearty wishes for a happy meeting. I need not tell you that we shall keep you among us as long as we can. Pray write again as soon as your day of departure is fixed that we may know when to expect you.

Believe me ever your
affec. Sister
D. Wordsworth

Saturday 7th Green Bank.

563. W. W. to GEORGE HUNTLY GORDON

Address: G: Huntly Gordon Esq. [*In Dora W.'s hand*]
MS. Cornell.
Mem. (—). *Grosart* (—). *K* (—). *LY i. 504* (—). *Broughton, p. 41.*

[mid-Aug. or later, 1830]

My dear Mr Gordon,

As W^m is on the move from Neuwied, will you be so kind as to forward this Letter direct, by the Post. We heard from him yesterday—he says he is well; but is far from having recovered the strength he lost at Bremen.—

I hope that your Father and Mother have not suffered from the commotion at Brussels.[2] I cannot but deeply regret that the late King of France and his ministers should have been so infatuated. Their stupidity not to say their crimes, has given an impulse to the revolutionary and democratic spirit, throughout Europe, which is premature, and from which much immediate evil may be apprehended, whatever things may settle into at last. Whereas had the government conformed to the encreasing knowledge of the People, and not surrender[ed] itself to the Councils of the Priests and the

---

[1] James Farmer Lloyd (1801–81), second son of Charles and Sophia Lloyd, and brother of Grosvenor (1800–40), Owen, Edward (1804–65), and Arthur Lloyd. There were five daughters of the marriage: Mary, Sophia, Priscilla, Agatha, and Louisa.

[2] Shortly after the July revolution in Paris (see previous letter), the people of Brussels rose in protest against the local system of taxes, established a provisional government, declared the separation of the Netherlands from Holland, and set about the election of a new King, excluding the House of Orange from the throne.

bigotted royalists, things might have been kept in an even course to the mutual improvement and benefit of both governed and governors.

In France incompatible things are aimed at; a monarchy and democracy to be united without an intervening aristocracy to constitute a graduated scale of power and influence. I cannot conceive how an hereditary monarchy can exist, without an hereditary peerage, in a country so large as France, nor how either can maintain their ground if the Law of the Napoleon Code compelling equal division of property by will, be not repealed. And I understand that a vast majority of the French are decidedly adverse to the repeal of that Law—which I cannot but think will erelong be found injurious both to France, and in its collateral effects to the rest of Europe. But why fatigue you with these dry speculations—

Mr Quillinan favored me a few days ago with an interesting Letter from Paris. You probably will be falling in with him shortly, as he was to set off from Paris last Wednesday. He will have much to tell you—Ever dear Mr Gordon, cordially and faithfully yours

Wm Wordsworth

564. W. W. to HENRY NELSON COLERIDGE

Address: Henry Nelson Coleridge Esqre. [*In M. W.'s hand*]
MS. *Victoria University Library, Toronto.*
LY i. 505.

[early Sept. 1830]

My dear Mr H. Coleridge,

I have long been in your debt, and having the advantage of a Frank, I sit down to *acknowledge* at least my obligation.—I have another motive for writing at present—to let you know that we have had the great pleasure of seeing here the other day your Father,[1] and Sister[2] and Mr Pattison etc. The weather was beautiful and they saw this place to the utmost advantage and seemed not a little delighted with it. Your Father I had never met before and I assure you I was highly gratified with making his acquaintance. We had all heard much of him from your Uncle S.[3] We found him however

---

[1] Col. James Coleridge, S. T. C.'s elder brother.
[2] Frances, married to John Patteson, the lawyer (see L. 482 above).
[3] Southey.

a very different man (at least I did) from what we had expected—
frank cordial and familiar in his manners—with nothing of the
stiffness of his Profession—it would have done you and Sara good
to see how happy he was, and what pleasure he found in talking
about you all.—I directed them where to find Hartley, who is in
his better way—dining about in respectable Houses—but he does
not come here. He has not been *formally*, though generally, invited
but he must know that he would be welcome as long as his conduct
is at all regular.—[1]

You will naturally expect some account of the Impression your
Book[2] made upon me. Where then shall I look for an apology
when I tell you what I must in truth do, that I have read it so
slightly as to feel myself scarcely at liberty to pass more than a
general judgement upon it, which is that it is creditable to the
author, and will I think do good to those for whom it is principally
intended. If I am not mistaken you and I had some talk about
Homer, when you were here, so that possibly you will not be at a
loss as to how far I am likely to agree with you. My own judgement I feel to be of no *especial* value, for I cannot pretend to have
read those Poems *critically*; and *scholastically* know little about
them,—but speaking from general impression and results I should
say that the Books of the Iliad were never intended to make one
Poem, and that the Odyssey is not the work of the same man or
exactly of the same age. These are startling things to affirm, but
as in respect to Ossian, to Rowley[3] etc, etc. there is or may be on
my mind a feeling and conviction, but slightly affected either for or

---

[1] Hartley's view of W. W. is given in his letter to Derwent Coleridge of
30 Aug.: 'Of Westmorland and the *old familiar faces*, what shall I say? All
are not gone—but most are changed. The Rydal Mount family perhaps the least
of any, tho' W. W. to me seems yearly less of the Poet, and more of the
respectable, talented, hospitable Country gentleman. Unfortunately, his
weakest points, his extreme irritability of self-approbation and parsimony of
praise to contemporary authors are much *in statu quo.* This is a little ungrateful,
for he always applauds my attempts; but what he would do, if they were favor-
ites with the public, no matter.' He adds later: 'I am afraid there is little hope
at present of another portion of the *Recluse*, but it must delight every lover of
mankind to see how the influence of Wordsworth's poetry is diverging, spreading over society, benefitting the heart and soul of the Species, and indirectly
operating upon thousands, who haply, never read, or will read, a single page of
his fine Volumes.' (*Letters of Hartley Coleridge*, ed. Griggs, pp. 111, 112.)

[2] *Introductions to the Study of the Greek Classic Poets. Designed Principally
for the Use of Young Persons at School and College*, 1830. This volume the first of
a projected series, dealt with Homer, and set out Henry Nelson Coleridge's
theory (which he shared with his father-in-law) that the *Iliad* was the work of
several poets. See S. T. Coleridge's *Table Talk* for 12 May 1830 and 9 July
1832.

[3] For Chatterton's authorship of the 'Rowley Poems', see L. 447 above.

against by such particulars of scholarship as I am at all competent to judge of. As to the merits of the Poetry, it is in my judgement only second to Shakespeare; at the same time I cannot but think that you in some points overrate the Homeric Poems, especially the manners. The manners are often to me an encumbrance in reading Homer as a *Poet*, using here (not very justifiably) manners, for designating customs, rules, ceremonies, minor incidents and details, costume etc. and for almost every thing, except natural appearances, that is not passion or character, or leading incident. As *history* those particulars are always more or less interesting, but as *Poetry*, they are to me often barely tolerable and not for their own sakes, but for the evidence they give of a mind in a state of sincerity and simplicity.

For the last five months I have lived in a constant bustle to which at present I see no termination. Give our kindest love to dear Sara—our thoughts are often and much with her and our best wishes to Mrs Coleridge also—and believe me my dear Sir

ever faithfully your obliged Wᵐ Wordsworth

565. W. W. to GEORGE HUNTLY GORDON

MS. Cornell.
Mem. (—). Grosart (—). K (—). LT i. 505 (—). Broughton, p. 42.

[Sept. 1830]

My dear Mr Gordon,

How sorry we are that you have had so much trouble about the Books—Before this is closed I shall see Mr [Troughton][1]—the direction I received from himself—I suppose the case is, that Parcels are forwarded to him not directly, but through the hands of Troughton's Kendal Correspondent—but I shall learn—

We have had more favorable Accounts of Wᵐ—in as much as he appears from his Letters to be in excellent spirits, and is silent upon the subject of his health—so that we doubt not that he is recovering his strength.—Thanks for your hint about Rhenish, strength from wine is good—from water still better.

One is glad to see tyranny baffled, and foolishness put to shame. But the French King and his Ministers will be unfairly judged by all those who take not into consideration the difficulties of their

---

[1] *MS. obscure.*

position.[1] It is not to be doubted, that there has long existed a determination, and that plans have been laid, to destroy the Government which the French received, as they felt, at the hands of the Allies —and their[2] pride could not bear—Moreover, the Constitution, had it been their own choice, would by this time have lost favor in the eyes of the French; as not sufficiently democratic for the high notion *that* People entertain of their fitness to govern themselves— Nous verrons—but for my own part, I'd rather fill the office of a Parish Beadle, than sit on the throne where the Duke of Orleans has suffered himself to be placed.—

The heat is gone and but that we have too much rain again, the Country would be enchanting—

With a thousand thanks I remain ever yours

Wm Wordsworth

[*M. W. writes*]

Parcels for Rydal Mount must be directed to Mr Troughton, Ambleside, *to the care of* Mr Richardson, Bookseller, *Kendal*, and sent to Whittaker and Co Ave Maria Lane to be forwarded by their first Parcel.

566. W. W. to WILLIAM ROWAN HAMILTON

MS. Cornell.
Hamilton. K (—). *LY i. 508* (—).

Thursday—9th Sep^br 1830.

My dear Mr Hamilton,

I deferred writing till I could procure a Frank from Mr W. Marshall; and this morning a party of us were to have crossed Kirkstone to spend two days in Patterdale; but the weather will not allow us to stir from here.—Tomorrow I hope will prove more favorable—

We were much pleased to learn from Miss E. Hamilton that your journey and voyage terminated so favorably so that your pleasurable remembrances will be unmixed with disagreeable ones—

We have had my Brother's company for a fortnight—and who do you think dined with us yesterday but Professor Airey and his *Bride*;[3] for so I will call her still though they were married last

---

[1] See L. 562 above. [2] their *written twice*.
[3] Professor Airy (see pt. i, L. 8) had married Ricarda, eldest daughter of the Revd. Richard Smith, rector of Edensor, near Chatsworth, on 24 Mar. 1830.

March. The P^r had hoped to meet with you in this country, which would have been highly gratifying to him. He looks forward to the pleasure of seeing you some time or other at Cambridge. His Bride is very pretty and an agreeable woman, and their mode of seeing the Country is judicious—She rides a pony—and he walks by her side—A few days ago we had a Letter from my Son W^m— the following is an Extract. 'The Book Mr Hamilton wishes for Pastor Keck[1] tells me is exceedingly difficulty to be met with, and the Gedanken[2] are not to be had singly, being but a small part of a work published in three small volumes, printed at Leipsic—The Bookseller here has written to Leipsic for the Book, which he promised me if it were to be had there, should be here in one month—or intelligence that it was not there; in the latter case I shall look for it on my travels. If the Book comes in time for Mr Hymers[3] (his Cambridge Friend) it shall be sent with him.'— We have had a great deal of Company since you left us—among others who have called was a fine old Gentleman Col: Coleridge, eldest Brother of the celebrated Mr C.—He had his only Daughter and her husband Mr Patteson a distinguished Lawyer likely ere long to be a judge,[4] along with him. The day before yesterday I dined at Calgarth, Mrs Watson's, where we met Professor Wilson; and your Bishop of Down Dr Mant,[5] and the P^r dined next day at Mr Bolton's, Storrs, where my Br and I met them and a large party. Miss Curwen is now with us as is her future Husband. Yesterday we called at the Barberini palace[6]—found it barricaded and had to wait 60 minutes before admittance; after all the Lord of the Palace could not be seen, he was in higher grounds, with Mr Cooper[7] the Clergyman of Hawkshead, recently come to the Living, and with this newly-arrived he seems to be in hot friendship. We live in a strange sort of way in this country at the present

---

[1] A German acquaintance of W. W. jnr.'s.

[2] *Gedanken von der wahren Schätzung der lebendigen Kräfte*, [*Thoughts on the True Estimation of Living Forces*], 1746–7, one of Kant's early scientific works, published in *Immanuel Kant's Sämmtliche Kleine Schriften*, 3 vols., Königsberg and Leipzig, 1797. See also L. 582 below.

[3] For John Hymers, see L. 562 above.

[4] See L. 482 above. He was appointed a judge in November.

[5] Richard Mant (1776–1848), from 1823 Bishop of Down and Connor, with which the bishopric of Dromore was united in 1842: a prolific writer of verse and prose, and author of a good *History of the Church of Ireland*, 2 vols., 1840. See also next letter.

[6] i.e. at Gell's Cottage, home of Samuel Barber, the eccentric bachelor whose behaviour caused such amusement in the neighbourhood.

[7] The Revd. Thomas Lovick Cooper (1802–92), vicar of Hawkshead, 1830–4: rector and patron of Mablethorpe, Lincs., and vicar of Empingham, Rutland, 1831–92.

season. Professor Wilson invited thirty persons to dine with him the other day, though he had neither provisions nor cook—I have no doubt, however, that all passed off well; for contributions of eatables came from one neighbouring house, to my knowledge, and good spirits, good humour, and good conversation would make up for many deficiencies. In another house, a Cottage about a couple of miles from the Pr's were fifty guests—how lodged I leave you to guess—only we were told the overflow after all possible cramming was received in the offices, farmhouses etc, adjoining.—All this looks more like what one has been told of Irish hospitality, than aught that the formal English are up to.

I received duly your very friendly Letter—be assured that I shall be most happy to have Letters from you at any time upon the terms proposed. You will make I doubt great allowances for me—my pen has little or no practise, and I have ever been a poor Epistolarian. With kindest regards to your Sister, and to all your family, I remain my dear Mr Hamilton your sincere friend

Wm Wordsworth

567. W. W. to EDWARD QUILLINAN

Address: Edward Quillinan Esqre, 12 Bryanston Sq^{re}, London.
Franked: Penrith Sept. eleven 1830 J. Marshall.
Postmark: 13 Sept. 1830. *Stamp*: Penrith.
MS. WL.
LY i. 508.

Sept. 10 1830

My dear Mr Quillinan,

Dora has already by a short note thanked you for bearing us in mind while you were in Paris, and for your interesting Letter. My own notions of the late changes in France, you will be at no loss to form an opinion about. From what you have heard me say upon Politics and government, reform and revolution, etc, you will not doubt but that I must lament deeply that the Ex-King of France[1] should have fallen into such a desperate course of conduct, and given his enemies so much the advantage over him. He has done much harm to the cause of rational monarchy all over the world by placing himself in the wrong; to a degree that one would have thought impossible. As to the future, fair and smooth appearances are not to be trusted, though the French, having passed

---

[1] For the deposition of Charles X, see L. 562 above.

lately through so many commotions and disappointments, may be in some degree checked in this democratical career by their remembrance of those calamities.

For the last two or three months we have been in a continual crowd and bustle, and are likely to be so for five or six weeks more, when a portion of us will move off to Cambridge for rather a lengthy visit to Dr Wordsworth, who has been making us happy with his Company for the last fortnight. We had Professor Hamilton and his Sister for three weeks, and many other visitors. Miss Curwen and John are now both with us, and Dr W. does not depart till a week hence. Today we were to have gone to Patterdale to Mr Marshall's, but it rains most forbiddingly, and the visit must be put off. Orson the hairy, alias, Professor Airey, dined with us yesterday, and his Derbyshire Bride,[1] a pretty woman to whom he was married last spring. Her profile reminded Miss Stanley[2] and her cousin Miss Hughes also (who is staying at the Hall) of poor Margaret Stanley,[3] but she is far from being so handsome. We have had Mr and Mrs Sharpe,[4] and the delightful Miss Kinnaird with us; if ever you happen to meet with her beg that for my sake, if not for yours or any one else that might be present, she would say for you Auld Robin Grey; if you dont like, if you are not in raptures with her performance, set me down as a Creature not without ears (that is nothing for I have not a good pair) but without a soul.

The wedding[5] takes place on the 11th of next month at Workington Hall—the more we see of Miss Curwen the more are we pleased with her, and the higher are our hopes. Another year, I hope, we may see you here—this I cannot wish it—for I am up to the neck in engagements, and have not seen the Lonsdales except for a couple of days at the close of the election,[6] when I found them at the Castle without expecting it. My visit was to Lord Lowther—I took Professor Hamilton along with me, who was much pleased with both the Person and the place.

I leave the rest of the sheet to the Ladies; remaining, my dear Friend, very sincerely yours

Wm Wordsworth

[1] See previous letter.
[2] Miss Stanley from Ayrshire, whose visit is recorded in *RMVB*, was a cousin of Isabella Curwen.
[3] Unidentified.
[4] Richard Sharp and his sister-in-law: Miss Kinnaird (see pt. i, L. 79) was his adopted daughter.
[5] The wedding of John W. and Isabella Curwen at Old Church, Workington (see *Cumberland Pacquet* for 12 Oct. 1830).
[6] The Westmorland election at Appleby. See L. 562 above.

10 September 1830

I dined at Mrs Watson's[1] and at Mr Bolton's[2] with the great Blackwoodite of Elleray,[3]—he came down for the Regatta, with his two sons and eldest daughter. Bp Mant[4] was also present at Mr B's—he was said to be the Author of a forgotten Poem called the Simpliciad—the principal butt of which was to ridicule me, so that I was somewhat drolly placed in such company.

[*S. H. adds a brief note*]

568. W. W. to WILLIAM ROWAN HAMILTON

MS. untraced.
Mem. (—). *Grosart. Hamilton. K* (—). *LY i. 510.*

Lowther Castle, Sunday Mor[ning]
[26 Sept. 1830]

My dear Mr Hamilton,

I profit by the frank in which the letter for your sister will be enclosed, to thank you for yours of the 11th, and the accompanying spirited and elegant verses.[5] You ask many questions, kindly testifying thereby the interest you take in us and our neighbourhood. Most probably some of them are answered in my daughter's

[1] At Calgarth, on Windermere. Mrs. Watson died the following April at the age of 83.   [2] Storrs Hall.

[3] i.e. Professor Wilson. His two sons were John, later a clergyman of the Church of England; and Blair, for a short time (unsuccessfully) Secretary to the University of Edinburgh. His eldest daughter Margaret, married in 1837 her cousin James Frederick Ferrier (1808–64), the philosopher. His second daughter, Mrs. Mary Gordon, provides a lively picture of the professor's multifarious activities in Ambleside this autumn ('*Christopher North*', *A Memoir of John Wilson*, 1862, ch. xiii).

[4] See previous letter. *The Simpliciad; a Satirico-didactic Poem, containing Hints for the Scholars of the New School* . . ., and addressed to Messrs W-ll—m W-rds-w-rth, R-b-rt S--th-y, and S. T. C-l-r-dg- (1808) had made fun of W. W.'s *Poems in Two Volumes*, 1807, deploring particularly the 'itch for simpleness' in W. W.'s early pieces, and remarking, e.g. of lines in the poem to the Daisy, 'I known not whether a more perfect instance of silliness is to be detected in the whole farrago of the School . . .' (p. 17). But while deploring certain tendencies in their poems, the author paid tribute in his Dedication to the personal characters of the two poets: 'With the friends of humanity and virtue, I venerate your humane feelings and your virtuous principles: with the generality of our countrymen, I acknowledge and admire your talents: but at the same time, with most men of discernment and cultivated minds, I lament the degradation of your genius, and deprecate the propagation of your perverted taste.' *The Simpliciad* appeared anonymously, but (as de Selincourt observes) there is no reason to doubt W. W.'s attribution of it to Mant.

[5] *Farewell Verses to William Wordsworth, At the Close of a Visit to Ryda Mount in 1830* (*Hamilton*, i. 369).

letter to Miss E. H.[1] I will, however, myself reply to one or two at the risk of repeating what she may have said: 1st Mrs Hemans has not sent us any tidings of her movements and intentions since she left us, so I am unable to tell you whether she means to settle in Edinburgh or London.[2] She said she would write as soon as she could procure a frank; that accommodation is, I suppose, more rare in Scotland than at this season in our neighbourhood. I assure you the weather has been so unfavourable to out-door amusements since you left us (not but that we have had a sprinkling of fine and bright days), that little or no progress has been made in the game of the Graces, and I fear that amusement must be deferred till next summer, if we or anybody else are to see another. Mr Barber has dined with us once, and my sister and Mrs Marshall, of Halsteads, have seen his palace and grounds, but I cannot report upon the general state of his temper. I believe he continues to be enchanted, as far as decayed health will allow, with a Mr Cooper,[3] a clergyman who has just come to the living of Hawkshead (about five miles from Ambleside). Did I tell you that Professor Wilson, with his two sons and daughter, have been, and probably still are, at Elleray? He heads the gaieties of the neighbourhood, and has presided as steward at two regattas. Do these employments come under your notions of action opposed to contemplation? Why should they not? Whatever the high moralists may say, the political economists will, I conclude, approve them as setting capital afloat, and giving an impulse to manufacture and handicrafts—not to speak of the improvement which may come thence to navigation and nautical science. I have dined twice along with my brother (who left us some time ago) in the Professor's company—at Mrs Watson's, widow of the Bp,[4] at Calgarth, and at Mr Bolton's. Poor Mr B.! he must have been greatly shocked at the fatal accident that put an end to his friend Huskisson's[5] earthly career. There is another acquaintance of mine also recently gone—a person for whom I never had any love, but with whom I had for a short time

[1] Eliza Hamilton.
[2] Mrs. Hemans finally settled in Dublin (see L. 546 above).
[3] See L. 566 above.
[4] i.e. Richard Watson, Bishop of Llandaff (see *EY*, p. 662).
[5] William Huskisson (see also pt. i, L. 330), statesman and 'Canningite': Treasurer of the Navy and President of the Board of Trade, 1823-7, and Colonial Secretary under Goderich and Wellington, until he resigned (1828) over the question of the redistribution of the disenfranchised seats of East Retford and Penryn. As M.P. for Liverpool (since 1823), he attended the opening of the Liverpool–Manchester Railway on 15 Sept. 1830: catching sight of Wellington he started to meet him, and fell on the rails in front of an on-coming engine: the train ran over his leg, and he died a few hours later.

a good deal of intimacy—I mean Hazlitt, whose death[1] you may have seen announced in the papers. He was a man of extraordinary acuteness, but perverse as Lord Byron himself, whose life by Galt I have been skimming since I came here. Galt[2] affects to be very profound, though [he][3] is in fact a very shallow fellow,—and perhaps the most illogical writer that these illogical days have produced. His 'buts' and his 'therefores' are singularly misapplied, singularly even for this unthinking age. He accuses Mr Southey of pursuing Lord B— with *rancour*. I should like a reference to what Mr S— has written of Lord B—, to ascertain whether this charge be well founded. I trust it is not, both from what I know of my friend, and from the aversion which Mr G— has expressed towards the *Lakers*, whom in the plenitude of his ignorance he is pleased to speak of as a *class* or *school* of Poets.

Now for a word on the serious part of your letter. Your views of action and contemplation are, I think, just. If you can lay your hands upon Mr Coleridge's 'Friend', you will find some remarks of mine upon a letter signed, if I recollect right, 'Mathetes',[4] which was written by Professor Wilson, in which, if I am not mistaken, sentiments like yours are expressed; at all events, I am sure that I have long retained those opinions, and have frequently expressed them either by letter or otherwise. One thing, however, is not to be forgotten concerning active life—that a personal independence must be provided for—and in some cases more is required, ability to assist our friends, relations, and natural dependents. The party are at breakfast, and I must close this wretched scrawl, which pray excuse.

Ever faithfully yours,
Wm Wordsworth

[1] Hazlitt died on 18 Sept. 1830 at his lodgings in Frith St., London.
[2] John Galt (1779–1839), Scottish novelist: his *Annals of the Parish* appeared in 1821, *The Entail* in 1823, and the *Life of Byron* in 1830.
[3] *Word dropped out.*
[4] See *Reply to 'Mathetes'* (*Prose Works*, ii. 3 ff.) and *MY* i. 378, 381, 388. In his letter of 11 Sept. (*Hamilton*, i. 395) Hamilton had written: 'I adopt here the common distinction of phrase between thought and action, and cannot quite avoid being influenced by the common opinion, which prefers the latter to the former, and condemns as even criminal the abandonment of action for thought. But is not thought, in truth, the highest action? And if anyone, endeavouring to be impartial, conscientiously believes that he has power of original thought, that he can discover new fountains, however small, at which the minds of men may drink and be refreshed, does not that person, in devoting himself to such a search, in following with entire submission the guidance of his inward light, and seeking to accomplish the task assigned to him from within, fulfil his highest duty, not to himself only, but to other men?'

Pray continue to write at your leisure. How could I have forgot so long to thank you for your obliging present,[1] which I shall value on every account?

569. W. W. to EDWIN HILL HANDLEY[2]

Address: Edwin Hill Handley Esq, 6 Grey's Inn, London. [*readdressed to*] Revd J. Turnbull, Mason's hill, Bromley, Kent.—
Postmark: 6 Oct. 1830.
MS. Harvard University Library.[3]
K (—). *LY ii. 513* (—).

Rydal Mount, Kendal
Oct. 4th, 1830

Dear Sir,

I lose no time in replying to your communication, and will proceed to the point without ceremony or apology.

I protest on your behalf against the competence of the Tribunal whose judgement you are content to abide by. A question of this moment can be decided only by and within the mind that proposes it.—Allow me to say that you have reversed the order of judicial proceedings by appealing from the higher (higher assuredly 'quoad hoc') to the lower power.—What more then shall I say?— that your interesting Letter evinces an extraordinary power would be obvious to the dullest and most insensible. Indeed I may declare with sincerity, that great things may be expected from one capable of feeling in such a strain and expressing himself with so much vigor and originality. With your verses upon Furness Abbey I am in sympathy when I look on the dark side of the subject—and they are well expressed, except for the phrase that 'Superstitions damn' (if I read aright) which is not to *my* taste.

And now for the short piece that contains the 'thoughts of your whole life'. Having prepared you for the conclusion that

---

[1] A presentation copy of one of Hamilton's recent works, the first supplement of his *Essay on Systems of Rays*, published in the *Transactions of the Royal Irish Academy*, vol. xvi (July 1830).

[2] Edwin Hill Handley (1806–43), second son of Thomas Handley, solicitor, of Gray's Inn: educated at Harrow and Trinity College, Cambridge: admitted to Gray's Inn, 1828: later lived at Bracknell, Berks. He was apparently the author of *An Appeal to Englishmen on behalf of the Polish Exiles, with a brief statement of their claims upon our generosity* [? 1838], the British Library copy of which contains W. W.'s autograph.

[3] There is also a transcript of this letter with a few minor variations in Dora W.'s Commonplace Book in the *WL*.

neither my own opinion nor that of any one else is worth much in deciding the point for which this document is given as evidence, I have no scruple in telling you honestly that I do not comprehend those Lines, but coming from one able to write the letter I have just received, I do not think the worse of them on that account. Were any one to shew an acorn to a Native of the Orcades who had never seen a shrub higher than his knee, and by way of giving him a notion or image of the Oak should tell him that its 'latitude of boughs' lies close folded in that 'auburn nut', the Orcadian would stare, and would feel that his Imagination was somewhat unreasonably taxed. So it is with me in respect to this germ; I do not deny that the 'forest's Monarch with his army shade' may be lurking there in embryo, but neither can I undertake to affirm it. Therefore let your mind, which is surely of a higher order, be its own oracle.—

It would be unpardonable were I to conclude without thanking you for not having abstained from expressing your sense of the value of my imperfect, and, comparatively, unworthy writings. The true standard of poetry is high as the Soul of man has gone, or can go. How far my own falls below that, no one can have such pathetic conviction of as my poor Self.

With high respect I remain, dear Sir,
Sincerely yours,
Wm Wordsworth

570. W. W. to SIR GEORGE BEAUMONT

MS. Pierpont Morgan Library.
K. LY i. 515.

Whitehaven Castle,[1] Oct^{br} 19th [1830]

My dear Sir George,

I have this moment received your obliging Letter, forwarded to me from Rydal Mount, whither I hoped to have returned before this time. Unexpected delays have arisen, and I now fear that we shall scarcely be able to start in time for reaching Coleorton till the first week in Nov^{br}. But, not to shackle Lady Beaumont and you in the least, we will let you know the day of our departure when it is fixed—and pray do not scruple to let us know if this unavoidable delay has rendered it inconvenient for you to receive us.

---

[1] W. W. was staying with Lord and Lady Lonsdale and some of the Lowther circle, including Lady Frederick Bentinck, Miss Thompson, Miss Grisedale, and the Hon. George O'Callaghan.

In fact we have been obliged to take another House for the new-married pair,[1] the one which my son had hired, and which we had half furnished, being pronounced by the medical attendant of the Curwen family much too cold for her health; which is too probable, as it is no less than 500 feet above the level of the sea, to which it is completely exposed, and indeed to all winds. I long to see your little Boy,[2] and believe me, dear Sir George, with kindest remembrances to Lady Beaumont,

Faithfully yours
Wm Wordsworth

571. W. W. to EDWARD QUILLINAN

Address: Edward Quillinan Esq, Bryanston Street, London.
MS. WL.
LY i. 516.

Whitehaven
Oct[r] 19th. [1830]

My dear Mr Quillinan,

I cannot suffer a Frank to go from this place for London without a scrawl for you, by the twopenny Post.—The marriage was celebrated as the papers perhaps have told you last Monday. The pair set off immediately for Edinburgh—the Bride I trust as happy as sorrow at parting from her excellent Parents would allow her to be. She is a sweet Creature, and were the body as strong as the mind is amiable, John would have a prospect before him truly and above measure enviable. I know you admire this young person as does everyone who has the happiness of knowing her—

Dora is at Workington Hall—where she officiated as one of three Bridesmaids. As to health she is in her better way, though having caught a slight cold.

I am now with Lord and Lady Lonsdale at their Residence here; and Mrs Wordsworth busy in fitting up John's House—we hope all three to return to Rydal in a couple of days—and soon shall start for Coleorton, and Trin: Lodge, Cambridge—I hope to have a peep at you in town before our return.

This is merely scrawled to shew that you were not out of mind—during a business so interesting to our family as John's Marriage.

---

[1] John and Isabella W.
[2] Sir George's heir, George Howland Beaumont (b. 1828).

Pray give a kiss for me to my God child[1]—and to Jemima if not too much of a young Lady for such a token of affection.

Miss Hutchinson has been suffering from an inflammation in her eyes caught I believe by over use of her needle in working for the Bride.

From ever yours
W W.

572. W. W. to SAMUEL ROGERS

Endorsed: not to be published S. R.
MS. Sharpe Collection, University College, London.
Rogers. K. LY i. 514.

Castle Whitehaven
October 19th—[1830]

My dear Rogers,

Not according to a cunning plan of acknowledging the Receipt of Books before they have been read, but to let you know that your highly valued Present of three Copies[2] has arrived at Rydal, I write from this place, under favor of a Frank. My Sister tells me that the Books are charmingly *got up*, as the Phrase is, and she speaks with her usual feeling of your kind attention; so does my Daughter, now at Workington Hall, where she has been officiating as Bridesmaid to the Wife of her happy Brother. The Embellishments, my Sister says, are delicious, and reflect light upon the Poetry with which she was well acquainted before.—

Lady Frederick[3] is here with her Father and Mother.[4] She is among your true Friends. Lord and Lady L. are quite well. In a couple of days I hope to return with Mrs Wordsworth and Dora to Rydal, we then go to Coleorton, and so on to Trinity Lodge Cambridge, where Dora will pass the winter. I shall take a peep at London; mind you be there, or I will never forgive you. Mrs Wordsworth sends her kind wishes to yourself and Sister, in which I cordially unite, not forgetting your good Brother. When you see the Sharps, and that most amiable person Miss Kinnaird, thank them for giving us so much of their company;[5]

---

[1] Rotha Quillinan.
[2] Of the illustrated *Italy* (see L. 538 above). Part I of the poem had appeared in 1822, and Part II in 1828.
[3] Lady Frederick Bentinck.   [4] i.e. Lord and Lady Lonsdale.
[5] During the previous month: see L. 567 above.

and believe [me][1] my dear Friend, eager to have your Book in my hand, much of the contents being in my heart and head,

> ever faithfully yours
> Wm Wordsworth

Lady Frederick begs me to say she is sorry they have not seen you in the North this year—We also had looked for you anxiously, at Rydal.

573. D. W. to MARY ANNE MARSHALL[2]

Address: Miss Marshall, by favour of Miss Askews.[3]
MS. WL.
LY i. 517.

> Sunday Evening. [24 Oct.[4] 1830]

We are sorry, my dear Mary Anne, that you will not have time tomorrow to turn aside to Rydal Mount, as I learn by a letter from your Mother, for which, should we not have the pleasure of seeing you on your return from Ulverston, I now commission you to give her my best thanks with an assurance that she shall hear from me when I have any thing new or interesting to communicate. At present, being very much occupied, she must consider *this* as a sort of answer to hers.

My Brother, Sister and Dora arrived at home yesterday—all well—But I think the Females look a little worn by excitement of various kinds not unattended with fatigue. Dora has, however, much happiness and enjoyment, and her Mother as much as could be expected amid the confusion and bustle of furniture unplaced and all its attendant arrangements with no constant companion but a servant of our own, (the cook) whom we shall be obliged to spare to the Moresby Establishment till Mrs John W.'s servants can come to her.

We have had very pleasant letters from the young couple. They have exceedingly enjoyed their travels, the fine weather, and the sights to be seen in and near Edinburgh. They were in comfortable lodgings where they intended to remain till tomorrow,

---

[1] *Word dropped out.* [2] Eldest daughter of John and Jane Marshall.
[3] Daughter of the Revd. Henry Askew of Greystoke and Glenridding (see L. 463 above).
[4] This letter was written the day after W. W., M. W., and Dora W. finally returned to Rydal. According to L. 571 of 19 Oct., they were expecting to return on the 21st.

when they will turn their faces homewards; and probably will reach Moresby about Thursday or Friday.

My Sister is very glad, as we all are, that Mrs W. Marshall got well through her long journey, and was in better plight for her approaching trial[1] than when I saw her at Paterdale Hall. We rely on being informed by my dear Friend your Mother or you or some one of your Sisters as soon as the great event is over. Poor little John William![2] I do not wonder that he was a little unhinged by the loss of fresh air and liberty and all the pretty playthings afforded by a garden at his own door; but I have seen as ruddy healthy-looking *gentlemen's* Children in London as anywhere else which I suppose is chiefly owing to the peculiar care there taken to give them all possible air and exercise, so I hope that he may return to the mountains as blooming as when he left them.

I saw Miss Askews at Chapel this morning; but had not time to make particular inquiries, which I expected to have an opportunity of doing this afternoon; but am prevented, by rain, from going to Mrs Luff's—and therefore I know not which of you or how many are going to Ulverston. No doubt you will attend the Ball, and if Julia[3] be there she will recognise our Friend Mrs Benson Harrison ('Cousin Dorothy') but if Julia be not of your party I hope you and Cordelia,[4] or you and Susan[5] will get introduced to her. She is rather of a shy character and therefore might not of herself (though Mrs Marshall called on her at Ambleside with me) make advances to you. I assure you Mrs B. Harrison is a thoroughly amiable Woman, and when you visit us I should like you to see something more of each other than can be seen in a Ball-room.

I have already through Mrs Marshall thanked Julia for the pleasure she has given me by confiding some of her poems to me; but I must beg you to do it again for me, telling her that when we meet again on the Banks of Ulswater I will repay her to the best of my power by pointing out what seems to me amiss in any of her poems. I must, however say that the simplicity with which in general she expresses herself in metre appears to me very extraordinary in so young a Writer.

You cannot think what pleasure it gave me to hear that your recollections of Switzerland and of the little bit of Italy which

---

[1] Mrs. William Marshall of Patterdale Hall was expecting her second child, a son Samuel.
[2] Mrs. William Marshall's baby son, John William.
[3] Mary Anne's younger sister, later Mrs. Venn Elliott (see L. 790 below).
[4] The third of the Marshall girls, later Mrs. Whewell.
[5] Mary Anne's youngest sister, later Mrs. Myers (see L. 483 above).

you and I have seen were revived in reading my Journal.[1] Adieu my dear young Friend.

Believe me ever
Your affect^e,
D. Wordsworth

When I began the sentence about Miss Askews I intended to go on with saying We should be very glad if you can come to see us on your return. Should my Brother and Sister and Dora not be actually gone to Cambridge you may find us in a little bustle; but we can make up three Beds for you without trouble. Now when I reckon days I find they will certainly *not* be gone, as they cannot leave us before the beginning of next week; and you will hardly stay more than three or four days at Ulverston.

If you can do no more, perhaps you will contrive to spend an hour with us—but the days are sadly shortened and there is the Mountain to cross.

Adieu.

Dora's very kind love to you all. It would give her great pleasure to see you again before her Flight to Cambridge.

574. D. W. to CATHERINE CLARKSON

Address: Mrs Clarkson, Playford Hall, Ipswich, Suffolk.
Endorsed: John Wordsworth's wedding.
Postmark: 6 Nov. 1830. *Stamp*: Kendal Penny Post.
MS. British Library.
LY i. 519.

[<i>c.</i> 5 Nov. 1830]

My dear Friend,

The Newspapers have no doubt informed you that John Wordsworth and Isabella Christian Curwen were married at Workington on the 11th of last month; but this you ought to have heard from one of ourselves, and I am that one who have failed in duty—but I will not tire you with excuses or confessions.—It is enough that I have not forgotten you, that I have been much occupied—(and more than I liked in letter-writing) and that from day to day—not without severe self reproaches have put off. I will give you a brief summary of what has happened among us—Ten days previous

---

[1] D. W. had lent Mary Anne her MS. Journal of a Tour on the Continent 1820 (*DWJ* ii. 7 ff.).

to the great day (the 11th) Mary went to Moresby to prepare and arrange her Son's house—On the 5th Isabella called here in a little carriage given her by her Father to take up Dora, and she (the Bride elect) and Bridesmaid proceeded to Workington Hall. They both looked very pretty and very interesting—seated side by side and driven by a servant on one of the horses. The Rest of Isabella's family followed and on Saturday, the 9th my Brother joined them—Sara H and I being left at home—unwilling to crowd Workington Hall with any *unnecessary* addition of numbers, and not sorry to have so good an excuse for avoiding a bustle and ceremony which to say the best of it—is but a *melancholy* pleasure. This wedding, however, was to be a gay one if a large assemblage of affectionately attached Relatives could make any wedding gay.—Uncles—Brothers—three Bridesmaids—with their attendant grooms—Children and grandchildren of attendant Friends—two Fathers and one Mother—with all the Servants of Workington Hall—and one of ours (who was at Moresby assisting her Mistress with the House) drew up round the altar in as regular order as the Bell's School[1] or the Military—Five carriages conveyed the Parties to Church—Servants perched outside—Mr Curwen, Dora and Isabella in the first carriage—postilions and Servants wore favours. All Workington was abroad making a lane for the carriages to drive through—some on house-tops—all the windows crowded—The people shouted Hurra! Curwen for ever! and the two Young Brothers[2] of the Bride outside her Carriage kept off their hats smiling and bowing all the way.—Not a tear shed at Church—or till they reached home—When as Dora says (who wrote us an account of the day) 'We all had a good cry'—Fifty people sate down to Breakfast. Then departed the Bride and Bridegroom for Scotland. By the Bye I should have told you that on their way from church they scattered silver among the people according to the Family Custom at W. Hall. Guns were fired and ships in the harbour hoisted their flags. Poor Mrs Curwen could not bear to go to church, and there was a sad parting when Isabella bade Farewell. Never did a Bride leave her Father's house more beloved and more regretted. I had a letter from her yesterday—a sweet one—I wish you could see it—you would be so delighted with the purity, innocence, good-sense, love and happiness which it displays—

---

[1] i.e. as in a school organized on Andrew Bell's principles (see *MY* i. 269).

[2] Probably Henry Curwen's second and third sons, Edward Stanley Curwen (1810–75) and Henry Curwen jnr. (see L. 482 above).

without a word of display. They spent 10 days at Edinburgh and have since made a charming Highland Tour, and expected to reach Workington Hall this evening. I am sorry to add that they have not yet a house ready for them. The one taken by John with Mr Curwen's decided approbation has been found out to be placed in a situation not favorable for Isabella's health—They are about taking another if the Bishop consents to her living a *mile out* of their Parish—a house very suitable but John and Isabella greatly object to not being *in* their parish. It is thought the Bishop cannot refuse as there is none vacant in the parish except the condemned one already taken. This affair has grieved all parties not a little and especially the young ones, who had set their hearts on returning to a fireside of their own. They must now remain at Workington Hall till the house is ready—I hope not long—as everything else is *quite* ready—William and Mary and their Daughter returned to us last Saturday but one—and again they have left us—Mary and Dora are now at Manchester and William on his travels on horse-back. They are to meet at Derby to-morrow, and proceed thence to Coleorton, where they will stay till the end of the week, and then go to Cambridge where they will all remain at least a month. Whether M and D will get to London or not I cannot say, but William certainly *will*—and when they will all reach home again I can as little guess, though Mary did say 'Before Christmas'. This I confess I do not look to. William rides Dora's pony, she and her cousins[1] wishing much to ride together, and horse exercise being more beneficial to her health than anything else. Thank God she is in great measure recovered from the very serious illness she had in the Spring—and, woeful as the parting is for two or three months at the least, *at our age*,—I am glad they are gone from this moist climate. *They* have had nothing but good weather since last Monday—*we* nothing but bad—and a damp or rainy atmosphere always affects Dora's throat. They will soon be but fifty miles from you. Fain would I persuade myself that the meeting will be effected—perhaps in London—perhaps in Cambridge—nothing known is planned—nothing was talked of beyond the month at Cambridge and William's trip to London. *I* much wish that Dora would resolve, or be prevailed on, to spend the remainder of the winter in a trial of the Cornish air. Miss Trevenan of Hilliston,[2] Derwent's faithful and opulent Friend—the Godmother of his child—she who after a stay in the Lakes conveyed Mrs Coleridge to her Son's

[1] i.e. C. W.'s sons, John, Christopher, and Charles Wordsworth.
[2] For Emily Trevenen of Helston, see L. 463 above.

house—she who delighted us all with her pleasing manners, her kindness, her goodness and good sense (I *must* have mentioned this Lady to you before)—*She* has invited and urged Dora to go to her —and if *that* air were to agree with her she could not have a more pleasant and comfortable place to stay at than under Miss Trevenan's Roof.—You will have rejoiced with us on John's and Chris's election to Fellowships[1]—and you may guess that the Uncle, Aunt and Cousin will have great joy in congratulating them and in being with all the 3 young men under their Father's Roof, previous to their going out—no one knows whither—to take care of themselves. *I* too should have liked well to have been of the party and my Brother Christ[r] much wished it, but I could not well have left dear Sara at home alone at this season of the year—or for me it is, perhaps, the safer plan to stay quietly here another winter. *Last* winter I was in no condition for travelling—Now I am quite another creature—going on thus well I trust that next year my friends may dismiss all anxiety on my account. We are truly comfortable together—and since they left us I have often felt thankful at being out of the way of temptation to over exertion or excitement. Sarah's health is on the whole excellent. She has a pony and is as fond of riding as ever, and it agrees with her as formerly, sometimes she rides alone sometimes Owen Lloyd is her companion. You will be glad to hear that he is well—has recovered from the dismal shock of his mother's death,[2] and makes an excellent parish priest.—Mrs Coleridge is the proudest and busiest of Grandmothers Sarah—[3] an excellent nurse and her husband the most contented of men—if we may judge from his letters. Poor S. T. C. declining in Body, but they tell us is as vigorous as ever in mind. I am happy to think that William and he will meet together yet once again. Southey and Bertha are going to London. Edith engaged to be married to a Mr Warter[4] now Chaplain to the Embassy at Copenhagen. Hartley goes on as usual—leaves his comfortable home about once in three months wandering about no one knows where

[1] At Trinity College, Cambridge.
[2] Mrs. Sophia Lloyd had died in France the previous August. See *Letters of Hartley Coleridge* (ed. Griggs), p. 120 for a generous tribute to her character.
[3] Sara Coleridge had just given birth to her first child, Herbert (1830–61), a brilliant scholar who died young.
[4] John Wood Warter (1806–78) married Southey's eldest daughter Edith, on 15 Jan. 1834. He was chaplain to the English embassy at Copenhagen, 1830–3, and vicar of West Tarring, Sussex, from 1834. He edited Southey's *Common Place Book*, 1849–50, and in 1856 brought out four volumes of Southey's *Letters*, supplementing Cuthbert Southey's *Life and Correspondence* of 1849–50. See Curry, ii. 505–6.

—sleeping in Barns etc etc.—When you meet him smiles and talks away as if all were right—how busy he is—what he is writing for—this Annual or that Magazine—but alas! no money comes in— and his Friends through me, pay for his Board etc. This however is a secret—so do not mention it. Did I tell you that Miss Barker[1] wrote to me to inform us that she was going to be married to a young man of not more than thirty-five—desperately in love with her? This was early in the summer—and we have heard no more— so I hope it will come to nothing—We suspect the youth to have been a Boulogne Swindler—I wrote my mind counselled inquiries and settlements etc etc—perhaps not very palateable—as no notice has been taken of my letter. What an illegible scrawl! Do tell me if you still can read my writing. How are the Hardcastles?[2] It is five weeks since we heard from Willy—Then at Heidleberg— uncertain where to settle for the winter. We trust he has the providence to keep out of danger; but are anxious—No place seems secure and I almost wish his resolve may be to come home. His health is improved—Pray write as soon as you can. I have no room for inquiries—Sorry Tom[3] did not get to see us—Love to Mr Clarkson. God Bless you my dearest Friend

ever yours
D. W.

Sara's Love——. Speak particularly of your health

575. W. W. to D. W.

MS. WL.
LY i. 523.

Coleorton[4]—Monday Mor:
[8 Nov. 1830]

My dear Sister

Yesterday at eleven a.m. I reached this place, after a pleasant journey, in spite of a tremendous heavy rain the whole of Sat: afternoon, which wet everything upon me, and in my portmanteau, so that I had nothing to do at Derby, but to go instantly to bed. Here I found Sir G. and Lady B.,[5] and their noble little Boy,

---

[1] Lately of Borrowdale: now resident in Boulogne. See also L. 590 below.
[2] Friends of the Clarksons.   [3] Tom Clarkson, C. C.'s son.
[4] W. W., M. W., and Dora W. left Rydal Mount for Cambridge on Monday, 1 Nov. James Dixon had ridden Dora W.'s pony 'Billy' to Lancaster, whence W. W. rode it to Cambridge, via Coleorton, as described in this letter and L. 582 below. The Wordsworths remained a week at Coleorton.
[5] Sir George and Lady Beaumont.

quite well; and a Letter from dear Willy, forwarded from Cambridge. W. is quite well; has got his money and our Letters, and means to stay at Heidelberg; but the letter will be forwarded to you. He treats the disturbances lightly, so that I hope his poor Mother's fears will abate.—This is a bright day, and they[1] will have a pleasant ride through Darley-dale by the Lord Nelson; a chaise from Derby, 16 miles, will bring them hither by five. They shall speak for themselves,—I will now say a word on my own journey—Did they tell you that I reached Preston before them, and slept at S. Horrocks's?[2] Mrs Sinclair[3] was luckily from Home, as was also the old Gentleman—S's wife is a very pleasing Woman, and plays upon the harp powerfully—her Father, Miller,[4] is a native of Whitehaven, and but of vulgar manners. At Chorley I called on Mrs Master, formerly Alice Horrocks[5]—her husband a creditable Clergyman—and she has a nice little girl. Lancashire is but a dull county, and in my long ride I saw nothing that pleased me so much as a sweet little Gainsborough cottage girl with a tiny wheelbarrow which she was guiding along the Causeway, filled with dung collected on the road, with a little basket enclosed in a red handkerchief and slung upon one of the handles of the Barrow, in which she had carried dinner to her Father in the fields.—I gave her a penny for her industry, and she said, 'Thank you Sir', in the prettiest manner imaginable—I regret I did not ask her whether she had learned to read.—Perhaps Mary has told you that on Friday morning John Cookson[6] rode my pony forward to Bullock Smithy (10 miles). I had set off from Manchester at 8 by coach, mounted at B. Smithy, and proceeded (look, dearest D. at the Map—Sarah I know does not matter[7] such details—the map I mean prefixed to that Book about Derbyshire, which Chris: left) by Chapel le Frith, Peak Forest, Tideswell, Cressbrook, and Ash-ford in the Waters to Bakewell where I slept. This road led me through the central Hills of Derbyshire. At Chapel, while my Pony was baiting I strolled into the Church-yard as usual. There was one, and only one monument of the Dumfries character, a

[1] M. W. and Dora W. who were following by coach.
[2] Samuel Horrocks jnr., the Preston manufacturer (see pt. i, L. 71). See also *MW*, p. 133.
[3] Formerly Sarah Horrocks (see pt. i, L. 199). The 'Old gentleman' is presumably her husband Dr. Sinclair, or rather St. Clare.
[4] i.e. the father-in-law of Samuel Horrocks jnr.
[5] For Alice Horrocks, see pt. i, L. 149.
[6] Younger son of the Cooksons of Kendal, now working in Liverpool (see *SH*, p. 377).
[7] So *MS*. Sarah is S. H., now at Rydal with D. W.

white and shewy Obelisk; I walked up towards it, commenting with too much self-complacency upon the vanity of Man, and received a sudden shock from these words engraven on the side that faced me—'The Lord will deliver thee into the hands of Death, and erelong O Reader thou shalt be with me'. At the Village of Peak Forest I saw fields of corn in the Sheaf, and ascending with the road to the highest and bleakest point that it crossed, I found a newbuilt Inn, called, as its Inscription of invitation tells the Traveller, *Mount Pleasant*, 'our first best country ever is at home'.—A starveling field or two of corn, intersecting stone walls without number, and few neighbouring eminences as unattractive, made all the prospect of Mount Pleasant. At Tideswell is a noble Church for its sequestered site; I regretted that my time did not allow me to enter it. Mounted a hill, and descended upon the Village of Cressbrook, where is a large Factory—but the Wey,[1] which I here first came in sight of, is singularly beautiful both above and below the Village. It winds between green lawny hills and limestone steeps, through a narrow trough, and twists its way in some places through slips of meadow-ground as rich in verdure as Nature's bounty can make them. I was charmed with the mile and a half of this Stream along which my road took me, wished for you both a hundred times. I would gladly have continued to follow the river, which I was told was possible, but along a rugged track that might have lamed my Pony, and the day was too far advanced, so I yielded to necessity, and turned up the main road after halting often to look back upon this happy and holy seclusion, for such I could not but think it. I clomb the hill, descended, and joined the Wey again at Ashford; a pretty spot, but twilight was coming on.— The firing of guns startled me every now and then, for it was the fifth Nov: and I thought it prudent to dismount, and walked most of the 2 miles into Bakewell.—Rose early—rode down the valley with Haddon Hall in view, and at the point where Wey and Derwent unite, turned up towards Chatsworth—rode a mile, and leaving my pony to bait, walked up the valley and through Chatsworth Park to the House—splendid and large, but growing larger every year.[2] The trees in this valley are still in many places clothed with rich variegated foliage—and so I found many all the way almost to Derby. My feelings at Chatsworth as contrasted with

[1] Generally written Wye.
[2] The sixth Duke of Devonshire (1790–1858) had added a new north wing to the late seventeenth and early eighteenth century mansion in 1820, to the designs of Sir Jeffry Wyatville (1766–1840). Further additions followed later, including the orangery (1827).

those which had moved me in the higher part of the Peak Country will be best given in the following, for which, as fresh from the brain, make such allowance as you can:

> Chatsworth! thy Park, and Mansion spreading wide
> And towering high, strange contrast do present
> To the plain treasures of that craggy Rent
> Which late I saw, where Wey's blue waters glide;
> A Dell whose native Occupants abide
> As in a dear and chosen banishment
> With every semblance of entire content,
> So kind is simple Nature, fairly tried!
> Yet he, whose heart in childhood gave her troth
> To pastoral dales thin-set with modest Farms,
> May learn, if judgement strengthen with his growth,
> That not for Fancy only Pomp hath charms;
> And, diligent to guard from lawless harms
> The extremes of favour'd life, may honor both.—[1]

Descending Darley dale I went into Darley Church yard and found by measure that its tall yew tree is in girth eleven times the length of my arm; but the tree in the expression and character of its trunk and arms is not to be compared to the best of those in Borrowdale. A mile below, upon an eminence to the right I recognized the two Trees that gave occasion to my Sonnet[2] on the parting of the two Brothers—I could not hear of any such tradition from the people whom I questioned, but a little Boy told me that the trees, two sycamores, were called Wm Shore's trees from the name of the man who had planted them above 200 years ago; and that a woman had been buried near them. The same Informant told me that two very large Willows had stood close by where we were, called Scotch Trees; and that the spot which he pointed to was called Scotchman's Turn, from a Scotchman who had been murthered there.—Matlock looked charming with its hoary, dove-coloured rocks, its ivy, its eugh-trees, its elms retaining much of their faded foliage, and several of its other trees as green as in Summer. I never saw such a beautiful decoration of China roses and pyracanthus as upon one cottage at the entrance of this place. The berries were in the utmost profusion, and brilliant as gems; I thought with regret of the poor appearance of our tree when I

---

[1] See *PW* iii. 49 and app. crit. The first five lines of the sonnet were later considerably altered.

[2] *A Tradition of Oker Hill in Darley Dale, Derbyshire* (*PW* iii. 49).

left it. Dear Sara, what is the cause? Billy's quondam owners were delighted with news of him. I found he is of Welch breed, and cost them 7 pound. Incessant rain to Derby, but the rich woods and green lawns made some amends—a high wind also.—Started a little after six—baited at Swarkstone Bridge upon Trent, and halted again at Breedon for the sake of mounting the Rock which I had never done before. The view very confined on account of mist and vapour, though the morning was bright. In the Church many monuments of the Shirley family, Earls of Ferrers;[1] and directly over the baptismal font, a skeleton, large as life or rather Death, painted on the wall, with a dart in one fleshless hand, and a spade in the other; below, this inscription—*Vive memor lethi*— Here also is a monument to a William Shakespeare killed by a fall from his Horse near Paris—I observed to the Clerk and a farmer who were with me that a very eminent person bore that name— the Clerk answered he only knew John Shakespear—'O but', said I, 'I mean a great dramatic Poet'—The farmer knew nothing of him, but the Parish Clerk recollected himself with a lively 'yes'.— 15 houses of the town below have each a right to send three sheep up to graze upon the unenclosed part of the hill. The Farmer told me that 14 persons had been killed in his memory in blasting the limestone Rock—I have now done.

The changes at Coleorton will in time prove decisive improvements—at present parts are cold and bare. Sir George took me round—when I sate down in Lady B's[2] grotto near the fountain I was suddenly overcome and could not speak for tears.

Now for business; tell John Carter to write most urgently to Slee,[3] and demand an immediate answer; I rather think I undertook to do this. His negligence is shameful. I had some other point of business to mention, though of little consequence, but I have forgotten. Yesterday afternoon I attended with Sir G. and Lady B. the Chapel on the Moor, and heard from the Clergyman of Ashby a sermon in support of the Charity School. The Chapel was full almost as it could hold—I gave my two shillings—13 pounds were collected. Tell John[4] this, and also what you will be sorry to hear that Mr Prickett[5] has lately shown symptoms of mental and bodily

---

[1] Of Staunton Harold, near Ashby de la Zouch.
[2] i.e. the late Lady Beaumont.
[3] Isaac Slee of Tirril, near Penrith, who managed the late R. W.'s estate at Sockbridge.
[4] John W., who had been curate at Whitwick, near Coleorton, the year before.
[5] For Mr. Prickett, the new curate, see L. 482 above.

irritability amounting to flightiness—The Merryweathers are not
here—

[cetera desunt]

576. D. W. to MRS. S. T. COLERIDGE

MS. Victoria University Library, Toronto.
LY i. 528.

[8 Nov. 1830]

My dear Friend,

We have heard this morning that Bertha[1] is to set off tomorrow,
and will call here on her way, so though you will hear all *news*
more pleasantly from herself I cannot let her go without a written
word of Love and good wishes to you and dear Sara and Henry and
the youngest born[2] of the Coleridge Race. How I should like to see
the busy Grandmother and the young Mother and the dear little
One, not forgetting papa and Grandpapa also! At least I *hope* my
Brother will ere long have that happiness, and much wish that my
Sister and Dora may also—but for their journeying further than
Cambridge no plans were arranged when they left home: however,
when but fifty miles from London I cannot but expect and wish
that they may travel thither. They left us this day week, halted
with Miss Jewsbury at Manchester, and if nothing prevented
were to reach Coleorton on Saturday; and we expect that *next*
Saturday they will reach Trinity Lodge; William rode his Daughter's pony—and as far as Manchester, Steed and Rider performed
to admiration; and if weather continue to favour them I trust the
journey on to Cambridge will be accomplished with equal satisfaction. Ever since they left us, until to-day, the weather, as Bertha
will tell you, has been in our worst mountain fashion; but as they
fared so well in their road to Manchester we persuade ourselves
that the torrents which have continued to pour down here have
been confined to our quarters. John and Isabella are safely returned
to Workington Hall after a charming Tour in the Highlands.
The house that John (with Mrs Curwen's especial approbation)
had taken was found to be in too high and exposed a situation for
Isabella's health—Fathers Mothers etc etc decided that they *must
not* live in it through the winter—None other was vacant in the
parish but an excellent house (far too grand in the exterior at least

---

[1] Bertha Southey, who was setting out to join her father in London.
[2] Herbert Coleridge (see L. 574 above).

for their desires) distant from the Parish a mile *was* vacant. These tidings cast a sad damp over the young People's pleasure—but they submitted and the Bishop was written to for permission—which, of course, he granted; but when they arrived at Workington on Friday evening to their great joy they found that another house in Moresby, and very near the Church, had become vacant, that it was exactly suitable as to size and every thing else, and that in a fortnight their furniture may be removed thither. Their present house (Croft Hill) will be on their hands four years; but Mr Curwen undertakes that loss, and we hope it may be let. Mrs Wordsworth went thither before the marriage with our Cook (Anne) and shortly after the marriage her proceedings were stopped, but Anne is still there, taking care of the furniture, and when the other place is ready Sara H. will go to assist in the removal, and the arrangement of it in its second new place. All's well that ends well; but truly this has been a troublesome and vexatious business, yet no one was to blame, and *that* being the case our mortification that poor Mary Wordsworth's labours were thrown away is the more bearable, and we are all so well satisfied with the present plan that we do not lament over the past. Isabella writes in excellent spirits and seems perfectly happy.

You have heard that poor Miss Cookson[1] has been unwell. She continues so, though much better, and I hope she will be able to come and stay with me during S. H.'s absence. Anne is to stay till they get into the house.

Have you seen Charles and Mary Lamb lately? Pray give our kind love to them and tell us all you know concerning them. We have heard that they have removed back again to London[2] and I am glad of it; for it is their natural place. We have not heard again of, or from, poor Miss Barker. I think, and may say hope, that her marriage will never take place. Owen Lloyd heard in passing through Boulogne that the young man was gone upon business to England, and it was even there thought that he was a mere adventurer. Were not you shocked to read of the death of Bishop Hobart?[3] and what dismal tidings from every part of the Continent! We are anxiously expecting letters from William. It is more than five weeks since his last—written at Heidelberg—then uncertain where to settle for the winter. Joanna writes that your sister[4] is

---

[1] Elizabeth Cookson.
[2] The Lambs had mostly been living in Holborn in recent months, but Charles Lamb moved his sister back to Enfield in November, following her renewed mental instability (see *Lamb*, iii. 293).
[3] For Bishop Hobart see pt i, L. 141.   [4] Mrs. Lovell.

well and happy at Douglas. She and Henry[1] are settled for the winter at Ramsey.

It is time I should turn to poor Hartley. He never comes near us, though I have sent word I have a parcel for him, which I shall only give to himself. It is from Liverpool—a Winter's break I suppose, and am afraid without money—or surely he would have come. When I last called (a few weeks ago) he held out fair promises, and spoke gaily of his doings—said he was very busy etc etc and promised to come and see us—and promised money. Since that time he has had another ramble; but is now at home and as well and as happy as usual. It is a sad sad thing but really I fear he will never pay any part of his debts either to you or others. Ben Hunter[2] came to me last week with a Bill for making up his last black cloaths (At that time H. was on the wander). I refused to pay, telling him he must apply to Mr C. at his return. Now as I have heard nothing I am not *quite* hopeless as to this little affair. Hartley *may* have got money somewhere and may have paid Ben Hunter. I enclose a statement of accounts as they now stand—You will perceive that another quarter's pay is due, or nearly so, and ere long I shall be called upon for at least a part—What is to be done? Grievous it is to go on in this way but how to get out of it I cannot tell. He might be *cheaper* lodged; but no where else so respectably. He *might* be cast upon his own resources. But what would follow? I fear wandering and starvation—unless his Friends could suffer him to be arrested. My dear Friend, these are hard words to say to a Mother and I cannot express the pain it gives me to write them. Mrs Carter[3] was with us lately. She read part of a letter from Mrs Fox[4] speaking in the highest terms of Derwent and Mary and Miss Trevenan. She had spent a day with them and stayed all night.

[*cetera desunt*]

[1] Joanna and Henry Hutchinson, S. H.'s sister and brother.
[2] Benjamin Hunter, the Ambleside tailor.
[3] Mrs. Jane Carter, the Quaker lady, of Dale End, Grasmere.
[4] Formerly Sarah Hustler (d. 1882), of Ulverston; wife of Charles Fox (1797–1878), of Perran and Trebah, Falmouth, and aunt of Caroline Fox, the diarist. The family was connected with the Lloyds of Birmingham, the Crewdsons of Kendal, the Gurneys of Earlham, and the Hoares of Hampstead, and Mrs. Fox had recently been visiting her Quaker connections in the north, calling on the Wordsworths at Rydal Mount. Charles and Sarah Fox visited Rydal Mount several times subsequently (*RMVB*).

577. W. W. to GEORGE HUNTLY GORDON

MS. Cornell.
Broughton, p. 43.

Coleorton Hall
Near Ashby de La Zouche
Nov^{br} 9th [1830]

My dear Mr Gordon,

It is a long time since we had an exchange of Letters—I am now able to say that W^m is settled for the Winter at Heidelberg where he has entered himself a Student of the University. The last Letter which you kindly forwarded lay long at the Hague for non-payment of frontier postage—it was obligingly released by Mr Grattan[1] author of Highways etc whom I had the pleasure of being introduced to by the Father at Brussels. To this Gentleman I owe a Letter—not on this account merely, and if you could favor me with his present address I should be thankful—

Pray how is Major Gordon and your amiable Mother? I have often thought of them during the sad disturbances at Brussels[2] and wished to know if they had escaped without injury or loss of property or if they were still there.—Mrs W. my Daughter and I are now upon a short visit to Sir George and Lady Beaumont, who is daughter of the present Archbishop of Canterbury[3]—next Monday we move for Trin Lodge, Cambridge—before my return to the North I shall take a peep at London—and promise myself much pleasure in the renewal of our acquaintance. If you see Mr Quillinan tell him where we are.—My own journey is performed on Horseback—and I deviated a little for the sake of some of the beauties of Derbyshire. The enclosed for W^m is to go viâ Paris—can you forward it thither—Mrs W. and my Daughter join me in kind remembrances

ever faithfully yours Wm Wordsworth

---

[1] Thomas Colley Grattan, the novelist, whom W. W. had met on the Continent in 1828 (see pt. i, L. 346). See also L. 587 below.

[2] See L. 563 above.

[3] Dr. William Howley. See pt. i, L. 175.

578. D. W. to WILLIAM PEARSON

MS. untraced.
Pearson. LY i. 531.

Rydal Mount,
11th Nov. [1830]

My dear Sir,

A pannier of beautiful apples is arrived with your signature, and I lose no time in returning you Miss Hutchinson's best thanks, and my own. I have not seen *such* apples this year, and as our orchard has produced none, they are particularly valuable.

I am ashamed of not having written to you for so long a time. The truth is, that at any time, if you had taken your chance, you would have been welcome, and would have found some one of us at home; but I was to write when we had no company, and no engagements. This I never could do, as we have had a constant succession of visitors ever since we had last the pleasure of seeing you, and this served me as an excuse for not writing: and I am now very sorry it did so, as my Brother, Sister, and Niece are gone away for a great part of the winter, and they would have been happy to see you before their departure. They are now at Coleorton, and next week will go to Cambridge. Whenever the weather changes for the better, and you are disposed to take a ride, Miss Hutchinson and I will be very glad to see you.

My Brother rode into Leicestershire on his Daughter's pony, and much enjoyed the journey through Derbyshire. They are all well; as *we* are at home, and our Bride and Bridegroom are returned to Moresby in good health and spirits, after a delightful tour in Scotland.

William intends to winter at Heidelberg. His health is much improved, and he writes in excellent spirits, making light of the disturbances in that part of Germany.[1]

Our man, James, desires me to request you, if you can, to procure us our straw, which he will be much obliged if you will send as before; and when the staw comes, we will return your hamper. James did not state his quantity, but no doubt he wishes for as much as heretofore.

I hope you have been in your usual comfortable state of health, since I last saw you and heard from you.

---

[1] There had been disturbances this autumn in Leipzig, Dresden, Hamburg, and other German cities, following the revolutions in Paris and Brussels.

Lamenting that you have not, in spite of my silence, dropped in during the Autumn and Summer to take your chance,

I remain, dear Sir,
Yours truly,
Dorothy Wordsworth.

579. D. W. to JANE MARSHALL

Address: Mrs Marshall, Hallsteads, Penrith.
Stamp: Kendal Penny Post.
MS. WL.
LY i. 532.

[12 Nov. 1830]

My dear Friend,

Having pen in hand, as is often my way, I will go on, and write a few lines to you—assured that, though accustomed so long to franks,[1] you will not grudge the postage, but, on the contrary will be pleased that I do not wait for something particular to communicate.

My Brother, Sister, and Dora left us in a post-chaise last Monday but one. It was one of our true mountain days of pouring rain. They stayed all night at Kendal, and next morning went on, per Coach, to Lancaster. There my Brother mounted his Daughter's pony, and he joined the Ladies at Manchester the following evening, delighted with his own prowess and that of the steed. On Friday morning (i.e., this day week) he left them at M., and pursued his journey through some of the wildest and most romantic parts of Derbyshire, to Coleorton, where he arrived on Sunday morning—in perfect health, and not at all fatigued. On Sunday he wrote to us, knowing how anxiously we were expecting tidings of this his grand equestrian exploit. The next day he expected to see his Wife and Daughter. They had remained behind at Manchester with Miss Jewsbury.

We hope for equally good news of *them* in the course of two or three days, as my Brother promises to forward to us a letter which he found at Coleorton from William—a letter anxiously expected by us all—and especially by his poor Mother who had been vexing her mind with all sorts of apprehensions. His previous letter (received 6 weeks ago) was from Heidelberg; and there he now remains, and *intends* to remain through the winter. His health is

[1] John Marshall had resigned his seat in Parliament (see L. 554 above).

restored, and he is perfectly satisfied and happy, resolved to make the best use of his time for general improvement, and, in short, seems to be undisturbed except by *one care.* What is to become of him at his return? How is he to maintain himself? What employment shall he find? To this I reply 'Sufficient unto the day is the evil thereof'. *His* business is to get knowledge, and if possible bodily strength. The healthy, the well-instructed, and even the well-befriended at this day know not whither to turn for profitable employment, and as for poor William, of this I am sure that six months' confinement in a Merchant's Counting-house or a Lawyer's Chambers would be the death of him.

I cannot but rejoice that Dora is removed, for a season, from this wet corner of England. Day after day since they left us have we had ceaseless rains, and *but one* fine day. On the contrary they write that they have been favored by weather, and my Brother had only one wetting. It was among the Derbyshire Hills, and he was completely soaked, but went to Bed and rose uninjured. I would fain hope that Dora may gather permanent strength. Before she left us, she ailed nothing except in the throat; but every damp or showery day (and what had we else?) brought on the uneasiness there, and thickness in the voice.

I *had* some longings when they left us to be one of the happy party at Trinity Lodge; but am quite satisfied that it is, for this one winter more, the safest plan to stay in quiet at home; and Miss Hutchinson and I are truly comfortable together.

We enjoy a quet fireside, both in itself, and as a preparation for still higher enjoyment of the more busy and chearful one which we trust again to have when we shall once more be all assembled together.

I look upon the *time* of their return as very uncertain, no less so than their route; but I hope they will have a meeting with you and yours either in London or at Leeds. My Brother found all well at Coleorton—Sir G. and Lady B. are most friendly towards us all. I have not seen much of Lady B.; but like exceedingly what I *have* seen.

Your Daughters would tell you in what discomfort they found Rydal Mount. It has since come into my mind that perhaps they intended to stay all night—though they did not confess to it. Now if that were the case I should be very sorry they did not do so; for, whatever might seem our bustle and confusion, we could soon have contrived for their comfort and for the pleasant enjoyment of their company.

John and Isabella were sadly grieved when informed that the house taken by John (with Mrs Curwen's especial approval) was pronounced unfit for their residence—and another in the next parish, in a situation which they disliked for various substantial reasons was to be taken—for not one house was vacant in the parish of Moresby except Croft Hill, which it was said would be the Death of Isabella if she should go to it. Well! Sorrow comes to one Family to bring joy to another. A Captain Dawson dies suddenly—His Widow wishes to part with her house —It exactly suits John and Isabella—They take it—and in a fortnight it will be ready to receive them and their furniture.

How fortunate that the Bishop did not answer John's letter immediately! The House, *out* of the *parish*, which so little for various other reasons suited their inclinations, could not be taken without the Bishop's consent, and had *that consent* arrived three days earlier, they must either have had three houses on their hands, or fixed themselves where they would never have been satisfied to be.

Isabella writes as if she were perfectly contented with her lot, and so I trust she will continue to be. She is a dear sweet creature. They had a charming Tour in the Highlands.

You must not forget our scheme of meeting at Keswick next spring or summer to go to Scale Hill, or of your coming hither to visit *us* and taking *me* up to go with you by this Road. It is very long since Mr Marshall was at Rydal, and my Brother much wishes him to pay us a visit—and this we now hope he will easily find time to do being released from parliament—and, dear Jane, if you can both contrive to come at the same time so much the better, and the more pleas[ant][1] for all parties.

I hope you have satisfactory [news] from dea[r] Julia, with as favorable reports from her Sister's Bed-chamber as we have any right to look for. I often think of Ellen[2] and the thoughtful and affectionate Julia by her side. To both pray when you write give my kind Love. I hope Julia will let me see more of her verses. Miss H. and I delight in them. One, upon 'poesy'—had been left by me unread and unseen in my drawer—I found it two days ago— and you cannot think with what pleasure Miss H. and I have read it. There is such rectitude of sentiment and feeling in whatever Julia writes that it is very satisfactory to read; and with respect to style and composition, her defects are marvellously few; and having the good sense not to be vain she will go on improving.

---

[1] *MS. torn.*   [2] Mrs. Marshall's fifth daughter, an invalid.

I *must* tell you that our industrious and simple-hearted Serving-man, James, who can do all sorts of little jobs, mend chair-bottoms, weave garden nets, make mats, list shoes, etc., etc., has made cap stands for the Ladies of this house and for Mrs John Wordsworth after the model of the one which you gave me to put into my Trunk when I left you. By the Bye, his *wedding*-present to Mrs J. W. was a paste-pin, turned by himself, and a potato bruiser, both made of wood grown in Rydal Mount grounds.

Give my kindest love to your Sisters. I am glad that Ellen had so pleasant a visit. What a nice opportunity that *might* have been for my going to see our good Aunt.[1] Ellen, I know, would have been glad to take me as far as our Roads lay together, and to have received me again to bring me back on her return! But at that time there was no thinking of it. I have had a letter from Mrs Rawson. Alas! it showed more symptoms of failure than any I ever before received from her.

What sad doings in London, in Kent, in Sussex![2] How is all this to end? And poor Antwerp![3] How distressing the outrages.

God bless you my dear Friend. Ever your affec^te

D. W.

Miss Hutchinson's kind Love. Pray write soon.

580. W. W. to EDWARD QUILLINAN

Address: Edward Quillinan Esq., 12 Bryanston Street, Portman Sq^re, London.
Postmark: 18 Nov. 1830. *Stamp*: Charles St. Westminster.
MS. WL.
LY i. 536.

Coleorton Hall
Monday 16th Nov^br [1830]

My dear Mr Q.

I scribble a word to say with many thanks, that you must on no account forbear to let your House; as the time of my going to

---

[1] Mrs. Elizabeth Rawson.

[2] The current of liberalism was flowing more freely in the new parliament, and Wellington's outspoken commitment to the existing system of representation caused great resentment and uncertainty. Owing to this, and to the popular dislike of Peel's newly-formed police force, London was anticipating a serious riot; the king declined to come to the Guildhall on 9 Nov., and the Funds fell. In Kent and Sussex there had been widespread firing of ricks and smashing of machinery as a result of the distressed state of agriculture. On 15 Nov. the government was defeated on the civil list and resigned.

[3] The independence of Belgium, since 1815 a part of the United Netherlands (see Ls. 416 and 563 above), had been declared on 4 Oct. But Antwerp remained for a time in the hands of Dutch troops, and was the scene of much slaughter.

London or even my going at all is uncertain. And certainly I shall come unencumbered with females.

Mrs W and Dora present their kindest regards and wish to know what you mean to do with your little lasses.—We depart in a few minutes for Leicester, I go to Market Harborough this evening on Dora's pony which I have ridden from Lancaster, saving one short stage on this side Manchester, and to-morrow evening the Ladies count upon reaching Cambridge by Coach. I shall be very proud if I arrive there on Tuesday evening without harm to the Creature that will convey me.

Thanks for your spritely verses, and your account of the London Mob.

The Bride cake being sent from the Bride's house and not ours we could not remind you of our proceedings in that way, which would on no account have been omitted had the parties been married from my House—

ever faithfully

my dear Mr Quillinan

yours

Wm Wordsworth

[For 580a, see Addendum, p. 755]

581. W. W. to JOHN ABRAHAM HERAUD[1]

Address: John Ab: Heraud Esqre, Hope Cottage, White Hart Lane, Tottenham.
  [In M. W.'s hand]
Postmark: 29 Nov. 1830.
MS. Harvard University Library.
Edith Heraud, Memoirs of John A. Heraud, 1898, p. 52 (—).
K (—). *LY i. 536.*

Trinity Lodge, Cambridge,

Nov^br 23^d, [1830]

Dear Sir,

It gives me much concern that you should have occasion to write to me again, and the more so because the wish which you have done me the honor of expressing, it is out of my power to gratify.

---

[1] John Abraham Heraud (1799–1887), a prolific poet and dramatist, and friend of the Carlyles. In verse he aimed at epic grandeur. The poem referred to here is *The Descent into Hell*, 1830 (see L. 514 above), which he followed up by another epic, *The Judgment of the Flood*, 1834. He edited *The Sunbeam, A Journal devoted to Polite Literature*, 1838–9, and the *Monthly Magazine*, 1839–42, and thereafter regularly contributed to the *Athenaeum* and the *Illustrated London News*.

Since your former letter reached Rydal I have been at home only for a short time, and there was much engaged. But to say the truth I read so little and am so very much less addicted to writing especially upon any formal subjects, that though I should not be without a strong wish to serve you were I able to do so, I am conscious that I could not undertake the task you would put me to, with the least prospect of benefit to either of us. I am not a Critic—and set little value upon the art. The preface which I wrote long ago to my own Poems[1] I was put upon by the urgent entreaties of a friend,[2] and heartily regret I ever had any thing to do with it; though I do not reckon the principles then advanced erroneous.

Your Poem is vigorous, and that is enough for me—I think it in some places diffuse, in others somewhat rugged, from the originality of your mind. You feel strongly; trust to those feelings, and your Poem will take its shape and proportions as a tree does from the vital principle that actuates it. I do not think that great poems can be cast in a mould.—Homer's, the greatest of all, certainly was not. Trust, again I say, to yourself.

By the bye you have fallen into an error in the 2nd page where you make Cerberus of the feminine gender and speak of the pangs of whelp-birth.

Believe me with sincere respect
your admirer
Wm Wordsworth

582. W. W. to WILLIAM ROWAN HAMILTON

MS. WL transcript (—).
Grosart. Hamilton. K (—). *LY i. 537.*

Trinity Lodge, Cambridge,
November 26, 1830.

My dear Mr Hamilton,

I reached this place nine days ago, where I should have found your letter of the 28th[3] ult., but that it had been forwarded to Coleorton Hall, Leicestershire, where we stopped a week on our road. I am truly glad to find that your good spirits put you upon writing what you call nonsense, and so much of it, but I assure you it all passed with me for very agreeable sense, or something better, and continues to do so even in this learned spot; which you

---

[1] i.e. to *Lyrical Ballads*, 1800.   [2] S. T. C.
[3] Hamilton's letter is actually dated the 25th (see *Hamilton*, i. 398).

will not be surprised to hear, when I tell you that at a dinner-party the other day I heard a Head of a House, a clergyman also, gravely declare, that the rotten boroughs, as they are called, should instantly be abolished without compensation to their owners; that slavery should be destroyed with like disregard of the *claims* (for rights he would allow none) of the proprietors; and a multitude of extravagances of the same sort. Therefore say I, Vive la Bagatelle; motley is your only wear.

You tell me kindly that you have often asked yourself, Where is Mr Wordsworth? and the question has readily been solved for you. 'He is at Cambridge'—a great mistake! So late as the 5th of November, I will tell you where I was; a solitary equestrian entering the romantic little town of Ashford-in-the-Waters, on the edge of the wolds of Derbyshire, at the close of day, when guns were beginning to be let off and squibs to be fired on every side, so that I thought it prudent to dismount and lead my horse through the place, and so on to Bakewell, two miles farther. You must know how I happened to be riding through these wild regions. It was my wish that Dora should have the benefit of her pony while at Cambridge, and very valiantly and economically I determined, unused as I am to horsemanship, to ride the creature myself. I sent James with it to Lancaster; there mounted; stopped a day at Manchester, a week at Coleorton, and so reached the end of my journey safe and sound—not, however, without encountering two days of tempestuous rain. Thirty-seven miles did I ride in one day through the worst of these storms. And what was my resource? guess again: writing verses to the memory of my departed friend Sir George Beaumont,[1] whose house I had left the day before. While buffetting the other storm I composed a Sonnet upon the splendid domain at Chatsworth,[2] which I had seen in the morning, as contrasted with the secluded habitations of the narrow Fells in the Peak; and as I passed through the tame and manufacture-disfigured country of Lancashire I was reminded by the faded leaves, of Spring, and threw off a few stanzas of an ode to May.[3]

But too much of self and my own performances upon my steed—a descendant no doubt of Pegasus, though his owner and present rider knew nothing of it. Now for a word about Professor Airey; I have seen him twice, but I did not communicate your message;[4]

[1] i.e. W. W.'s patron and friend, the late Sir George Beaumont. See *Elegiac Musings* (*PW* iv. 270), published 1835.

[2] See *PW* iii. 49 and L. 575 above.

[3] *To May* (*PW* iv. 118), published 1835. The earliest version in 4 stanzas (*WL MSS.*) is dated 1829.

[4] About a second supplement to Hamilton's *Essay on Systems of Rays*.

it was at dinner and at an evening party, and I thought it best not to speak of it till I saw him, which I mean to do, upon a morning call. There is a great deal of intellectual activity within the walls of this College, and in the University at large; but conversation turns mainly upon the state of the country and the late change in the administration.[1] The fires have extended to within 8 miles of this place; from which I saw one of the worst, if not absolutely the worst, indicated by a redness in the sky, a few nights ago.

I am glad when I fall in with a member of Parliament, as it puts me upon writing to my friends, which I am always disposed to defer, without such a determining advantage. At present we have two members, Mr Cavendish,[2] one of the representatives of the University, and Lord Morpeth,[3] under the Master's roof. We have also here Lady Blanche, wife of Mr Cavendish, and sister of Lord Morpeth. She is a great admirer of Mrs Hemans' poetry. There is an interesting person in this University for a day or two, whom I have not yet seen—Kenelm Digby,[4] author of the 'Broad Stone of Honor', a book of chivalry, which I think was put into your hands at Rydal Mount. We have also a respectable show of blossom in poetry. Two brothers of the name of Tennyson in particular, are not a little promising.[5] Of science I can give you no account;

---

[1] After Wellington's defeat and resignation, Lord Grey had become Prime Minister on 16 Nov., stipulating that Reform should be a Cabinet measure. His ministry including several Canningites, and Henry Brougham as Lord Chancellor.

[2] For William Cavendish, see L. 451 above. He had married in 1829 Lady Blanche Georgiana Howard (d. 1840), younger daughter of the 6th Earl of Carlisle. See also *RMVB* for 1832 and 1834.

[3] George William Frederick Howard, Lord Morpeth, later 7th Earl of Carlisle (1802–64), Whig politician and miscellaneous writer: M.P. for Morpeth (1826–30), for Yorkshire (1830–2), and for the West Riding (1832–41); supporter of Catholic Emancipation and the Reform Bill; Chief Secretary for Ireland, 1835–41.

[4] For Kenelm Henry Digby, see pt. i, L. 376, and L. 418 above. '. . . Digby is here, he ran over from Paris or Rome per⌈haps⌉ for two days and remains two days longer on purpose to meet my Father at dinner and this my Father considers a great Compliment as it is said he would have done so for no body breathing but Mr Wordsworth and the Pope.' (*Letters of Dora Wordsworth*, p. 78.)

[5] *Hamilton* reads, 'one not a little promising'. Alfred Tennyson (1809–92) and his younger brother Charles (1808–79) both matriculated at Trinity in Feb. 1828: *Poems by Two Brothers* had been published anonymously at Louth the previous year. Alfred Tennyson went on to win the Prize Medal at Cambridge in June 1829 for his poem *Timbuctoo*, and published *Poems, Chiefly Lyrical* shortly before this letter was written. W. W. probably met Tennyson during this visit to Cambridge, when he stayed in James Spedding's rooms and became acquainted with all the Cambridge 'Apostles' (see also L. 784 below). Tennyson called at Rydal Mount in May 1835 (*RMVB*), while he was staying with the Speddings at Mirehouse.

though perhaps I may pick up something for a future letter, which may be long in coming for reasons before mentioned. Mrs W. and my daughter, of whom you inquire, are both well; the latter rides as often as weather and regard for the age of her pony will allow. She has resumed her German labours,[1] and is not easily drawn from what she takes to; therefore I hope Miss Hamilton will not find fault if she does not write for some time, as she will readily conceive that with this passion upon her, and many engagements, she will be rather averse to writing. In fact she owes a long letter to her brother in Germany, who, by the bye, tells us that he will not cease to look out for the Book of Kant[2] you wished for. Farewell, with a thousand kind remembrances to yourself and sister, and the rest of your amiable family, in which Mrs W. and Dora join.

Believe me most faithfully yours,
Wm Wordsworth

583. W. W. to EDWARD QUILLINAN

Address: Edward Quillinan Esq[re] 12 Bryanston Street, Portman Sq[re]. [*In M. W.'s hand*]
Postmark: 14 Dec. 1830. *Stamp*: Oxford Street.
MS. WL.
LY i. 540.

Trin: Coll. 13th Dec[br] [1830]

My dear Mr Q:

Mr Southey who has been here a few days with Bertha is bearer of this to the Twopenny.—

This day week we all start for London on our way to D[r] Wordsworth's Living in Sussex.[3] Mrs Wordsworth and Dora will be at Hampstead, Mrs Hoare's, while my B[r] and I are at Mr Joshua Watson's[4] Westminster. We shall not stay more than two or

---

[1] Assisted by Julius Charles Hare, with whom W. W. renewed his warm friendship during this visit.

[2] See L. 566 above. Willy W. was now enrolled as a student at the University of Heidelberg for the winter (see *MW*, p. 131).

[3] Buxted near Uckfield.

[4] Joshua Watson (see *MY* ii. 605 and pt. i, L. 134) was the leading Anglican layman of the day. W. W. and C. W. dined with him on 22 Dec. According to Mrs. Watson's Journal, 'The poet . . . was most eloquent on the subject of the times: very high-minded, but very gloomy in his anticipations.' (Churton, *Memoir of Joshua Watson*, ii. 1.)

three days in London. I should have gladly profited by your kind invitation and taken up my abode in Bryanston Street, but I left Wes^nd at this season expressly to hold a consultation with Mr Watson on some private affairs of my B^r. Mr Watson was unable to meet me here as was intended, so I go to his house in Town for the purpose. On my return from Sussex, I hope to pass a few days with you if you are in Town; but I beg you would not forbear letting your House with any view of that kind—it would hurt me much were you to do so; and do not check or alter your own movements on my account. I will write to Bryanston Street on our arrival, in the mean while it may be as well to mention that Mr Watson's House is No. 6 Park Street Westminster. Kindest remembrance from Mrs W and Dora who I am sorry to say has got a bad cold.

ever yours,
W W.

[*M. W. adds*]

I hope an opportunity will be afforded to Dora and myself to have a peep at you and y^rs. I enclose this in a frank to-night—Southey does not go till tomorrow. Ever my d^r Friend,

Y^rs

M Wordsworth

584. D. W. to WILLIAM PEARSON

MS. untraced.
Pearson. LY i. 542.

Saturday Morning [18 Dec. 1830]

My dear Sir,

I am much obliged for the potatoes, and shall pay the man. Miss Hutchinson is not yet arrived, but we expect her to-day.[1] All distant friends well. Mrs Luff is still with me, but walking out, otherwise I should have a message from her.

We shall be very glad to see you whenever you come. I am going to-morrow to spend a few days with Mrs B—— H——,[2]

---

[1] According to D. W.'s MS. Journal (*WL MSS.*), S. H. returned from Moresby and Keswick on 18 Dec.

[2] Mrs. Benson Harrison.

Green Bank, Ambleside, and should I not happen to be at Rydal Mount when you come, pray call on me at Mr B—— H——'s.

In greatest haste, with wretched pen,
Yours truly,
D. Wordsworth.

I am quite well, and take care of exposure to cold.

585. M. W. to LADY BEAUMONT

MS. Pierpont Morgan Library.
LY i. 541.

Trinity Lodge Dec. 21ˢᵗ [1830]

My dear Lady Beaumont

Mr W. sends a revised copy of the verses,[1] with which it gave him pleasure to find Sir Geo. and you had been pleased. Dora and myself were very much affected when he poured them out to us on his arrival—we were affected by the verses for their own sake, thinking them characteristic of our lamented friend—and not a little from the consideration of their having been composed thro' such a storm—on a day when our great comfort for his sake had been 'that the weather was so bad no one could think of venturing out on horseback'. We are all apprehensive that the composition will be found too long for an inscription—but do not see how it could be shortened. I do not like to mention the subject to Mr W. at present —but I should rather wish him to recast something shorter, than attempt to reduce the verses which, as they stand, appear to me to be so happy.

On Wednesday we all leave Cambridge—Dr Wordsworth has induced us to prolong our absence from home, and accompany him to his Living in Sussex, where we shall pass a few weeks. On going or returning, thro' London, Mr W. hopes he may have an opportunity of paying his respects to the Archbishop and Mrs Howley.[2]

---

[1] The *Elegiac Musings* in memory of the late Sir George Beaumont, mentioned in L. 582 above.

[2] Lady Beaumont's father and mother. W. W., C. W., and Joshua Watson dined at Lambeth Palace with the Archbishop on 23 Dec., Southey also being of the party. On Christmas Eve W. W. visited Coleridge at Highgate, and on 27 Dec. he was in Hampstead, meeting Joanna Baillie (see F. V. Morley, *Dora Wordsworth, Her Book*, 1924, pp. 60, 70). He also had an invitation (*WL MSS.*) to stay with Blomfield, Bishop of London, at Fulham Palace, and according to E. Q.'s MS. Diary (*WL MSS.*), he took this up on 1 Jan. 1831 while staying with E. Q. in Bryanston Street.

We have since we left you, been more or less in a state of excitement from the disturbances of the neighbourhood;—and our Politicians are in very bad spirits at the prospect of Public affairs. For my part I am willing to hope all will go well, and that we shall be, as we have hitherto been, preserved from those evils that have more often been anticipated than felt.

Mr W. and Dora beg to join me in affectionate regards to Sir G. and yourself—and with the best of wishes of the season to you and yours, believe me my dear Lady Beaumont to remain very sincerely

Yours
M. Wordsworth

Mr W. desires me to say that he has spoken to Mr Southey (who was at Trinity Lodge last week) about your intended Spanish Library, and he will have great pleasure in making out a list as soon as he returns to Keswick where he can best do it, from his own Library.

586. D. W. to WILLIAM PEARSON

MS. untraced.
Pearson. LY i. 542.

Rydal Mount,
Wednesday. [?29 Dec. 1830]

My dear Sir,

I am glad to hear that you had not a troublesome journey home, and were no worse for it in health.

My Brother and Sister write from London and Hampstead, in good spirits. All three are well. No fresh news from Heidelberg or Moresby. This weather is charming for the young and strong—Moonlight and at Christmas used to be delightful, thirty years ago. I now enjoy a short, sharp walk in the garden, and a peep out of doors, on the Evergreens and sunshine, from a warm fire-side. Many thanks for the straw, I shall pay the bearer.

Believe me, my dear Sir,
Truly yours,
D. Wordsworth.

587. W. W. to THOMAS COLLEY GRATTAN[1]

Address: T. C. Grattan Esq., The Hague.
Endorsed: Wm Wordsworth Jany 5th 1831.
MS. Cornell.
T. C. Grattan, Beaten Paths and Those Who Trod Them, 2 vols., 1862, ii. 141.

Bryanston Street
Port^n Square
Jan^ry 5th 1831

My dear Sir,

Your very obliging Letter, Feb^ry 28th 1830, is now lying before [me]; both as an agreeable Memorial of your regard, and in some degree as a reproach for my delay in not sooner thank[ing] you for it. The fact is that I waited for a sight of the present that it announces, that my Letter might have some value from the Report which any work of yours would I am sure enable me to make of the pleasure I and mine had derived from it. Month passed on and Month and the Book never reached me—at last I enquired but without success—then came the unhappy Revolution of Brussels—which I was sure would drive you—whither I could not guess. I came to London about ten days ago, and have since been tossed about at Hampstead, Fulham,[2] etc—but your Book I am happy to say is on its way to Rydal and will in a few days I trust contribute to the amusement of my Sister and such of my family as are at Home. My Wife and Daughter whom you mention with an interest flattering to my paternal affection, not to say vanity, came with me to Town, and are now in Sussex where I join them tomorrow.

I am sorry to say that I have been so hurried during my short stay here that I could not possibly have read your Work; I foresaw this and sent it down the moment it came into my hands, with other Books, for my leisurely perusal. Be assured that I think with much pleasure of the two days we passed together—of the entertaining conversations we had—of the droll adventure of the Diligence—

---

[1] T. C. Grattan, the novelist (see pt. i, L. 346), whom W. W. had met on the Continent in 1828: author of the popular *Highways and Byways, or Tales of the Roadside*, 1823 (2nd series, 1825; 3rd series, 1827). He had written to W. W. on 28 Feb. 1830, recalling their meeting on the Meuse, and promising to send a copy of his forthcoming historical romance *The Heiress of Bruges*, 1831 (*WL MSS.*). Grattan was driven from Brussels by the revolution of 1830, but later returned to the new kingdom of Belgium to write on European affairs for the British and foreign reviews.

[2] W. W. returned from Fulham Palace to E. Q.'s on 3 Jan. and that evening, according to E. Q.'s MS. Diary (*WL MSS.*), they dined with Rogers and Allan Cunningham.

and of the image of that Castle on the Hague where your scene is laid[1] and which I would gladly have visited. You described it with animation, and surely I saw it among the shadows of Evening —or is this an Imagination? I wished you *had* touched, I never shall I fear, on the rude Chapel and Cross which we sate under looking down upon Dinant.

I have now to thank you for what I and all my family regard as a great favor, and indeed a kindness for which we are truly grateful, though in a small matter; I mean your releasing the Letter addressed to my Son from its durance at the Hague.[2] I consider myself in your debt for the postage and I should be happy to repay you through Mr Gordon or in any other way.

I hope neither yourself nor Mrs Grattan nor any of your family suffered injury during the Commotions at Brussels, either in person or property. To be driven away from a place of Residence by popular revolution must always be melancholy, and mostly perilous. You are no doubt aware of the alarming state in which Great Britain and Ireland are—What is to be the end of it no one can foresee—all are full of fears that take the trouble of thinking—

> Believe me my dear Sir
> very faithfully yours
> Wm Wordsworth

588. D. W. to GEORGE HUNTLY GORDON

Address: G. H. Gordon, Esq[re].
MS. WL. Hitherto unpublished.

Rydal Mount 18th Jan[ry]—1831

My dear Sir,

Again I trouble you with an enclosure for France, and am really half ashamed of myself for so speedily calling upon you to repeat your former kindness; but you have so often assured me of your good-will, and desired me not to entertain any scruples, that I

---

[1] In *Beaten Paths* (ii. 121), Grattan describes his trip from Namur with W. W. and S. T. C. in 1828: 'We drove to Dinant along the banks of the river which presents a succession of very lovely views. These called forth... nothing worth recording, if I may be allowed to except the fact that my fixing on the ruins of Poilvache Castle as the scene of part of my novel of *The Heiress of Bruges*, which I was then employed on, arose from a joking conversation between us, as to our separate appropriation of various scenes on the river for literary purposes.' The river is the Meuse; and Grattan converted the name of Poilvache Castle into Welbasch. [2] See L. 577 above.

will forbear making any apology, only I must say that if it be inconvenient to you to forward my letter as heretofore I beg you will be so kind as to send it to the post office, and call upon my Brother (whom no doubt you will see again) for the postage.

I was much obliged to you for the pleasant communication you made to me concerning your Father; and very glad that he had not been a sufferer in the commotions at Brussels.

My Brother and Sister and their Daughter write chearfully from Buxted in Sussex. My Niece's health seems to be quite re-established; but I need not enter into particulars, as no doubt you have heard from them, so will conclude with assuring you that I am with much respect

Your obliged Friend
Dorothy Wordsworth

589. W. W. to JOHN KENYON

Address: John Kenyon Esqre, 16 Regency Square, Brighton [*In M. W.'s hand*]
Stamp: Uckfield Penny Post.
MS. Cornell. Hitherto unpublished.

Buxted Rectory
Wednesday 19th [Jan. 1831]

My dear Sir,

I am glad my Letter found you, having begun to fear that you were gone from B.[1]

It will suit us to act upon you kind invitation, this day Week. The Ladies will take the Coach that passes through Uckfield about half past two, if there be room, if not they will try another day—and I will accompany them—or ride on my Daughter's Pony which I brought from Rydal for her use. I do not know which Inn the Coach drives to, nor can learn here, but you may easily know at Brighton; I suppose it will arrive about five.

It gives us all great pleasure to know that you enjoyed yourselves so much while abroad. Much do I regret that circumstances did not allow me and mine to join your party.

With very kind remembrances to yourself and Mrs Kenyon in which Mrs W. and Dora unite, I remain

faithfully and affectionately
yours
Wm Wordsworth

[1] Brighton.

590. D. W. to SARA COLERIDGE

Address: To Mrs H. N. Coleridge.
Endorsed: very kind letter of dear Miss Wordsworth—account of Hartley and family matters. I am burning old letters, but am loth to burn all hers and Miss H.'s, they are indeed most good and kind to me.
MS. Victoria University Library, Toronto.
LY ii. 545.

20th Jan^ry [1831]

. . . at supper time. I should *not* have mentioned these facts, but to prevent your good mother from building too much on the improved reports I have lately been enabled to make. For a while, at least, she must be contented if he[1] goes on as at present— making a little money perhaps—working by fits—and not wandering about in publick houses or Barns.—The affection the Flemings[2] feel for him, and their patience and kindness are admirable, and this I am convinced of—that go the world through he could not find a place where he would be likely to do so well. Harshness and excessive strictness would only drive him further from the right course, and I do believe that notwithstanding Mrs F.'s indulgence he stands in some awe of her.

Give my kindest love to your Mother. My next shall be addressed to her—after Blackwood's second payment,[3] and I shall then be able to state the use that can be made of the money—I fear *none* will go to the liquidation of the present debt to her.

Miss H. and I are very well in [? health][4] and spending a quiet and comfortable winter. Now and then we long for a few chearful family faces; but are quite reconciled to their long absence, and not impatient for their return as the party have all enjoyed themselves and the improvement in Dora's health has been marvellous since she went into Sussex. Their plans are yet unsettled, and what further stay will be made at Cambridge or elsewhere I know not. Mrs Slade Smith[5] has promised me a letter from her own Chateau. Poor Soul! She had a wretched journey, and one cannot but regret that she ever came, as no good was done. Miss H. joins with me in kindest Love to you all. Tell Grandmama *she* must kiss the Baby[6]

---

[1] Hartley Coleridge.
[2] For the Flemings, with whom Hartley Coleridge lodged, see L. 507 above.
[3] With the help of Professor Wilson, Hartley was now writing for *Blackwood's*. The three parts of *Ignoramus on the Fine Arts* (*Essays and Marginalia*, ed. Derwent Coleridge, 2 vols., 1851, i. 178 ff.), appeared in the issues for Feb., Mar., and Oct. 1831.
[4] *Seal*.
[5] Formerly Miss Barker of Borrowdale, and later, Boulogne.
[6] Sara's son, Herbert.

for us. Dora gives us charming accounts of him. Your poor Father—
I fear he is very weak in Body for they speak of a great change in
his appearance. Pray give him my most affectionate remembrances,
and my regards to Mr and Mrs Gillman. I should have liked well
to have seen your table spread at the christening dinner. You
cannot think how comfortably Miss H. has sate fixed to netting her
Doileys (I spell the word guessing) day by day. Again my Love to
your Mother. God bless you all. Yours ever

D W

My Love to Bertha—all well at Keswick.

The Introduction to Bishop Coleridge[1] not wanted. Capt Manning's[2] regiment does not go to the West Indies. Thanks etc from
Mr Harrison of the Green.

591. W. W. to WILLIAM ROWAN HAMILTON

MS. untraced.
Hamilton (—). *K* (—). *LY ii. 546* (—).

Buxted Rectory, near Uckfield, Sussex.
January 24, 1831.

I am two letters in your debt, which I must pay poorly enough
with one. Yours followed me to London and to this place, where
we have been for some time under the roof of my brother. . . . I am
glad to find from your letters that you are in such high spirits. The
lady[3] you name is known to Mr Rogers, who speaks of her in terms
of praise that accord with your own. I am sorry that you are so ill
supplied with my poems. Upon inquiring of my publisher I find
that there are still a hundred copies upon hands: when these shall
be somewhat reduced, I shall proceed to a new edition with additions, and I shall then beg your acceptance of a copy as a very
inadequate mark of my affection and esteem. Here let me say that I
found lying for me at Mr. Moxon's, Bookseller, Bond-street, a

---

[1] William Hart Coleridge, Bishop of Barbados (see *MY* ii. 235, 597).

[2] A relative or connection of John Harrison of the Green, Ambleside (to be
distinguished from Benson Harrison of Green Bank).

[3] Hamilton's close friend Pamela, Lady Campbell (d. 1869), whose husband,
Sir Guy Campbell, Bart. (d. 1849) was Quartermaster-General in Dublin.
Her father was Lord Edward Fitzgerald (1763–98) the unfortunate Irish
patriot, who died while resisting arrest on a charge of high treason; her mother
was supposedly the daughter of the Duc d'Orléans. See *Hamilton*, i. 359–60,
404.

N

copy splendidly bound of your Mathematical Treatise.[1] I forwarded
it with other books to Rydal, where I hope it is arrived by this
time; pray accept my thanks for it. In the *Quarterly Review* lately
was an article, a very foolish one I think, upon the decay of Science
in England,[2] and ascribing it to the want of patronage from the
Government—a poor compliment this to Science! her hill, it seems,
in the opinion of the writer, cannot be ascended unless the pilgrim
be 'stuck o'er with titles, and hung round with strings,' and have
the pockets laden with cash; besides, a man of science must be a
Minister of State or a Privy Councillor, or at least a public func-
tionary of importance. Mr. Whewell, of Trin. Coll. Cambridge,
has corrected the mis-statements of the reviewer in an article printed
in the *British Critic*[3] of January last, and vindicated his scientific
countrymen. But your higher employments leave you little leisure
to take interest in these things. How came you not to say a word
about the disturbances of your unhappy country? O'Connell[4] and
his brother agitators I see are apprehended; I fear nothing will
be made of it towards strengthening the Government; and if the
prosecution fails, it cannot but prove very mischievous. Are you
in the habit of seeing your cousin Hamilton?[5] What does he think
of the aspect of affairs among you? Are you not on the brink of a
civil war? Pray God it be not so! You are interested about Mr.
Coleridge; I saw him several times lately, and had long conversations with him. It grieves me to say that his constitution seems
much broken up. I have heard that he has been worse since I saw
him. His mind has lost none of its vigour, but he is certainly in that

---

[1] See L. 568 above.

[2] 'Decline of Science in England', *Quarterly Review*, xliii (Oct. 1830),
305–42. The author was Sir David Brewster (1781–1868), the natural philosopher. In the article he contrasted the liberal treatment traditionally accorded
to scientists in other European countries with the lack of recognition they received in Britain.

[3] 'Transactions of the Cambridge Philosophical Society', *British Critic*,
ix (Jan. 1831), 71–90: a discussion of recent advances made by Cambridge
scientists, many of them acquaintances of W. W. It seems unlikely that Whewell
was the author of the article, which criticizes his recent *Mathematical Exposi-
tion of some Doctrines of Political Economy*.

[4] Daniel O'Connell was returned for Waterford at the general election of
1830, and continued to agitate for parliamentary reform and the repeal of the
Union. The Marquess of Anglesey, Lord Lieutenant of Ireland, failing to win
his support for the administration, adopted tougher tactics, and on 19 Jan.
O'Connell was arrested and charged with conspiracy to violate and evade the
recent proclamations against his political activities. But his case was never
brought to trial, and the prosecution was quietly dropped through the influence
of the English reformers who hoped to secure his support at the next general
election (in the following spring).

[5] For Arthur Hamilton, see L. 488 above.

state of bodily health that no one who knows him could feel justified in holding out the hope of even an introduction to him as an inducement for your visiting London. Much do I regret this, for you may pass your life without meeting a man of such commanding faculties. I hope that my criticisms have not deterred your sister from poetical composition. The world has indeed had enough of it lately, such as it is; but that is no reason why a sensibility like hers should not give vent to itself in verse.

Parliament is soon to meet, and the Reform question cannot be deferred.[1] The nearer we come to the discussion, the more am I afraid of the consequences. O that the stars and the Muses might furnish at least a few with a justification for shutting their eyes and ears to political folly and madness, two relatives as near each other as sisters, or rather parent and child. What misery they may speedily bring upon this fair island I fear to calculate. But no more. I hear you are going to be married,[2] and I suspect there may be some foundation for the report, as you talk in your letter of *the comfortable state* of the great married astronomers. We had the report from a countrywoman of yours, and a friend—you will guess whom, when I add that she is a person of great literary distinction. It is high time to stop, or write better. Farewell then, and believe me with kindest regards to yourself and sisters, in which my wife and daughter join . . .

[*unsigned*]

592. W. W. to JOHN KENYON

Address: John Kenyon Esqre, 16 Regency Square, Brighton.
Stamp: Uckfield Penny Post.
MS. untraced.
Transactions of the Wordsworth Society, no. 6, *p.* 105. K. *LY ii.* 547.

[Buxted]
Saturday [late Jan.–early Feb. 1831]

My dear Sir,

It was taking no small liberty to entangle you and Mrs Kenyon in our little economical arrangements. I am pleased, however, with

---

[1] See L. 607 below.
[2] Hamilton did not marry till Apr. 1833. W. W. had heard the unfounded rumour from Maria Edgeworth who was staying in London. See *Hamilton*, i. 427.

having done so, as it has been the occasion of my hearing from you again. Your eloquence, as the heart has so much to do in it, has prevailed, and we will order a chaise to be here on Wednesday next time for our reaching Brighton[1] by five—perhaps earlier—but if the day prove fine I should like to stop an hour at Lewes to look round me.

You seem to lead a dissipated life, you and Mrs Kenyon; but I have no right to reproach you. I have left my Brother's quiet fireside for the last two days to dine with two several Magistrates at Uckfield, where, of course, I heard rather too much of obstinate juries, grand and Petty; burnings, poor rates, cash-payments, and that everlasting Incubus of universal agricultural distress.

Five times have I dined while at Buxted at the table of an Earl[2]—and twice in the company of a Prince.[3] Therefore let you and Mrs Kenyon prepare yourselves for something stately and august in my deportment and manners. But King, Queen, Prince, Princesses, Dukes etc are common articles at Brighton [so] that I must descend from my elevation, or pass for a downright Malvolio.

I congratulate you upon being *un*radicalized. I wish however the change had taken place under less threatening circumstances. The idle practice of recrimination is becoming general. The Whigs upbraid the Tories as authors of the mischief which all feel, by withstanding reform so obstinately; and the Tories reproach the Whigs with having done all the harm by incessant *bawling* for it. . . .

[*cetera desunt*]

[1] The Wordsworths remained several days at Brighton. They met Harriet Douglas and her brothers there.

[2] Charles Cecil Cope Jenkinson, 3rd Earl of Liverpool (see pt. i, L. 76), half-brother of the Prime Minister. Buxted Place came to him through his wife, Julia Evelyn Medley (d. 1814), daughter and sole heiress of Sir George Shuckburgh-Evelyn, 6th Bart., whom he had married in 1810. On 23 Jan. C. W. reported to Joshua Watson that W. W. was 'out frequently, particularly at Lord Liverpool's, with whom he walks and talks and dines continually'. They had tried to persuade him to write on the political crisis, but without success: 'Christopher and he have a great deal of talk, and he is murmuring a great deal by himself; but that is, I know, in part, poetical murmuring.' (Churton, *Memoir of Joshua Watson*, ii. 2–3.) Early the following month, on 4 Feb., Dora W. wrote to C. W. jnr.: 'Father has dined once this week with Ld Liverpool, but brought home no news—he bids me say he misses you very much and is more and more convinced that he cannot write any better than anyone else on the present affairs.' (*WL MSS.*)

[3] Probably Prince William Frederick, 2nd Duke of Gloucester (see also *MY* ii. 648), Chancellor of Cambridge University. Knight states that W. W. also dined with William IV and Queen Adelaide at Buxted, but cites no authority for this.

593. W. W. to C. W. JNR.[1]

Address: C. Wordsworth Esq., Trin: Coll: Cambridge.
Franked: Uckfield Feb. seventeen 1831. *Liverpool*.[2]
Postmark: 18 Feb. 1831. *Stamp*: Uckfield.
MS. WL. Hitherto unpublished.

[*In Dora W.'s hand*]

[Buxted]
Thursday [17 Feb. 1831]

Sir John Walsh[3] in Bull[4] takes the same view of the Ballot that I
have been accustomed to do, his thoughts are just, it is only to be
regretted that his expression of them is not more easy and popular.
I cannot however concur with him in opinion that the Ballot was
beneficial to France in saving the Electors from an unwarrantable
influence of the late government. The factious dispositions of the
Electors became I believe much more formidable to the monarchy
in consequence of this mode of voting: and the ill judging ministers
of Charles the 10 were accordingly driven upon those violent
measures which ended in the loss of his [crown.][5]
A man must be blind as a mole who cannot see that the revolutionary movements of the present day are pointed for their ultimate
aim against social inequality as based upon and upheld by accumulated Property. For many reasons I detest the ballot and not the
least of these is a conviction that armed with this instrument the
enemies of the present social system would be irresistible. Do not
infer from this that I am reconciled either to those vast capitals and
very great inequalities of *landed* property in particular which exist

---

[1] A postscript added to a long letter from Dora W. to C. W. jnr. describing
their activities at Buxted.
[2] i.e. Lord Liverpool, the owner of Buxted Place.
[3] Sir John Benn Walsh, 2nd Bart. (1798–1881), later 1st Baron Ormath-
waite, of Warfield Park, Bracknell, Berks.: M.P. for Sudbury, 1830–4 and
1838–40, and thereafter for Radnorshire for nearly 28 years. He wrote several
pamphlets, including *Popular Opinions on Parliamentary Reform, considered . . .,
Fourth edition, with additions, and a postscript to the Ballot*, 1831, a conciliatory
statement of the conservative case against sudden political innovation, which
won the admiration of Coleridge. 'Plain good sense, enriched as well as
enlightened by observation, and History', was his comment in his own copy,
now in the British Library.
[4] The weekly paper *John Bull*, edited by Theodore Hook, consistently
opposed the Reform Bill. The extract from Walsh's pamphlet (p. 69) appeared
on 14 Feb.
[5] *Dora W. draws a crown*. The remainder of this text is on a separate sheet
(which includes the address) that has become detached from the earlier section,
but the two parts appear to belong together.

in these Islands but all this might be brought within reasonable
bounds in due course of time without incurring the mischiefs
which must inevitably arise out of the principles of [? another]
system; mischiefs incalculably greater [   ]¹ which the
liberals are set upon removing at [any] cost.

Ever your affectionate uncle
Wᵐ Wordsworth²

I should like to see Sir John Walsh's Pamphlet but at present
unfortunately I can neither read nor write, nor scarcely venture to
think.

[*Dora W. adds*]

Poor man he is to be pitied! but those who are obliged to listen
to his hooping cough still more so I tell him. For you must know his
cold is turned into this baby's disease—are not you sorry for him.
There are symptoms too of incipient consumption. This is very
wicked in me, as he bears this deprivation most patiently indeed.

[*C. W. adds*]

Send the inclosed to the Bursar and to Mr Thorp³ immediately.

Ever most affect^ly   C. W.

I am afraid the accounts of Mrs Watson⁴ are much worse, and
very unpromising.

594. D. W. to MRS. S. T. COLERIDGE

Address: To Mrs S. T. Coleridge at H. N. Coleridge's Esqʳᵉ, Hampstead.
MS. Victoria University Library, Toronto.
LY ii. 548.

[Rydal Mount]
March 7ᵗʰ [1831] Monday.

My dear Friend,
    We think it very long since we heard from—or even *of* you and
I am glad of the means of sending a *wee* note free of cost, especially

---

¹ *Hole in MS.*   ² Not signed by W. W.
³ The Revd. Thomas Thorp (1797–1877), Fellow of Trinity College,
Cambridge, since 1820, and at this time Junior Dean: Archdeacon and Chan-
cellor of Bristol, 1836–73, and rector of Kemerton, Glos., from 1839: first
President of the Cambridge Camden Society.
⁴ Mrs. Joshua Watson died later this year. She was Mary, daughter of
Thomas Sikes, a London banker, and niece of Charles Daubeny, Archdeacon of
Salisbury and one of the forerunners of the Tractarians.

368

as I have good news of Hartley. He received a second £10 from
Blackwood the week before last and paid up his quarter's Board till
March, leaving a small surplus in James Fleming's[1] hands to be
called for when wanted. J. Fleming wrote to tell me the above
good news, and last Friday I called at the house. I was sorry not to
find H. at home, and more sorry to hear that he had drawn out
5/- at two different times, but it might mainly be to pay small
debts, for on the whole he has been pretty regular—even for a long
time, and James Fleming assured me that he was very busy and he
thought would soon have earned more money—so he hoped that
in future Mr Coleridge would be able himself to pay for his lodgings etc. It is very pleasing to hear how affectionately James
Fleming and his Wife speak of Hartley—indeed I never go without
feeling thankful that he is in so respectable a home. My Brother in a
letter received to-day tells me he has received £20 from H. N.
Coleridge on Hartley's account. Now my Sister mentioned the
like Sum a good while ago. Does my Brother mean the same twenty
pounds or have you paid them that sum twice over? At all events it
is ready to meet Hartley's wants, but if he goes on as he has lately
done it will not be needed, and truly thankful shall we all be if it
prove so. We were exceedingly glad to hear of the accession to
Mrs Coleridge's property by the death of her Sister[2] (I suppose *her*
Sister, but mean Henry's aunt). With a share of such a fortune in
prospect Henry and Sara need not now have any care for the
Future.—Poverty is never likely to stare *them* in the face, and truly
do I rejoice in this both for their sakes and yours. We really long
to hear from you—and pray give us one of your old-fashioned
letters, tip-top full of domestic news and indeed of whatever news
comes into your head. My Brother has, I find, seen H. N. C. but he
says not yet S. T. C., and as he does not mention you I fear he has
not seen either you or Sara since his return to London.

Last news from Keswick good—all well—Southey very busy.
This is a sad scrawl to send so far; but I have not time for more or
better. Going to tea with Mrs Luff, who comes home to-night
having spent the winter at Graystoke. Love to S. and Henry—
Pray mention all that concerns yourself in particular—health and

---

[1] Hartley Coleridge lodged with James Fleming at Town End.
[2] Mrs. Brown, formerly Dorothy Ayer Taylor (1755–1831), sister of Col.
Coleridge's wife and widow of Henry Langford Brown of Combesatchfield,
Silverton, Devon, had died on 11 Jan., leaving her considerable fortune to her
sister. She had helped to finance her nephew Henry Nelson Coleridge's education at Eton. See Lord Coleridge, *The Story of a Devonshire House*, 1905, pp. 68,
173, 299.

every thing else. Good news from Joanna of sister Martha.[1] We are all well—a comfortable winter in all respects we have had [?][2] for our health has been very good—only at one time S. H. suffered from weak eyes. A letter from Mrs Slade Smith[3] but not one word of Borrowdale or debts—only she is charmed with her Lover of a Husband. God bless you all, ever your affect^e

D Wordsworth

We sent a packet some time ago to H. N. C. by Mrs Cookson, in which I enclosed a letter for Sara.

595. W. W. to GEORGE HUNTLY GORDON

Address: G: Huntly Gordon Esqre, Treasury Chambers. [*In Dora W.'s hand*]
MS. Cornell.
Broughton, p. 43.

[*In E. Q.'s hand*]

[Bryanston Street]
[early Mar. 1831][4]

My dear Sir,

  Mr Quillinan, who holds the pen for me, can testify how much mortified I was when I heard that you had come over to breakfast here by my own appointment on a morning (a very wet one too) when I was out, the engagement having escaped my recollection. You would not wonder at this if you had as many proofs as Mr Q. has of what a state this faculty of mine is in amid the hurry of this great city.[5]

---

¹ Probably Martha Ferguson, Mrs Rawson's niece.
² *MS. cut away.*   ³ Formerly Miss Barker.
⁴ W. W. had been called to London on 21 Feb. on business connected with the future of his Distributorship, the Distributor for Cumberland, Mr. James of Penrith, having died suddenly; and on 25 Feb. Lord Lonsdale wrote promising to help W. W. secure a better financial return if the proposed enlargement of his district took place (*WL MSS.*). Dora W. wrote to C. W. jnr. from Buxted on the 26th: 'My Lord Althorp [the new Chancellor of the Exchequer] has been most liberal, just gives him *double risk, double duty*, and *no more pay*, whilst he has doubled the pay of my father's Subs. . . . The Distributorships of the two counties Cumberland and Westmorland are consolidated—and this ridding away of a "Place Man" made a grand sound in the newspapers, whilst in fact it will be no saving, or very little at least, to the country . . .' (*WL MSS.*)
⁵ W. W. dined with Archbishop Howley on 1 and 12 Mar., and with Lord Liverpool on the 13th. Writing to Dora W. at Buxted on 3 Mar., E. Q.

It will give me the greatest pleasure (and *this* I will *not forget*) to mention all that you wish to Sir James Macintosh:[1] and let me add that I feel obliged by your giving me this opportunity of doing any thing that wears a probability of serving you. Sir James Macintosh resides so very near that I am sure of having a good opportunity of speaking to him on this or any other point if a dinner party should not afford one.

In the commerce of good offices I am greatly in your debt, and am not unwilling to be more so, as you will see when I ask you to speak a good word in *my* behalf with Mr Ellice;[2] my friend Mr Sharpe[3] has already applied to him, but two friends are better than one however good. All that I would wish you to say is that you are pretty sure from your private knowledge of me that I would not make a request to government that was unreasonable. Should your friendship induce you to add more of course I could have no objection. All this alludes to the memorial[4] to the Treasury which you mentioned to Mr Quillinan. I have not yet recd an answer to that request.—I shall call upon you either at the Treasury or in Cannon Street on Friday.—

Yours most faithfully
[*signed*] Wm Wordsworth

Mr Quillinan's best regards—

described W. W.'s busy life: 'His time is swallowed up in swallowing break-fasts, making morning visits (where he gets cold collations) devouring dinners, and thundering denunciations against reform: and now and then "brooding over his own sweet voice" and Sir George Beaumont.' Dora W. told C. W. jnr. on 7 Mar. that her father was 'employed chiefly as he tells us, in conversing with men of all parties hearing their opinions and endeavouring to correct the bad ones—he is busy is he not?' (*WL MSS.*)

[1] For Sir James Macintosh, see *MY* ii. 45, and pt. i, L. 195. For Francis Jeffrey's meetings with W. W. at Mackintosh's, see L. 602 below, and Lord Cockburn, *Life of Lord Jeffrey*, 2 vols., 1852, i. 322: 'He is not in the very least Lakish now, or even in any degree poetical, but rather a hard and a sensible worldly sort of a man'. Another visitor whom W. W. met at Mackin-tosh's was the Irish dramatist and politician Richard Lalor Sheil (1791–1851).

[2] Edward Ellice (1781–1863), M.P. for Coventry, 1818–26, and from 1830 onwards: Secretary to the Treasury and Government Whip from Nov. 1830 until 1832, and Secretary at War, 1832–4: an influential politician (his wife was Lord Greys' youngest sister), and associate of Joseph Hume (see pt. i, L. 27).

[3] Richard Sharp.

[4] W. W. jnr. was now returning from Germany with no further prospects of gainful employment, and W. W. was canvassing the possibility of his appointment as his sub-distributor at Carlisle. See L. 615 below.

Address: W. C. Macready Esq^(re)., 37, Weymouth St., Portland Place. [*In Dora W.'s hand*]
MS. Hudleston family archives. Hitherto unpublished.

[? Wandsworth]
[? *c.* 14 Mar. 1831]²

My dear Sir,
    I much regret that a previous engagement will prevent me having the pleasure of dining with you as you propose, and the more so as you are going out of Town so early. Believe me I should be happy to see more of you at any time when Fortune may be kind enough to throw us together.

I am, my dear Sir,
sincerely yours
Wm Wordsworth

Turn over

Could you breakfast with us tomorrow at nine oclock.

597. W. W. to JOHN MITCHINSON CALVERT

Address: Dr Calvert, 3 Sackville Street [*delivered by hand*]
MS. Yale University Library. Hitherto unpublished.

12 Bryanston Street
17^(th)—[Mar. 1831]

My dear Sir,
    I am sorry that I was not at home when you called.—I have not forgotten my breakfast engagement, but my mornings have been occupied very much, and among other ties I have one with a portrait painter³—

Believe me ever faithfully
yours
Wm Wordsworth

---

¹ William Charles Macready (1793–1873), the celebrated actor, whom W. W. had met in 1823 (see pt. i, L. 102).
² This note cannot be dated with certainty. It was perhaps written on 14 Mar. 1831, while W. W. was staying the night at East Hill, Wandsworth, as the guest of John Jebb (1775–1833), Bishop of Limerick, a noted High-Churchman, whom he had met recently at Sir Robert Inglis's. Jebb's invitation of 7 Mar. is preserved among the *WL MSS.*: 'You have, in the true sense of the word, consented to an act of charity,—in thus coming to an invalid, who wishes that he could receive you,—in a way more expressive of his great respect and veneration. He has nothing to offer, but a cordial welcome, a well-aired bed, and a bishop's blessing: and these he trusts, indeed, he may venture to say, he knows, you will not despise.'
³ William Boxall. See L. 603 below.

598. W. W. to D. W. and S. H.

Address: Miss Wordsworth, Rydal, Westmorland.
Franked: London April one 1831 Wᵐ J. Bankes.[1]
Postmark: 1 Apr. 1831.
Stamp: Keswick.
MS. Manchester University Library. Hitherto unpublished.

[Bryanston Street]
[1 Apr. 1831]

Dearest Dorothy and Sarah

Wᵐ looks well, for him![2]—but is not so strong for walking as one would wish.—I am sitting for my Bust to Mr Macd[on]ald.[3] I hope you will like it. I am much mistified not to hear from the Stamp off[ice].[4]

Farewell—in a great Hurry

W W

[*W. W. jnr. adds*]

I forgot that I could enclose Mother's last letter   WW Jʳ.

599. W. W. to ALEXANDER DYCE

Address: The Rev. Alexander Dyce, Gray's Inn Square.
Postmark: 7 Apr. 1831. *Stamp*: Oxford [? Street].
MS. Victoria and Albert Museum.
K. LY iii. 1072.

12 Bryanston Street, 7ᵗʰ April (my birthday 61) [1831]

My dear Sir,

When you read the Excursion do not read the Quarto—it is improved in the 8ᵛᵒ Ed:[5]—but I thought the Quarto might have its value with you as a Collector.

Believe me,
faithfully yours
W. Wordsworth

[1] William John Bankes of Kingston Lacy, Dorset, formerly M.P. for Cambridge University (see pt. i, L. 212), and now for Marlborough.
[2] Willy W. returned to London from Germany on 26 Mar.
[3] There is a blot on the MS. but the name is legible. Lawrence Macdonald (1799–1878) practised in Edinburgh and London, and latterly in Rome. His bust of W. W. has not apparently survived. See *Letters of Dora Wordsworth*, p. 86, and Blanchard, *Portraits of Wordsworth*, p. 155. W. W. met Macdonald on 12 Mar.; the sittings seem to have begun around the 25th, according to E. Q.'s MS. Diary (*WL MSS.*).
[4] *MS. indistinct.*   [5] i.e. the edition of 1827.

373

600. W. W. to SAMUEL CARTER HALL[1]

Address: S. C. Hall Esqre, 59 Sloane Street.
Postmark: 12 Apr. 1831.
MS. Mr J. M. Edmonds.
LY ii. 549.

[Bryanston Street]
[12 Apr. 1831]

My dear Sir,

I hope I may be able to see you again before I quit Town, next
Monday. If convenient, which you can let me know by the twopenny post, Mr Quillinan and I and my younger son, fresh from
Germany, will breakfast with you either on Thursday or Friday
as you may fix—Thursday I should prefer.—

ever sincerely yours
Wm Wordsworth

601. W. W. to ALLAN CUNNINGHAM

MS. Cornell. Hitherto unpublished.

12 Bryanston Street
April 14th 1831

My dear Sir

You will remember our talk at [? Liv][2] about the Busts[3] in
which you were so kind as to say that you would meet my wishes.
Two are for my Nephews John and Christopher Wordsworth, and
may be directed to Dr Wordsworth,

Trin Lodge
Cambridge.

The Third is for my Daughter in Law, late Miss Curwen of Workington Hall Cumberland, and I wish to be directed to the

Revd John Wordsworth
Moresby
Whitehaven
Cumberland.

---

[1] For S. C. Hall, editor of *The Amulet*, see pt. i, L. 285. W. W. breakfasted
with him on 14 Apr., and the two went on to visit a bookshop in Piccadilly to
look into the sales of Galignani's edition. W. W. was impressed by its
popularity, and all the more convinced that he should himself produce a cheap
edition of his works. (See S. C. Hall, *Retrospect of a Long Life*, 2 vols., 1883,
ii. 37 n., 39 n.)

[2] It seems that W. W. was meaning to write Liverpool, and then became
uncertain whether that had been the place. He had met Cunningham several
times recently, however, in London.

[3] Copies of Chantrey's bust of W. W., executed in 1820. It appears that the
busts were not sent to their destinations until more than three years later.
See L. 828 below.

374

This last, could you be so kind as to send, by any ship going to Whitehaven.

With many thanks for this trouble you are about to undertake upon this occasion believe me

dear Sir

very faithfully

yours

Wm Wordsworth

602. W. W. to HENRY TAYLOR[1]

Address: Henry Taylor Esq. [*delivered by hand*]
MS. Mr. W. Hugh Peal. Hitherto unpublished.

[Bryanston Street]

[*c.* 15 Apr. 1831]

My dear Mr Taylor,

Tomorrow I am engaged to breakfast at home—pray come here —On Sunday I purpose to go to Enfield Chase to see my friend Charles Lamb,[2] and I do not think it likely I shall return the same night. If I do I will breakfast with you on Monday.

Could you contrive to forward the enclosed franked.

Ever sincerely

your obliged

W Wordsworth

[1] For Henry Taylor of the Colonial Office, see pt. i, L. 120. Taylor wrote to Isabella Fenwick in May: 'I have seen a good deal more of Wordsworth than I ever saw before; I feel as if one could have a great deal of regard for him. I have had three or four breakfasts for him, and he is as agreeable in society as he is admirable in his powers of talking, so perfectly courteous and well-bred and simple in his manners. He met Jeffrey the other day at Sir J. Mackintosh's, and at Jeffrey's request, they were introduced. Lockhart beheld the ceremony, and told me that Wordsworth played the part of a man of the world to perfection, much better than the smaller man, and did not appear to be conscious of anything having taken place between them before.' (*Correspondence of Henry Taylor*, ed. Edward Dowden, 1888, p. 38). It was at one of these breakfasts, on 27 Feb., that W. W. and Southey were fellow guests with John Stuart Mill (see also L. 633 below), Edward Strutt, Charles Villiers, and other 'philosophical radicals'. (See *The Greville Memoirs*, ed. Lytton Strachey and Roger Fulford, 8 vols., 1938, ii. 122.)

[2] See *Lamb*, iii. 307. W. W. was accompanied by Edward Moxon.

603. W. W. to SAMUEL ROGERS

Address: Samuel Rogers Esqr, St James's Place.
MS. Mr. Basil Cottle.
Basil Cottle, 'Wordsworth and His Portraits', NQ ccxviii (Aug. 1973), 285–6.

Tuesday Noon. [19 Apr. 1831]

My dear Friend

With a thousand good wishes for your speedy recovery I take my departure this day.

Mr Boxall[1] the Painter would be proud and happy to make your acquaintance. I know him to be a most amiable Man, as he is a very promising Artist. I should have requested permission to introduce him personally, but this cannot be, and I have to request that if he should call at your Door, you would receive him as cordially as you are accustomed to do my Friends.

My Sister never writes without sending her love to you and Miss Rogers; to whom also I beg my farewell remembrances.

Ever my dear Friend
most faithfully yours
W Wordsworth

---

1 William, later Sir William, Boxall, R.A. (1800–79), painter, who specialized in portraits: Director of the National Gallery, 1865–74. The Boxall portrait was, as E. Q. wrote to Dora W., 'perhaps not the most striking likeness in the world, but it is a likeness, thoughtful and poet-like'. (*WL MSS.*) See Blanchard, *Portraits of Wordsworth*, pp. 70–1, 154–5. The portrait seems to have been finished before 6 Apr., on which date, according to E. Q.'s MS. Diary (*WL MSS.*), Macdonald the sculptor, Allan Cunningham, and Boxall dined with W. W. and E. Q. Just before this, on 30 Mar., W. W. had sat to Wilkin (see L. 639 below).

604. W. W. to HANNAH HOARE[1]

MS. Cornell. Hitherto unpublished.

12 Bryanstone Street
[? Apr. 1831]

Dear Mrs Hoare,

The Enclosed is for Mr Hall[2] who will call upon me about 4 oclock; pray be so kind as to let him have it—

faithfully your
much obliged
Wm Wordsworth

We shall be at Hampstead by the same time—

605. W. W. to BENJAMIN ROBERT HAYDON[3]

Address: B. R. Haydon Esqre, 4 Burford Place, Connaught Terrace.
MS. untraced.
LY ii. 550.

Trinity Lodge Cambridge
Ap. 23^d [1831]

Dr Haydon

I had not time to answer your friendly notes.[4] If I can command my thoughts I will write something about your Picture,[5] *in prose,*

---

[1] Mrs. Hoare, the Wordsworths' Hampstead friend (see pt. i, L. 1). M. W. and Dora W. arrived at her house from Buxted on 18 Apr., and on the 19th they joined W. W. at E. Q.'s in Bryanston Street. The Wordsworths returned to Mrs. Hoare's that evening to prepare for their departure north, and this letter may belong to that day.   [2] Samuel Carter Hall.

[3] W. W. and Haydon had been estranged since 1823, after Haydon had taken offence at some imagined slight to his wife at their last meeting, and in a letter to Mary Russell Mitford of 12 Feb. 1824 (*British Library MSS.*) he had not scrupled to accuse W. W. in the most general terms of meanness, egoism, and servility (see pt. i, L. 97). But W. W. now seems to have taken the initiative in healing the breach, by calling on Haydon on 12 Apr. (see *Diary of Benjamin Robert Haydon*, ed. Pope, iii. 515).

[4] In his letter of 15 Apr., Haydon had written: 'You must not think us disrespectful if we do not pay you the comp^t of an invitation as we used to do. Since I last saw you I have lost all—in fact nothing is left to us but the clothes on our backs and if we asked you to dine, the chance is, you must turn up your plate to eat your pudding on the back, if you wanted a clean one . . .' And he added a comment on Hazlitt's recent death: 'He used us like a Fiend. He had been treated with marked kindness, assisted with money and without cause, turned round and assailed me for hire!—He was a most entertaining Fiend— but still his humour was Fiendish.' (*WL MSS.*)

[5] 'Napoleon on the Island of St. Helena.' 'He spoke of my Napoleon in high poetry of language', Haydon wrote in his *Diary*, 'with his usual straight forward intensity of diction.'

for the Muse has forsaken me—being scared away by the vil-
lainous aspect of the Times.

I regret I saw so little of you—which was in some degree my
own fault. With best wishes for your success in y^r Art—and for
happiness in life I remain faithfully y^rs

W. Wordsworth

I hope to be at home next Wed.—

606. W. W. to JOHN KENYON

MS. Mr. W. Hugh Peal. Hitherto unpublished.

[*In M. W.'s hand*]

Trinity Lodge Cam
April 23^d. [1831]

My dear Friend,

I was hurried out of Town by business—and Mrs W. and Dora
only passed thro', so that they could not call upon you and Mrs K.
which they very much regret. We expect to reach Rydal by next
Wed. When may we look for the pleasure of seeing you and Mrs
K?

We all unite in kind regards to you both, and believe me

faithfully y^rs
W Wordsworth[1]

607. W. W. to HENRY TAYLOR

MS. Harvard University Library.
K (—). LY ii. 550.

[*In M. W.'s hand*]

Trinity Lodge Cambridge
Ap. 23^d [1831]

My dear Sir

Thus far am I on my way to the North—being suddenly called
out of Town. On Sunday I visited Ch: Lamb and did not return
till 4 o'c. on Monday afternoon, so that I could not breakfast with

---

[1] Not signed by W. W.

you either day, every hour of Tuesday I was engaged, and slept at Hampstead, and on Thursday arrived here. I have been thus particular to shew that it was no fault of my own that deprived me of the pleasure of giving you a farewell shake by the hand. Pray express my regrets to Mr Steven[1] that I could not see him again—being absolutely hurried far beyond my powers.

I have taken the liberty of addressing the enclosed to you for the 2ᵈ Post—they are parting notes to such friends as I had not time to see.

Of the Dissolution,[2] or *desolation* of Parᵗ as the Gips here call it, I shall [say][3] nothing. You know what I must think of it—and our poor Jack Tar of a King.

God have mercy upon him, and us all! I calculate upon reaching Rydal next Wed: and to start next day for Carlisle. If any thing remarkable occurs that the Papers do not notice—pray tell me.

Ever faithfully yours
[*signed*] W Wordsworth

[1] James, later Sir James, Stephen (1789–1859), Henry Taylor's colleague at the Colonial Office, and Under-Secretary of State for the Colonies, 1836–47, and according to Henry Taylor (*Autobiography*, 2 vols., 1885, i. 123), virtual ruler of the Colonial Empire. As a nephew of Wilberforce, he took a strong interest in the Slavery question and drafted the measure passed in 1833: he also had much to do with the development of responsible government in Canada. His contributions to the *Edinburgh Review* formed the basis of *Essays in Ecclesiastical Biography*, 2 vols., 1849. Thereafter he was Regius Professor of Modern History at Cambridge. For some account of his political and literary friendships, see *The Right Honourable Sir James Stephen . . . Letters, with Biographical Notes, By His Daughter Caroline Emelia Stephen* (privately printed), 1906.
[2] The Reform Bill was introduced in the House of Commons on 1 Mar. by Lord John Russell, and carried on the second reading (22 Mar.) by 302 to 301. On 19 Apr., however, during the committee stage, the ministry found themselves in a minority of 8 on an amendment that the number of M.P.s for England and Wales should not be diminished; and after a second adverse vote they resigned. Their resignation not being accepted by the King, they appealed to the country, and Parliament was dissolved on 22 Apr. amid mounting excitement.
[3] *Word dropped out.*

608. W. W. to EDWARD QUILLINAN

Address: Edward Quillinan Esqre, Bryanston Street, Portman Square, London.
[*In S. H.'s hand*]
Postmark: 2 May 1831. *Stamp*: Kendal Penny Post.
MS. WL.
'Some unpublished Letters of William Wordsworth', Cornhill Magazine, xx
(*1893*), *257–76. K. LY ii. 551.*

[Rydal Mount]
[29 Apr. 1831]

My dear Friend,

I cannot suffer this Letter[1] to go without a word from me. And first of dear Mrs Wordsworth—her complaint is lumbago and sciatica, the younger sister and scarcely distinguishable from tic-douloureux. But here my poetical Reputation served us. I knew no one in Notingham, but bethought me of the Howitts.[2] There are two Brothers of them; on one I called to state my situation and found that there was a third Brother, a Physician. Him I sent for, and W^m and Mary Howitt insisted upon the invalid being brought to their house, which was a great comfort on the eve of an Election. We made one attempt to move her in vain—in the afternoon we succeeded, and she passed through the wide market-place of Notingham, wrapped in a blanket, she could not be dressed, and in a chair, followed by a 100 boys and curious persons. So that she preceded Sir Thomas Denman[3] and Ferguson[4] in the honour of

[1] A joint letter from Rotha to Jemima Quillinan and S. H. to E. Q. (see *SH*, pp. 379–81). Rotha had accompanied the Wordsworths on their journey north in order to spend some time at Rydal Mount.
[2] For William and Mary Howitt, the Quaker poets, see pt. i, L. 293. The other two brothers were Richard Howitt (1799–1869), author of *Antediluvian Sketches, and other poems*, 1830; and Dr. Godfrey Howitt, author of *The Nottinghamshire Flora*, 1839. 'Christopher North' alludes to the family in his discussion of 'Quaker Poets' in *Noctes Ambrosianae*, no. lvi, *Blackwood's Magazine*, xxix (Apr. 1831), 699 ff. Dora W. (left behind with M. W. at Nottingham) wrote this same day to C. W. jnr. about the election fever there and the hospitality of the Howitts: 'Nothing can exceed the kindness of our Host and Hostess. They are "Friends" not tho' in the least rigid ones. Mrs Howitt is a charming Creature, much the most fascinating of the Authoresses I have seen—but alas she is a red hot Reformist, and we are in a hot bed of Reformists—in a wasps nest positively . . .' (*WL MSS.*)
[3] Sir Thomas Denman, 1st Baron Denman (1779–1854), the distinguished lawyer, who came into prominence along with Brougham in the defence of Queen Caroline in 1820 (see *MY* ii. 643), and was thereafter associated with him in his reforming programme: Whig M.P. for Wareham, 1818, and for Nottingham, 1820–6, and 1830–2: Attorney General from 19 Nov. 1830, responsible for drafting the Reform Bill; and Lord Chief Justice from 1832 to 1850. Denman was an enthusiastic admirer of Wordsworth's poetry, and they met occasionally in the later years (see *RMVB* for 1841).
[4] General Sir Ronald Craufurd Ferguson (1773–1841), M.P. for Kirkcaldy, 1806–30, and for Nottingham, 1830–41. Denman and Ferguson were returned unopposed at the election on 29 Apr.

being chaired, and was called by us Parliament woman for the loyal Borough of Notingham.

As to Rotha she is a sweet clever child and we were the best companions in the world. As Miss H. says, we must take care not to spoil her. She is wonderfully intelligent.

God bless you. I am called away.

Ever faithfully and gratefully yours
W. Wordsworth

Love to Jemima.

609. D. W. to WILLIAM PEARSON

MS. untraced.
Pearson. LT ii. 552.

Thursday, 5th May [1831]

My dear Mr Pearson,

You must have thought me very slow in writing, but the truth is, that I have waited for definite intelligence; and even yet am not enabled to give it. My Brother reached home this day week (Thursday) in good health, and as good spirits as an anxious mind would allow of—for he is very anxious concerning the passing of this Bill.[1] He and his Wife and Daughter left Cambridge on Monday, and grievous to relate! Mrs Wordsworth had a wretched journey to Nottingham, where she was fast bound, by the excruciating torture of the Lumbago; and there my Brother was obliged to leave her, with his Daughter. Happily, they are under the roof of the kindest of Friends,[2] and in the care of a most judicious physician; but you may judge of their eagerness to be at home: however, when they wrote (last Sunday) they could not venture to fix a time for their departure. Thank God! the complaint is not a dangerous one, and she is decidedly recovering, though slowly. We are now chiefly anxious lest they should venture too soon, and suffer a second detention, with the additional misfortune of being among strangers. It was very unfortunate that my Brother's Stamp Office business obliged him to leave her. He reached home in good health, as I have said, and was again compelled to leave us on Sunday afternoon. He and Mr. Carter are now at Carlisle, and are intending to

---

[1] The Reform Bill, which Lord John Russell was to reintroduce in the House of Commons on 24 June.

[2] The Howitts (see previous letter).

go the rounds of his new district,[1] and we cannot guess the time of
their return; only I do not expect them before the end of next
week. Whether he will be preceded by my Sister and Niece it is
not possible to conjecture. My Nephew William (from Germany),
arrived at Rydal last Monday.—He is quite well, and much improved by his travels, and very happy to find himself, once again,
at his own home.

I will write to you again when my Brother returns, and then
hope to be able to say when he will be settled at home, and glad to
see you. In the mean time, conclude that 'no news is good news'.

It will please you to hear, that at his first dinner, my Brother
ejaculated 'What excellent potatoes!' Miss Hutchinson is well,
and joins me in best regards. I need not add how glad I shall be
to see you after we are settled.

I remain, dear Sir,
Yours truly,
D. Wordsworth

610. W. W. to D. W. to C. W. JNR.

Address: To Chris^r Wordsworth Esqre, Trinity College, Cambridge. [*In
D. W.'s hand*]
Stamp: Kendal Penny Post.
MS. WL. Hitherto unpublished.

Rydal Mount. Monday, May 9th [1831]
My dear Chris,
A thousand thanks for your successive Letters. I am more than
satisfied with the majority,[2] considering the difficulties you had to
contend with.—I certainly approve of your view of the Compro-
mizers—as I have said in my Letter to Mr Rose.[3]—He will shew

[1] Cumberland, now combined with the Distributorship for Westmorland
(see L. 595 above and next letter).
[2] The election for Cambridge University had taken place on 6 May, and
Henry Goulburn (see L. 419 above) and William Peel had been elected, with
806 and 805 votes respectively, defeating William Cavendish (see L. 451
above) and Palmerston, who received 630 and 610. William Yates Peel
(1789–1858), Sir Robert Peel's younger brother, had sat with him as M.P.
for Tamworth, 1818–30, and was his Under-Secretary in the Home Department in Wellington's administration. He sat for Cambridge University until
1833.
[3] Hugh James Rose. W. W.'s letter has not survived.

you my Letter, with some notices of the Carlisle election.[1] Do give my congratulations to your dear Father. Mr Rose tells me that he has been very active.

We had a sad journey from Cambridge, for Mrs W's tortures were almost insupportable. But Dora told you all. I left Notingham with an anxious mind, and have since had a slavish journey among the wilds of Cumberland and part of Northumberland upon Office business, which I heartily wish I was rid of—seeing nothing but confusion and disorder, and being dismayed with the responsibilities of the situation. I have no less than 21 Agents to look after, whose circumstances must more or less be thrown into confusion by the revolutionary dis[as]ter impending over us.—I wish I could write you an entertaining Letter; but my loss of spirit takes away my power. It seems ungrateful to talk of low spirits after the good and great news of your letter—pray excuse me. Isabella is here—and John would have been so too but for the Cumberland election.[2] Her father in law has subscribed £500 for the Radical Candidate—feeling I suppose that his Estate has been unreasonably long in his family, into which it came at the Conquest; yet he disapproves of the Bill[3] in his private conversation. What ails this unhappy nation that what used to be called principle seems utterly to have deserted it!

Do you hear of John?[4]—good news I hope. My dear wife looks

---

[1] In the Carlisle election the sitting Tory member, General Sir James Lushington (d. 1859), was defeated amid widespread accusations of intimidation of voters. Philip Henry Howard (1801–83) of Corby Castle, the other sitting member, a Whig and Roman Catholic, was re-elected, and he represented Carlisle until 1847, and again 1848–52, when he retired in the face of the agitation over the Ecclesiastical Titles Bill. He was now joined as the other member for Carlisle by William James (1791–1861) of Barrock Park, a wealthy radical, who retained his seat until 1834.

[2] In Cumberland a new situation was created by the withdrawal after thirty-five years of Sir John Lowther (see *MY* ii. 581) and the nomination in his place of Lord Lowther, who had already issued an address to the electors of Westmorland. The radical candidates were Sir James Graham (see *MY* ii. 536 and L. 419 above), who had represented Cumberland since 1829; and William Blamire (1790–1862) of Thackwood Nook, near Dalston, connected through his mother and his wife with the Curwens and Christians: later (1836) head of the Tithe Commutation Commission, and of the Copyhold and Inclosure Commissions. (See Henry Lonsdale, *The Worthies of Cumberland*, 6 vols., 1867–75, i. 207 ff.) Henry Curwen supported both candidates and nominated Blamire when the Poll opened on 5 May. Lord Lowther's candidacy was fatally damaged by his switch of constituency, and he withdrew from the contest on the fourth day, having polled 454 votes to Graham's 1196 and Blamire's 1170. (See *Cumberland Pacquet* for 3 and 10 May 1831.) In July he was brought forward for the Irish borough of Bandon but was again defeated, and remained out of active politics until Feb. 1832 (see L. 662 below).

[3] The Reform Bill.

[4] i.e. his nephew, C. W.'s son, whose health was increasingly precarious. He was now on holiday in France.

much better than one could have expected after so severe an illness. W^m reached Rydal last Monday morning, having been precisely a week on the road—he was sadly tired the first two days, as no doubt was the pony, having his long legs and so many years of its own to bear. I hope your father has not suffered in health by his exertions—ever most affectionately, my dear nephew

Yours Wm Wordsworth.

Mr Rose says that the young men were decidedly with you. This is hopeful—I ought to have told you that I did all in my power, short of *asking* Mr Hudson[1] (which the Law forbad) to go to Cambridge. I fear I did not prevail—he pleaded indisposition etc, etc. Sir Richard[2] went. Farewell.

W. W.

[*D. W. writes*]

My dear Chris,
Your uncle has put his letter into my hands to fold and direct it with all this blank paper, so I cannot help sending a word of my own of congratulation, to the Master of Trinity in the first place, then to you who have been so zealous in the cause. We know nothing of the Poll in Cumb^d—except that on the 2nd Day Lord L[3] was sadly in the rear—and *I* expect nothing but final defeat. As to Westmorland, though now only two candidates have come forward, Miss Hutchinson and I expect that two Reformers will rush to the Contest, and throw out Col L. and Mr Nowel[4]—though it appears that Mr N. is, or professes to be, a Reformer. I only regret that Lord Lowther did not come forward *at first* for Cumberland, and that he ever put forth any address for Westmorland.

¹ The Revd. John Hudson (1773–1843), educated at Heversham School, Fellow of Trinity College, Cambridge, from 1798 and vicar of Kendal, 1815–43. As a Government official, W. W. was not allowed to canvass.

² Sir Richard le Fleming, rector of Grasmere, formerly of Trinity Hall, Cambridge.

³ On the second day of the poll Lord Lowther had received 165 votes to Graham's 324 and Blamire's 317.

⁴ The Lowthers sustained a second defeat in Westmorland, but by a compromise a poll was avoided. Col. H. C. Lowther stood again, and W. W. Carus Wilson of Casterton Hall (see *MY* ii. 419) took the place of Lord Lowther when he elected to contest Cumberland. The 'blue' candidates were Alexander Nowell (d. 1842) of Underley Hall, near Kirkby Lonsdale, younger son of Ralph Nowell of Gauthrop Hall, Lancs., and formerly an officer in the Indian army; and William Crackanthorpe of Newbiggin Hall, W. W.'s cousin (see *MY* ii. 82, 405). By an arrangement arrived at before the nomination on 4 May, Wilson and Crackanthorpe withdrew, and Col. Lowther and Nowell, one from each party, were returned. (See *Westmorland Gazette* for 14 May 1831.)

I confess, dear Chris, that, notwithstanding the many causes we have for thankfulness in our own little domestic circle, I am in bad spirits. Your uncle has but confirmed our fire-side fears. I mean Miss Hutchinson's and mine—for many an hour has been passed by us during our solitary six months in gloomy forebodings. But to turn to the parlour below stairs, where my dear Sister is sitting with her own chearfullest countenance, and wonderfully well considering the past, and Dora and Isabella are as happy as possible. You have very much improved Dora's health and strength. Miss Hutchinson begs her kindest remembrances. Believe me, dear Chris, Ever your affectionate Aunt

D Wordsworth

Thanks for the Cambridge Paper!

611. S. H. and D. W. to EDWARD QUILLINAN

Address: Edward Quillinan Esqr, 12 Bryanston Street, Portman Square, London.
Postmark: 12 May 1831. *Stamp*: Kendal Penny Post.
MS. WL.
SH, p. 381.

May 10th [1831]

My dear Friend

I know you will be glad to hear that my Sister and Dora are at last safe at home again—tho' detained until last Saturday at Nottingham—My Sister is much better than we could have hoped after such a severe attack, and bore her journey very well—indeed she says she improved during her progress—Dora quite well—and much the better for her wintering in the South—Your Darling[1] well also—and very happy—and in as great favor with all the House as ever—a better and sweeter Child cannot be—My Sister and Dora and myself are all decided in our *opinion* that you *ought* not to take Jemima to Portugal, which we take the liberty of giving as you ask it—My Sister bids me say that you had best leave her at School—if you are not satisfied to leave her in Town—or at Hendon[2] bring her to Miss Dowlings[3]—This is all that I have to say—Rotha, who is now taking her music Lesson, is to fill up the paper which I guess she will do in a more entertaining strain than

[1] Rotha Quillinan, now staying at Rydal Mount.
[2] At Mrs. Gee's school.
[3] Elizabeth Dowling's school in Ambleside.

I can—for we are all in the Dolefuls—I have not had a drop of comfort, except the Camb. Election, in our cups since the return of Mr W.—Miss W. and I dolorus enough before—but he has made us ten times worse. We are very sorry for your friends, the Wakes,[1] and for your disappointment in consequence—*that* trip for Mima would have been both pleasant and useful to her—but, poor Thing! why toss her about on the Seas *for nothing*—No such duty, I trust, will devolve upon us—but, should it, most faithfull will it be performed to this dear little creature.

All send their best love to you and Mima—and believe me ever most truly. Your friend S. H.

[After a note from Rotha to her father, D. W. adds]

Here is a Blank space (left for Dora I suppose) but I cannot help saying one word—that your little Daughter is writing beside me—copying a poem for her own pleasure—that I *delight* in having her beside me; for she is the best and pleasantest and happiest Child I ever knew—In this judgment of her we all agree—adieu my dear Friend—Yours ever D. W. Sen[r].

612. W. W. to GEORGE HUNTLY GORDON

MS. Cornell.
Broughton, p. 44.

Monday Noon
[23 May 1831][2]

My dear Sir,

I was glad to hear of you through the hands of your Cousin. Unluckily he was stinted for time; and could only call on Sunday just, as it happened at our 1 o clock Sunday meal, which he could not partake of having only break[f]asted late.—I sent him around the walks of my little Policy, and joined him after dinner, and walked with him a mile and a half on his way to Keswick, giving him the best Instructions, I could.—I was pleased with his Conversation.

We have had a hand bill and Placard circulated in this neighbourhood calling upon the Friends of the Bill to massacre its

---

[1] For Mr. and Mrs. Charles Wake, see pt. i, L. 364. Later on this summer E. Q. joined them in France, where he remained for much of the rest of the year. Rotha was left in the charge of Dora W.

[2] This letter was written the day following M.W.'s departure for Cheltenham on 22 May, as recorded in D. W.'s MS. Journal (*WL MSS.*).

opponents—the expression used, is to give them 'war to the Knife'[1]—Take this as an answer to your hopes that society has not been Disturbed by reform, among our mountains—

Pray hear it's very much my wish to see you here when it suits you, yet you must not be sure that we can at all times accommodate you with a bed—at present we are full to overflowing—and are often so during summer—you must take your chances—but at the worst we can lodge you near us.—

Mrs Wordsworth left us yesterday for Cheltenham to visit our friend Dr Bell[2] who is lying there in a helpless state, a Sister with him as helpless. Mrs W had only been a fortnight at home; a most severe attack of Sciatica and Lumbago compelled her to stay behind at Notingham, I myself being under the necessity of proceeding to Carlisle—Her Daughter remained with her—

ever faithfully yours
W Wordsworth

612a. W. W. to WILLIAM HAZLITT JNR.[3]

MS. untraced.
W. Carew Hazlitt, Four Generations of a Literary Family, 2 vols., 1897, i. 233;
* W. Carew Hazlitt, Memoirs of William Hazlitt, 2 vols., 1867, i. 103 n.[4]*

[23 May 1831]

[Hazlitt] . . . was then[5] remarkable for analytical power, and for acuteness and originality of mind; and that such intellectual qualities characterized him through life, his writings, as far as I am acquainted with them, sufficiently prove.

I cannot recollect that I ever saw him but once since the year 1803 or 1804,[6] when I passed some time in this neighbourhood. He was then practising portrait-painting, with professional views. At his

---

[1] See *SH*, p. 383, where the authorship of the handbill is ascribed to Captain Mark Beaufoy (1774–1834) of Bowness. He had served with the Coldstream Guards at Waterloo.

[2] Dr. Andrew Bell, the educationalist, who had visited the Wordsworths the previous summer (*RMVB*).

[3] William Hazlitt jnr. (1811–93), a journalist on the *Morning Chronicle*, edited his father's *Literary Remains* (1836), and became Registrar of the Court of Bankruptcy in 1854.

[4] Each of these works quotes a single paragraph of this fragmentary letter.

[5] i.e. at Nether Stowey in 1798.

[6] For Hazlitt's visit to the Lakes in the autumn of 1803, see *EY*, pp. 446–7. W. W. had met him subsequently in London in 1808 (see *MY* i. 221), by which time their relationship had cooled considerably.

desire, I sat to him, but as he did not satisfy himself or my friends, the unfinished work was destroyed.¹

[*cetera desunt*]

613. W. W. to MRS. RICHARD LOUGH²

MS. WL. Hitherto unpublished.

[*In John Carter's hand*]

Rydal Mount
23 May 1831.

Madam,

With reference to my letter of March last, and that of the 12ᵗʰ ult: requiring certain particulars to be furnished me relating to the recent change in the Proprietorship Etc. of the 'Westmorland Advertiser'—I beg to say that unless such particulars are forwarded to me within a week from this date, I shall be under the necessity of calling the attention of the Solicitor of Stamps to the subject.

I am Madam
Your obᵗ Servant,
[*signed*] Wᵐ Wordsworth

614. W. W., DORA W., and D. W. to CHARLES WORDSWORTH

Address: Charles Wordsworth Esqʳᵉ, Christ Church, Oxford [*In Dora W.'s hand*]
Endorsed: 1831. On my gaining the Oxford Latin Essay Prize.
MS. Mr. Jonathan Wordsworth. Hitherto unpublished.

Rydal Mount
June 6ᵗʰ
1831

My dear Nephew,

Most sincerely and heartily do I congratulate you upon your success,³ which was amply deserved as the reward of your talents your attainments and matchless industry.

---

¹ Both Coleridge and Southey found the portrait 'dismal'. For a full discussion, see Blanchard, *Portraits of Wordsworth*, pp. 43–6, 142. W. W.'s letter to Charles Lamb of 21 Nov. 1818, which has just (1978) come to light, confirms that the portrait was indeed burnt, and is therefore no longer in existence.

² Richard Lough, proprietor of the *Westmorland Advertiser and Kendal Chronicle* since 1820 (see *MY* ii. 576), had died recently, and the proprietorship had passed to his widow on 12 Feb.

³ Charles Wordsworth had won the Chancellor's Essay Prize at Oxford on the subject, *Quaenam fuerit oratorum Atticorum apud populum authoritas.* See his *Annals of My Early Life*, pp. 370 ff.

Mind you contrive to keep a copy of it for my perusal—and send it me by an early opportunity. You did well also in not leaving us to hear the news through the public Papers.

The Democracy has been going on Infamously since you and I met. No more infamous day than that of Lord Grey will be found in English [History];[1] because there never was a Minister that put so much to hazard for the maintenance of his own vile, and as it must prove, short-lived Power.[2]

Your Aunt (my Wife I mean) [is] at Cheltenham. But here comes Dora and to her I surrender the pen. Farewell and God bless you and prosper your endeavours, and let me hear by and bye (now that you have gotten almost all the prizes you can contend for) that you love Books and Study for their own sakes.

Your affectionate Uncle
Wm Wordsworth

[*Dora W. writes*]

Most sincerely do I rejoice in your success my dear Charles and in the improved taste of the Oxford Examiners or Prize deciders or what ever you call them—Your aff^{te} Cousin

Dora Wordsworth

[*D. W. writes*]

Knowing my gladness to be equal to her own, Dora brings the letter for me to add my congratulations, which I do most heartily. I had been often sending good wishes; but having once met with a disappointment after witnessing your industry week after week, had had many apprehensions in the present case. I assure you I am not a little proud of my Nephews.

Your Aunt and Mr Southey will both be at Cheltenham about the time of your commemoration, and how nicely they might visit you! But they are to visit Brinsop Court (Herefordshire) on their homeward journey, and I fear Mr Southey cannot spare the time; but Suppose, however, that you *try* them by addressing a letter to Mrs Wordsworth at the Revd Dr Bell's, Cheltenham. I am called to Tea—and it is near post-time, and to scribble these few lines have laid down Mr Hine's Selection[3] from Wordsworth's poems which I am reading through to detect errors. Some I have already discovered of the most cutting kind for the Author and Lovers of his poems.

I rejoice to hear from many quarters, better accounts of your

---

[1] *Word dropped out.*

[2] Lord Grey, the Prime Minister, was already an old man. He retired in the summer of 1834 at the age of 70.   [3] See L. 617 below.

dear Father's health, and good ones of John's—Adieu dear Charles, God bless and prosper you in all your undertakings as in this last most honorable one

Yours ever Affecly
D Wordsworth Senr.

I hope you can read my sad scrawl—no time for pains-taking.

615. JOHN W. and D. W. to FRANCIS MEREWETHER

Address: To The Revd Francis Merewether, Coleorton, Ashby de la Zouche, Leicestershire.
MS. WL. Hitherto unpublished.

Rydal Mount
June 6th [1831]

My dear Sir,

I deferred answering your last kind letter which I received at Moresby till my visit here, that my Aunt who is so good a letter-writer might by additions and news make my letter better worth the postage. Our whole family is now at home except my mother, who is gone to Cheltenham to attend upon an old Friend Dr Bell[1] who is fast declining. You have perhaps heard that by deed of gift he has disposed of 120,000 £ to build or endow Schools at St Andrews[2] where Professors are to lecture according to his system. We think that he might have disposed of his money more judiciously and as it all came out of England and the English Church if some of it had returned thither it would have been as well, especially as it is half of it likely to be wasted among Scotch Lawyers. My Brother is much improved by his residence upon the Continent, he is likely to be placed for the present at Carlisle as one of my Father's Sub-distributors[3] as there is a tolerable good situation there, considering the times. He will be a near neighbour of ours as a Carlisle Coach passes our door every day which comes in a few hours. I go on much in the old way at Moresby, and am perfectly happy except that the delicate state of my wife's health

---

[1] Andrew Bell.
[2] In successive wills Bell varied his testamentary intentions, and at one point considered leaving his fortune to benefit the Church of England (he had been a Prebendary of Westminster since 1819). But he finally transferred £120,000 to trustees, half to go to his native city of St. Andrews for the foundation of Madras College, the other half to be divided equally between Edinburgh, Glasgow, Leith, Aberdeen, Inverness, and the Royal Naval School in London. See Robert Southey and C. C. Southey, *The Life of the Rev. Andrew Bell*, 3 vols. 1844, iii. 367 ff.   [3] See L. 595 above.

causes me some uneasiness, and our visit here I am sorry to say has not done her much good. We are going to Gilsland,[1] a watering place in the north of Cumberland, to try if drinking the waters there will be of service to her.—

[*D. W. writes*]

So far had John proceeded when he was summoned to the coach at the foot of the Hill. In confirmation of what he has said of his own happiness I may truly say that as far as his Wife is concerned there is not a single drawback saving her present delicate present state of health, and in *that* there is not cause for serious alarm. She only wants strengthening and is, I trust, taking the right course, in trying the Gillsland water. She has won her way in this house by her sweet temper, aimiable manners and good sense insomuch that we are attached to her as if she had been born among us; and at parting from her I did indeed feel as if we were losing one of our own Family. Was it not a pity that my poor Sister, after twelve days detention at Nottingham, under the tortures of Sciatica and Lumbago should be obliged to undertake another long journey. She had not been at home quite a fortnight when a letter so urgent arrived from Dr Bell entreating *me* to go to him that it was not possible to resist, especially as we considered it as the last request of a dying man. My Friends, however, would not allow *me* to go on account of the danger to my health. So my dear Sister chearfully undertook the office, and we hope that the Baths, Waters, etc may be of use to her poor Back, which is still very rheumatic and stiff. Thank God! she is in other respects quite well, and writes in good spirits, though her situation is, as far as may be, removed from quiet comfort. True it is one would not be surprized any day to hear of the poor old Gentleman's death; but he may yet live many months—nay years. His bodily health is as good as usual; but there is a palsy of some of the muscles of his throat, so that he is obliged to write all his wishes. Judge of this affliction to an impatient spirit like *his*. Then he has most of his worldly affairs yet to settle, except the £120,000 already given away. But concerning *that*, the perplexities are overwhelming. The good Folks at St Andrews are absolutely confounded with the *monstrous grandeur* of the Gift, and know not what they shall do with it. Hence letters, consultations, etc etc without end.—Dear Friends, this has often made me think

---

[1] The spa on the bank of the River Irthing had been a popular place of resort since the end of the eighteenth century. It was while staying there in 1797 that Sir Walter Scott met his future wife, Charlotte Carpenter.

it is a blessing to have no worldly wealth to dispose of, nothing to think of but the narrow slip of earth which is quietly to receive our remains!—No accounts to settle but with our Maker and merciful Judge, and our own consciences. I fear there is no chance of a cure for D^r B's afflicting malady, and very much do I feel for him. Mr Southey[1] is going to Cheltenham for a few days, and he and Mrs Wordsworth will return together. We have good accounts from Cambridge—the Master much better—John (at Versailles) quite well—Charles successful at Oxford—and dear Chris with all youthful ardour gone or going in quest of knowledge to foreign countries. My Brother William is in sounder [?].[2] In spite of all that he has suffered from the madness of the Reformers, and of all that he dreads may happen to our long-favoured country and its glorious institutions, he is strong in health and even in spirits chearful. He now no longer discusses, or attempts to *persuade.* He finds it all in vain, and now he endeavours to wait in patience, trusting that by the wisdom and providence of God some changes (which he cannot foresee) may be wrought in the minds and actions of the infatuated multitudes, high and low, rich and poor.

The weather has been charming for many weeks, and is so still but the grass is beginning to pine for rain. So are all other fruits of the earth. This place (would that you and Mrs Merewether could see it) is enchanting. We have made great improvements, and the growth of the trees is astonishing. My Brother and his son William are fellow-labourers, and the Father almost as active as the Son, in lopping trees, making Seats, for sunshine or shade, a pool for the gold-fishes etc etc etc. These my Brother finds very worthy employments after the Turmoils of London in the late stormy times. How gloriously have our friends combated at Cambridge! I trust they will have their reward, by opening the eyes of some who are now in power, and thus arrest the calamity which seems to threaten that venerable Establishment, and all others resembling it. I suppose Sir G. and Lady Beaumont are at Coleorton. Pray give my kind regards to him, and my love to Lady B. for she was kind enough to send a message to me couched in those same kind words.—How beautiful your small garden and the Lawn at the Hall must now be looking, with all their Rhododendrons!

---

[1] Bell, who died the following January, had just made a new will, and named his old friend Southey as an executor. He was also proposing to bequeath a thousand pounds each to Southey and W. W. on condition that they prepared a complete edition of his works (see Southey, vi. 153), but the plan was dropped. Southey wrote the first volume of *The Life of the Rev. Andrew Bell*, but the rest of the work was completed by Cuthbert Southey.   [2] *Hole in MS.*

My dear Mrs Merewether, I ought to have thanked you for your last kind letter long ago. Pray forgive me. Taking up John's unfinished paper I have addressed you both, and both together may be able to decypher my scrawl, Such it is, for I have been much hurried to save the posting.

I often think of you all, and dear Whitwick. Remember me to Mrs Wright[1] and Joseph[2] and all Friends, and give my especial regards to Emily and Frank.[3]

God bless you all, and believe me
ever your affectionate Friend
D Wordsworth

Dora is quite well. She sends best love to you both. My Brother sends his sincerest good wishes and William Jr. begs to be recalled to your recollection.

616. W. W. to ROBERT JONES

Address: The Revd Robert Jones, Plas yn llan, Ruthin, N. Wales.
MS. WL. Hitherto unpublished.

Rydal Mount
June 7th [1831]

My dear Friend,

Many thanks for your congratulations,[4] I wish there had been more cause for them—these are not times when much is likely to be add[ed] to the Emoluments of public officers. The fact is that by uniting a neighbouring District with mine, my responsibility has been nearly doubled my trouble very greatly increased, scarcely more addition to my profits than one year with another will suffice to pay the additional expense incurred. Do not imagine however that I complain—though after 18 years service this is not the way one would treat a Friend in a concern of private life.

I am much concerned to hear of the decease of your Brother.[5] Your family has been so much united that he must have proved a

---

[1] A Coleorton acquaintance.
[2] One of the Coleorton servants.
[3] Daughter and son of Francis Merewether. Francis Lewis Merewether (b. 1811) had been at Trinity College, Cambridge, since 1830. He eventually went out to Australia, became an immigration agent and public official, and finally Chancellor of Sydney University.
[4] On the extension of W. W.'s Distributorship to include Cumberland.
[5] Edward Jones.

great loss to you all. His life was a quiet and to all appearance a useful and a happy one; but men of our age are little disposed to [? doubt]¹ that such a change, however Friends may grieve for it at the time, is for the better—

It rejoices me much that you have made up your mind to visit us this summer, but pray do not let the hope end in disappointment as it did before. The way you propose to come is much the best; and as an additional motive for taking it, I must mention that my Son John lives within two miles of Whitehaven, his home close by the side of the Way between Whitehaven and Rydale. You must contrive to give at least one day to him—were it only that he may have the pleasure of introducing you to his most amiable wife. She is the eldest Daughter of Mr Curwen of Belle Isle Windermere, and of Workington Hall.

I do not recollect whether you know that my Sister had a severe illness about two years ago, inflammation of the bowels, which put her life in great danger and the effect of which upon her strength she will never I fear perfectly recover. This makes it doubtful whether we shall ever think it prudent for her to venture much upon Touring—at all events for this summer it is out of the question, so that we cannot encourage my favorite hope of shewing her North Wales—at least during this summer.

Your nephew Mr Cartwright² made a noble stand for Northamptonshire—I wish you had had a vote to give him, and that I had one also.

Mrs Wordsworth is at Cheltenham now, called there by the illness of our Friend Dr Bell of the Madras system.

Pray along with mine give my sister's and daughter's kind regards to your sisters, accept them also yourself—

and believe me my dear Jones

your very faithful Friend
Wm Wordsworth

These are sad Times!
My nephew Charles has just got the prize for the Latin essay at Oxford.—

¹ *MS. obscure.*
² In the recent election for Northamptonshire the successful candidates were Lord Althorp, later 3rd Earl Spencer (1782–1845), a Whig of advanced views, and Chancellor of the Exchequer and Leader of the House of Commons under Lord Grey; and William Ralph Cartwright (1771–1847) of Aynhoe, Northants.: M.P. for Northamptonshire, 1797–1832, and thereafter for South Northants. No information is forthcoming about Jones's relationship (if any) with the latter, but it is clear from pt. i, L. 212 that he had some connections with the county.

617. W. W. to EDWARD MOXON[1]

MS. untraced.
K. LY ii. 555.

[*c.* 9 June 1831]

My dear Sir,

On the other side see a list of *errata*, some of which are so important and so mischievous to the sense that I beg they may be struck off instantly upon a slip of paper or separate leaf, and inserted in such books as are not yet dispersed. For one of these *errata*, perhaps more, I am answerable.

Tell Mr Hine,[2] to whom I wish to write as soon as I can find

[1] Moxon was about to publish *Selections from the Poems of William Wordsworth, Esq., Chiefly for the use of Schools and Young Persons*, 1831. This was the first selection of W. W.'s poetry to be published, the earlier proposals of James Dyer (see pt. i, L. 332), and of Allan Cunningham (see pt. i, L. 369), having fallen through. It was more comprehensive in scope than Cunningham's scheme (see pt. i, Appendix II), and marked a new stage in W. W.'s popularity.

[2] The editor of the *Selections* was Joseph Hine, a schoolmaster in Brixton, who had visited W. W. the previous summer (*RMVB*). His Preface was a somewhat effusive plea for the use of poetry in the classroom, and W. W.'s in particular. 'His was the only school I ever heard of which the *curriculum* was almost made up of English literature. I suspect he was a self-taught man . . . Mr Hine had a personal and intimate acquaintance with the poet Wordsworth, and was, I think, one of his earliest admirers, and communicated his admiration to his pupils and to all who came under his influence in very early days . . .' (*Life of John Hullah, LL.D., By his Wife*, 1886, pp. 3–5). In his letter to Dora W. of 3 Mar., E. Q. had described his recent visit with W. W. and Captain Todd (see pt. i, L. 103) to see Hine at his school: 'This broad shouldered muscular Theban had an advantage over us besides his learning. His eyes are so arranged that you never know when he is looking at you; so that he may be staring hard at you all the time that he seems to look quite the other way. . . . He received us all three with the most earnest cordiality, and gave us glasses of sherry and pound-cake. But to Mr Wordsworth he was crushingly affectionate. . . . After wine and cake we were ushered into the schoolroom. . . . The boys rose and bowed, sate and gazed; pencils and slates were brought out at word of command; pedagogue gave out, line by line, the Sonnet supposed to be written on Westminster Bridge. All the boys wrote it, one echoing the Master, as the clerk . . . does the clergyman. When finished, several boys in turn read it aloud: very well too. They were then called upon to explain the meaning of "the river glideth at its own sweet will". One boy, the biggest . . . made a dissertation on the influence of the moon on the tides etc etc and seemed rather inclined to be critical; another said there was no wind, another that there were no water breaks in the Thames to prevent its gliding as it pleased; another that the arches of the bridge had no locks to shut the water in and out: and so forth. One boy said there were no boats—that was the nearest. Poet explained: was then called upon by Pedagogue to read his Sonnet himself; declined: Ped. entreated: Poet remonstrated: Ped. inexorable: Poet submitted. I never heard him read better. The Boys evidently felt it; a thunder of applause; Poet asked for a half-Holiday for them—granted—Thunders on Thunders . . . *Seriously speaking* the whole scene was indescribably animated and interesting.' (*WL MSS.*) A proof-sheet of Hine's Preface, with corrections and revisions by W. W., is preserved at the Huntington Library. See Paul M. Zall, 'Wordsworth Edits his Editor', *Bulletin of the New York Public Library*, lxvi (1962), 93–6.

395   o

time, that I think the collection judiciously made. When you mentioned 'notes', I was afraid of them, and I regret much the one at the end[1] was not suppressed; nor is that about the editorial nut-cracks[2] happily executed. But Mr Hine is an original person, and therefore allowance must be made for his oddities. He feels the poetry, and that is enough. His preface does him great credit.

ever and most truly yours,
Wm Wordsworth

618. W. W. to BENJAMIN ROBERT HAYDON

Address: B. R. Haydon, Esq., Connaught Terrace, Burford Place, London.
MS. untraced.
Haydon. K (—). *LT ii. 553.*

Rydal Mount, Kendal
11th June, 1831.

My dear Haydon,

On the other side is the Sonnet,[3] and let me have your 'Kingdom' for it.[4] What I send you is not 'warm' but piping hot from the brain, whence it came in the wood adjoining my garden not ten minutes ago, and was scarcely more than twice as long in coming.— You knew how much I admired your Picture both for the execution and the conception.—The latter is first-rate, and I could dwell upon

---

[1] On p. 365, at the end of selections from *The Excursion*, the note reads: 'I am sorry that space will not allow me to give the reader more of this Divine Poem. "The Excursion" will take rank with the first productions of the British muse. With the Faery Queen, Paradise Lost, The Essay on Man, The Seasons, The Task, and whatever is worthy of praise and admiration.'

[2] The note, p. 286, at the close of the Sonnets to Liberty, reads: 'We have plucked handfuls of these Sonnets for our readers, with a somewhat greedy grasp; where there is plenty it is a sin to starve, and where the plenty is good, it is difficult to come away unsatisfied . . . Having thus collected with no unsparing hand, from the author's Miscellaneous Sonnets, and from his Sonnets to Liberty . . ., there remain three other clusters to which we should like to apply our editorial nutcrackers: "The River Duddon", "Memorials of a Tour on the Continent", and the "Ecclesiastical Sketches": from each of which we dare take only a few for our own modest share; and refer the wholesale lovers of *kernels* to satisfy themselves in the author's poetical works, 5 vols., Longman and Co.'

[3] *To B. R. Haydon, on seeing his picture of Napoleon Buonaparte on the island of St. Helena.* According to de Selincourt, who examined the MS. of this letter, the text of the sonnet is as in *PW* iii. 51, except for punctuation.

[4] Haydon had written on 30 May in answer to W. W.'s letter of 23 Apr. (L. 605 above): 'I cant let you off in dull prose—though your prose is poetry— you know "High is *our* calling"! I must have a specimen of yours and shall enclose you a fair proof that you may look at it occasionally and wait for Inspiration. People are Napoleon mad—I have two more commissions—depend on it, it is a subject worthy of your muse. . . . Adieu my dear Friend. My Kingdom for a Sonnet.' (*WL MSS.*)

it a long time in prose without disparagement to the former; which I admired also having to *it* no objection but the Regimentals —they are too spruce and remind one of the Parade, which the Wearer seems to have just left.—One of the best Caricatures I have lately seen is that of Brougham, a single figure upon one knee, stretching out his arms, by the sea shore, towards the rising Sun (Wm the 4th) which, as in duty bound, he is worshipping.[1] Do not think your excellent Picture degraded if I remark that the force of the same principle, 'simplicity', is seen in the burlesque composition as in your Work, with infinitely less effect, no doubt, from the inferiority of style and subject; yet still it is pleasing to note the under currents of affinity in opposite styles of art.—I think of Napoleon pretty much as you do, but with more dislike probably; because my thoughts have turned less upon the flesh and blood man than yours and therefore have been more at liberty to dwell with unqualified scorn upon his various liberticide projects and the miserable selfishness of his spirit.—Few men of any time have been at the head of greater events; yet they seem to have had no power to create in him the least tendency towards magnanimity.—How, then, with this impression, can I help despising him? So much for the Idol of thousands!—As to the Reformers, the folly of the ministerial Leaders is only to be surpassed by the wickedness of those who will speedily supplant them. God of Mercy have Mercy upon poor England!—to think of this glorious Country lacqueying the heels of France in religion (that is *no* religion) in morals, government and social order! It can not come to good, at least for the present generation, they have begun it in shame and it will lead them to misery.

God bless you, remember me to Mrs Haydon of whom I am sorry to have seen so little—Do not forget the Print which might be sent me directed as below, ever faithfully

Yours
Wm Wordsworth

You are at liberty to print the sonnet with my name where and when you think proper.—If it does you the least service the end for which it is written will be answered.—Call at Moxon's Bond Street, and let him give you from me, for your children, a copy of the Selections[2] he has just published from my poems.

[1] Henry Brougham had become Lord Chancellor in Nov. 1830, and was raised to the peerage as the 1st Baron Brougham and Vaux.
[2] Joseph Hine's *Selections*. See previous letter.

Would it not be taken as a compliment to Sir Robert Peel, who you told me has purchased your picture[1] if you were to send him a Copy of the Sonnet before you publish it?

619. W. W. and D. W. to WILLIAM ROWAN HAMILTON and ELIZA HAMILTON

MS. untraced.
Hamilton (—). *K* (—). *LY ii. 556* (—).

Rydal Mount, 13 June 1831.

I prepared you for my not being much of a correspondent, but I have been so unpardonably long silent, that I am almost afraid to appear before you. My daughter has given, I see, an account of our movements, and alluded to a subject[2] which was in no small degree the cause of my seeming to be unmindful of you as well as my other friends. I know not at present where to look for your last letter, but it is upon my conscience for putting off a commission of Mr. O'Sullivan's[3] with which it charged me. For this I have no excuse, therefore my hope is that the business was not urgent—at all events mention it, I pray, in your next, lest I should not be able to find your letter, which may possibly be mislaid among the mass of my London papers: I saw little or nothing of Cambridge on my return—which was upon the eve of the election—but I found that the Mathematicians of Trinity, Peacock,[4] Airy, Whewell, were taking what I thought the wrong side: so was that able man, the Geological Professor, Sedgwick. But 'what matter'! was said to me by a lady—'these people know nothing but about stars and stones;' which is true, I own, of some of them. Your University, I am proud to see, keep to members[5] that do it credit, and it was to me a great satisfaction to find the opinions of the cultivated classes

---

[1] The picture remained at Drayton Manor, Staffs., until the turn of the century when it was sold to America.

[2] The reference is probably to the enlargement of W. W.'s Distributorship, which preoccupied him while he was in London. Dora W.'s part of this letter is missing.

[3] Samuel O'Sullivan, a friend and neighbour of Hamilton's—'a clergyman of some standing in our Church, and a graduate of our University'—whom W. W. had met on his visit to Dublin in 1829. He wished to find out the conditions under which he could be incorporated as a graduate of Cambridge.

[4] The Revd. George Peacock, D.D., F.R.S. (1791–1858), educated at Sedbergh, Fellow of Trinity (1814), Tutor (1823–39), Lowndean Professor of Astronomy and Geometry (1837–58), and Dean of Ely from 1839.

[5] After the elevation of William Plunkett, M.P., later 1st Baron Plunkett (1764–1854), to the office of Lord Chief Justice of Ireland in 1827, Dublin

in England and Ireland so decidedly pronounced through the organs of their respective Universities against this rash and unprincipled measure[1]—you, I trust, will be glad also to hear that a large majority of the *youth* both of Cambridge and Oxford disapprove the measure; and this proof of sound judgment in them I think the most hopeful sign of the times. . . . Is your pupil Lord Adare[2] still with you, and do you continue your observations together? I wish I could tell you that I had been busily employed in my own art; but I have scarcely written a hundred verses during the last twelve months; a sonnet, however, composed the day before yesterday,[3] shall be transcribed upon this sheet, by way of making *my* part of it better worth postage. It was written at the request of the Painter Haydon, and to benefit him—*i.e.*, as he thought. But it is no more than my sincere opinion of his excellent picture, of which there is a very good print, which ought to find its way to Ireland. By-the-bye, I was much pleased with your sister's poem, pray tell her so: that the portrait is true, we have a striking proof in one of our intimate friends, who might have sat for it. Have your sisters any interest with schoolmasters or *mistresses?* A selection from my poems has just been edited by a Dr. Hine for the benefit chiefly of schools and young persons, and it is published by Moxon, of Bond-street, an amiable young man of my acquaintance, whom I wish to befriend, and of course I wish the book to be circulated, if it be found to answer his purpose; 1500 copies have been struck off. . . The retail price (bound) is only 5s. 6d., and the volume contains, I should suppose, at least 1100 verses . . . and it would be found a good travelling companion for those who like my poetry.

[D. W. writes]

As you, my dear friends, Mr. and Miss Hamilton, may have discovered by the slight improvement in legibility of penmanship, [other hands] have been employed to finish this letter, which has

University was represented by John Wilson Croker, Secretary to theAdmiralty, until 1830, and then by Thomas Langlois Lefroy (1776–1869), of Carrigglas Manor, Co. Longford, another distinguished lawyer, who held the seat until his appointment in 1841 as a Baron of the Irish Court of the Exchequer. He was Lord Chief Justice of Ireland, 1852–66.

[1] The Reform Bill.
[2] Edwin Richard Wyndham Quin, later 3rd Earl of Dunraven (1812–71), had been Hamilton's pupil at the Dunsink Observatory since Feb. 1830. He was M.P. for Glamorgan, 1836–50, and a noted antiquary.
[3] See previous letter. Some months before this, probably before he left Rydal Mount the previous autumn, W. W. had written *The Armenian Lady's Love* (*PW* ii. 96), suggested by an anecdote in Kenelm Henry Digby's *Orlandus*, and *Presentiments* (*PW* ii. 305).

been on the stocks half as long as a man-of-war. I cannot but add from myself that Miss Hutchinson and I, by our solitary winter's fireside, often remembered you—talked of 'the Graces'[1]—and all pleasant forms and faces that flitted about before our windows every sunny day of that gloomy summer. This very moment a letter arrives—very complimentary—from the Master[2] of St. John's College, Cambridge (the place of my brother William's education), requesting him to sit for his portrait to some eminent artist, as he expresses it, 'to be placed in the old House among their Worthies.' He writes in his own name, and that of several of the Fellows. Of course my brother consents; but the difficulty is to fix on an artist. There never yet has been a good portrait of my brother. The sketch by Haydon,[3] as you may remember, is a fine drawing—but what a likeness! all that there is of likeness makes it to me the more disagreeable. Adieu! believe me, my dear friends, yours truly, etc.

620. W. W. to EDWARD MOXON

Address: Mr Edward Moxon, 64 New Bond Street, London. [*In M. W.'s hand*]
Postmark: 13 June 1831. *Stamp*: Kendal Penny Post.
MS. Henry E. Huntington Library.
K (—). *LY ii. 556.*

Rydal Mount
June.—Wednesday 13th [1831]

My dear Sir,
I am sorry to incur the expense of another Letter[4] but on the other side I have sent a more correct list of Errata for two of which at least I know that your printer is not answerable.—But some of these blunders destroy the sense entirely—for example 'the' for 'thy'—page 97 lawful for lawless 109.—If we are to talk about cancelling, the passage page 51 I could wish most to be cancelled is the last with the note about the Excursion—it would hurt Mr Hine's feelings perhaps to tell him so—but really the note ought not to be there.—As to improving the Selection in another Edition,

1 Some kind of game which the Hamiltons had played with the Wordsworth household during their visit the previous summer.
2 For Dr. James Wood, W. W.'s former tutor, see *MY* ii. 653. His letter of 8 June is among the *WL MSS.*
3 The chalk drawing that hung in the dining room at Rydal Mount during the poet's lifetime, but eventually found its way to the National Portrait Gallery. See *MY* ii. 577.
4 About Joseph Hine's *Selections*. See L. 617 above.

I am very sceptical about that. Mr Quillinan talks of omitting the Idiot Boy—it was precisely for his perception of the merit of this Class of Poems that I allowed Mr Hine to make the Selection. You would find no two Persons agree [with you][1] what was best; and upon the whole tell Mr H[ine] that I think he has succeeded full as well if not better than most other Persons could have done.— There is another Note which I also object to much—it is about Editorial Nutcrackers—but perhaps I mentioned this before—I wish I could have sent this letter through a Frank but I cannot without loss of one post, probably two. Mr Leigh Hunt[2] is a Coxcomb, was a Coxcomb, and ever will be a Coxcomb.

ever faithfully yours
W. W.

621. W. W. to SAMUEL ROGERS

Address: Samuel Rogers Esq^e, St James Place, London.
Postmark: 16 June 1831. *Stamp*: Kendal Penny Post.
Endorsed: not to be published S. R.
MS. Sharpe Collection, University College, London.
Rogers. LY ii. 558.

Rydal Mount
June 14th [1831]

Let me, my dear friend, have the benefit of your advice upon a small matter of taste. You know that while I was in London I gave more time than a wise man would have done to Portrait-painters and Sculptors[3]—I am now called to the same duty again. The Master and a numerous body of the fellows of my own College, St. John's Cambridge, have begged me to sit to some Eminent Artist for my Portrait, to be placed among 'the Worthies of that House' of Learning, which has so many claims upon my grateful remembrance.—I consider the application no small honor, and as they have courteously left the choice of the Artist to myself I entreat you would let me have the advantage of your judgement.

---

[1] *MS. torn.*
[2] In *The Tatler* for 4 June 1831, Leigh Hunt had poked fun at one of Moxon's publishing ventures, the anonymous satire *Mischief*. W. W. did not apparently know at this stage that Edward Quillinan was the author. See L. 622 below.
[3] See Ls. 598 and 603 above.

Had Jackson[1] been living, without troubling you, I should have inquired of himself whether he would undertake the task; but he is just gone, and I am quite at a loss whom to select. Pray give me your opinion. I saw Pickersgill's[2] Pictures at his own house, but between ourselves I did not much like them. Philips[3] has made Coxcombs of all the Poets, save Crabbe, that have come under his hands, and I am rather afraid he might play that trick with me, grey-headed as I am. Owen[4] was a manly painter, but there is the same fault with him as the famous Horse one has heard of—he is departed. In fact, the art is low in England, as you know much better than I—don't, however, accuse me of impertinence, but do as I have desired.

We stayed three or four days at Cambridge, and then departed for the North; but I was obliged to leave dear Mrs Wordsworth at Nottingham, suffering under a most violent attack of sciatica. Her daughter was left with her. We fell among good Samaritans,[5] and in less than a fortnight she was able to renew her journey.

Her stay here, however, was short. My Sister was summoned to Cheltenham by our old Friend Dr Bell,[6] and as we did not dare to trust *her* so far from home on account of her delicate state of health, Mrs W. was so kind and noble-minded as to take the long journey in her stead. The poor Doctor thought himself dying—but he has rallied—and we expect Mrs W. back with Southey, who left us this morning for the same place. Southey is gone upon business connected with the Doctor's affairs. Excuse this long story, but I know you are kind enough to be interested about me and my friends in every thing. Dora is writing by me, both she and my sister and W^m join me in kindest regards to yourself and your Sister, most faithfully yours   Wm Wordsworth

[1] John Jackson (1778–1831), befriended in his youth by Sir George Beaumont, was elected R.A. in 1817, and became one of the most famous portrait painters of his day. He had died on 1 June.

[2] Henry William Pickersgill, R.A. (1782–1875), a competent, successful, but undistinguished artist, exhibited 363 pictures in the Academy. Among his famous portraits (besides that of W. W.) are those of Bentham, Crabbe, Godwin, 'Monk' Lewis, Hannah More, and Talfourd, all in the National Portrait Gallery. Rogers in his reply of 25 June considered Pickersgill on the whole the best choice, but he had reservations. 'P. may fail altogether. Nothing should induce me to sit to Phillips.' (*WL MSS.*)

[3] Thomas Phillips, R.A. (1770–1845). His well-known portraits of Blake (1807) and Byron are in the National Portrait Gallery. He also painted, among others, Lord Thurlow, Lord Lyndhurst, Scott, and Sir Humphry Davy.

[4] William Owen, R.A (1769–1825), portrait painter to the Prince of Wales, 1810. He also painted Pitt, Lord Grenville, and Viscount Exmouth, and his portrait of John Wilson Croker is in the National Portrait Gallery.

[5] The Howitts.   [6] See L. 615 above.

622. W. W. to EDWARD QUILLINAN

Address: Edward Quillinan Esq^e, 12 Bryanston Street, Portman Square.
Postmark: 8 July 1831.
MS. WL.
LY ii. 559.

[In Dora W.'s hand]

Rydal Mount, July 4th [1831]

My dear Friend,

The Master of the Coll: of St John's Cam: to which as you know probably I belonged, has written to me on the part of a numerous body of the fellows requesting that I would sit for my portrait to be placed among the Worthies of that house: the Master kindly seconds this request in terms very flattering to me; they have courteously left to myself the choice of the Artist and as I could not depend on my own judgement I referred the matter to Rogers who fixes on Pickersgill as the best upon the whole. Now for the point— you know Pickersgill pretty well and perhaps might ascertain for me whether he gives any part of the summer or year to recreation, and if so whether he could be tempted to come as far as the Lakes and make my house his head-quarters, taking my portrait at the same time; if you do not object to sound him upon such a subject I should thank you to do so, as a reply in the negative might be given with less of a disagreeable feeling thro' a third person than directly to myself. You must be well aware how inconvenient it would be to me after so long an absence to make a second visit to town. Considering that Parliament is likely to sit great part of the summer and that many engagements must have devolved upon Mr P. by the death of Sir T. Lawrence[1] and Mr Jackson,[2] I do not think it probable that anything will come of this proposal, but as one of the fellows[3] of the Coll: told me yesterday they wish the thing to be done as soon as may be, I have thought that Mr P. will excuse the liberty I have taken. I ought to add they wish for a half-length, as a size which may range best with the Portraits of the Coll:. When you call at Moxon's pray tell him that I begged Lady Frederick Bentinck w^d send for a copy of the Selections[4] to be

---

[1] Sir Thomas Lawrence (1769–1830), the celebrated portrait painter: President of the Royal Academy from 1820.
[2] John Jackson. See previous letter.
[3] According to the *RMVB*, this was John Hymers (see L. 562 above).
[4] Joseph Hine's *Selections*.

considered as a present from me to her son;[1] request him to send also a copy to Colbourn's the bookseller for Wm Howitt Esq^e, Nottingham—now Dora writes as you will guess from the impudence which follows. I hope you are not answerable for the sin of being the author of 'Mischief'.[2] Father says there are some lines far too pretty and pure to have been found in such company. Now comes Daddy back again. Rotha continues to gain upon us (indeed she does) and we hope that the place with all the entertaining objects and employments about it will stir her mind profitably. She is very clever like her father but with some of his flibertygibertism. Farewell. Yours affe^ly

Wm Wordsworth[3]

But see P. as soon as you can as I wish to write to the Coll:[4]

623. W. W. and D. W. to LADY BEAUMONT

Address: To Lady Beaumont, Coleorton Hall, Ashby de la Zouch, Leicestershire.
Stamp: Kendal Penny Post.
MS. Pierpont Morgan Library. Hitherto unpublished.

Rydal Mount
July 8th [1831]

Dear Lady Beaumont,

I am sorry to have been prevented answering your acceptable Letter by yesterday's post.

We are glad to hear such favorable accounts of your own health and that of the Children, and as you do not say any thing to the contrary we hope that Sir George is well also.

---

[1] George Augustus Cavendish Bentinck (1821–91): later on, Parliamentary Secretary to the Board of Trade, 1874–5, and Judge Advocate-General, 1875–80.

[2] *Mischief*, a tale of amorous intrigue, obviously suggested by *Beppo*, and imitative of the style introduced into English poetry by John Hookham Frere (1769–1846) in his *Monks and the Giants*, 1818, but written in the Spenserian stanza. The poem shows some metrical skill and felicities of phrasing, as de Selincourt notes, but as a satire it is feeble and pointless. E. Q. published the first section (anon.) with Moxon in 1831, and the second (anon.) in 1834 with a Preface defending himself from the charge of plagiarism from Byron. In his reply of 8 July E. Q. defended the work, but submitted to Dora W.'s judgement in a fit of abject abasement: '. . . if I lose your friendship I shall never gain any thing in this world that can be a compensation.' (*WL MSS.*)

[3] Not signed by W. W.

[4] Crossed over the first page, Dora W. adds a note to E. Q. about Rotha's activities at Rydal Mount, where young Mary Hutchinson was also staying, newly arrived in the company of M. W. from Brinsop.

—You have thought of me and mine upon a very interesting occasion. Be assured it will give me great pleasure to be God-father to the Little William.[1] I need not repeat how much I am attached to Coleorton—the place and its Inhabitants—departed and present—and how sincerely I wish the welfare of your family. God grant that this little-one may prove a blessing to his Parents.

We have at present under our Roof a God child of mine—called Rotha[2]—after one of our beautiful Streams upon the banks of which her Mother Mrs Quillinan died under melancholy circumstances soon after giving birth to this Daughter.[3] The little Girl (she is about 8 years old) came down with me in the Coach from Nottingham. At Kendal we took an open Car, a noisy sort of vehicle, and as we were travelling along I said to her, 'You know that I am your God father, and it is part of my duty to be sure that you can repeat the Lords prayer—let me hear you, and we will say it together'. When we had done, she looked up saying with a smile, 'I hope the Driver did not hear us.' The Story seems scarcely worth the trouble of reading—but it is for you as a Mother; and I never shall forget the mixture of archness and simplicity in the Child's Countenance.

I am not sorry that Sir George is not in the present parliament; and do let him beware of contested elections—they entail incalculable expense, and are mostly attended with mortification that no one can foresee.

Your account of poor Mr Merewether concerns us much. I had a letter from him a little time ago, which I hope to answer in a few days.

The Article in the Quarterly Review which you mention,[4] I have not read. It is monstrous to affirm with Mr Malthus, that the World is overpeopled—yet they err grievously on the other side who talk as if there were no obligations upon people to reflect

[1] Lady Beaumont's second child, born on 13 Mar. 1831, who in due course became rector of Coleorton and Canon of Peterborough, and died in 1901. Lady Beaumont had written on 2 July asking W. W. to stand as his godfather: 'We are particularly anxious that our children should always remember how old and valued a friend you were of our late Relations and how inseparably this place must to the latest ages owe its name to your beautiful records of it.' (*WL MSS.*)

[2] Rotha Quillinan.   [3] See pt. i, L. 70.

[4] 'Malthus and Sadler—Population and Emigration', *Quarterly Review*, xlv (Apr. 1831), 97–145: a discussion of Malthus's *Essay on Population* in the light of recent studies by Nassau Senior (1790–1864), the economist, and Michael Thomas Sadler, M.P. (1780–1835), the social reformer. The author was George Poulett Scrope (1797–1876), economist and M.P. for Stroud from 1833. In her letter Lady Beaumont had expressed agreement with this critique of Malthus: 'I think his doctrines the most selfish that the rich ever propounded for the poor.'

before marriage how their children are to be maintained. If impolitic or unjust laws stand in the way of the earth being as productive as it might be, and impediments are thus thrown in the way of marriage, that is no reason why poor people should go about marrying as fast and as recklessly as they can—still less is it a reason, as Mr M lays down, that they should not marry at all—farewell—give my kindest regards to Sir George and a kiss to each of your little one[s] for my sake

ever faithfully yours
W Wordsw[orth][1]

[*D. W. writes*]

My dear Lady Beaumont, My Brother has left me but small space for reply to your very kind letter and most kind invitation to visit you and dear Coleorton in September. It would have given me true pleasure and the resolve would have been made without much 'thinking about it' if the various circumstances which have determined me not to move southward this year were not such as to stifle all hesitation even in this case where I should have had such strong impulses to give up pre-concerted schemes of quiet and home-staying. I will not trouble you with particulars, only pray accept my hearty thanks, and believe me I shall never lose sight of the privilege afforded me by your frequent and kind invitations of looking to Coleorton as a place where I should be welcome if you were at home and disengaged, and as it lies in the way to most others where I have friends or connexions, it should not be through any fault of mine that I missed the gratification of seeing you and yours upon your own ground. I would inform you of my movements or intentions, trusting to your sincerity and frankness. Do not suppose however that in the present or any other case I should *need* any other *inducement* to lead me from home, beyond that which you kindly offer me—but at my time of life one always feels it a duty to snatch at opportunity. My Sister is returned from Cheltenham. I wish I could add that she had there left her rheumatic pains and Lumbago. Since her return she has had another sharp attack; the lumbago is, however, subdued but the rheumatism is still flying about her limbs. She begs her kindest remembrances to you and Sir George; and with me heartily congratulates you on the happy prospects you have in both your Children. What a Blessing that the Birth of your younger Darling, 'William', should have been so speedily and happily got over! but how dreadfully some

MS. torn.

Ladies would have been alarmed in such a case!!—Mr Merewether wrote in bad spirits to my Brother, and spoke of his own state of health pretty much as you have done. I am very sorry both for himself and for his amiable Wife. It seems that the perils into which our rash Governors are leading this long-favoured Country oppress his mind.

I trust the Archbishop[1] is well as you say nothing to the contrary; but he must needs feel the weight of his high station, and the numerous extra cares now forced upon him—My dear Lady Beaumont, pray excuse this poor return for your interesting letter. I have been interrupted, and am called away by visitors—but *must* add that there was no need of *my* pleading to move my Brother to take upon him the office of God-father to your Child—Will you give my love to Mrs Merewether when you see her and say I shall write ere long—and believe me ever your much obliged and affectionate

Dorothy Wordsworth

624. W. W. to BENJAMIN ROBERT HAYDON

Address: B. R. Haydon Esqᵉ, Connaught Terrace, Edgware Road.
Postmark: 8 July 1831.
MS. untraced.
Haydon (—). *LY ii. 561.*

[*c.* 8 July 1831]

My dear Haydon,

I have to thank you for two Letters—I am glad you liked the Sonnet.[2] I have repeated it to one or two Judges whom it has pleased.—You ask my opinion about your daughter learning Music. If she had an independent fortune I should say no, unless she have a strong inclination to the Study. I am aware that such a natural bent is by no means necessary for the attainment of excellence both in playing and singing,—I know one striking instance to the contrary—still I am not friendly to the practice of forcing music upon females—because I think their time might be better employ'd; but if you look to the situation of a Teacher or Governess for any of your Daughters Music would serve them much in procuring such situation. I know several persons otherwise well qualified who are unemployed solely from their want of that accomplishment.

You ask my opinion about the Reform Bill.—I am averse

[1] Dr. Howley, Lady Beaumont's father.
[2] *To B. R. Haydon, on seeing his picture of Napoleon Buonaparte on the island of St. Helena.* See L. 618 above.

(with that wisest of the Moderns Mr Burke)[1] to all *hot* Reforma-
tions; i.e. to every sudden change in political institutions upon a
large scale. They who are forced to part with power are of course
irritated, and they upon whom a large measure of it is at once
conferred have their heads turned and know not how to use it. To
the *principle* of this particular measure, I object as *unjust*; and by its
injustice opening a way for spoliation and subversion to any extent
which the rash and iniquitous may be set upon.—If it could have
been shewn of such or such a Borough that it claimed the right to
send Members to Parliament, upon usurpation, or that it had made
a grossly corrupt use of a legal privilege—in both these cases I
would disfranchise—and also with the consent of the owners of
burgage Tenure, but beyond this I would not have gone a step.
As to transferring the right of voting to large Towns; my conviction is that they will be little the better for it—if at all—but een
let them have their humour in certain cases and try the result.
In short the whole of my proceedings would have been *tentative*,
and in no case would I have violated a principle of justice. This is the
sum of what I have to say. My admirers, as you call them, must have
been led (perhaps by myself) to overstate what I said to Lord
John Russel.[2] I did not conceal from him my utter disapprobation of
the Bill; and what I said principally alluded to its effect upon the
Aristocracy. I remember particularly telling him that the middle
and lower classes were naturally envious haters of the Aristocracy—
unless when they were *proud* of being attached to them—that there
was no *neutral* ground in these sentiments—the Mass must either
be your zealous supporters, said I, or they will do all in their power
to pull you down—that power, all at once, are you now giving
them through your ten pound renters who to effect their purpose
will soon call in the aid of others below them till you have the
blessing of universal suffrage; and what will become (I might
have said in that case, I did hint it) of Covent Garden[3] and

---

[1] W. W. had gradually come round to the philosophy of Burke's *Reflections
on the French Revolution* (1790). His growing veneration was reflected in the
tribute to the 'Genius of Burke' added some time before this (the exact date is
uncertain) to *The Prelude*. See *Prel.*, pp. 251, 565.

[2] 'What are your distinct objections to the Bill?', Haydon had asked in his
letter of 28 June, '. . . I understand at Lord Holland's you had a fierce argument
with Lord John, and your admirers say gave it him—Will you tell me what you
said?' (*WL MSS.*) W. W. had dined and slept at Holland House on 4 Apr.
during his London visit, according to E. Q.'s MS. Diary. (*WL MSS.*)

[3] Originally the garden of the Abbey at Westminister, granted to the Russells, Earls of Bedford, in 1552. Bedford House was later built on the site, and
after its demolition in 1704 the temporary market which had grown up there
was extended by the ground landlords, the Dukes of Bedford.

Wooburn[1] etc etc. I am called off and you must accept the wretched
Scrawl poor return as it is for your [   ] letters—

[*a line or two, and the signature, torn away*]

625. D. W. to EDWARD MOXON

Address: To Mr Edward Moxon Bookseller, New Bond Street, London.
Postmark: 19 July 1831. *Stamp*: Kendal Penny Post.
MS. WL. Hitherto unpublished.

Rydal Mount, July 16th—1831

My dear Sir,

When your letter of the 10th (which Mrs Wordsworth opened)
reached Rydal, my Brother was on a visit to his Son in the neighbourhood of Whitehaven, and as we expected him at home by the
middle of last week we did not think it necessary to forward your
letter to him. Receiving no tidings from my Brother we have continued daily to expect him until this morning when he informs us
that he will not reach home before next Thursday; and not only this,
but that he is going on a Tour among the mountains: so there is
little or no chance that any communication we might send would
reach him at all. This we very much regret, as if it should be in his
power to comply with your request it seems that there would not
be time for it.

Mrs Wordsworth begs me to offer her kind regards, to which
allow me to add my own good wishes, and believe me, dear Sir,

Yours respectfully
Dorothy Wordsworth

626. W. W. to EDWARD MOXON

Address: To Mr Moxon, 64 New Bond Street, London.
Postmark: 23 July 1831. *Stamp*: Kendal Penny Post.
MS. Henry E. Huntington Library.
K (—). LY ii. 562.

Rydal Mount near Kendal
July 21st [1831]

My dear Sir,

Your letter of the 19th has been received—As you *know well*
that I am anxious to serve you I have the less pain in saying that I

[1] Woburn Abbey in Bedfordshire, the magnificent eighteenth-century seat
of the Russells.

cannot do it in this way.[1] I have an aversion little less than insurmountable to having any thing to do with periodicals—and nothing but a sense of duty to my family would have induced me to treat with Mr Hall.[2] If I could bring myself out of personal kindness for any Editor or proprietor of a Periodical to contribute, it would be to the Annual of Alaric Watts[3] who has a sort of claim upon me for some literary civilities and intended services, some time ago.— I not only feel this aversion myself but Mrs W has it in so strong a degree that, for the present, I put away all thoughts of looking for pecuniary emolument, from that way of publication, which is tantamount to abandoning such expectation from any other.

And now may I take the liberty of expressing my regret that you should have been tempted into this experiment at all? It must be attended with risk; and *risk* I am most anxious you should avoid.—You *were sure* of succeeding if you had adhered to the Rules of Prudence we talked over together; but if you yield to these temptations, the hazard may hurt you in a thousand ways.— Allow me to say also, that I fear the proprietorship of a Magazine may tempt you to write yourself, which will take your thoughts off from business, in a greater degree than you would be inclined to suspect. It strikes me also that there is something like attempting to take the public by storm in putting forth your distinguished personal friends in the way you propose to do. The Public is apt to revolt at any such step and the Contemporary Journals might be inclined to resent it, and fall upon you, in consequence—Indeed my good friend on whichever side I look at this project I dislike it.

It costs me something to write this Letter, but I do it out of sincere friendship. Be assured that I shall do all I *can* to serve you, but in this way you must excuse me.

I am glad the Selections[4] sell—

ever faithfully yours
Wm Wordsworth

Thursday.

The Sonnet on viewing Mr Haydon's picture was sent to him with permission to present it when, where, and how he liked. I

---

[1] In Apr. 1831 Moxon started under his own editorship the *Englishman's Magazine*, but abandoned the venture the following October. He had recently asked W. W. for a contribution. See Merriam, *Edward Moxon, Publisher of Poets*, pp. 30–5.

[2] Samuel Carter Hall. It seems that after their recent meetings in London, Hall had again approached W. W. for a contribution to *The Amulet*, which, however, he declined to provide.

[3] *The Literary Souvenir*. For Watts's negotiations on W. W.'s behalf with Hurst and Robinson in 1825–6, see pt. i, L. 182.

[4] Hine's *Selections*.

wrote it to serve *him*, but I had nothing to do with its appearance in Mr Hall's Journal.¹

627. W. W. and D. W. to FRANCIS MEREWETHER

Address: To The Revᵈ. Francis Merewether, Coleorton, Ashby de la Zouche.
 [*In D. W.'s hand*]
Stamp: Kendal Penny Post.
MS: *WL. Hitherto unpublished.*

[*c.* 22 July 1831]

My dear Sir,

Your Letter of the 13ᵗʰ June ought to have been answered long ago, but my aversion to the Pen, aware as I am how ill I write, encreases every year; besides, after so long an absence I was necessarily much in arrear with engagements of every kind. It concerns us much to have so unfavorable an account of your health, and as you attribute your disease in part to the times, which are not likely to mend, it is to be feared, it may still hang upon you. My own health suffered not a little from the same Cause and from the exertions I made during my stay in London against this rash and unjust measure.

—The Verses you send had previously been shown me by Dr Wordsworth at Cambridge; though they are scarcely correct in metre I liked them much both in sentiment and expression, with the exception of the Phrase 'quaffed the Cup of conjugal felicity.' The subject you propose² as an additional Sonnet to the Ecclesiastical Sketches would certainly be in its place there, but I cannot *engage* to throw it into verse. In these matters so much depends on happy impulse which one cannot command.

—You will be pleased to hear that, having just returned from a visit of a week (my first) to John and my daughter in Law, I can, except in the point of her health or rather her strength, report most favorably. Never in my life did I make so interesting a visit, or sojourn: they are so happy and with so much good sense attached to each other. You know that John's manners are mild, and her affections are the very pattern of what a woman's ought to be. The neighbourhood, as to society, is not very much to

¹ The sonnet appeared first in the *New Monthly Magazine*, xxxii (July 1831), 26. S. C. Hall had taken over the editorship for a time in 1831 when Thomas Campbell retired. Later in the year, he reverted to his former position as sub-editor, this time under Lytton Bulwer.
² Lay patronage: see L. 640 below.

boast of, but the beauties of the country make amends in no small degree for the want, a very common one in country places, of intellectual Society. My Son Wᵐ was with me there, and we spent much of our time together in rambling by the sea-shore and diving not into the waters, though he did bathe more than once, but into the beautiful and wild clefts or dingles, formed by little rills and streams that work their way to be swallowed up by the neighbouring sea. You perhaps know that the Parish Church of Moresby stands upon the site of a Roman encampment,[1] a few hundred yards from the edge of a high Cliff against which the waves are ever breaking. The population of the Parish is for the most part very respectable, and amounts to about 800.

Mrs Wordsworth is much obliged by Mrs Merewether's regrets and her kindness, but she knew from your son whom she saw the day before we left Cambridge that you were absent at the time of her seizure. It grieves me to say that since her return she has been again very unwell with Lumbago, influenza, and a general attack of Rheumatism, which have confined her a good deal to her room and bed; but she is I hope better, being now walking about the Room down stairs; she sends her love as do we all. My sister is well.—John was much concerned that you were so unwell and talked of writing to you, indeed we purposed writing a joint Letter from Moresby, but engagements sprang up and prevented it, and you know that like myself he is dilatory in his epistolary duties. We were rejoiced to learn at Cambridge that Frank[2] was so very near obtaining the Bell Scholarship.—I will bear in mind your proposal about the Sonnet.

I hope every one is well at the Hall. Pray give our kindest remembrances there. And believe me my dear Mr Merewether

Very faithfully yours
Wᵐ Wordsworth

[*D. W. writes*]

I cannot perform my office[3] without a word of affectionate remembrance to yourself and Mrs Merewether, and poor old Whitwick, a place I always think of with great interest, and with many a pleasing remembrance.—May God speedily restore you to your former health and chearfulness. But as to chearfulness there can be none in the present aspect of public affairs except through

---

[1] The Roman fort of Arbeia, dating from the second century A.D.
[2] Francis Merewether's son of the same name, now an undergraduate at Trinity (see L. 615 above).
[3] i.e. to address the letter.

reliance in an overruling providence that works by means and
for ends one cannot fathom.

> Believe me my dear Friends
> ever your obliged and affectionate
> Dorothy Wordsworth Senr.

I congratulate you on your son's good doings at Cambridge. D. W

628. W. W. to ALEXANDER DYCE

MS. Victoria and Albert Museum.
Mem. Grosart. K. LY ii. 563.

> Lowther Castle, near Penrith
> 23^d July,[1] [1831]

My dear Sir,

I have put off replying to your obliging Letter till I could
procure a Frank; as I had little more to say than to thank you
for your attention as to Lady Winchelsea, and for the Extracts
you sent me.

I expected to find at this place my Friend Lady Frederick
Bentinck, through whom I intended to renew my request for
materials, if any exist, among the Finch family, whether MSS
poems or anything else that would be interesting; but Lady F.,
unluckily, is not likely to be in West^nd. I shall, however, write to
her. Without some additional materials, I think I should scarcely
feel strong enough to venture upon any species of publication
connected with this very interesting woman, notwithstanding
the kind things you say of the value of my critical Remarks.[2]

I am glad you have taken Skelton[3] in hand, and much wish I
could be of any use to you. In regard to his life, I am certain of
having read somewhere (I thought it was in Burns's *Hist. of
Cumberland and West^nd*,[4] but I am mistaken), that Skelton was born

---

[1] Septemb^r *written by mistake.*
[2] Dyce had written on 3 July about the projected publication: 'The most
interesting part of the volume . . . will be your Essay on her Genius; and in
the present day (now that the influence of the Edinburgh Review has completely
died away) I am certain that poetical criticisms from your pen will be read
with eagerness.' (*WL MSS.*)
[3] Dyce's edition of Skelton was not published until 1843.
[4] Joseph Nicolson and Richard Burn, *The History and Antiquities of the Counties of Westmorland and Cumberland*, 2 vols., 1777.

at Branthwaite Hall,[1] in the County of Cumberland. Certain it is that a family of that name possessed the place for many generations; and I own it would give me some pleasure to make out that Skelton was a Brother Cumbrian. Branthwaite Hall is about 6 miles from Cockermouth, my native place. Tickell[2] (of the Spectator, one of the best of our minor Poets, as Johnson has truly said) was born within two miles of the same Town. These are mere accidents it is true, but I am foolish enough to attach some interest to them.

If it would be more agreeable to you, I would mention your views in respect to Skelton to Mr Southey. I should have done so before, but it slipped my memory when I saw him. Mr Southey is undoubtedly much engaged, but I cannot think that he would take ill a Letter from you on any literary subject. At all events I shall in a few days mention your intention of editing Skelton, and ask if he has anything to suggest.

I meditate a little tour in Scotland this autumn, my principal object being to visit Sir Walter Scott; but as I take my Daughter along with me, we probably shall go to Edinburgh, Glasgow, and take a peep at the Western Highlands. This will not bring us near Aberdeen.[3] If it suited you to return to Town by the Lakes, I would be truly glad to see you at Rydal Mount, near Ambleside. You might, *at all events*, call on Mr Southey on your way; I would prepare an introduction for you by naming your intention to Mr S. I have underlined the above Sentence,[4] because my Scotch tour would, I fear, make it little likely that I should be at home about the 10th of Sepbr. Your return however may be deferred.

Believe me, my dear Sir,
very respectfully, your obliged
W. Wordsworth

P.S.—I hope your health continues good. I assure you there was no want of interest in your conversation on that or any other account.

---

[1] One tradition associates John Skelton with the Cumberland branch of the family and with Armathwaite Castle on the Eden; but it is now more usually held that he was a native of Norfolk, where he was rector of Diss from about 1504.
[2] For Thomas Tickell, see pt. i, L. 201.
[3] Where Dyce then was.
[4] i.e. the phrase *at all events*.

629. W. W. to SIR JOHN STODDART[1]

MS. untraced.
John Davy, Fragmentary Remains, Literary and Scientific, of Sir Humphry Davy, Bart . . ., 1858, p. 255.

[23 July 1831]

. . . I became acquainted with Sir Humphry Davy when he was a lecturer at the Royal Institution;[2] and have since seen him frequently at his own house in London, occasionally at mine in the country and at Lord Lonsdale's, at Lowther, where I have been under the same roof with him several days at a time. Of his scientific attainments I am altogether an incompetent judge; nor did he talk upon those subjects except with those who had made them their study. His conversation was very entertaining, for he had seen much, and he was naturally a very eloquent person. The most interesting day I ever passed with him was in this country.[3] We left Patterdale in the morning, he, Sir Walter Scott, and myself, and ascended to the top of Helvellyn together. Here Sir H. left us, and we all dined together at my little cottage in Grasmere,[4] which you must remember so well. When I last saw him, which was for several days at Lowther[5] (I forget the year), though he was apparently as lively as ever in conversation, his constitution was clearly giving way; he shrank from his ordinary exercises of fishing and on the moors. I was much concerned to notice this, and feared some unlucky result. There were points of sympathy between us, but fewer than you might perhaps expect. His scientific pursuits had hurried his mind into a course where I could not follow him; and had diverted it in proportion from objects with which I was best acquainted . . .

[cetera desunt]

---

[1] Stoddart (see *MY* i. 12; ii. 651), now Chief Justice of Malta, had written to W. W. on 7 Apr. asking him to furnish materials for his friend Dr. Davy's biography of his brother, and recalling their friendship many years before. ' "Old men forget, yet do not all forget"—and I certainly have not forgotten either Grasmere or Rydale . . .' (*WL MSS.*) For Dr. John Davy, see L. 921 below.

[2] See *EY*, p. 289.

[3] In Aug. 1805. See the I. F. note to *Musings near Aquapendente* (*PW* iii. 490–1).

[4] Dove Cottage.

[5] Probably in Sept. 1825.

630. W. W. to MISS CARLYLE[1]

Address: Miss Carlyle, Carlisle.
Stamp: Kendal Penny Post.
MS. Tullie House, Carlisle.
LY ii. 565.

[*In Dora W.'s hand*]   Rydal Mount
                                 Wednesday July 25th [1831]

My dear Miss Carlyle,

I have to thank you for two most obliging letters, and the great trouble you have taken on my son's account. As I knew you would give me credit for being sensible of your kindness I did not think it right to trouble you with an acknowledgement till the second letter which you promised, might reach me. I have taken a day to consider along with my son, the offer of Mrs Carrick.[2] The lodgings seem in all respects suitable but I must own that the terms strike me as high. Suppose the case of a young clergyman lodging at Carlisle: had he to pay £30 a year for lodging without any beverage to his meals but water found him, he would have little left to supply himself with other necessaries if £80 be demanded on account of the additional small room—that seems to me more than is reasonable. I should therefore think that £80 would be a handsome remuneration for the whole, the care of such small portion of the Stamps as would devolve upon Mrs Carrick included. If Mrs C. consents to this my son would be glad to take the lodgings three months hence if they should then be at liberty. I think he will benefit by another quarter's residence here under my clerk, and his Mother is very anxious to see a little more of him, after his long absence in Germany, than her engagements have allowed, she only returned the other day from Cheltenham where she has been several weeks—not I might say on account of her own ill-health but to attend a sick friend.[3]

I am concerned to hear of Mrs Lodge's[4] indisposition.—With best wishes for her recovery and remembrances to both your Aunts, I remain dear Miss Carlyle yours very much obliged,

[*signed*] Wm Wordsworth

---

[1] Of Abbey Street, Carlisle: a friend of the Wordsworths (mentioned in *MW*, p. 123), whom W. W. had consulted about lodgings for Willy W., who was about to take up his sub-distributorship at Carlisle: probably a relation of the Revd. Joseph Carlyle (1759–1804), Chancellor of Carlisle and Professor of Arabic at Cambridge.

[2] Probably Mrs Sarah Carrick, of Eden Terrace, on the north side of the city.   [3] Dr. Andrew Bell.

[4] Mrs. Sarah Lodge, a neighbour of Miss Carlyle's in Abbey Street.

Be so good as to thank Miss Grisdale[1] for interesting herself in my concerns. I regretted much her absence from Carlisle when I was there.

Mrs. Carrick will understand that my son would not be justified in taking the lodgings for *a year*, as circumstances might call him from Carlisle, or in these retrenching days, the situation be so reduced as not to be worth holding—in such case a month's notice he hopes will satisfy Mrs Carrick.

631. W. W. to SAMUEL BUTLER[2]

Address: Revd Dr Butler etc etc, Shrewsbury.
MS. Royal Institution of Cornwall, Truro.
Samuel Butler, Life and Letters of Dr Samuel Butler . . ., 2 vols., 1896, ii. 2.

Rydal Mount
Augt 3^d—[? 1831][3]

My dear Sir,

Mr Harrison[4] having requested of me a line of Introduction I willingly comply with his wish, both on his and his Son's account, and as it furnishes me with an occasion of being brought to your recollection.—

Mr. H. is in a still greater degree than Parents ordinarily are, anxious for the well-doing of his Son; and is much pleased with the report which from time to time having examined his Son during the last two years, I have been able to make of his progress. He is still however in point of accuracy, and habits of strict attention, far from what one would wish to find in a boy of his years; and this I take the liberty of mentioning in order that you may not be disappointed in him. I trust however, with the benefit of your care that he will in the end do his duty to his Teachers, his Parent and himself.

Mr Tillbrook's[5] pretty place continues unoccupied; nor do we hear either of himself or any of his Friends coming to it during the remainder of the Summer.

---

[1] Miss Caroline Grisedale, also of Abbey Street: perhaps identical with the Miss Grisedale who was one of the Lowther Castle circle.

[2] Headmaster of Shrewsbury (see pt. i, Ls. 180 and 356a).

[3] In the British Library transcript of this letter, the year has been added, perhaps by Butler himself.

[4] Benson Harrison of Green Bank. His son John was at Shrewsbury, 1830–2.

[5] The Revd. Samuel Tillbrooke, owner of Ivy Cottage.

Poor Margaret[1] suffered much in her long and wasting illness. You will be pleased to hear that, through the exertion of this family, she was induced to make a Will by which her small property was better disposed of than in strict course of law it would have been. Mr. Carter, my clerk, was so kind as [to] undertake the office of Ex[r]—

I remain dear Sir
sincerely yours
W. Wordsworth

632. W. W. to BASIL MONTAGU

Address: Basil Montagu Esq[re], Lincolns Inn.
Stamp: Bond St.
MS. Cornell. Hitherto unpublished.

8th August [1831]
Rydal Mount
Kendal.

My dear Montagu,

On my return from London and Cambridge some time ago I found upon my Shelf the Vol: of Lord Bacon;[2] but having not been told of your Present of your tract upon Punishment of Death[3] I was not aware of it, till your last note reached me.

I have read the Tract with much pleasure. You have treated the subject with your usual ability—and I own it does surprize me that the Experiment is not *tried* of abolishing the punishment of death in the case of Forgery; as if it were not found to answer, men would surely be ready enough to recur to it, as they are sufficiently careful about their property.—

You would have received this acknowledgement earlier, but I waited for an opportunity to send my note to London without expence of Postage.

ever faithfully yours
W[m] Wordsworth

[1] Margaret Wilkinson, housekeeper at Ivy Cottage (see L. 477 above).
[2] Vol. xiii (1831) of Montagu's edition of *The Works of Francis Bacon*, which consisted of a further collection of letters and legal tracts.
[3] *Thoughts upon Punishment of Death for Forgery*, 1830. In this and other tracts Montagu was exploring the possibility of reducing the number of offences to which the death penalty still applied. On 31 July 1832 a bill to abolish the death penalty for certain types of forgery was given a third reading in the House of Commons and passed by the Lords subject to certain amendments. W. W.'s own views on the subject of capital punishment were finally embodied in the *Sonnets upon the Punishment of Death* in 1839 (see *PW* iv. 135, 433).

633. D. W. to WILLIAM PEARSON

MS. untraced.
Pearson. K (—). LY ii. 573.

Rydal Mount,
[11 Aug. 1831][1]

My dear Sir,

My Nephew, being particularly engaged with office business during Mr Carter's absence, who is keeping holiday at Liverpool, has desired me to return you his best thanks for your letter, and for all the pains you have taken to procure a horse.

As perhaps you may have heard, William and his Father set off a few days ago to look after one or more of the horses you had mentioned; and fortunately fell in with the *Grey*, and its owner. In some respects they were much pleased with it; but the man asked for it £30, which they thought too much, and besides, he was not ready to *warrant* its soundness, but only said, he 'would pass it'. These considerations induced my Brother, with his Son, to go to Crook[2] yesterday, and there they actually made a bargain, not for the Crook Hall *Grey*, but for a bay horse, which they hope will answer their purpose.

It is an admirable walker, but unused to trotting, having only been put to carting and ploughing. We expect the horse to-day, and as soon as it has had a fair trial it is to be sent to Moresby to bring home Mrs Wordsworth; and soon after her return it may possibly have the honour of conveying the Poet and his Daughter to Abbotsford, to visit Sir Walter Scott! This visit has long been promised, but the late accounts of Sir Walter's health having been very bad, we were fearful that the visit might never be accomplished. I am happy, however, to tell you that a friend of ours, who has just been on a visit at Abbotsford, informs us that Sir Walter is much better at present, and quite able to enjoy the society of friends. This information has determined my Brother to think

---

[1] Incorrectly dated to 20 Oct. in *Pearson*, and to early Sept. by de Selincourt: correct date established from D. W.'s MS. Journals (*WL MSS.*) which record W. W.'s purchase of the bay horse on 10 Aug. The Journals also establish that John Stuart Mill's visits to W. W. described in his MS. Tour to the Lakes (*Bodleian Library MSS.*), and the conversations recorded in his letter to John Sterling on 20 Oct. (*Collected Works of John Stuart Mill*, vol. xii: *Earlier Letters of John Stuart Mill, 1812–1848*, ed. Francis E. Mineka, 1963, pp. 74 ff.), took place just before this, on 4–7 Aug., and not afterwards, on 11–14 Aug., as suggested by Anna J. Mill, 'John Stuart Mill's Visit to Wordsworth, 1831', *MLR* xliv (1949), 341–50.

[2] A village near Crosthwaite, where Pearson lived.

seriously of the journey; and if Sir Walter continues as well as he is at present, it will probably be accomplished during the Autumn.

You will be glad to hear that the sea air has proved very beneficial to my Sister, and that Mrs John Wordsworth's health is improved. Miss Hutchinson is at Keswick, and will probably remain there till Mrs Wordsworth's return.

My Brother and William would have been very glad to call on you yesterday, but the additional three miles would have made the ride too long for him. As it was, he was a good deal fatigued, not being so clever on horseback as on foot.

My Brother and his Daughter unite their thanks, with William's —It is very long since we have heard of, or seen you,—I hope you have been in good health. My Brother begs his kind regards.

I am, dear Sir,
Yours sincerely,
Dorothy Wordsworth.

634. W. W. to EDWARD QUILLINAN

Address: E. Quillinan Esqre, Bryanston Street, Portman Sq^re, London.
Franked: Penrith August Twenty Four 1831 Mexborough.[1]
Postmark: (1) 24 Aug. 1831 (2) 26 Aug. 1831. *Stamp*: Penrith.
MS. Lilly Library, Indiana University.
Russell Noyes, 'Wordsworth and Pickersgill', NQ cciv (Mar. 1959), 86–7.

Lowther Castle
Wednesday 23^d
August [1831]

My dear Mr Quillinan,
Did I ever thank you for the manner in which [you] managed the rather delicate business with Mr Pickersgill.[2]—I have nevertheless, being as you know of an anxious temper, had some little uneasiness about one point—viz the Expense which the College may be put to.—I thought I had expressed myself so in making the proposal through you; that Mr P. would consider it so much in the light of a recreation, that a journey to the Lakes, or rather a little tour among them, would be a recompense for his trouble and fatigue, and that no additional charge for the Picture would be made on this account.—I thought I had put this as delicately as I could,

[1] John Savile, 3rd Earl of Mexborough (1783–1860), of Methley Park, Leeds: Irish peer, and M.P. for Pontefract, 1807–26, and 1831–2.
[2] See L. 622 above.

nevertheless for this very reason I fear the expression may have been left short. Could you set me at ease on this particular; for I could not think myself justified in putting the College to an expense which they might not be prepared for when they made the request which of course I must consider as an honor.—

There is also another point—Could you learn when it would suit Mr. P— to come.—I had the other day an affectionate message from Sir Walter Scott, adding that if I did not come soon to see him it might be too late. This was said in allusion to his delicate state of health. I am therefore anxious to go and fulfill an engagement of many years standing.—Dora will go along with me and as we should certainly proceed as far as Edinburgh and not improbably farther, I should be glad to leave my proceedings to Mr. P's convenience.

You know that the Lakes are very beautiful in October, perhaps as much so as at any time—but the days are short. I wish you could make Mr P. understand that I was sincere in my wish to see him at my House, and that the invitation was not one of favor—

Thanks for your news of France—I wish to hear more. When are we to see you[1]—

Rotha[2] is a delightful creature, and I love her very much—

Ever affectionately yours
Wm Wordsworth

635. W. W. to SIR WALTER SCOTT

Address: Sir Walter Scott Bart, Abbotsford, Melrose, N.B. [*In M. W.'s hand*]
Stamp: Kendal Penny Post.
Endorsed: Wordsworth Augt. 1831.
MS. National Library of Scotland.
LY ii. 566.

Rydal Mount, Kendal
29th August 1831.

My dear Sir Walter,

I received your kind message through Mr Taylor;[3] it has decided me to fulfill an engagement which has long pressed upon my

---

[1] E. Q. went back to France soon after this, and did not revisit the Lakes until the new year.

[2] Rotha Quillinan was being looked after by Dora W. while E. Q. was in France.

[3] Henry Taylor visited the Lakes in July–August, staying with Southey at Keswick and spending several days at Rydal Mount with Miss Fenwick (see L. 680 below) in early August, when J. S. Mill was also there (see D. W.'s MS. Journals and *RMVB*).

mind, viz to set off for Abbotsford with my Daughter in ten days, if you could receive us with comfort to your self, and Miss Scott.[1]— As we shall travel with a young Horse our day's journies will be short; and we mean also to stop a day on the road so that it will take us six days at least to reach you.

If it do not suit you my dear friend to receive us, pray do not let this offer embarrass you, but say frankly what you feel, or how you are circumstanced.

I hope that your health is not worse, that Miss Scott is well, and Mr and Mrs Lockhart with you.

I am in sad spirits about public affairs. The Whigs have I fear subverted this antient and noble Government—God protect us—

> Ever my dear Sir Walter
> Your affectionate friend
> Wm Wordsworth

I presume we must go to Hawick—which is our best way after we leave that place?

636. W. W. to LORD LONSDALE

MS. Lonsdale MSS. Hitherto unpublished.

[*In M. W.'s hand*]

Tuesday Aug 30th [1831]

My Lord,

On behalf of my Nephew Charles Wordsworth of Christ Church and my younger Son, I take the liberty of requesting that your Lordship would allow them a couple of days Shooting on any moor where their presence might not interfere with your arrangements. I may add that they are both Novices, and are not likely to commit any great Slaughter. My Son having only been out 2 days, (2 years ago, at Ravenstonedale, by Col: Lowther's permission) and my Nephew not at all.

You will perhaps recollect that I mentioned Mr Westall's panoramic Views[2] of this Country. The one that is finished—that

---

[1] Scott replied on 2 Sept.: 'Nothing in the world can be more convenient than your own visit and your sisters here and as many of your family as you find it convenient.' (*Letters of Sir Walter Scott*, ed. Grierson, xii 30.)

[2] For William Westall the artist, see *MY* ii. 362, 510. He had made another tour of the Lakes this month and was working in the neighbourhood (see Warter, iv. 236).

of Windermere—pleased much. They are not published by Sub[n] but if y[r] Ldship would allow me to give in your name to Mr W. for the whole set as they come out—he would reserve for you one of the earliest Impressions.

On Sunday last, being at Bowness Church, I saw Mr and Mrs Bolton—who are both in their better way; I dined at the Island, and for the first time had a long conversation with Mr Curwen upon the Reform Bill—I gave him unreservedly my views on its character and tendency. He regretted much that the change had been pushed so far—he said that there was an intention (which I believe has been mentioned in the Papers) in Cumberland, to petition against the division of the County as tending to place them[1] under nomination; and as to his own views, he observed, that he had no objection to two Members being returned by the great landed Proprietors, provided that two others were a fair representation of the landed Interest of the county in general.

At Halsteads I found the Fairfaxes[2] of Gilling Castle. Mrs F. is a thoughtful and clear-headed woman—the young man seemed much pleased with what I said to Mr Marshall on the Reform Bill, a subject which I should have been loth to introduce but Mr M. asked me, if my opinion had undergone any change in its favour.[3]

I ought to add that the days which would suit my Nephew are Friday and Saturday next.

I have the honor to be
your Ldshp's faithful St.
[*signed*] Wm Wordsworth

[*W. W. adds*]

An inflammation in my eyes has obliged me to employ Mrs W.'s pen.

---

[1] i.e. the four new seats which, under the Reform Bill, were to come from dividing Cumberland into two new constituencies, the eastern and western divisions.

[2] Charles Gregory Piggott of Gilling Castle, near Helmsley, Yorks., assumed the name of Fairfax by Royal Licence in 1793, and the following year married Mary, sister of Sir Henry Goodricke, Bart., of Ribston, Yorks. Their son was Charles Gregory Fairfax (b. *c.* 1795).

[3] In his reply of 6 Sept. Lord Lonsdale wrote: 'Lord Althorp goes blundering on with his Reform Bill, which appears to approach its end . . .', and in a further letter on 30 Sept. he predicted that the Bill would be rejected in the Lords. (*WL MSS.*) See L. 645 below.

637. W. W. to JOHN MARSHALL

Address: John Marshall Esqre, Hallsteads, Penrith.
Stamp: Kendal Penny Post.
MS. WL.
LY ii. 567.

[*In M. W.'s hand*]

Friday [2 Sept. 1831]

My dear Sir,

What a pity that we cannot turn this beautiful weather to better account by setting out on our journey today or tomorrow, as we had intended—but business has unexpectedly sprung up in the office, for which my presence is indispensable, and I have little hope of being at liberty in less than ten days. I thought it right to let you know of this disappointment, as you and Mrs Marshall would have been looking for us.

My Sister is on a visit to Mr and Mrs Curwen at the Island, where are also my Son and his wife. Pray mention to your young Ladies that it is regretted in this house, that we cannot have their Company to add to what is elegantly called a *cram*, which is to take place at Rydal Mount on Monday evening—*they* perhaps will not be sorry to be absent, as it is apprehended the fiddlers will not have room to move their elbows.

Say to Miss M.[1] that we were all much delighted with the verses she put into my hands—Mr S. thought highly of those addressed to his Daughter,[2] which were shewn him by Miss Hutchinson—they are *we think* eminently characteristic and tender.

I am suffering from my eyes, which obliges me to employ Mrs W.'s pen.

Ever very sincerely yours
[*signed*] Wm Wordsworth

[1] Julia Marshall.
[2] 'My Sister Julia's lines on Kate Southey'—note by Mary Anne Marshall, later Lady Monteagle.

638. W. W. to JOHN KENYON

Address: John Kenyon Esqre, St. Leonards, near Hastings.
Postmark: 13 Sept. 1831.
MS. untraced.
Transactions of the Wordsworth Society, no. 6, p. 101. K (—). *LT ii. 570.*

[*In M. W.'s hand*]

Rydal Mount, Septr 9th. [1831]

My dear Mr Kenyon,

Your letter, which reached me at the breakfast Table, as my letters generally do, was truly acceptable to myself and to all of us. You ask how we are in health, I will therefore briefly despatch that subject first of which I have nothing but well to say, except that I am now suffering from an inflammation in my eye (which obliges me to make use of my wife's pen) and that she, on our journey from Cambridge had a violent attack of Sciatica and Lumbago which obliged me to leave her with Dora at Nottingham. *There, that* poetry, upon which you are so good-naturedly copious, stood me in good stead; I had not an acquaintance in that large Town, but I introduced myself, and told our distresses to a Brother and Sister of the Lyre, William and Mary Howitt, and they were as kind to us as all Poets and Poetesses ought to be to each other; offering their house as a place of retreat from the noise and tumult of the Elections which were to begin the next day.[1] In twelve days Mary and Dora followed me home. And here we are with William, who is to be fixed at Carlisle as my Sub-distributor in about a month from this time. John and his wife have been with us and have just departed for a Tour in N. Wales; and Dora and I are going to see Sir Walter Scott at Abbotsford, before his departure for Naples, where he intends to winter for the benefit of his health. Had I not feared that you might have left St. Leonards, I would have kept this letter, with the hope of making it more interesting to you and Mrs K. by some account of that great man, and the many things and objects he has about him, which you would have been pleased to hear of, and which he is going to leave so soon upon what may prove a melancholy errand.

The summer that is over has been with us as well as with you a brilliant one, for sunshine and fair and calm weather—brilliant also for its unexampled gaiety in Regattas, Balls, Dejeuners, Picnics by the Lake side, on the Islands, and on the Mountain tops— Fireworks by night—Dancing on the green sward by day—in short

[1] See L. 608 above.

a fever of pleasure from morn to dewy eve—from dewy eve till break of day. Our Youths and Maidens, like Chaucer's Squire, 'hath slept no more than doth the nightingale', and our Old Men have looked as bright as Tithonus when his withered cheek reflected the blushes of Aurora upon her first declaration of her passion for him. In the room where I am now dictating, we had, three days ago, a dance—forty beaus and belles, besides Matrons, ancient Spinsters, and Greybeards—and to-morrow in this same room we are to muster for a Venison feast. Why are you not here, either to enjoy or to philosophise upon this dissipation? Our party to-morrow is not so large but that we could find room for you and Mrs Kenyon. The disturbed state of the Continent is no doubt the reason why, in spite of the Reform Bill, such multitudes of Pleasure Hunters have found their way this Summer to the Lakes.

After so much levity, Mary shall transcribe for you a serious Stanza or two, intended for an Inscription in a part of the grounds of Rydal Mount with which you are not acquainted, a field adjoining our Garden which I purchased two or three years ago.[1] Under the shade of some Pollard Oaks, and on a green Terrace in that field, we have lived no small part of the long bright days of the summer gone by; and in a hazel nook of this favourite piece of ground is a Stone, for which I wrote one day the following serious Inscription, you will forgive its Egotism.

> In these fair Vales, hath many a tree
> At Wordsworth's suit been spared,
> And from the builder's hand this Stone,
> For some rude beauty of its own,
> Was rescued by the Bard;
> Long may it rest in peace! and here
> Perchance the tender-hearted
> Will heave a gentle sigh for him
> As One of the Departed.[2]

I have heard something like what you say of Campbell[3] before, but in that case I partly suspected that the admiration might in some degree be affected to ingratiate himself with the Individual who was a friend of mine. By the bye, let you, and every other Person who has a *pet Poet* be on your guard agst that trick. How

---

[1] Actually in 1825 (see pt. i, L. 206).
[2] See *PW* iv. 201. The poem was composed on 26 June 1830.
[3] Thomas Campbell the poet.

sorry I am that Mr Bailey[1] should have gone as far as Ceylon ignorant of the fact that I never have received his book, nor before the receipt of your letter was aware of the intended favour. How came your Brother to go from Manchester into Scotland without taking us by the way? but perhaps he *steamed it* from Liverpool. Tillbrook has offered his House[2] and furniture for sale by private Treaty—the price two thousand Guineas, entre nous, 8 hundred more than its worth, except for fancy. Adieu—every one here—to wit Self and Spouse, Son and Daughter, Sister and Sister in something better than Law, join in kindest regards to you and Mrs Kenyon, and to your brother when you write to him. Farewell again,

Very aff[ly] yours
[*signed*] Wm Wordsworth

We shall always, not merely 'now and then', be glad to hear from you. You asked how I had 'things from London'. Pamphlets, etc., sent to J. Richardson, 91 Royal Exchange, are forwarded if directed to me under cover to Hudson and Nicholson, Booksellers, Kendal.

639. D. W. to CATHERINE CLARKSON

MS. untraced.
K. LY ii. 568.

concluded on Friday, the 9th of September [1831]

My dear Friend,

. . . There is just come out a portrait of my Brother, for which he sat when last in London. It is a lithograph of a chalk drawing by

---

[1] Benjamin Bailey (1791–1853), Archdeacon of Colombo: the friend of Keats, as de Selincourt notes, and from his Oxford days a great admirer of W. W. In 1831 he published *Poetical Sketches of the South of France*, which contained forty sonnets and fifteen other poems, several of which borrow from W. W. or are obviously written under his influence. When Mrs. Fletcher (née Jewsbury) went to India in 1833 she stayed with Bailey and wrote to Dora W. that he was 'such a Wordsworthian as I have rarely if ever met: every edition of your Father is here, filled with MS. notes—Sonnets, remarks etc.' (Gillett, pp. lxi–ii). In 1835 a small anonymous book entitled *Lines addressed to William Wordsworth Esq.* was printed by the Wesleyan Mission Press at Ceylon. It contains 84 sonnets and two poems of eight lines, signed B. and obviously written by Bailey. He also published *The Duties of the Christian Ministry*, 1840 (*R.M. Cat.*, no. 187), and translations of the Old and New Testaments into the Malayalam language.   [2] Ivy Cottage.

Wilkins,[1] and may be had in London. I think it a strong likeness, and so does every one. Of course, to his own family something is wanting; nevertheless I value it much as a likeness of him in company, and something of that restraint with chearfulness, which is natural to him in mixed societies. There is nothing of the poet. . . .

Saturday. This letter was interrupted three weeks ago, or thereabouts; and afterwards being unexpectedly called away to Belle Isle,[2] while John and Isabella were there, I left it unfinished. I stayed there ten days. It is a splendid place for a visit such as mine; but compared with Rydal Mount dull, and to the feelings confining, though persons who live there persuade themselves there is no more trouble in being ferried over to the shore than in continuing uninterruptedly to walk on.

But what I like least in an island as a residence is the being separated from men, cattle, cottages, and the goings-on of rural life. John and Isabella are on a tour in North Wales, and my Brother, Dora, and Charles Wordsworth hope to set off next week on a few days visit to Sir W. Scott; and, if weather allow, a short tour— Edinburgh, Glasgow, Stirling, Loch Lomond, Inverary, Loch Awe, Loch Etive, and the isle of Mull. We have friends[3] at that island. Stamp-office business prevented their setting off some days ago. . . . Dora is to drive her father in a little carriage of our own, with a very steady horse. Charles will travel by coach, and on foot, or as he can. He is a fine, chearful fellow, and rejoices in the hope of this little tour, being very fond of both his uncle and cousin, and glad of the opportunity of seeing a person of so much importance as Sir Walter. Poor man! his health is shattered by a recurrence of slight paralytic strokes, but his mind is active as ever. He would write eight hours in the day if allowed by the physicians, but it is the worst thing he can do; and most likely it is rather to divert him from study, than for benefits expected from the climate, that he has been advised to winter in Italy. He has fixed on leaving Abbotsford at the end of this month to proceed to Naples. The young William is still here; but on the 20th of next month is to begin residence at Carlisle as sub-distributor there—a good putting on (for it is about

---

[1] Francis William Wilkin (1791–1842), who specialized in portraiture in chalk. The original is now in the Museum of Fine Arts, Boston. The lithograph was published in a series called *Men of the Day*: W. W. himself spoke of it as the portrait of the Stamp-Distributor. See Blanchard, *Portraits of Wordsworth*, pp. 68–70, 153–4.

[2] The Curwen residence on Windermere.

[3] Col. and Mrs. Campbell, formerly tenants of Allan Bank (see L. 432 above), who revisited the Lakes this summer (*RMVB*).

£180 per annum) till something better fall out, or as long as things are allowed to remain as they are. But, to tell you the truth, so many changes are going on, I consider nothing as stable; and do expect that the sovereign people to whom our rulers bow so obsequiously will not long endure the stamp office, and its distributors, or the national debt, or anything else that now is.

In October we expect Mr Jones,[1] the companion of my Brother forty years ago over the Alps. He looks back to that journey as the golden and sunny spot in his life. It would delight you to hear the pair talk of their adventures. My Brother, active, lively, and almost as strong as ever on a mountain top; Jones, fat and roundabout and rosy, and puffing, and panting while he climbs the little hill from the road to our house. Never was there a more remarkable contrast; yet time seems to have strengthened the attachment of the native of Cambrian mountains to his Cumbrian friend. We also expect Mr Quillinan in October. Whether he will leave his daughter Rotha (his youngest born) with us for the winter, or take her to school, I know not. Jemima is at school near Paris, and as Dora does not like to part with her godchild, perhaps it may be settled that she remain here till spring. She is an interesting and very clever child, the image of her father. We never saw the Tillbrooks[2] but at church, and did not exchange a word with either of them. It is of no use to enter on a painful history; enough to say that both Tillbrook and his wife so misrepresented the truth in regard to Dora's refusal of Mr Ayling's offer of marriage,[3] that we could have no satisfaction in holding intercourse with them, and therefore we never entered their door. For your own private ear I will just say that Mrs T. is what the world calls a fascinating woman, and that there is an appearance of simplicity and frankness about her

[1] Robert Jones.

[2] The Revd. Samuel Tillbrooke, who was now trying to sell Ivy Cottage, had resigned his fellowship at Peterhouse in 1828, and the following year married Frances, daughter of John Ayling of Tillington, Sussex, and became rector of Freckenham, Suffolk. The cottage was let later this year to Thomas Hamilton (see L. 673 below).

[3] Frances Ayling and her sister had been pupils of Charlotte Lockier at Hendon, and came to Spring Cottage in the summer of 1824 with an introduction from her to the Wordsworths. Their brother, the Revd. William Ayling (b. 1793), an unbeneficed clergyman, who had graduated at University College, Oxford, some years before, accompanied them. The Aylings seem to have made a very favourable impression in local society: Miss Ayling and her brother returned to Spring Cottage in Sept. 1826, and William Ayling took up residence in Ivy Cottage for the following winter. It was about this time that he proposed marriage to Dora W., who had become intimate with his sister, but was refused. (See *MW*, pp. 110–11; *SH*, pp. 285, 328–9, 333; and *Letters of Dora Wordsworth*, pp. 89–90.)

which won Dora's heart, and we all liked her much. During the intercourse which continued a little while between Dora and her, after D.'s refusal, we had cause to think her a person whom we should not desire to be closely connected with. . . . If you would come next summer for one month, two, or three—or as long as you liked—Mrs Luff would consent chearfully to let you keep house,[1] and would be your guest. Now, is it not possible that the thing might be? Surely it is. But I feel inclined neither to talk, think, nor plan about such a scheme. If circumstances favour, no need of planning. You would have only to resolve and propose, and the thing is done. At sixty years of age, scheming is not the amusement one is inclined to resort to. The certainty of death, its near approach, and the sudden changes continually happening among those who were young when we were, absolutely check in me all disposition to form plans. . . . My Brother was lately at Lowther, and called with Lord Lonsdale on Thomas Wilkinson.[2] He was chearful, though quite blind. . . .

[*cetera desunt*]

640. D. W. to FRANCIS MEREWETHER

Address: To The Rev^d. Francis Merewether, Coleorton, Ashby de la Zouche.
    [*readdressed to*] Mrs Ways, Spaynes Hall, Yildham Hasted, Essex.
Postmark: 16 Sept. 1831. *Stamp*: Kendal Penny Post.
MS. WL. Hitherto unpublished.

Tuesday 13th September [1831]

My dear Mr Merewether,

Numerous engagements were pressing on my Brother at the time he received your letter of the 3rd of August, to which he was desirous to give, not a hasty but a thoughtful and full reply; and therefore he waited for a day of leisure, and when *that* came he was utterly unable to use a pen himself; and for many days suffered so much from an excessive inflammation in his eyes that it was injurious to him even to dictate to another person. This inflammation

---

[1] In her letter to D. W. of *c.* 30 July, C. C. stated that the Clarksons could not afford to take Fox Ghyll for the summer. Her letter reflected her political anxieties ('The madness of the people does not seem to be appeased. Oh the folly of yielding to intimidation!'); but it also brought further confirmation of W. W.'s growing reputation, in the remarks of a friend about *The Excursion*: 'It has been my comfort, it has been to me instead of country air, and song of birds and green fields this last month . . .' (*WL MSS.*)

[2] Thomas Wilkinson of Yanwath, the Quaker.

could hardly have come at a worst time: it retarded his setting off for Scotland to visit Sir Walter Scott, who before the end of this month intends leaving Abbotsford to winter at Naples for the benefit of his health. For some days, however, the poor afflicted eyes have been mending; and though one of them is nearly closed up, he has ventured to depart this morning, intending to proceed by very short day-journeys. When once decidedly convalescent he has always hitherto found benefit from travelling, and we hope, though not without some degree of anxiety on that score, that he may in the present instance experience the like good effects from change of air and gentle exercise. His Daughter drives him in a little carriage of our own with a very steady horse. Charles Wordsworth who is now at Rydal Mount, will leave us tomorrow for Newcastle, whence he will join his Uncle and Cousin at Sir Walter Scott's next Tuesday; and after a few days' Stay there, the party will proceed to Edinburgh, Glasgow, and a part of the Western Highlands, weather permitting.

I must now assure you that it concerns me much to be obliged to act as my Brother's deputy in the present case, as I cannot be an efficient one, but I will endeavour, to the best of my power, to convey my Brother's sentiments to you on the subject on which you consulted him; and as I trust I can accurately report the general tenor of them, will hope that you may not be dissatisfied when you come to the end of my letter, though it must be a great disappointment to you to find that it is not even dictated by my Brother. Having, no doubt, heretofore received letters from him penned by one or another of us, the handwriting of this probably did not at first prepare you for any signature but his own; and it is a fact that till eleven o'clock last night, my Brother fully intended to employ me to take the words down according to his dictation; but his eyes became so uneasy that I insisted on his going to bed and leaving me to do as well as I could this morning.—And now to begin with the substance of what last night he desired me to say, and I will give it as nearly as I can in his own words. 'In the first place, explain to Mr Merewether how it happens that I have not written myself, and then tell him how sorry I am, now at last, to give up my intention of dictating tonight, and in the next tell him that in the sincerity of friendship I would dissuade him from printing the poems. The Sale *could* hardly be sufficient to defray expences: but, what is of more importance, the charm of verses such as these is almost destroyed by printing. A printed poem *invites* criticism. The Critic dwells on the faults, such as indifferent rhymes, imperfect metre, or it may be prosaic expression, and thus the sympathetic feeling with which such poems ought to be read is wanting, or it is disturbed. In the manuscript those poems are of value as containing pious sentiments and good thoughts, and to *Friends* those especially which speak of the Departed and of the Living, whose virtues they have known and do know.' Thus far, as concerns the publishing. We now come to the Lines sent in a previous letter,[1] I mean the *metre* of those lines. 'They sail'd together—together quaff'd the cup.' This line is irregular, one syllable redundant. 'May I but follow you! Father of Spirits hear.' In this line, two syllables are redundant. It would be a regular verse without the word 'Father.' But observe here my Brother remarked, 'this is not positively a *fault* but an *irregularity*, such as in a long poem may not only be tolerated but approved if not occurring frequently, yet in very short poems such irregularities are better avoided. There is no objection to the word 'equal.' With regard to the different poems I have only to say that my Brother read them all with much pleasure; but he more than once repeated to me that he should wish you to come to the determination not to publish them in the way you venture. I (DW) say *in that way*—i.e. as a publication by themselves with 'prose reflections,' because it strikes me that the sentiments of some one or more of the poems might fall in by the way of illustration hereafter, in case you should again be tempted to write for the press, but I do entirely agree with my Brother in the opinion that you would do well to retain them in your own possession in manuscript, by which means I feel assured that you would be enabled to give much more pleasure to your private Friends than by putting into their hands a printed Book.— I cannot dismiss this subject without saying that I was much affected by the opening of the poem which begins thus—'On thoughts and visions.' The subject of Lay Patronage is a good one and very well suited for a place in my Brother's Series of Ecclesiastical Sketches; and perhaps at some future time he may take it up; but he never does any thing suddenly at the suggestion of another.—

You and Mrs Merewether will be glad to hear that my Sister's rheumatism is much better, yet she is far from being free from occasional pain; nor will be, I fear, through the winter; but her general health is now very good, and her spirits and activity surprising. John and his wife have been paying a short visit to her Father and Mother at the Windermere Island, and on Wednesday they set off on a Tour in North Wales, which they hope will

---

[1] See L. 627 above.

entirely re-establish Isabella's health, already much improved. William is still at home; but on the 20th of next month he is going to Carlisle as Sub-distributor of Stamps, a place that is very well for a beginning; and we can hope that something better may fall out in a little time; but every thing is now in such an uncertain state that one cannot even calculate on his Father's place remaining *as it is*. I will not, however, turn to the gloomy subject of Reform or any other connected with the strange schemes of our present Rulers, or the Will of the Sovereign People.

I hope my dear Sir, that you and Mrs Merewether are returned to your pleasant home both benefited by sea, air and change of scene. What a pleasure would it have been for John, and for all of us if you could have turned your steps towards Whitehaven. You mention that Sir George and Lady B. are gone to Addington,[1] an intention mentioned to us by Lady B., and she added that the younger born Child was to be christened there by the Archbishop. If they are returned pray make Mrs Wordsworth's and my respectful and affectionate regards to them.

We were sorry to hear of good Mr Foster's dangerous illness. I hope he is now recovered; and beg to be remembered to him and his Sisters, to Mr and Mrs Knight, and to Joseph and Mrs Wright and all inquiring Friends at Whitwick. Mr Pricket[2] had been unwell when you wrote. I hope he is better, and continues to prosper at Whitwick and that Whitwick prospers under his care. I trust your Son continues to give and receive satisfaction at Trinity College.— It is long since we heard from D[r] Wordsworth; but his Son Charles brought a good report of his health. He seems pleased with Buxted; but I fear the place will be too solitary to be beneficial to him. I always fancy that an active Life best suits him. I suppose Emily[3] is still at school, but perhaps you will not part with her again after Christmas. Give our kind Love to Mrs Merewether, and believe me dear Sir,

your faithful and affectionate Friend
D Wordsworth.

[1] Addington Palace, Surrey, residence of the Archbishop of Canterbury, Lady Beaumont's father.
[2] John W.'s successor as curate of Whitwick.
[3] Francis Merewether's daughter.

641. W. W. to SIR WALTER SCOTT

Address: Sir Walter Scott Bart: Abbotsford, Melrose.
Postmark: 16 Sept. *Stamp*: Carlisle.
Endorsed: Wordsworth Sept. 1831.
MS. National Library of Scotland.
K (—). *LT ii. 574.*

[*In Dora W.'s hand*]

Carlisle, Friday Eve^{ng} Sept. 16th [1831]

My dear Sir Walter,

'There's a man wi' a veil, and a lass drivin',' exclaimed a little urchin, as we entered 'merrie Carlisle' a couple of hours ago, on our way to Abbotsford. From the words you will infer, and truly, that my eyes are in but a poor state—I was determined however to see you and yours, and to give my daughter the same pleasure at all hazards; accordingly I left home last Tuesday, but was detained two entire days at Halsteads on Ullswater by a serious increase of my complaint—this morning I felt so much better that we ventured to proceed, tomorrow we hope to sleep at Langholm, on Sunday at Hawick, and on Monday, if the distance be not greater than we suppose, under your roof.

In my former letter I mentioned a nephew of mine, a student of Christ Ch:,[1] and I may add, a distinguished one, to whom (so far did I presume upon your kindness) I could not but allow the pleasure of accompanying us—he has taken the Newcastle road into Scotland, hoping to join us at Abbotsford on Tuesday, and I mention him now from an apprehension of being again retarded by my eyes, and to beg that if he should arrive before us he may be no restraint upon you whatever.—Let him loose in your library, or on the Tweed with his fishing-rod, or in the Stubbles with his gun (he is but a novice of a shot, by-the-bye) and he will be no trouble to any part of your family.

With kindest regards to Miss Scott and to M^r and Mrs Lockhart if still as we hope with you, in which my Daughter unites, and with the same for yourself and a thousand good wishes

I remain my dear Sir Walter
very affectionately yours
[*signed*] Wm Wordsworth

---

[1] Charles Wordsworth had been elected a Student of Christ Church in 1827.

642. W. W. to ROBERT JONES

Address: Revd Robert Jones, Plas yn Llan, near Ruthin, North Wales.
Postmark: (1) 27 Sept. 1831 (2) 29 Sept. 1831.
Stamp: (1) Falkirk (2) Birmingham.
MS. Cornell.
LY ii. *575* (—).

[*In Dora W.'s hand*]

Falkirk
Monday 26th Sep^t [1831]

My dear Jones,

My old complaint an inflammation in my eyes and official engagements compelled me to put off my journey to Sir Walter Scott's for nearly *3* weeks in consequence of which and the uncertainty my eyes have caused me to be in I have not been able to write to you sooner. We left (my Daughter and I)¹ Abbotsford last Thursday and a desire to shew her something of Scotland with a hope that travelling may be of use to myself has induced me to extend our tour so that I do not expect to be at home till the 22^d of next month. I shall take it as a very great favour if you will then come and see us and the longer you can stay the better and it would add much to my pleasure on reaching home to find you there—the season is so far advanced as to make a day or two, to travellers, of importance.

I should be able to be at home sooner had we your grey mare, our old friend, but unfortunately our horse is only rising four—much too young for such a journey, so that we can only travel [at the]² rate of *20* miles a day at the very utmost.

Sir Walter was to leave home last Friday for London—he is to embark in a King's Ship for Malta with the intention of wintering at Naples where his younger son³ is attached to the Embassy. His friends say that he is much better in health than he was some months and even weeks ago, and much good is expected from breaking his sedentary habits and application to writing more than from the change of climate.⁴

---

¹ left *written twice*. W. W. left a full account of his visit to Abbotsford, 19–22 Sept., in the I. F. note appended to *Yarrow Revisited, and Other Poems* (*PW* iii. 524–6). See also Charles Wordsworth, *Annals of My Early Life*, pp. 112 ff.
² *MS. torn.*   ³ Charles Scott.
⁴ W. W.'s sonnet *On the Departure of Sir Walter Scott from Abbotsford, for Naples* (*PW* iii. 265), was composed at Callander a few days after the visit to Abbotsford, as Charles Wordsworth makes clear.

He was *60* years of age in August, his complaint has been a succession of slight apoplectic shocks attended with paralysis that shews itself principally in his utterance—I have thought these particulars would interest you and have now to subscribe myself my dear Jones

Your faithful friend
[*signed*] Wm Wordsworth

My Daughter sends her kindest remembrances.

643. D. W. to WILLIAM PEARSON

MS. untraced.
Pearson (—). *LY ii. 576* (—).

Rydal Mount
Tuesday [? 4 Oct. 1831]

My dear Sir,

I have more than once said to you that we should be troubling you again for a supply of potatoes, after your last year's successful purchase of that article, and I now write, (I hope in good time) to beg that you will be so kind as to buy us . . .

My Brother and his Daughter are not expected home before the 25th.[1] They will meet William at Carlisle, who will be settled there as Sub. Distr. about that time. I am happy to tell you that travelling has agreed with my Brother's eyes, and that they were nearly well about ten days ago. The last tidings that have reached us were from Callendar.

They were going to Bonawe,[2] Oban, and the Isle of Mull. Thence to Glasgow and to Lanark, and home by Carlisle—Sir Walter Scott was much pleased to see them; but I am sorry to say his health seems to be much broken—great hopes, however, are entertained from a change of climate and of scene.

---

[1] They actually arrived home on Monday, 17 Oct., according to D. W.'s MS. Journal (*WL MSS.*). Charles Wordsworth had returned on his own at the beginning of the month.

[2] Brenane *Pearson*; but there is no such place. A letter from Dora W. to M. W. of 7 Oct. (*WL MSS.*) describing their itinerary, proves it to be Bonawe. Enclosed in her letter were copies of six sonnets, which were later included in *Yarrow Revisited, and Other Poems*: 'On the Departure of Sir Walter Scott for Naples, Sept. 28th 1831'; 'Composed after Passing some time in the Chapel of Roslin in a storm'; 'A Place of Burial in Scotland'; 'Composed in the Trossacks'; 'Composed in the Glen of Loch Etive'; and 'Composed in the same Place' (see *PW* iii. 265–9).

It is very long since you were at Rydal—To this I can say no more than that you have always been a welcome guest, and that it will give my Brother pleasure to see you popping in as formerly, when he has settled himself at home;—and I am sure you will be glad to inquire after his health, and to hear of their adventures.

I am, dear Sir,

Sincerely and respectfully,

your friend,

D. Wordsworth.

Sunday evening.

I kept back my letter, recollecting it might be likely that our horse-proprietors would wish to have more straw, and no one being at hand to direct me. I find that they will be much obliged if you will procure them a supply, to send along with the potatoes. . . .

Pray excuse the trouble I give you—but I know you will, having so often experienced your kindness that way. Mrs Wordsworth begs I will return her best thanks for the Partridges received whilst I was staying at Belle Isle.

644. W. W. to BASIL MONTAGU

Address: Basil Montagu Esqre, Bedford Sq^re, London.
Postmark: 22 Oct. 1831. *Stamp*: Kendal Penny Post.
MS. Berg Collection, New York Public Library.
K (—). *LY ii. 577* (—).

[In M. W.'s hand]

[19 Oct. 1831]

My dear Montagu,

On my return from an excursion in Scotland two days ago I found the 14th vol of Bacon,[1] together with your note of the 9th of Aug, left here by Mr Romilly:[2] and yesterday arrived by Post

---

[1] Vol. xiv (1831) of *The Works of Francis Bacon* consisted of translations of the *Instauratio Magna* and 'Thoughts on the nature of things'.

[2] John, later Sir John, Romilly, 1st Baron Romilly (1802–74), second son of Sir Samuel Romilly (see *MY* ii. 303, 485, 507), friend of J. S. Mill and the 'philosophical radicals': M.P. for Bridport, 1832–5 and 1846–7, and for Devonport, 1847–52; Solicitor General (1848), Attorney General (1850), and Master of the Rolls (1851).

your letter announcing your Son's[1] intention of visiting this neighbourhood. It will give me great pleasure to see him both on his own account and yours, and to shew him every attention in my power. But as we have at present two little Girls[2] in the house beyond our own family, and are daily expecting my old College Friend Robt Jones, and my nephew John of Trinity Col. also, I fear he cannot be accomodated with a bed in our small House—indeed had the truth been told to my nephew in this matter, I am sure he would have turned his steps elsewhere.

Letters of acknowledgment I always send with as little charge of Postage as I can. Accordingly under cover to a friend in London, a note[3] was sent to you several months ago thanking you for the 13th vol, and the Tract upon the Pun^t: of Death, which letter by some mischance you do not appear to have rec^d. On the question of the Pun^t: of Death, you have written with much ability. For my own part, I am decidedly of opinion that in the case of forgery, both humanity and policy require that an experiment should be made to ascertain whether it cannot be dispensed with.

I am glad that you are proceeding with the life of Lord Bacon.[4] You say that he was sacrificed to Buckingham;[5] have you read a letter of Buckingham to him in which he charges him with the intention of sacrificing him, Buckingham, as he had betrayed all his Patrons and friends in succession? B——m enumerates the cases. It has always appeared to me that much of the odium attached to Lord B's name on account of corrupt practices, arose out of ignorance respecting the Spirit of those times, and the way in which things were carried on. Did I mention to you that there are serious errors of the Press in your Ed: much to be regretted as the work is so valuable.

Your Augt note speaks of your intention of proceeding fr. Bolton to the Lakes. Unluckily I should have been absent, but as

---

[1] Charles (b. 1810), fifth and youngest son of Basil Montagu by his third wife Anna, widow of Thomas Skepper (see *MY* i. 63, 212). Charles Parr Montagu was educated at Caius College, Cambridge, from 1826, entered Lincoln's Inn, 1829, and was called to the Bar in 1834—but he died soon afterwards.

[2] Little Mary Hutchinson from Brinsop, and Rotha Quillinan.

[3] L. 632 above.

[4] This occupied the sixteenth and last volume of Montagu's edition, and appeared in 1834. His attempts to rehabilitate Bacon's reputation were not successful, and prompted Macaulay's trenchant article in the *Edinburgh Review* for July 1837.

[5] George Villiers, 1st Duke of Buckingham (1592–1628). In 1621, when charges of corruption were brought against Bacon, Buckingham was less than whole-hearted in defending him.

you were not heard of, I suppose you changed your purpose. You say your disinclination to move encreases every year—it is not so with myself—travelling agrees with me wonderfully. I am as much Peter Bell as ever, and since my eyelids have been so liable to inflammation, after much reading especially, I find nothing so feeding to my mind as change of scene, and rambling about; and my labours, such as they are, can be carried on better in the fields and on the roads, than any where else.[1]—

I shall be much disappointed if we do not see your Son Charles.

Believe me to be d^r Montagu
very faithfully yours
[*signed*] Wm Wordsworth

645. W. W. to WILLIAM ROWAN HAMILTON

MS. Cornell.
Mem. (—). *Grosart. Hamilton. K* (—). *LY ii. 578.*

[*In M. W.'s hand*]

Rydal Mount, Octr. 27th [1831]

My dear Mr Hamilton,

A day or two before my return from Scotland arrived your letter and verses, for both of which I thank you, as they exhibit your mind under those varied phases which I have great pleasure in contemplating. My reply is earlier than it would have been, but for the opportunity of a frank from one of the Members for the University of Oxford[2]—a friend of Mr Southey's and mine; who by way of recreating himself after the fatigues of the last Session, had taken a trip to see the Manchester railway,[3] and kindly and most unexpectedly came on to give a day apiece to Southey and me. He is like myself in poor heart at the aspect of public affairs; in his opinion the Ministers when they brought in the Bill neither

---

[1] On 20 Oct. Dora W. wrote to Mrs. Fletcher (*née* Jewsbury): '. . . the best of all was I took dear daddy away almost blind and brought him home with eyes as bright as any of my little Turkies that you knew some 6 or 7 years back—and what was more surprising he was busy composing most of the time and he promises that the Recluse shall be his winter's employment—but entre nous I think his courage will fail him when winter really arrives.' (*Letters of Dora Wordsworth*, p. 91.)

[2] Sir Robert Inglis (see L. 418 above).

[3] Opened in Sept. 1830 (see L. 568 above).

expected nor wished it to be carried.[1] All they wanted was an opportunity of saying to the People, 'behold what great things we would have done for you had it been in our power—we must now content ourselves with the best we can get.' But to return to your letter. To speak frankly you appear to be at least three fourths gone in love; therefore, think about the last quarter in the journey. The picture you give of the Lady[2] makes one wish to see her more familiarly than I had an opportunity of doing, were it only to ascertain whether, as you Astronomers have in your Observatories magnifying glasses for the Stars, you do not carry about with you also, when you descend to common life, coloured glasses and Claude Loraine mirrors for throwing upon objects, that interest you enough for the purpose, such lights and hues as may be most to the taste of the Intellectual vision.—In a former letter you mention Francis Edgeworth. He is a Person not to be forgotten, if you be in communication with him pray present him my very kind respects, and say that he was not unfrequently in my thoughts during my late poetic rambles;[3] and particularly when I saw the objects which called forth a Sonnet that I shall send you. He was struck with my mention of a sound in the Eagle's notes, much and frequently resembling the yelping and barking of a Dog, and quoted a passage in Eschylus[4] where the eagle is called the flying hound of the air, and he suggested that Eschylus might not only allude by that term to his being a Bird of Chase or Prey, but also to this barking voice, which I do not recollect ever hearing noticed. The other day I was forcibly reminded of the circumstances under which the pair of Eagles were seen that I described in the letter to Mr Edgeworth, his brother.[5] It was the Promontory of Fair-head

---

[1] The Reform Bill, altered only in minor detail, was introduced by Lord John Russell for the second time on 24 June: it passed the Commons on 22 Sept., but was rejected by the Lords on 8 Oct. after a five-day debate. On 12 Dec. the Bill was introduced into the Commons for the third time. See G. M. Trevelyan, *Lord Grey of the Reform Bill*, 1920, pp. 311 ff.; and J. R. M. Butler, *The Passing of the Great Reform Bill*, 2nd edn., 1964, pp. 277 ff.

[2] Hamilton had fallen in love with Ellen, daughter of Sir Aubrey de Vere, Bart. W. W. had met her in Dublin in 1829, and was soon to form a close friendship with her brother Aubrey, the poet (see L. 739 below). She eventually married Robert, fourth son of Sir Edward O'Brien of Dromoland, in 1834 (see *Recollections of Aubrey de Vere*, 1897, pp. 76 ff.).

[3] i.e. the recent Scottish tour, commemorated in *Yarrow Revisited, and Other Poems*, published 1835.

[4] Δίος . . . πτηνὸς κύων, δαφοινὸς ἀετός, 'the winged hound of Zeus, the ravening eagle', *Prometheus Vinctus*, ll. 1021–2. Cf. *Agamemnon*, l. 136.

[5] Lovell Edgeworth (see L. 466 above), proprietor of Edgeworthstown. See also the additions to *On the Power of Sound* mentioned in L. 559 above, and the I. F. note to *Eagles* (*PW* iii. 529).

on the coast of Antrim, and no Spectacle could be grander. At
Dunally Castle, a ruin seated at the tip of one of the horns of the
bay of Oban, I saw the other day one of these noble creatures
cooped up among the ruins, and was incited to give vent to my
feelings as you shall now see—

[*There follows Eagles as in PW iii. 268, but ll. 5–6*
  '*and struck my Soul with awe | Now wheeling low, then with a
  consort paired,*'
  l. 8 'Flying' for 'Flew high' and l. 12
'*In spirit, for a moment he resumes'.*]

You will naturally wish to hear something of Sir Walter Scott,
and particularly of his health. I found him a good deal changed
within the last three or four years, in consequence of some Shocks
of the apoplectic kind; but his friends say that he is very much
better, and the last accounts, up to the time of his going on board
were still more favourable. He himself thinks his Age much against
him, but he has only completed his 60th year. But a friend of mine
was here the other day, who has rallied, and is himself again, after
a much severer [shock, and at an age several][1] years more advanced. So that I [trust the] world and his friends may be hopeful,
with good reason, that the life and faculties of this man, who has
during the last six and twenty years diffused more innocent pleasure
than ever fell to the lot of any human being to do in his own life-
time, may be spared. Voltaire no doubt was full as extensively
known, and filled a larger space, probably, in the eye of Europe—
for he was a great theatrical writer, which Scott has not proved
himself to be, and miscellaneous to that degree, that there was
something for all classes of Readers—but the pleasure afforded by
his writings, with the exception of some of his Tragedies and minor
Poems, was not pure, and in this Scott is greatly his Superior.
As Dora has told your Sister, Sir W. was our guide to Yarrow.[2]
The pleasure of that day induced me to add a third to the two
Poems upon Yarrow[3]—*Yarrow Revisited*. It is in the same measure
and as much in the same Spirit as matter of fact would allow. You
are artist enough to know, that it is next to impossible entirely to

---

[1] *MS. cut away*: words in brackets added in another hand.
[2] In her letter to Eliza Hamilton, sent under the same cover (*Hamilton*,
i. 471), Dora W. mentioned their expedition with Sir Walter Scott to Newark
Castle on the Yarrow on 20 Sept.
[3] *Yarrow Unvisited* (1803) and *Yarrow Visited* (1814): see *PW* iii. 83, 106.
See also *EY*, pp. 531, 553; *MY* ii. 166–7, 170.

harmonize things that rest upon their poetic credibility, and are idealized by distance of time and Space, with those that rest upon the evidence of the hour and have about them the thorny points [of] actual life.

I am interrupted by a Stranger and a gleam of fine weather reminds me also of taking advantage of it the moment I am at liberty, for we have had nearly a week of incessant rain.

[signature torn away]

646. D. W. to WILLIAM PEARSON

MS. untraced.
Pearson (—). *LY ii. 580* (—).

Saturday Morning [29th October, 1831][1]

My dear Sir,

We are exceedingly obliged for the potatoes and apples, and are, I assure you, much too selfish to desire to part with any of the latter, to our friends. . . . It is quite a treat to look at the apples, they are so beautiful.

This fine morning has tempted my brother on a walk to Grasmere with his friend Mr Jones,[2] otherwise, I should have had a message from him—but I know he will at any time be glad to see you, though we may have other visitors;—and I hope it will not be very long before fine weather and leisure tempt you to ride over into these parts. My Brother continues quite well, and my Niece much improved by her journey, in health and strength.

As to the poor horse, I did not name him, because not able to give a good account, though *through no fault of his.* My Brother had injudiciously put him to a journey too long and too heavy for his years; and they were obliged to leave him, in comfortable quarters, to winter at Bonawe,[3] and to hire horses for their return. The horse, however, is a very good one; and judges pronounced that no harm had been done, and that a *winter's run*, and *small labour next summer*, would make him an excellent beast.—It was a great pity that he was so soon put upon a journey—however, the human creatures' tour was a delightful one.

---

[1] Date apparently added by Pearson.
[2] Robert Jones, who arrived from Wales on 23 Oct., and according to D. W.'s MS. Journal (*WL MSS.*) stayed until 7 Nov.
[3] See L. 643 above.

We are daily expecting my eldest Nephew John.[1] William[2] is at Carlisle, and we hope very comfortable. With many thanks,

I am, dear Sir,
Yours truly,
D. Wordsworth.

647. W. W. to HENRY TAYLOR

Address: Henry Taylor Esq[e]. [*delivered by hand*]
MS. Chicago University Library. Hitherto unpublished.

Rydal Mount
nr. Kendal
Thursday
[late Oct. 1831]

My dear Sir,

The two enclosed Letters, being for persons who have sent me their Books, I have taken the liberty to forward them through your kind offices to the 2 penny Post.

My daughter and I were not able to set off for Abbotsford as we hoped. We however saw Sir Walter Sco[tt][3] and had a pleasant tour in the Highlands—pleasant because no Newspaper ever came near us—

Most sincerely your most obliged
W[m] Wordsworth

[1] John Wordsworth had been visiting his Lloyd relatives at Bingley, Birmingham, and arrived on 6 Nov. He remained at Rydal Mount over the winter, as C. W. reported to C. W. jnr. (*British Library MSS.*) on 18 Apr. 1832: 'They were very loath to part with him at Rydal for he has been of great value to all the family—more especially to your uncle—who having John to talk to in his walks, was very industrious through the whole winter at all other times of the day—and worked very hard, specially in the revising and finishing of his long autobiographic poem [*The Prelude*—see L. 658 below].'

[2] W. W. jnr.

[3] *MS. torn.*

648. W. W. to JOSEPH HUNTER[1]

Address: The Rev[d] Joseph Hunter, Belvidere, Bath.
MS. WL.
Henry Julian Hunter, Old Age in Bath . . . , 1873, p. 70 (—).

[*In M. W.'s hand*]

Rydal Mount,
October 31st, 1831.

My dear Sir,

I feel truly obliged by the pains you have taken in sending me so many notices of the apparently respectable, tho' somewhat obscure family from which I am descended. I have no doubt but that you are right in your conjecture as to the branch from which we come; I have been told that my Grandfather came into West[d] as a Law Agent of the Lowther family, probably thro' some connection with the Lowthers of Swillington. He had practised as an Attorney in London, where he married his first wife, who died without children. He purchased lands at Sockbridge West[d],[2] which now belong to my Nephew, and went first to London in consequence of his Father having been obliged to sell his family Estate thro' embarrassment arising out of Suretyships and speculation in Mines. This latter gentleman was of Normanton and was probably the Son of the Richard who sold Wraith house. My Grandfather's name was Rich[d], which is the name of the Individual who sold the lands—as mentioned in your statement. The Wordsworths of Normanton were connected with the Favells of that place or neighbourhood. My Father's elder Brother[3] married a Miss Favell, who was a first Cousin of his. In connection with the Lands sold by my great Grandfather, (whatever was their name) I may observe, that my

---

[1] The Revd. Joseph Hunter (1783–1861), antiquary and author of numerous works on genealogy, topography, and antiquities. Since 1809 he had been minister of a Presbyterian congregation at Bath: in 1833 he moved to London to take up a post in the Public Record Office. In his *South Yorkshire: The History and Topography of the Deanery of Doncaster* . . . , 2 vols., 1828–31, he discussed W. W.'s descent from the Wordsworths of Peniston and Falthwaite, Yorks., and it was presumably his genealogical interest in the family that prompted his call at Rydal Mount this summer. Subsequently, on 27 Oct., he addressed to W. W. a long letter (see *Mem.* ii. 512) amplifying certain points about his ancestry.

[2] The Sockbridge estate, which consisted of a mansion house and nearly 200 acres of farmland, had been acquired by W. W.'s grandfather (see *EY*, p. 344), and descended through R. W. to his son John, for whom it was now held in trust. On his coming of age in 1836, it was sold.

[3] Richard Wordsworth, Collector of Customs at Whitehaven (see *EY*, p. 11).

Father's elder Brother Richard, who was Collector and Comptroller
of the Port of Whitehaven, having learned that the Mansion and
some part of the lands were on Sale, employed a Person to re-
purchase them for him; but, as I have heard in the family, the
Agent thought he had made so good a bargain that he kept it for
himself. Could it be ascertained whether the Almorie[1] you mention
is still extant?—those things are interesting memorials of past
times, and as it was made at the expence of a *William Wordsworth*,
and the Inscription carries the family far back, I should be very
happy to possess it.

As you have taken so much trouble about the Wordsworths on
my account you may perhaps take some little interest in knowing
from what other Stocks I am descended. My *Grandfather* R[d] W.
married a Miss Robinson[2] of Appleby, Aunt to the famous *Jack
Robinson*,[3] who represented the County of West[d], was Col: of the
West[d] Militia, and having borne an active part in Lord North's
administration, died Surveyor of the Woods and Forests. This
family was originally called Robertson of the Robertson of Struan—
Perthshire—and if John Robinson had had a Son, he himself
would have taken the title of Lord Struan—his only daughter[4]
married the present Earl of Abergavenny, who was then a Baron,
and as I have been told, probably owed his elevation in the Peerage
(great as his family was) to his Father in law. The Robinsons came
into West[d] in the time of Henry 8th. My maternal Grandfather was
William Cookson[5]—this family were of consideration in Newcastle
upon Tyne, and in other parts of England—one of that name, in the

---

[1] This aumbry, which was described by Hunter in his *History* (ii. 334), has
on its front the inscription HOC OPUS FIEBAT AO DNI MOCCCCCOXXVO EX SUPTU
WILLMI WORDESWORTH FILII W FIL IOH FIL W FIL NICH VIRI ELIZABETH FILIE ET
HEREDS W PCTOR DE PENYSTO QORU AIABUS PPICIETUR DEUS. (This work was
made in the year of our Lord 1525 at the expense of William Wordsworth son
of William son of John son of William son of Nicholas husband of Elizabeth
daughter and heiress of William Proctor of Penyston on whose souls may God
have mercy.) It remained in the possession of the Wordsworths of Peniston,
Yorkshire, till 1780–90, when it was sold to Sir Thomas Blackett; his daughter
Diana who inherited it married Col. T. R. Beaumont (1758–1829), and their
son Thomas Wentworth Beaumont (see L. 672 below) eventually gave it to
the poet after some protracted negotiations through Mrs. Benjamin Gaskell.
See letters of 9 Jan., 25 Mar., 23 May, and 18 June 1840 (in next volume).
The aumbry, which is now in the Dove Cottage Museum, is not now thought
to be earlier than the eighteenth century in its present form.
[2] Mary Robinson (see Genealogical Table. *EY*, p. 695).
[3] See *EY*, p. 57.
[4] Mary. For her husband, the 2nd Earl of Abergavenny, see *EY*, p. 25.
It was his father, the 17th Baron, who was raised to an earldom in 1784, the
year before he died.
[5] See *EY*, p. 2.

time of my youth, was distinguished upon the Turf at Newmarket. My Grandfather Cookson was a Mercer in the Town of Penrith—at a time as you well know when that calling was very different from what it now is. He inherited a good Property, and married Miss Crackenthorpe¹—a family that have represented the borough of Appleby and County of West^d from very early times. Their principal Estate, Newbiggen Hall, is now in the possession, and is the residence of my first Cousin William Crackenthorpe.² I have written down these particulars as the only return I could make, in the genealogical way, for your attention. And have only to add that I should be much obliged by any further particulars which might happen to fall in your way respecting the descent of the Wordsworths. If [I] ever have an opportunity I shall make a point of consulting the Parish Register of Normanton. In consequence of my eyes, tho' much better, being still disordered, I am obliged to employ an Amanuensis—hence the interlineations, which you will excuse. You have settled the point as to the Xtian name of the Author³ of the Memoir of Wolsey.

Believe me my dear Sir, to be faithfully your much obliged

Wm Wordsworth

P.S. Are you aware of a notice of the name Wordsworth in the Introduction or Notes to the Ballad of the Dragon of Wantley, in Percie's Relics of Ancient Poetry? and if so of any connection of the individual there named with the others of the name.⁴

¹ Dorothy Crackanthorpe (see *EY*, p. 2).
² William Crackanthorpe, a staunch supporter of the radical cause in Westmorland elections.
³ In a tract published in 1814 (reissued 1825) entitled *Who wrote Cavendish's Life of Wolsey?*, Joseph Hunter had shown that George, elder brother of William, was the author. He was the Cardinal's gentleman usher. The *Life* was included in the first volume of C. W.'s *Ecclesiastical Biography*.
⁴ In his reply of 23 Nov. (*Mem.* ii. 509), Hunter was able to identify the person named. This P.S. is missing from the MS. (which is probably a copy of the letter actually sent), and has been restored from the published text.

649. W. W. to SAMUEL ROGERS

Address: Sam¹ Rogers Esqre, St James' Place, London.
Postmark: 10 Nov. 1831. *Stamp*: Kendal Penny Post.
Endorsed: not to be published S. R.
MS. Sharpe Collection, University College, London.
Rogers. LY ii. 583.

[*In M. W.'s hand*]

Rydal Mount Novr 7th [1831]

My dear Rogers,

Several weeks since I heard, thro' Mr Quillinan, who I believe had it from Moxon, that you were unwell, and this unpleasant communication has weighed frequently on my mind; but I did not write, trusting that either from Mr Q. or Moxon I should hear something of the particulars. These expectations have been vain, and I now venture, not without anxiety, to make enquiries of yourself. Be so good then as let me hear how you are, and as soon as you can.

If you saw Sir Walter Scott, or have met with Mr and Mrs Lockhart since their return to town, you will have learned from them that Dora and I reached Abbotsford in time to have two or three days of Sir Walter's company before he left his home. I need not dwell upon the subject of his health, as you cannot but have heard as authentic particulars as I could give you, and of more recent date.[1]

From Abbotsford we went to Roslin, Edinburgh, Sterling, Loch Kettering, Killin, Dalmally, Oban, the Isle of Mull—too late in the season for Staffa—and returned by Inverary, Loch Lomond, Glasgow, and the falls of the Clyde. The foliage was in its most beautiful state; and the weather, though we had five or six days of heavy rain, was upon the whole very favourable; for we had most beautiful appearances of floating vapours, rainbows and fragments of rainbows, weather-gales, and sunbeams innumerable, so that I never saw Scotland under a more poetic aspect. Then there was in addition the pleasure of recollection, and the novelty of showing to my Daughter places and objects which had been so long in my remembrance.

---

[1] Rogers replied on 16 Nov. that he had seen Scott in London before he boarded the *Barham* at Portsmouth on 29 Oct.: 'He is gone, poor fellow; and whether we shall live to see each other again is very doubtful.' Lord Lonsdale also wrote on 14 Nov. to say that he had seen Scott: 'He seem'd better than your account gave me Reason to expect. He was very cheerful during the short Time I was with him.' (*WL MSS.*)

About the middle of summer a hope was held out to us that we should see you in the North, which would indeed have given us great pleasure, as we often, very often, talk, and still oftener think, about you.

It is some months since I heard from Moxon. I learned in Scotland that the Bookselling Trade was in a deplorable state, and that nothing was saleable but Newspapers on the Revolutionary side. So that I fear, unless our poor Friend be turned Patriot, he cannot be prospering at present.

We, thank God, are all well, and should be very glad to hear the same of yourself, and Brother and Sister. My Son William is gone to Carlisle as my Sub-distributor, how long to remain there, Heaven knows! He is likely to come in for a broken head, as he expects to be enrolled as a Special Constable, for the protection of the Gaols and Cathedral at Carlisle, and for Rose Castle—the Bishop's country residence which has been threatened. But no more of these disagre[eables.]¹ My heart is full of kindness towards you, and I wish much to hear of you. The state of my eyes has compelled me to use Mrs W's Pen. Most affectionately yours

[*signed*] Wᵐ Wordsworth

[*W. W. adds*]

Notwithstanding the flourish above, I have written to my Son to stay at home and guard his Stamps.

650. W. W. to LADY FREDERICK BENTINCK

MS. untraced.
Mem. Grosart. K. LT ii. 584.

Rydal Mount, Nov. 9. [1831]

My dear Lady Frederick,

. . . You are quite right, dear Lady Frederick, in congratulating me on my late ramble in Scotland. I set off with a severe inflammation in one of my eyes, which was removed by being so much in the open air; and for more than a month I scarcely saw a newspaper, or heard of their contents. During this time we almost forgot, my daughter and I, the deplorable state of the country. My spirits rallied, and, with exercise—for I often walked scarcely less than twenty miles a day—and the employment of composing verses amid scenery the most beautiful, and at a season when the foliage

---

¹ *MS. torn.*

was most rich and varied, the time fled away delightfully; and when we came back into the world again, it seemed as if I had waked from a dream that was never to return. We travelled in an open carriage with one horse, driven by Dora; and while we were in the Highlands I walked most of the way by the side of the carriage, which left us leisure to observe the beautiful appearances. The rainbows and coloured mists floating about the hills were more like enchantment than anything I ever saw, even among the Alps. There was in particular, the day we made the tour of Loch Lomond in the steamboat, a fragment of a rainbow, so broad, so splendid, so glorious with its reflection in the calm water, that it astonished every one on board, a party of foreigners especially, who could not refrain from expressing their pleasure in a more lively manner than we are accustomed to do.

My object in going to Scotland so late in the season was to see Sir Walter Scott before his departure. We stayed with him three days, and he quitted Abbotsford the day after we left it. His health has undoubtedly been much shattered, by successive shocks of apoplexy, but his friends say he is so much recovered that they entertain good hopes of his life and faculties being spared. Mr Lockhart tells me that he derived benefit by a change of treatment made by his London physicians, and that he embarked in good spirits.

As to public affairs, I have no hope but in the goodness of Almighty God. The Lords have recovered much of the credit they had lost by their conduct in the Roman Catholic question.[1] As an Englishman I am deeply grateful for the stand which they have made, but I cannot help fearing that they may be seduced or intimidated. Our misfortune is, that those who disapprove of this monstrous bill give way to a belief that nothing can prevent its being passed; and therefore they submit.

As to the cholera,[2] I cannot say it appals me much; it may be in the order of Providence to employ this scourge for bringing the nation to its senses; though history tells us in the case of the plague at Athens, and other like visitations, that men are never so wicked and depraved as when afflictions of that kind are upon them. So that, after all, one must come round to our only support, submission

---

[1] See L. 645 above.
[2] There was a serious outbreak of cholera this autumn at Sunderland, which spread to Gateshead and Newcastle, and by Christmas the *Kendal Chronicle* and *Westmorland Gazette* were expressing alarm that it might spread to Cumberland and Westmorland. There were outbreaks in Workington and Kendal the following summer.

to the will of God, and faith in the ultimate goodness of His dispensations.

I am sorry you did not mention your son,[1] in whose health and welfare and progress in his studies I am always much interested. Pray remember me kindly to Lady Caroline.[2] All here join with me in presenting their kindest remembrances to yourself; and believe me, dear Lady Frederick,

Faithfully and affectionately yours,
Wm Wordsworth

651. W. W. and M. W. to EDWARD QUILLINAN

Address: Edward Quillinan Esq^e, N° 7. Rue des Bucherons, St Germain-en-Laye *Via Paris*.
Postmark: 21 Nov. 1831
Endorsed: 1831 Wordsworth Nov^br 14. The difficulty of teaching Rotha to reflect.
MS. WL. Hitherto unpublished.

[In M. W.'s hand]

[14 Nov. 1831[3] or later]

My dear Mr Quillinan,

Your letter has given us all much concern—for myself tho' thoroughly aware how difficult to be resisted are the temptations which beset needy men, I had always made an exception in favor of Col. B.[4] and even now would gladly hope that there was no act of willful deception on his part, which painful as the business is, and nearly as it concerns those most dear to you, would I am sure be felt as the worst portion of it. I have long been convinced that the Family[5] was going to utter ruin—except as far as the barriers of preexisting legal Instruments might interpose for the preservation of its inheritances. Mr Wake[6] has given you good advice when he tells you 'do not trust mortal man.' In what concerns your children, in fact, you have no right to do so. And if any Steps can be taken

---

[1] See L. 622 above.
[2] Lord Lonsdale's fourth daughter (see pt. i, L. 76).
[3] This letter is written at the end of a letter from Rotha Quillinan to E. Q. and Jemima Q. bearing this date.
[4] Col. Barrett.
[5] i.e. the Brydges family, whose finances were in a tangled and parlous state. See Ernest de Selincourt, *Wordsworthian and Other Studies*, 1947, p. 39.
[6] E. Q.'s friend Charles Wake.

to recover what they may claim as their Mother's fortune, it is your duty to proceed with strictness: Moreover the fearful times in which we live, tho' they impose upon us the necessity of making up our minds to do with very little, precisely on that account, do they make it incumbent upon Fathers to guard what belongs to their children, as far as they are able, from private waste or Spoilation. With this I dismiss the painful subject. Do not make yourself anxious about dear Rotha—She is very well and happy, growing quite fat and taller withall. She is advancing with her books, and above all with the culture of the *power of thought*, in which she was exceedingly difficient,—being *very* quick and disposed to learn by the eye without reflexion. I must own to you that I think some disadvantage attends the pains that are here taken with her, inasmuch as she must feel herself of more importance than if she was learning the same sort of things with other pupils in a School. And this I have always considered as the great objection to private education. It unavoidably makes Children of too much importance in their own eyes—and if they be quick and clever will be apt to make them vain.

We had a very pleasant ramble in Scotland, of which you shall hear the details when we meet, which we hope will be on your return to England—We passed 3 days with Sir Walter Scott at Abbotsford immediately before his departure. His friends said his health was *much* improved, therefore we may have hopes of its being reestablished. He went with us to Yarrow, which tempted me to write a third Poem *Yarrow revisited*.[1] It has I fear one fault, being longer than either of the others. Lady F. Bentinck tells me by letter the other day, that she saw Rogers looking very ill—after severe illness—I have written to himself to make enquiry.[2] Of Moxon I have heard nothing, since I refused to contribute to his Magazine.[3] Truly sorry was I that he ventured upon any such undertaking.

I will say nothing of either Cholera or public Affairs—you will be well aware that I dread the moral and Political disease infinitely more than the natural. If you are in the way of hearing any thing about the comforts or expences of living on the French Side of the Pyrenees—about Pau or elsewhere—pray attend to the Subject and let me know what you learn.

ever affectionately yours
[*signed*] W. W.

[1] See L. 645 above.   [2] See L. 649 above.
[3] *The Englishman's Magazine* (see L. 626 above).

[*M. W. writes*]

My dear Friend,

Should you be again in the neighbourhood of Bolougne, Miss W. desires me to tell you that Mrs Slade Smith's (formerly Miss Barker)[1] residence is, 'Villa de la Motte, a Hardinghen, près de Marquise,' and she wishes you would if you conveniently can, call upon her, and signify that you will convey letters or message to us—and further if you can *hear* any thing of Mr S. S. and his goings on. We thank you for your offer of services in the way of nick-nacking—but have no need to trouble you. Some trifling notes of commissions I believe would reach Bryanston St. after you had left—especially one from Willy to bring him a Coat—Now that your visit is so provokingly deferred, we have told him to be contented with his Carlisle Tailor and order it there. You will be glad to hear he is very happy in his new Situation[2]—tho' he left us in bad Spirits—feeling such an uncertainty in the continuance of his office, and of all other things in our poor Country. Dear Rotha is most happy to learn that Mimma is to return with you—She was often sad lately at the thought of their being parted long enough for a change to take place in either of them—'I would not like to see Mimma, *nor any of them* different from what they were' were her words to me the other day. She is a sweet Darling! and we shall be very sad when the time comes for us to part with her—We shall for *our own sakes* be apt to wish she had never come. But it would be cruel to wish to separate the darlings—and upon this account like Rotha I am glad you do not mean to leave Mimma in France. If you return soon after Xtmas the Season will be unfavorable, or it would be a pleasant thing if you brought Mima with you when you come. As to sending Eloiza for R. [that][3] is an absurd thought—A pretty creature like Eloiza—a nice Governess for R. in a Public Coach truly—Nay we shall keep her for a better escort I assure you. But I hope no impediment will prevent your fetching her yourself. With every good wish, for the termination of y^r perplexities believe me to be most faithfully yours

M. Wordsworth

[*There follows in M. W.'s hand Gold and Silver Fishes in a Vase, as in PW iv. 151, except in 1.37 read 'When they abate their fiery glare' and in 1.38 'Shapes' for 'forms'; and To Sir Walter Scott On his quitting Abbotsford for Naples, as in PW iii. 265, except in 1.1 read 'nor' for 'or'.*]

---

[1] Of Borrowdale. [2] As W. W.'s sub-distributor at Carlisle.
[3] *Word dropped out.*

652. W. W. to GEORGE HUNTLY GORDON

Endorsed: Visit to Scott.
MS. Cornell.
Broughton, p. 45.

[*In M. W.'s hand*]

Rydal Mount Nov 16 [1831]

My dear Sir

I am glad of the opportunity, such as you have kindly allowed, to assure you that I am still in the land of the living. The enclosed single sheet holds, is stuffed with, at least four letters to Mr. Q.[1] who is detained in France much against his will. We expected a visit from him this Autumn, but he will scarcely be here before Xtmas, if then.

My daughter and I have been touring in Scotland this Autumn. Our motive for leaving home was, to see Sir Walter Scott before his departure from home, for Naples. We were with him three days, and left Abbotsford the day before he quitted it. His friends told us that his health was much improved, so that we have good reason to hope he may do well. Our tour was confined to the line of Edinborough, the Trossachs, Killin, and the Western Highlands, as far as the Isle of Mull—returning by Loch Lomond, Glasgow and the Falls of the Clyde. The Autumn was in great beauty, and the weather upon the whole not unfavourable.

I hope you have had good health since I last saw you, and that your Father's health continues to improve.

William, to whom you were so kind is at Carlisle, acting [as my Sub-distributor.]

[*The last few lines of the letter and the signature have been cut away. The postscript continues*]

Can you procure for me at your leisure (for a friend), The Literary Gazette[2] for Sepr 25th 1830 No. 714.

---

[1] Quillinan.

[2] Edited at this time by William Jerdan (see *MY* ii. 547). The number W. W. asks for contained (among other items) reviews of Hazlitt's *Conversations of James Northcote, R.A.* and of Scott's *Letters on Demonology and Witchcraft*, and articles on America and the Slave Trade.

653. W. W. to WILLIAM ROWAN HAMILTON

Address: Professor Hamilton.
MS. Cornell.
Mem. (—). *Grosart. Hamilton. K* (—). *LY ii. 586.*

[*In M. W.'s hand*]

Novr. 22^d—[1831]

My dear Mr Hamilton,

You send me Showers of verses,[1] which I receive with much pleasure, as do we all; yet have we fears that this employment may seduce you from the path of Science which you seem destined to tread with so much honour to yourself and profit to others. Again and again I must repeat, that the composition of verse is infinitely more of an art than Men are prepared to believe, and absolute success in it depends upon innumerable minutiae, which it grieves me you should stoop to acquire a knowledge of. Milton talks of 'pouring easy his unpremeditated verse.'[2] It would be harsh, untrue and odious to say there is any thing like cant in this; but it is not *true* to the letter, and tends to mislead. I could point out to you 500 passages in Milton upon which labour has been bestowed, and twice 500 more to which additional labour would have been serviceable: not that I regret the absence of such labour, because no Poem contains more proofs of skill acquired by practice. These observations are not called out by any defects or imperfections in your last pieces especially, they are equal to the former ones in effect, have many beauties, and are not inferior in execution—but again I do venture to submit to your consideration, whether the poetical parts of your nature would not find a field more favourable to their exercise in the regions of prose: not because those regions are humbler, but because they may be gracefully and profitably trod with footsteps less careful and in measures less elaborate. And now I have done with the Subject, and have only to add, that when you write verses you would not fail, from time to time, to let me have a sight of them; provided you will allow me to defer criticism on your diction and versification till we meet. My eyes are so often useless both for reading and writing that I cannot tax the eyes and pens of others with writing down observations which to indifferent persons must be so tedious.

[1] Hamilton had written on 29 Oct. and again on 11 and 17 Nov. enclosing some translations from the German and several sonnets of his own (see *Hamilton*, i. 478–81, 486–91).

[2] See *Paradise Lost*, ix. 23–4.

Upon the whole, I am not sorry that your project of going to London[1] at present is dropped. It would have grieved me had you been unfurnished with an introduction from me to Mr Coleridge, yet I know not how I could have given you one—he is often so very unwell—A few weeks ago he had had two attacks of cholera,[2] and appears to be so much broken down, that unless I were assured he was something in his better way, I could not disturb him by the introduction of any one. His most intimate friend is Mr Green,[3] a man of Science and a distinguished Surgeon. If to him you could procure an introduction, he would let you know the state of Coleridge's health, and to Mr Green whom I once saw, you might use my name, with a view to further your wish, if it were at all needful.

Shakespeare's Sonnets (excuse this leap) are not upon the Italian model, which Milton's are; they are merely quatrains with a couplet tacked to the end; and if they depended much upon the versification they would unavoidably be heavy.

One word upon Reform in Parliament—a Subject to which somewhat reluctantly you allude. You are a Reformer! Are you an approver of the bill as rejected by the Lords?[4] or, to use Lord Grey's words, any thing 'as efficient'? he means, if he means any thing, for producing change. Then I earnestly exhort you to devote hours and hours to the study of human nature, in books, in life, and in [your][5] own mind; and beg and pray that you would mix with Society, not in Ireland and Scotland only, but in England; a Fount of Destiny, which if once poisoned, away goes all hope of quiet progress in well doing. The Constitution of England which seems about to be destroyed, offers to my mind the sublimest contemplation which the History of Society and Govern[t] have ever presented to it; and for this cause especially, that its principles have the character of preconceived ideas, archetypes of the pure intellect, while they are in fact the results of a humble-minded experience. Think about this, apply it to what we are threatened with, and farewell.

[*signed*] W[m] Wordsworth

---

[1] To attend the opening by the Duke of Wellington of an equatorial telescope in the observatory of Sir James South at Kensington. Owing to technical difficulties the ceremony was postponed until the following spring.
[2] See Griggs, vi. 874.
[3] Joseph Henry Green (1791–1863), surgeon: Coleridge's literary executor, and author of *Spiritual Philosophy: founded on the teaching of the late S. T. Coleridge*, 2 vols., 1865.
[4] See L. 645 above.
[5] *MS. torn.*

654. W. W. to FELICIA DOROTHEA HEMANS

Address: Mrs Hemans, Dublin. [*In M. W.'s hand*]
Endorsed: From Mr Wordsworth. Novr 22/31 or 32.
MS. Harvard University Library.
Mem. Grosart. K. LY ii. 588.

Rydal Mount, Novr 22^d, [1831]

Dear Mrs Hemans,

I will not render this sheet more valueless than at best it will prove, by tedious apologies for not answering your very kind and welcome letter long and long ago. I received it in London when my mind was in a most uneasy state, and when my eyes were useless both for writing and reading, so that an immediate reply was out of my power; and since, I have been doubtful where to address you. Accept this and something better as my excuse, that I have very often thought of you, with hundreds of good wishes for your welfare and that of your fine Boys, who must recommend themselves to all that come in their way.—Let me thank you in Dora's name for your present of the Remains of Lucretia Davidson[1]—a very extraordinary young Creature of whom I had before read some Account in Mr Southey's Review of this Volume. Surely many things not often bestowed must concur to make genius an enviable gift. This truth is painfully forced upon one's attention in reading the effusions and story of this Enthusiast hurried to her grave so early. You have I understand been a good deal in Dublin. The Place, I hope, has less of the fever of intellectual or rather literary ambition than Edinburgh, and is less disquieted by factions and cabals of *persons*—as to those of parties, they must be odious and dreadful enough—but since they have more to do with religion, the adherents of the different creeds perhaps mingle little together, and so the mischief to social intercourse, though great, will be somewhat less.

I am not sure but that Miss Jewsbury has judged well in her determination of going to India.[2] Europe is at present a melancholy Spectacle, and these two Islands are likely to reap the fruit of their own folly and madness in becoming for the present generation the two most unquiet and miserable spots upon the Earth. May you,

---

[1] *Amir Khan and other poems: the remains of Lucretia Maria Davidson* ..., *with a biographical sketch by Samuel F. B. Morse*, New York, 1829. The book was reviewed by Southey in the *Quarterly Review*, xli (Nov. 1829), 289–301. The early death of Lucretia Davidson (1808–25), child poet, who died of tuberculosis just before her seventeenth birthday, caught the imagination of her generation in America, and much was written about her.

[2] Maria Jewsbury, now Mrs. Fletcher (she was married on 1 Aug.), was preparing to go to India with her husband, who had been appointed chaplain of the East India Company. They finally sailed from England on 19 Sept. 1832. See Gillett, pp. lv ff.

456

my dear Friend, find the advantage of the poetic Spirit in raising you, in thought at least, above the contentious clouds! Never before did I feel such reason to be grateful for what little inspiration Heaven has graciously bestowed upon my humble Intellect. What you kindly wrote upon the interest you took during your travels in my verses could not but be grateful to me because your own show that in a rare degree you understand and sympathise with me. We are all well, God be thanked. I am a wretched Correspondent as this Scrawl abundantly shews. I know also that you have far too much both of receiving and writing Letters, but I cannot conclude without expressing a wish that from time to time you would let us hear from you and yours, and how you prosper. All join with me in kindest remembrance to yourself and your Boys, especially to Charles, of whom we know most. Believe me, dear Mrs Hemans, not the less for my long silence,

faithfully and affectionately yours,
Wm Wordsworth

655. W. W. to LORD LONSDALE

MS. Lonsdale MSS.
K (—). *LY ii. 589* (—).

My Lord, Nov. 29th [1831]

A few days ago I had a note from Mr Southey, which led me to expect another upon the same subject, but as he does not appear to have gained the information he wished I will transcribe from the Note before me. 'Baily[1] is not the guilty person about the Black List.[2] It was brought to his House here, to be printed in his absence;

[1] Thomas Bailey, printer and bookseller, of Keswick.

[2] The Black List was a handbill edged with black and circulating widely that purported to give the names of the majority in the House of Lords opposed to the Reform Bill with 'the annual amount of their pickings' from the public purse. John Wilson Croker, who had retired from the Admiralty to concentrate on opposition to the Bill, discussed the Black List in 'State of the Government', *Quarterly Review*, xlvi (Nov. 1831), 274–312. Among many other allegations, it was suggested that the Earl of Lonsdale received £14,000 as Colonel of the Cumberland Militia. But this was specifically denied in the *Cumberland Pacquet* for 1 Nov.: Lord Lonsdale was *not* the Colonel, and in any case the position carried no emoluments apart from allowances for training exercises. Lord Lonsdale expressed his misgivings about the List in his letter to W. W. on 14 Nov.: 'It might not be amiss to give a Hint to the Keswick Printer as to [the] use to which his Press is applied. He must know, as far as regards me, in particular, that He is giving currency to a falsehood. These Statements have been contradicted in many of the Country Papers—but the Keswick Printer is a most impudent Varlet, to put forth such a Scandal. I am much obliged to Mr Southey for the notice he has taken of this Handbill.' (*WL MSS.*) See also Warter, iv. 249.

and I hear that he is displeased with his young man for having executed such an order. The Bellman was no doubt employed by the Fellow who ordered the printing, and I shall endeavour to find him out, having indeed a strong suspicion already.'

At the suit of two or three labourers in this neighbourhood I have written the Enclosed to Mr Benn;[1] as one of my Sons has some little interest in the application, I did not like to forward the Letter without begging your Lordship would be so kind as to cast your eyes over it.

The nation will soon know what Lord Grey meant by his expression 'A measure equally efficient'. If he means efficient for a change as great, as sudden, and upon the same principles of Spoliation and disfranchisement in the outset as the former Bill, and the new constituency to be supplied by its coarse and clumsy contrivances, not to speak of the party injustice of their application, then it must be obvious to all honest men of sound judgment that nothing can prevent a subversion of the existing Government by King, Lords and Commons, and the dissolution of the present order of society, in this Country. Such, at least, is the deliberate opinion of all those friends whose judgment I am accustomed to look up to. One of the ablest things I have read upon the character and tendency of the Reform Bill is in the North American Review, of four or five months Back.[2] The Author lays it down, and I think gives irrefragable reasons for his opinion, that the numerical principle adopted, and that of property also, can find no rest but in Universal Suffrage. Being a Republican and a professed Hater and Despiser of our modified feudal institutions, he rejoices over the prospect, but his views, though in some points mistaken, for want of sufficient knowledge of English Society, are entitled to universal consideration.

Excuse me my Lord for writing at such length; but I cannot conclude without thanking you, as a Member of the house of Peers, for the Vote you gave.[3]

> Believe me
> gratefully your Lordship's
> most obliged
> Wm Wordsworth

[1] Joseph Benn (1788–1860), Lord Lonsdale's principal agent at Lowther.
[2] 'The Prospect of Reform in Europe', *North American Review*, xxxiii (1831), 154–90. The author was Edward Everett (1794–1865), the American statesman, formerly editor of the Review and now Congressman for Massachusetts. W. W. was to meet him frequently later on at Henry Taylor's when he was American minister in London (1841–5).
[3] Against the second reading of the Reform Bill in the House of Lords (see L. 645 above).

656. D. W. to H. C. R.

Address: To Henry C. Robinson Esqre, Plowden's Buildings, Middle Temple Lane, London.
Postmark: 5 Dec. 1831. *Stamp*: Kendal Penny Post.
Endorsed: 1st Dec. 1831, Miss Wordsworth.
MS. Dr. Williams's Library.
K (—). *Morley, i. 224.*

Friday December 1st [1831]

My dear Friend,

Had a rumour of your arrival in England[1] reached us before your letter of yesterday's post you would ere this have received a welcoming from me in the name of each member of this family; and further, would have been reminded of your promise to come to Rydal as soon as possible after again setting foot on English ground.—When Dora heard of your return and of my intention to write, she exclaimed after a charge that I would recal to your mind your written promise, 'He must come and spend Christmas with us—I wish he would!' Thus you see; notwithstanding your petty jarrings Dora was always, and now is, a loving Friend of yours—I am sure I need not add that if you can come at the time mentioned, so much the more agreeable to us all, for it is fast approaching; but that *whenever* it suits you—(for you may have Christmas engagements with your own Family) to travel *so far* Northward we shall be rejoiced to see you; and whatever other visitors we may chance to have, we shall always be able to find a Corner for you.— At present, though our Nephew John of Cambridge is here, we have a vacant spare Room which will most likely, if you do not come to occupy it, remain so during most part of the winter.—We are thankful that you are returned with health unimpaired—I may say, indeed amended; for you were not perfectly well when you left England—You do not mention rheumatic pains so I trust they have entirely left you.—As to your being grown older—if you mean to say *feebler* in mind—my Brother says 'No such thing—your judgment has only now attained autumnal ripeness.'—Indeed my dear Friend I wonder not at your alarms or those of any good Man, whatever may have been the course of his politics from youth to middle age and onward to the decline of Life—but I will not enter on this sad and perplexing subject. I find it much more easy to look with calmness on the approach of pestilence or any affliction which it may please God to cast upon us without the intervention

---

[1] H. C. R. had been on the Continent for over two years, mainly in Italy, where he had seen much of Landor. He returned to London on 7 Oct.

of man—than on the dreadful results of sudden and rash changes—
whether arising from ambition—or ignorance—or brute force,—
but I am getting into the subject without intending it—so will
conclude with a prayer that God may enlighten the heads and hearts
of our Men of power—whether Whigs or Tories—and that the
madness of the deluded people may settle.—This last effect can
only be produced I fear, by exactly and severely executing the Law[1]
—seeking out and punishing the guilty—and letting all persons
see that we do not *willingly* oppress the Poor. One visible Blessing
seems already to be coming upon us through the alarm of the
Cholera. Every rich man is now obliged to look into the miserable
bye-lanes and corners inhabited by the Poor; and many crying
abuses are (even in our little Town of Ambleside) about to be
remedied—But to return to pleasant Rydal Mount—still cheerful
and peaceful. If it were not for the newspapers, we should know
nothing of the turbulence of our great Towns and Cities. Yet my
poor Brother is often heartsick and almost desponding—and no
wonder—for until this point at which we are arrived he has been
a true prophet as to the course of events—dating from the 'Great
Days of July'[2] and the appearance of the Reform Bill, 'the whole
Bill and nothing *but* the Bill'—It remains now for us to hope that
Parliament may meet in a different Temper from that in which they
parted[3]—and that the late dreadful events may make each man
seek only to promote the peace and prosperity of the country.—
You will say that my Brother *looks* older—He is certainly thinner—
and has lost some of his teeth; but his bodily activity is not at all
diminished; and if it were not for public affairs his spirits would be
as chearful as ever. He and Dora visited Sir Walter Scott just before
his departure, and made a little Tour in the Western Highlands
—and—such was his leaning to old pedestrian habits—he often
walked from 15 to 20 miles in a day following or by the side of the
little carriage of which his daughter was the Charioteer. They both
very much enjoyed the Tour and my Brother actually brought home
a Set of poems,[4] the product of that journey—When they left

---

[1] 'Of late the greatest criminals have gone on undiscovered—or if discovered
unpunished.' (Note by D. W. at bottom of MS.)
[2] The revolution in Paris in July 1830.
[3] Parliament was prorogued on 20 Oct., and the new session opened on 6
Dec. On 12 Dec. Lord John Russell introduced the Reform Bill in the House of
Commons for the third time.
[4] The poems that made up *Yarrow Revisited, and Other Poems.* See L. 645
above. Two sonnets in the collection were composed later (in 1833): *On the
Sight of a Manse in the South of Scotland* and *Fancy and Tradition* (*PW* iii.
266, 277).

home my Brother's eyes were much inflamed—and had been worse than useless to him for more than a fortnight; but, according to expectation change of air and the pleasant exercise of travelling soon abated the inflammation; and he has since his return suffered but little, though he is not able to read by candle-light or to use his eyes for a long time together for any purpose. My dear Sister is now perfectly well; but in the Spring she had a severe attack of Lumbago and Sciatica, and the effects hung upon her for some time; at present, however, she looks as well as she has done for many years—and is strong and active—You will be glad to hear also that my health is good; and that my Niece is grown strong and healthy.—Her Brother John is happily married, and lives at Moresby, near Whitehaven, being rector of M.—His Wife is one of the best of good creatures—William returned from Germany much improved, and with strong likings to that Country. He is now living at Carlisle very contented if our Financiers will suffer him so to remain, on an Income of 150£ per ann^m as his Father's Subdistributor. Miss Hutchinson is well and begs her kind regards to you. It reconciled me in some degree to my misdoings to hear that some of your Friends' letters had miscarried during your wanderings. The truth is that in spite of wishes and intentions, and of gratitude and pleasure for your most interesting letter from Rome I did not once write. The causes of this you may easily grasp, therefore I will not trouble you with them—You have forgiven me, though I have not quite forgiven myself. We were glad you had seen Charles and Mary Lamb[1]—and Mrs Clarkson— and thankful for as good a report of them as we had a right to expect —You do not mention *Mr* Clarkson, nor your Brother. My Brother, Dr Wordsworth, is in *much* better health than last winter— His son John was ill for some time after getting his Fellowship: but is now in tolerable health, and seems to be very happy among us—though we have each and all our share of apprehension and uneasiness.—Fires—Riots—and Burking[2]—not to speak of the Cholera—*will* haunt every Family circle.—This morning is so warm and sunny that I now sit opposite to an open window. Were you here on this day you would say our country wants not summer and leafy trees to make it beautiful.—

—We shall expect, and wish for your promised long letter if

---

[1] See *HCR* i. 392.

[2] William Burke was executed in 1829 for smothering people in order to sell their bodies for dissection. The local newspapers were full of horrific cases of alleged 'burking' at this time. The *Westmorland Gazette* for 3 Dec. protested that all missing persons were automatically thought to have been 'burked'

you do not write a short one to tell us that you are coming.—
I could fill my scraps of paper—under the Seal, etc but am called
away,—So God bless you—Ever your affec^te Friend

D Wordsworth

Chris^r Wordsworth is in Italy—Charles has pupils[1] at Oxford.
The Hardens[2] will be glad to hear of you

657. W. W. to ALARIC WATTS

MS. untraced.
Alaric Watts, ii. 189. K (—). *LT ii. 637* (—).

[early Dec. 1831]

My dear Sir,

I have to thank you, I presume, for a copy of the *Souvenir* for
1832, just received.[3] My eyes are so subject to inflammation that
I can read but little, so that I have yet only been able to cast my
eyes over this elegant volume, with the exception of three pieces,
with all of which I have been much pleased; namely; Mrs Watt's
Choice;[4] Mrs Howitt's *Infancy, Youth, and Age*; and your own
Conversazione—a great deal too clever for the subjects which you
have here and there condescended to handle. The rest of the
volume I shall hope to peruse at leisure. I fear the state of the
times must affect the annuals, as well as all other literature. I am
told, indeed, that many of the booksellers are threatened with
ruin. I enclose a sonnet[5] for your next volume, if you choose to
insert it. It would have appeared with more advantage in this
year's, but was not written in time. It is proper I should mention
that it has been sent to Sir Walter Scott and one or two of my other

[1] Some of the most distinguished men of the age were pupils of Charles
Wordsworth at Christ Church, including Gladstone and Manning in 1830 and
Charles J. Canning in 1831. See Charles Wordsworth, *Annals of My Early
Life*, pp. 80 ff.
[2] John Harden and his family, formerly of Brathay Hall.
[3] W. W. received his copy from the editor, Alaric Watts, at the beginning of
December. (see *Letters of Dora Wordsworth*, p. 94).
[4] Mrs. Priscilla Watts (d. 1873), who edited *The New Year's Gift and
Juvenile Souvenir* (1829–36), was the sister of the Quakers Jeremiah Holmes
Wiffen (1792–1836), the translator of Tasso (1824), and Benjamin Barron
Wiffen (1794–1867), writer on Spanish history. The two brothers had visited
W. W. at Rydal Mount in 1819. See S. R. Pattison, *The Brothers Wiffen:
Memoirs and Miscellanies*, 1880.
[5] *On the Departure of Sir Walter Scott from Abbotsford, for Naples.* The
sonnet was duly published on p. 1 of the *Literary Souvenir* for 1833.

friends; so that you had best not print it till towards the latter sheets of your volume, lest it should steal by chance into publication, for which I have given no permission. Should that happen I will send you some other piece.

I remain, my dear sir,
Sincerely your obliged,
Wᵐ Wordsworth

P.S.—The compliment with which you had distinguished me I had seen in several of the newspapers before the *Souvenir* reached me.[1] Allow me to express my pleasure at a notice so flattering.

658. W. W. to JOSEPH KIRKHAM MILLER[2]

MS. untraced.
Mem. Grosart. K. LY ii. 590.

Rydal Mount, Kendal, Dec. 17, 1831.

My dear Sir,

You have imputed my silence, I trust, to some cause neither disagreeable to yourself nor unworthy of me. Your letter of the 26ᵗʰ of Nov. had been misdirected to Penrith, where the post-master detained it some time, expecting probably that I would come to that place, which I have often occasion to visit. When it reached me I was engaged in assisting my wife to make out some of my mangled and almost illegible MSS,[3] which inevitably involved me in endeavours to correct and improve them. My eyes are subject to frequent inflammations, of which I had an attack (and am still

---

[1] 'Sketches of Modern Poets: 1. Wordsworth', *Literary Souvenir*, 1832, pp. 289–90.

[2] 'The Vicar of Walkeringham (in Nottingham), a much valued friend, who, together with some other correspondents, particularly the late revered and lamented Hugh James Rose, had urged Mr. W. to exercise those powers, in writing on public affairs, which he had displayed twenty years before, in his "Essay on the Convention of Cintra".' (*Mem.*) J. K. Miller (1785–1855) had been a Fellow of Trinity College, Cambridge, from 1808, and held his living in Notts. for some thirty-six years.

[3] W. W. was now preparing for the thorough revision of *The Prelude* which can be dated to early 1832. The work had started by 3 Dec. (see *Letters of Dora Wordsworth*, pp. 94–5) and was well under way by 17 Feb. 1832, as Dora W. reported to Miss Kinnaird: 'Father is particularly well and busier than *1000* bees. Mother and he work like slaves from morning to night—an arduous work—correcting a long Poem written thirty years back and which is not to be published during his life—"The Growth of his own Mind"—the "Ante-Chapel" as he calls it to the Recluse . . .' (*WL transcript*). See also *Prel.*, p. xxiii.

suffering from it) while that was going on. You would, neverthe-less, have heard from me almost as soon as I received your letter, could I have replied to it in terms in any degree accordant to my wishes. Your exhortations troubled me in a way you cannot be in the least aware of; for I have been repeatedly urged by some of my most valued friends, and at times by my own conscience, to under-take the task you have set before me. But I will deal frankly with you. A conviction of my incompetence to do justice to the momen-tous subject has kept me, and I fear will keep me, silent. My sixty-second year will soon be completed, and though I have been favoured thus far in health and strength beyond most men of my age, yet I feel its effects upon my spirits; they sink under a pressure of apprehension to which, at an earlier period of my life, they would probably have been superior. There is yet another obstacle: I am no ready master of prose writing, having been little practised in the art. This last consideration will not weigh with you; nor would it have done with myself a few years ago; but the bare mention of it will serve to show that years have deprived me of *courage,* in the sense the word bears when applied by Chaucer to the animation of birds in spring time.

What I have already said precludes the necessity of otherwise confirming your assumption that I am opposed to the spirit you so justly characterise.[1] To your opinions upon this subject my judgment (if I may borrow your own word) 'responds'. Providence is now trying this empire through her political institutions. Sound minds find their expediency in principles; unsound, their principles in expediency. On the proportion of these minds to each other the issue depends. From calculations of partial expediency in opposi-tion to general principles, whether those calculations be governed by fear or presumption, nothing but mischief is to be looked for; but, in the present stage of our affairs, the class that does the most harm consists of well-intentioned men, who, being ignorant of human nature, think that they may help the thorough-paced reformers and revolutionists to a *certain* point, then stop, and that the machine will stop with them. After all, the question is, funda-mentally, one of piety and morals; of piety, as disposing men who are anxious for social improvement to wait patiently for God's good time; and of morals, as guarding them from doing evil that good may come, or thinking that any ends *can* be so good as to justify wrong means for attaining them. In fact, means, in the concerns of this life, are infinitely more important than ends, which

---

[1] As revolutionary. (*Mem.*)

are to be valued mainly according to the qualities and virtues requisite for their attainment; and the best test of an end being good is the purity of the means, which, by the laws of God and our nature, must be employed in order to secure it. Even the interests of eternity become distorted the moment they are looked at through the medium of impure means. Scarcely had I written this, when I was told by a person in the Treasury, that it is intended to carry the Reform Bill by a new creation of peers. If this be done, the constitution of England will be destroyed, and the present Lord Chancellor,[1] after having contributed to murder it, may consistently enough pronounce, in his place, its *éloge funèbre!*

I turn with pleasure to the sonnets you have addressed to me, and if I did not read them with unqualified satisfaction, it was only from consciousness that I was unworthy of the encomiums they bestowed upon me.

Among the papers I have lately been arranging, are passages that would prove, as forcibly as anything of mine that has been published, you were not mistaken in your supposition that it is the habit of my mind inseparably to connect loftiness of imagination with that humility of mind which is best taught in Scripture.

Hoping that you will be indulgent to my silence, which has been, from various causes, protracted contrary to my wish,

Believe me to be, dear sir,
Very faithfully yours,
Wm Wordsworth

[1] Lord Brougham.

659. W. W. to JOHN FORSTER[1]

Address: John Forster Esqre, 4 Burton St., Burton Crescent, London.
Postmark: 22 Dec. 1831. *Stamp*: Keswick.
MS. Cornell.
LY ii. 592.

[*In M. W.'s hand*]

Rydal Mount Decr 19th, 1831

Sir,

I was much concerned to learn from your letter and its inclosure that Mr L. Hunt[2] was suffering from ill health and embarrassed circumstances; to the relief of which I should be happy to contribute as far as my Subscription goes, and regret that from my sequestered situation here, I can do little more. The consideration of Mr Hunt being a Man of Genius and Talents, and in distress, will, I trust, prevent your proposal being taken as a test of opinion, and that the benevolent purpose will be promoted by men of all parties.

I am Sir, sincerely yours
[*signed*] Wm Wordsworth

660. W. W. to ROBERT SOUTHEY

Address: Robt Southey Esqre.
MS. Cornell. Hitherto unpublished.

[*In M. W.'s hand*]

[19 Dec. 1831]

My dear S.

Probably you have received a Copy of the enclosed[3]—if you have not, pray look them over, and also my Answer—and if you approve

---

[1] John Forster (1812–76), the biographer and essayist, was editor of *The Examiner* (1847–55), secretary to the lunacy commission (1855–61), and a lunacy commissioner (1861–72), and published lives of his friends Landor (2 vols., 1869) and Dickens (3 vols., 1872–4). He became friendly with Leigh Hunt in 1829.

[2] Leigh Hunt was over-taxing himself with his daily sheet *The Tatler*, which ran from 4 Oct. 1830 till 13 Feb. 1832 (see also L. 620 above). Forster's 'proposal' was that Hunt's financial difficulties should be relieved by the publication, by subscription, of an expensive edition of his *Poetical Works*. This appeared in the following year from Moxon.

[3] John Forster's appeal on behalf of Leigh Hunt. See previous letter. W. W. shared Southey's anxiety (see Warter, iv. 253–4) that support of the subscription should not be taken as implying approval of the radical causes which Hunt had espoused.

of the latter, seal and send it to the Post off: otherwise tell me what you think I ought to do—Strongly desirous as I am to relieve a distressed Man, I should deny myself that pleasure, if thereby I seem to be committed to an approval of the use which Mr H. may have made of his talents.

Ever faithfully yours
[*signed*] Wm Wordsworth

661. W. W. to JOHN GIBSON LOCKHART

Address: J. G. Lockhart Esq, Sussex Place, Regents Park, London.
Postmark: 24 Dec. 1831. *Stamp*: Kendal Penny Post.
MS. National Library of Scotland.
LY ii. 593.

Storrs near Bowness, 21 Dec^{br} [1831]

My dear Sir,

The Newspapers report that your Son, who has languished under so long an illness, is no more.[1] Pray excuse my breaking in upon you and Mrs Lockhart with my condolences and those of Mrs W. and my family, upon this occasion. Of the measure of your parental grief, or of the degree to which you may have cause for being thankful to the Almighty for this removal, it is impossible that I or anyone can judge; but I know that it is some comfort under such trials to be assured of the sympathy of friends; and I trust that mine will not be unacceptable.

How will this event affect Sir Walter? is a question many will put to themselves, as I have often done.

We should be glad to hear at your leisure and entire convenience how Mrs Lockhart supports herself under this loss, and also if you have heard of Sir Walter.[2]

Believe me my dear Sir
very faithfully yours
Wm Wordsworth

[1] John Hugh Lockhart (the Hugh Littlejohn of Scott's *Tales of a Grandfather*) had died on 15 Dec.

[2] In his reply of 27 Dec. (*WL MSS.*), Lockhart described Scott's arrival at Malta on 22 Nov., and the pleasure which W. W.'s sonnet (see L. 642 above) had given him. By 13 Dec. Scott had moved on to Naples for the winter.

662. W. W. to LORD LONSDALE

MS. Lonsdale MSS.
K (—). *LY ii. 596* (—).

[*c.* 23 Dec. 1831][1]

My Lord,

The accompanying Paper is the one I mentioned to you some time ago. As the Person[2] who, no doubt, is the Author of it still resides at Bowness, and may be prepared to act in the spirit of it, it cannot be considered as altogether without interest even now: I had it from Mr Bolton whom with a part of my family I have just been visiting for a few days. He and Mrs Bolton are both in pretty good health.—

The altered Bill does little or nothing to prevent the dangers of the former. The principle of disfranchisement without proof or charge of wrong acquisition or corrupt use of the franchise is retained, and though the violation of the right is not now to be extended to Freemen, what follows from that but a still more democratic Representation.

The mischief already done can never be repaired. The scheme of regulating representation by arbitrary lines of property or numbers is impracticable; such distinctions will melt away before the inflamed passions of the People. No Government will prove sufficiently strong to maintain them till the novelty which excites a thirst for further change shall be worn off and the new constituency have a choice of acquiring by experience the habits of a temperate use of their power. A preponderance so large being given to ten pound Renters, the interest and property of the large towns where they are to vote will not be represented, much less those of the community at large, for these ten pound Renters are mainly men without substance who live, as has been said, from hand to mouth. Then will follow frequent parliaments, triennial perhaps, at first, which will convert the Representatives into mere slavish Delegates as they now are in America, under the dictation of ignorant and selfish numbers, misled by unprincipled journalists who as in France, will, no few of them, find their way into the House of Commons; and so the last traces of a deliberative assembly will vanish.—

But enough my Lord of this melancholy topic.—

---

[1] Probably written from Storrs Hall, where W. W. was staying just before Christmas. The 'altered Bill' is almost certainly the third Reform Bill introduced into the House of Commons on 12 Dec.

[2] Captain Beaufoy. See L. 612 above.

I resided fifteen months in France during the heats of the Revolution, and have some personal experience of the course which these movements must take if not fearlessly resisted, before the transfer of legislative power takes place.

I have not heard again from Mr Southey.

Poor Thomas Wilkinson[1] I am sorry for him.

Ever my Lord
most faithfully
your Lordship's
much obliged
Wm Wordsworth

How sorry I am that Lord Lowther is not in the House.[2]

663. W. W. to JOHN GARDNER[3]

Address: John Gardner Esqr, 16 Foley Place, Portland Place, London.
[*In M. W.'s hand*]
Postmark: 29 Dec. 1831. *Stamp*: Kendal Penny Post.
MS. Miriam Lutcher Stark Library, University of Texas.
LY ii. 593.

Rydal Mount Kendal 27th Decb—[1831]

My dear Sir,

I thanked you through Mr Boxall[4] for an obliging Letter received some months ago. I now write from a hope that you may be able to assist me in a matter which *I* am able to make little progress in; I have a Nephew[5] who must now be settled in a profession—he has chosen the medical one—Surgeon and Apothecary probably; and my wish is to place him in the House and under the care of some respectable Practitioner—in a large Town, not excluding London—if that should be thought advisable by those of my Friends who are judges in the case. Do let me know what you

---

[1] Thomas Wilkinson of Yanwath had become blind.

[2] Lord Lowther had been defeated in the Cumberland election the previous summer (see L. 610 above). He was returned for the pocket borough of Dunwich at the beginning of Feb. 1832, and was re-elected for his old seat, Westmorland, at the general election which followed the passing of the Reform Bill.

[3] The London physician. See L. 515 above.

[4] William Boxall, who had painted W. W.'s portrait the previous spring. See L. 603 above.

[5] R. W.'s son, 'Keswick John', a pupil at Hawkshead Grammar School. W. W. and C. W. were his guardians.

think best—and at what rate annually he might be placed in London. I have long had this matter upon my mind—this day I have written to a Friend in Birmingham,[1] who promised some time ago to make inquiries, and also to Dr Calvert[2] of London.—

How is Mr Boxall—and how are you yourself going on. I had a most charming Tour of 5 autumnal weeks in Scotland especially in the Highlands. My Daughter was my sole Companion, she driving a little four wheeled Phaeton, and I mainly walking by her side at the rate of 15 or 20 miles a day. The weather was a good deal broken but the appearances most exquisite of faded and fading foliage and of mists rainbows and sunbeams. We went as far as the Isle of Mull, but the Season was too far advanced for Staffa. We stopped three days with Sir Walter Scott—but now it strikes me that I told you all this through Mr Boxall.—

Lord Grey cleaves obstinately to what he calls the principle of his Bill, in other words to his presumptive rashness, which will throw the whole Country into Confusion. The preponderance in the Constitution given to the ten pound Raters or Renters, call them what you may, is irreconcileable with a representation of the property even of the several places for which they will have to [   ],[3] and if so, still more is it incompatible with a representation of the other interests of the Country. Let but short Parliaments follow, as they must, and there will be an end to all traces of a *deliberative* assembly, the nominal Representatives will become mere delegates or tools of the narrow views of the most selfish, perhaps, and ignorant class of the community—I say ignorant because half knowledge in matters of this kind is worse than no knowledge. Remember me kindly to Mr Boxall and believe me faithfully your obliged

Wm Wordsworth

I am sorry to send this Letter unfranked—but I am afraid of its being detained, on account of the Holidays, should I enclose it in an official one.

---

[1] Probably one of the Lloyds.
[2] For Dr. John Calvert, see L. 403 above.
[3] *Word missing*.

664. W. W. to JULIUS CHARLES HARE[1]

MS. untraced.
Philological Museum, i. 382 (—). K (—). LY ii. 611.

[Rydal Mount]
[late 1831 *or* early 1832]

. . . Your letter reminding me of an expectation I some time since held out to you, of allowing some specimens of my translation from the *Æneid* to be printed in the *Philological Museum*, was not very acceptable; for I had abandoned the thought of ever sending into the world any part of that experiment—it was nothing more—an experiment begun for amusement, and, I now think, a less fortunate one than when I first named it to you. Having been displeased, in modern translations, with the additions of incongruous matter, I began to translate with a resolve to keep clear of that fault, by adding nothing; but I became convinced that a spirited translation can scarcely be accomplished in the English language without admitting a principle of compensation. On this point, however, I do not wish to insist; and merely send the following passage, taken at random, from a desire to comply with your request. . . .

W. W.

665. W. W. to JOHN GARDNER

Address: John Gardner Esq. 16 Foley Place.
MS. Pierpont Morgan Library.
LY ii. 596.

[*In M. W.'s hand*]

Rydal Mount Jan^{ry} 4th [1832][2]

My dear Sir,

Having reason to expect other letters upon the same subject,[3] and especially one from a valued Friend of mine, a Physician in

---

[1] Julius Hare (see pt. i, L. 123), who had visited W. W. the previous summer (*RMVB*), was now editing the *Philological Museum*, 2 vols., 1832–3, with the aim of introducing the latest German Classical scholarship to English readers, and his first issue appeared in Nov. 1831. In Feb. 1832 he published a specimen passage from W. W.'s translation of Virgil's *Aeneid* (see *PW*, iv. 286; and pt. i, Ls. 124 and 127–8), consisting of ll. 901–1043 from Book I (*Aen.* i. 657–756). D. W.'s MS. Journal (*WL MSS.*) shows that she had been preparing a fair copy of W. W.'s translation in the autumn of 1831 (see entries for 31 Oct. and 7 Dec.). Hare also included in his first volume some of Landor's Latin poems and his dialogue *Solon and Pisistratus*.

[2] 1831 *written by mistake.*   [3] See L. 663 above.

Town[1]—who I hope will find leisure to confer with you; I delayed to answer your friendly letter as soon as it deserved. For the attention you have paid to my wishes I feel truly obliged.

Is the *premium* a compensation in the case of an apprentice for board and lodging? I suppose it is, and if so the expence is not more than would be met without difficulty. As to the question of an open Shop, I am incompetent to judge, but I agree with my Friend in thinking that *hard work* and what he calls *blind labour*, may be attended with advantages which are apt to be underrated. At the same time I should have no satisfaction in thinking my nephew should be engaged in that Profession, unless his mind were likely to be cultivated, and he were led, and taught by example, to regard the practice of medicine as an intellectual pursuit.

I should greatly prefer his being placed in the Family of a married Man for the sake of his manners, and the kindly influence of some portion of domestic female society. Nevertheless this might be waived in favour of his being placed, were that possible, with some younger unmarried Person, who as being single, might be likely to take more interest in him as a friend and companion.

My nephew[2] is 17 years of age, I think has good dispositions, fair talents and a strong desire to improve himself—and likely to take a lively interest in his profession, which is entirely his own choice—but he is shy and awkward in his manners, tho' tall and well looking. He is not a good Scholar, but I cannot think justice has been done him at School. And I trust as he is fond of miscellaneous reading, that hereafter he will do justice to *himself* by proper application.

You will let me hear from you again as soon as you have leisure, and any thing further to communicate. Give my kind regards to Mr Boxall and believe me very sincerely your much obliged

[*signed*] Wm Wordsworth

666. W. W. to LORD LONSDALE

MS. Lonsdale MSS. Hitherto unpublished.

Rydal Mount
14th Janry 1832

My Lord,
There can be no doubt that it is as you say; the Electors of Westnd must be guided not only by what they would wish to do

---

[1] Dr. John Calvert.   [2] R. W.'s son John.

but by considerations of what they are able to do. As to their wish—if one may judge from a communication made the other day by Mr Daniel Harrison[1] to Mr Partridge[2] of Ambleside the wish and *expectation* of our Friends at Kendal is, that Lord Lowther will sit for West[nd].[3] Mr D. Harrison states this and adds, that in consequence of such belief, though Mr Barham's[4] Partizans are active, the Yellows at Kendal are resting on their oars. In the event of Lord Lowther's preferring to sit for West-Cumberland, the prevalent wish of the Yellows judging from what I know, I should say would undoubtedly be for a staunch though not for a bigoted Conservative. And here is the difficulty. As you say we want *'the Material'*—the Person fit to support the Cause. Col: Howard[5] is not more liked even by his own people than you represent; if these reports are not in some degree exaggerated by persons at Kendal to whom his habits of life have prevented him paying as much attention as they may require. At all events the indisposition to take an active part in promoting his own election puts him out of the Question; for activity in that way is indispensible. Connected with your Lordship's family there are Mr Lowther,[6] late Candidate for York, and Sir John Beckett,[7] but to both these would the objection apply that now does to the two Brothers,[8] without the counterbalancing advantage which the cause derives from having two persons so nearly connected in blood with the Head of the Lowther family as one of the present members. Whom

---

[1] The Kendal wine merchant, a prominent Lowther supporter (see *MY* ii. 417).

[2] Robert Partridge, of Covey Cottage.

[3] As the Reform Bill crisis approached its climax, the Yellows were actively planning their dispositions in Westmorland and Cumberland in the event of another general election. Lord Lowther had been defeated in Cumberland the previous year (see L. 610 above), and the point at issue now was whether he should contest the new division of West Cumberland proposed in the Bill, or return to his former safe seat in Westmorland alongside his brother. See L. 675 below.

[4] John Foster Barham (d. 1838) of Trecwn, Pembrokeshire, nephew of Charles Tufton, 10th Earl of Thanet (see pt. i, L. 180), and of his brother Henry Tufton, 11th and last Earl. At present M.P. for Stockbridge, he unsuccessfully contested Westmorland against the Lowthers later this year, but won Kendal (a new division created by the Reform Bill) in 1833, on the death of James Brougham. His younger brother Charles Henry Barham was the last M.P. returned for Appleby, being elected in May 1832, on the succession of Henry Tufton to the Thanet peerage.

[5] Col. Fulke Greville Howard of Levens.

[6] John Henry Lowther (1793–1868), later Sir John Lowther, 2nd Bart., of Swillington: at present M.P. for Cockermouth, and later for Wigan and York.

[7] Lord Lonsdale's son-in-law (see *MY* ii. 515), at present M.P. for Haslemere.

[8] i.e. Lord Lowther and Col. H. C. Lowther.

can the Requisitionists turn to? Mr Wilson of *Rigmaiden's* Son,[1] though from his Father's property well qualified, is I apprehend not the Person. The two Individuals that have struck me as of most promise, are either Mr Hasell[2] of Dalemain, or Mr Braddyll[3] who has lately shown so much spirit and activity in the County of Durham; but perhaps he may consider himself pledged to his supporters there. Mr Braddyll's Father has a property in West^nd and his Residence near the County makes his name *well* known all over this side of it. With regard to Mr Hasell he is by all Parties allowed to be an intelligent and diligent Magistrate, and is personally much respected; but speaking in confidence I must say to your Lordship that the Blues in his neighbourhood talk of him as having a strong reforming bias, saying in the common phrase that he is *turned.* Indeed upon the Hustings he said more in favor of the Reform Bill than was called for, or than many liked, and also he spoke most pointedly of Col: Wilson's[4] fitness to represent the County! Now as to Col: Wilson, if he be thought of generally as he is among all educated Conservatives in this neighbourhood, he would certainly lose his election if started against Barham, unless he were supported, which is not probable, by many Blues. As I have said in other Letters, no one here has confidence in Col: Wilson—his original connections they say are Whiggish, he would be mixed up with that Party in London and the hopes of the Conservatives would be sacrificed by his return. I need not say my Lord how much I regret both on your own account and upon every other this interminable warfare. But I cannot see how we are to get out of it. Should Mr Barham succeed in obtaining *one* seat in West^nd the Party thus far supported by the Thanet interest would soon clamor for *two.* The Head of that Family, at least the present Lord,[5] might be content with dividing the County—but his

[1] For Edward Wilson of Rigmaden, banker and landowner, see *MY* ii. 493, 513.
[2] Edward W. Hasell of Dalemain (see *MY* ii. 537), Receiver General for Westmorland.
[3] Edward Stanley Richmond Gale Bradyll (d. 1874), elder son of Thomas Richmond Gale Bradyll (1776–1862) of Highhead Castle, between Carlisle and Penrith, and Conishead Priory, near Ulverston, where some years before this he had built himself an ambitious mansion in a flamboyant Gothic style.
[4] Col. George Wilson of Dallam Tower (see pt. i, L. 233), who had played a less than enthusiastic role in the Westmorland election of 1826. Lord Lonsdale, in a later letter to W. W. (6 Jan. 1833), saw Col. Wilson's candidacy as a means of destroying Broughamite influence: '. . . I think the Blues of Kendal would support Him, and by that means the Brougham Faction would be extinguish'd, which has been the cause of all the Irritation which has existed for so many years.' (*WL MSS.*)
[5] i.e. the 10th Earl of Thanet.

Kendal Friends, the Dissenters of all denominations, and the Liberals of all classes, would not. They would cry out that the County was worse enslaved than ever, as divided between two great families. There cannot be a doubt that now when the expense of elections though great, is reduced, a *third* party would either spring up or the Thanet Interest would be seduced to lend its aid for the return of two radicalized Members. My conclusion then is that the gentlemen of West^nd ought to imitate their Brethren of West C: and subscribe for the return of the best Conservative that can be found either in the County, or, by Property or family, connected with it. This plan would not want support in our neighbourhood, but I regret to say that when a few weeks ago it was proposed by my Friend Mr Harrison, to the Gentlemen of Kendal, through the means of a Letter to Mr Daniel Harrison, that Letter was, and still is, unanswered. Mr D. Harrison is to be at Ambleside in a day or two and I will see him if possible. From what I have written, the length of which demands an apology, you will infer my Lord that in my opinion a Stranger from a distance would not be successful. And as to Mr Sadler[1] in particular, I am sure that to one wealthy family his introduction into the County would be so obnoxious that they would carry their hostility to the Yellows, which is strong enough at present, to the utmost point.

As to West Cum^nd did you take the trouble of reading in the last Carlisle Patriot the Report of Mr Blamire's[2] Speech at a dinner given to Mr P. Howard?[3] It shows how much the Party are galled by their failure which they ascribe in no small degree to Mr Curwen having acted on the novel doctrine of not canvassing the electors; this may however be only a cloak for their defeat.—If I had any influence over the Editor of the Cumberland Pacquet I should strongly advise him to abstain from *personal reflections* on Mr Curwen, a Gentleman of most honorable character. His eldest Son[4] is on the point of marriage, and about to settle at Workington—both he and his brothers differ widely from their Father upon politics, *at present*; but certainly to have their father contemptibly spoken of by the public organ of the other Party

---

[1] Michael Thomas Sadler, the social reformer (see also L. 623 above), author of *Ireland: its Evils and their Remedies*, 1828, and *Law of Population*, 1830: Tory M.P. for Newark, 1829 and 1830, and for Aldborough, Yorks., 1831–2, and a leader of the movement to limit child labour in factories.

[2] William Blamire, at present M.P. for Cumberland (see L. 610 above).

[3] Philip Henry Howard, M.P. for Carlisle (see L. 610 above).

[4] Edward Stanley Curwen. See L. 574 above, and L. 748 below.

would be more likely than anything to dispose their minds for a change.

It is high time to release you—believe me ever most faithfully

Your Lordship's much obliged
Wm Wordsworth

667. W. W. to LORD LONSDALE

MS. Lonsdale MSS. Hitherto unpublished.

15th Jan^{ry} [1832]

My Lord,

Though my Letter of yesterday was so long I must trouble you again.—Supposing an eligible Candidate could be found even in the county in Lord Lowther's place, for Westnd there would be no time to make his pretensions or person known to a large body of the Electors, and the following further considerations would make his return very difficult if not impossible.

1st—The withdrawing of Lord Lowther from a County which has a prior claim upon him, and which would undoubtedly offend many of his active Supporters.

2nd Notwithstanding all that is against two Brothers for one County, the loss of the Lowthers name in one Candidate; which I cannot but think would lessen the number of Votes.

3rd The larger number of non-residents on *our* side, many of whom would scarcely come again so soon

4th The *possibility* of Col: Wilson being actively hostile; thus far, with few exceptions, the Persons over whom he has influence, have I understand been with us—

5th and lastly—The Superior zeal and activity which they always have who *are* bent upon change, and take the popular side.

Acknowledging, as every one must do, the extreme desirableness of Lord Lowther's sitting for West Cumberland, could Barham and the Brougham faction[1] be kept out of *this* county; the above considerations lead me to think it very probable that if Lord Lowther *should* determine to sit for Cumberland, the other Party would triumph, and ere long would try for two members. It is not to be concealed, that a young man who could stir himself (on this

---

[1] Now led by James Brougham, the Lord Chancellor's brother, who had made himself popular during previous contests in Westmorland, and was returned for Kendal after the passing of the Reform Bill.

side of the County especially) is wanted to support the Yellows. The others are gaining ground by their incredible activity, and it is painful to observe, what unreasonable things are expected from the Lowther family even by their Friends. Little or no allowance is made for the vast expense, already incurred, nor for the weariness and disgust which the Representatives must feel after so much trouble, and so many mortifications. Yet still, men being what they are, if the interest is to be maintained, the Electors must be seen from time to time by the Candidates, and on this account it appears most desirable that some young person connected with this side of the County should hereafter be brought forward, at present there is no time, either for Mr Braddyll,[1] or any one else. Watson of Calgarth[2] were he a few years older, might perhaps be proposed with advantage. At present the difficulty as to a fit Person seems nearly unsurmountable.—

Since the above was written this morning I have seen at Ambleside Mr Daniel Harrison.—He is decidedly against Lord L. giving up Westnd—he insists upon this county's prior claim, and has declared to Mr Benson Harrison which he did not to me, that he will stir no more if Lord Lowther leaves them; to me he said that many Friends would take offense; and the sum of his opinion was, that Barham would be returned should another Contest now take place. When I asked him his reasons he named first, the offense that would be taken, then the want of a person fit to be proposed, and next the want of time. To my question whether he thought Col. Wilson would be openly hostile, he replied, no one could know. And when I spoke of the non-resident voters, he said that not many had been brought from a distance, but that undoubtedly there would be considerable falling off in that portion of the Electors, especially if the weather should prove severe with snow. Nothing could be more decided than his opinion. I was glad to find from him however, that he did not think that there was foundation for the report of Col. Howard's unpopularity; the objection was, his not being known in the County, and his unwillingness to exert himself.— The people of W. Cumberland, said he in conclusion, must take Mr Irton[3] and we keep Lord Lowther at least *for the present.*—

[1] i.e. the younger Mr. Bradyll (see previous letter).

[2] Richard Luther Watson (b. 1811), eldest son of Col. Charles Luther Watson (1774–1814), and grandson of the late Bishop of Llandaff. He was at this time an officer in the Rifle Brigade: on attaining his majority in 1832, he became the owner of Calgarth. He was a frequent visitor at Rydal Mount in the later years (*RMVB*).

[3] Samuel Irton (1796–1866), of Irton Hall, near Ravenglass, the present representative of an ancient Cumberland family. In the election that followed

After leaving Mr Daniel Harrison I called upon Mr Benson Harrison; from whom I learned that Mr D. H. had not replied to Mr B. H's letter proposing a subscription for a new Conservative West^nd Candidate, because he did not know what to say. The people of Kendal like most Tradesmen are loth to part with their money. Mr Benson Harrison says, (what a pity the opinion is not general!) that the Yellows should take up their cause with a spirited subscription, which would do more to discourage their opponents than any thing else.

Thus my Lord at the risk of being very tiresome, I have written all that strikes me as bearing upon the subject locally considered. When I extend my views, the general aspect of affairs quite appals me. Clear it is, that never was it so incumbent upon the Landed Aristocracy to exert themselves as now. After Lord Grey has trampled upon the House of Lords,[1] as he has done, where are they to exert themselves for the maintenance of their property and rights but through their influence whatever it may be in stemming the revolutionary torrent in the House of Commons. All may be unavailing, but they will have the consolation of having done their duty.

ever faithfully your Lordship's much obliged
W Wordsworth

P.S. I have just reperused your Lordship's last Letter. What I have written rather serves to shew that Lord Lowther, if possible, should not decline West^nd, than how Mr Barham is to be met, should he present himself again, as he certainly would. *Hereafter* Mr B. might be opposed with greater advantage. Besides, as the Blues of Cumberland appear persuaded that Lord L: *will* prefer that County, they are perhaps not so well prepared, and Mr Irton might take them by surprize; in the meanwhile the Conservative cause is suffering in West^nd from no canvassing going forward, while the Blues are very active.

the passing of the Reform Bill, Lord Lowther was returned for both West Cumberland and Westmorland, and on his choosing to sit for the latter, Irton was returned for West Cumberland at a by-election in 1833, and represented the division until 1847, and again from 1852 to 1857.

[1] Lord Grey had already made it known that should the Reform Bill be thrown out for a third time, he would recommend the King to make a sufficient number of peers to carry it through the Lords.

668. W. W. to LORD LONSDALE

MS. Lonsdale MSS. Hitherto unpublished.

Friday morning
18th [Jan. 1832][1]

My Lord,

Apprehending that in my last letter I might have overrated the probable Reduction of the majority in favor of a second Conservative Candidate for West[nd] in case of Lord Lowther making his Election for Cumberland, I was glad yesterday of an opportunity of talking upon this subject with Mr Tatham[2] of Kendal.—

I found him as afraid as Mr Daniel Harrison of another Election; but he said that perhaps neither he nor any Inhabitant of Kendal could be an impartial judge, because they had perpetually before their eyes the bitterness and activity of the Quakers and other Dissenters of the opposite Party, and because the Riot at the Election had alarmed so many. But after all he dwelt most on the difficulty of finding at present a proper person; and he thought that offense would be taken if Lord Lowther should desert them after being elected under circumstances which took away from all rational Men the plea of objection to two Brothers.

Though I wrote in a desponding tone as to the probable reduction of Votes, should an election take place immediately, I think that with due firmness, on this side of the County, the interest might *hereafter* be much strengthened, on the supposition that the Reformed Parliament does not alter the Constituency and even without that step a Clause requiring the attendance of non-residents at the Registration of the Votes would be to us very injurious. But what we chiefly want is a young active member who by his personal qualities would recommend himself to the Electors in the Wards on this side of Shap-fell, and would move about among them.

Mr Tatham said Col. Wilson[3] would undoubtedly vote regularly with Ministers.

Ever faithfully your Lordships   W Wordsworth

[1] But Friday was the 20th.
[2] Edward Tatham the Kendal attorney (see *MY* ii. 419), now Deputy Recorder of Kendal.
[3] Col. George Wilson of Dallam Tower. See L. 666 above.

669. W. W. to JOHN GARDNER

MS. *Harvard University Library.*
LY ii. 598.

Rydal Mount,
Friday Jany 19th [1832]

My dear Sir,
Having the opportunity of a Frank, I merely write a line, to say, that having taken my Nephew from School I am anxious to learn whether you are likely to procure a situation for him. I have said nothing about taking him yourself, because this was placing you in a delicate situation; this business is mainly for Dr Calvert who I am very sorry, is not likely to see you. On this point I will only state my firm belief, that you would not take him yourself if you thought he could do better elsewhere—Being therefore easy as to that consideration, I will say nothing upon the subject, nor press a matter which might be inconvenient to you

farewell—

[*unsigned*]

I am going to press with another edition of poems to be sold for 24 shillings in 4 Vols—would that answer?[1]

670. W. W. to JOHN HYMERS[2]

Address: John Hymers Esqr, St. John's College, Cambridge.
Stamp: Kendal Penny Post.
MS. *St. John's College, Cambridge.*
LY ii. 598.

[*In M. W.'s hand*]

Rydal Mount, Jany 26th [1832]

My dear Sir,
The proposal to paint my Portrait was made to Mr Pickersgill thro' my friend Mr Quillinan,[3] and an answer received thro' the

---

[1] i.e. Gardner's plea for a cheap edition, referred to in L. 515 above. Writing on 16 Jan. 1832, Longman's had proposed a four-volume edition of 1,500 copies, which if sold at £1.4s., could yield a profit of about £650. See W. J. B. Owen, 'Letters of Longman and Co. to Wordsworth, 1814–36', *The Library*, 5th Series, ix (1954), 25–34.

[2] For John Hymers, see L. 562 above. This letter was first printed in *The Eagle*, the St. John's College magazine.

[3] See L. 622 above.

same channel, which led me to expect Mr P. at Rydal in October last. I had deferred answering your obliging Letter a few days in the expectation of hearing that Mr Quillinan had returned from Paris to London, and would be able to tell me why I had neither seen Mr P. nor heard from him. All that I know is that about the time he was expected here, he was at Paris painting several distinguished Persons there, La Fayette[1] and Cuvier[2] among the number—these engagements probably detained him longer than he expected, as I am this moment told that it is only about a week since he returned to London. I have no doubt but that as soon as Mr Quillinan returns he will see Mr P. and I shall be able to answer more satisfactorily the enquiries which yourself and other Fellows of yr Col: have done me the honor to make upon the subject.

Your message has been communicated to William who is well, and not discontented with his situation at Carlisle. The obliging reference in your Letter to Henry Cookson[3] was mentioned to his Mother, who is at present at Ambleside with her Daughters. We were glad to see his name so high after the fears which had been felt by his friends lest he should break down altogether. I congratulate you upon one of your Pupils being so high upon the Tripos—and notice with regret that St John's has not made so great a figure as usual.

Would you be so kind as to let me know, at your leisure, what advantages, on the score of economy, a sizar has at St John's— and whether there are any *serious* objections to a person entering and remaining in that rank? My Brother-in-Law Mr Thos Hutchinson is about to send his Son[4] to Sedbergh School with a view to his going to St John's and would be glad, as we all would be, to be able to form an estimate of the expense, and particularly as compared with that of a Pensioner.

The state of my eyes (tho' not bad) obliges me to use an amanuensis which I hope you will excuse. The Ladies beg their kind remembrances of you.

and I am my dr Sir very truly yours
[*signed*] Wm Wordsworth

[1] Marie Joseph, marquis de Lafayette (1757–1834), the French revolutionary leader. He had helped Louis Philippe to ascend the throne in 1830.
[2] Georges, Baron Cuvier (1769–1832), French zoologist and statesman.
[3] Henry, eldest son of the Cooksons of Kendal, took his B.A. at Peterhouse this year and was 7th Wrangler.
[4] Thomas Hutchinson jnr., of Brinsop, entered Sedbergh this February and went on to St. John's in 1834. He was curate of Hentland, Hereford, 1839–41, vicar of Kimbolton from 1841, and lived latterly at Grantsfield, Leominster.

671. W. W. to JOHN KENYON

Address: John Kenyon Esqre, John Curteis Esqre, 39 Devonshire Place, London.
Postmark: 30 Jan. 1832. *Stamp*: Kendal Penny Post.
MS. untraced.
Transactions of the Wordsworth Society, no. 6, p. 106. K (—). LT ii. 599.

[*In M. W.'s hand*]

Rydal Mount, 26th Jan^y, [1832]

My dear Mr Kenyon,

You have enriched my house by a very valuable present, an entire collection of all that it is desirable to possess among Hogarth's Prints—the Box also contained a quarto volume, 'Hogarth Illustrated,'[1] and 3 Vols of a French work for Mr Southey, which shall be forwarded to him. I have been thus particular as because there was no Letter within the Box perhaps it was not made up under your own eye—and I am now at a loss where to direct to you.

We are great admirers of Hogarth, and there are perhaps few houses to which such a collection would be more welcome; and living so much in the Country, as we all do, it is both gratifying and instructive to have such scenes of London life to recur to as this great master has painted.

You are probably aware that he was of Westmorland extraction,[2] his name is very common hereabouts, and it is amusing to speculate on what his genius might have produced if, instead of being born and bred in London, whither his Father went from West^d, he had been early impressed by the romantic scenery of this neighbourhood, and had watched the manners and employments of our rustics. It is remarkable that his pictures, differing in this from the Dutch and Flemish Masters, are almost exclusively confined to indoor scenes or city life. Is this to be regretted? I cannot but think it is, for he was a most admirable *painter*, as may be seen by his works in the British Gallery; and how pleasant would it have been to have had him occasionally show his knowledge of character, manners, and passion by groupes under the shade of Trees, and by the side of Waters in appropriate rural dresses. He reminds me both of Shakespeare and Chaucer; but these great Poets seem happy in softening and diversifying their views of life, as often as they

[1] Probably *The Works of William Hogarth; containing one hundred and fifty-nine engravings, by Mr. Cooke, and Mr. Davenport . . .* , London and Glasgow, 4to, 1821.
[2] Hogarth's family reputedly came from Kirkby Thore, and the artist's father from Bampton, near Lowther (see pt. i, L. 201). But see Ronald Paulson, *Hogarth: His Life, Art, and Times,* 1971, ii. 475 ff.

can, by metaphors and images from rural nature; or by shifting the scene of action into the quiet of groves or forests. What an exquisite piece of relief of this kind occurs in The Merchant of Venice—where, after the agitating trial of Antonio, we have Lorenzo and Jessica sitting in the open air on the bank on which the moonlight is sleeping—but enough.

Since I last heard from you I have received, and carefully read with great pleasure, the poems of your friend Baillie.[1] The scenes among which they were written are mainly unknown to me, for I never was farther south in France than St. Valier on the Rhone, where I turned off to the Grand Chartreuse,[2] a glorious place—were you ever there? I think you told me you were.

Mr B. has, however, interested me very much in his sketches of those countries, and strengthened the desire I have had all my life to see them, particularly the Roman Antiquities there, which H. C. Robinson tells me are greatly superior to any in Italy, a few in Rome excepted. I do not know where Mr Baillie is now to be addressed, and beg, therefore, if you be in communication with him, or with any of his friends who are, you would be so kind as to have my thanks conveyed to him, both for his little volume and the accompanying letter.

It is now time to say a word or two about ourselves. We are all well, except my Sister, who, you will be sorry to hear, has been five weeks confined to her room by a return of the inflammatory complaint which shattered her constitution three years ago. She is, God be thanked, convalescent, and will be able to take her place at our fireside in a day or two, if she goes on as well as lately.

We long to know something about yourself, Mrs Kenyon, and your Brother. Pray write to us soon.

We have had a most charming winter for weather—Hastings[3] could scarcely be warmer, and as to beauty the situation of Rydal Mount at this season is matchless. I shall direct to your Brother-in-law's House, as the best chance for my letter reaching you. Mrs Wordsworth, sister, daughter and Miss Hutchinson join me in kindest remembrances to yourself and Mrs Kenyon.

Farewell, and believe me, with every good wish,

faithfully yours,
[*signed*] Wm Wordsworth

[1] i.e. Benjamin Bailey. See L. 638 above.
[2] In Aug. 1790, during his 'pedestrian tour' to the Alps with Robert Jones (see *EY*, pp. 32–3; *Prel.*, pp. 196 ff.).
[3] Where the Kenyons were staying.

My son Wm is at Carlisle, as my Sub-Distributor, and pretty well. John quite well, and happy with his excellent and amiable wife—a better Living would not be amiss—but where is it to come from? We Conservators are out of date.

W. W.

672. W. W. to JOSEPH HUNTER

Address: The Rev. Joseph Hunter, Bath.
MS. untraced.
Hunter, Old Age in Bath, p. 73.

Rydal Mount
January 30, 1832.

My Dear Sir,

I have long wished to write to you to thank you for an unanswered letter, and I now have an additional obligation, having received another interesting one yesterday.[1] The information contained in the former induced me to apply to Mr. Beaumont,[2] he referred me to his Steward at Bretton Hall, from whom I heard that the Almory was there and in good condition, but as from the tenor of my letter to Mr. B. and his answer I had some reason to expect a second letter from him I deferred writing to you. Thus far I have been disappointed, and I have therefore this day written to the Steward to enquire if that article is to be sold, and proposed taking it at a valuation if agreeable—otherwise I must employ some one to bid for me, standing my chance at a public sale. Another reason for my not writing was that I had made application to one of my oldest relatives[3] on my father's side for particulars which I hoped she might be able to furnish, but she has been too ill to allow her mind to enter on the subject.

Pray accept my very sincere thanks for the interesting memoranda with which you have furnished me. The habits of mind seem to be changing fast that induce people to look back upon their ancestors,

---

[1] Joseph Hunter (see L. 648 above) had written on 23 Nov. and again on 27 Jan. (*Mem.* ii. 509, 516) with further elucidations of W. W.'s ancestry.

[2] Thomas Wentworth Beaumont (1792–1849), of Bretton Hall, near Wakefield, the present owner of the Wordsworth family aumbry. He was M.P. for Northumberland (1818–26), for Stafford (1826–30), again for Northumberland (1830–2), and for S. Northumberland (1833–7).

[3] Probably W. W.'s cousin Mrs. Elizabeth Barker of Rampside (see *EY*, p. 121; *MY* ii. 567), sixth child and eldest daughter of Richard Wordsworth, the Collector of Customs at Whitehaven. She survived until 1834, having been a widow for some thirty-seven years.

especially if, like mine, they have been obscure in their condition. But I am so old-fashioned as to take some little concern in such matters—therefore if you should hit upon anything in future that throws light upon this humble genealogy I should be glad of an occasion to hear from you. From a copy of Dugdale's Visitation in 1666,[1] find in the account of the Favell family that Redman Favell, of Normanton, married Ann, daughter of Richard Wordsworth, of Normanton, which marriage according to a memorandum sent me by my relative just mentioned took place about 1714. This Ann Wordsworth, I conclude, must have been sister to my grandfather, and I conceive that by consulting the Parish Register of Normanton, one might learn when the family came there and whence, so as to connect it with the other documents. If I succeed in obtaining the relic I will not fail to let you know. With many thanks believe me most sincerely yours,

William Wordsworth

673. W. W. to GEORGE HUNTLY GORDON[2]

MS. Cornell transcript.
Broughton, p. 47.

[Jan.—Feb. 1832]
... We have some pleasant strangers in this neighbourhood at this time; to which I wish you could be added—Mr. Hamilton[3]

---

[1] Part of the visitation of his northern province (1662–70) by Sir William Dugdale (1605–86) Norroy King of Arms, extracts of which were given by Hunter in his letter of 23 Nov.

[2] This fragment was sent to C. W. jnr. when he was compiling the *Memoirs* with the following note: 'The subjoined copy of part of a note from Mr W. is under a Portrait and I cannot remove it. It is written on half a sheet of paper—enclosing some letters, and the part preceding the fragment, and hidden by the print, merely states that he sends some letters to be forwarded. It is without date, but I dare say you and Mrs Wordsworth will remember not only the year but the month. G H Gordon.'

[3] Captain Thomas Hamilton (1789–1842), brother of Sir William Hamilton, the metaphysician, and a friend of Scott's, had joined the *Blackwood's* circle on his return from the Peninsula, and published a popular novel *Cyril Thornton* (1827), *Annals of the Peninsula Campaign* (1829), and *Men and Manners in America* (1833). This winter he was living in the Ivy Cottage: later he settled at Elleray, John Wilson's house on Windermere, and married (1834) as his second wife Maria (d. 1875), widow of Sir Robert Townsend Farquhar (see pt. i, L. 131).

(Cyril Thornton) and Dr Arnold of Rugby and his family,[1] also a nephew[2] of mine, an excellent scholar and amiable man.

Ever faithfully your's
W. W.

674. W. W. to JOHN GARDNER

Address: John Gardner Esqre, 16 Foley Place, Portland Place, London.
Postmark: 3 Feb. *Stamp*: Kendal Penny Post.
MS. Miriam Lutcher Stark Library, University of Texas.
LY ii. 602.

[*In M. W.'s hand*]

[*c.* 2 Feb. 1832]

Your very acceptable letter I sit down to answer, as soon as I am able—not having seen my Nephew till yesterday. I am very much gratified by the prospect of his being placed under your care being assured that he will find protection and instruction in a situation most favourable to him—and were he my own Son I should send him off to you at once. But my position in regard to him is a delicate one. His Mother is living, and married to a Person[3] with whom I have no intimacy—and she hesitates about his being sent to London, preferring his being placed for a couple of years in some country Town, naming Carlisle—to this I decidedly object, as would his other Guardian Dr Wordsworth. And as I do not find that his Mother is disposed to press the point of his not going to London—I consider *that* at present as his destiny, and am truly happy at the thought of his being placed with you, as I have said before.

Previous to this however, circumstanced as I am in respect to him—something is due to form, and I am sure that your delicacy will not be wounded when I state, that I should be obliged if you would furnish me with a reference to any Practitioner, or Person of note, who would give me such Testimony, (as might go further than my own opinion) of your merit and character, towards satisfying his Mother, and my fellow-guardian (who has not yet been consulted) that I had not taken so important a step without due precaution.

---

[1] For the visit of the Arnolds, see L. 680 below.
[2] John Wordsworth, C. W.'s son.
[3] Lightfoot, the Keswick attorney.

I have examined the youth this day in Latin. Justice cannot have been done to him at School, or he would have known more—I am afraid you will find him very backward. Hence I have great pleasure in the plan you propose in having a Teacher for him together with your own Nephew—to whom I hope he may recommend himself, as I believe him to be of an amiable disposition: and well inclined to improve himself.

I should be glad to write more but I am very much tired having had a series of hard work for the last two months. Of course no time must be lost—and he shall be prepared to go to London as soon [as]¹ this point is settled.

> With great respect I remain dᵣ Sir
> faithfully yours
> [*signed*] Wm Wordsworth

Give my kind regards to Mr Boxall.—

675. W. W. to LORD LONSDALE

MS. Lonsdale MSS. Hitherto unpublished.

> Rydal Mount
> 7ᵗʰ Febry [1832]

My Lord,

Mr Curwen² has informed me by message that he does not mean now, or at any future time to come forward as a Candidate for Cumberland. Being much interested for Mr C's personal welfare I am truly glad of this determination. The fact is communicated to me solely from the family connection, but I feel there is no breach of confidence in naming it to your Lordship; and though not improbably you may have heard it from some other quarter, and it may even have been publicly declared, yet I should not wish it to be mentioned as coming from me.

Let me congratulate your Lordship, as I do most cordially, upon your recovery from the late severe accident.

Lady Lonsdale will accept of my sincere thanks for the truly welcome Letter with which she favored me the other day.

¹ *Word dropped out.*
² Henry Curwen.

I hope that Lord Lowther is arrived, and that circumstances may allow him to decide for Westmorland.[1]

> ever most faithfully
> Your Lordship's
> much obliged
> Wm Wordsworth

676. W. W. to LORD LONSDALE

Address: The Earl of Lonsdale, Cottesmore, Greatham, Grantham.
Stamp: Kendal Penny Post.
MS. Lonsdale MSS.
Mem. (—). *Grosart* (—). *K* (—). *LY ii. 603* (—).

[*In M. W.'s hand*]

> Rydal Mount
> Feb 17th 1832

My Lord,
As you have done me the honor of asking my opinion on Lord H's[2] letter, I will give it without reserve premising only, that I have a high respect for his Lordship's judgment, and am aware how far his opportunities for forming right notions of points respecting this Question in its present state, are better than any which I can have. The facts upon which Lord H's proposal of compromise is grounded are an increased Majority in the Commons in favor of the Bill, and a belief that the Ministers have Carte Blanche for creating Peers to carry it. I am not aware of the amount of this increase, nor on what occasions the opinion of the House upon the general character of the Bill is to be collected from it—but be the fact what it may, does not its importance mainly depend upon the degree to

---

¹ See L. *666* above.
² Dudley Ryder, 1st Earl of Harrowby (1762–1847), Foreign Secretary under Pitt, 1804–5, and Lord President of the Council, 1812–27. A Canningite conservative with liberal leanings, he refused the premiership in 1827 on the death of Canning and retired from office. Believing by the autumn of 1831 that some measure of reform was inevitable, he tried to bring about a compromise between Lord Grey and the Tory peers in the winter of 1831–2, whereby a fresh creation of peers might be averted, and issued a circular letter with that aim in the December. But his efforts failed, and he and those who acted with him became known as the 'waverers'. In his later years W. W. came to know both Lord Harrowby and his brother Henry Ryder (1777–1836), Bishop of Lichfield and Coventry from 1824 (see also *MY* ii. 286). See *RMVB* for 1838 and 1840; and for 1834.

which it may be deemed an index of the People's dispositions being more favourable towards the Bill. Now I cannot think that they are so: there may not be a reaction, but there is a great slackness, and the Mass could not be made to stir as they did at the first outbreak. Nor do I believe that an excitement comparable to the former could be produced, till the legislative Power shall get fairly into the hands of the Radicals—by a Parliament reformed upon the Whig principle—then indeed the Mass of the People may be excited to anything—beginning with tithes—the funds—Public establishments—feudal rights and all the most assailable rights of private property which in course of time would be got at—either with, or without, ballot—and a constituancy ending in universal suffrage. I agree however with Lord H. that it is impossible for any Ministry to stand without Reform, which however guarded, must be carried I apprehend to an extent that must prove dangerous. But to this I will recur after considering the Carte Blanche. Lord H. does not affirm that this is *certain*; and I would ask is it not within the Power of any Councillors having access to the King, to convince him not only of the ruinous tendency of such a step—but to make him feel, as a point of duty, that whatever Power the forms of Law may give him, to create Peers for setting aside their deliberate resolve—the *spirit* of the Constitution allows him no right to do so: for the application of such Power to particular emergencies is subversive of the principle for which the Peers mainly exist. Again, the Ministers opened the Question of Reform with a most solemn declaration, that it was a measure indispensible for the preservation of the Constitution, and adopted in order to preserve it. Yet for the sake of carrying their Bill they are prepared to destroy a vital organ of that Constitution. A virtual destruction it certainly would be, for it would convert the house of Lords into a mere Slave of any succeeding Ministry; which, should it not bend to threats, would immediately create new votes, to counterbalance the Opposition. Cannot then Lord Grey and his coadjutors be brought, by a respect for reason or by a sense of shame from being involved in such a contradiction and absurdity, to desist from that course? Presuming that they can not, and that the K's mind is not to be changed, then occur the dangers foretold by Lord H. in a prophecy, which it is too probable might be fulfilled.

As to the Alternative of Compromise, I agree with Mr Southey in thinking that little is to be gained by it, but time for profitting by contingencies. Would the H. of L's be sure of making such alterations in their Committee as would render the Bill much less mischievous? Or if they should, would the lower House pass the Bill so amended? The manner in which the Committee of the Commons dealt with it is far from encouraging.[1] For my own part, I cannot see that upon the whole the present Bill is better than the former; unless it be an advantage, that the provisions respecting the most important part of it, the £10 voters cannot be carried into effect, and that therefore the Bill is self-destructive in its main principle. In litigated questions of settlement, the Law, I am told, has twice declared the criterion of actual value to be impossible. We will suppose however the Bill to be much improved in passing thro' the Committee of the Lords, and accepted by the Commons. How do we stand then? We have a House of Lords not overwhelmed indeed by new Members, but in spirit broken and brought down upon its knees. The bill is passed, and parliament, I presume, speedily dissolved; for the Agitators of the Political Unions would clamour for this, which neither the present, nor any Ministry likely to succeed them, would resist, even did they think it right to do so. Then comes a new House of Commons—to what degree radical under the best possible modification of the present Bill, one fears to think of. It proposes measures which the House of Lords would resist as Revolutionary, but dares not, for fear of being served in the way that was threatened to secure the passing of the Reform Bill—and so we hasten step by step to the destruction of that Constitution in form—the spirit of which has been destroyed before. We should perish, but somewhat more slowly than possibly or too probably we might have done if the Lords had resisted in the present stage of the Bill.

There is no part of Lord H's letter which gives me so much concern as the statement that neither the Duke of Wellington nor Sir Rt Peel would undertake the responsibility of a new Bill. This does not surprise me though I lament it exceedingly. Should contingencies of any sort—death—or alienation of mind in certain quarters—aggravated blunders on the part of Ministers, in finance and other matters—the spread of pestilential disease—or any other concurrence of causes, make an opening for the return of a Conservative Ministry—then if a new Reform Bill cannot be brought forward and carried by a strong Appeal to the sense, and not to the passions of the Country, there is no rational ground, I think, for hope. And here one is reminded of the folly and the rashness, not to touch upon the injustice, of creating such a gap in

---

[1] The Committee stage of the (third) Reform Bill had opened in the Commons on 20 Jan. and lasted till 10 Mar.

the Old Constituency, as it is scarcely possible to fill up without endangering the existence of the State. Nevertheless I cannot but think that the Country might still be preserved from Revolution— by a more sane Ministry, which would undertake the question of Reform with prudence and sincerity; combining with that measure, wiser views in Finance—for this Question is pressing into a frightful importance, which will throw that of Reform into the back ground, unless with those who regard Reform as an indispensible introduction to the right treatment of the Finances.

If after all, I should be asked how I would myself vote if it had been my fortune to have a seat in the House of Lords—I must say, that I should oppose the 2^d reading—tho' with my eyes open to the great hazard of doing so. My support however would be found in standing by a great Principle: for without being unbecomingly Personal I may state to your Lordship, that it has ever been the habit of my mind, to trust that expediency will come out of fidelity to principles, rather than to seek my principle of action, in calculations of expediency.

With this observation I conclude, trusting your Lordship will excuse my having detained you so long.

> I have the honor to be most faithfully
> Your much obliged
> [*unsigned*]

677. W. W. to SIR ROBERT INGLIS

Address: Sir R. H. Inglis, Bart., M.P., Manchester Buildings, Westminster, London.
Postmark: 20 Feb. 1832.
MS. untraced.
LY ii. 605.

Rydal Mount [*c.* 19] Feb^{ry} [1832]

My dear Sir,

I am not sure that I am doing right by troubling you with the enclosed, especially as I have the intention of following it up successively with two or three of its fellows, but I wish to spare the Com^{tee} the expense of postage, and I hope by this precaution your privilege will not be drawn too much upon—and that you will excuse me giving you the trouble of transmitting the Papers to their proper destination, when the rest shall have been received.

The Declaration[1] has had very good success among the scattered population of our extensive Parish—we have no dissenting place of Worship among us, and had it not been that the minds of some are poisoned by a Radical Whig and Dissenting Journal[2] printed at Kendal, the Papers would have been signed by almost every one.

I hope that your own health, and that of Lady Inglis,[3] are good. I have not seen Mr Southey for a long time but I understand that he is more than usually well.

Believe me d[r] Sir Rob[t]
very faithfully yours
Wm Wordsworth

678. W. W. to JOHN GARDNER

Address: J. Gardner Esq[e], 16 Foley Place. [*In M. W.'s hand*]
Postmark: 22 [   ] 183 [ ]. *Stamp*: [   ] St. West[r].
MS. Cornell.
Broughton, p. 68.

[*c*. 20 Feb. 1832]

My dear Sir,

I have seen my Nephews Mother,[4] and she is quite reconciled to my opinion and that of my Brother Dr Wordsworth that her Son will be better placed in London than in the Country. It gives me pleasure to state this at the time that I have to thank you for your Letter, and the enclosed Testimonial,[5] with which I am quite satisfied.

You may therefore expect my Nephew though I am not yet able to name the time precisely, because Mr Quillinan being here, I wish the Yo[u]th to accompany him to Town, as he has never been from home.—

I think I told you how my Nephews property is circumstanced— his Estate is respectable but there is a good deal of debt upon it; and Dr Wordsworth and I cannot raise money upon it on account of the terms of my Brothers Will, but we shall be responsible for our

---

[1] Lowther supporters in Cumberland and Westmorland had been active for nearly a month getting up petitions and circulating a Declaration against Reform (see *Westmorland Gazette* for 18 Feb.).

[2] *The Kendal Chronicle.*

[3] She was Mary, eldest daughter of Joseph Seymour Biscoe of Pendhill Court, Bletchingley, Surrey, and had married Sir Robert Inglis in 1807.

[4] Mrs. Lightfoot, mother of 'Keswick John'.

[5] The testimonial which W. W. had asked Gardner to supply. See L. 674 above.

Nephews maintenance. Under these circumstances you probably would not object to being paid by annual Installments; say 50 or 60 pounds per ann.

I have yet another proposal to make—Would it not be better before he is bound that he should stay a month with you by way of trial—of course I should not mention this to him, but I think such an arrangement would be better for both Parties.—Being at present in extreme haste—I have only to thank you again for your obliging Letter and to beg you would say to Mr Boxall[1] that I have received Mr Judkins[2] beautiful Picture, and his two interesting prints and Letter, for which I beg my sincere thanks—and say that I shall write to both in a few days

Ever faithfully yours
Wm Wordsworth

679. W. W. to SIR ROBERT KER PORTER[3]

Address: Sir R. Ker Porter, Caracas. [*In M. W.'s hand*]
MS. Berg Collection, New York Public Library. Hitherto unpublished.

Rydal Mount
Kendal
23^d Feb^{ry}, 1832.

My dear Sir,

Along with your obliging Letter of Dec^{br} 5th—31 I received a communication from Mr Mocatta[4] which decided me to leave the

---

[1] William Boxall, the artist.

[2] The Revd. Thomas James Judkin (1788–1871), perpetual curate of St. Mary's, Somers Town, 1828–68: a competent amateur painter and friend of Turner and Constable, and author of *Church and Home Psalmody*, 1831 (7th edn., 1851).

[3] Sir Robert Ker Porter (1777–1842), brother of Jane Porter the novelist, was a man of many parts—painter, traveller, writer. After some success as an artist in London, he travelled extensively in Scandinavia, Spain, Russia, and the East, publishing *A Narrative of the Campaign in Russia during 1812*, and *Travels in Georgia, Persia, Armenia, Ancient Babylonia, 1817–1820*, 2 vols., 1821–2. He was appointed British Consul in Venezuela in 1826, and thereafter lived for fifteen years at Caracas. He married a Russian princess, and died at St. Petersburg. W. W. had met him some time before this, probably when he visited the Lakes, and had sought his advice in Sept. 1831 about investment in Columbian bonds; for he was apprehensive about his European securities and, as Southey noted, 'invested all the money he could command in the American funds'. (Warter, iv. 225.) The venture was not a success; and S. H. lost even more heavily on her Columbian bonds.

[4] A banker at Caracas. He called at Rydal Mount in 1833 (*RMVB*).

bonds in his hands.—Accept my thanks for the opinion you have so kindly given respecting their probable value. The Sum is so small that I shall abide by the speculation though certainly not very promising, and one which I should never have thought of but for the unsettled State of Europe.—

It grieves me to hear that the climate where you are tells upon your constitution, and I sincerely join in the wish that some turn of official good fortune might bring you back to Europe; though England certainly does not promise to be a happy place of residence what with threatened political convulsions, and with the Cholera actually among us. But of these things the public Papers will inform you.—

If you recalled much of the neighbourhood of Keswick, being as you are a lover of the picturesque and beautiful in Nature, it may interest you perhaps to be told that the Estates[1] (formerly Lord Derwentwater's and forfeited) which lie in that neighbourhood are about to be sold. This Event will throw on the market some of the finest situations for rural Mansions in Great Britain. I often think how poor Mr Green[2] would have trembled for the issue, as the passing of this beautiful Property into many hands may exceedingly disfigure a neighbourhood, which he poor Man often busied his fancy in beautifying.

We have delightful Accounts of the benefit which Sir Walter Scott has derived in his health from change of place,[3] and the interest he takes in I hope objects, that are quite new to him.—

Our neighbourhood has through the course of this winter been very beautiful, the weather of the finest temperature, and most favorable both to the Scenery and to health for enjoying it—

Mrs Wordsworth joins me in good wishes, and believe [me] my dear Sir

Sincerely your obliged
Wm Wordsworth

[1] See L. 682 below.
[2] William Green, the Ambleside artist (see *MY* i. 195, 258).
[3] Scott was now wintering at Naples. See Sir William Gell, *Reminiscences of Sir Walter Scott's Residence in Italy, 1832* (ed. James C. Corson, 1957).

680. W. W. to HENRY TAYLOR

Address: Henry Taylor Esq^e. [*In Dora W.'s hand*]
MS. Pierpont Morgan Library.
K (—). *LY ii. 606* (—).

Rydal Mount, Kendal
Feby 23^d [1832]

My dear Sir,

When I was over at Southeys the other day he enquired about two Vols. of Tiraboschi[1] supposed to be left with us by you or your Father;[2] if we received them which no doubt you will distinctly remember pray let us know. They cannot be found in our House after the most diligent search—and I conclude if they were left with us they must have been sent to S.—but none of us recollect any thing about the matter.

Will you have the kindness to two penny Post the enclosed— I hope your Father and Mother, and Miss Fenwick[3] are well—We have had Dr Arnold[4] and his family staying his Christmas Vacation,

---

[1] Girolamo Tiraboschi (1731–94), Italian scholar and Jesuit. His *Storia della Letteratura Italiana* was published at Modena in 11 vols., 1772–81, and quickly became a standard work.   [2] For George Taylor, see pt. i, L. 120.

[3] Isabella Fenwick (1783–1856), the devoted friend of W. W.'s later years, was the daughter of Nicholas Fenwick, of Lemminton Hall, Edlingham, near Alnwick, and his wife Dorothy Forster, first cousin of Henry Taylor's stepmother. W. W. had met Miss Fenwick by 1830, if not earlier, for Henry Taylor brought her to Rydal towards the end of that year (*RMVB*), and according to D. W.'s MS. Journal she returned with Mr. and Mrs. George Taylor on 2 Aug. 1831 (*WL MSS.*), while Henry Taylor was also visiting the Lakes (see L. 635 above). For a generous tribute to her qualities of mind and character, see *Autobiography of Henry Taylor*, i. 52 ff.

[4] Thomas Arnold (1795–1842), the celebrated headmaster of Rugby (since 1828), had first met W. W. during a tour of the Lakes in Sept. 1818, two years before his marriage to Mary (1791–1873), youngest daughter of the Revd. John Penrose, rector of Fledborough, Notts., and his wife Jane Trevenen. Some six years later he paid another call at Rydal Mount with his family, as his wife recalled in a letter of 23 July 1824: 'I was agreeably surprised in Mr W. I had somehow expected to see a sentimental wild looking person, instead of which I found him mild and gentlemanly with considerable dignity in his appearance and manner.' The Arnolds had called again on 7 Aug. 1831, and arranged to rent Spring Cottage; and the success of this Christmas holiday at Rydal finally cemented W. W.'s friendship with Thomas Arnold, in spite of their political and religious differences. As Arnold wrote to his sister Susannah on 12 Jan. 1832, '. . . We have plenty of society and the Time only passes too quickly;—though in Truth the Delights of Rydal are rather too great for this workday world, and with so much Evil and Misery in the country, one seems unjust to be enjoying such perfect Peace and Delight for oneself and one's own Household.—I rejoice therefore in my sober mind that I have got more stirring Employment at Rugby,—and then as a Refreshment, such a Place as Rydal is quite delicious.' (*WL MSS.*) See also his letter to J. T. Coleridge in A. P. Stanley, *Life and Correspondence of Thomas Arnold*, 2 vols., 1844, i. 284; and Norman Wymer, *Dr Arnold of Rugby*, 1953, pp. 80, 147–8.

at the foot of our hill—they enjoyed themselves mightily—the weather having been delightful.—The Lords being threatened with destruction I say nothing of Politics

ever faithfully yours
W Wordsworth

Could you be of any use in returning for [   ]¹ or [?
printing]² these Proofs; if you can pray let [Mr] Longman know—if not dont trouble yourself about the matter.

681. W. W. to LORD LONSDALE

MS. Lonsdale MSS.
K (—). *LY ii. 606* (—).

[*In M. W.'s hand*]

Rydal Mount Feb 24th '32
My Lord,
Lord H's letter³ was returned by the same Post as my last, but unluckily under the cover for Lady Frederic: after reading it 3 times over I came to the conclusion that the hope expressed in it would prove fallacious; but, situated as I am at a distance from the Scene of Action, I did not presume to lay before your Lordship my reasons in detail. As you honor me by wishing I should do so, I now regret that Lord H's letter is not before me.

The Ministers have declared over and over that they will not abate a jot of the principle of the Bill. Thro' the whole of the debates in both Houses, but particularly in the Commons, there has been a confusion between principle, and the rules and measures of applying principle: the main or fundamental principle of this Bill, is an assumed necessity for an increase of democratic power in the Legislature; accordingly, the Ministers have resolved upon a sweeping destruction. This, which may be called a rule, or subsidiary principle, has been applied to the existing Constituency in its 3 great branches,—the Burgage Tenures, the Freemen, and the Freeholders. What havoc has been made in the first we all know—the 2ᵈ, the Freemen, were destroyed, and are restored; but upon

---

¹ *MS. torn.*
² *MS. illegible.* The new edition of the *Poetical Works* was now going through the press.
³ For Lord Harrowby's circular, see L. 676 above.

the 3ᵈ I cannot speak with the precision which I could wish, not distinctly recollecting the manner in which the votes of a portion of this Body are to be affected, by the Franchise conferred upon them as £10 Voters, in Towns; or retained as Freemen; but none of this class of Voters have been deprived of their right of voting without an equivalent. So that the change which time has effected in making, by the reduction in value of money, the Body of Freeholders so democratic, is left in its full force; and made more dangerous by new circumstances. Now, is it to be expected that the Lords in Committee could succeed in a scheme for a less sweeping and less unjust destruction in the old Constituency? Lord H. himself does not seem to expect it.

The only source then, to which we can look for any improvement must be in supplying the gap in a less objectionable way; numbers and property are the principles here. In order to foresee how the Ministry are likely to act here, we must enquire how their power is composed: they know themselves that if it were not for the Reform Bill, they must [go] out instantly. As Constitutional Whigs, then supposed to be actuated by a sincere wish to preserve the British Constitution, the Leaders of them are already as a Party annihilated—they are the tools of men bent on the destruction of Church and State. Even in their opinions, many who continue to call themselves Whigs, are scarcely by a Shade distinguishable from the Radicals. But tho' such is the character of so many of their prominent Leaders, there is diffused thro' the Country a large Body of Whig Partisans, who, could their eyes be opened, would cease to support them; especially if they had hopes of a more moderate measure from other quarters—but they are not likely to be undeceived till too late. The Ministry, I repeat, are under Radical dictation; does not the mere act of the late Appointment to the Secretaryship of War[1] shew it? Still further to propitiate the Political Unions, Hume[2] and Warburton[3] will follow him into office, who can say how soon? Whatever therefore the Ministry in conscience think prudent and Proper, they would not have the courage to act upon it: even supposing, as Lord H. suggests, that

[1] Sir John Cam Hobhouse, 2nd Bart., 1st Baron Broughton (1786–1869), the friend of Byron, was Secretary at War, 1832–3, and then briefly Chief Secretary for Ireland. He was President of the Board of Control in 1835–41 and 1846–52.

[2] Joseph Hume, the radical politician (see pt. i, L. 27) was at this time M.P. for Middlesex.

[3] Henry Warburton (? 1784–1858), the 'philosophical radical': M.P. for Bridport, 1826–41, and for Kendal, 1843–7. He specialized in medical reform. W. W.'s fears that Hume and Warburton would soon take office were unfounded.

the more moderate men in the House, and those who have the fear of a Radical Parliament hanging over their heads, should support such improvement coming from the Lords. The Ministry would act, as your Lordship anticipates, by creating new peers, by seduction and I lament to say, by intimidation, and encouraging or conniving at agitation out of doors.

But to come to particulars. Could the £10 franchise be altered, or the Delegation—for I will not call it representation—from London and its neighbourhood? As to the large Towns all over the Country, a worse source for a new Constituency than the £10 Voter, they do not—in my judgment—contain. But, take smaller places, and less populous districts. Mr Senhouse thinks £10 not a bad qualification for Cumb[nd]. Look then at Cockermouth, and read Mr Green's[1] late Advertisement—he may be a Man of poor Talents, and sorry discretion, but he is no stranger there—he was born, bred, and has long been a resident in the Place. He may therefore reasonably be supposed acquainted with the present opinions and dispositions of the £10 renters in that Town, to whom he would recommend himself, in the event of the Bill passing. He tells them 'that he has for many years been reproached for being a Jacobin, a Radical, and a Leveller'—unjustly, he insinuates,—that a reform is wanted for making *a great change* in the present state of things. 'Do not, however, suppose,' he adds, 'that I wish to see Reform run into Revolution. The conduct of the King, forming as it does a glorious contrast to that of most of the Sovereigns that for half a Century have appeared in Europe, *has justly entitled him to the preservation of his Crown*, etc. The conduct of the Ministers, too, who have aided and counselled him in his efforts for the public good, must not be forgotten; they all, or nearly all, belong to—or are connected with—the hereditary Aristocracy, and by their Services have at once entitled themselves to our gratitude,' etc, etc. Now what is all this but to say that the moment the King or the Aristocracy do not please Mr G. and his future Constituents he will turn upon them, and, if he can, will destroy the Monarchy and Peerage together. Judge, my Lord, of my indignation when I read this trash—contemptible, were it not so pernicious in this emergency—addressed to the Inhabitants of my Native Town.

Now for the Delegation of London, etc, with the vast population there and in its neighbourhood, to back the Agitators whenever

[1] Andrew Green (1774–1847), woollen manufacturer and radical candidate for Cockermouth (see *MY* ii. 590). He was at Hawkshead Grammar School just after W. W. left, and followed him to Cambridge (Trinity College) in 1793.

they shall choose to call upon it. Can Lord H. expect that the Ministry would consent to any improvement in this department? Yet nothing is more clear to a sane mind than that the Gov^t by King, Lords, and Commons, and not only *that*, but that the property, in a state of society so artificial as ours, cannot long stand up against such a pressure. When I was in London last Spring, I mixed a good deal with the Radicals,[1] and know from themselves what their aims are, and how they expect to accomplish them. One Person at least, now high in Office, is looked up to as their future Head and allowed at present to play a false part. It is not rationally to be expected that the present Ministry would allow the Delegation, as I have called it, of London and its neighbourhood, to be of a less obnoxious construction than the Bill makes it.

Let us now look at the other side—the uncompromising Resistance and its apprehended consequences in swamping the House of Lords, and passing the Bill in its present State, not perhaps without popular commotions. The risk attending such resistance with this, or any Ministry, not composed of firm-minded and truly intelligent Men is, I own so great as to alarm any one; but I should have no fear of popular commotion were the Gov^t what it might and ought to be. The overthrow of the government of Charles 10th, and the late events in Bristol,[2] prove what mischief may be done by a mere rabble, if the executive be either faithless or foolish. Seeing the perilous Crisis to which we are come, I am nevertheless persuaded that, could a conservative Ministry be established, the certain ruin that will await upon the passing of this Bill might be avoided: thousands of respectable People have supported both bills, not as approving of a measure of this character or extent, but from fear that otherwise no Reform at all would take place. Such Men would be ready to support more moderate plans if they found the Executive in hands that could be relied upon. Too true it is, no doubt, as Lord H. has observed, that opinions as to the extent and nature of advisable reform differ so widely as to throw great difficulties in the way of a new Bill. But these in my humble opinion might be got over so far, as to place us upon ground allowing hope for the future.

In looking at the Rule of applying the principle of Numbers to

---

[1] See L. 602 above.

[2] During three days of disturbances the previous autumn (29–31 Oct.), the Bristol mobs had sacked the Mansion House, and forced the Recorder, Sir Charles Wetherell (1770–1846), an anti-reformer, to escape by the roof. They also broke into the gaols, and burnt the Bishop's Palace. Order had to be restored by the cavalry.

supply a part of the New Constituency, or govern the retention of the old, I have only considered London and its neighbourhood. As far as I know, this principle is altogether an innovation, and what contradictions and anomalies does it involve? The Lords would not probably attempt an improvement here. Had such a rule come down to us from past times, had we been habituated to it, it might have been possible to improve its application. But how could any thinking Man expect that with the example of America and France before us—not deterring the People, but inciting them to imitation—this innovation can ever find rest but in universal Suffrage. Manchester is only to have two Members, with its vast population, and Cocker-mouth is to retain one with its bare 5,000! Will not Manchester and Birmingham, etc, point on the one hand to the increased representation of London and its neighbourhood, and on the other to the small places which, for their paltry Numbers, are allowed to retain one or two Votes in the House; and to towns of the size of Kendal and Whitehaven, which for the first time are to send each a Member; will Manchester and Birmingham be content? Or is it reasonable that they should be content with the principle of Numbers so unjustly and absurdly applied? This anomaly, which is ably treated in the American Review,[1] which I named to your Lordship some time ago, brings me to the character and tendency of this Reform.

As Sir J. B. Walsh observes in his Pamphlet, from which I saw an extract the [other][2] day in a Newspaper: 'Extensive, sudden, and experimental innovation is diametrically opposed to the principle of progressiveness, which in every art, science, and path of human Intellect is gradual and reposes upon the foundation of what has been already accomplished.'[3] The result of the last election has proved, that the quantum of democratic power is at present rather too great than too small; so that the only real improvement that could be made would be not by adding to the sum but by a change in the distribution of it.

Our Constitution was not preconceived and planned beforehand— it grew under the protection of Providence—as a skin grows to, with, and for the human body. Our Ministers would flay this body,

[1] i.e. Edward Everett's article in the *North American Review*, referred to in L. 655 above.
[2] *Word dropped out.*
[3] Sir John Walsh (see L. 593 above), *On the Present Balance of Parties in the State*, 1832, p. 130. In the passage quoted, Walsh was answering Macaulay's contention that political reform was part of the history of progress and civilization.

and present us, instead of its natural Skin, with a garment made to order, which, if it be not rejected, will prove such a Shirt as, in the Fable, drove Hercules to madness and self-destruction. May God forgive that part of them who, acting in this affair with their eyes open, have already gone so far towards committing a greater political crime than any recorded in History.

In the foregoing notices I have not let loose my Pen, but have written coldly and under great restrictions; being apprehensive that what I might say upon the details of Lord H's letter, not having it before me, would not answer the purpose for which you did me the honour of asking my opinion—besides, there are many minor points of detail, as to Persons, Parties or Factions, of which, living where I do, and seeing few new Publications of any account, I cannot be supposed capable of judging as well as others. But I reckon this no disadvantage upon the whole; being unincumbered and unobstructed by these subordinate parts of the Question, I can look at it in its main principles with a more distinct view of their character and tendency.

It would give me great pleasure to meet any further wishes of your Lordship upon this subject—and this I say without any reference to considerations of personal esteem. As an Englishman I am grateful for what you have already done, by opposing this measure, and whatever course you may take at this Crisis, I am confident will be chosen from the purest motives.

I have the honor to be, my Lord,
Ever faithfully yours,
[*signed*] Wm Wordsworth

[*W. W. writes*]

To save your Lordship's eyes I have taken the liberty of employing a better pen than my own, Mrs Wordsworth's.

682. W. W. to JOHN MARSHALL

MS. WL.
LY ii. 611.

[*In M. W.'s hand*]

[late Feb. 1832]

My dear Sir,

I have much pleasure in answering your letter, and will begin with the latter part first.

Were it not for the State of the Times, I should say without scruple that unless the price were very high with reference to the present rents the purchase of the Derwentwater Estate,[1] to sell out again in parcels, would be a promising speculation—provided the Purchaser did not care about disfiguring the Country when he came to divide it. If he should have any reserve of that kind, even in favourable times—there might be a doubt then of his making much of his bargain. One of my own neighbours, and a friend, has an eye to purchase with *that view*—and whether he or any one else should succeed, in such a plan, the beauty of that neighbourhood would be destroyed. Two or three Gentlemen's Houses might be erected under good taste with advantage, because it would lead to the preservation of the woods and other improvements. But if the most beautiful and commanding sites were broken up for paltry Cottages, rows of lodging houses, and inns with stables etc., which would be the most likely way to make money of the thing, the Lake and neighbourhood would be ruined for ever. Summarily I should say that if the Property could be bought, so as to pay a tolerable interest at present, it would be an advisable purchase for any one who had money to command: except for the political convulsions with which we are threatened, and especially as far as the rents are dependent upon feudal claims, which is a species of private property, that the Revolutionary spirit now at work, will not long keep its hands off. The land lying so near the town will be likely to keep up its price more than other lands that have not that advantage; the future value of the woods, which is now low, one can only guess at. The Derwentwater Estate at Keswick is as to picturesque beauty above all praise—but for a Gentleman's residence its neighbourhood to the town would be a strong objection and especially for the case you mention—viz. the people and strangers having been used to range over it in all directions. A house of moderate size would stand most charmingly, even magnificently, upon a field flanked by Friar's Crag on the right, with Cockshot hill, and Castlet, two beautifully wooded hills, behind and on the left. Upon this spot I stood a few days ago: but there may possibly, tho' I think not likely, be still better situations on the property.

[1] The Derwentwater Estate was confiscated from Sir James Radcliffe, Bart., 3rd and last Earl of Derwentwater (1689–1716), who was beheaded for his part in the first Jacobite rebellion, and transferred by Act of Parliament to Greenwich Hospital. It was bought in Apr. 1832 by John Marshall for his son John for 30,000 guineas, two-thirds of its estimated value (see Warter, iv. 314), and remained in the family for almost a century. See also L. 699 below.

Lady W. Gordon's[1] property I know very well, tho' I never went over it with a view to a choice for sites for building. But speaking from my recollection I should say that the Greenwich H. Estate has upon the whole finer views. The Lake never presents itself with that dignity from the Gordon Grounds, which lie towards the middle of it, and it being only 3 miles long there is not that stretch of view which you would have from the other Property— but the Gordon property abounds in beauty and is unannoyed by the Town. Your Son[2] would observe that the woods upon it are much inferior in character to the other, having few trees that can be called Timber.

As to my own opinion, if my fortune were equal to erect a House correspondent to the dignity of the situation, and sufficient to give me considerable influence over the Town, I should prefer the G^{ch} H^l Estate. Lyulph's Tower,[3] on account of its noble views with the adjoining Dell, I have always reckoned the first situation among the Lakes, but its timber is poor compared with the Keswick Property, and the *mere ground*, excepting the dell, is in its features, greatly inferior.

I agree with your Son John that the Gordon Estate is overplanted, and might be exceedingly improved by taste and judgment —he would observe, however, that part of it, and the part which is nearest Keswick, looks directly over to the only weak part of the Vale, that which opens to the Ambleside and Penrith roads— lying between Wallacrag and Laterigg—the site he mentions probably looks on Skiddaw.

In all that I have said, having reference to profit, I reckon my own opinion, or indeed any one else's, of little value—but one thing is clear that if the democratic spirit be organized in Legislation to the extent now wished for, and aimed at by many, the pecuniary value of every thing in the world of Taste will sink accordingly; and its intellectual estimation also will erelong be proportionably affected. Men will neither have time, tranquillity, or disposition to think about any such thing. A few years ago, tho' always apprehensive of a storm, I should have advised you or any friend of whose taste and feeling I think so highly as of yours, to purchase this Property, from a belief that it would be profitable to yourself, and a certainty that it would be a great advantage to the beauty of the neighbourhood, had you kept it in your own hands.

---

[1] Lady William Gordon owned Derwent Bay and Derwent Bank in the village of Portinscale, near the foot of Derwentwater.
[2] i.e. John Marshall jnr.
[3] On Ullswater.

At present no doubt it will be bought much lower than at that time, but who can form a conjecture of its value three years hence?

My poor Sister has been confined at least 10 weeks to her room in consequence of another, tho' slighter, attack of inflammation.[1] She has been for some time convalescent, and were it not from apprehension of relapse we should be full of hope that the warm weather would restore her strength which is all that she wants. Her friends might suppose that having been so fond of the country, its prospects, and exercise, she would have been in bad spirits under confinement, but it is not so—she finds compensation in reading, and her time never hangs heavy.

We are pleased to learn from Mrs M. that Ellen's[2] health was so good during the early part of the winter—and that all your family are pretty well; faithfully yours

[*signed*] W. Wordsworth

Mrs W. joins me in best regards—My Sister writes a few lines to Mrs M.—

683. W. W. to GEORGE HUNTLY GORDON

MS. Cornell.
Broughton, p. 46.

[Mar. 1832]

My dear Sir,

I am ashamed to trouble you so often without a word, but I know you will give me credit for thinking of you with interest and pleasure—

I have been much out of heart for a long time on account of the long and threatening illness of my dear Sister, and as you know my opinion upon the reform Bill, you will not wonder when I add that the weight of my private anxieties is not at all relieved but much the contrary by my apprehension for the Country. If this bill passes in any thing like its present shape a subversion of the Constitution and

---

[1] D. W. had been ill since Dec. 1831 (see *SH*, p. 386), when she abandoned her MS. Journal for a long period. On 17 Feb. 1832 Dora W. reported to Miss Kinnaird that 'for nine weeks past she has scarcely left her room, indeed scarcely her bed', while W. W. was busy revising *The Prelude*. 'His eyes keep quite well, in spite of us he often and often pores over his MSS by candle light, but we cannot be sufficiently thankful that his mind has been so much occupied during Aunt W.'s illness, had it not been so he w^d have been almost as ill as she.' (*WL MSS.*)

[2] The Marshalls' invalid daughter.

a correspondent shock to all institutions, (to say nothing of private fortunes,) is in my judgement inevitable.

My Son Wᵐ who acts as my Su[b-]distributor at Carlisle was here on a short visit lately—he is quite well and happy. How are your father and mother?

ever faithfully
Your much obliged
Wᵐ Wordsworth

684. W. W. to ROBERT SOUTHEY

Address: R. Southey Esqᵉ.
MS. Lilly Library, Indiana University.
Russell Noyes, 'Two Unpublished Wordsworth Letters', NQ ccix (Jan. 1964),
17–18.

[Mar. 1832]

My dear!

Though, having been very busy, I have not had time to read more than one of your Essays[1] I cannot let this parcel go without thanking you for your valuable present; which I hope will be read by many.—What is to become of this poor Country—I have no hope but in the reflections which your mind rests on as expressed in your Dedication to our worthy Friend.—[2]

My poor Sister is recovering but very slowly; because she has bilious attacks rising from confinement, Mr. Carr says, in a warm room.—

Have you heard any thing from the Friends of Dr Bell—we have had barely a Letter from his Man, written immediately after his death.[3]—

Dora is well but lean as a rake.—

God bless you
affectionately yours
W Wordsworth

[1] *Essays, Moral and Political*, 2 vols., 1832.
[2] In the course of his Dedication to Sir Robert Inglis, Southey wrote: 'We who know in W H O M we believe, and on *what* our principles are established, shall neither lose heart nor hope.'
[3] Dr. Andrew Bell had died at Cheltenham on 27 Jan. He was buried in Westminster Abbey.

685. W. W. to MRS. ROSE LAWRENCE[1]

MS. untraced.
LY ii. 614.

Rydal Mount 2nd March [1832]

My dear Mrs Lawrence,

You have gratified me much by the kind Present of your two elegant Volumes,[2] which I received the day before yesterday by Mr Bolton's Servant; and as Mr B—is only to stop a day or two, and I am going to call upon him this morning I shall request him to be the Bearer of this short note of thanks.—Why did you humble yourself to apologize for what I must deem an honor, your selecting a few of my Pieces for your Cabinet.—Almost the whole of yesterday I was engaged with Friends so that I have scarcely had time to glance an eye over the Contents of your little Volumes, but I promise myself much pleasure from perusing them at leisure, for your taste may be depended upon and the object is a judicious one. I am glad there [are many][3] pieces from your own pen.

Allow me to turn to another Subject. It is true that I had been furnished with your address when I was in Town last Spring, but I could neither profit by that nor any good thing, for they were all driven out of my Mind, by the Reform Bill, inflammations in my eyes and the stupid occupation of sitting to four several Artists.—[4] I can assure you that from these and other causes I was in anything but a comfortable state of feeling; and should have proved very sorry company, so that you had a lucky escape in not seeing me.—

Mr Bolton has been so kind as to urge me several times to visit him during this Spring at Liverpool; but I fear I shall not have courage to quit home. Surely you will be tempted to visit our Lakes erelong—the Boltons often mention you with great interest, and I should be truly happy my dear Mrs Lawrence to shew you

---

[1] Of Liverpool (see *MY* ii. 587).

[2] *Cameos from the Antique; or, The Cabinet of Mythology. Selections illustrative of the mythology of Greece and Italy, for the use of children* . . . , Liverpool, 1831 (other edns. 1833, 1834: 2nd edn. revised, 1849), and *Pictures, Scriptural and Historical, or, The Cabinet of History: with poetical selections, religious and moral* . . . , *for the use of children* . . . , Liverpool, 1831 (reissued 1834). The first included W. W.'s *Laodamia*: the second, the cottager's funeral from *The Excursion*.

[3] *Written* may.

[4] i.e. Lawrence Macdonald the sculptor (see L. 598 above), and the portrait-painters Boxall (L. 603 above) and Wilkin (L. 639 above). The fourth artist was a 'Mr Gardener', almost certainly an amateur (see *Letters of Dora Wordsworth*, p. 86), and perhaps to be identified with John Gardner the physician.

something of the beauties of our neighbourhood—But I must leave off—Mr Hamilton[1] is my Companion to Storrs, and the Carriage is getting ready

farewell most sincerely
your obliged
W. Wordsworth

686. W. W. to JOHN BOLTON

Address: John Bolton Esqre, Liverpool.
Endorsed: Mr Wordsworth.
Stamp: Kendal Penny Post.
MS. Cornell. Hitherto unpublished.

Rydal Mount March 5th [1832]

My dear Sir,

On Friday last I set off to pay you a visit at Storrs, having arranged with my neighbour Mr Hamilton that he was to follow in His Gig, and take me up. I got on foot as far as Ambleside—a Servant of Mr Hamilton's overtook me and said that a Shower of Rain had frightened his master who thought it would prove a bad day and he had gone back. I was a good deal mortified, but it could not be helped; I was so beaten with my walk to and from Ambleside in a heavy Greatcoat that I was forced to give up the plan. Next day it was so wet that we could not go as we intended; but yesterday we got as far as Bowness and learned to our great disappointment that you had returned to Liverpool on Saturday.—Mr Hamilton was a great deal vexed at being the occasion of my not seeing you at Storrs.

I had also prepared a Letter of thanks for Mrs Lawrence's little present[2] to go by you—it is not worth sending by Post—pray tell her this when you see her. I may however send it by Post.

My poor Sister amends but slowly.—You will be rather shocked to hear that our Neighbour Mr Barber[3] was found at 7 oclock this

---

[1] Capt. Thomas Hamilton (see L. 673 above).   [2] See previous letter.
[3] The follies and extravagances of Samuel Barber of Gell's Cottage had long been the subject of amused comment in the Wordsworth household. E. Q., who was a guest at Rydal Mount from 10 Feb. until 13 Mar., summed up Barber's unhappy career in his MS. Diary: 'The story of poor Barber—his origin—his London and Paris life—his foppery—his goodness to his mother and sister, yet making them miserable by his jealousy and temper—his romantic friendships violent and easily checked by the least symptoms of neglect, his first appearance at the Lakes with his Pylades, with Mr Campbell a hotel adonis—his purchase of Sir Wm Gell's cottage—his professions of flattery to

morning dead in his Bed.—I have been over to his House; where
I found our two medical men, Mr Carr and Mr Fell, and Mr B's
neighbour Mr Greenwood.[1] He had left papers of written directions
to be opened by Mr Greenwood after his Decease.—He appears to
have died without any pain. His Servant slept in an adjoining Room,
and found him dead at the usual time of entering his apartment.
He made a Will in —31, but nothing is known of the disposition
of his property. With kindest regards from every one here to
yourself and Mrs Bolton and Miss Dixon

> I remain dear Sir,
> very faithfully yours
> W Wordsworth

687. M. W. to LADY BEAUMONT

MS. Pierpont Morgan Library. Hitherto unpublished.

Rydal Mount March 5th [1832]

My dear Lady Beaumont,
  Your Kind letter was received by us all with much pleasure—
more especially as it not only conveyed good news from dear
Coleorton, but from Lambeth also—whence, in this time of excitement, we could scarcely hope for so favourable a report of the
Archbishop's health. We are very thankful it is so, and none more
earnestly wish for its continuance than this household. Mr W. bids
me say that he has long wished for some report from you of his
Godson[2] and his not having made enquiries after him must be set
down to his procrastinating habits (where letter-writing is concerned) and not to a want of interest in you and yours, and a feeling

friends—his cottages—his flowers—his taste—his fantastic dresses—caps,
boots, wigs . . . his violence in politics—Mr Canning's visits to him—his fatal
intimacy with Smith . . . the manner in which this man bewitched him—his
blind abandonment of his property to him—the man's ingratitude—the ruffian
bully Fletcher—Barber's agony—the ride on the mountain—the end.' (*WL
MSS.*) According to Dora W.'s MS. letter to Emily Trevenen of 23 Mar.
(*Victoria University Library, Toronto*), W. W. and M. W. had known Barber
for thirty years, but the exact circumstances in which they first met have not
yet been established.

  [1] James Greenwood (1788–1845) of the Wyke: buried in Grasmere church-
yard.
  [2] The Beaumonts' younger son William (see L. 623 above).

of the relation he stands in to the dear little Boy. We rejoice too once more to hear of George,[1] and congratulate you on the promise he gives of quickness at his lessons. This is such a comfort to mother and child as none can appreciate sufficiently who have not had experience of the contrary.

Mr W. and indeed all of us would much like to see the improvements at Coleorton, and the comforts he[2] is spreading among the Whitwickers. John often wished for the allotment of Gardens to some of the more industrious among his Parishioners, and he will be very glad to hear that his wish has been fulfilled.—The individual you mention was a suspected Person even when I was at Whitwick, on John's first being there. It is well for the Place that he has removed himself, and it is to be hoped no more may be heard of him. For I fear seldom any good comes of the *exposure* of such wickedness, if it can be otherwise got rid of. It makes one shudder to think of having lived next door to such a wretch.

You will be sorry to learn that Miss W. has been confined to her room, since the latter end of Dec^r—at that time she had a return, tho' a less violent one, of the attack which took such hold upon her constitution during her residence at Whitwick. She is now so far strengthened, as to come downstairs for $\frac{1}{2}$ an hour, perhaps twice in the day—but tho' we have had most delightful weather during her confinement we are afraid to trust her to drive out—and until the season is further advanced so as to allow of this, we do not look to her perfect recovery. Except for fits of toothache, Dora has been quite well, and she charges me with her love and thanks for the interest you express for her.

Mr W. has not at present the least intention of being in Town this Spring. So, dear Lady B., unless you should be tempted to visit the north I fear we have little chance of meeting this year. It would indeed be a great delight to us all to see Sir G. and you among the mountains—Nor would the two Darlings be out of place gathering primroses and following with their eyes at least, the lambs racing round the rocky knolls—This journey should be made before the bands strengthen, that will keep you at home—But one need not fear this, recollecting that during the Xtmas vacation D^r and Mrs Arnold (of Rugby) brought no less than their eight children,[3] and passed 6 happy weeks in a cottage at the foot of the

---

[1] The elder son and heir.
[2] The reference seems to be to Mr. Merewether, or his curate.
[3] Including Matthew, the eldest (b. 1822), and Thomas (b. 1823). Mary Arnold wrote to her sister-in-law from Rydal on 2 Jan.: 'All the chicks have

hill upon the side of which our house stands. All, except Mrs A. whose health and situation confined her very much within doors, became complete mountaineers, and few Summer Tourists left the Lakes better satisfied with their excursion, than these winter sojourners.—The weather of course greatly favoured them.

The Cholera *is* indeed a perplexing subject—but the thought disturbs us less than that of Reform. By the bye, may I ask if the Queen made the reply to the Archbishop's congratulatory address on her birth-day, as was reported in the newspapers. Do not reply to this if the question is an improper one.

With our joint respectful regards to the Archbishop and Mrs Howley, and affectionate remembrances to Sir Geo and yourself, believe me my dear Lady B.

to be very truly yours
M. Wordsworth.

I take the liberty to enclose a note, which do not trouble yourself to forward till it is perfectly convenient to you.

688. W. W. to JOHN GARDNER

Address: John Gardner Esqre, 16 Foley Place, Portland Place. By Favor of Mr Wordsworth.
MS. Carl H. Pforzheimer Library.
K (—). *LY ii. 615* (—).

[*In M. W.'s hand*]

Rydal Mount Mar: 12th —32.

My dear Sir,

Mr Quillinan has staid longer here than he intended, or you would have seen the Bearer of this, my Nephew,[1] earlier. I cannot let him depart without a few words, in which I may perhaps repeat something I have said before. He seems in good spirits, and I hope will

found the advantage of the Wordsworths' pleasant neighbourhood as well as ourselves—for they have two girls staying with them of ten and fourteen [Rotha Quillinan and young Mary Hutchinson], and are themselves so fond of Children and know so well how to amuse them, that I never saw the four Eldest in higher Spirits than they were a few nights ago after drinking tea and spending the Evening at the Mount.' (*WL MSS.*)

[1] R. W.'s son.

take with zeal and firmness to the course of life which he has chosen. I believe his principles and dispositions to be very good, but as to deportment, forms of manners, and Scholarship he is deficient, from want of opportunity, for the causes I mentioned to you before I have not seen as much of him as I could have wished. I trust however he will improve under your care: and am very glad that he will have the opportunity of benefitting by your nephew's example, and the advantages he will have in common with him, under the Instructor whom you spoke of. I hope he will so conduct himself, so that after a few weeks probation, there will be no difference on either side, in fixing him with you by Indenture.

I have not many Acquaintances or friends in London whom I could *at present* trouble with Introductions in his favour. To a Mr Addison[1] of Gray's Inn who was his Father's Partner in business, and the youth's Godfather, I have given him a letter, but I understand that this Gentleman has lately fallen into bad health, and I fear cannot notice him as much as he would wish. Some of his Uncle Dr Wordsworth's friends also may, at present, or hereafter, be induced to pay him attention, but his main dependance must be upon your care and superintendence.

Mr Q. will confer with you about having some Clothes made, which he will require immediately. Such Books also as he may want you will be kind enough to recommend, and they shall be paid for directly.

The Cholera does not appear to spread so much in London as was apprehended. I have always seen the disease in the same light as you do. A friend has told me this evening, that there is a report in Sydenham's miscellaneous works,[2] of a disease resembling this in *his* time, which was very fatal in London.

The intended Ed: of my Poems[3] is to be compressed into four volumes—there will be no additions, beyond what appeared in the Keepsake two or three years ago.[4] And a Sonnet or two which have already seen the light. The books cannot be afforded under 24/- to leave a tolerable profit to the Author and Publisher. It is therefore to be apprehended, that the French Ed: will still continue to injure much the English Sale.

[1] Richard Addison (see *MY* i. 366).
[2] Thomas Sydenham (1624–89), author of *Observationes Medicae*, 1676, a landmark in the history of medicine, was an early authority on epidemic diseases. His complete works were published in Latin in Amsterdam (1683) and London (1685), and in English in 1696 (11th edn., 1740).
[3] The edition of 1832, now going through the press.
[4] See pt. i, L. 327.

I say nothing of Politics—the Foolish and wicked only appear to be active, and therefore it is plain, that confusion and mischief will follow.

I remain my d^r Sir

very faithfully yours

[*signed*] Wm Wordsworth

689. W. W. to JOHN MITCHINSON CALVERT

MS. untraced.
LY ii. 617.

Rydal Mount, [March][1] 13th [1832]

My dear Sir,

The bearer is my nephew, John,[2] whom you have kindly interested yourself about—for which I heartily thank you, as no doubt he would do if his shyness did not prevent him.

I cannot presume, knowing how much you are engaged, to recommend him in any way to your notice—but I could not let him go to London without your being told that when this is delivered he will be with Mr Gardner upon trial, which I hope may end by his being regularly indentured with him.

I am not aware of any news from this quarter that will interest you. Your mother[3] will be concerned to hear that my sister, though we hope convalescent, recovers slowly. Your sister Mary[4] must have been sorry to learn from the papers that poor Mr Barber is dead.[5] His health was never good, but his end has been hastened by exasperation of mind from pecuniary dealings with a professed friend.

With the joint remembrance of all to all believe me

My dear Sir, your much obliged,

Wm Wordsworth

---

[1] Dated to April by de Selincourt, but in fact written just before 'Keswick John' left Rydal on 13 Mar.
[2] R. W.'s son.
[3] For Mrs. William Calvert, see *EY*, p. 515. She lived till 1834.
[4] Now Mrs. Joshua Stanger.
[5] See L. 686 above.

690. W. W. to JOHN WORDSWORTH[1]

Address: John Wordsworth, Esqre.
MS. British Library. Hitherto unpublished.

Tuesday Morn: [13 Mar. 1832]

My dear John,

Mr Quillinan will have to stop a couple of days perhaps more at Doncaster.—Should it be your intention to proceed immediately to Cambridge, it strikes me that it would be better that John[2] should go along with you thither, and after stopping two or three days to see his Uncle should proceed to his destination; taking a Hackney Coach instantly upon his arrival in London.—If you mean to diverge or stop on the Road let him by all means wait with Mr Quillinan at Doncaster.

Perhaps upon the whole it was better that you did not return to Rydal—especially on your poor Aunt's account.—She is not suffering much perhaps not at all at present; but I fear she has not gathered strength since you left us.

God bless you my dear Nephew—
ever affectionately yours
Wm Wordsworth

691. W. W. to LORD LONSDALE

MS. Lonsdale MSS.
K (—). *LY ii. 576* (—).

[*c.* 17 Mar. 1832]

My Lord,

Perhaps the fate of the Bill[3] is already decided or will be so before this reaches your hands. I cannot forbear however, writing once more upon a subject which is scarcely ever out of my Thoughts.

---

[1] C. W.'s son, who had spent the winter at Rydal Mount, and was now about to depart for Cambridge in the company of E. Q., Rotha Q., and R. W.'s son. 'What a contrast are his [John Wordsworth's] modesty and courtesy to the manners of that little queer will o the wisp of conceit Hartley Coleridge', E. Q. noted in his MS. Diary (*WL MSS.*).

[2] 'Keswick John', bound for Mr Gardner's in London.

[3] The third Reform Bill. De Selincourt mistakenly supposed that this letter refers to the second Bill, and dated it to Sept.–Oct. 1831.

By the John Bull of last Monday[1] I see, that a writer in the *Quarterly Review*, probably the same who has written before so ably on the Reform Question, is most decidedly against the Bill going into Committee: he appears convinced, as thousands are, that no good would arise from it, and that the destruction of the Constitution must follow; adding that if the Lords resist they will at least fall with honor. In this I perfectly concur with him. In the two Letters[2] which I had the honor of addressing to your Lordship I dwelt principally upon the utter improbability that any changes of importance, affecting the *principle* of the Bill, that is, making it less *democratic* could be effected. Mr Southey was of the same opinion as I mentioned. The other side of the question, the dangers of resistance, I did not dwell upon. Lord H.[3] seemed to take it for granted that the Place would, as he expressed it, 'be taken by Storm and immediately given up to Pillage.' Would this be worse than what *must* follow if the Bill be so far sanctioned as to pass through the Lords?—Residing at a distance from Town I can form no distinct notion of the mischief which might immediately arise with an Executive such as now afflicts this Kingdom. But I do confidently affirm (with the Editor of the Standard)[4] that there are materials for constructing a Party, which if the Bill be not passed, might save the Country. I have numerous acquaintances

[1] *John Bull* for 11 Mar. printed an extract from 'The revolutions of 1640 and 1830', *Quarterly Review*, xlvii (Mar. 1832), 261–300. This article was written by John Wilson Croker (with help from J. G. Lockhart); but W. W. may here be attributing it to another writer in the *Quarterly* on the Reform question, John Fullarton (? 1780–1849), the merchant banker, whose articles had already impressed him, as Dora W. had mentioned to C. W. jnr. on 26 Feb. 1831 (*WL MSS.*).

[2] Ls. 676 and 681 above.

[3] Lord Harrowby. Lord Lonsdale wrote at length on 18 Mar. about Lord Harrowby's behaviour over the second reading of the Reform Bill, and deploring 'the stupendous change, which, under any much more moderated Views, this measure will produce on the whole Frame of Society. It is most fearfull to see an order of things establish'd, the probable effects of which, it is impossible for any man to foresee, and this all for the Sake of what is call'd Consistency. When you see a Minister sacrificing that consistency, which had for years made Him the Stay and Hope of his Party, to effect a great national change, which He deem'd necessary to preserve the Peace and even the entirety of the Empire, and another, in order to preserve it, introducing all the visionary Schemes He had cherish'd when He saw no Prospect of enforcing them, what Hope is there of Stability in any Quarter? We are left to wander without a Guide, or at least without any rallying Point around which the scatter'd Forces can collect themselves. What you say of the pervading Sentiments of the several Classes you refer to, I believe to be perfectly just, and I believe the same Feeling begins to pervade all Classes—but it comes too late . . .' (*WL MSS.*)

[4] The evening paper edited by Stanley Lees Giffard (1788–1858) from 1827.

among men who have all their lives been more or less of Reformers, but not One, unfastened by party engagements, who does not strongly condemn this Bill. Take the Profession of the Law for instance—three Gentlemen, distinguished upon the Northern Circuit, were here the other day. They all, though Reformers, condemned it severely as tending to subvert the Government, and one of them assured me that, out of eleven Lawyers he had dined with, ten were against it. In the Universities the proportions are I am told scarcely less than five to one. People in trade are much misled by the Journals which they read—and the great majority of the journals are democratic, but trade and revenue have already suffered so much that their eyes would be opened, could the Ministry be changed; and the House of Commons would change with the People. There is one point also delicate to touch upon and hazardous to deal with, but of prime importance in this Crisis. The question, as under the conduct of the present Ministers, is closely connecting itself with Religion. Now, after all, if we are to be preserved from utter confusion it is Religion and Morals and Conscience which must do the Work. The religious part of the Community, especially those attached to the Church of England, must, and *do* feel that neither the Church as an Establishment, nor its points of Faith as a church, nor Christianity itself as governed by Scripture ought to be left long, if it could be prevented, in the hands which now manage our affairs.

But I am running on at unpardonable length. I took up the pen principally to express a hope that your Lordship may have continued to see the question in the light which affords the only chance of preserving the nation from several generations perhaps of confusion and crime and wretchedness.

Excuse the liberty I have taken
and believe me most faithfully
your Lordship's
much obliged
W Wordsworth

692. W. W. to C. W.

Address: The Rev^d. Dr Wordsworth, Joshua Watson's Esq^e, Park St, West-
minster [*In Dora W.'s hand*]
Postmark: 3 Apr. 1832. *Stamp*: Kendal Penny Post.
MS. British Library.
Mem. (—). *LY ii. 616* (—).

April 1st [1832][1] Rydal Mount.

My dear Brother,

I write on consequence of a Letter just received from your Son
John, in which he says you are going to buy into the Danish funds.
Pray inquire further about these funds, whether you have bought in
or not.—Somewhat unfortunately I think I advised Miss Hutchinson
the other day to buy Danish Stock. I mentioned this to Mr Southey
who has been here a couple of days.—Mr Jacob,[2] a well known
political writer and Government Agent, assured him that the
Danish Government is extremely poor and only pays the interest of
its debt by fresh borrowings.—Mr Warter[3] the young Man who is
engaged to Edith Southey, is now at Copenhagen, as Chaplain to
the Embassy there. Southey inquired of him as to the resources of
that Government and the standing of its funds—he confirms Mr
Jacob's account; and adds that the Danish Revenue proceeds principally from the Sound Duties, and that its credit is maintained by
the extreme frugality and economy of the King:[4] but that the
Crown Prince[5] has a taste for expense. My Letter to save the
Post might close here, as I could not be easy without naming to
you what I had just heard.

Our dear sister makes no progress towards recovery of Strength.
She is very feeble, never quits her room, and passes most of the day
in, or upon, the bed. She does not suffer pain except now and then
from wind and stitches. She is very chearful, and nothing troubles
her but public affairs and the sense of requiring so much attention.
Whatever may be the close of this illness, it will be a profound
consolation to you, my dear brother, and to us all, that it is borne
with perfect resignation; and that her thoughts are such as the
good and pious would wish. She reads much, both religious and
miscellaneous works.—

If you see Mr Watson, remember me affectionately to him.

I was so distressed with the aspect of public affairs, that were it

[1] Year added by C. W.   [2] William Jacob (see L. 416 above).
[3] For John Wood Warter, see L. 574 above.
[4] Frederick VI (1768–1839), King since 1808.
[5] Frederick's cousin, later Christian VIII (1786–1848).

not for our dear Sister's Illness, I should think of nothing else.— They are to be envied, I think, who, from age or infirmity, are likely to be removed from the afflictions which God is preparing for this sinful nation. God bless you, my brother. John says you are well; so am I, and every one here except our Sister: but I have witnessed one revolution in a foreign Country, and I have not courage to think of facing another in my own. Farewell. God bless you again.

Your affectionate B^r
W. W.

693. W. W. to EDWARD QUILLINAN[1]

Address: Edward Quillinan Esq^e, 4 Ryder Street, St James—
Postmark: 17 Apr. 1832. *Stamp*: Charing Cross.
MS. WL.
LY ii. 617.

[*In Dora W.'s hand*]

[Rydal Mount]
[14 Apr. 1832]

Of Hogg's silly story[2] I have only to say that his memory is not

---

[1] Written by Dora W. in the middle of a letter of her own to E. Q., dated 12 Apr., and introduced with the words: 'Saturday—I have got hold of Father for 5 minutes, and now he speaks.'

[2] In his *Autobiography* Hogg records 'an affront which I conceived had been put on me' at Rydal Mount. 'It chanced one night, when I was there, that there was a resplendent arch across the zenith, from the one horizon to the other, of something like the aurora borealis, but much brighter.... Well, when word came into the room of the splendid meteor, we all went out to view it; and, on the beautiful platform at Mount Ryedale, we were all walking, in twos and threes, arm-in-arm, talking of the phenomenon, and admiring it. Now, be it remembered, that Wordsworth, Professor Wilson, Lloyd, De Quincey, and myself, were present, besides several other literary gentlemen, whose names I am not certain that I remember aright. Miss Wordsworth's arm was in mine, and she was expressing some fears that the splendid stranger might prove ominous, when I, by ill luck, blundered out the following remark, thinking that I was saying a good thing:—"Hout, me'm! it is neither mair nor less than joost a treeumphal airch, raised in honour of the meeting of the poets." "That's not amiss—eh? eh?—that's very good," said the Professor, laughing. But Wordsworth, who had De Quincey's arm, gave a grunt, and turned on his heel, and leading the little opium-chewer aside, he addressed him in these disdainful and venomous words:—"Poets? poets? What does the fellow mean? Where are they?" Who could forgive this? For my part I never can, and never will! I admire Wordsworth; as who does not, whatever they may pretend? but for that short sentence I have a lingering ill-will at him which I cannot get

the best in the world, as he speaks of his being called out of this room when the arch made its appearance; now in fact, Wilson and he were on their way either to or from Grasmere when they saw the arch and very obligingly came up to tell us of it, thinking, w^h was the fact, that we might not be aware of the phenomenon. As to the speech, which galled poor Hogg so much, it must in one expression at least have been misreported, the word 'fellow' I am told by my family I apply to no one. I use strong terms I own, but there is a vulgarity about that, w^h does not suit me, and had I applied it to Hogg there w^d have also been hypocrisy in the kindness, w^h he owns I invariably shewed him, wholly alien, as you must know, to my character. It is possible and not improbable that I might on that occasion have been tempted to use a contemptuous expression, for H. had disgusted me not by his vulgarity, w^h he c^d not help, but by his self-conceit in delivering confident opinions upon classical literature and other points about w^h he c^d know nothing. The reviving this business in this formal way after a lapse of nearly 18 years does little credit to Mr Hogg and it affords another proof how cautious one ought to be in admitting to one's house trading Authors of any description, Verse men or Prose men.

I was at Corby[1] and Rose Castle[2] and much pleased with both, the horse performed well. W.[3] and I left Carlisle at 20 m: past Six and reached home ¼ before 4.

I ought to thank you for flogging Mr Mitchell[4] so openly. Who is he? I dont disapprove of Dora's sending the sonnet[5] tho' the Editor may not think it worth while to insert it. The great resort to the places of Worship on that day through the whole Island as far as I can learn gave me more pleasure than anything that has

---

rid of. It is surely presumption in any man to circumscribe all human excellence within the narrow sphere of his own capacity. The "*Where are they*" was too bad! I have always some hopes that De Quincey was *leeing*, for I did not myself hear Wordsworth utter the words.' (*The Works of the Ettrick Shepherd*, ed. T. Thomson, 2 vols., 1865–6, ii. 464.) Hogg's story appeared in the *Noctes Ambrosianae*, and was apparently the subject of much comment.

1 Corby Castle, on the Eden opposite the village of Wetheral: residence of Henry Howard (see *MY* ii. 610), and his son Philip (see L. 610 above).
2 The residence of the Bishop of Carlisle.
3 W. W. jnr.
4 According to E. Q.'s letter to W. W. of 4 Apr. (*WL MSS.*), one Nicholas Mitchell had written a 'conceited, stupid, incredibly weak, and impudent' volume entitled *Poets of the Age*, lauding L. E. L., Mrs. Hemans, and Campbell, and abusing Coleridge, Southey, and W. W. E. Q. found the book lying on the table at his club and wrote two bad quatrains of satiric doggerel in it. On his next visit to the club the book had disappeared.
5 *Upon the Late General Fast. March 1832* (*PW* iv. 128). A General Fast was enjoined on 21 Mar. on account of the cholera epidemics.

occurred for a long time. What a state they are in [in] Paris—how thankful you must be for having Jemima in England. I am in poor heart about the bill—farewell. Love to Rotha,

[*signed*] W. W.

694. W. W. to HENRY WILLIAM PICKERSGILL

Address: H. W. Pickersgill Esqr, Soho Square, London. [*In M. W.'s hand*]
Postmark: 30 Apr. 1832. *Stamp*: Kendal Penny Post.
MS. St. John's College, Cambridge.
LT ii. 619.

Thursday [26 Apr. 1832]
Rydal Mount near Kendal

My dear Sir,

I learn with much and unexpected pleasure, that there is a prospect of our seeing you here, and that you purpose to leave London for Manchester on Monday next.—On that very day, however, I must unfortunately be at Carlisle on account of public business. I will strain every point to return on Thursday at the latest.—Possibly this being Easter holidays, you may have a little leisure now, which you cannot command afterwards, otherwise I should have been startled by your coming so far when your engagements must be so pressing. When I took the liberty through Mr Quillinan of making the proposal,[1] it was with a view of its taking effect, if acceded to, during the Summer Vacation, when a little recreation and a ramble in this fine Country during the season of its beauty might recompense you for so long a journey. At present the Spring is not so far advanced as might be wished, and your allowance of time will probably be short.—I allude to these particulars both as affecting your own gratification while here, and also a point of some delicacy to myself in relation to the College for whom and at whose expense the Portrait is to be executed. The College handsomely gave me the choice of an artist but it was at a time when it was scarcely in my power, on account of official engagements, to go back to London from which I had just returned after a long absence; I therefore wrote to Mr Quillinan, submitting to him whether, if you were in the habit of giving any portion of your time to summer recreation, you might not be determined, by

---

[1] The proposal that Pickersgill should visit the Lakes as W. W.'s guest, in order to paint his portrait for St. John's. See L. 622 above.

the consideration of obliging me in this way, to prefer the Lakes and give me the pleasure of your Company. I felt there was a good deal of delicacy in that proposal, which I was induced to make, not thinking myself justified in putting the College to any further expense than a Portrait from so distinguished an Artist must necessarily impose under ordinary circumstances. I may add that I never could have presumed to propose your coming so far at this season of the year, or any other than the Summer Vacation. The above particulars having been frankly and cordially stated, they may be left to our joint consideration when I have the pleasure of seeing you here, if they should make no change in your obliging purpose.

I remain my dear Sir faithfully yours Wm Wordsworth

If you reply immediately to this Letter direct to me Stamp Off: Carlisle.—

695. W. W. to HENRY WILLIAM PICKERSGILL

MS. St. John's College, Cambridge.
LY ii. 620.

Rydal Ambleside
May 5th [1832]

My dear Sir,

Many thanks for your obliging Letter and your friendly Invitation, of which, during the painting of the Portrait, I should have been happy to avail myself had it been in my power to go to London. Unfortunately, for this purpose, and alas for me and my family, a most distressing circumstance.[1] My Sister, the only one I ever had, and who has lived with me for the last 35 years, is now in so weak and alarming [a] state of health that I could not quit home, except under absolute necessity. We must therefore wait for some more favorable opportunity. Let me add that I entirely release you from any engagement to come hither in consequence of what has passed between us; for such a proposal would have never been made but upon a supposition, which proves not to be the fact, that you were in the habit of allotting (as almost all professional men who have leisure, do) a small portion of the Summer to recreation, and I thought that the beauty of the Country, with the opportunity of working at the Portrait without interruption,

---

[1] *So MS.*

might induce you to come so far.[1] I repeat therefore that I have no claim upon you whatever in consequence of your having given me some reason to expect you. I attach, however, so much interest to the Portrait being from your pencil, that I hope many months may not pass without the College being gratified with a Production which many of its Members are so desirous of possessing.

If I should be able to come to London hereafter, I should be happy, as I have said, to be under your Roof, till your task was accomplished, and I am sure you would not take it ill if after that I removed into some Lodging; for all Persons *in the least known* are troublesome visitors in London; but till the Portrait were finished I should call upon very few of my Friends

I remain, my dear Sir,
Very faithfully yours
Wm Wordsworth

Mr Quillinan did not speak *positively* that you would be able to come.

696. W. W. to C. W.

Address: The Revd. the Master of Trinity, Lodge, Cambridge.
Stamp: Kendal Penny Post.
MS. British Library. Hitherto unpublished.

May 5th [1832]

My dear Brother,

I cannot but write you a short Letter on our Dear Sister's account: I grieve much to say that after she had been going on well for a fortnight and we were full of heart and hope about her, she was seized ten days ago with a Relapse which left her extremely weak, and so she continues; without having, I think recovered any strength to speak of. I cannot conceal from you that this last attack has alarmed me much more than any other—not for its violence—for it was less violent much than the others she has had; but her recovery from each attack is slower and slower—indeed, except that her pain is only occasional, proceeding from extreme flatulence, she can yet be scarcely said to have rallied at all. In the midst of all this we have a paramount consolation—that she is in a happy and chearful state of mind—her thoughts, as seems, just what they should be. Mary and I received the Sacrament with her, she being in bed, last

---

[1] Pickersgill was finally able to come to Rydal at the beginning of September. See L. 715 below.

Sunday.—I will say no more on this affecting subject, but commend her to your prayers.—

We have this morning heard of the Death of Elizabeth Hutchinson,[1] Mary's Sister: she has always been of weak faculties; and latterly her mind was disordered; so that it is a happy deliverance. Sarah and Joanna her Sisters, both went from this place about six weeks ago to attend upon her, near Stockton.—

We thank John for his very interesting Letter; and are delighted to hear so good an account of your health. Had my Sister been well I should have been induced (taking Cambridge in my way or return) to go to London to have my Portrait painted as Pickersgill's engagements do not allow him to come down hither.—

It was well that I wrote what I had heard of the Danish Funds. What a state the world is in. I have just heard that the *Drapeau Blanc* is hoisted in Marseilles.—

I was gratified the other day by receiving under cover of the Marques of Bristol,[2] two Copies of his admirable Speech, which I had previously read in the Standard. I wrote to thank him, and have had an amiable Note in return, this morning, with a Copy of the 2nd Edition. Dora is just returned from Carlisle, where she has had several teeth extracted. She is well but woefully thin and eats little or no animal food.—

If the Constitution is to be subverted and the Country thrown into utter confusion, we may blame Lords Harrowby, Wharncliffe,[3] the Bp of London,[4] and id genus omne; firmness might have saved us.—

This is a shabby letter; but what with private and public apprehensions, I cannot command my thoughts to write about any thing.

Love from us all—to yourself and John and Charles

ever affectionately and faithfully yours

W Wordsworth

---

[1] M.W.'s invalid sister Betsy (see *EY*, p. 335; *MY* i. 463; ii. 121).

[2] Frederick William Hervey, 5th Earl and 1st Marquess of Bristol (1769–1859), of Ickworth Park, Bury St. Edmunds: M.P. for Bury St. Edmunds, 1796–1803, Under-Secretary of State for Foreign Affairs, 1801–3. See also next letter.

[3] James Archibald Stuart-Wortley-Mackenzie, 1st Baron Wharncliffe (1776–1845), a Canningite, opposed Reform, but considering resistance hopeless, he joined with Lord Harrowby and others (see L. 676 above) in trying to effect a compromise, and advised his friends to support the second reading of the Bill in the House of Lords (see next letter) in the hope that it could be amended in Committee. He became Lord Privy Seal in Peel's ministry, 1834, and President of the Council, 1841.

[4] W. W.'s friend C. J. Blomfield, who was under constant attack in the

697. W. W. to LORD LONSDALE

MS. Lonsdale MSS. Hitherto unpublished.

May 11th [1832]
Rydal Mount

My Lord,

I must break in upon you for a moment in consequence of the news of this morning.—The King I suppose has refused to overwhelm the House of Lords with a new Creation.[1] This surely is a revolution to be rejoiced over. But what sort of a Ministry are we to have in place of the one that has resigned. Staunch Tories with Waverers? or Moderate Whigs with Waverers—or how is the government to go on with the present parliament—and can the people be trusted for returning a better, in case a dissolution should be ventured upon? These points must agitate the mind of every sincere and reflecting Lover of his Country.

If the Country cannot be governed but by irrational concessions to popular clamor, or to clamor of any kind, or from any quarter, our prospects are hopeless.

I am almost ashamed of having directed your Lordship's thoughts at this time, as in my last, to any personal interests or feelings of my own.[2] Since I wrote I have seen my Son. He came over to see his Aunt who has been languishing five months under an Illness from which there is too much reason to fear she will not recover. But for this cause I should probably have been in Town at this moment. The College of St John's some time since did me the Honor of asking me to sit for my Portrait to be placed among their 'Worthies', as the Master was good enough to say. For this purpose Pickersgill was to have come down according to his obliging

Tory press for betraying the Church. He had been active in pursuing a compromise along with Harrowby and Wharncliffe, and voted with the Government. See Alfred Blomfield, *Memoir of Charles James Blomfield, D.D.*, 2 vols., 1863, i. 167–73.

[1] The second reading of the Reform Bill had been carried in the Lords on 14 Apr. by a majority of nine, and on 7 May it was proposed that the whole House should go into committee on the Bill; but Lord Lyndhurst successfully blocked this move with his motion to postpone the disenfranchising clauses, and Grey's ministry resigned two days later. The King was urged after this defeat to create sufficient new peers to pass the Bill, but he declined to do so, and after Wellington and Lyndhurst failed to form an alternative ministry (and Peel refused to join them), Grey's ministry was recalled. On 17 May the King finally agreed to create the necessary peers, and the threat of this was enough to overcome the opposition of the Lords and the Bill was passed. It received the royal assent on 7 June.

[2] Lord Lonsdale was about to offer the living of Brigham to John W. See next letter.

promise, but his engagements do not allow him to quit Town: whither I cannot go. So the thing must stand over. But to return to my Son. The Paper from which I gave your Lordship the account of Moresby Living I had from him several months ago. It referred to the Proceeds of *1831*—he has since let the glebe for ten pounds per ann: more, and mentions certain particulars in which he thinks the Living might be improved, which I will lay before your Lordship when we meet. Last year also there fell in a fine of six pounds from a small Manor belonging to the Living.

I find from my son that a Son of Mr Leach[1] has officiated as his Father's Curate—and also that he is a married Man with a family. Had I been aware of this, I do not know that I should have directed your Lordship's attention to my Son's situation at Moresby, well assured as I am of the very kind interest you take in my family.—

I have the honor to be most faithfully your Lordship's

obliged Ser[nt]
W[m] Wordsworth

(please to turn over)

P.S. If Lord Ellenborough's speech[2] be faithfully reported, and he utters the opinion of a numerous Body in the two Houses, there appears to me to be no cause for rejoicing in the resignation of Ministers. Lord Ellenborough is said to be prepared for a disfranchisement to the Extent of Schedule A,[3] and the Borough of Weymouth, 113 Members, and not to object to the £10 franchise on account of its *uniformity.*—If we are to have a Bill from men with these views, it is to be feared nothing can prevent a speedy subversion of the Government. Well has Lord Bristol[4] protested in his

---

[1] The Revd. William Henry Leech was the resident curate of Brigham on behalf of his father, the Revd. John Leech (see also pt. i, L. 236), who held the living along with that of Askham, near Lowther, until his death on 28 Apr.

[2] In the House of Lords on 7 May, conceding the right of the large towns to enfranchisement. Edward Law, 2nd Baron Ellenborough (1790–1871), son of the Lord Chief Justice, was President of the Board of Control, 1828–30, 1834–5, 1841, and 1858; Governor General of India, 1841–4; and was created 1st Earl of Ellenborough, 1844.

[3] The first Reform Bill proposed to abolish under Schedule A some sixty closed boroughs with populations of less than 2,000 (like Appleby), to which the aristocracy had acquired the right of nomination. As a concession, this number was reduced to fifty-six in the third Bill. Under Schedule B, forty-seven towns of less than 4,000 inhabitants (like Cockermouth) were to lose one of their two members. This number was also reduced (to thirty) in the third Bill. In addition, Weymouth was to lose two of its four members. On 21 May, during the Committee stage in the Lords, Lord Ellenborough tried to amend the enfranchisement provisions by producing a revised list of new towns for enfranchisement under Schedule C.   [4] See previous letter.

admirable speech against the 'adoption of one *uniform right*' of *election* in all the Towns of England, as of most dangerous tendency.

698. W. W. to C. W.

Address: To the Revd The Master of Trinity, Cambridge.
Stamp: Kendal Penny Post.
MS. British Library. Hitherto unpublished.

Rydal Mount May 19th ⌈1832⌉

My dear Brother,

In answer to John's Letter for which I feel much obliged I will say a few words to you. Our excellent and dear Sister, since her last Relapse has certainly been mending though slowly, yet we think gradually. Nevertheless she had a return of pain yesterday that alarmed us in some degree. On reading the above to Mary, she corrects the term *slowly*, and says that her course of Recovery has been more rapid since her last attack, than after the former One— and she seems now about as well as when John left us.[1] What I am in fear of is these Relapses, coming from no assignable external cause. I have another pleasing piece of domestic news—Lord Lonsdale will present John[2] to the Vicarage of Brigham; on the Derwent two miles below Cockermouth. It is now worth £190 per annum—of which 160 arises from Glebe. When Mr Fleming[3] held it, it was worth £360. Unluckily there is no parsonage House. Could one be erected he would instantly give up Moresby, which *now* (after deductions) produces £100 per Ann—out of which he has thirty one pounds to pay for the House he lives in. Could you point out any way in which he could be helped in erecting a parsonage House at Brigham. The situation is beautiful, and he wishes much to reside, giving up Moresby,—to keep which would in no sense be an advantage to him, if he had a house at Brigham. At present he is hampered with two leases of houses in Moresby— losing 7 pounds per ann by that which he could not live in, on account of his wife's health. I will now try to write better, but I must have a better pen—

---

[1] John Wordsworth, C. W.'s son, had left Rydal to return to Cambridge on 13 Mar. See L. 690 above.
[2] i.e. W. W.'s son John.
[3] John Fleming of Rayrigg, W. W.'s old school-friend (see *EY*, p. 343; *MY* ii. 427), had been vicar of Brigham, 1813–14.

Mr Goulburn[1] says, 'the state of the Country and of the H. of C. infuriated as both have been by the reason of a democratic administration *put out of question* any attempt to make an anti reform —or *even a moderate* reform administration even if the King etc.'— Did it put out of the question the attempt to make an administration with a plan of reform if not moderate *absolutely*, yet moderate *relatively* to the present Bill? I say decidedly not—very many even of the existing House of Commons who have voted for the bill having seen its dangerous tendency and condoned it utterly in their hearts. And if the conservative party had been manfully and fearlessly headed by the Government, a strength might—and I think would have displayed itself, of which they who have looked at the question as Mr Goulburn has done appear to have no conception. When this ruinous Bill was first proposed, it would have been kicked out of the House of Commons by acclamation if a motion in that spirit had been made by Mr Peel—yet how soon was a change effected in the mind of that Body, when they found the people intoxicated with the sudden offer of political power to that extent. In like manner no inconsiderable degree of a counter movement would have appeared even in the House as now constituted, had the new Government boldly appealed to the great Body of people prepared to support them out of doors. The difficulty most insurmountable in its nature, (provided Mr Peel and others had been gifted with courage and fortitude) lies in the pledged word of the King—viz to what extent he was committed with Lord Grey, when he consented to the dissolution of the late Parliament. Pray look again at Mr G's Letter in the sentence following the one above remarked upon. 'The only alternative *then*, 'etc., the premises being not admitted the conclusion of course is rejected by all who take the view I do of the subject—'To such few of those could accede' etc.,— Well it is that they *were* few—And I own I am astonished that after the Duke of Wellington's protest,[2] he could ever think of taking up a Government prepared to carry the *Reform* Bill and with such

[1] Henry Goulburn, M.P. for Cambridge University.

[2] Immediately after the second reading of the Bill in the Lords on 14 Apr., Wellington had tabled his objections to it in principle on the grounds that it undermined the rights of the monarchy and the influence of the landed interest. He was supported by Lord Lonsdale among others. The Protest was, according to *The Courier* for 17 Apr., 'false in position, inconclusive in argument, and weak in words', and destroyed his credibility as the head of an alternative government. Peel, while accepting the need for some measure of reform, thought it dishonourable for anti-reformers to pass the Bill as the price of office, and refused to co-operate with Wellington in the formation of an alternative ministry. See Norman Gash, *Sir Robert Peel*, 1972, pp. 30–4.

modification as would be acquiesced in by the House of C., if he means the House in *its present temper*. But did not the reduced majority on Ebrington's motion[1] show the House to be mutable— and might it not have been expected to be much more so had the New Government bold[ly][2] and candidly appealed to the people for support? And after all could a manly resistance have put the King and the Constitution and the people in a worse position than Mr G. acknowledges they are brought to? Timidity has destroyed us. A King's *honor* is not to be stained—but when an error has been committed (which we will suppose in this case) is there no retracting? *Is* an ancient people to be condemned to generations of Misery because a King may have made an ill-advised promise? I put this only as a question but am prepared with the answer. My dear Brother—adieu—

[unsigned]

[*M. W. writes*]

Doro will write to John as soon as she can announce the arrival of his Parcel—Sister has been up 5 hours today, and was not much tired, but she is at this moment suffering somewhat from flatulence—

699. W. W. to JOHN MARSHALL

MS. WL.
LY ii. 636.

[? late May 1832]

My dear Sir,

It gives me much pleasure to learn that you are the Purchaser of the Derwentwater Estate,[3] and I sincerely congratulate you on the acquisition which you have made, I should think, upon very reasonable terms. Having never seen a plan of the Estate I do not exactly know its limits, but for beauty and grandeur of situation it has no

---

[1] On 11 May the House of Commons carried by a majority of 80 Lord Ebrington's motion regretting the resignation of Grey's ministry, upholding the principles of the Bill, and calling for the return of a ministry that would carry it into effect. Lord Ebrington, later 2nd Earl Fortescue (1783–1861), was M.P. for Devonshire.

[2] *MS. torn.*

[3] See L. 682 above. John Marshall's purchase of the estate was announced in the local press on 5 May, so that this letter must be considerably earlier than Dec. 1832 to which de Selincourt assigns it.

parallel.—Great mistakes may be made in valuing the wood; so that it is of the utmost consequence that persons should be employed who can estimate fairly its value *on the Spot*. My Neighbour Mr Harrison[1] not long ago purchased a very extensive fall of timber and other wood in Scotland. The Vendor had employed a Valuer from a distance, one of whose items was a 1,000 pounds for broom for besoms, which broom in that remote part of the Highlands was of *no value whatever*, and the Item was accordingly struck out of the Estimate.

—It will give me much pleasure to go over the Estate, with you, and together we certainly might hit upon improvements of its Beauty. I shall most likely be at Keswick before you come down, and if I can learn any thing there that will be worth naming to you I shall write. Mr Southey will be pleased to hear that you are the Purchaser, as will all men of taste, especially when they know your chief inducement for buying the property.

—Will you excuse my expressing a wish that you would procure the Conveyance Stamp through my Son William, at Carlisle.—Solicitors in cases of so large a purchase often interfere, to prevent, for the sake of a small benefit of their own, the Distributor of Stamps and his Sub—getting their regular profit.—If got through my Son it would throw a few pounds into his pocket, and be a little encouragement in his humble situation—

ever faithfully yours
Wm Wordsworth

700. W. W. to LORD LONSDALE

MS. Lonsdale MSS. Hitherto unpublished.

Moresby
June 12th 1832

My Lord,
    Your letter followed me to this place. It gives me great pleasure that you are satisfied with the Duke's conduct,[2] and to your

---

[1] Benson Harrison.

[2] i.e. the Duke of Wellington, who had attempted to form an alternative ministry in mid-May on the resignation of Lord Grey (see L. 697 above). W. W. had apparently hoped for the return of a Tory ministry which would bring in a limited measure of Reform on different principles from those implied in the Reform Bill (see L. 681 above). But Wellington had undermined such a

judgement I defer till an opportunity shall occur of discussing it with your Lordship.

Yesterday I saw Mr Curwen.[1] He introduced the subject of the Representation for Cumberland; and said that if the Freeholders should call upon him, and upon enquiry there should appear good grounds for a hope of success, he should then come forward as a Candidate for the western division. But thinking that Lord Lonsdale and his political Friends were fully entitled to send a member for that division he would in no way countenance or cooperate with any attempt to return two Blues or Reformers for that portion of the Country. With Mr C's permission, I have reported this determination to your Lordship. He further observed that if an attempt should be made to bring in two Conservatives or Tories, or anti-Reformers, or by whatever name they were called, for the West, his present determination was to oppose that measure in coalition with another Candidate, who he doubted not would come forward.[2] The above is all that your Lordship need be troubled with, as little importance can attach to the endeavour which I made to show how little moderation there was in this and the tendency of such a course at the present time, on the part of the Reformers, their Bill being passed and there being no probability of a Tory candidate in the East.[3] I have seen Henry Lowther[4]—but have heard little respecting Whitehaven[5] except from him; only Mr Bell[6] told

possibility in advance by his rash commitment to the existing system of representation in Nov. 1830 (see L. 579 above), and by his more recent 'Protest'; and, as Lord Lonsdale explained in his letter of 12 May (*WL MSS.*), Peel declined to join any alternative administration; so that in the end the return of Grey's ministry and the passing of his Reform Bill seemed almost inevitable.

[1] Henry Curwen. See also L. 675 above.

[2] In the general election in the December following the passing of the Reform Bill, the Tories in West Cumberland carried both their candidates, Lord Lowther (who was also returned for Westmorland, and elected to sit for that division), and Edward Stanley of Ponsonby (see *MT* ii. 490). They were at first opposed by two Blues, Henry Curwen and Sir Wilfred Lawson, Bart. (1795–1867), younger son of Thomas Wybergh (see *MT* ii. 442), but the latter withdrew.

[3] East Cumberland returned Sir James Graham and William Blamire, who had represented the undivided county in the previous Parliament (see L. 610 above). No Tory candidates were brought forward, though the names of Edward W. Hasell (see L. 666 above) and Sir Francis Fletcher Vane, 3rd Bart. (1797–1842) were at one time canvassed.

[4] The Revd. Henry Lowther of Distington.

[5] The new constituency of Whitehaven returned Matthias Attwood (d. 1852), the Birmingham banker and economist, who had previously represented Callington and Boroughbridge. He was opposed in the Lowther interest by Isaac Littledale, the Whitehaven banker.

[6] Probably Charles Bell, surveyor of taxes at Whitehaven.

Mr. Harrison[1] of Ambleside when he was here lately, that a requisition from a commanding Body, a majority indeed of the Voters, had been made to Mr Isaac Littledale, who, however, was not likely to stand. If my Sister's health should not prove worse, I shall remain here till the end of next week. I need not say how happy it would make me could I be of any use to the good cause.

I grieve to hear so unfavorable an account of Lady Frederick's Lameness.

Henry Lowther tells me it is not improbable Lord Lowther may be coming down very shortly. I deferred writing to him having a visit here in prospect, and thinking I might obtain information that might be useful.

ever faithfully your Lordship's

W. W.

701. W. W. to FRANCIS MEREWETHER

Address: The Rev[d] F: Merewether, Coleorton Rectory, Ashby de la Zouch.
Postmark: [   ] 1832. *Stamp*: Whitehaven.
MS. Cornell.
LY ii. 621.

[*In Dora W.'s hand*]

Moresby June 18th 1832.

My dear Sir,

Your two letters reached me duly but at times when my mind was so occupied with anxiety on private and public accounts that I could not muster courage to thank you for those marks of friendly attention.—The Reform bill being passed my *anxiety* for that cause is over but only to be succeeded by dejection to despondency— the Parliament that has past this bill was in profligacy and folly never surpassed since the parliament that overthrew the monarchy in Charles the first's time; and it is to be feared that it will give birth to a Monster still more odious than itself. Of nine members to be returned by the county from which I write, seven will to a certainty be, either down right Jacobin Republicans, or of a class, in the present stage of our revolution, still more dangerous—rash or complying Whig Innovators: of the other two members one will

---

[1] Either Benson Harrison or John Harrison of the Green (see L. 590 above).

probably be a Conservative and the ninth is in doubt,[1] but I fear the good cause in this instance also will not prevail.

The private anxiety to which I alluded is caused by the very feeble and alarming state of my dear Sister's health which received at Whitwick a shock it never recovered from. She has been upwards of six months almost perpetually confined to her room and the greater part of the day through weakness tho' thank God not thro' pain to her bed.—We thought her something better and in consequence my daughter and I ventured a week ago upon a visit to John and his amiable Wife; and here I shall remain if we have no bad news from Rydal a week longer—John is well and no doubt would send his affect[e] regards but he is gone over to his new vicarage of Brigham, the Church of w[h] is 9 miles hence; the parish is of vast extent having under it several chapelries inclusive of the town of Cockermouth (5000 inhabitants) but those under the care of the *vicar* amount only to 1500—the situation is most beautiful —rich sloping or meadowy grounds with the fine river Derwent winding thro' them, and Skiddaw with other lofty mountains in full view at the distance of 6 or 7 miles: unluckily neither in this little rectory of Moresby nor at Brigham is there a parsonage: he has some thoughts however of building at Brigham—

It is now high time to turn to your letter. I am much pleased that your residence by the sea-side proved so beneficial to your health of body and as your verses shew must have given an impulse to your mind—you were mistaken in supposing that it would be any task to me to peruse your short metrical compositions—the lines on the sea are good and you succeed best as must be the case with every one where the subject is most poetical—but as to the Reform bill and Reform the genius of Milton himself could scarcely extract poetry from a theme so inauspicious.

I was much concerned to learn from the Archbishop[2] that Sir George Beaumont had been very poorly: pray present my kind regards to him and to Lady Beaumont and say that I shall not visit London without turning aside to Coleorton either going or

---

[1] W. W.'s pessimistic fears were not entirely confirmed at the Cumberland elections at the end of this year. East Cumberland returned two reformers (see previous letter); Carlisle returned for the second time Philip Henry Howard, a moderate reformer, and William James, the radical (see L. 610 above); the new enlarged division of Cockermouth returned two reformers, Henry Aglionby (1790–1854) and Frecheville Lawson Ballantyne Dykes (1800–66) of Dovenby, and rejected Andrew Green the radical (see L. 681 above); and Whitehaven returned a radical (see previous letter). But two conservatives were elected for West Cumberland, Lord Lowther and Edward Stanley.

[2] Dr. William Howley, Sir George Beaumont's father-in-law.

returning—but for my Sister's illness I should have been in town this spring for a short time—

I am glad to learn that my dear brother's health is upon the whole better in spite of public affairs, but he tells me that that most excellent man Mr Joshua Watson is declining and that his daughter also is far from well. This if news to you will grieve you much. Mr Watson is perhaps the ablest supporter the Church has out of her own bosom—indeed he is the friend and support of all that is virtuous and rational in the country—Dora joins with me in kindest remembrances and best wishes to Mrs Merewether and yourself and believe me ever faithfully yours

[*signed*] Wm Wordsworth

702. W. W. to JOHN GARDNER

Address: J. Gardener Esqᵉ 16 Foley Place, Portland Place.
MS. Harvard University Library.
LY ii. 623.

[*In Dora W.'s hand*]

Moresby June 22ᵈ '32

My dear Sir,

You will think I have been lost—I could not write sooner not having heard from Dʳ Wordsworth who has been dancing about between London and Cambridge. He has undertaken to advance £100[1] and I will advance another £100; the precise sum you named for a fee, if any were fixed upon, I do not recollect—but if it exceed £200 my brother and I will provide it, also between us.— My Nephew's situation is unfortunate as to his Father's Will; which was made before the rapid decline of land and stock prices, wʰ made the sum allotted for the payments of his debts, much short of what was required, and no land can be sold till he is of age without an expensive process in chancery.

You mention bills—would one payable at three months suit you for £100 and another for a like sum at *6* or *9*? by that period money would be due to my family from which without inconvenience I could advance my portion—I hope you continue to be satisfied with

[1] C. W. wrote on 7 June: 'John's interests and education must not be neglected . . . and when you have made the necessary arrangements with Mʳ Gardiner and will let me know, an instalment of £100 shall be ready, as a *gift* from me.' (*WL MSS.*)

John, and I was pleased to find you did not think me mistaken in my estimate of his character—he writes in good spirits, seems very happy and thankful for your kindness.—May I beg of you to exhort him to frugality; not that I ever saw anything to the contrary in him: —whatever is necessary for books, dress and other expenses, will be supplied as wanted.

The printing of my new Edition[1] is finished, I promised a copy to John and beg you will accept another, which Longman shall be directed to send to Foley Place when ready—it contains nothing but what has appeared either in the last Ed: or some Miscellany since.—I return to Rydal in a few days and shall be happy to hear from you.

Remember me most kindly to Mr Boxall[2]—my brains have been racked in vain for a title to his series of paintings—w^h I am persuaded will do him much honor; the specimen he kindly sent me is very much admired and improves upon acquaintance. Mr Quillinan tells me that the engraving[3] from his portrait of me is beautifully done and with the picture will be very acceptable at Rydal.

Believe me dear sir

Ever very faithfully yours
[*signed*] Wm Wordsworth

Love to John from his Uncle and his three Cousins—his dear Aunt, he will be sorry to hear, continues in a very languishing state.

Not knowing the Revd Mr Judkin's[4] address I have desired my publishers to enclose three copies to you one of w^h Mr Boxall will be kind enough to take charge of for the said M^r J:—

[1] The four-volume edition of 1832.
[2] E. Q. wrote to Dora W. on 4 Apr.: 'Boxall is doing a series of paintings to be engraved, an attempt to give the varieties of expression of poetical female beauty—for instance he is doing one on the expression "Quiet as a nun Breathless with adoration". He wants a title for the work. Can or will Mr W. suggest a title? It is said that B. is the *best* painter of abstract female beauty among the artists.' (*WL MSS.*)
[3] By William Bromley (1769–1842).
[4] For T. J. Judkin, see L. 678 above.

703. W. W. to GEORGE HUNTLY GORDON

Address: G: Huntly Gordon Esq^e, Treasury Chambers.
MS. Cornell. Hitherto unpublished.

[*In Dora W.'s hand*]

Moresby
n^r Whitehaven
June 23^d —32.

My dear Sir,

My last dispatch was sent under a mistake, and I trouble you with this to let you know it: as the printing of different Vols: was going on at the same time it had escaped my notice that the whole was finished, otherwise I should have thanked you in my last for y^r service in helping me thro' this expensive publication,[1] from w^h as it will be sold at a low price, my gains will be small—Longman will be directed to send you a copy of w^h I beg your acceptance, less as an acknowledgement for y^r aid than as a memorial of my regard. I understand from Mr Quillinan that you flitted lately to the Stamp Office or at least such was the intention; if a change is to take place thought I, I am glad, as a Distributor, to have another friend in the Office, but to tell you the truth I had not the least thought that a new Ministry would be formed.

Farewell—I do not trust my pen to the state of public affairs, besides would it not be indelicate to let out what I think, feel, and fear, under a Treasury Cover.

God bless you and believe me faithfully your obliged friend

[*signed*] Wm Wordsworth

I return to Rydal in a few days.

Would you be kind enough to fill up the address of Mr Lockhart's note.[2]

---

[1] The four-volume edition of 1832.

[2] Probably a letter of inquiry about the health of Sir Walter Scott, who had arrived back in London on 13 June.

Address: Professor Hamilton, Observatory, Dublin.
Postmark: 28 June 1832. *Stamp*: Whitehaven.
MS. Cornell.
Mem. (—). *Grosart. Hamilton. K* (—). *LY ii. 625.*

[*In Dora W.'s hand*]

Moresby
June 25th 1832.

My dear Mr Hamilton,

Your former letter reached me in due time; your second from Cambridge two or three days ago.[1] I ought to have written to you long since, but really I have for some time from private and public causes of sorrow and apprehension been in a great measure deprived of those genial feelings which thro' life have not been so much accompaniments of my character, as vital principles of my existence. My dear Sister has been languishing more than seven months in a sick-room nor dare I or any of her friends entertain a hope that her strength will ever be restored; and the course of public affairs, as I think I told you before, threatens, in my view, destruction to the institutions of the country; an event which whatever may rise out of it hereafter, cannot but produce distress and misery for two or three generations at least. In any times I am but at best a poor and unpunctual correspondent, yet I am pretty sure you would have heard from me but for this reason, therefore let the statement pass for an apology as far as you think fit.

The verses called forth by your love[2] and the disappointment that followed I have read with much pleasure tho' grieved that you should have suffered so much; as Poetry they derive an interest from your philosophical pursuits which could not but recommend the verses even to indifferent readers and must give them in the eyes of your friends a great charm. The style appears to me good and the general flow of the versification harmonious—but you deal somewhat more in dactylic endings and identical terminations than I am accustomed to think legitimate. Sincerely do I congratulate you upon being able to continue your philosophical pursuits under such a pressure of personal feeling.

It gives me much pleasure that you and Coleridge have met[3] and that you were not disappointed in the conversation of a man

---

[1] Hamilton had written twice from Cambridge, on 13 Apr. and 15 June. See *Hamilton*, i. 551, 566.

[2] For Ellen de Vere. The verses are given in *Hamilton*, i. 560–4.

[3] On 20 and 23 Mar. See *Hamilton*, i. 536, 538–42; and Griggs, vi. 893, 896–8.

from whose writings you had previously drawn so much delight and improvement. He and my beloved Sister are the two Beings to whom my intellect is most indebted and they are now proceeding as it were pari passu along the path of sickness, I will not say towards the grave but I trust towards a blessed immortality.

It was not my intention to write so seriously: my heart is full and you must excuse it. You do not tell me how you like Cambridge as a place, nor what you thought of its buildings and other works of art. Did you not see Oxford as well?[1] Surely you would not lose the opportunity; it has greatly the advantage over Cambridge in its happy intermixture of Streets, Churches and collegiate buildings.

I hope you found time when in London to visit the British Museum.

A fortnight ago I came hither to my son and Daughter who are living a gentle, happy, quiet and useful life together. My daughter Dora is also with us. On this day I should have returned but an inflammation in my eyes makes it unsafe for me to venture in an open carriage, the weather being exceedingly disturbed. A week ago appeared here M[r] W. S. Landor[2] the Poet and author of the *Imaginary Conversations*, which probably have fallen in your way. We had never met before tho' several letters had passed between us, and as I had not heard that he was in England my gratification in seeing him was heightened by surprise. We passed a day together at the house of my friend M[r] Rawson,[3] on the banks of Wastwater. His conversation is lively and original, his learning great tho' he will not allow it and his laugh the heartiest I have heard for a long time. It is I think not much less than 20 years since he left England for France and afterwards Italy where he hopes to end his days, nay [he has] fixed n[r] Florence upon the spot where he wishes to be buried. Remember me most kindly to y[r] Sisters. Dora begs her love and thanks to y[r] Sister Eliza for her last most interesting letter w[h] she will answer when she can command a frank.

Ever faithfully yours
[*signed*] W[m] Wordsworth

---

[1] Hamilton was in Oxford by 16 June for the meeting of the British Association, at which he was reading a paper.

[2] This was Landor's first visit to England for some eighteen years. He crossed the Channel on 10 May, and after some days in London, and a visit to Cambridge to see Julius and Augustus Hare, he went on to stay with his friends the Abletts (see next letter) in North Wales. It was from there that he set out, by steamboat from Liverpool to Whitehaven, to visit Wordsworth and Southey. Landor left England again at the end of September. See R. H. Super, *Walter Savage Landor, A Biography*, 1957, pp. 226–32.

[3] Stansfeld Rawson of Halifax, who owned an estate at Crookhead, in Nether Wastdale.

I have desired Messʳˢ Longman to put aside for you a copy of the new Ed: of my poems compressed into 4 vols. It contains nothing but what has before seen the light but several pieces wʰ were not in the last. Pray direct yʳ Dublin publisher to apply for it.

705. W. W. to EDWARD QUILLINAN[1]

Address: Edward Quillinan Esqᵉ, George Watson's Esqᵉ, Bronsil, nʳ Ledbury, Herefordshire.
Stamp: Cockermouth.
MS. WL. Hitherto unpublished.

[*In Dora W.'s hand*]

[Moresby]
[26 June 1832]

Dora has promised an addition to this letter from me, but really I have nothing to say. I mean to present Rotha with a copy of my Poems[2] bound, wʰ would have been sent to her immediately but that we all know that the printing of a book is injured by the pressure in binding if done before time has hardened the ink. I have therefore requested Messʳˢ Longman to put aside a copy for her to be bound at a proper time when I must throw the choice of the execution upon your taste.

I wish you to have a copy yourself also, and you may apply to Longman for it on your returning to town.

You kindly propose certain Autographs for Dora's book, and every person you name on the score of genius is worthy of being there, and could you come at Landor before his departure for Italy we should be particularly glad if he would write in that book the few lines that Dora already possesses of his penmanship, and wʰ last should he[3] have forgotten them she will transcribe in this letter. You will be surprised when I tell you that this very gentleman was a few days ago in the house where we are now writing along with Mʳ Rawson and a gentleman of the vale of Clwyd. He came by steam fʳ Liverpool to Whitehaven. I had not heard of his being in England and was of course much gratified by the

---

[1] Written over a letter of Dora W. to E. Q.
[2] The new four-volume edition.
[3] *Written* he should. For Landor's contribution to Dora W.'s autograph album, see F. V. Morley, *Dora Wordsworth, Her Book*, 1924, p. 113 and facsimile.

interview. I passed a day with them at Mr Rawson's very pretty residence among the sublimities of Wastdale. Mr L. and his Clwyd friend, Mr Ablet[1] I think is his name, went over the Lake thro' Borrowdale to visit Southey at Keswick and on to Rydal which Mary tells me they preferred to any thing they had seen in our country.

⌈Have⌉ you ⌈been⌉[2] told that the green terrace has been lengthened towards the church 34 level feet so as to make a charming quarter deck walk; and at the termination will be a seat and in time an arbour if the wind will permit. Landor's conversation is lively and animated. We talked principally about Literature for as to politics any thing of that kind between him and me as matter of friendship at least w^d have been like an endeavour at shaking hands from the Poles. From the little that was dropt (à la Julius Hare whom we have been studying) I suspected ⌈him⌉[3] to be in opinion as wild as infidelity and radicalism can make any man, and therefore not quite as wise notwithstanding his great talents as humblemindedness might make the simplest artisan or the rudest hind of this or any other parish. But keep this to yourself for he appears to think of me much more highly than I deserve. By the bye he is the heartiest laugher I have ever heard. Such a laugh c^d not be maintained long I think in our foggy climate and in the midst of our raucous politics, but he has expatriated himself and chosen n^r Florence the place where he means to be buried. As to Crabbe Robinson whom I look upon as one of the best natured and friendliest men in the world I can neither account for his not calling upon you, nor for his not writing to us. Since you were at Rydal he was told[4] of my Sister's deplorable weakness and dangerous illness. As he has a sincere regard for her I am inclined to impute his silence to unwillingness to face the pain of writing in answer to our last melancholy letter. In that I also touched upon politics and strongly, considering I was writing to one who had sent from abroad 20 or 30 £ in aid of the reform bill.—C^d he be offended at that? We poor

---

[1] Joseph Ablett (d. 1848), of Llanbedr Hall, near Ruthin, Denbighshire, whom Landor had met in 1828: son of a prosperous Manchester merchant. Landor was indebted to him for securing the Villa Gherardesca at Fiesole. According to a letter he wrote to his sister from Llanbedr on 6 June, Ablett was 'of all the men living . . . the very best, the most modest and soberminded'. See Landor's tribute in his *Ode to a Friend* (*Complete Works of Walter Savage Landor*, ed. T. Earle Welby and Stephen Wheeler, 16 vols., 1927–36, xv. 270).

[2] *Written* here you told   [3] *Word dropped out.*

[4] W. W.'s letter to H. C. R. of c. 20 Mar. (see *HCR* i. 405) has not survived.

conservatives of the old school should make a sad figure in Cumber-land.[1] 7 out of the 9 members will certainly be either down right revolutionary radicals, flaming reformers, or Whigs of a class in the present stage of our revolution still more dangerous. Isabella's cousin Stanley of Ponsonby is of the conservative side and in the Lowther interest, her Father the candidate on the reforming side for the same division viz: the western. Her Cousin Blamire with Sir James Graham will I suppose be returned for the eastern. L. Lowther appears to be sick of the country and declines standing.

I envy you the sight of the beautiful country you are now in, and of my excellent friends, in that neighbourhood. John and Isabella are quite well and happy as the day is long.

Dora reads me that part of your letter marked 'private'—In conjunction with her Aunt[2] I doubt not she would be happy in doing all that could be done for your children. Trusts are delicate things but I suppose will have nothing to do with the management of property. That which your children would inherit is put I fear thro' the misconduct of the Brydges into a very simple state. But in case of Barrett's[3] death without issue there w^d arise claims of a very complex kind and matters in which justice c^d not be done to your children but by a man of experience, integrity and ability. Henry Coleridge[4] has all these qualities and is young, and it would be a happy thing if he would protect *their rights* should you be taken away.

Ever faithfully yours, with love to your little Girls,
Wm Wordsworth[5]

Your beggar Girl is I suppose kindly intended as a preparatory hint of what the gentry of England including those of Rydal Mount and its Visitors are to be brought to by the sage [? misanthropy][6]

---

[1] See Ls. 700 and 701 above.

[2] i.e. S. H., whom E. Q. had asked to be joint guardian with Dora W. of his two children in the event of his death. In her section of this letter Dora W. wrote: 'Father has answered the main points of your very kind letter but you must now allow me to assure you (which I think I need not scruple to do after the very flattering mark which you have given of the unbounded confidence you place in me) of what I have so long and so often thought and felt—that long as life is given to me your Darlings will have one friend who must always think of them with a Mother's anxiety and love them with a Mother's love and whose only regret will be or rather is that her power of serving them falls so far short of her desire to serve—and what I say of my own feelings towards y^r children applies I know with equal force to Aunt Sarah.' (*WL MSS.*) See also next letter.   [3] Col. Brydges Barrett, E. Q.'s brother-in-law.

[4] Henry Nelson Coleridge.   [5] Not signed by W. W.

[6] *MS. illegible*. The reference is perhaps to the print sent by William Boxall (see L. 702 above).

of a 10 £ rent legislature. The admonition will be borne for the
sake of the Donor and the painter.

706. W. W. to EDWARD QUILLINAN

Address: Edward Quillinan Esqre, Mr George Benson's, Fern Hill, Malvern,
   Worcestershire.
Stamp: (1) Kendal Penny Post (2) Malvern Penny Post.
Endorsed: 1832—July. Mr Wordsworth to me on the subject of Guardians for
   my children.
MS. WL.
LY ii. 627

[*In S. H.'s hand*]

July 10th [1832]

My dear Friend,
   (I hold the pen for Mr W., whose eyes, I grieve to say, do not
serve him for this and scarcely any other purpose at present. S.H.).
From your Letter I am sorry to learn that you have been led to
entertain so confident an expectation that Dora would undertake
the charge of Jemima and Rotha, in case of their standing in need
(which God forfend) of guardianship.[1] The part of her letter which
I dictated was meant to set you at ease upon the point that in the last
necessity your Children would not be left unprotected—even by
her—as far as circumstances might allow. My wish was that Miss
H. and she, who were named together, should have written you a
joint letter, stating their views of the proposal, but that was impossible, and when Dora wrote Miss H. had not even seen the
proposal—there having been no communication between them.
I therefore wished that the Letter written from Moresby should
merely aim at setting you at ease upon the main point, but from
the language of your last letter (in which you say 'accept my
thanks') I infer that her feelings must have betrayed her into the
expression of sentiments on this point very different from what
would find sanction from her own understanding, uninfluenced by
such feelings or rather unblinded by them. It is incumbent on me,
as her Father, and as the Friend of the Children and yours, to
assure you that she is utterly unfit both from her health, strength,
temper, and circumstances to stand pledged for such an anxious

---

[1] See previous letter.

responsibility. In the last necessity, and under no other, should I approve of her undertaking it, but you named Mr and Mrs Wake,[1] and from what I have heard you say of her and her Family I thought that she would be likely to undertake the office and felt convinced that your Children would be infinitely better under her super-intendence than any protection that my Family could afford. I will not advert to our situation—it is enough for me to know that the ardent and anxious temper of my Daughter in conjunction with her weak frame disqualifies her from such an office—and that it ought not to be undertaken unless where it devolves upon her as an imperious duty. You say that the 'expression of your will' binds no one, but how ungracious would it be for her, the first person named, to decline the charge, and how painful, you having gone out of the world with the expectation that she would accept it. I am persuaded that such an alternative would prey upon health and do her the greatest injury.[2]

Thanks for your amusing letter. I am truly glad that you and the dear children are enjoying yourselves so agreeably in that beautiful country.—We have had a round of visitors—Dr Arnold[3] and his family are at Brathay for 6 weeks—and yesterday we had Mr Carr[4] of Bolton Abbey and his two nieces—young enthusiasts, and he a handsome fresh, prosing old man of 70—with a fine feeling, a lively enjoyment, and just discrimination of nature. Mr Julius Hare—a friend of Landor—is here also, and several promising Cantabs.[5] I could tell you much about certain Syrens of the name of Wynyard who haunt the Islands of Winandermere, and the perplexity of the young mathematicians—and are also a good deal

[1] E. Q.'s friends, Mr. and Mrs. Charles Wake.

[2] E. Q. replied on 18 July: 'What you say will make no difference as to my arrangements, because it will still be a matter perfectly optional; and as I have the agreement of *one* of the other parties that the trust will be accepted if declined by my friends at Rydal . . . my mind will be at ease as to the main object of securing my children from the wolf-guardianship of the Brydges. . . . I have only to make my apologies for having started the subject at all, and I am sure you will all forgive me for having suffered my feelings for my children to overrule some other considerations which might have made me silent. I am glad that I *have* mentioned my intentions and wishes, because, as you say, I shall now not go out of the world self-deceived.' (*WL MSS.*) See also *SH*, p. 389.

[3] Thomas Arnold had written from Rugby on 11 May asking W. W. to arrange for him to rent Brathay from John Harden (*WL MSS.*). See also Moorman, ii. 485.

[4] For the Revd. William Carr (1763–1843), see *MY* ii. 335. He was rector of Aston Tirrold and Tubney, Berks., as well as incumbent of Bolton.

[5] Julius Hare was accompanied by another Fellow of Trinity, Joseph Williams Blakesley (1808–85), Tennyson's friend, later Dean of Lincoln. Other visitors from Trinity this summer included Thorp (L. 593 above) and Peacock (L. 619 above). See *RMVB*.

about Rydal not perhaps without views upon the Ivy Cot[1] that I leave you to guess at. In the Mitchell affair[2] you did well to keep your own counsel, but he is too great a booby for notice from any quarter—such trash nature intended should come into the world still born. Boxall's Picture[3] and Prints[4] have not yet reached us— we will do our best to procure subscribers, but we have no chance of succeeding except in summer time, therefore the delay is unlucky. Mr Hare named the picture but did not relish it, seeming to hint it was nothing of a likeness. Farewell! very faithfully yours

[*signature cut away*]

[*There follows S. H.'s letter to E. Q. of the same date, as in SH, p. 387*]

707. W. W. to JOHN GARDNER

Address: John Gardner Esq[re], 16 Foley Place, Portland Place.
MS. Henry E. Huntington Library.
LY ii. 629.

[*In M. W.'s hand*]

Rydal Mount July 16th [1832]

My dear Sir

I have been much distressed by an inflammation in my eyes and engaged almost every hour since I rec[d] your letter. Pray draw upon D[r] W. at Buxted near Uckfield for a 100gs at 3 months, and upon myself for a hundred and twenty pounds at 6 mo: that will meet the expense of the Indentures etc.[5] Mr Addison of Grey's Inn, is John's Godfather, a Solicitor and an excellent Man—and it would interest him in John's welfare if *he* should be applied to to execute the Indenture.

I have a small favor to beg of you. My eyelids have sometimes suffered from exposure to sudden changes of wind, which may be guarded against by spectacles with side-glasses—I should not wish them to be green nor ordinary glass—but there are a kind that

---

[1] i.e. on Mrs. Tillbrooke's brother, Mr. Ayling (see L. 639 above), an eligible bachelor.
[2] See L. 693 above. E. Q. naturally kept secret his defacing of a club book.
[3] His portrait of W. W. (see L. 603 above), which he had retained while an engraving was being prepared.
[4] Probably the engravings mentioned in L. 702 above.
[5] For their nephew, R. W.'s son, now entrusted to John Gardner's care.

subdue the glaring light, of a cold bluish tint, would you be so kind as purchase a pair for me at Dollands.[1]—Observe my eyes, tho' so long harrassed by inflammation, are not *aged*, so that without being the least short-sighted I *can* read the smallest print without spectacles—tho' I have for some time used the first size.

The Spectacles must have a proper case, directed to me and be taken (which John can do) to Rob[t] Hook Esq[re],[2] 18 King Street St James's, who has instructions to forward them to me.

> Ever faithfully your's
> [*signed*] Wm Wordsworth

708. W. W. to EDWARD MOXON

MS. Henry E. Huntington Library. Hitherto unpublished.

[*In M. W.'s hand*]

Rydal Mount July 19th [1832]

My dear Sir

I thank you cordially for the books you sent me thro' Mr Southey. Having been for some weeks unable to read, from an inflammation in my eyes, and every body about me much engaged, I can yet say nothing of their contents. But when I have the pleasure of seeing you here, I hope to be able to tell you how I like them—Pray continue your journey so as that you may be able to stay a few days with us. My Poems[3] are out, I bear 2.3[ds] of the expence to receive 2.3[ds] of the profits—but I shall have a large sum to advance, unless a number of Copies go off in the course of[4] a twelvemonth—therefore pray push me where you can.

Remember me most kindly to Mr Rogers, and tell him that we hope to see him during the course of the Summer. He will grieve to hear that my poor Sister makes no progress towards the recovery of her strength.

> Ever faithfully your
> much obliged Friend
> [*signed*] Wm Wordsworth

[1] George Dollond, optician, of St. Paul's Churchyard.
[2] Probably Robert (1799–1873), younger brother of Walter Farquhar Hook and grandson of Lady Farquhar (see Ls. 726 and 727 below).
[3] The fourth collected edition, 4 vols., 1832.
[4] of *written* for.

709. W. W. to ALEXANDER DYCE

Address: Mr Pickering, Bookseller, Chancery Lane. *For The Revd Alex. Dyce*
Postmark: 24 July 1832.
MS. Victoria and Albert Museum.
LY ii. 629.

[In M. W.'s hand]   Rydal Mount July 21st [1832]

My dear Sir,
   I ought to have written to you before to say that I had not
forgotten your request concerning Skelton.¹ Mr Southey, to
whom I have several times named the subject, was pleased to hear
that you had undertaken the work; but had nothing to communicate further than that in Mr Heber's² Library were certain
printed poems of Skelton not to be found in any collection of his
works. Mr Heber is now in England, and, as we all know, is very
liberal in giving Editors the use of anything in his Library. I
observed that Mr Southey in his extracts from Skelton affirms that
he was born at Dis in Norfolk, but I have heard, or read, that he was
born at Branthwaite Hall near Cockermouth in Cumberland which
place was undoubtedly possessed for many generations by a family
of his name—but on the above I lay no stress as I have no means of
verifying the report.
   Pray let me hear how you come on with your work and believe
me faithfully yours   [signed] Wm Wordsworth

710. W. W. to H. C. R.

Address: H. C. Robinson Esqre, Plowden Buildings, London.
Postmark: 23 July 1832. *Stamp*: Kendal Penny Post.
Endorsed: 21 July 1832 Wordsworth.
MS. Harvard University Library.
K (—). Morley, i. 230 (—).

[In M. W.'s hand]   Rydal Mount,
                                        July 21st, [1832]

My dear Friend,
   We were truly glad to hear from you³ after so long a silence.

---

¹ See L. 628 above.
² For Richard Heber, the bibliophile, see *MY* ii. 152, and pt. i, L. 200.
³ Extracts from H. C. R.'s letter of 13 July are given by Morley, i. 229. He
was preoccupied with the recent death of Goethe.

The Ladies you mention[1] are distant relations of ours, and we should have been glad to serve them had it been in our power. One of them wrote to my Sister above a year ago, and several letters passed between them. Long after my Sister had fallen ill, ie a few weeks ago, Mrs. Wordsworth took up the correspondence, and told them, in reply to a like request, that there were no collections of pictures in this neighbourhood that she was acquainted with save the Earl of Lonsdale's which by the bye is very small. Mrs. W. added such observations as she thought right upon the subject. Mr. Bolton, of Storrs (upon Windermere) has also some pictures, and I am told that a Mr. Brancker[2] of Liverpool, who has lately settled near Ambleside, has also some good ones, but I have never seen them. I regret not being able to do anything to further the views of these Ladies. This country holds out little temptation in their way. Should it suit them to take a lodging at Bowness, there would be no difficulty in getting access to Mr Bolton's Pictures; nor, were the Ladies at Ambleside, to Mr Brancker's, though I cannot say he is of my acquaintance. As to the pictures at Lowther, they could only be copied by some person staying in the House, there being no accommodation for Lodgers in the neighbourhood. There used to be a few Claudes at Lord George Cavendish's[3] (Holkar Hall), near Cartmell, not far from their present abode; and, as the family are seldom there, these might easily be got at.

You will grieve to hear that your invalid friend, my dear Sister, cannot be said to be making any progress towards recovery. She never quits her room but for a few minutes, and we think is always weakened by the exertion. She is, however, God be praised, in a contented and happy state of mind, and though subject frequently to pain wears it so well that she seems to have little to complain of but debility. I have not told her that I am writing to you, or she would have sent her affectionate remembrances. The rest of the family are well, save that my eyes seem every year more and more subject to protracted inflamation.

To my great surprize and pleasure Landor appeared at Moresby

---

[1] H. C. R. had been informed by a friend of his that one of W. W.'s distant relatives, the widow of a clergyman lately deceased, had herself died and left orphan daughters, 'both in delicate health, but anxious to employ their cultivated talents usefully. They copy ancient paintings.' (*Dr. Williams's Library MSS.*) These ladies have not been identified.

[2] For James Branker of Croft Lodge, see pt. i, L. 372.

[3] Lord George Augustus Henry Cavendish (b. 1754), recently created 1st Earl of Burlington. His seat, Holker Hall, which was considerably enlarged in the Victorian period, was noted for its fine collection of pictures.

near Whitehaven (having come by steam from Liverpool), when I was on a visit there to my Son.[1] I followed him to Wastdale next day, where I spent a day with him in the same house. We went on thro' Borrowdale to Mr. Southey's. He appears to be a most warm-hearted man, his conversation very animated, and he has the heartiest and happiest laugh I ever heard from a man of his years.

You designate yourself 'a conservative Whig'. I could not but smile at both substantive and adjective. You and men of your opinions have piloted the Vessel, and navigated her into the Breakers, where neither Whig nor Tory can prevent her being dashed to pieces. I shall look out for the quietest nook I can find in the center of Austria, where I shall be glad to give you welcome to a crust when you shall be tired of improving a thankless world.

You would observe that a cheap edition of my poems is advertized in 4 Vols. Help the sale, if you can, till I get back my own money, which I shall have to advance to the amount of 4 or 500 £. My terms of publication are 2 thirds of the risk and expense for what the Publishers calls two thirds of the profit—but this if I recollect right I told you before.

Yesterday, notwithstanding the state of my Eyes, I was on the top of Helvellyn with my friend Mr. Julius Hare of Trinity Col: Dr Arnold, Master of Rugby,—as keen a reformer as yourself, or any other dissenting Whig,—and Mr Hamilton,[2] author of Cyril Thornton, etc., etc., also a Brother of Professor Buckland.[3] We tempered our Brandy with water from the highest, and we will therefore infer the purest, Spring in England, and had as pleasant a day as any middle-aged Gentlemen need wish for, except for certain sad recollections that weighed upon my heart. Once I was upon this summit with Sir H. Davy and Sir W. Scott;[4] and many times have I trod it with my nearest and dearest relatives and friends, several of whom are gone, and others going to their last abode. But I have touched upon too melancholy a String. Life is at

---

[1] See Ls. 704 and 705 above.

[2] For Capt. Thomas Hamilton, see L. 673 above.

[3] The Revd. John Buckland (b. 1786), a college friend of Thomas Arnold, who had married his sister Frances in 1816. He ran a preparatory school at Laleham, at first in partnership with Arnold, and then independently. He was the brother of the Revd. William Buckland, D.D., F.R.S. (1784–1856), Professor of Mineralogy at Oxford from 1813, who wrote a notable Bridgewater Treatise on *The Power, Wisdom, and Goodness of God as manifested in the Creation*, 1836, and became Dean of Westminster in 1845.

[4] In 1805.

best but a dream, and one in times of political commotion too often crowded with ghostly images. God preserve us all!

affectionately yours,
[*signed*] Wm Wordsworth

711. W. W. to ROBERT JONES

Address: The Revd Robt Jones, Plas yn Llan, near Ruthen.
MS. WL. Hitherto unpublished.

Rydal Mount July 22^d [1832]

My dear Jones,

Your letter, dated a month ago, reached this place when I was absent on a visit, together with Doro, to my Son at Moresby; it gave us all much pleasure as containing favourable accounts of yourself and family. I wish I could return you the same; but alas! my poor dear Sister has been for nearly 8 months confined to her room by sickness and debility. In Decr last she was seized again with internal inflammation, which attack, tho' far less violent than that from which she suffered 2½ years ago, has produced more serious effects, as acting upon a frame so much weakened. But I will not dwell on this affecting subject; and will only add that she bears her confinement, and what she has not unfrequently, of pain and her debility with entire resignation; and most admirable cheerfulness. Her mind is rich in knowledge, and pleasing re-membrances; in which, and her religious faith, she finds thro' the blessing of God, abundant consolation. From her state, were there no other reason, you see that we cannot avail ourselves of your very kind and pressing invitation, to visit you during the present summer.

With much concern I have observed in the Papers that the Cholera has been fatal in the Town of Denbigh. Your Brother's family I hope have escaped. We have the disease on all sides of us at Carlisle, Maryport, Workington—and so near as Kendal. So that Ambleside can scarcely escape. I ought to tell you that except for the complaint in my eyes, I have been in perfect health since you left us;[1] and that Mrs W. Miss H. and Doro are also very well. Mr Fleming[2] has been absent some time, having been called into the South to attend a dying B^r. The duty of his Church for the

---

[1] On 9 Nov. 1831, at the end of his last visit to Rydal Mount.
[2] The Revd. Fletcher Fleming, incumbent of Rydal.

last 4 Sundays has been performed by Dr Arnold, Master of
Rugby, who has taken a House for the holidays at Brathay—two
miles off.

The Mr Landor[1] you mention came by Steam from Liverpool to
Whitehaven, and called upon me at my Son's—and next day I
joined him at Wastwater where we spent a day together in a House
that Mr Stansfield Rawson of Halifax has built there—Mr Landor's
companion was Mr Ablett, a neighbour of yours in the Vale of Clwyd.

Did you observe that my Son had got another living,[2] to which
he was kindly presented by the Earl of Lonsdale—it is a vicarage
of something less than £200 a year—beautifully situated on the
banks of my native stream the Derwent, 2 miles below Cockermouth. Unluckily there is no Parsonage—he thinks of building
one, and in that case will give up Moresby, which clear of deductions does not bring him in £100 a year. My son W^m is in good
health at Carlisle—but this day we learn from him that the Cholera
is not abated there. My eldest Brother's Son,[3] whom I think you
saw, is with a Surgeon in London, and we have very favourable
accounts from his Master of his behaviour etc. D^r W's youngest
Son Chris. is now travelling in Greece—he is very industrious as we
hear and makes friends wherever he goes—and if his life be spared
will return home an accomplished Person. John and Cha:[4] talked of
going this summer to Paris—but as the Cholera is broken out again
they may perhaps be deterred. Mr Julius Hare, late of Trin. Coll.[5]
will be the Bearer of this letter to St Asaph.—he has been staying
10 days with us. Dr Arnold he and I and two other Friends clomb
to the top of Helvellyn last Friday; and tomorrow we mean, before
the Coach takes Mr H. from us at 4 o'c, to ascend Fairfield, the
Mountain immediately behind our House. I once was upon the top
of Helvellyn with Sir Humphrey Davy—and Sir Walter Scott now
languishing under paralysis[6]—they were both younger then than

---

[1] For Landor's recent visit, see L. 704 above.   [2] Brigham.
[3] R. W.'s son, John, now studying with Mr. Gardner.
[4] i.e. C. W.'s other sons, John and Charles.
[5] Now rector of Hurstmonceaux, Sussex. Writing on 4 Aug. to thank W. W.
for his hospitality, Julius Hare expressed the hope that Landor and he might
have W. W.'s company on their journey back to Italy: 'How overjoyed we
should both be if you could join our party! One should look on the wreck of a
former civilization with increast interest now that ours seems to be passing
away from us, and that the nation seems to be on the point of sinking into its
second savagehood, now that our aristocracy has been deprived of its power by
Lord Grey, and that the House of Peers is headed by Lord Billingsgate.'
(*WL MSS.*)
[6] Scott had set out by steamboat from London on his last journey home on
7 July, arriving at Abbotsford on the 11th.

myself—Sir H. many years younger; and when I trod that elevated ground, where I had stood with them, I felt cause to be grateful to Almighty God for still preserving to me my faculties both of body and mind. I am glad that your Sisters were pleased with the *Excursion*—a new Ed: of my Poems has just been published in 4 Vols—the price only 24/-.

I shall receive with great pleasure your Welsh and English Dictionary. Remember me most affly to your Family—not forgetting your Brother and his family—and believe me with best regards from every one here

your faithful Friend   Wm Wordsworth

Pray let me hear from you.

712. W. W. to DAVID LAING

Address: D. Laing Esqr, South Bridge S^t, Edinburgh.
Franked: Penrith July twenty eight 1832 Lonsdale.
Postmark: (1) 28 July 1832 (2) 29 July 1832. *Stamp*: Penrith.
MS. Edinburgh University Library.
Geoffrey Bullough, 'The Wordsworth–Laing Letters', MLR xlvi (1951), 1–15 (—).

[*In M. W.'s hand*]

Rydal Mount July 27th [1832]

My dear Sir,

I have been waiting more than 3 weeks with the hope that an inflammation in my eyes would subside, and allow me to thank you with my own hand for the letter and the valuable present which accompanied it—but I am notwithstanding still obliged to employ an Amanuensis.

A good part of the Drummond Papers has been read to me,[1] and I find them both curious and interesting. The Volume of loco-descriptive Poetry[2] I value much: and the Editor's own Poem of the

---

[1] See 'A Brief Account of the Hawthornden Manuscripts in the possession of the Society of Antiquaries of Scotland; with Extracts, containing several unpublished Letters and Poems of William Drummond of Hawthornden', read to the Society by David Laing in 1828, and published in *Archaeologia Scotica: or, Transactions of the Society of Antiquaries of Scotland*, iv (1857), 57–116.
[2] *Scottish Descriptive Poems; with some illustrations of Scottish Literary Antiquities*, Edinburgh, 1803. W. W.'s copy is now in the British Library. The editor was Dr. John Leyden (see pt. i, L. 201), Scott's helper in the earlier volumes of the *Border Minstrelsy*, who became an expert on Eastern languages and died in Java. He also published *Scenes of Infancy: descriptive of Teviotdale*, Edinburgh, 1803 (*R.M. Cat.*, no. 582).

same class 'Scenes of Infancy' I happen to possess. If the Collection should ever be re-printed, it would be well to add that, and some others, perhaps, that have since appeared.

You would probably notice an announcement of a new Ed: of my Poems, with some additions, *compressed* into 4 vols. As I shall have to advance a considerable sum of money towards the Work, you would serve me by helping an *early* Sale, if it be in your power.

I was much concerned to learn from your letter, that your worthy Father was no more. When I had the pleasure of seeing him last Autumn, he appeared in good health, and vigorous for his years. My Sister, Daughter and myself sympathize with you and your Family upon this sad occasion.

Miss Laing and you will be grieved to hear, that my Sister, whose health received a great shock two or three years ago, has for these last 8 months been in a languishing condition, and in a great measure confined to her room. If she knew I were writing she would beg her kind remembrances. My Daughter and I had a very agreeable tour in the Highlands—tho' the Season was so late and the weather very unsettled: but the vapours and the rainbows and the rich tints of the decaying foliage made us ample amends. We slept two nights in the Isle of Mull, but it rained all the time we were there.

Poor Sir Walter is returned to Abbotsford, the hopes of his Friends unhappily disappointed.

Believe me to be with kind regards to your Sister and Mother, very truly yr obednt

[*signed*] Wm Wordsworth

713. W. W. to THOMAS HAMILTON

Address: T. Hamilton Esqe. [*In Dora W.'s hand*]
MS. Mr. W. Hugh Peal. Hitherto unpublished.

Rydal Mount
Sat. Morn. [? Summer 1832]

My dear Sir,
Miss H. and I mean to ride—will you accompany us as soon after eleven as may suit you—

ever yours
WW.

714. W. W. to C. W.

Address: Revd Dr Wordsworth, Buckstead, Uckfield, Sussex.
Franked: Penrith August Five 1832 H. C. Lowther.
Postmark: 6 Aug. 1832. *Stamp*: Penrith.
MS. British Library. Hitherto unpublished.

Lowther Saturday
[4 Aug. 1832]

My dear Brother,

My eyes have been and still are in such a state that I must write you but a short Letter, and on business merely.

Your acceptance of Mr Gardner's draft at six months will be for 100 *guineas* and not pounds. I have very good accounts of Sockbridge John,[1] so that appears ground for fair hopes of him.—

I trust your Vote for West^nd will not be wanted,[2] but one ought to be prepared, and I therefore beg you would be so kind, as to write me here, by return of post under cover to Lord Lonsdale with your name in the *middle* of half a sheet of paper, so that we can fill up the form and have it presented to the overseer where your freehold lies. I left Rydal yesterday—all well except our dear Sister, who though suffering less than she has often done, neither gathers strength nor flesh, but I should fear is weaker every month: She was out in a closed carriage a few days ago, and was certainly rather better for the ride—but what one dreads is a relapse, and every relapse however slight, finding her weaker, leaves her more and more so.

Dear Isabella also has been and is very unwell. She has had a case of severe English Cholera in the house, which agitated her much—and she is very weak from constant sickness, being in a family way. One of the servants of Workington Hall has died of the malignant cholera, which has been very bad at Maryport, Workington, and Carlisle—it is now a bit abated at Kendal.

We are very anxious to hear about Chris:[3] where are John and Charles; give my kindest love to them all.

ever your affectionate Br
Wm Wordsworth

---

[1] R. W.'s son.

[2] C. W. had a vote by virtue of his share in the Ivy How syndicate (see *MY* ii. 509). At this stage in the run-up to the elections to the reformed Parliament, it was not yet clear whether Westmorland was again to be contested by the two Lowther brothers standing against John Foster Barham (see L. 666 above).

[3] C. W. jnr. was travelling in Greece in the company of a Trinity friend Richard Monckton Milnes, later 1st Lord Houghton (1809–85), the poet and

715. W. W. to HENRY WILLIAM PICKERSGILL

Address: H. W. Pickersgill, Esq^e, 18 Soho Square, London [*In Dora W.'s hand*]
Postmark: 25 Aug. 1832. *Stamp*: Kendal Penny Post.
MS. Mr. W. Hugh Peal. Hitherto unpublished.

Rydal Mount
near Ambleside
Thursday noon
[23 Aug. 1832]

My dear Sir,

It gives me great pleasure to learn that we shall see you here so soon;[1] but I regret to say that your precursor, has not yet reached us. I should have answered your Letter yesterday but from the hope that to day I might have had it in my power to tell you that the Canvass had arrived. Remember that my House is only a mile and a half beyond Ambleside, so that if you come by a Chaise or Car from Kendal you will have no occasion to stop at Ambleside.

The Coach leaves Kendal every morning between 7 and 8 oclock, and passes just under my House a little after ten. If you come by that Conveyance and the morning prove fine, by all means travel on the outside for the sake of the fine views.

I remain dear Sir
very faithfully yours
Wm Wordsworth

Pray remember that you are to be my Guest, on this point we must insist.—And if possible make such arrangements as will allow you time to see, under my guidance, something of the beauties of this charming Country—

politician, who published in 1834 his *Memorials* of the tour. C. W. jnr.'s *Athens and Attica: Journal of a Residence There* appeared in 1836. See James Pope-Hennessy, *Monckton Milnes, The Years of Promise*, 1949, pp. 54 ff.

[1] See L. 695 above. After a long period of uncertainty, Pickersgill had written on 20 Aug. promising to come within a fortnight in order to paint W. W.'s portrait for St. John's. 'I am detained in Town by the Speaker of the House of Commons, but the moment I have obtained all that is necessary from him . . . I shall put myself in the Mail, nor shall I rest until I reach Rydal.' (*WL MSS.*) See also L. 717 below.

716. W. W. to SIR GEORGE BEAUMONT

Address: Sir G. H. W. Beaumont Bart, Coleorton Hall, Ashby de la Zouch
[*In M. W.'s hand*]
Stamp: Kendal Penny Post.
MS. Pierpont Morgan Library. Hitherto unpublished.

Rydal Mount
Kendal. August 27th [1832]

My dear Sir George,

It is a long time since we heard from Coleorton. I have just read in the Papers that Lady B. has brought you another Son[1]—if this be so, accept our sincere congratulations upon the event; and be assured of our best wishes for the health of Mother and child.— It is time too that I should inquire after my little Godson;[2] Mr Longman, my Publisher, has been directed to prepare a Copy of the new edition of my Poems in 4 Vols and to send it to Lambeth[3] for him. I hope the time will come when he will value the Contents more as coming from one who stood in the Relation to him in which I stood, with but little hope, from my age and other circumstances, of being as useful to him as I could wish to be.

Having had the honor of a Letter from the Archbishop some time ago I learned with much concern that you had been unwell while in London during the Spring season. I hope that all traces of your Complaint are vanished; and that you and Lady Beaumont take much pleasure in your improvements at Coleorton. May I beg that when either of you write to the Archbishop or to Mrs Howley you would present Mrs Wordsworth's and my respectful remembrances. Judge of our indignation and sorrow when we read of the outrage[4] at Canterbury from which neither the Archbishop's exalted office, nor the admirable manner in which he fills it, nor his piety, nor his learning, nor his mild manners could protect him. But these are sad times, and all reflecting Men must tremble at the prospect before us. But it is our duty as Christians and Englishmen to *hope*, and not to abandon any effort to stem the evil Spirit of the age.

In the course of this week I hope to see Mr Pickersgill here. He is coming down to paint my Portrait for St John's Coll: Cam: the

---

[1] There is no record of the survival of this son born on 15 Aug. Presumably he died in early infancy.   [2] The Beaumonts' younger son, William.
[3] i.e. to Lambeth Palace, residence of the little boy's grandfather, Dr. William Howley.
[4] On 7 Aug. the Archbishop was mobbed and his carriage stoned while he was on his way to the Deanery. He had made himself unpopular with the masses for his opposition to the Reform Bill.

Master and Fellows having honoured me by requesting I would sit for the purpose of having the Picture placed among their Worthies. Whatever success Mr P. may have, he will not, I fear, come near the bust,¹ a cast of which we have, and it is greatly admired by every one. Remember me kindly to the Merewethers and pray my dear Sir George, let me hear from you at your early convenience. I ought to have told you that my dear Sister, though still very poorly, is something better.

With kindest remembrances to Lady Beaumont, in which all unite, ever faithfully Yours   W Wordsworth

717. W. W. to EDWARD MOXON

Address: Mr Moxon Bookseller, Bond Street.
Postmark: 14 Sept. 1832. *Stamp*: [   ] St. Soho.
MS. Henry E. Huntington Library.
K (—). *LY* ii. 630.

Wednesday 12th Sept^r [1832]
Rydal Mount

Dear Mr Moxon,

Mr Pickersgill is the Bearer of this to London, he has been painting my Portrait²—We all like it exceedingly as far as it is carried—it will be finished in London—Should you wish to see

¹ The Chantrey bust, commissioned by the late Sir George Beaumont.
² Pickersgill had now completed a preliminary chalk drawing of W. W.'s head (see *Frontispiece*), and prepared the ground for the half-length portrait in oils for St. John's, which was completed in the artist's studio in London by the following May (*HCR* i. 426). 'Only the face is finished,' Dora W. wrote to Mrs. Rose Lawrence on 27 Sept., 'and the figure just rubbed in. He is placed on, or rather reclining upon, a rock on his own terrace with his cloak thrown over him, and a sweet view of Rydal Lake in the distance. The attitude is particularly easy and the whole thing perfectly free from anything like affectation.' (*K* ii. 503). See Blanchard, *Portraits of Wordsworth*, pp. 74–8. Pickersgill had spent ten days at Rydal Mount. 'Our garret was the only corner of the house that afforded a high light,' Dora W. explained to Maria Kinnaird on 15 Oct., 'so there the picture was painted, and as Mr P. liked to have people with him to keep the Poet from thinking of where he was and what he was doing every one that came was introduced into the garret and great fun we had.' (*WL MSS.*) Pickersgill's likeness was at first highly praised in the Wordsworth circle: 'All that I need say is none of the females of this house could gaze upon it for 5 minutes with eyes undimmed by tears . . .', was Dora W.'s verdict in the same letter. And her feelings were echoed by W. W. himself in his sonnet, 'Go, faithful Portrait!' (*PW* iii. 50). But though the portrait remained the best-known likeness of W. W. during his lifetime, the initial enthusiasm of the family cooled off somewhat: perhaps when it became clear that the refinement and sensitivity of the preliminary drawing had not been recaptured in the finished oil painting.

it in the present State you can call at his House; but not till a month hence, as it will remain here some little time.—

I have to ask of you a favor; in all probability it will be engraved,[1] but not unless we could secure before-hand 150 Purchasers. I do not say *Subscribers* for it would not be asked as a favor. To further the intent may I beg of you to receive the names of such persons as it *might* suit, to write them down in your Shop?

I hope your tour in Scotland proved agreeable—my dear Sister does not recover her strength.—All send their kind regards.

ever faithfully yours
W Wordsworth

Pray mention the Contents of this Letter to Mr Rogers with my affectionate remembrances.

I ought to have said that it is not wished to have a *Board* or Advertisement of this intention in your Shop, but merely that you should receive such Names as might offer.

718. W. W. to THOMAS ARNOLD[2]

MS. untraced.
K. LY ii. 631.

Rydal Mount, Tuesday, Sept. 19th, 1832.

My dear Sir,

Yesterday Mr Greenwood[3] of Grasmere called, with a letter he had just received from Mr Simpson—the owner of Fox How —empowering Mr G. to sign for him an agreement, either with yourself or any friend you may appoint, for the sale of that estate for £800; possession to be given, and the money paid, next Candlemas. . . . I need not say that it will give me pleasure to facilitate the purchase, as far as is in my power. . . .

Faithfully yours,
William Wordsworth

---

[1] The first of the three known engravings of Pickersgill's portrait was by William Henry Watt (b. 1804). It was used as the frontispiece to the *Poetical Works* of 1836–7.

[2] Earlier this year Thomas Arnold had written to W. W., 'We are quite earnest in our Request that you will remember our wish to become Inhabitants of your neighbourhood, when any Thing likely to suit us presents itself . . .' (*WL MSS.*); and he was now negotiating, through W. W., for the purchase of the Fox How estate on the bank of the Rotha, adjoining Fox Ghyll, with a view to building a holiday house on it. See also L. 721 below.

[3] James Greenwood of the Wyke (see L. 686 above).

719. W. W. to JOHN GIBSON LOCKHART

Address: J. G. Lockhart Esqre, Abbotsford, Melross. [*In M. W.'s hand*]
Stamp: Kendal Penny Post.
MS. National Library of Scotland.
LY ii. 631.

Rydal Mount
September 24th [1832]

My dear Sir,
  Many thanks for your Letter. Sir Walter's death[1] is indeed a 'Release', so that the language of condolence would be out of place here. Be assured however that every member of my family sympathizes deeply with you and Mrs Lockhart and Miss Scott— above all I cannot but feel for her upon whom her poor Father for the latter years of his life must have leaned so much.[2]—I am very loth to be troublesome to you upon an occasion that will involve you in so many occupations and engagements, but allow me to say that we should be thankful if you let us know by and bye how Mrs Lockhart and Miss Scott support their loss, and how as to health and spirits you all are.
  Believe me with kind remembrances from all here
faithfully your obliged
Wm Wordsworth

Mr Hamilton[3] is in the Highlands.

720. W. W. to ROBERT EAGLESFIELD GRIFFITH[4]

Address: Robt Griffiths Esqre, Philadelphia. [*In M. W.'s hand*]
Endorsed: Mr Wordsworth Rydal Mount Oct 6. 1832.
MS. Historical Society of Pennsylvania.
LY ii. 632.

Rydal Mount Oct^br 6th [1832]

My dear Sir
  My Sister begs that I would write you a few words, as she was obliged to close her Letter abruptly. Not knowing what it con-

---

[1] Sir Walter Scott had died at Abbotsford on 21 Sept.
[2] Anne Scott did not survive her father for long: she died the following June.
[3] Capt. Thomas Hamilton.
[4] W. W.'s second cousin, the Philadelphia merchant (see *EY*, p. 12).

tained, and unwilling to burthen you with repetitions, I must confine myself to assuring you that we shall be glad to hear from you at all times, and happy to pay attention to any of your friends whom curiosity may lead to visit this interesting part of England. My dear Sister may not have entered into particulars of her long—but you will be happy to hear, not at all times painful illness. She is often, and for several days together, though weak, free from painfull sensations; and being fond of reading she supports confinement with chearfulness. During the summer also, and up to this time, when the air has not been damp, she has ridden out regularly in an open Carriage—but her Constitution has had a severe shock, we have however great cause to be thankful.—

The health of all the rest of my family is good, and the portion of happiness which God has voutchsafed to grant us, appears to exceed the common lot of mankind. May we be duly sensible of his goodness! For my own private concerns, except my dear Sister's illness, I have nothing to lament; on *public* accounts however I am troubled with much anxiety. A spirit of rash innovation is every where at war with our old institutions, and the habits and sentiments that have thus far supported them; and the ardor of those who are bent upon change is exactly according to the measure of their ignorance.—Where men will not, or through want of knowledge, are unable to, look back they cannot be expected to look forward; and therefore, caring for the present only, they care for *that* merely as it affects their own importance. Hence a blind selfishness is at the bottom of all that is going forward—a remark which in other words was made by Mr Burke long ago—farewell believe me my dear Sir, faithfully yours

Wm Wordsworth

P.S. My Sister did not know that Miss Douglas[1] was coming back this way or she would not have closed her Letter so hastily.

---

[1] Harriet Douglas was about to return to America. She was still being courted by Francis Ogden (1783–1857), the steam engineer, American consul at Liverpool from 1830, who called at Rydal Mount this month (*RMVB*); but soon after her return home she was married to Henry Cruger, a New York lawyer. The marriage was not a happy one, and broke up a few years later. For a full discussion of W. W.'s American friends and visitors, see Alan G. Hill, 'Wordsworth and His American Friends', *Bulletin of Research in the Humanities*, lxxxi (1978), 146–160.

721. W. W. to [? JAMES GREENWOOD][1]

MS. Harvard University Library.
LY ii. 633.

[*In M. W.'s hand*]

[9 Oct. 1832][2]

My dear Sir

Yesterday I rec^d a letter from Dr Arnold, who begs me 'to ask you, or Mr Simpson's Solicitor at Ambleside, to send up an abstract of the Title and of the terms of the Contract of the Sale to Messrs Jones and Ward, No 1 St John St, Bedford Row, London'. He adds, 'I have no objection to the Property continuing with Mr Simpson till Candlemas; but I suppose we might begin any Improvements which we might wish to make on the Rock when I am down there in the Winter, as so long an Interval must take place between my Visits'.

The weather and other causes prevent my calling upon you—Perhaps you will communicate direct with D^r A, if any thing has to be said to him on the Subject.

Very sincerely y^{rs}
[*signed*] W. Wordsworth

722. W. W. to HENRY PHILLPOTTS[3]

MS. Cornell.
Broughton, p. 69.

Rydal Mount
24th Octr 1832.

My Lord

It gives me pleasure to comply with the request your Lordship and Miss Philpot have honored me with, and the more so, because the amended state of my eyes enables me to send a fairer sample of my handwriting than any scraps of Mss would have allowed. The

---

[1] James Greenwood was acting for Mr. Simpson, the owner of Fox How, in his negotiations with Dr. Arnold (see L. 718 above). Arnold had written to W. W. on 3 Oct.: 'I was delighted to find myself in a fair way of becoming a Proprietor of Land in Westmoreland', and he discussed at length the impending general election and his plans for Rugby. 'We are still going on most comfortably in the School, both as regards the Health of the Boys and their moral State. In both we must be prepared for Clouds and Storms,—but I shall be sorry to be insensible to the Delights of the present fair weather, though it were to change tomorrow.' (*WL MSS.*)   [2] Date added in another hand.
[3] Henry Phillpotts (1778–1869), Bishop of Exeter from 1830: a High-Churchman and disciplinarian of uncompromising views. W. W. had probably attended his consecration during the London visit of 1830–1.

558

passage is from the Excursion and will at least be recommended by
its moral.

I have the honor to be faithfully and with high respect

Your Lordship's

Ob^nt Servant

Wm Wordsworth

To Miss Philpot

As the ample Moon,
In the deep stillness of a Summer Even,
Rising behind a thick and lofty grove
Burns like an unconsuming fire of light
In the green trees; and, kindling on all sides
Their leafy umbrage, turns the dusky veil
Into a substance glorious as her own,
Yea with her own incorporated—by power
Capacious and serene; like power abides
In Man's celestial Spirit; Virtue thus
Sets forth and magnifies herself, thus feeds
A calm a beautiful and silent fire.
From the incumbrances of mortal life,
From error, disappointment—nay from guilt,
And sometimes, so relenting Justice wills,
From palpable oppressions of despair.

Excursion 4th Book[1]

Rydal Mount
23^d Oct^br—1832.

Wm Wordsworth

723. W. W. to JOHN MARSHALL

Address: John Marshall Esqr. Senr.
MS. Stephen Marshall MSS., Record Office, Preston.
Chester L. Shaver, 'Three Unpublished Wordsworth Letters', NQ ccxii (Jan.
1967), 14–18.

[Autumn 1832]

My dear Sir,

Bad spirits, and innumerable interruptions prevented my seeing
the property[2] upon Windermere again till about a fortnight ago.

---

[1] ll. 1062–77 (*PW* v. 142). As Broughton points out, the passage shows
numerous variations from the established text in punctuation, capitalization
and spelling.

[2] This estate is unidentified. John Marshall was investing money in land on
behalf of his sons at this time and had already bought the Derwentwater
Estate at Keswick (see also L. 699 above).

I did not find the owner at home, but I left your Queries at his House. He called on me next day and brought certain answers, but not to the most important points. He promised to call again with these answers and to let me see a plan of the Estate, but he has failed to do either, and yesterday I was told that he had sold 20 acres of the property lying along the lake at 100 £ an acre, an extravagant fancy price. The inquiries which I had made in other quarters respecting the farming value of the Estate, and the mode in which it had been treated for some time past made me rather indifferent about it, as it was clear that it could not answer for anyone but as a fancy-purchase, and in that light, as your Letter told me, you were not disposed to regard it. I begged the Man to fix his price, and his unwillingness to do this was probably the cause of his not keeping his engagement with me.—Upon the whole I feel, however, a little mortified that the Estate is not, after these 20 acres have been cut off, worth your looking at, as the situation though out of the way, and difficult of approach and the Land without a stick of timber is truly magnificent. The owner however from the first as it appears other persons had been looking after it was set upon a fancy-price.

You have heard me speak of the Estate of Brathay at the Head of Windermere—it is in point of beauty and appeal for this Country a fine property and must come into the Market if the present owner[1] has the power of selling it, which depends upon the Will of Mr Law of Brathay who died some 20 years ago I think. If any of your sons should like this part of the Country it would be well worth their ascertaining that point which might be done by inspecting that old Gentleman's Will. He left the Estate to a Brother who died not long ago at Ulverstone. I am sorry I do not recollect their christian names.

Believe me ever faithfully yours

W. Wordsworth

Betholme is the name of the present owner of the Brathay Hall Estate.

[1] As Shaver notes, this was John Law Beethom, nephew of George Law (1776–1802), who had acquired the estate not long before 1787 from the trustees of Gawen Brathwaite (d. 1772). Under Law's will of 21 Aug. 1802, the property went to his brother Henry (1745–1830) for life and was then to be held in trust for Beethom, son of Law's sister Sarah, until he came of age. Beethom was perhaps John, son of John Beethom of Heversham, who matriculated at Queen's College, Oxford, in 1806 at the age of sixteen. From 1804 Henry Law had rented the newly enlarged Hall to John Harden, but now the whole estate, including Brathay Hall and Old Brathay, was about to come on the market, and the Hardens were soon to move to Hawkshead (see L. 758 below).

724. W. W. to C. W.

Address: The Master, Trinity College, Cambridge.
Franked: Penrith November eight 1832 Lonsdale.
MS. British Library. Hitherto unpublished.

Lowther Castle
Thursday [8 Nov. 1832]

My dear Brother,

Since I left home last Monday with Mary and Dora who are now at Mr Marshalls at Halsteads upon Ulswater, a Requisition has been set on foot calling upon Lord Lowther to stand with his Brother as a second Conservative for the County of West[nd].[1] On casting up the Votes after a Registration it has been found that there is a decided Majority leaving no doubt of success for two Conservatives: and certain Gentlemen having called at Rydal Mount during our Absence from Rydal to request the signatures of our friends residing at a distance, Miss Hutchinson tells me that not doubting of your opinion upon this matter she has ventured to sign for you, and she begs me to let you know this in order that you may not be surprized to hear of it or at seeing the list. She has signed for my two Sons, and her own two Brothers[2] also.

Our dear Sister has been in but a languishing way for some time —the weather affects her greatly. Miss H. however, in her Letter of yesterday says that she was unusually well on Tuesday. She still rides out when the weather will allow. Isabella has been at the Island of Windermere during great part of the summer at first for ill health and afterwards to keep out of the way of the Cholera, which was severe at Whitehaven, with several deaths in John's own Parish. He had himself about the same time a severe attack of the Bowels. His wife is a good deal better but she is I think of a very weakly constitution. Dora has a severe cough and cold, which I think she does not manage well.—

I understand from the Blues of this neighbourhood that the Lord Chancellor[3] has prepared a Church Reform Bill upon a sweeping plan. No good can come from that quarter.—The politics of our two Counties stand thus[4]—two Conservatives for West[nd] one for

---

[1] See L. 714 above.
[2] Henry Hutchinson, now resident in the Isle of Man, and Thomas Hutchinson of Brinsop both had votes by virtue of their share in the Ivy How syndicate (see *MY* ii. 509).   [3] Lord Brougham.
[4] For the candidates and results in the impending elections in Cumberland and Westmorland, see Ls. 700 and 701 above. The two local reformist candidates, J. F. Barham (for Westmorland) and James Brougham (for Kendal), both called on W. W. during the election campaign (*RMVB*).

Cumberland, one through Lord Lonsdale's influence for Whitehaven. For Kendal—a Whig tending to Radicalism in James Brougham and Do two at Cockermouth, do two at Carlisle, do three for the County of Cumberland—that is in the two Counties 7 to 4: only I ought to observe that one of the Carlisle members James is an infidel Radical. He however I am told by an intelligent professional Gentleman of Carlisle might be turned out if [only some]¹ respectable Reformer would offer himself but there is not he tells me [the] least chance or possibility of a Tory being elected at Carlisle nor do I believe either at Cockermouth, Kendal nor I fear in any of the Towns of the new Constituencies in England where there does not happen to be, as at Whitehaven, a most powerful family, and then you must have a firm Man at the head of it. Sir John Ramsden² who has the command of Huddersfield has been driven out (though himself a high-flying Whig) from the place for fear of the Radicals of the place and neighbourhood who have no [Votes].³

Kindest love to John. Glad [? of news] of Chris and Charles

Affectionately Yours
W. W.

P.S. Parliament, it is thought, will be dissolved early next month— You must come down give your Vote and see our dear Sister—

725. W. W. to JOHN SPEDDING⁴

Address: John Spedding, Esq, Mirehouse, Keswick.
Franked: Penrith Nov ten 1832. W. Marshall.
Endorsed: Wᵐ Wordsworth.
Postmark: 10 Nov. 1832. *Stamp*: Penrith.
MS. Major J. H. F. Spedding. Hitherto unpublished.

Halsteads—Saturday.
[10 Nov. 1832]

My dear Spedding,

I am going to trouble you about a concern of mine upon which I cannot enter without first offering you and Mrs Spedding my sincere condolence upon the affliction you have lately had to sustain

¹ *MS. torn.*
² Sir John Ramsden, 4th Bart. (1755–1839), of Byrome Hall, Yorks. His son John Charles Ramsden (1788–1836) was one of the M.P.s for Yorkshire.
³ *MS. torn.*
⁴ W. W.'s school friend (see *EY*, p. 116; *MY* ii. 525), now living at Mirehouse on the shores of Bassenthwaite.

in the loss of a Son[1] whose Character is highly spoken of by every one who knew him—

The business upon which I hope you will excuse my troubling you relates to your late Uncle's Will Mr Gibson's;[2] it has struck me that you or one of your Sons might be an Ex^r, in which case, considering you as Resident at Mirehouse, you might benefit me considerably by paying the Duties through my office, which would be in due course of business. I may add that nothing is gained to the Estate of a Testator by paying the Legacy Duty into the Head-office London, while the Distributor of the District is deprived of his regular emoluments.—

My Son W^m resides at Carlisle as my Sub^{dr} and if these Duties could be paid to him, he would receive 30 Shillings per Cent and I shall receive 35 for the same. I need not say more to induce you to do any thing you can to serve me upon this occasion.

With Kindest [remembrances][3] to Mrs Spedding, I remain

faithfully yours
Wm Wordsworth

Mr Wm Marshall who franks this sends his Comp^{ts}.—

726. W. W. to WALTER FARQUHAR HOOK[4]

MS. untraced.
W. R. W. Stephens, Life and Letters of Walter Farquhar Hook, 2 vols., 1878, i. 238.

[Rydal Mount]
[*c.* 12 Nov. 1832]

Dear Sir,

I cannot but avail myself of the present opportunity to thank you for the very valuable volume of lectures[5] which I have had the

[1] John Spedding's youngest son Edward (b. 1811) had died in London on 24 Aug. at the age of 21. He is commemorated in Tennyson's lines *To J. S.*, addressed to his elder brother James.

[2] John Spedding had married (1799) Sarah, eldest daughter of Henry Gibson, surgeon, of Newcastle upon Tyne. The reference is to one of his brothers. [3] *MS. obscure.*

[4] The Revd. Walter Farquhar Hook (1798–1875), elder son of Dr. James Hook (1771–1828), Dean of Worcester, and nephew of Theodore Hook the journalist: incumbent of Holy Trinity, Coventry, 1828–37; vicar of Leeds, 1837–59; and thereafter Dean of Chichester: a High-Churchman of remarkable energy, author of *Lives of the Archbishops of Canterbury*, 12 vols., 1860–76. He met W. W. at Rydal Mount the following Aug. (*RMVB*), and called several times thereafter.

[5] *The Last Days of Our Lord's Ministry*, 1832, sent at the request of his mother who had been staying in Rydal (see next letter). Southey expressed

honour of receiving from you through the hands of your excellent mother. Having been absent from home I have not had opportunity yet to read more than the two first discourses, with the matter and manner of which I have been exceedingly pleased. The first and paramount importance of the subject cannot but recommend to general notice, at least so I trust a work executed with so much sincere piety and fervour, and with learning and ability of so high an order. Wishing you earnestly success in the labours of your ministry, and health and life to prolong them,

I remain, dear Sir,
Faithfully your obliged,
Wm Wordsworth

727. D. W. to JANE MARSHALL

Address: To Mrs Marshall, Headingley.
MS. WL.
LY ii. 634.

Rydal Mount, Tuesday 20th Nov^r, [1832]

My dear Friend

Dora is writing to Mary Anne,[1] and I cannot miss the opportunity of slipping a few lines into the frank, for though M. A. herself may be the Bearer of good news of me I know you will like still better to receive it from my own hand. I will not trouble you or myself with particulars. Enough to say that I am very much better—have now no regular or irregular maladies except the flatulence and pains in the Bowels—and I am certainly much stronger, less susceptible of changes in the atmosphere. My horrid cravings have quite left me.—It is true I have *sinkings* now and then; but any thing is better than the gnawing appetite with which I was for many days afflicted.

Dora's cough is still very troublesome; but her breathing is better; and with due care I trust she is in the road to perfect recovery. How unlucky that the pleasure of her very pleasant visit to Hallsteads should have been diminished by so troublesome a companion! Poor thing! the morning after her return she was very

his high opinion of the volume, in thanking Mrs. Hook for his copy on 24 Dec.: 'It will be placed upon the same shelf as the Bishop of Limerick's Sermons, the Bishop of Durham's, and John Miller's.—In these evil days it is well that we have such fruits of the present generation to produce.' (*MS. Mrs. Ann Coatalen.*)

¹ The Marshalls' eldest daughter.

ill, and was right glad to apply to a blister, though it always has a very weakening effect upon her.

Every day I am anxious till the letters arrive—Mr Ferguson[1] no doubt knows that my Friends were with you when the affecting tidings reached you, and no change having since taken place either much for the better or the worse is, I suppose, the reason of his not having written to me. My daily prayer for that best of Women[2] is now but that she may be spared from much bodily suffering. One cannot wish her life to be prolonged under the present decay of her mental powers; for there cannot be a hope remaining that *they* will be restored to her; but on the contrary her memory must daily become weaker. Do let us hear from you as soon as you have leisure, and tell us all you have heard from Halifax. Perhaps you and your Sister may yet once again see our beloved Friend. Your Sister, in a most kind letter which I received from her mentions that she had such a hope. Probably your Sisters did not tell you in what way they intended to administer to my pleasures and comforts, but *I* cannot help saying to you that so far from being ashamed of receiving such a Gift from *such* Friends I am proud of it. Already I have schemed for the supply of several small—*wants* I will not call them—but gratifications, such as I might otherwise have scrupled to indulge myself with. I will not trouble you with more on this subject, which is an affecting one to me.

We were much gratified by Mary Anne's letter, and especially her account of your delightful meeting at Headingley—the Grand-child's[3] joy—and above all poor dear Ellen's[4] happiness and her improved looks after such an attack of severe pain. Dear Creature! often have I thought of her when I felt the bliss of lying down upon my bed—worn out—yet free from pain. I have thought of *her* and of her grievous sufferings compared with mine. That difficulty in breathing is what I grieve for most in thinking of her. The contrast of my own easy breath makes it doubly felt by me when I lie down. Indeed I have often said that till within the last year I never knew what was the Blessing of a good bed to lie upon. Pray give my tender love to Ellen with sincerest wishes that she may be enabled to enjoy her Mother's company as long as you remain with her. When you write tell me all particulars concerning her, whether she leaves her room, if she can bear the society of the

---

[1] Edward Ferguson, Mrs. Rawson's nephew.
[2] Mrs. Rawson had been seriously ill, but she survived till 1837.
[3] William Marshall's son, John William: or possibly John Marshall jnr.'s son Reginald, b. 8 July.
[4] The Marshalls' fifth daughter.

Family, and whatever occurs to you as likely to interest me in regard to her.

Lady Farquhar etc. did not leave Fox Ghyll[1] till the Friday after my Friends parted from you. I hope they will all come again; for they are very amiable Women, and they so much enjoyed the Country. My Brother's severe cold left him marvellously. The ride outside the Chaise over Kirkstone instead of giving him cold tended to his cure—indeed I always hold that the Inside of a Coach or hack-chaise is the most cold-catching place in the world. My dear Sister is quite well. She and Miss Hutchinson have been happily and busily employed in knitting garters for you and your Sisters. How I have wished that *I* also could have sent my contribution!

I must have done, for I have another letter to write, and, believe me, I am grown so careful of myself that I endeavour always to prevent fatigue by leaving off writing while I have yet a hundred things to say. Adieu my dear Friend. With affectionate regards to Mr Marshall, and love to all the young ones, believe me ever your grateful and loving Friend

D. Wordsworth

I have never sent my thanks to Julia[2] for her very interesting letter. The feelings and sentiments she expresses meet with my entire sympathy. Will you tell her so?

728. W. W. to JULIET SMITH[3]

MS. Lilly Library, Indiana University. Hitherto unpublished.

⌈*There follows* To the Author's Portrait, *as in PW iii. 50, except that in l. 6 read 'In the hot crucible of change, wilt seem', in l. 8 'To think', and in l. 10 'a starting tear'.*⌉

Rydal Mount
28 Nov^{br} 1832.

My dear Madam,

Pray accept the above—a little stiff in the hand-writing which is partly owing to inexpertness in managing the horizontal Pen you

---

[1] Lady Farquhar, widow of Sir Robert Townsend Farquhar, had spent about ten weeks this autumn at Fox Ghyll with her daughter Anne (d. 1844), widow of Dr. James Hook, and her granddaughter Georgiana. D. W.'s MS. Journal (*WL MSS.*), which she was now well enough to resume, records their growing intimacy with the Rydal Mount household.

[2] The Marshalls' sixth daughter.

[3] Mrs. Juliet Smith, of Tent Lodge, Coniston (see *MY* ii. 409), mother of Elizabeth Smith, the scholar and translator (see pt. i, L. 317).

were so kind as to give me during my late very agreeable visit at
Tent Lodge.

ever sincerely yours
Wm Wordsworth

729. W. W. to RICHARD PARKINSON[1]

Address: The Rev^d. R. Parkinson, St. Bees. [*In Dora W.'s hand*]
Postmark: 6 Dec. 1832. *Stamp*: Whitehaven.
MS. Cornell.
Broughton, p. 70.

Rydal Mount
Tuesday evening [4 Dec. 1832]

Dear Sir,

I should have thanked you earlier for the agreeable Present of
your Vol: of Poems,[2] if I had not wished to peruse it first. I have
done so and with much pleasure. The principal I had read before,
and found it very interesting.—

The Legend of St Bega's Abbey[3] is well treated, and with the
concluding allusion to the College I was particularly pleased. The
feeling and expression are both excellent. Permit me to observe
that the agreeable lines upon the hermitage,[4] would be improved by
the omission of the stanza beginning Such was his life and also that
which follows. They distort the quiet tenor of the Poem. The line,
'Of[5] friend untimely snatched above,' is but a bad one, and might be
altered with advantage.

Excuse this hasty scrawl and believe me dear Sir

Your obliged Ser^{vnt}
Wm Wordsworth

---

[1] The Revd. Richard Parkinson, D.D. (1797–1858), was educated at
Sedbergh and St. John's College, Cambridge, and practised journalism for a
time in Lancashire before his ordination in 1823. Three years later he was
appointed theological lecturer at St. Bees College, and he remained there for
the rest of his life, becoming Principal in 1846. He was a Canon of Manchester
from 1830, and one of the founders of the Chetham Society. W. W.'s friendship with him seems to date from the summer of 1830 (*RMVB*).
[2] *Poems Sacred and Miscellaneous*, 1832. The volume included Parkinson's
Seatonian Prize Poem of 1830, *The Ascent of Elijah*.
[3] *A Legend of the Foundation of Saint Bega's Abbey*, op. cit., pp. 135–44.
W. W. was to take up the story of St. Bega himself the following year: see
Stanzas Suggested in a Steamboat off Saint Bees' Heads, on the Coast of Cumber-
land (*PW* iv. 25, 402–3).
[4] *The Hermitage*, ibid., pp. 121–3.
[5] W. W. misquotes, as Broughton notes. The text reads 'Or friend . . .'

730. W. W., D. W., and DORA W. to
JOHN WORDSWORTH

Address: John Wordsworth Esqre, Trin: Coll: Cambridge. [*In Dora W.'s hand*]
Stamp: Kendal Penny Post.
MS. British Library.
K (—). *LY ii. 679* (—).

[*W. W. writes*]

Wednesday December 5 [1832]

My dear John
    The last Cambridge paper proved to us very interesting, especially to your dear Aunt my Wife who is a keen Electioneerer.—
Who is to be set up against Lubbock now that Peel is retired?[1]
We of this family will be mortified above measure if you do not
triumph over this upstart. Here follows an Epigram for you,
allusive to the testimonials of the Astronomical Professor[2] *in
favor of J. Lubbock Esq^e as a Candidate to represent the University
of Cambridge in Parliament.*

> For Lubbock vote—no legislative Hack
> The dupe of History—that 'old almanack';
> The Sage has read the *stars* with skill so true
> The Almanack he'll follow, must be *new*.

    Now for Domestics—Your dear Aunt Dorothy is upon the whole
decidedly [*D. W. adds*: very much] better than she was three
months ago and looks [*D.W. adds*: much] better, [*D.W. adds a
footnote*:* I have been growing fatter regularly for many weeks.
D.W.] though she still suffers sharp pain occasionally; and is now
and then troubled with sickness. Dora has had a severe cold which
has reduced her a good deal but we hope she has seen the worst of
it. Her Mother started this morning in our Carriage for Moresby.

---

[1] William Peel (see L. 610 above) had retired from the Cambridge University
representation, and in the contest now impending, John William
Lubbock, F.R.S. (1803–65), later Sir John Lubbock, 3rd Bart., was offering
himself in the Whig interest. Banker, astronomer, and mathematician, he was
a man of many parts, prominent in the Society for the Diffusion of Useful
Knowledge, and later the first Vice-Chancellor of London University (1837–
42). He was opposed by Charles Manners-Sutton (see pt. i, L. 151), Speaker
in six successive parliaments, who had not yet received the peerage which was
his due, and by Henry Goulburn. Lubbock retired before the Poll closed on
14 Dec. and Manners-Sutton and Goulburn were returned without opposition.
    [2] George Airy (see pt. i, L. 8).

James[1] drives her. She will be a fortnight about. Mr. Hamilton[2] is gone to Edinburgh for 4 months. We expect Dr and Mrs Arnold[3] on the 22nd. As far as I could judge by a Letter received from him sometime ago he was much disgusted with the Radicals in his neighbourhood.[4] Politics are but gloomy in our two Counties. Lord Lowther is absent in Italy. The Whigs are about starting a second Candidate to turn out the Conservative for the West.[5] How Mr. Curwen will behave on this occasion is to be seen. He has been strictly catechized in a Meeting at Keswick and the like at Cockermouth. The Report of the latter Meeting has not transpired. But at Keswick in answer to the question about Church Reform, he declared that he would vote for a *thorough* Reform in the Church, a commutation of Tithes, better protection for the poorer orders of the Clergy, some *other* appropriation for the property of Deans and Chaplains and other clerical Bodies upon the Demise of the respective Holders and would enforce the Residence of Bishops in their several Dioceses, *they ceasing to be Members* of Parliament; Will you vote for Triennial Parliaments? Yes? Will you *obey* the intreaties of your *Constituents*? Yes if they come from a *County Meeting*, for if I do not obey I will resign. You know my dear Nephew what such things County Meetings are and have long been—Does not all this convince you that a thoroughpaced Whig whatever may be his intentions, will prove in conduct a Revolutionist? In justice however to Mr Curwen I must say that he declared upon questions being put he was against annual Parliaments and universal suffrage. In Westmorland we are most awkwardly situated—Tell your Father that a most powerful Requisition has been forwarded to Lord Lowther[6]—but he may not receive it in time; nor is it absolutely certain that he will comply with it. I

[1] James Dixon, the gardener and handyman.
[2] Capt. Thomas Hamilton.
[3] The Arnolds had taken Fox Ghyll for the Christmas holidays.
[4] In his letter from Rugby on 3 Oct., Thomas Arnold had written: 'I often think of your Sonnet on the French Revolution, "France, 'tis strange, has brought forth no such minds as we had then, etc"—and I fear the same may be said at this moment of England.—We have clever Men in Plenty, but a sad Lack of great ones,—by which I mean Men who can at once look above them and around them, who fear God, and have at once the ability and the will to serve him faithfully in guiding this great Nation through its most complicated difficulties.' He deplored the recent loss of Sir Walter Scott, 'his hankering after feudal Times, and Kings, and Barons, being a wholesome counteraction to the utilitarian Folly of the opposite Party'. (*WL MSS.*)
[5] i.e. in West Cumberland. Sir Wilfred Lawson, Bart. was proposing to stand in the Whig interest along with Henry Curwen, but he later withdrew (see L. 700 above).
[6] To persuade him to stand in Westmorland as well as West Cumberland. See L. 714 above.

cannot get up my Spirits; everything seems going *against* sober sense, against patience and justice.

Should the Epigram give you no pleasure—the following which I threw off this morning may perhaps make a little amends— [*In D.W.'s hand. She adds in the margin*: If you please, you may print this in the Chronicle immediately after the Epigram.]

addressed to Revolutionists of all Classes

If this great World of joy and pain
Revolve in one sure track,
If what has set, will rise again;
And what is flown, come back;
Woe to the purblind crew that fill
The heart with each day's care,
Nor learn, from past and future, still
To bear and to forbear.

Pray find a moment to tell us how you all are. Love to yourself and Charles, and to your dear Father—God bless him—he's a good man and true. If you think it worth while to print the Epigram don't tell that I wrote it.

Your most affectionate friend and Uncle
[*signed*] W. Wordsworth

Poor Owen[1] is not in the best way. He returned hither some time ago.

[*D.W. writes*]

My dear John: I cannot close up this half legible scrawl without a word to you and my dear Brother—I heartily wish you well through the troubles of your own Election and am selfish enough to wish that ours might bring him down to give us a helping hand— But I know not that so patriotic a wish can be called selfish, and much I fear that our languid Conservatives will let Barham[2] step in. Dear John I have often regretted that you were not a Freeholder of Westmorland.

Pray come down and make yourself one as fast as you can. My best love to Charles: yours ever D.W.

Ask Charles if my unfortunate present has ever yet been sent to my Herefordshire God-daughter?[3] I fear not—but tell him I should

---

[1] Owen Lloyd, John Wordsworth's cousin.
[2] John Foster Barham (see L. 666 above).
[3] Elizabeth Hutchinson.

THOMAS HUTCHINSON
from a portrait at Rydal Mount

like to add to its value by a small addition to the Gift (now it has been so slow in going). You would do me a kindness by selecting one other book—about 5/- value.

[*Dora W. writes*]

Father brings this to me to 'mend' but really I have not courage to try to decypher this *scrawl*. So you must make the best of it. I trust you and dear Uncle keep your health to help you somewhat thro' your troubles. How I wish you could have come to us this Xmas[1] when we have a quieter fireside to offer you than last year. Only Father and Mother and Daughter for Aunt W. still keeps upstairs and Aunt Sarah is going to leave us. We have had an account of your money paid into Masterman's Bank.

[*unsigned*]

731. W. W. to JOHN WORDSWORTH

Address: John Wordsworth Esqr, Trin. Coll. Cambridge.
Postmark: 8 Dec. 1832. *Stamp*: Penrith.
MS. British Library. Hitherto unpublished.

Lowther Castle 7th Dec^br
[1832]

My dear Nephew,

Knowing how much your Father is engaged I do not like to break in upon him, but through you. Pray let him know that the West^nd Election is fixed for Tuesday and Wednesday, 18th and 19th instant.[2] Lord Lowther along with his Brother will be put in nomination—in consequence of a Requisition to Lord L. signed by nearly 1,800—and accompanied with several hundred promises from men who did not sign the Requisition. The presence of all Friends who are not better employed for the cause elsewhere is wished for. Therefore if my Brother could come we should be glad. I have written to two of Mary's Brothers[3] and to Mr. Monkhouse[4]—to appear. My two sons[5] will be there—so that we should

---

[1] C. W. was induced to come to Rydal Mount later this month (*RMVB*), in time for the election on 18 Dec.

[2] The voting in the Westmorland election was as follows: Lord Lowther 2061, Col. Lowther 1953, John Foster Barham 1612. The Lowther candidates were therefore returned.   [3] Henry and Thomas Hutchinson.

[4] John Monkhouse of Stow. All three attended the election (see *RMVB*).

[5] John W. and W. W. jnr. had both been equipped with freeholds in Westmorland. John W.'s position in West Cumberland as the son-in-law of the

be quite a family party—and your dear aunt Dorothy would be so glad to see her Brother. The Whigs and Radicals having started another Candidate[1] for the West of Cumberland—the Conservatives are determined to oppose them with another also—and we have little or no doubt that we can bring in two so that the Conservative cause is looking up a little. As the Expense of both these Contests will fall upon the Lowther family, your Father will agree with me that after having spent nearly 160,000 pounds in resisting the enemy in this County they deserve the generous support and the personal exertions of all friends to good order and the British Constitution.—

I left here yesterday at one o'clock; and had the Moon for my Companion all along Ulswater side. My love of nature and the works of God in his Creation grows with my years. Riding tires my body, but my mind was soothed and happy.—

I see that the Speaker[2] stands for Cambridge University—I hope with every prospect of success. The last of the Squibs on the other side, was composed on horseback yesterday—you may burn them or do what you like with them, only don't let be known that I wrote them.—

Colonel Lowther is here—his B[r] still in Italy. Believe [me] my

> dear John John
> Your affectionate friend and Uncle
> W[m] Wordsworth

I have just seen that the University election takes place on the 12th so that there will be quite time for the Master to come to Rydal—

> For Lubbock vote—no legislative Hack
> The dupe of History—that old Almanack!
> The Sage has read the Stars with skill so true
> That Men may trust him, and be certain, too,
> The Almanack He'll follow must be *new*

Whig candidate was not easy. As Lord Lonsdale remarked to W. W. on 6 Jan. 1833: '. . . Your Son is one of those who must have felt the Embarrassment of his Situation, but Mr Curwen does not seem to be a Person of such austerity as to insist on carrying all the Members of his own Family along with Him on this occasion—indeed I should wonder if He did, as his Ideas on political matters don't seem to be accurately defined . . .' (*WL MSS.*)

[1] Sir Wilfred Lawson, Bart. See L. 700 above.
[2] Charles Manners-Sutton. See previous letter.

Now that Astrology is out of date,
What have the Stars to do with Church and State?
In Parliament should Lubbock go astray;
Twould be an odd excuse for Friends to say,
'He's wondrous knowing in *The Milky Way*!'

Question and Answer
'Can Lubbock fail to make a good M.P.
A Whig so clever in Astronomy?'
'*Baillie*,[1] a Brother-sage, went forth so keen
Of charge—for what reward?—the Guillotine:
Not Newton's Genius could have saved his head
From falling by the *Mouvements* he had led.'

Is the name of the french Astronomer spelt right? I have no
means of ascertaining, and rather think not.

Now for something more suitable to [your] [?][2] and taste. The
following was [com]posed in the Summer house at [Rydal at]
the end of the Terrace, whe[n the] wind was blowing high the
other Evening. Pray if you can find a moment's leisure read it to
your Father—

A Thought Upon the Seasons[3]

1

Flatter'd with promise of escape
   From every harmful blast,
Spring takes, O genial May! thy shape,
   Her loveliest and her last.

2

Less fair is Summer riding high
   In full meridian flower,
Less fair than when a lenient sky
   Brings on her parting hour—

[1] Jean Sylvain Bailly (1736–93), the French astronomer, took a prominent
part in the early stages of the French Revolution, and was elected President of
the National Assembly and Mayor of Paris in 1789; but he later fell into
disfavour, and was arrested and guillotined.

[2] *MS. torn*.

[3] See *PW* iv. 107. There are significant differences between the version
given here and the printed text, as published in 1835. In the I. F. note, the
poem is wrongly attributed to 1829.

When fields repay with golden sheaves
    The labour of the plough,
And, daily, fruits and forest leaves
    Are brightening on the bough,

What pomp what beauty, Autumn shows
    Before she hears the sound
Of Winter rushing in—to close
    The emblematic round!

Such be our Spring, our Summer such;
    So may our Autumn blend.
With hoary Winter; and Life touch
    Through heav'n-born hope, her end!

732. W. W. to VINCENT NOVELLO[1]

Address: Vincent Novello, Esqre, 67 Frith St, Soho Square, London [*In M. W.'s hand*]
Stamp: Kendal Penny Post.
MS. Cornell.
LY i. 507.

[? mid-Dec. 1832]

My dear Sir,
    There was not the least occasion to make an apology for your letter to which I reply by return of post, the Master of Trinity being now under my roof. I have put your letter into his hands, and he will take it with him to Cambridge whither he goes in a few days. He bids me say that your application and letter will be treated with due consideration and respect; that the election will take place early in Febry and that application and testimonials ought to be addressed to the Master's Lodge, Trin: Coll. Cambridge, on or before the 20th of Jan^ry. He adds that the choice will be made without favor or partiality, nothing being attended to but professional skill and character. I may add however on my own part

---

[1] It is impossible to be sure about the date of this letter. De Selincourt assigned it to Aug.–Sept. 1830; but it seems more likely to belong to Dec. 1832, when C. W. paid a brief visit to Rydal Mount, and to refer to the election of Thomas Attwood Walmisley (1814–56) as organist of Trinity early in 1833. Vincent Novello (1781–1861), organist, composer, and editor, author of the *Life of Purcell*, founded, with his son, the famous firm of musical publishers. He lived in Frith St. from 1830 to 1834. W. W. had probably already met him in London, for he had a wide circle of friends, including the Lambs (see Elia's 'Chapter on Ears') and the Leigh Hunts. His daughter Mary Cowden-Clarke wrote *The Life and Labours of Vincent Novello*, 1864.

that a testimonial from a gentleman so distinguished for professional abilities and Genius as Mr Novello will hardly fail of being duly appreciated.

Excuse extreme haste to [? serve]¹ the Post, and believe me very

Sincerely yours
Wᵐ Wordsworth

733. W. W. to DERWENT COLERIDGE²

Address: The Revᵈ Derwent Coleridge, No 12 Frankfort Street, Plymouth.
Stamp: Kendal Penny Post.
Endorsed: From Wᵐ Wordsworth Esqʳ. Stamford School.
MS. Miriam Lutcher Stark Library, University of Texas. Hitherto unpublished.

[28 Dec. 1832]

My dear Derwent,

It is an awkward thing to give the testimonial you request; I am far from being satisfied with what you will find on the other side.

—My poor Sister continues very feeble—and I am sorry to say that Dora whom you so kindly invite is far from well. She has had an ugly cold for nearly three months—and I do not think her at all likely to throw it off speedily. Mrs W. and Miss H. are well.

It grieves us all to hear that Miss Trevennon³ is in weak health. All beg their love to her—and believe us with kind regards to yourself and Mrs C from all

faith. yours
W W.

I gave a Letter of Introduction to you, to Mr Tatham⁴ who has lately been presented by Lord Grenville⁵ to the Rectory of Bradock etc. You will find him an aimiable young man of sound principles.

¹ *MS. illegible.*
² Derwent Coleridge, headmaster of Helston Grammar School, was now applying for a similar post at Stamford School, Lincs., and wrote to W. W. for a testimonial. See next letter.　　³ For Emily Trevenen, see L. 463 above.
⁴ The Revd. Arthur Tatham (1809–74), of Magdalene College, Cambridge, rector of Boconnoc with Bradoc, Cornwall, from 1832. He had spent the previous summer in the Lakes and made the Wordsworths' acquaintance. See M. W.'s MS. letter about him to Emily Trevenen on 16 Sept. (*Victoria University Library, Toronto*).
⁵ For Lord Grenville, see pt. i, L. 233. He had married in 1792 the Hon. Anne Pitt (1772–1864), only daughter of Thomas, 1st Lord Camelford (1737–93), and sole heiress of her brother Thomas (1775–1804) the 2nd and last Baron, through whom she had inherited the Boconnoc estate.

734. W. W. to DERWENT COLERIDGE

Endorsed: Testimonial—From Wm Wordsworth Esqr.
MS. Miriam Lutcher Stark Library, University of Texas.
*Testimonials of the Rev. Derwent Coleridge, A.M. Head Master of Helleston
Grammar-School, Cornwall, 1840, p. 19.*[1] *The Wordsworth Circle, Summer, 1976.*

Rydal Mount
28th Dec^br 1832

My dear Sir,
It is to be feared that with reference to the office you are soliciting
you overrate my good opinion, not only from partiality towards
your old Friend, but also because I have seen little of you since
you left the North, for College. Up to that time from your infancy
you were almost constantly under my eye and I can affirm conscientiously that I had always a high opinion of your abilities, that
your temper was aimiable, and your conduct most praise-worthy.

It gives me great pleasure to add, that by estimable Persons
living in the neighbourhood of Hells[ton] where you have resided
for some years I have repeatedly heard you spoken of in high terms
of respect; both as a Member of Society; a Preacher of the Gospels,
and a diligent able and successful Schoolmaster.

Happy should I be to hear that you were elected to the office of
Head Master of Stamford School, for which you tell me you are a
Candidate, and believe me my dear friend

faithfully yours
Wm Wordsworth

735. W. W. to EDWARD MOXON

Address: Mr Moxon, Bookseller, New Bond S^t. [*In Dora W.'s hand*]
Postmark: [   ] 183 [?]. *Stamp*: Fleet St.
MS. Cornell. Hitherto unpublished.

[Dec. 1832]

My dear Sir,
I wish to make a Present of a Copy of my Selections[2]—be so
good as to send one handsomely bound to me through the address I

---

[1] Derwent Coleridge was not appointed to the post at Stamford, but he kept
W. W.'s testimonial by him, and it was published eight years later when he
was nominated by the Professors of London University for the headmastership
of the City of London School.
[2] Published by Moxon the previous year.

576

gave you—Whitakers through Hudson and Nicholson[1] to Troughton Ambleside. Pray send also through Whitaker Keith[2] on the
Prophecies—Waugh and Innes Edinburgh Whitaker London
ever faithfully yours
W. Wordsworth

Along with these books pray give a Short Note telling how the
Bookselling trade goes on especially any thing in which you
yourself may be concerned. We were most grieved to see in the
Paper, the Death of Mr Henry Rogers.[3] Pray how does our common
friend the Poet bear this serious loss?—My Sister continues very
poorly.

I hope you are quite well as I and Mrs W. and Miss H. all
are. My Daughter has been suffering from a severe Cold.

736. W. W. to JOHN GARDNER

Address: Mr Gardner [*delivered by hand?*]
MS. Cornell. Hitherto unpublished.

[*In M. W.'s hand*]

[late 1832 or early 1833]
My dear Sir

Tho' I have had no communication with yourself, it always gives
me pleasure to hear by my Nephew's[4] letters that Mrs G. and you
are well.—I have been made somewhat uneasy, from Mr Lloyd's[5]
report of John's appearance—his remarkable growth, and extreme
thinness,—more especially as he had himself mentioned the return
of his cough—At the same time I feel assured that if any thing
serious threatened his health I should have heard from you. I would

---

[1] The Kendal booksellers.
[2] Dr. Alexander Keith (1791–1880), writer on prophecy. W. W. is either
referring to his *Evidence of the Truth of the Christian Religion from the Fulfilment of Prophesy*, 1828, or *The Signs of the Times; illustrated by the Fulfilment of
Historical Predictions*, 1832.
[3] Youngest brother of Samuel Rogers. He died this December, which settles
the date of the letter.
[4] R. W.'s son, John.
[5] Owen Lloyd.

however be much obliged to you when he next writes to his Cousin if you would add a word on this subject.

If you hear any tidings of Mr Boxall from Italy be so good as tell me about him, and how long he means to be absent. It has mortified me much that I cannot get any of my Friends and Acquaintances to be pleased with his Portrait of me as a likeness—or with the Print[1]—both of which they say are much too dark and gloomy, and they do not think the likeness happy—tho' on the other hand I have great pleasure in saying that the best judges of Painting as an art, speak of its execution in very high terms. With very kind regards and high wishes to Mrs G.

believe me d^r Sir

sincerely y^{rs}

[*signed*] Wm Wordsworth

737. W. W. to MR. BRAY[2]

Address: The Rev^d—Bray, Vicarage, Brigham, Cockermouth.
Postmark: 8 Jan. 183 [? 3]
Stamp: (1) Ambleside Penny Post. (2) Kendal·
MS. Cornell. Hitherto unpublished.

[*In M. W.'s hand*]

Rydal Mount Jan^{ry} 7th [? 1833]

Revd Sir,

As I understand from my Son, that (as his Curate, for the time being at Brigham) a Q^{rs} Salary, will be due to you on the 10th inst, at the rate of £75 a year; I have, according to his request, desired Mr Sanderson[3] my Subdistributor at Cockermouth, to pay you the sum of £18–15 upon your calling upon him for that purpose. Your receipt thro' Mr Sanderson will be a sufficient acknowledgment to my Son.

I am Sir Yours etc

[*signed*] Wm Wordsworth

---

[1] See L. 702 above.
[2] Unidentified: perhaps the Revd. Joseph Bray, of St. John's College, Cambridge, who at different times held curacies in Gloucester and Market Bosworth.
[3] A draper.

738. W. W. to ALEXANDER DYCE

Address: Revd Alex^r Dyce, 9 Grays Inn Square.
Postmark: 12 Jan. 1833. *Stamp*: Fleet St.
MS. Victoria and Albert Museum.
Mem. (—). *Grosart* (—). *K* (—). *LY ii. 637.*

> Rydal Mount,
> Kendal,
> 7th Jan^ry, 1833.

My dear Sir,

Having an opportunity of sending this to Town free of Postage, I write to thank you for your last obliging Letter. Sincerely do I congratulate you upon having made such progress with Skelton, a Writer deserving of far greater attention than his works have hitherto received. Your Edition will be very serviceable, and may be the occasion of calling out illustrations perhaps of particular passages from others, beyond what your own Reading, though so extensive, has supplied. I am pleased also to hear that Shirley is out.[1]

You mention with commendation the last Edition of my Poems. It gives me pleasure to learn that you approve it. It was my intention to send it to you, and unless some mistake prevented it, you must have received the work: if you have not pray send to Mr Longman the Slip of Paper on the opposite Page and he will forward a copy to your Address.

I lament to hear that your health is not good; my own, God be thanked, is excellent, but I am much dejected with the aspect of public affairs, and cannot but fear that this Nation is on the brink of great troubles.

Be assured that I shall at all times be happy to hear of your studies and pursuits, being, with great respect,

> sincerely yours,
> Wm Wordsworth

---

[1] *Dramatic Works and Poems of James Shirley*, 6 vols., 1833, the completion of Gifford's edition. As de Selincourt notes, Dyce edited part of Vol. vi, and wrote the Memoir. See also L. 752 below.

Address: Miss E. Hamilton, Observatory, Dublin.
Franked: Stamford January Fifteen 1833—Lonsdale.
Postmark: 15 Jan. 1833. *Stamp*: Stamford.
MS. Cornell. Hitherto unpublished.

Rydal Mount
Thursday—
Jan^ry 10th 1833

My dear Miss Hamilton,
   Your Letter has occasioned me much concern. You know how unwilling I am that Females of delicate mind should open their hearts to the rude breath of the Publick, by their Poetry or in any other way.—If therefore your motive for going to Press is *benevolence* merely that you may assist the distressed of your own unhappy Country, I should certainly say do your utmost to serve them in any other manner, by exertion among your wealthier friends, by writing exhortations in the Newspapers, or other Periodicals, and pointing out how the misery may be relieved. But if unfortunately you are induced to think of publishing by private expediencies or necessities, allow me first to express my sympathy, and to add that my objections to Publication in that case, fall to the ground: To come then to the point of your request—permission to transcribe from my Letters. I cannot bring my mind to consent to this—it is attaching far too much importance to words dropped in that way. [? There are] other objections also, and I think I could serve you better, by writing directly to my Friend, Mr Hamilton, Author of Cyril Thornton, who is now in Edinburgh. Let me observe with frankness and in the spirit of true Friendship to you my dear Miss Hamilton, that my name has often been treated with such Disrespect in the Magazine[1] alluded to, that I could not be persuaded to ask a *favor* from the Proprietor[2] who is at the same time the Conductor of it; but I will gladly mention to Mr Hamilton what your wishes are, and at the same time state how much I admire your genius, and have been touched with your sensibility. I am persuaded however that the rate of payment in that, and all other magazines, is small, especially to Authors *entering* the field. I have heard from Mr Hamilton that it would perhaps be worth the Proprietors while to pay *Mrs Hemans* well, provided she confined her productions to

---

[1] *Blackwood's Magazine*, for which Miss Hamilton wished to write.
[2] William Blackwood (1776–1834), the publisher. His son visited W. W. in May (*RMVB*).

their Magazine, but as they [   ] among many
periodicals,

[part of the page cut away]

and also I am deeply in debt to Sir Aubrey V. Hunt for a Poem[1]
addressed to me, and transmitted by your Brother. This communication would have been noticed with due respect almost immediately
after the Receipt of theirs, but the Letter was unfortunately mislaid,
and could not be found for several weeks—it is now recovered and
I hope to reply to it soon, but really I have been so dejected in
mind, by some private distresses, and still more by the alarming
State of public affairs in the two Islands, that I have not been able
to take the least pleasure in Poetry, or in my ordinary pursuits.—
In my Youth I witnessed in France the calamities brought upon all
classes, and especially the poor, by a Revolution, so that my heart
aches at the thought of what we are now threatened with—farewell.

[signature cut away]

740. W. W. to JOHN JEBB[2]

Address: The Right Revd The Bishop of Limerick, East Hill, Wandsworth,
    London.
Postmark: 28 Jan. 1833. *Stamp*: Kendal Penny Post.
MS. Mr. R. Jebb.
LY ii. 638.

Rydal Mount
Ambleside [c. 27 Jan. 1833]

My Lord,
    A short time since I received through the hands of Mr Southey,
your Reprint of Burnet's Lives[3] Etc, with Preface and Notes, a

---

[1] According to *K*, W. R. Hamilton had sent W. W. a copy of Aubrey de
Vere's madrigal, beginning 'May is the bridal of the year', which W. W.
mistakenly supposed was the work of his father. Aubrey de Vere (1814–1902),
the poet, third son of Sir Aubrey de Vere, Bart. (see L. 464 above), had recently entered Trinity College, Dublin, and was already an enthusiastic admirer
of W. W.

[2] Bishop of Limerick. See L. 596 above.

[3] *Lives, Characters, and An Address to Posterity, by Gilbert Burnet, D.D.,
Lord Bishop of Sarum, with the two Prefaces to the Dublin Editions*, edited by
John Jebb, 1833. The volume included Bishop Burnet's *Life of Sir Matthew
Hale* and *Life of John, Earl of Rochester*, and character sketches of (among
others) Archbishop Leighton and Robert Boyle from Burnet's *History of
His Own Times*, and was a reprint of the Dublin editions of 1803 and 1815.

valuable token of your regard for which I beg you to accept my sincere thanks.

The Prefaces by Mr Knox[1] were new to me; and I have read them with greater interest because they recall to me, along with your Lordship's account of the same Individual, an interview which I had with him at Dublin three years ago. I was introduced to him by Professor Hamilton of Trinity College Dublin, and was much delighted with his eloquent, philosophical and truly christian tone of conversation.

If Bishop Burnet's Life of Bishop Bedell[2] could have been abridged without material injury, it would have given me pleasure to see it in the Collection.

Scarcely any man has done more honor to the Episcopal office, and these times require as much as any ever did to be reminded of what a Blessing to a Country a good Bishop is. I have often expressed to D[r] W. my regret that Bp. Bedell's Life was not included in his ecclesiastical Biography.[3]

Pray present my kind regards to Mr Forster,[4] and believe me my Lord with sincere respect

most faithfully
your obliged Ser[nt]
W[m] Wordsworth

[1] Alexander Knox (1757–1831), for many years Jebb's friend and correspondent, was a lay theologian who in much of his teaching anticipated the Oxford Movement. His *Remains* were published in 4 vols., 1834–7.

[2] William Bedell (1571–1642), chaplain to Sir Henry Wootton when Ambassador to the Venetian Republic, became Provost of Trinity College, Dublin, in 1627, and two years later Bishop of Kilmore and Ardagh, where he worked energetically to reform ecclesiastical abuses. Burnet's *Life* (1685) won the admiration of Coleridge: 'What a picture of goodness! I confess, in all Ecclesiastical History I have read of no man so spotless: tho' of hundreds in which the Biographers have painted them as masters of perfection . . .' (R. F. Brinkley, *Coleridge on the Seventeenth Century*, Duke University Press, 1955, p. 374).

[3] C. W.'s *Ecclesiastical Biography* had appeared in 1810 (see *MY* i. 388).

[4] The Revd. Charles Forster, Bishop Jebb's chaplain, Chancellor of Ardfert, and later perpetual curate of Ash, near Sandwich: editor of *Thirty Years Correspondence between J. Jebb . . . and A. Knox . . .*, 2 vols., 1834, and author of *The Life of John Jebb, Bishop of Limerick*, 2 vols., 1836.

582

741. W. W. to C. W.

Address: The Revd Dr Wordsworth, Trin: Coll: Cambridge. Single. [*In M. W.'s hand*]
Stamp: Kendal Penny Post.
MS. British Library. Hitherto unpublished.

Tuesday 29th Jan^ry [1833]

My dear Brother,

You will grieve to hear that our dear Sister is very poorly and seems to grow weaker every day. It was a month on Sunday since she left her room—perhaps she caught some cold then—at all events she had an unusually bad night and has never rallied since. Her legs began to swell—and the swelling is accompanied with black spots, which alarm Mr Carr much; and he has ordered her allowance of brandy and opium to be considerably increased, apprehending mortification. She is not at all aware of this danger, and I am happy to say that though unable now to rise from her bed she is in a quiet state of mind. I will harrass you no more with particulars, but will conclude with recommending her to your prayers. It cannot be long before we must follow in course of Nature all those whom we love, who are gone before us. When you write, do not let it appear that I have sent you a desponding account.

Give our united love to John and Charles[1] if with you. Letters from both I believe remain unanswered, which they will excuse. Dora is better of her cold; but she eats so little, that I cannot help being uneasy on her account. W^m[2] was knocked down while skating on the Ice, and remained senseless for 10 minutes—he has a severe cut upon the forehead: but he apprehends no further mischief than a mark for life. If I do not hear from Cottesmore today I shall be fearful that Lord Lonsdale's accident (a fall with or from his horse) has been very severe. This is a gloomy Letter, but I have no good news further than that the rest of the family are well.—

God bless you my Dear brother, and with kindest love from all, I have not mentioned to our Sister that I am writing, believe me most affectionately your Brother

Wm Wordsworth

[1] C. W.'s sons.
[2] W. W. jnr.

583

742. W. W. to MARIA KINNAIRD[1]

Address: Miss Kinnaird
MS. WL transcript (—).
LY ii. 639.

Rydal Mount
30th Jan^ry, 1833

My dear Miss Kinnaird,

It was very kind in you to avail yourself of your amiable Friends[2] application as an occasion for writing to me with your own hand: Be assured that I take a lively interest in all that concerns you, and that I regret much we are not likely to see you in the North, during the ensuing Summer. As Dora means to write, I need not say any thing of or about the Poem, of which we know more than you do.—

It gives me the sincerest Pleasure to learn that the Winter has dealt mildly with Mr Sharp, and that Mrs Sharp[3] is so well.— Poor Mr Rogers and Miss Rogers! how sorry am I for their recent loss,[4] especially for hers.—And then and at the same time, (mercifully one may say if it was to be published) comes that execrable Lampoon of Lord Byron.[5]—What a monster is a Man of Genius whose heart is perverted! The weather with us has been charming through the winter, with the exception of some half a dozen foggy days. As Dora will tell you how feeble my dear Sister is I shall not dwell upon her state which weighs incessantly upon every thought of my heart. Believe me my dear Miss Kinnaird with sincere affection

most faithfully yours
Wm Wordsworth

---

[1] Richard Sharp's adopted daughter.
[2] Mary Spring Rice. See next letter.
[3] Widow of Richard Sharp's brother William.
[4] The death of their brother Henry the previous month.
[5] 'To Lord Thurlow', who had written some feeble lines *On the Poem of Mr Rogers entitled 'An Epistle to a Friend'*. The poem was first printed by Thomas Moore in his *Works of Lord Byron: with his Letters and Journals, and his Life*, 17 vols., 1832–3, ix. 41, and he gives an account of the circumstances in which it came to be written (ii. 196–200). See also Byron's *Letters and Journals* (ed. Prothero), ii. 211–12. Edward Hovell-Thurlow, 2nd Baron Thurlow (1781–1829) nephew of Lord Chancellor Thurlow, published *Poems on Several Occasions* in 1813.

743. W. W. to MARY SPRING RICE[1]

MS. Cornell.
Broughton, p. 70.

Rydal Mount Ambleside
Jan^{ry} 30th 1833

Dear Miss Rice,

Understanding from my amiable Friend Miss Kinnaird, that you wished for my opinion of a Poem[2] addressed to myself, which she has kindly forwarded, I would readily venture to give it you, did I not feel that the subject disqualifies me from speaking impartially.

I ought to tell you that the Poem, several months ago, was transmitted to me by Professor Hamilton of Trin: Coll: Dublin, and to my shame be it said, I have only acknowledged the Receipt of it through the hands of Miss Eliza Hamilton the Professor's Sister. This apparent neglect, be assured, was not owing to a want of a due sense of the value of the Complement paid me, or of the talent and Genius displayed in the Composition, but to the accident of mislaying the MS; I am however now in possession of two Copies, the former having been found. It may, perhaps be enough for me to say of the merits of this Ode that at the age of eighteen I could not have written half so well.—

I remember the evening when I sat by you at dinner at Mr Marshall's. Was not Mr Robert Wilson[3] on my left hand, you on my right? If I ever have the pleasure of meeting you again I shall profit more I trust by the opportunity. My mind was then entirely absorbed by the Measure before Parliament, which was spoken of at table in a strain little accordant to my apprehensions. Schedule A and Schedule B[4] etc were upon many tongues with gaiety sincere or simulated,—for your poor Neighbour, and he could not help thinking of that passage in the second book of Paradise Lost where the Author says—of a formidable Phantom and certain Gates which need not be named—

---

[1] Mary (d. 1875), eldest daughter of Thomas Spring Rice, 1st Lord Monteagle (see L. 464 above) by his first marriage, and cousin of Aubrey de Vere, married John Marshall's third son James (see L. 453 above) in 1841. Sir Henry Taylor, who married her sister Theodosia, said of her: 'She has Wordsworth at her fingers' ends and is full of poetry from her fingers' ends to her toes.' (*Autobiography*, i. 210.)

[2] Aubrey de Vere's madrigal. See L. 739 above.

[3] Unidentified: probably a Yorkshire friend of the Marshalls.

[4] The schedules of those towns, the representation of which had been abolished or reduced under the Reform Bill. See L. 697 above.

30 January 1833

'She opened, but to shut
Excelled her power'[1]

But surely this is out of place—believe me dear Miss Rice

sincerely yours
W Wordsworth

744. W. W. to JOHN SPEDDING

Address: John Spedding, Esq., 14, Queens Square, Westminster.
Endorsed: William Wordsworth 1833.
Postmark: 4 Feb. 1833. *Stamp*: Kendal Penny Post.
MS. Major J. H. F. Spedding. Hitherto unpublished.

Rydal Mount
Sat. 2nd Febry [1833]

My dear Spedding,
Many thanks for your friendly Letter, and kind compliance with my request.[2]

If you had now been at Mirehouse and had the Probate with you we could have easily prepared the Receipts in this off: but as you are in London it would probably suit yourself and the other Exrs to have the Forms filled up by your Solicitor there, and accordingly I have sent a supply by Coach (carriage paid), by the *Union* from Kendal to Leeds and thence by the *Express*. The Forms when filled up and executed by the Parties, viz. the Legatees and Exrs you will be so kind as to forward (together with the Forms—if any— that may not be required) to Wm Wordsworth, Stamp off. Carlisle. As soon as the Papers are so forwarded you will please to pay the Duty into the hands of Masterman and Co Lombard Street, for my account with Wakefield, and Sons Kendal.

Permit me to observe that the Act requires the duty to be paid within 21 days after Receipt of the Legacies, otherwise a penalty of 10 per cent will be incurred.

You will be sorry to hear that my poor Sister has long been in a languishing State, and is now confined to her bed with little or no hope of Recovery.

---

[1] *Paradise Lost*, ii. 883–4.
[2] See L. 725 above.

586

Pray present my kind remembrances to Mrs Spedding and believe me

dear Spedding

faithfully your obliged Friend

Wm Wordsworth

P.S. The Forms will be stamped in about six weeks after you forward them to Carlisle, and will be returned to you, as you may direct.—

745. W. W. to H. C. R.

Address: H. C. Robinson Esqre, 2 Plowden Buildings, Temple, London. [*In M. W.'s hand*]
Postmark: 6 Feb. 1833. *Stamp*: Kendal Penny Post.
Endorsed: 5 Feb: 1833, W. Wordsworth, Opinion on the Reform bill.
MS. Dr. Williams's Library.
K (—). *Morley, i. 232.*

Feb. 5th 1833.

My dear Friend,

On the other page you have Extracts[1] from one of your Letters and from one of Mr Courtenay—The number of shares is small;—more I suppose could not be procured.—

Many thanks for your Letter—we had frequently been wondering and regretting why we did not hear from you, and asking ourselves where you could be—My Son as you conjecture has no desire to be a member of the U: Club,[2] so let his name be struck off. There must I think be some mistake in your account of poor Coleridge—He is *still* confined to his bed you say—Perhaps the word ought to have been he is *again* confined etc—for not long ago he was at Highgate New Church, attending divine service the day it was consecrated—We have also heard of his being out several times. His Daughter Mrs Henry Coleridge has been for some time suffering from a sad derangement of nerves.—

We rejoice to hear that the Lambs are well—pray give our kindest love to them—Mr Clarkson has long been looking very old, as we knew, but we were not aware that Mrs Clarkson had been so unwell—, it is long since we heard of them.

---

[1] Details, copied by M. W., of stocks bought on W. W.'s behalf, but registered in the name of the Pattisons (see below), so that W. W. could hold more than the maximum allowed.
[2] The University Club.

587

U

I am now brought to my own family. My Daughter caught cold in the beginning of the Winter, and has been very unwell, but is recovered in a great measure—but for my poor dear Sister, she has not left her room for five weeks and scarcely her bed—but merely to return to it. She is you will grieve to hear deplorable weak; and cannot we fear remain long with us. But do not speak of this to any body, further than to say that she is very poorly. For she anxiously inquires after all the Letters that come to the house, and depressing allusions to the state of her health would be made; therefore, in your reply, do not write in a desponding tone.—The origin of her complaint was an inflammation in the Bowels, caught by imprudent exposure, during a long walk, when she lived with her Nephew in Leicestershire three years ago. She had a relapse above 12 months past and never has been well or strong since.— But no more of this sad subject. I am come to that time of life, when I must be prepared to part with or precede my dearest Friends; and God's will be done—

The fate[1] of your poor Friend Pattison I had noticed as every body did, with sincere sympathy, but I was ignorant that either you or I had any connection with her whatsoever.

You mistake in supposing me an Anti Reformer—*that* I never was—but an Anti-Bill man; heart and soul.—It is a fixed judgement of my mind, that an unbridled Democracy is the worst of all Tyrranies. Our Constitution had provided a check for the Democracy, in the regal prerogative influence and power, and in the house of Lords acting directly through its own Body and indirectly by the influence of individual Peers over a certain portion of the House of Commons—the old system provided in practise a check— both without and *within*. The extinction of the nomination-boroughs has nearly destroyed the internal check. The House of Lords, as a body, have been trampled upon, by the way in which the Bill has been carried, and they are brought to that point that the Peers will prove useless as an external check—while the regal power and influence has become, or soon will, mere shadows—

'She opened—but to shut

Excelled her power,' as your friends, the Bill-men of all denominations have found or soon will find. ever affectionately yours

W Wordsworth

---

[1] W. Pattison jnr. and his bride, while upon their honeymoon, were drowned in the Lac de Gaube. The lady was a Miss Thomas, a sister of a partner in Esdaile's bank. (Morley's note.)

In passing thro Soho Sq. it may amuse you to call in upon Mr Pickersgill the Portrait Painter where he will be gratified to introduce you to the face of an old Friend[1]—take Ch. and M. Lamb there also.

This Household all send affec. remembrances

746. W. W. to WILLIAM ROWAN HAMILTON

Address: W. R. Hamilton Esqre, Observatory, Dublin [*In M. W.'s hand*]
Postmark: 9 Feb. 1833. *Stamp*: Kendal Penny Post.
MS. Cornell.
Hamilton (—). *K* (—). *LY ii. 640* (—).

Rydal Mount
8th Feb^ry—[1833]

My dear Sir,

Your very friendly Letter and the accompanying Lecture,[2] would have been acknowledged instantly, but I have been looking every day for a reply to the one I wrote to Mr Hamilton now in Edinburgh, in consequence of your Sister's application.[3] My Letter was addressed to him at his Brother's[4] Sir Wm Hamilton's, and I begin to fear that it has not reached him; the purport of it was simply to request that he would mention to Mr Blackwood my opinion of Miss Hamilton's productions, and to know whether upon the strength of that he would wish to see a Specimen of them, so that if approved of some terms of publication in his Magazine might be entered upon. If I do not hear from him shortly, I shall write again—

---

[1] Pickersgill was now putting the finishing touches to his portrait of W. W. for St. John's. See L. 717 above. H. C. R. went to see the portrait on 30 May, but had some reservations about it: 'It is in every respect a fine picture, except that the artist has made the disease in Wordsworth's eyes too apparent. The picture wants an oculist.' (*HCR* i. 426) E. Q. saw it on exhibition a year later, and was on the whole impressed, as he reported to Dora W. on 9 May, 1834: 'The hands are too black; I do not like the cap in his hand, nor the dandy military sort of cloak—All the rest I like exceedingly. The likeness capital, the attitude thoughtful and characteristic, and the background bold and appropriate.' (*WL MSS.*)

[2] An introductory lecture on Astronomy, given by Hamilton in Trinity College, Dublin, on 8 Nov. 1832. See *Hamilton*, i. 640 ff.

[3] See L. 739 above.

[4] Sir William Hamilton, 9th Bart. (1788–1856), the philosopher, contributed to the *Edinburgh Review*, and was Professor of Logic and Metaphysics in the University of Edinburgh from 1836.

In reply to the communication made me in your last, let me express my fervent wishes that your marriage[1] may be attended with all the blessings you expect from it; and in this wish my family unite, not excepting my poor Sister, whose life is but a struggle from day to day.

In my Letter to Miss Hamilton I sent you a message of thanks for the Poems, and Mr De Vere's Ode.[2] Pray assure him that I am duly sensible of the honour he has done me in his animated verses; a copy of which was also sent me by Miss Rice.[3]

Your Lecture I have read with much pleasure. It is philosophical and eloquent, and instructive, and makes me regret—as I have had a thousand occasions of doing—that I did not apply to Mathematics in my youth. It is now, and has long been, too late to make up for the deficiency.

I fear that Mr Coleridge is more than usually unwell: a Letter from a London Friend informs me that he is still confined to his bed. I hope, however, there is some mistake here, as not very long ago he attended at the Consecration of Highgate church, and had a long conversation with the Bp of London[4] who officiated upon that occasion.

It seems a shame to tax you with Postage for this Letter, and I know not how to get it franked; and even still less do I feel able to make it interesting by any agreeable matter. With regard to P[oetry][5] I must say that my mind has been [kept] this last year and more in such a state [of] anxiety that all harmonies appear to have been banished from it except those that reliance upon the goodness of God furnishes:

Tota de mente fugavi
Haec studia, atque omnes *delicias* animi.[6]—

This must be my excuse for writing after so long an interval a letter so dull. But believe me under all circumstances

your faithful Friend
Wm Wordsworth

Affectionate regards to your Sister.

---

[1] On 9 Apr. 1833 Hamilton married Helen Maria (1804–69), daughter of the Revd. Henry Bayly, rector of Nenagh, Tipperary.
[2] See L. 739 above.   [3] Mary Spring Rice (see L. 743 above).
[4] Charles James Blomfield.   [5] *MS. torn.*
[6] Catullus, *Carm.* lxviii, *Ad Mallium*, l. 25: lines peculiarly appropriate for W. W. to recall as they express Catullus's grief for the untimely death of his brother.

747. W. W. to THOMAS HAMILTON

Address: T. Hamilton Esqᵉ, 4 Atholl Place. [*In Dora W.'s hand*]
MS. Bookfellow Foundation Collection, Knox College. Hitherto unpublished.

Monday—18ᵗʰ febʳʸ [1833]

My dear Sir,

Having an opportunity of writing free of postage, I thought you would be pleased to hear about your property.[1]—Mr Tatham[2] has not yet applied for the money, so that some thing must yet be wanting for his satisfaction.—He was here not long ago and surveyed the property, and had a plan made of it which will be attached to the Deeds.—Fleming of whom Mr Tillbrooke bought it as a parcel of another property, has entered into a covenant for the production of the original deeds which he retains, when required. This Mr Tillbrooke neglected to stipulate for.—Backhouse[3] and his wife have also signed the conveyance for the part purchased of them. So that I hope the Deeds will soon be executed to your satisfaction. The next Manor court that is held, Mr Tillbrooke will of course be set on Tenant, and you can be so at the same time.—

I often look in upon your ground, where I have not any fault to find—

My poor Sister has now been confined seven weeks to her bed. Mr Carr a few nights ago prepared us for her Dissolution before morning. It pleased God to give her a respite; and though very very languid, she is a good deal better.—

Backhouse's Mother died last night at his house, in her 87ᵗʰ year; and poor Hayes[4] a fine looking man who farms the small Estate behind Rydal Moun[t][5] [i]s we apprehend dying from a neg[lect]ed inflammation of the lungs. W—[6] thinks him however a little better today.

The Paisleys[7] are well at present—but Sir Thomas has been a good deal disordered. They have had Mr and Mrs Carpenter[8]

[1] Capt. Thomas Hamilton was apparently negotiating for the purchase of the Ivy Cottage from Samuel Tillbrooke.
[2] Edward Tatham, the Kendal attorney (see *MY* ii. 419).
[3] James Backhouse, farmer at Rydal.
[4] Richard Hayes, the Ambleside gardener, who had helped W. W. with the construction of his terraces.   [5] *Hole in MS.*   [6] W. W. jnr.
[7] Admiral Sir Thomas Sabine Pasley, 2nd Bart. (1804–84), an amateur artist, and his wife Jane (d. 1869), eldest daughter of the Revd. Montagu Wynyard, rector of St. Martin's, Micklegate, York, were staying in Grasmere this year. For their daughter Jane, see L. 753 below.
[8] Mr. and Mrs. George Charles Carpenter, presumably tenants of the 3rd Marquess of Waterford (1811–59), owner of Ford Castle, between Wooler and the Scottish border.

who live at Ford Castle Northumberland staying with them, and also a Brother of Lady Paisley.—I saw Archer[1] yesterday, his novel is finished, but he will have the labor of transcribing it—he has been confining himself too much, and if he does not take care, will surely be tortured by a stomach complaint.

I am pleased to learn from Archer that your American Book[2] advances so rapidly.—I have scrawled you two Letters before this one about my friend Miss Hamilton of Dublin and her wish to dispose of some poems for Blackwoods Mag—

With kindest remembrances from all
faithfully yours   W.W.

748. W. W. to EDWARD STANLEY CURWEN[3]

Address: Edward Curwen Esqre, Workington Hall, Workington. [*In M. W.'s hand*]
Stamp: Kendal Penny Post.
MS. Curwen MSS., Record Office, Carlisle. Hitherto unpublished.

Rydal Mount
Ambleside
20th Febry 1833.

My dear Sir,

Having heard that you and your Bride are arrived at Workington Hall, I cannot deny myself the pleasure of joining my own congratulations with those of my family and offering them to you upon this Event. May it prove a source of happiness to yourself, your wife, and all your family. Your dear Sister[4] with whom I have the satisfaction of being so nearly connected speaks feelingly of her new Sister, and rejoices in the union.—The state of my poor Sister's health does not allow me to see at present any of our Friends under our roof, but I need scarcely say how happy we should be under more favorable circumstances to have you and Mrs E.C. and to

---

[1] Edward Archer (see *Addendum*, L. 580a) had returned from Dublin to lodgings in the neighbourhood.
[2] *Men and Manners in America*, published later this year.
[3] Henry Curwen's eldest surviving son (see L. 574 above), an officer of Dragoons. On 22 Jan. he married Frances Margaret, daughter of Edward Jesse (1780–1868), the naturalist, of Hampton Court, Middlesex.
[4] W. W.'s daughter-in-law, Isabella.

show her the beauties of this neighbourhood. Mrs W. and all here unite in kindest regards and believe me my dear Sir very faithfully

yours

Wm Wordsworth

[M. W. writes]

Mr Wordsworth having desired me to put up his letter, I cannot do so without repeating with my own hand my sincere congratulations to you and M^{rs} Ed: Curwen upon your Union; and to add how happy I shall be when circumstances will allow us the pleasure of seeing you both at Rydal Mount. With aff. regards to your Father, Mother and Sisters, believe me to be very

Sincerely yours

M Wordsworth

749. W. W. to JOHN SPEDDING

Address: John Spedding Esqre
Endorsed: Feby. 1833 Wm Wordsworth.
MS. Major J. H. F. Spedding. Hitherto unpublished.

Rydal Mount

20th Feb^{ry} [1833]

My dear Spedding,

I should have replied to your last instantly but I thought it best as the case was not urgent to wait for a Frank.—The matter[1] can be arranged just as well at your perfect convenience when you return into the Country.

You are perhaps aware that the payment of the office which I hold is by rate of poundage, and that this rate has been reduced more than one half, after 20 years of service; the duties and responsibilities being nearly doubled at the same time. I do not complain of this, but I feel that it gives me an additional claim for requesting my Friends who may happen to be Ex^{rs} to pay to me such duties as in course of business, and by the rules of the Head-office would fall into *mine*. With this feeling I made to you the application which you have so readily met.

Believe me with Kind regards to Mrs Spedding ever faithfully yours

Wm Wordsworth

---

[1] See L. 744 above.

The Newspapers announce that your eldest Son is just married[1]— allow me to congratulate you and Mrs Spedding upon this event, and to express my wishes for the happiness of the Bride and Bridegroom.

750. W. W. to EDWARD QUILLINAN[2]

Address: E. Quillinan Esq^e, Lee Priory, Wingham, Canterbury.
Franked: London February Twenty five 1833 J. Marshall.
Postmark: (1) 25 Feb. 1833 (2) 26 Feb. 1833. *Stamp*: Canterbury.
Endorsed: 1833 Feb^ry 22 Mr Wordsworth etc.
MS. WL.
LY ii. 641 (—).

[*In Dora W.'s hand*]

Saturday, Feby 23^d
C^d not get a frank before.

My dear Mr Quillinan,

I hope you will find some amusement in angling during your solitude at melancholy Lee. I should like to be there a few days with you tho' my eyes would not allow me to gaze upon dazzling water; however dull the place you are surely better there than in Oporto at this time. A friend of mine in this neighbourhood occasionally sees the Athenaeum but has not the No. which contains your contribution[3] for which I thank you; the suppressed vow is quite characteristic of the Ed^r of the Keepsake.[4] I dont mention my poor Sister[5] who we hope is getting better tho' slowly. We have now in the room a beautiful bunch of Primroses, which is full of promise for her, transplanted from our green terrace. I am much mortified about

[1] Thomas Story Spedding (1800–70), barrister, and Fellow of Trinity Hall, Cambridge, 1825–33, had married Frances Elizabeth, daughter of the Ven. John Headlam, Archdeacon of Richmond, Yorks.
[2] Written by Dora W. in red ink, crossing a letter of her own to E. Q.
[3] This item cannot be identified with any certainty.
[4] F. Mansel Reynolds.
[5] D. W. was now past the worst crisis in her illness. Dora W. wrote this same day to Maria Kinnaird: 'Monday week, neither we nor our medical attendant had the slightest hopes that another Sun w^d rise upon my dear Aunt. The Cross was in mercy allowed to pass from us, and since that trying night she has rallied slowly but regularly. . . . Father was mercifully supported that sad sad night when he thought he had taken leave of his sister for the last time— indeed all through this trying winter—but surely such love as he bears to her is of no common nature, and when the separation does take place it will be hard to support . . .' (*WL MSS.*)

Boxall's print of me,[1] for except my sister I cannot get any one to look at it with pleasure. How kind Rogers is to Moxon, but I remember with some apprehension that when my good friend 'Joseph of Bristol, the brother of Amos'[2] went from just such a pigmy shop as Moxon's late one the change did not prove advantageous, an instance that Ambition in small matters as well as great is apt to play false with her Votaries. As you dont mention the complaint in your head I hope it is better—one is sometimes ungrateful for not thanking diseases for taking their departure. Did I tell you that your binding of my Poems was much admired by the several parties young and old who have seen the book.—Politics are too dismal to advert to. Principles are kicked out of the House of Commons and Oaths Nuts to them cracked with derision and merriment; in the meanwhile nevertheless there is a God in Heaven, as the British Empire will learn to its cost.

Be assured that in the midst of my public and private anxieties I reserve a corner of my heart for yours, and earnestly wish you were out of them. I am glad that the 4ᵗʰ book of the Excursion has contributed to your support. A year has elapsed since I wrote any poetry but a few lines, and I have rarely even read anything in verse till within the last week, when I have begun to accustom my ear to blank verse in other Authors with a hope they may put me in tune for my own. The Hounds are this moment making a most musical cry, which penetrates the sick room, but the silent looks of our little friend the Primrose are still more agreeable as they announce that the winter music must be near its close. Thanks for Charles Lamb's verses[3] wʰ are characteristic, and believe me with love to the young Ones—my dear friend, faithfully yours

⌈*signed*⌉ Wm Wordsworth

⌈*D. W. adds*⌉

One word of love from me to yourself and dear Girls especially my sweet Rotha, whose still ⌈? form⌉ I have often wished to see, whose quiet smiles to see. The worst of my late illness has been spasms in the legs, excessive langour and ⌈? avoidance⌉ of noise. Add to these I could neither write, read nor listen to anyone, Thank God I can now do all tho' very little. Always loving my Friends I am ever yours D.W.

Dora is the tenderest of nurses.

---

[1] The engraving by William Bromley of the Boxall portrait.
[2] i.e. Joseph Cottle.
[3] 'To Dora W.', Lamb's contribution to her autograph album, *Works* (ed. Lucas), v. 73; F. V. Morley, *Dora Wordsworth, Her Book*, 1924, pp. 87–8.

751. W. W. to ELIZA HAMILTON

Address: Miss Hamilton, Observatory, Dublin.
Franked: [   ] March one 1833. [? J. Marsh] all.
Postmark: 1 Mar. 1833.
MS. Cornell. Hitherto unpublished.

Rydal Mount
Ambleside.
26th Feb^{ry}. [1833]

My dear Miss Hamilton,
The above is an extract from Mr Hamilton's Letter,[1] received yesterday. I am sorry that the prospect it holds out is not more favorable. You have not I hoped been inconvenienced by delay in receiving this Intelligence. In respect to Blackwood's Magazine, it is true that it often speaks of me and my writings in a panegyric strain but it is equally true that articles have often appeared in it of a spirit quite the contrary; and some time ago, indeed several years since appeared one[2] intended to be so offensive, though indeed utterly contemptible, that I never could condescend to ask a personal favor of the Conductors of that publication. This determination ought not and should not affect you in any way; for you will observe that all that I have done in consequence of your request, has been simply to beg Mr Hamilton to report my favorable opinion of your Genius, and your productions.
—The proceedings in Parliament as affecting the protestant Church of Ireland,[3] and the cause of true religion in that country, must I infer, have been painful to you as to every friend of institutions favorable to piety and Liberty. But all is in the hands of a good God, and we must hope, and each do the best in his several Sphere to withstand the Torrent that is sweeping among every thing that genuine Patriots have been accustomed to venerate.— I hope that you are all well and that your Brother's intended marriage[4] may make him as happy as he deserves to be! My dear Sister has now been confined nearly ten weeks to her bed. A fortnight since we thought we should have lost her; but she is better, and we

[1] i.e. the extract printed below, the last lines of which are copied in at the top of p. 1 of the MS.
[2] The reference is probably to the articles by Chauncy Hare Townshend in 1829, which gave W. W. such offence. See L. 498 above.
[3] On 12 Feb. the Government introduced a measure for reforming the Established Church of Ireland, which proposed the abolition of ten bishoprics. The move was viewed with alarm by High-Churchmen, and was one of the contributory causes of the Oxford Movement.
[4] See L. 746 above.

hope though timidly that she may still be spared to us at least for some time, but her frame seems almost worn out. Pray remember us all most kindly to your Brother and Sister.

[*signature cut away*]

[*In M. W.'s hand*] Extract from Mr Hamilton to Mr W.

'I spoke about Miss Hamilton's Poems to Blackwood. He stated in reply that the excellence of any poems coming armed with a recommendation from Mr Wordsworth would of course not admit of dispute, and he will be glad to receive any with which Miss H. may favor him. He says however, what I believe is very true that the existence of high merit in a poem does by no means imply adaptation to produce effect in a popular miscellany. In truth in most cases is inconsistent with it, for the readers of such works demand something racy and highly peppered, a sort of poetical *devil*, and stimulate their jaded palates. In short, *Magazine* poetry must deal in Exaggeration, or in other words must be written in vicious taste to suit the diseased craving of the public. They want something of strong and stirring incident, the display of furious passion; and are peculiarly delighted with a gentleman of 'one virtue and a thousand crimes.' I only mention this that Miss H. may not imagine that any judgment which the Editor of a periodical may form abt her poems, will have any thing to do with their real merit. If she chuses to send any of them to B. they will be recd with all the deference due to yr recommendation but he says it is impossible without seeing them to make any promise as to their insertion.[1] So much for the commission. My own opinion is, that B's Mag: is not a good vehicle for poetry, for it is principally circulated among the mercantile part of the population. Several of the London ones I should think are better; but wherever Miss H. may send her poems she will probably find that she is casting pearls before swine. The public appetite is in a most depraved state.'

[1] Eliza Hamilton eventually had two poems published in *Blackwood's*, xxxviii (July 1835), 93–5.

752. W. W. to ALEXANDER DYCE

MS. Victoria and Albert Museum.
Mem. (—). *Grosart* (—). *K* (—). *LY ii. 643* (—).

Rydal Mount,
March 20th, [1833]

My dear Sir,

I have to thank you for the very valuable Present of Shirley's works, just received.[1] The Preface is all that I have yet had time to read. It pleased me to find that you sympathized with me in admiration of the Passage from the Dutchess of N[ewcastle]'s poetry;[2] and you will be gratified to be told that I share the opinion you have expressed of that cold and false-hearted Frenchified Coxcomb —Horace Walpole.

Poor Shirley! what a melancholy end was his,[3] and then to be so treated by Dryden.[4] One would almost suspect some private cause of dislike, such as is said to have influenced Swift in regard to Dryden himself. Shirley's Death reminded me of a sad close of the life of a literary person, Sanderson[5] by name, in the neighbouring County of Cumberland. He lived in a cottage by himself, though a man of some landed estate; his cottage, from want of care on his part, took fire in the night—the neighbours were alarmed— they ran to his rescue, he escaped, dreadfully burnt from the flames; and lay down (he was in his seventieth year) much exhausted under a tree a few yards from the Door. His friends in the meanwhile endeavoured to save what they could of his property from the flames. He inquired most anxiously after a box in which his MSS and published pieces had been deposited, with a view to a publication of a laboriously corrected edition, and upon being told

---

[1] See L. 738 above. [2] See L. 521 above.

[3] Shirley and his wife were driven from their home near Fleet Street by the Great Fire in 1666, and died on the same day two months later: 'being in a manner overcome with affrightments, disconsolations, and other miseries occasion'd by that fire and their losses', as Anthony Wood puts it.

[4] In *Mac Flecknoe*, 1682, Dryden ridicules Shirley's work as anticipating the reign of Shadwell:

> Heywood and Shirley were but Types of thee,
> Thou last great Prophet of Tautology. (ll. 29–30)

[5] Thomas Sanderson (1759–1829), schoolmaster and poet, taught at Greystoke and Blackhall, near Carlisle, and spent his last years in retirement at Kirklinton. He was a close friend of Robert Anderson, the ballad-writer. Sanderson contributed to the *Cumberland Pacquet* and the *Carlisle Patriot*; published *Original Poems* in 1800, and a *Companion to the Lakes* in 1807. See *Life and Literary Remains of Thomas Sanderson*, ed. the Revd. J. Lowthian, 1829

that the box was consumed—he expired in a few minutes, saying or rather sighing out the words 'Then I do not wish to live'. Poor man! Though the circulation of his works had not extended beyond a circle of 50 miles diameter, perhaps, at the most, he was most anxious to survive in the memory of the few who were likely to hear of him.

The publishing trade, I understand, continues to be much depressed, and authors are driven to solicit or invite subscriptions, as being in many cases the only means for giving their works to the world.

I am always pleased to hear from you; and believe me, my dear sir,

faithfully your obliged friend,
Wm Wordsworth

P.S. I have not yet received Sir E. B.'s work[1] or heard of it from any one but yourself.

753. W. W. to HIS FAMILY AT RYDAL

MS. WL.
LY ii. 644 (—).

[Moresby]
Monday Ev§. [1 Apr. 1833]
My dearest Friends,

You will be disappointed as I am grieved that you will only have this parcel instead of my body. But the urgent entreaties of Mrs Curwen and Isabella have prevailed on my stay. All was fixed for departing tomorrow, but Mrs C has got a severe fit of the Lumbago, John is too lame to walk about, and obliged to pass so much of his time alone that I thought it common charity to give him this week. Besides I am anxious to have everything determined about the building[2] that can be, and for this purpose Mr Peele, the Surveyor or Architect, and John and I go to Brigham tomorrow. It was our intention that this should be done, and I proceed to Keswick to be with you on Wednesday; but, as I have said, if I am [not][3] called home before, I shall prolong my stay here till next Monday, when I shall depart without fail, God willing. Let me express my heartfelt pleasure (after telling you that except for a

---

[1] Sir Egerton Brydges's edition of *The Poems of William Collins*, 1832.
[2] The building of a rectory for John W. at Brigham.
[3] *Word dropped out.*

slight cough Isabella is going on well—she has been downstairs
in the large room all day, and the Baby[1] well also and thriving)
for the good accounts of dearest Dorothy,[2] and let me thank you,
Mary and Dora, for your interesting Letters, to dearest Dora in
particular I felt especial obligation, for you know it an *imperative*
duty for a wife to write to her absent Husband. For myself I have
executed all commissions—ordered the stove, got the Mat as I
said, for though I fear you wont like it, it is of Cocoa tree or nut
material and may not perhaps be lasting, got a new tooth put in the
lower range, a new coat and pantaloons, sent you the pattern from
King,[3] in short neglected nothing. I have walked and ridden a
great deal, almost the whole day and part of the night, having
dined at Dr Ainger[4] at St Bees, and been twice in the evening at
Workington, once to dine out with Mr Curwen, and yesterday at
seven to hear the famous Calvinistic preacher [? Dr Essex][5] and
one day with another, I have scarcely walked less than 12 miles.
The sea is a delightful companion and nothing can be more charming, especially for a sequestered Mountaineer, than to cast eyes
over its boundless surface, and hear as I have done almost from
the brow of the steep in the Church field at Moresby, the waves
chafing and murmuring in a variety of tones below, as a kind of
base of harmony to the shrill yet liquid music of the larks above. I
took yesterday five minutes of this [   ][5] before going into the
Church, and surely it was as good a prelude for devotion as any
Psalm, though one of the Moresby female songsters has a charming
voice and manages it well. But concerning my employments I have
a communication for Dora especially—shall I let it out, I have
composed since I came here the promised Poem upon the birth of
the Baby,[6] and thrown off yesterday and today, in the course of a

[1] W. W.'s granddaughter, Jane Stanley Wordsworth (1833–1912).
[2] Dora W. had written to Miss Kinnaird about the improvement in D. W.'s
health on 22 Mar., just after W. W. left for a stay of nearly three weeks at
Moresby: 'Our beloved Invalid sits up for an hour or two with little or no
fatigue, can read to herself for a considerable time, and can listen to reading for
hours, the blackness about the ancles which alarmed us so very much is all but
gone. She cannot however yet attempt to stand, tho' in other respects her
strength has returned to her amazingly.' (*WL MSS.*) But Southey took a
gloomier view of D. W.'s 'premature old age'. See Curry, ii. 398.
[3] Probably William King, cabinet maker and looking-glass manufacturer at
Whitehaven.
[4] The Revd. William Ainger, D.D. (1785–1840), educated at Sedbergh and
St. John's College, Cambridge, of which he became a Fellow: perpetual curate
of St. Bees, and first Principal of the Theological College, 1816–40, and Canon
of Chester from 1827.   [5] *MS. obscure.*
[6] *To——Upon the Birth of Her First-Born Child, March, 1833* (*PW* iv.
107).

ride to Arlecdon (Mr Wilkinson's),[1] a sober and sorrowful sequel[2] to it which I fear none of you will like. They are neither yet fairly written out but I hope to send them for your impressions in this parcel. Mr Wilkinson we did not see, he was in bed with an inflammatory cold. I do not think Isabella will get rid of her cough till milder weather comes for a continuance. The Dr (Mr Dickinson)[3] says the overflow of milk she has proceeds from weakness and that if she could get into the fresh air it would brace her, and the milk would be reduced in quantity and better in quality. The day we dined at W— Hall, I got Mr D. to look at John's ancle about which I was not a little uneasy, but he most confidently assured me that nothing was amiss with the bones and that time, bandages, and cold water would set all to rights. It appears from John that the Surgeon called in from Whitehaven directed his attention almost entirely to the ugly gash in the knee which was cured in a fortnight, and neglected or rather scarcely thought at all about the ancle from which real and permanent mischief was to be apprehended. Had this been treated with proper care and resolution, the Dr says, it could have been healed in a month—now it will take many to make the leg useful. I dined twice with Lord Lowther[4] and went with him to the play, he went away the next day; as there have been no franks in this neighbourhood since I received your letter for Mrs A.[5] I sent it back—You will find some legacy Receipts for Mr Carter in the parcel.—Lord L. is very gloomy about public affairs, thinking that as this reformed Parliament cannot be altered for the better, nothing can prevent an explosion and the entire overthrow of the Institutions of the Country. He appears to have been gratified by his tour in Italy, and I believe at the bottom of his heart would return there and give up public anxieties and cares, for ever at any sacrifice. Not that he said anything of the kind to

---

[1] George Wilkinson, formerly curate of Moresby (see pt. i, L. 393), was now incumbent of Arlecdon, a few miles further inland.

[2] *The Warning* (*PW* iv. 110) represents, as de Selincourt remarks, the lowest depths of depression to which W. W. sank in the months following the Reform Bill crisis. For the cancelled MS. passage in the *Postscript, 1835* referring to this poem, and the cancelled note, see *PW* iv. 426–7 and *Prose Works*, iii. 260–1, 284.

[3] William Dickinson, the Workington surgeon.

[4] After being for long undecided whether to sit for West Cumberland or Westmorland (and having contemplated resigning both), Lord Lowther finally opted for the latter early in March, and this necessitated a by-election in Cumberland (see L. 667 above), which took place at the end of the month. Lord Lowther left Cumberland for London early in April, in the company of William Holmes, the Tory whip (see pt. i, L. 240).

[5] Probably Mrs. Arnold.

me, but from the hopeless tone of his language I draw this inference. I have now scribbled so much that I must leave off or my eyes will scarcely serve for transcribing the Poems which are rather long for such occasion. Bear in mind with respect to 2nd especially that this will be its first appearance on paper and no doubt it will require altering. One word for dearest Sister—how shall I rejoice to see her; if any mischief come to her I shall never forgive myself for staying so long beyond the intended time.—My love would be sent to Jane Pasley[1] but no doubt they are gone. Love, kindest love to you all with blessings innumerable. I send remembrances to all the Servants and neighbours, Mrs Luff not forgotten. Tell Miss B. Harrison[2] that I called yesterday, Sunday afternoon, upon the Browns,[3] thinking that a favorable time, but they were gone to Hensingham.[4] At Dr Ainger's I met, with his lady, Mr Parkinson,[5] a lively man who seemed pleased with the notice I had taken of his Poems. John who is sitting beside me—we have both been some time with the ladies—sends his kindest love. Mr Curwen has been here twice but I was gone, again farewell most tenderly yours W. W. Pray write, best perhaps by the coach as you might send any Letters beside. Remember me to Mr Hamilton and Mr Archer,[6] Mr Robinson[7] etc.

P.S. You will observe that the Pillars in Mr King's plan are both longer and much more [? ornamental] both at the Capitals and base. As he says, the proportions only are true, although these I have not nor shall I have time to measure, but I will bring them with me.—I ought to have said how much I liked Dora's elegant present, and how much cloak and hood were admired and also James' knitting shoes.—When I called at the Book-keepers that time to pay for your parcel charged one shilling he said it was the regular charge for a parcel however small, and that they charged no more for anything under a stone-weight. Tell this with my kind regards to John Carter, surely it is not correct, they never

[1] Jane Pasley (1827–95), only daughter of Admiral Sir Thomas Sabine Pasley (see L. 747 above), and, like her father, an artist. Much later, in 1845, she made an etching of W. W., a signed copy of which is in the *WL*. (See Blanchard, *Portraits of Wordsworth*, p. 172.)

[2] Benson Harrison's only daughter Dorothy.

[3] Probably a Whitehaven family of that name.

[4] A village just south of Whitehaven.

[5] Richard Parkinson of St. Bees (see L. 729 above). His wife was Catherine (d. 1860), daughter of Thomas Hartley the Whitehaven banker, of Gillfoot, Egremont.

[6] See L. 747 above.

[7] W. W.'s cousin, Capt. Charles Robinson.

charge the Legacy parcels at this rate. I have written all the above and transcribed the Poems by candle-light this Monday evening. I was at prayers this morning at John's Church.

754. W. W. to ALEXANDER DYCE

Address: The Revd Alex. Dyce, 9 Grey's Inn Sq^re, London.
Postmark: 23 Apr. [? 1833]. *Stamp*: Kendal Penny Post.
MS. Victoria and Albert Museum.
Mem. Grosart. K. LY ii. 651.

[*c.* 22 Apr. 1833]

My dear Sir,

The dedication[1] which you propose I shall esteem as an honor; nor do I conceive upon what ground, but an over-scrupulous modesty, I could object to it.

Be assured that Mr Southey will not have the slightest unwillingness to your making any use you think proper of his Memoir of Bampfylde:[2] I shall not fail to mention the subject to him upon the first opportunity.

You propose to give specimens of the best *Sonnet-writers* in our language. May I ask if by this be meant a Selection of the *best Sonnets*, *best* both as to *kind* and *degree*? A Sonnet may be excellent in its kind, but that kind of very inferior interest to one of a higher order, though not perhaps in every minute particular quite so well executed, and from the pen of a writer of inferior Genius. It should seem that the best rule to follow, would be, first to pitch upon the Sonnets which are best *both* in kind and perfectness of execution, and, next, those which, although of a humbler quality, are admirable for the finish and happiness of the execution, taking care to exclude all those which have not one or other of these recommendations, however striking they might be as characteristic of the age

---

[1] Of Dyce's *Specimens of English Sonnets*, which appeared later this year (see also L. 792 below). He included fifteen of W. W.'s, speaking of them as 'in power and poetic feeling superior to all similar compositions in the language, save those of Shakespeare and Milton' (p. 222).

[2] John Codrington Bampfylde (1754–96) quitted his native Devon for London, and failing to secure the patronage of Sir Joshua Reynolds, he fell into dissipation, was confined in a madhouse, and finally died of consumption. In 1778 he published a quarto volume of *Sixteen Sonnets*, which Southey called 'some of the most original in our language'. See Southey's *Specimens of Later English Poets*, 3 vols., 1807, iii. 434 for his Memoir of Bampfylde, and his letter to Sir Egerton Brydges (1809) quoted in *The Autobiography of Sir Egerton Brydges*, 2 vols., 1834, ii. 257–61. Dyce included eleven of Bampfylde's sonnets, *Specimens*, pp. 140–50.

in which the author lived, or some peculiarity of his manner. The tenth sonnet of Donne, beginning 'Death, be not proud', is so eminently characteristic of his manner, and at the same time so weighty in thought, and vigorous in the expression, that I would entreat you to insert it,[1] though to modern taste it may be repulsive, quaint, and laboured.

There are two sonnets of Russell,[2] which, in all probability, you may have noticed, 'Could, then, the Babes', and the one upon Philoctetes, the last six lines of which are first-rate. Southey's Sonnet to Winter[3] pleases me much; but, above all, among modern writers, that of Sir Egerton Brydges, upon Echo and Silence.[4] Miss Williams's Sonnet upon Twilight is pleasing; that upon Hope of great merit.[5]

Do you mean to have a short preface upon the Construction of the Sonnet? Though I have written so many, I have scarcely made up my own mind upon the subject. It should seem that the Sonnet, like every other legitimate composition, ought to have a beginning, a middle, and an end—in other words, to consist of three parts, like the three propositions of a syllogism, if such an illustration may be used. But the frame of metre adopted by the Italians does not accord with this view, and, as adhered to by them, it seems to be, if not arbitrary, best fitted to a division of the sense into two parts, of eight and six lines each. Milton, however, has not submitted to this. In the better half of his sonnets the sense does not close with the rhyme at the eighth line, but overflows into the second portion of the metre. Now it has struck me, that this is not done merely to gratify the ear by variety and freedom of sound, but also to aid in giving that pervading sense of intense Unity in which the excellence of the Sonnet has always seemed to me mainly to

---

[1] Dyce took W. W.'s advice and printed the sonnet, *Specimens*, p. 108.

[2] Thomas Russell (see pt. i, L. 61), *Sonnets and Miscellaneous Poems*, 1789, pp. 10, 13. Dyce included W. W.'s two suggestions and three other sonnets by Russell, *Specimens*, pp. 161–4.

[3] 'A wrinkled, crabbed man they picture thee, Old Winter', *Poetical Works*, 10 vols., 1838, ii. 97. The sonnet was written in 1799. Dyce included it in his *Specimens*, p. 185.

[4] Sir Egerton Brydges, *Sonnets, and other poems*, 1785, p. 5. The sonnet is dated 20 Oct. 1782. Dyce included it in his *Specimens*, p. 160. W. W. wrote the following note at Lee Priory on 16 May 1823: 'I cannot resist an impulse to record my admiration for this Sonnet. In *creative* imagination it is not surpassed by any composition, of the kind, in our Language. The *feelings* of melancholy and joyousness are most happily contrasted; and the intermediate line that describes the evanescence of Silence, is sublime.' (See *Cornell Wordsworth Collection*, no. 2222.)

[5] Helen Maria Williams, *Poems on Various Subjects*, 1823, pp. 203–4. Dyce included *To Hope* (*Specimens*, p. 172), but not *To Twilight*.

consist. Instead of looking at this composition as a piece of architecture, making a whole out of three parts, I have been much in the habit of preferring the image of an orbicular body,—a sphere—or a dew-drop. All this will appear to you a little fanciful; and I am well aware that a Sonnet will often be found excellent, where the beginning, the middle, and the end are distinctly marked, and also where it is distinctly separated into *two* parts, to which, as I before observed, the strict Italian model, as they write it, is favorable. Of this last construction of Sonnet, Russell's upon Philoctetes is a fine specimen; the first eight lines give the hardship of the case, the six last the consolation, or the *per-contra*.[1] Ever faithfully,

> Your much obliged Friend and Ser[nt],
> W. Wordsworth

Do not pay the postage of your letter to me.

In the case of the Cumberland poet,[2] I overlooked a most pathetic circumstance. While he was lying under the tree, and his friends were saving what they could from the flames, he desired them to bring out the box that contained his papers if possible. A person went back for it, but the bottom dropped out and the papers fell into the flames and were consumed. Immediately upon hearing this the poor old Man expired.

755. W. W. to BENJAMIN DOCKRAY[3]

MS. untraced.
K. LY ii. 647.

Rydal Mount, April 25, [1833]

My dear Sir,

Your *Egeria* arrived on the morning when I was setting off to visit my son,[4] with whom I stayed nearly three weeks. This must be my apology for not thanking you for the valuable present

---

[1] Dyce replied on 5 July: 'The remarks on Sonnet-writing with which you favoured me are very interesting: the consciousness that I should be able to offer only *commonplace observations* on that subject deterred me from attempting the Essay with which I originally intended to usher in the volume.' (*WL MSS.*)

[2] Thomas Sanderson. See L. 752 above.

[3] For Benjamin Dockray, see pt. i, Ls. 253 and 380. His *Egeria; or Casual Thoughts and Suggestions* was made up of contributions to the provincial press between 1831 and 1843. The dates of the three parts are, respectively, 21 June 1831, 21 June 1832, and 4 Sept. 1840.

[4] i.e. John W. at Moresby.

somewhat earlier. The strain of your thoughts is, I think, excellent, and the expression everywhere suitable to the thought. I have to thank you also for a most valuable paper on Colonial Slavery.[1] In your view of this important subject I entirely coincide. Fanaticism is the disease of these times as much or more than of any other; fanaticism is set, as it has always been, whether moral, religious, or political, upon attainment of its ends with disregard of the means. In this question there are *three* parties,—the slave, the slaveowner, and the British people. As to the first, it might be submitted to the consideration of the owner whether, in the present state of society, he can, as a matter of private conscience, retain his property in the slave, after he is convinced that it would be for the slave's benefit, civil, moral, and religious, that he should be emancipated. Whatever pecuniary loss might, under these circumstances, attend emancipation, it seems that a slave-owner, taking a right view of the case, ought to be prepared to undergo it. It is probable, however, that one of the best assurances which could be given of the slave being likely to make a good use of his liberty would be found in his ability and disposition to make a recompense for the sacrifice should the master, from the state of his affairs, feel himself justified in accepting a recompense. But by no means does it follow, from this view of individual cases, that the *third* party, the people of England, who through their legislature have sanctioned and even encouraged slavery, have a right to interfere for its destruction by a sweeping measure, of which an equivalent to the owner makes no part. This course appears to me unfeeling and unjust. . . .

What language, in the first place, would it hold out to the slave? That the property in him had been held by unqualified usurpation and injustice on the part of his master alone. This would be as much as to say, 'We have delivered him over to you; and as no other party was to blame, deal with your late oppressors as you like.' Surely such a proceeding would also be a wanton outrage upon the

[1] The slave trade with the West Indies had been prohibited to British subjects and British ships in 1807, and by 1830 France, Portugal, and Spain had followed this lead. But the trade still continued, and prohibition was made more difficult by lack of co-operation from the United States. A policy of 'melioration' of the slave's status, as a prelude to emancipation, was put in hand; but it was opposed by the planters. In Apr. 1833 Edward Stanley, later 14th Earl of Derby (1799–1869), the Victorian Prime Minister, became Secretary for War and the Colonies, and introduced a measure of emancipation embodying a transitional period in which slaves would be apprenticed to their masters before they attained their freedom; but the scheme soon broke down under pressure from the abolitionists that complete emancipation should be granted without delay.

feelings of the masters, and poverty, distress, and disorder could not but ensue.

They who are most active in promoting entire and immediate Abolition do not seem sufficiently to have considered that slavery is not in itself at all times and under all circumstances to be deplored. In many states of society it has been a check upon worse evils; so much inhumanity has prevailed among men that the best way of protecting the weak from the powerful has often been found in what seems at first sight a monstrous arrangement; viz., in one man having a property in many of his fellows. Some time ago many persons were anxious to have a bill brought into Parliament to protect inferior animals from the cruelty of their masters. It has always appeared to me that such a law would not have the effect intended, but would increase the evil. The best surety for an uneducated man behaving with care and kindness to his beast lies in the sense of the uncontrolled property which he possesses in him. Hence a livelier interest, and a more efficient responsibility to his own conscience, than could exist were he made accountable for his conduct to law. I mention this simply by way of illustration, for no man can deplore more than I do a state of slavery in itself. I do not only deplore but I *abhor* it, if it could be got rid of without the introduction of something worse, which I much fear would not be the case with respect to the West Indies, if the question be dealt with in the way many excellent men are so eagerly set upon. I am, dear sir,

Very sincerely, your obliged
Wm Wordsworth

756. W. W. to GEORGE WILLIAMS FULCHER[1]

Address: D. W. Fulcher Esq[re], Sudbury, Suffolk.
Postmark: 29 Apr. 1833.
MS. Cornell. Hitherto unpublished.

Rydal Mount
near Ambleside
April 26th 1833

Sir,

I have to return you thanks for the obliging Present of your Sudbury Memorandum Book and extracts; in which I find many

---

[1] George Williams Fulcher (1765–1855), publisher and writer, issued from 1825 an annual called the *Sudbury Pocket Book*, in which he included poems by Bernard Barton, William and Mary Howitt, and James Montgomery, as well

pleasing performances. The Book is elegantly got up and does great credit to a provincial Press.

Believe me to be
sincerely
Your obliged Servant
Wm Wordsworth

757. W. W. to H. C. R.

Address: Henry Crabbe Robinson Esqʳᵉ, Athaeneum, London. [*In M. W.'s hand*]
Postmark: 6 May 1833. *Stamp*: Kendal Penny Post.
Endorsed: 5ᵗʰ May 1833. Wordsworth Politics Verses "Avaunt this economic rage."
MS. Dr. Williams's Library.
K (—). *Morley, i. 236.*

[5 May 1833]

My dear Friend,

I sit down to thank you for your last with so much uneasiness in one of my poor eyes that I know not how soon it may be necessary or at least proper to lay down the pen—We are much obliged by your care of our little money concern; and before I proceed let me beg of you to do me a small service in one of your walks, and as early as convenient. This morning I have received a Letter from a Mr Dewhurst 16 Willm Str Waterloo Bridge, Lambeth who gives a wretched account of himself and his affairs, and requests me to subscribe to a book of his upon Whales,[1] and other creatures of the Ar[c]tic Regions. I have no money that can be well spared, and nothing can be more out of my way—but the poor Man seems so heavily distressed, not being able to pay even the postage of his Letter, that I beg you would call at his house, and put my name down—and you shall be repaid by the first opportunity—How he has fallen into such distress, I cannot guess as his subscription is numerous and of the first respectability—But could you previously

as some of his own. A collection of these contributions was published in 1841 as *Fulcher's Poetical Miscellany*. Fulcher also brought out a volume of his own pieces *The Village Paupers, and other Poems*, 1845, in imitation of Crabbe and Goldsmith, and began a *Life of Thomas Gainsborough*, which was completed by his son and published in 1856.

[1] Henry William Dewhurst, *The Natural History of the Order Cetacea, and the oceanic inhabitants of the Arctic regions . . . Illustrated* (published by the author), 1834.

enquire into the case, and use your discretion whether I ought to subscribe or not.[1]

We are thankful with our whole hearts, and we do hope for further improvement—but that is all I dare venture to say—It is in the hands of God and we must be prepared—I do not think that she has any organic disease—but the functions of the stomach and bowels are pitiably impaired—her Ancles are still a good deal swoln but the blackness from which the medical attendant apprehended gangrene and mortification has entirely disappeared. I have been thus particular to you, knowing how strong a friendship you have for this excellent Person, and how much we all must feel on her account.

Public affairs are going on just as I apprehended. Nothing, I am persuaded but a course of affliction will bring back this Nation to its senses. And when it recovers then it will be a long time under the necessity of sacrificing liberty to order, probably under a military government but at least under one unavoidably despotic. It would give me much pleasure to talk over these matters with you, and some, to write upon them if my eyes were better, and my scrawl legible. And this—[2]

What think you of 'Columbian'[3] as a substitute for the faulty word—I was well aware of its impropriety—but the sweet sound and the want of a fit term seduced me into the use of it. The word Columbian is undoubtedly at present connected mainly in English ears with the sad sound of Columbian bonds, to which one of Mrs Wordsworths sisters[4] five or six years ago entrusted 1,500 pounds the better half of her fortune.

A neighbour of ours, Mr Hami[l]ton Author of a novel called Cyril Thornton, has in the Press, the result of a year's tour in America.[5] The subject is rather hackneyed—but I hope his Book,

---

[1] About two inches of the sheet has been cut away, destroying several lines of the text. It is resumed in the middle of a discussion of D. W.'s recent illness.
[2] There is another gap here, corresponding to the bottom of p. 2 of the MS.
[3] In his letter to W. W. of 28 Apr., H. C. R. had been critical of one point in the *Elegiac Stanzas* to Goddard (*PW* iii. 193): 'By the bye, reading over to a young Bostonian the beautiful lines on poor Goddard I was struck with the *impropriety* of "*Virginian*" dews. I now know more of the United States than I did—And holding as I do in extreme abhorrence all the Southern and slave-states of which Virginia is one—While Goddard was a New-Englander—I wish that you could find an appropriate word to designate his the better division of America his country—There ought to be a line of demarcation drawn between the Slave and free states—Indeed I think there ought to be at once a separation.' (Morley, i. 235.) In spite of the alternative W. W. suggests here, he retained 'Virginian' in the text (l. 45).
[4] Joanna H.　　　　[5] *Men and Manners in America*, 2 vols., 1833.

of which I have read the first Vol: will be of some use in correcting the errors of those, who are inclined to think that a Government such as the American might be advantageously adopted in our Country. Hume[1] may really believe this as he is a narrow-minded stupid Fellow, but Cobbet who is a most able and sagacious Man [when][2] he talks in that strain is a wilful deceiver, for selfish purposes. Cobbett was asked how he liked the Reform Bill—he replied I am more than satisfied—but I would say to the Minister—'Father forgive them for they know not what they do' But replied the Interrogator—I thought you were for triennial perhaps annual parliament, and universal suffrage. All that will follow and more if desirable, it is a Revolution, a bloody one would it have been if the Bill had not passed but a Revolution it is, to all intents and purposes.

Why should not you come down to see us during the summer? and let us talk about your travels.—Love to the Lambs and the Clarksons when you see them—pray tell them about my Sister. I saw Byron's execrable Lampoon[3]—what an unhappy mortal he was—With love from all here affectionately

yours
W. Wordsworth

To fill up the Paper a[ccept?][4] these verses composed or rather thrown off this morning.

[There follows To The Utilitarians, *as in PW iv. 388.]*

Is the above intelligible—I fear not—I know however my own meaning—and that's enough for Manuscripts.

758. W. W. to JOHN MARSHALL

MS. Stephen Marshall MSS., Record Office, Preston.
Chester L. Shaver, 'Three unpublished Wordsworth Letters', *NQ ccxii (Jan. 1967), 14–18.*

Rydal Mount
May 7th [1833]

My dear Sir,

I was most gratified by your account of your notices in France.—[5] I object to the evidence of La Fayette, as to the effect of the divi-

---

[1] Joseph Hume, the radical politician.
[2] *Word dropped out.*   [3] See L. 742 above.   [4] *MS. torn.*
[5] Which Marshall had recently visited.

sions of property.[1] In his early youth he commenced Republican, upon a slender stock of knowledge—and his personal vanity, of which he always had an inordinate share was gratified by the power and applause which attended his early exertions in support of democratic opinion, first in America and then in France. His imprisonment in Olmutz[2] might well strengthen his aversion to monarchical government,[3] and his subsequent disappointments and mortifications in point of personal ambition all contributed to keep him in error. The arrangements made in families to prevent an injurious splitting of property cannot meet the true exigencies of society. The number of men born to a state of leisure will always be too small for refined manners and elevated pursuits being held in sufficient esteem—not to speak of the want of sufficient capital for great enterprizes of art manufacture and commerce; this objection might however be in part obviated perhaps by joint stock companies—I should like much to know at what rate population in France has encreased. But enough of this. I write now to tell you that the Brathay Estate[4] is now surveying by the Proprietor with a view to its being offered for sale. The House is large and has been built at great expense, and if it be valued only according to its present rent it will be given away. As a Lake property the domain is entitled to great consideration.

Ever faithfully yours
W. Wordsworth.

Mrs. Wordsworth thanks Mrs. Marshall for her long and very interesting Letter. Pray tell her that my sister has been born round the terraces and one of the fields, from which she will see that the poor Invalid is going on well. We were truly glad to have so good an account of your sufferer[5] notwithstanding the Relapse. Dora is pretty well though looking deplorably thin—but your Son W^m would tell you about us all—

adieu—

[1] Lafayette (see also L. 670 above), had represented Meaux in the Chamber of Deputies since 1825, as Shaver notes. During a debate in 1832 he had spoken against the principle of a hereditary peerage.
[2] Declared a traitor by the National Assembly on 19 Aug. 1792, he fled to Liège, but was captured, and held in Prussian and Austrian prisons, chiefly Olmutz (in Moravia), until released by the Treaty of Campo Formio in 1797. (Shaver's note.)
[3] After the attempted assassination of Louis Philippe on 19 Nov. 1832 Lafayette refused to go to the Tuileries to congratulate him on his escape.
[4] See L. 723 above. The estate was sold later this year to Giles Redmayne (1782–1857), mercer, of Bond Street in London, whom W. W. had met in 1831 (*RMVB*), and the Harden family moved to Field Head, Hawkshead. Redmayne later (1836) built Brathay church on the estate.
[5] Probably the Marshalls' daughter Ellen, a chronic invalid.

759. W. W. to WILLIAM ROWAN HAMILTON

Address: Professor Hamilton, Observatory, Dublin.
Franked: London May nine 1833 J. Marshall.
Postmark: (1) 9 May 1833 (2) 11 May 1833.
MS. Cornell.
Mem. (—). *Grosart* (—). *Hamilton* (—). *K* (—). *LY ii. 654.*

Rydal Mount
8ᵗʰ May 1833

My dear Sir,

My Letters being of no value but as tokens of friendship, I waited for the opportunity of a frank which I had reason to expect earlier. Sincerely do we all congratulate you upon your marriage.[1] Accept our best wishes upon the event, and believe that we shall always be deeply interested in your welfare. Make our kind regards also to Mrs Hamilton who of course will be included in every friendly hope and expectation formed for yourself.

We look with anxiety to your Sister Eliza's success in her Schemes,—but for pecuniary recompense in literature, especially poetical, nothing can be more unpromising than the present state of affairs except what we have to fear for the future. Mrs Godwyn[2] who sends verses to Blackwood is our neighbour. I have had no conversation with her myself upon the Subject, but a friend of hers says she has reason to believe that she has got nothing but a present of Books. This however is of no moment, as Mrs G. being a person of easy fortune she has not probably bargained for a return in money. Mrs Hemans I see continues to publish in the periodicals. If you ever see her pray remember me affectionately to her, and tell her that I have often been and still am troubled in conscience for having left her obliging Letter so long unanswered but she must excuse me, as there is not a motive in my mind urging me to throw any interest into my Letters to friends beyond the expression of kindness and esteem, and *that* she does not require from me. Besides my Friends in general know how much I am hindered in all my pursuits by the inflammation to which my eyes are so frequently subject. I have long given up all exercise of them by candle light, and the evenings and nights are the seasons when one is most

---

[1] See L. 746 above.

[2] For Mrs. Catherine Grace Godwin, see L. 423 above. She was now living in a cottage under Loughrigg. 'She is an aspirant after literary reputation, and therefore a disappointed woman', was the comment of Mrs. Elizabeth Fletcher (later of Lancrigg), who kept a log-book of her holiday at Thorney How, Grasmere, this summer (*WL MSS.*).

disposed to converse in that way with absent friends. News you do not care about and I have none for you, except what concerns Friends. My Sister, God be thanked, has had a respite. She can now walk a few Steps about her room, and has been borne twice into the open air.—Southey to whom I sent your Sonnets,[1] had, I grieve to say, a severe attack of some unknown and painful complaint about 10 days ago. It weakened him much, but he is now, I believe perfectly recovered. Coleridge I have reason to think is confined to his bed, his mind vigorous as ever—Your Sonnets, I think, are as good as any thing you have done in verse.—We like the 2nd best, and I single it out the more readily as it allows me an opportunity of reminding you of what I have so often insisted upon, the extreme care which is necessary in the Composition of Poetry.

> The ancient images *shall not* depart
> From my Soul's temple, the refined Gold
> Already prov'd *remain*.

Your meaning is that it *shall remain* but according to the construction of our language, you have said 'it shall *not*.'

>   the refined gold,
> Well proved, shall then remain,

will serve to explain my objection.—

Could you not take us in your way when coming or going to Cambridge.[2] If Mrs H. accompanies you we should be glad to see her also. I hope that in the meeting about to take place in Cambridge, there will be less of mutual flattery among the men of Science than appeared in that of the last year in Oxford. Men of Science in England seem, indeed, to copy their Fellows in France, by stepping too much out of their way for titles, and baubles of that kind, and for offices of state and political Struggles which they

---

[1] Sonnets written by Hamilton the previous autumn as he recovered from his unsuccessful wooing of Ellen de Vere (see *Hamilton*, ii. 4).

[2] The British Association was meeting at Cambridge this summer, at the end of June. The visit was made memorable for Hamilton by his meeting with Coleridge. This was S. T. C.'s first visit since his undergraduate days, and the reception accorded to him was remarkable. See *Romilly's Cambridge Diary 1832–42*, ed. J. P. T. Bury, 1967, p. 36: 'Went with Hare to Thirlwall's dinner . . . to hear Coleridge talk:—a wonderful old man.' On 30 June Hamilton wrote to W. W. with a full account of the proceedings, 'where almost nothing was wanted, except yourself.' (*WL MSS.*)

would do better to keep out of. With kindest regards to yourself
and Mrs H, and to your sisters, believe me ever

My dear Mr H.
faithfully yours
W. W.

760. W. W. to MARY ANN RAWSON[1]

Address: Mrs W. B. Rawson, Joseph Read's Esq[re], Wincobank Hall, near
Sheffield. [*In M. W.'s hand*]
Stamp: Kendal Penny Post.
MS. John Rylands Library.
*N.B. Lewis, 'The Abolitionist Movement in Sheffield, 1823–1833', Bulletin of
the John Rylands Library, xviii (1934), 377–92. LT ii. 650.*

[? May 1833]

Dear Madam,

Your letter which I lose no time in replying to, has placed me
under some embarrassment, as I happen to possess some Mss
verses of my own[2] upon the subject to which you solicit my
attention. But I frankly own to you, that neither with respect to
this subject nor to the kindred one, the Slavery of the children
in the Factories,[3] which is adverted to in the same Poem, am I
prepared to add to the excitement already existing in the public

[1] Mrs. W. P. Rawson, daughter of Joseph Read of Wincobank Hall, Shef-
field, was an original member of the committee of the Sheffield Female Anti-
Slavery Society (1825). Since 1826 she had been compiling an anthology of
anti-slavery prose and verse, which was published in 1834 under the title
The Bow in the Cloud in a limited edition of 500 copies. Contributors included
Bernard Barton, William and Mary Howitt, Lord Morpeth, and James Montgomery. Among those who declined were Campbell, Moore, Macaulay, and
Southey (in a MS. letter of 4 May 1833 in the John Rylands Library). W. W.'s
reply, which echoes Southey's sentiments, was probably written at about the
same time.
[2] *Humanity* (*PW* iv. 102), written in the autumn of 1829 and published
1835.
[3] Under pressure from Michael Thomas Sadler (see L. 666 above), a
parliamentary commission of inquiry in 1832 produced evidence about child
labour in factories that profoundly shocked public opinion. A Royal Commission, which included Edwin Chadwick (1800–90), made further investigations.
The Act of 1833, which was vigorously promoted by Ashley, later 7th Earl of
Shaftesbury (1801–85), secured the exclusion of children under 9 from factories,
and limited the work of children under 13 to forty-eight hours a week, or
nine hours in any one day. Among other provisions, it enacted that children
under 13 were to attend school for not less than two hours a day; and it set up
a factory inspectorate to ensure the proper working of the Act. But it failed to
secure the ten-hour day for all persons under 18, as had been hoped.

mind upon these, and so many other points of legislation and government. Poetry, if good for any thing, must appeal forcibly to the Imagination and the feelings; but what at this period we want above every thing, is patient examination and sober judgement. It can scarcely be necessary to add that my mind revolts as strongly as any one's can, from the law that permits one human being to sell another. It is in principle monstrous, but it is not the worst thing in human nature. Let precipitate advocates for its destruction bear this in mind. But I will not enter farther into the question than to say, that there are three parties—the Slave—the Slave owner—and the imperial Parliament, or rather the people of the British Islands, acting through that Organ. Surely the course at present pursued is hasty, intemperate, and likely to lead to gross injustice. Who in fact are most to blame? the people—who, by their legislation, have sanctioned not to say encouraged, slavery. But now we are turning round at once upon the planters, and heaping upon them indignation without measure, as if we wished that the Slaves should believe that their Masters alone were culpable—and they alone fit objects of complaint and resentment.

> Excuse haste and believe me Dear Madam
> respectfully yours,
> Wm Wordsworth

P.S. Unwillingness to allude to my own writings, even though indirectly led to the subject, has prevented me from expressing the satisfaction which I felt from your Letter that they had afforded you so much pleasure.—

761. W. W. to ABRAHAM HAYWARD[1]

Address: A. Hayward Esqre, 1 Pump Court, Temple.
Postmark: 20 May, 1833. *Stamp*: Piccadilly.
MS. Carl H. Pforzheimer Library. Hitherto unpublished.

Rydal Mount
Sir,   14th May 1833.

I have to thank you for your valuable Present the translation of Faust; from which I promise myself much pleasure. I should have

---

[1] Abraham Hayward (1801–84), edited the *Law Magazine, or Quarterly Review of Jurisprudence* from 1828 to 1844, spent some time in Germany, and published his translation of Goethe's *Faust* into English prose in 1833. His *Biographical and critical essays*, a selection from his numerous contributions to the reviews, was published in 5 vols., 1858–74. See also *A Selection from the Correspondence of Abraham Hayward, Q.C.*, 2 vols., 1886. See L. 800 below.

deferred making my acknowledgments to you, if I had known enough of German to read the original, but the small acquaintance I have with that language would render any notices of mine upon a Translation from it, utterly insignificant.

I remain Sir
your Obliged Serv^{nt}
Wm Wordsworth

I ought not to have omitted to express the pleasure which I feel in being told that my writings had interested you so far as to call from you frequent allusions to them.

762. W. W. to EDWARD MOXON

Address: Mr Moxon, Bookseller, Dover S^t. [*In Dora W.'s hand*]
Postmark: 18 May 1833.
MS. Boston Public Library.
LY ii. 655.

Rydal Mount
May 14th [1833]

My dear Sir,
    My Daughter joins with me in thanks for your Sonnets[1] which we have both read with much pleasure. There is a great deal of sweet feeling and pleasing expression in them. In the 3^d there is a mistake, the River that flows through Rydal is not the Brathay but the Rothay—This is a good Sonnet. Were I asked to name a favorite or two, perhaps I should chuse 12,—18—23—28. In the cadence and execution of your Sonnets, I seem to find more of the manner of Bowles than my own, and this you must not think a disparagement as Bowles in his sonnets has been very successful. The principal fault in your style is an overfrequency of inversion. For example at the close of the first—the *fall of Man* is a phraze of meaning so awful, and so much in the thoughts and upon the tongue of every religious Person that the Dislocation of the words is to me a little startling—not that I have any wish that it should be altered. —As to the Selections,[2] I think you are a little too sanguine: a Collection from different Authors will always be preferred for schools, and if well done ought to be. In other times, however, I

---

¹ The first volume of Moxon's *Sonnets*, 1833.
² Hine's *Selections* of W. W.'s poems, 1831 (see L. 617 above).

think the one made from my Poems would sell, were it only for its cheapness; but as the whole of my Poems are sold at a much lower price than formerly, by means of the Pirated french Edition,[1] and my own last,[2] the Selections are not even in respect of price so well off as before.—It is a disgrace to the age that Poetry wont sell without prints—I am a little too proud to let my Ship sail in the wake of the Engravers and the drawing-mongers. Thank you for your kind offer of your House—and also for sending Lamb's Present,[3] most of the Essays I have read and with great pleasure —ever faithfully your friend W. Wordsworth

763. W. W. to JOHN PAGEN WHITE[4]

Address: John Paget White Esq^e, 48 St Anne S^t, Liverpool. [*In Dora W.'s hand*]
Stamp: Kendal Penny Post.
MS. Cornell. Hitherto unpublished.

Rydal Mount
14th May 1833.

Dear Sir,

Your courteous Letter and the accompanying Verses ought not to have been left so long unacknowledged. Be assured that I was not indifferent to the outpouring of your feelings in connection with a place, for innumerable reasons so dear to me. In apology for my silence I have only to say that your Pacquet reached me just on my return home after an absence which had caused a considerable arrear in my correspondence; and I put off my acknowledgements to yourself, till I had disposed of prior claims. Among the best rewards which a Poet can receive for his labours, may be reckoned such lively expressions of gratitude and heartfelt pleasure as those with which you have honored my endeavours to excite sympathies which, wherever they may be felt, will I hope prove salutary.—

I remain dear Sir,
sincerely yours
Wm Wordsworth

[1] Galignani's edition of 1828.
[2] i.e. the 'cheap' edition of 1832.
[3] See L. 765 below.
[4] Author of *Lays and Legends of the English Lake Country*, 1873.

764. W. W. to ROBERT SOUTHEY

Address: Robt Southey Esqre [*delivered by hand*]
MS. *Harvard University Library.*
LY ii. 649.

[May 1833]

My dear S—

I like your Book[1] much, and have only one objection to what I have seen: viz. the notice of Mr Wilberforce[2] by name. My wish is that you should adopt it as a general Rule, not to allude (in the mention of public men),—to their *private* habits, otherwise your book will be so far degraded to the level of the magazine-writers— but probably this may be the only instance, and as it is so good natured there is little or no harm in it. A public man's public foibles are fair game!—The Popes[3] allusion is also well struck out— it is astonishing how queerly in these fantastic times the sale[4] of a Book may be checked, by what might seem the arrantest trifle.—

I hope you have not forgot what I told you about the puppet-shows of Ingleton[5]—and that you will notice them in some way or other. The puppets are still to be seen there—which used to travel all England over, the great Master of the art living there.—

We are truly glad that you have had no return of your ugly attack[6]—

ever affectionately yours

Remember Dr Green[7] the famous quack—Doctor of Doncaster, of a gentleman's family and regularly educated, he flourished in the middle of the last century in all the Midland counties and used to prefer itinerancy with a stage and a zany to regular practice. So famous was he and so fortunate that his name was adopted for many years afterwards by many travelling Mountebanks, or rather by all of them, at least in these parts. Relatives of his own name still

---

[1] A draft of the first two volumes of *The Doctor*, which were published early in Jan. 1834 (Southey, vi. 226–8). Southey had been compiling the work over many years.

[2] The reference to Wilberforce, who seems to have kept snuff loose in his pockets, is to be found in *The Doctor*, i. 22.

[3] See *The Doctor*, i. 117, where Southey writes: 'Let not Protestants suppose that Nepotism is an affection confined to the dignitaries of the Roman Catholic Church. In its excess indeed it is peculiarly a Papal vice . . . but like many other sins it grows out of the corruption of a good feeling.' The MS. version of the passage may have been more severe.

[4] *Written* sail.   [5] See *The Doctor*, i. 213 ff.

[6] Almost certainly the illness mentioned in Southey's letter to John Rickman of 1 May (Warter, iv. 337), which helps to establish the date of this letter.

[7] See *The Doctor*, i. 227, where Southey gives an account of Dr. Green based on W. W.'s letter. See also *MY* ii. 447.

618

reside at Doncaster or near it. Old Wilsy[1] knew him well. Wilsy and all the old women used to look back with delight upon his exhibitions, and talk of them with profound reverence also for his medical skill.—

Many thanks for your Pamphlet[2]   W. W.

My Sister rather suffers from this raw and uncertain weather.

765. W. W. to CHARLES LAMB

Address: Charles Lamb Esqre, Care of Mr Moxon, Bookseller, Dover St. [*In M. W.'s hand*]
MS. Henry E. Huntington Library.
Mem. (—). *Grosart* (—). *K* (—). *LY ii. 656.*

Rydal Mount
Friday May 17th [1833] or thereabouts

My dear Lamb,

I have to thank you and Moxon, for a delightful Vol.—your last, I hope not, of *Elia*.[3] I have read it all, except some of the popular

---

[1] Mrs. Wilson, the old housekeeper at Greta Hall, beloved of Hartley Coleridge, who used to call her Wilsy (see *EY*, pp. 335, 447). She died in 1820. (de Selincourt's note.)

[2] *A Letter to John Murray Esq. 'touching' Lord Nugent, in reply to a letter from his Lordship touching an article in the Quarterly Review, by the author of that article* (anon.), 1833. George Nugent Grenville, Baron Nugent (1788–1850), an extreme Whig, one-time M.P. for Aylesbury, now Lord High Commissioner of the Ionian Islands, had published towards the end of 1831 *Some Memorials of John Hampden, his Party, and his Times*. The work was reviewed favourably by Macaulay, but Southey attacked it in the *Quarterly Review*, xlvii (July 1832), 457–519, comparing it unfavourably with Isaac D'Israeli's *Commentaries on the Life and Reign of Charles the First*. His review developed his favourite parallel between the age of the Civil War and the era of the Reform Bill, and ended by quoting W. W.'s sonnet *Upon the late General Fast* (see L. 693 above) as evidence that 'old English feeling and old English piety' were not yet dead. Nugent's reply, *A Letter to John Murray touching an Article in the last Quarterly Review . . .*, dated 18 Sept. 1832, attacked Southey's interpretation of seventeenth-century history, adverted to his political inconsistency with quotations from *Wat Tyler*, and described W. W.'s poem as 'a very sorry sonnet'. Southey had now launched his reply to this *Letter*. The MS. was sent to the printer in mid-February (Warter, iv. 329; Curry, ii. 393); and a month later Lockhart was planning to include it in the next *Quarterly* (Curry, ii. 396), but it eventually appeared as a separate pamphlet later in the spring (which confirms the dating of W. W.'s letter here). In his pamphlet, Southey castigated Nugent for sacrificing truth to party spirit, for concealing the shortcomings of his hero—and also for failing to identify the author of the sonnet, 'which no one having any pretensions to be conversant with the literature of the present age, could have failed to affiliate rightly'.

[3] *The Last Essays of Elia, Being a Sequel to Essays Published under that Name*, 1833.

fallacies which I reserve not to get through my Cake all at once. The Book has much pleased the whole of my family, viz my Wife, Daughter, Miss Hutchinson, and my poor dear Sister, on her sick bed; they all return their best thanks.—I am not sure but I like the Old China and The Wedding as well as any of the Essays.—I read Love me and love my Dog to my poor Sister this morning, while I was rubbing her legs at the same time.—She was much pleased, and what is rather remarkable, this morning also I fell upon an Anecdote in Madame D'Arblayes'[1] life of her father, where the other side of the question is agreeably illustrated. The heroes of the Tale are David Garrick and a favorite little Spaniel of King-Charles's Breed, which he left with the Burneys when he and Mrs Garrick went on their Travels. In your remarks upon Martin's pictures,[2] I entirely concur.—May it not be a question whether your own Imagination has not done a good deal for Titian's Bacchus and Ariadne?[3]

With all my admiration of that great artist I cannot but think, that neither Ariadne or Theseus look so well on his Canvas as they ought to do.—But you and your Sister will be anxious, if she be with you, to hear something of our poor Invalid.—She has had a long and sad illness—anxious to us above measure, and she is now very weak and poorly—though she has been out of doors in a chair three times since the warm weather came. In the winter we expected her dissolution daily for some little time.—She then recovered so as to quit her bed, but not her room, and to walk a few steps, but within these few days the thundery weather has brought on a bilious attack which has thrown her back a good deal and taken off the flesh which she was beginning to recover—Her Spirits however thank God are good, and whenever she is able to read she beguiles her time wonderfully.—But I am sorry to say that we cannot

---

[1] Frances Burney, later Madame d'Arblay (1752–1840), diarist and novelist: author of *Evelina* (1778), etc. She was the daughter of Dr. Charles Burney (1726–1814), the musicologist and traveller, and published her *Memoirs of Dr Burney* in 1832.

[2] John Martin (1789–1854), landscape and historical painter. He began to exhibit his spectacular canvases at the Royal Academy in 1811, and achieved an outstanding success with *Belshazzar's Feast* (1821), which was followed by *The Deluge, The Last Judgment*, and many other pictures on biblical subjects and by illustrations of the Bible and *Paradise Lost*. Many of his engravings were reproduced in the popular annuals. While his colossal 'romantic' conceptions enjoyed wide popularity, they were treated with a certain scepticism by professionals like Hazlitt and Wilkie, and Lamb took him as an example of the *Barrenness of the Imaginative Faculty in the Productions of Modern Art*.

[3] Painted in 1523, and now in the National Gallery. In his essay, Lamb had praised the picture for its harmonization of past and present.

expect that whatever may become of her health, her strength will ever be restored.—

I have been thus particular, knowing how much you and your dear Sister value this excellent person, who in tenderness of heart I do not honestly believe was ever[1] exceeded by any of God's Creatures. Her loving kindness has no bounds. God bless her for ever and ever!—Again thanking you for your excellent Book, and wishing to know how you and your dear Sister are,[2] with best love to you both from us all

I remain my dear Lamb
Your faithful Friend
W Wordsworth

766. W. W. to H. C. R.

Address: H. C. Robinson Esqre, 2 Plowden Buildings, Temple. [*In M. W.'s hand*]
Postmark: 18 [   ] 1833.
Endorsed: *May* 1833. Wordsworth.
MS. Dr. Williams's Library.
Morley, i. 238.

[18 May 1833]

My dear Friend

I have this moment received your Letter, and am induced to reply to it so speedily by the opportunity of sending my Letter to Southey, so that you may receive it with the twopenny Post charge only.—

We shall be most happy to see you whenever it suits you[3] and the sooner the better—And if my Sister should go on tolerable I will accompany you on your Hebridean Tour[4]—

My subscription I meant to be nothing more than the price of the Mans Book[5] one guinea I believe—but I did not wish even that this should be done unless the case would bear enquiry. His Letter

---

[1] *Written* never.
[2] Lamb replied at the end of May that his sister was ill again. 'In short, half her life she is dead to me, and the other half is made anxious with fears and lookings forward to the next shock.' (*Lamb*, iii. 371.) They had moved to Mr. Walden's house at Edmonton, where Mary Lamb, when deranged, was now always taken.
[3] *Written* it.
[4] H. C. R. set out from London on 6 June, and after intermediate stops at Liverpool and Manchester, arrived at Rydal Mount on the 14th. See *HCR* i. 427 ff.
[5] See L. 757 above.

has unfortunately been mislaid, or I could have put you in the way of hearing about the book at his Bookseller's—

In the extempore lines[1] I filled up the Corner of my paper with were two execrably bad, mere stop gaps, in which the word 'elevate' was used improperly.

—My poor Sister is better today, but for the last five or six days she has been losing ground; Thunder always used to disorder her, and we had some very hot weather which produced that state of Atmosphere.—I fear the Influenza on her account—At Ambleside are 40 people confined to Bed by it—

We will talk about your Lodging when you come. I must conclude to save the Coach for the parcel by which this goes.—

A Coach comes[2] here from Kendal and passes us every Monday Wednesday, and Friday at ten o'clock in the morning—ever faithfully yours

Wm Wordsworth

767. W. W. to H. C. R.

Address: Henry C. Robinson Esq, 2 Plowden's Buildings, Temple.
Postmark: (1) [? 26] May 1833 (2) 4 June 1833. *Stamp*: Piccadilly.
Endorsed: Wordsworth.
MS. Dr. Williams's Library.
Morley, i. 239.

Friday—
[? 24 May 1833]

My dear Friend,

Having an opportunity of sending this note to London, I write with a request from my Sister, that you would bring down for her a Copy of Whites Natural History of Selborne[3] which she has long wished to possess—The Book, as originally published was in Quarto entitled Natural History and Antiquities of Selborne, but the antiquities being of less general interest have not in many Editions been Reprinted. I think I have seen an Edition of the Natural History, alone, advertized, by Sir Wm Jardine,[4] with

---

[1] *To the Utilitarians.* W. W. never published the lines himself.

[2] The four words 'comes here', 'and', and 'every', are deleted in the MS.

[3] *The Natural History and Antiquities of Selborne* was first published by Gilbert White (1720–93) the naturalist, in quarto in 1789. It was based on his letters to Thomas Pennant and Daines Barrington.

[4] Sir William Jardine, 7th Bart. (1800–74), naturalist, published *Illustrations of Ornithology*, 1830, and edited the *Naturalists' Library*, 1833–45. His edition of *The Natural History of Selborne*, published by Constable in 1829, and

Notes and a few Engravings—this is probably the Book which would best[1] suit my Sister, and I believe it is not expensive. Before you come could you contrive to call at Longmans, and learn if the last Edition of my Poems has had a tolerable sale, also, if they have my parcel of books, or any Book, to send me be so kind as bring it.

Alaric Watts used to send me his Souvenirs,[2] and as the last year's contained a Sonnet of mine on the departure of Sir Walter Scott, for Naples, I hope[d][3] they would have sent m[e] a copy as an acknowlegement which they have not done—though I wrote a few weeks ago to tell them I have not received such a thing. Perhaps they have it prepared to send down if so, be so good as bring it.—The weather continues still unfavorable to my poor Sister—We have had thunder to day, and several times since. I wrote you a few days ago[4] and she is not yet any better—We shall be *most* happy to see you

faithfully your
W W

768. W. W. to H. C. R.

Address: H. C. Robinson Esq, Post office, Liverpool.
Stamp: Kendal Penny Post.
Endorsed: 7th *June* 1833. Wordsworth abot the Isle of Man.
MS. Dr. Williams's Library.
K (—). *Morley, i. 240.*

Rydal Mount
Wednesday—5th June [1833]

My dear Friend,

As Mrs Wordsworth and my Daughter are absent,[5] and will not return till this day week at the earliest, and they would wish to see as much of you as may be, while you are here, there is quite time enough for your trip to the Isle of Man, which my Sister thinks that for other reasons, as it falls in your way, it would be

---

reissued in succeeding years, omitted the antiquities, the poems, and many observations.

[1] *Written* besstt.
[2] The *Literary Souvenir*, which Alaric Watts edited. See L. 657 above.
[3] *Seal.*
[4] See previous letter.
[5] M. W. and Dora W. were away on a visit to Stockton-on-Tees (see next letter) to see John Hutchinson, M. W.'s eldest brother, who was seriously ill. See L. 778 below.

worth your while to make, only I must observe, that there is only one *fixed* conveyance, and that by Steam between the Isle of Man and Whitehaven, but there are fishing smacks, and private traders, going very frequently especially in the summer season—To us the sooner you come the better you would please us, only you *must* make your stay so much *longer* on account of Mrs W and D's absence.—

We are truly sorry for Mr Gilman's state of health,[1] and Charles Lamb's account of his Sister[2] is most deplorable. Poor Fellow what he has to endure; and surely, on his own account, his situation, so near his Sister in such a place must be doleful——My dear Sister, is upon the whole considerably better, but sadly subject to injury from the changes of the Weather. She can walk about 20 or 30 steps, but always with exhaustion—nevertheless when the weather is favorable she is always wheeled about in a chair, for an hour or two, in the Garden. Miss Hutchinson is here and quite well.— We shall have a bed for you, and cannot consent to your being at an Inn nearly 2 miles from us, unless something unforeseen should happen.—

To account for this wretched penmanship, I must tell you that I have been using a Hatchet this morning, for a long time, which has made my hand shake—ever affectionately yours

Wm Wordsworth

Isle of Man.

I write from my Sister's dictation, who has been there.[3]— Pleasant road from Douglas to Ramsey—Maughold head is on the right, go to the Church and along the cliffs or steeps. Go from Ramsey direct to Bishop's Court, avoiding the Point of Ayre, which is flat and wholly uninteresting—from Peele to Castle Town—Back to Douglas—which is all my sister has seen, but I should be inclined to ascend from Laxey to the Snow-Fell the highest point of the Island.—Our Sister Joanna Hutchinson is in Lodgings at Ramsey: it would give her and us great pleasure that you should see each other. Mr and Mrs Cookson Kendal Friends of ours, driven by Reverse of Fortune to the Island for economy's sake are now at Ballasalla near Castle Town, they would also be

---

[1] Coleridge's host had been ill: the following month the Gillmans went to Ramsgate, and S. T. C. accompanied them.

[2] See L. 765 above.

[3] D. W. visited the Isle of Man in the summer of 1828. See pt. i, L. 341, and *DWJ* ii. 401 ff.

glad to see you; but do not put yourself to inconvenience on either account. With respect to the attractions of the Isle of Man, my Sister does not think them sufficient to justify a long journey but as they fall in your way, she thinks the place worth looking at for you—My Son John lives at Moresby three miles on this side of Whitehaven; his house is small, and having Visitors he could not offer you a bed, but he and his amiable wife would be truly happy to see you, and make you acquainted with my Grandchild.[1] He would also, most likely, be able to accompany you on your way towards Keswick, in his little Carriage, if he be recovered from the Influenza. At Whitehaven by all means, see the new Pier—And as you were so unfortunate in weather the last time you were here, pray go to Keswick by way of Loweswater; Scale Hill, and Butter Mere and by Honister Crag into Borrowdale, at Scale Hill is a good Inn, and at Buttermere also, But John will direct you, and, I hope accompany you part of the way.—

769. DORA W. and W. W. to C. W. JNR.

Address: Christopher Wordsworth Esq, Trin. Lodge, Cambridge.
Stamp: Kendal Penny Post.
MS. WL.
Mem. (—). *Grosart* (—). *K* (—). *LY ii. 658* (—).

Rydal Mount
June 17th 1833

My dear Chris,

Both your letters were duly received and gave us much pleasure and are as much prized as you could wish. As you kindly expressed a desire to receive a Rydal letter at Paris[2] I ought to have sent one; the fact is, two sides of a sheet were filled but I was so disgusted with the stupidity of my epistle that instead of troubling you with it, it was thrown into the fire for which you may feel very thankful.

Dear Aunt continues tolerable. She has neither gained nor lost strength the last six weeks. She can walk a little by aid of two sticks, ride round the garden several times in her little carriage, work a little, talk a little, read a great deal, eat well, and sleep tolerably, and enjoy thoroughly the society of her Lover, for an hour together, Henry Crabbe Robinson who has been in this neighbourhood for a few days past and with whom my Father

---

[1] Jane.
[2] C. W. jnr. had stopped off at Paris on his way home from Greece.

hopes to visit Staffa and others of the Western Islands by and bye. She hopes too, you will come and reliven her chamber with pleasant histories of all you have seen and done since you quitted England. Father will thank you for the letter addressed to her from Paris and reply to it. We expected *the* Grandchild today with Papa and Mamma but they have put off their visit for a time much to our displeasure. M: K:[1] is still M: K: and the field *still* open to you, so dont go and make a monk of yourself if you please till you have seen her. If she be not à votre gout then I shall only pity your bad taste, and bear the disappointment as best I may. Your message was sent to Willy—he is not a despairing Lover as his love does meet with a return.

My mother and I have been travellers in a small way, and are just returned from a very pleasant visit to my uncle and cousins[2] who have been [at] Stockton on Tees. We drove ourselves in our little open carriage and had no servant or any body to help to take care of us. I assure you our names are up in this county and that as two independent and [? *fending*][3] females. We had no difficulty of any kind. The weather was beautiful but for one day. We went by Ullswater, Appleby, Greta Bridge, seeing Rokeby of course, and returned by Richmond and through that rich and beautiful vale of Wensley. We were absent from Rydal just three weeks. Pray thank John[4] for a kind letter which I received yesterday, brought by Mr Dawson.[5] I suppose uncle[6] is at Buxted now and Sockbridge John with him. We shall be anxious to hear what you think of his health as we are uneasy about him from his own report of himself tho' Mr Quillinan who has seen him does not think much ails him.

We are about to lose Aunt Sarah who goes into Herefordshire before the end of the month. My two cousins Hutchinson who are at Sedburgh school pass their holydays with us and are to be here on Thursday. The country is fuller than ever, quite disagreeably so every house and every lodging taken.

---

[1] An enigmatic reference by Dora W. as matchmaker.
[2] Thomas Hutchinson of Brinsop, and his two sons Thomas (see L. 670 above) and George, who were now, as Dora W. explains below, both at Sedbergh. George Hutchinson went on to St. John's College, Cambridge, and Wells Theological College, becoming curate of Chew Magna with Dundry, Somerset (1843–5), and perpetual curate of St. James's, Mathon, Hereford (1845–56), where the Wordsworths visited him. He later went out to Newfoundland and worked for the Church in Labrador.
[3] *MS. obscure.*
[4] C. W. jnr.'s brother.
[5] The new owner of Allan Bank.
[6] i.e. C. W.

We hear that Pickersgill is hard at work with *the* picture[1] and that it will be a splendid thing. If you are in Soho Square, pray step in and look at it. I don't think your brother John was satisfied with it. We are all more than satisfied. I beg pardon for daring this scrawl but as only half the sheet was mine I thought you would excuse it. Ever dear Chris your affectionate and grateful—grateful for my Parnassian letter—for both indeed but especially for that.

Dora Wordsworth

[*W. W. writes*]

My dear nephew Chris:

You are welcome to England after your long ramble.—I know not what to say in answer to your wish for my opinion upon the offer of the Lectureship.[2] The advantages and disadvantages of accepting you can weigh much better than I. Then comes the consideration how are you to do better? The principal objection seems to be, that if you pass any time in the office of a Lecturer, it will be so much lost for any other profession, and will *force* you into the Church; a profession which ought to be *chosen*, if entered into at all. The next objection which strikes me is the time which you will lose in going over and over the same ground as a Lecturer; but of the force of this you can judge much better than I, who probably overrate it. Then if you go into the Church, is it not probable that there will be three Brothers, saddling (you will excuse the expression) upon the profession, which with the father belonging to the same, is rather an objection. We have the like in Mr. Fleming's family[3] of Rydal.—But after all, what other line could you be happy, or equally useful in? I have only one observation to make on the subject, to which I should attach importance if I thought it called for in your case, which I do not. I mean the moral duty of avoiding to encumber yourself with private pupils, in any number. You are at an age when the blossoms of the mind are setting, to make fruit, and the practice of pupil *mongering* is an absolute blight for this process.—Whatever determination you come to, may God grant that it proves for your benefit: this prayer I utter with earnestness, being deeply interested, my dear Chris,

---

[1] His portrait of W. W. for St. John's (see L. 717 above).

[2] A Classical lectureship at Trinity, to which C. W. jnr. was appointed the following year. He was ordained in 1835.

[3] The Revd. John Fleming of Rayrigg had one son in the Church, Fletcher Fleming, curate of Rydal, and two sons at Cambridge destined for the Church, Thomas (1810–67) at Pembroke College, and George (1811–44) just entered at Christ's College.

in all that concerns you. I have said nothing of the uncertainty hanging over all the establishments, especially the religious and literary ones of the Country; because if, as is too probable, they are to be overturned, the calamity would be so widely spread, that every mode of life would be involved in it; and nothing survive for hopeful calculation.—In a letter to your Father, I begged that he would commission John to thank Professor Whewell for his valuable Present of his Bridgewater essay.[1] If this has not been done pray do it for me, and [? say] that I will write on some future occasion, when I have read at leisure his valuable work. If you see Professor Hamilton of Dublin at Cambridge,[2] tell him that I think of a Tour to the Hebrides and consequently may not be at home should he favor this Country with a visit as I invited him to do, some time ago, upon his marriage. Remember me most kindly to him.—I am truly glad to hear from John that your Father has returned to K. Charles's times. Only let him take care not to play the advocate, but keep strictly to the duty, strictly as he can to the duty of the Historian. Thank your brother John for his last Letter. We are always delighted to hear of any or all of you. God bless you my dear Chris:

most faithfully your affectionate Uncle
W. Wordsworth.

770. M. W. to H. C. R.[3]

Endorsed: 3 July 1833, Mrs Wordsworth.
MS. Dr. Williams's Library.
Morley, i. 242.

Rydal Mount
July 3^d [1833]

My dear Friend

The Staffa expedition has been the last thing, and you among the first, in our thoughts, during the miserable weather which has

---

[1] Whewell's *Astronomy and general physics considered with reference to Natural Theology*, the third of the Bridgewater Treatises, appeared this year. W. W. did not himself write to Whewell for nearly a year (see L. 819 below).

[2] W. R. Hamilton was attending the meeting of the British Association (see L. 759 above).

[3] H. C. R. had left Rydal Mount on 26 June on a visit to Southey at Keswick (see *HCR* i. 431–2). 'I have found *Southey* pretty much in the same mood as Wordsworth', he wrote to his brother on 4 July, '—with only that difference which flows from their personal peculiarities—There is a solemnity and an earnestness about W: which inspire respect; A more chearful and dashingly polemical tone in Southey, which provokes hostility. But I know on the other

passed since you left us—and though this day is very hopeful, W^m says he can come to no resolution until encouraged by a succession of at least three fine days. So that Saturdays being the only days for crossing to the Isle of Man—your departure cannot be *this* week. We therefore all join in the hope that you will meanwhile return to us[1]—I plead this in the name of all the Party—who last evening were planning a petition which was to be sent, to induce you to come to brighten our gloomy hall by your animating conversation. But of course if you have any strong inducement to ramble we are not so selfish as to wish to bring you here—only understand that we shall be delighted if it is otherwise.

Miss W. continues much the same as when you left her. She sadly fears, hearing that I am writing to you, that I am about fixing the time for your encountering these 'boisterous winds'—My Sister and Niece[2] left us yesterday.

With kindest remembrances from all believe me to be aff^ly yours

M Wordsworth

Will you tell Bertha S.[3] with my love that they are not to expect Janetta[4] till Friday. She has rather a large Parcel from Rydal for them.

771. W. W. to HIS FAMILY AT RYDAL

Address: Mrs Wordsworth, Rydal Mount, near Kendal.
Postmark: [? 17] July 1833. *Stamp*: Greenock.
MS. WL.
LY ii. 659.

Greenock Wednesday morn^g half past ten
[17 July 1833]

Dearest Friends one and all

Just arrived here from Ramsey, which we left yester Eve after a charming passage—no rocking of the vessel, no squeamishness.

side, no individuals so perfectly candid and essentially liberal as they are—' (Morley, i. 243–4).

[1] H. C. R. returned to Rydal Mount on 8 July, and left with W. W. and John W. for Whitehaven and the Isle of Man on Friday the 12th. They reached Staffa and Iona on the 20th. Their route is reflected in the *Poems Composed or Suggested During a Tour, in the Summer of 1833* (*PW* iv. 20 ff.), which were published in the volume of 1835.
[2] S. H. had accompanied young Mary Hutchinson (who had been staying at Rydal Mount) back to Brinsop.
[3] Bertha Southey.
[4] Daughter of Mrs. Gee, of Hendon.

Ailsa Craig the peaks of Arran and the whole land and sea views most beautiful in sunshine with curling vapours, and an eclipse of the sun[1] between 5 and 6 this morning into the bargain. I thought of Lugano. A boat sails for Oban this afternoon which we shall take and so proceed to Staffa—which way we shall take then will depend upon weather and opportunities. I fear we shall be unable to receive Letters from Rydal till we reach Carlisle—as I am quite unable to tell you where to address me. The weather has been enchanting—but had we gone to Liverpool last Friday we should have been here by three o'clock of last Sunday morning—but then we should not ever have touched at the Isle of Man. As John wrote on Sunday evening I need only tell you that between 7 and 8 that evening Mr R[2] and I reached Bala Sala.[3] Mrs C well, Mr C[4] with a touch of the Rheumatic gout causing lameness: Bala Sala is a little wood-embosomed Village by the side of a stream upon which stands the ruined walls of an old Abbey, a pretty sequestered place —thronged with Blackbirds and thrushes of extraordinary size and power of song—the upper part of the old Tower is overgrown with a yellow Lychen which has the appearance of a gleam of perpetual evening sunshine. In front of the Cottage where the Cooksons live is a narrow sloping garden richly stocked with the choicest flowers, many of them exotics. Next morning we walked from Castleton to the new College[5] finished all but the top of the tower and thence with the sea on our right walked to the extremity of the left Horn of the bay, where Mr C. told us we should see some *noble* rocks which did not prove quite so noble as good Mr Clarkson's Ducks, but we were recompensed by agreeable views of Castleton bay, town, church, castle, the College, one windmill, the only one of the Island, and the grand slopes backward to the South Barsul, the Manx[6] name for mountain.—all this is chiefly for dearest Dorothy. After breakfast took a car for six miles to the summit of the mountainous slope, on the road to Peel. When we had travelled in this wretched vehicle three miles, whom should we come upon but Mrs Cookson who started up like a

---

[1] See *In the Frith of Clyde, Ailsa Crag* (*PW* iv. 36).

[2] H. C. R.

[3] See *At Bala-Sala, Isle of Man* (*PW* iv. 34).

[4] The Cooksons of Kendal, who after some financial losses had retired to the Isle of Man. W. W.'s sonnet is supposedly written by a friend who has found repose in such retirement, close to the ruins of Rushen Abbey. Mr. Cookson died later this year. See L. 784 below.

[5] King William's College, originally founded by Isaac Barrow in 1668, and reconstituted in 1833.

[6] *Written* Manks.

Hare out of her Fern—and told us that she had been waiting there
an hour and a half beguiling the time with Peveril of the Peak.
She put into our hands a Letter for Joanna,[1] and we part[ed] much
too soon for our mutual wish, she returning to Bala Sala something
better than a mile off. From the sixth milestone where we had met
a fresh bracing mountain air, we found the road descending agreeably and rapidly towards St Johns. We halted under some sycamores beside a waterfall on our left; and there took a nap, to the
great delight of the neighbouring cottagers. Halted again at the
Tynewald,[2] St John's, and here eleven cottage children gathered
about us, and nearly on the top of Tynewald (dearest D. knows what
it is) sate an old Gullion with a telescope in his hand through which
he peeped occasionally having the advantage of seeing things
double, for as he frankly owned he had got a drop too much.
Arrived at Peel after five. Dined and went to the Castle which we
sailed round to the great dismay of my Companion though the sea
was calm as glass, but it broke unintelligibly with noise and foam
over the sharp black rocks on which the Castle stands. At 7 next
morning started and walked to Kirk Michael, 7 miles to breakfast,
crossed several deep ravines and one very near Kirk Michael very
beautiful. (D. will recall it). I was much pleased with Peel Bay,
especially on looking back from the slope of the hill which you
ascend on quitting the Town for Kirk Michael. Here about a quarter
of a mile from Peel stands a Farm house, with a Summer house, that
commands the Bay delightfully. From Kirk Michael walked to
Bps Court[3] and thence I proceeded to Ballaugh where I waited till
the coach overtook me. I had left Mr R. in the grounds of Bps
Court. Near the Deemster's[4] very handsome house I met John going to dine there—I *could not*—nor did he, but he joined me at the
Inn, and we went to Joanna's. She is looking not ill. We had luncheon and tea with her. The Deemster and his Lady came down to
the shore to see us embark. Margaret C.[5] *said* to be something
better. Upon the whole, Dearest D., I liked your Isle of Man
better than I expected. We had charming weather, which made
everything look bright. I am very anxious dearest Sister about

---

[1] Joanna Hutchinson, now resident (with her brother Henry) in the Isle
of Man. W. W. included Henry Hutchinson's sonnet *By a Retired Mariner*
among his 'Itinerary Poems' (*PW* iv. 34).
    [2] See *Tynwald Hill* (*PW* iv. 35).
    [3] Bishop's Court, the thirteenth-century palace of the Bishops of Sodor and
Man.
    [4] John Christian (see L. 539 above) of Milntown. His wife, mentioned below,
was Susanna (d. 1853), daughter of Lewis Robert Allen of Bath.
    [5] John Christian's second daughter.

you, and by far the worst thing about the Tour is not knowing
where you should direct to me—I will call however at the Post Off.
at Inverness in case we go there; also at Edinburgh and at Glasgow,
for we possibly may return this way. Tell Sir Thomas Pasley[1] that
the prices of Lodging vary according to the accomodation—at
Castle Mora, Table d'hote and lodging two guineas a head per
week, at the principal Inn Castleton, not half that money—I could
not learn that there are bathing Machines anywhere but at Douglas
—but both at Peel and Castleton gentlemen may bathe conveniently
on the shore—If Sir Thomas thinks of going, he had best repair
to Douglas where he could be at an hotel till he found a private
lodging to his mind. There is a very agreeable Hotel, as I am told,
called the Crescent near Castle, here the terms are 27 shillings a
head—Dearest Dorothy I thought far too much about your fatiguing walks in the Isle of Man and wished many times for you all to
see the objects which pleased me so much. John has told you about
shy Henry.[2] The view of Douglas Bay is much improved lately by
a new Church, by the Tower of Refuge[3] and a new Light house.—
I called both on Mr Gray the Postmaster and Mrs Puttenham[4]
who inquired with much interest after Dorothy. God bless you all—
the Baby included—How are the Invalids? I ask but can get no
answer, in the list both Dora and Julia[5] are included—Dearest
Mary, we must make a little Trip sometime to Mona—ever most
affectionately and faithfully yours W. W.

John and Mr Robinson are exploring the Town.—

[1] See L. 747 above.
[2] Henry Hutchinson.
[3] See *On Entering Douglas Bay, Isle of Man* (*PW* iv. 32). The Tower of
Refuge was built by Sir William Hillary in 1832.
[4] The Putnams were friends of Joanna and Henry Hutchinson. D. W. had
seen much of them during her visit to the Isle of Man in 1828.
[5] Dora W.'s cousin, Julia Myers (see pt. i, L. 2).

772. W. W. to H. C. R.[1]

Address: H. C. Robinson Esqr, Post off., Edinburgh.
Postmark: 30 July 1833. *Stamp*: Kendal Penny Post.
Endorsed: Jul 29th 1833, Wordsworth, Autograph.
MS. Dr. Williams's Library.
Morley, i. 246.

Monday
July 29th. [1833]
Reached home on Thursday last, our Invalid[2] much improved, unfortunately however had a seizure of spasm that night which weakened her much—she is rallying though slowly—every body else well—

773. W. W. to EDWARD MOXON

MS. Henry E. Huntington Library.
Mem. (—). *Grosart* (—). *K* (—). *LY ii. 663.*

Lowther Castle West^nd [*c.* 10 Aug. 1833]
My dear Mr Moxon
Accept my own hearty congratulations, and those of all my family upon the event announced by your bridal Present,[3] which along with one of the same purport for Mr Southey, reached Rydal just before I left it, to attend the Assizes at Carlisle.[4] As I expect[ed] to

---

[1] After their tour from the Isle of Man to Staffa and Iona (see *PW* iv. 40–3; Morley, i. 245–6), W. W. had left H. C. R. in Scotland and returned to Rydal Mount by way of Glasgow and Kilmarnock. He arrived home in time to entertain Sir Aubrey de Vere and members of his family (see *Hamilton*, ii. 65). H. C. R. reached Rydal on 13 Sept. after another extensive tour through eastern Scotland, the Highlands, and Edinburgh.

[2] D. W.

[3] Moxon had married Emma Isola, Lamb's adopted daughter, on 30 July (see *Lamb*, iii. 378, 380).

[4] Lord Lonsdale had sued several of the local newspapers for libel in consequence of their attacks on him for his involvement in the St. Bees charity (see *MY* ii. 486, 488, 492), and the case came up at the Carlisle Assizes in the first week of August. Wordsworth, as Distributor of Stamps, attended in court to prove the publisher's affidavit, and remained as an observer throughout the proceedings. During the trial his *Convention of Cintra* was quoted in favour of the thesis that abuse of charitable funds by the aristocracy was a signal proof of the moral degeneracy of a people. The cases against the *Kendal Chronicle* and the *Whitehaven Herald* (founded 1831) were not pursued, but a verdict was given against the radical *Carlisle Journal*, and one of its proprietors, Mrs. Jollie, went to prison for four months. See Sir Joseph Arnould, *Memoir of Thomas, First Lord Denman*, 2 vols., 1873, ii. 86. W. W.'s sonnet *To the Earl of Lonsdale* (*PW* iv. 49), which was composed during his visit to Lowther following the trial, was inspired by the vindication of Lord Lonsdale's character which it had produced.

procure a Frank there I deferred making my acknowledgements for your attention upon this interesting occasion, and I write from this place under cover, having been disappointed at Carlisle. —But too much of this, Be assured we all rejoice in the prospect before [you];[1] as I learned from Mr Lamb sometime since, who the Lady is, and also his high opinion of her deserts; and his favorable expectations for your then intended union. Pray present my very kind regards to your Bride, and add that we should be happy to see you both at Rydal, should it ever suit you to make so long a journey.

At Carlisle I had the pleasure of seeing in a Booksellers shop, the Illustrations of the forthcoming Edition of Mr Rogers Miscellaneous Poems.[2] As far as I could judge from a hasty inspection, without opportunity for comparison, I am inclined to think that the embellishments will be reckoned fully equal to those of the Italy.

There does not appear to be much genuine relish for poetical Literature in Cumberland; if I may judge from the fact of not a copy of my Poems having sold there by one of the leading Booksellers, though Cumberland is my native County.—Byron and Scott are I am persuaded the only *popular* Writers in that line, perhaps the word ought rather to be that they are *fashionable* Writers. My Poor Sister is something better in health. Pray remember me very affectionately to Charles Lamb, and to his dear Sister if she be in a state to receive such communications from her friends. I hope Mr Rogers is well. Give my kindest regards to him also

ever, My dear Mr Moxon
faithfully yours
W Wordsworth

774. W. W. to ROBERT JONES

MS. WL transcript. Hitherto unpublished.

Lowther Castle, West.d
11th August [1833]

My dear Jones,

As I am now paying one of my annual visits, in a House where, notwithstanding the Reform Bill, franks may still be procured, I

---

[1] *Word dropped out.*
[2] *Poems*, 1834. The plates were by J. M. W. Turner and Thomas Stothard.

avail myself of the opportunity to write you a few lines as I have often done before from the same place.—I shall confine myself to domestic particulars, which I know are always interesting to you as one of my oldest Friends.—And first, for my dear Sister:— During the course of the winter we feared we should have lost her. No one could scarcely be brought lower and yet survive, as God be thanked she has done.—She is never likely to be strong again, but after having been many months confined to her room, and almost to her bed, she can now walk about in her room a little, and when the weather is favorable, she is wheeled about out of doors every day for an hour or more. Having many resources and a devout spirit, she has supported this long illness with admirable patience and resignation, furnishing an example for us all.—My wife is well, and now with me here, after a little Tour, which on returning from Carlisle we have made together on the Banks of the beautiful river Eden.[1]—

My daughter is well, but not strong.—My elder Son and his wife have been staying with us several weeks—they brought their Baby a very fine girl of six months old. Her presence was a great treat to us all, and of course when they went away they were much missed. My younger son acts as my Sub-distributor at Carlisle. He is well, though in bad spirits, as the situation leads to nothing, and is wholly dependant, not merely on my life but on the temper of the Times which continues to be deplorable.—I have now told you all, and have only to request that you would give me a like Bulletin at your leisure. I hope your health, in particular, has been good. Mine continues excellent and I am active also; though I feel not so strong for bearing exertion as I have been. I got however pretty well this summer through a fortnight Tour in Scotland, when I had a good deal of walking, though our travelling was principally by steam, Staffa having been our chief object. Pray remember me kindly to your Brothers and Sisters. Mrs W. joins me in best remembrances.

ever faithfully yours
Wm Wordsworth

[1] See *PW* iv. 45–6, and the I. F. notes, p. 409, for the sonnets which were inspired by this tour of the Eden to Wetheral, Nunnery (see pt. i, L. 3), and Lowther.

775. W. W. to UNKNOWN CORRESPONDENT

MS. Cornell. Hitherto unpublished.

[*In M. W.'s hand*]

Aug. 12ᵗʰ [1833]

My dear Madam,
    Your obliging letter with its enclosure I did not receive till
very lately, and have since been from home, which has prevented
my returning the Poem earlier.
    It gives me pleasure to say that I have read the Work with
much admiration of the skill with which the Object of the Author
has been attained: the language is fresh and choice, and the versification carefully adapted to the thoughts and feelings; which in
the literature of these times too rarely happens—the knowledge of
the subject, and the accurate observation which appears throughout,
will be obvious to every one—and my remarks are purposely
confined to the style and execution as more peculiarly belonging
to my province as an Artist who has taken some pains with poetic
composition.
    May I beg you to present my thanks to Mr [   ]¹ for
this mark of his attention, and token of his remembrance.
    And believe me, with best Compᵗˢ to Mr and Miss [   ]
to be
                                    faithfully yours
                            [*signed*] W Wordsworth

776. W. W. to FELICIA DOROTHEA HEMANS

Address: Mrs Hemans.
Endorsed: Mʳ Wordsworth to Mʳˢ Hemans 1833.
MS. Harvard University Library.
K (—). *LY ii. 662.*

[*In M. W.'s hand*]

Rydal Mount Aug 20ᵗʰ [1833]

My dear Mrs Hemans
    It gave me much pleasure to hear from you once again, and by a
letter of which your Son Charles was the Bearer; we were all glad
to see how well he looks, how much he is grown, and what strength

---

¹ Here, and lower down, there are gaps left in the MS.

for walking and exercise he has acquired. It was agreeable to us also to make the acquaintance of Mr Graves,[1] who appears to be very amiable; and he is certainly a Man of gentlemanly manners, of talents and thoroughly well-informed. Had my eyes permitted, but they are in a state which compels me to employ an Amanuensis, I might have been tempted to write at some length, but I must be short, for our house is overwhelmed with engagements at this Season.

We are concerned to hear that your health has not been good; as far as its improvement might depend upon a change of residence, if this Country should be your choice, gratifying as it would be to see you here again, I must in sincerity say, that taking the year thro', you would not be much of a gainer by the exchange. Ireland is no doubt upon the whole a moister Climate than England—but the more level parts of Ireland are I apprehend dryer than the mountainous parts of England, Scotland and Wales. The whole of the Eastern coast of Great Britain is much less moist than the Western.

The visit which occasioned the Poem addressed to Sir Walter Scott,[2] that you mention in terms so flattering, was a very melancholy one—My daughter was with me; we arrived at his house on Monday noon, and left it at the same time on Thursday, the very day before he quitted Abbotsford for London, on his way to Naples. On the morning of our departure he composed a few lines for Dora's Album,[3] and wrote them in it; we prize this Memorial very much, and the more so as an affecting testimony of his regard at the time, when as the verses prove, his health of body and powers of mind were much impaired and shaken. You will recollect the little green book, which you were kind enough to write in on its first page.

[1] The Revd. Robert Perceval Graves (1810–93), son of Mrs. Hemans's Dublin doctor, was now completing his studies at Trinity College, Dublin. With his brother Charles (1812–99), later Bishop of Limerick, and Mrs. Hemans's son Charles (1817–76), the antiquary, Graves spent some time this summer in the Lakes, and got to know W. W. His letters to Mrs. Hemans of 12 and 18 Aug. (*WL MSS.*) paint an attractive picture of the Rydal Mount circle. Later, on 12 Oct., after his return to Dublin, he wrote to W. W. confessing his dislike of the 'uncongenial spirit' of the Irish Church and inquiring about the possibility of his obtaining a curacy in the Lake District. With W. W.'s help he eventually obtained the curacy of Bowness in Jan. 1835, which he happily occupied for thirty years, without seeking any further preferment, and became an intimate friend of the Wordsworths. See also Ls. 782 and 783 below. Graves later wrote the biography of his friend Sir William Rowan Hamilton, and some notable *Recollections of Wordsworth and the Lake Country* (1863).   [2] See L. 642 above.

[3] See F. V. Morley, *Dora Wordsworth, Her Book*, 1924, pp. 78–9.

Let me hope that your health will improve, so that you may be enabled to proceed with the Sacred Poetry[1] with which you are engaged—Be assured that I shall duly appreciate the mark of honor you design for me in connection with so interesting a work.

My Sister is much better than she was in the winter—being able to walk about in her room unsupported, and to take an airing in the carriage when the weather is favourable. She, Mrs W. and Dora all unite with me in kind remembrances, and good wishes for yourself and your Sons.

and believe me dear Mrs Hemans to be
ever your faithful Friend
[*signed*] Wm Wordsworth

777. W. W. to GEORGE HUNTLY GORDON

MS. Cornell.
Broughton, p. 46.

[*In Dora W.'s hand*]

Rydal Mount
Aug^st 24th 1833—

My dear Sir,

As you are so anxious for a speedy reply I regret much that I was unable to meet your wishes having been absent from home.

Like yourself I have been touring in Scotland and also in the Isle of Man and paying visits in the adjoining Counties. I s^d have regretted too very much, but for this cause, that you had not time to visit us in our beautiful neighbourhood.

The request that you make with respect to Mr Rogers I should have had no difficulty in complying with if a personal interview had allowed me to do so, but I have heard such unfavorable accounts of his health and spirits since the death of his last surviving brother that I am sure you will enter into my feelings when I say that I am loth to introduce a stranger however interesting to me to his acquaintance. I have been told that he barely shews himself at the Evening parties of his friends—therefore you must excuse me sending a formal letter which he might give way to tho' much

---

[1] Mrs. Hemans published her *Scenes and Hymns of Life, with other Religious Poems* in 1834. The volume was dedicated to W. W. See L. 817 below.

against his inclination and I beg that you would wait for some occasion when I might accidentally mention your wish in such terms as might lead most agreeably to its fulfilment.

Many thanks for your offer of receiving letters which I may probably avail myself of to the extent you mention.

Our common friend Mr Quillinan is I understand at Boulogne with his Daughters.

Staffa and Iona were my principal objects in going to Scotland but I renewed my acquaintance with several well known scenes and had the pleasure of passing for the first time through Burns' Country, Renfrewshire and Ayrshire and thro' some parts of Dumfries[s]hire I had not seen before.[1]

My Sister, about whom you kindly enquire, is something better, all the rest of my family including my Son William who is here, are well as I am except for an Inflammation in my eyes which obliges me to employ an Amanuensis. Believe me dear Sir

Faithfully yours
[*signed*] Wm Wordsworth

778. W. W. to JOHN KENYON

Address: John Kenyon Esqre, Twickenham, London.
Postmark: 24 Sept. 1833. *Stamp*: Keswick.
Franked: Keswick September twenty four 1833 J. Marshall.
MS. Mr. Arnold Whitridge.
Transactions of the Wordsworth Society, no. 6, p. 109. K. LY ii. 665.

[*In M. W.'s hand*]

Rydal Mount, Sept. 23d, [1833]

My dear Mr Kenyon,

Your letter was most welcome. It is truly agreeable to be told in this unexpected way that one still lives in the memory of one's friends. We should have replied earlier, but your letter reached us when Mrs W's mind was much depressed by the death of her eldest Brother,[2] and as for myself, I have been and still am unable to write because of my old enemy, inflammation in my eyes. The only

---

[1] See ' "There!" said a stripling', *PW* iv. 44 and the I. F. note, p. 408, discussing Burns and Nature.

[2] M. W.'s eldest brother, John Hutchinson, had just died, and she had recently been involved with her brother Thomas from Brinsop in settling the family affairs at Stockton-on-Tees. See L. 768 above, L. 780 below, and also *MY* ii. 118.

remarkable events that have occurred in my family since our last intercourse by letter are the dangerous illness of my Sister, and the addition to our family by the birth of a Grand-daughter, who as being the first of the 3ᵈ generation both by father and mother's side is highly thought of by both families. She is withal a nice little thing in herself; by name Jane Stanley Wordsworth, from her maternal grandmother. Upon the banks of the Derwent, 2 miles below Cockermouth, my native Town, her Father is now building a Parsonage house upon a living, somewhat under £200 a year, to which he was lately presented by my honored friend the Earl of Lonsdale; and I am still simple and fanciful enough to draw pleasure from the thought of the Child culling flowers and gathering pebbles upon the banks of the same stream that furnished me with the like delights 60 years ago.

> So in the passing of a day, doth pass
> Of mortal life the bud, the leaf, the flower.[1]

I congratulate you upon the noble conduct of your Br., which is quite of a piece of all we know of him. I wish he could have spared a fortnight for this country before his return to Germany—he would be welcome under this roof. Mr Southey also esteems him much, and would have been pleased to see him. May we not hope, upon some future occasion, when your Sister's health is recovered, that we may welcome you and Mrs K also? It is mortifying that so many Persons, indifferent, or disagreeable to us, should take furnished houses in this Vale, and we never have a glimpse of you here, in that way, or any other. There is an opening preparing, and let me tell you of it, with an entreaty that you and Mrs K would take it into serious consideration.

Within ¾ of a mile of Rydal Mount on the banks of the stream that flows between the Lakes of Rydal and Windermere, Dr Arnold, Master of Rugby School, is building a House[2] for himself and his family to retire to, during the Summer and Winter Vacations; so that it will not be wanted by the owner more than 10 weeks in the year; and I can scarcely doubt that he would let it on very reasonable terms, to an eligible Tenant, and none could be more so than yourselves, during the time he does not want it. You would then have every accommodation, and no obligation be incurred. The pleasure this would be to us, I need not speak of.

---

[1] Spenser, *The Faerie Queene*, II. xii. 75, misquoted.
[2] Fox How (see L. 718 above). The Arnolds had spent Christmas at Fox Ghyll, Easter at Old Brathay, and the summer at Allan Bank, while their new house was being built.

In the way of chat I may tell you that great changes are going on in the Proprietorships of the Lake district. Mr Marshall's 2d Son, as probably you know, the Member for Leeds, has purchased the Greenwich Hospital Estate at Keswick,[1] and is Lord of Derwentwater—and this morning has invited me to meet him at Keswick, which I cannot do, for my advice in some new Plantations which he meditates; so that we hope the beauty of the country will not suffer from this princely Estate falling into his hands. At the head of Windermere Mr Redmaine,[2] a Silk Mercer of Bond Street, has purchased 500 Acres, including the Residences of Brathay Hall, and Old Brathay once occupied by Sir G. Beaumont, and afterwards by Charles Lloyd—and previously, while the Lakes were an unvisited corner of the world, by two flashy Brothers, named Westren, who came hither to sculk, and were hanged for highway robbery. The silk mercer will have command of some miles of the shore of Windermere, and what he will do thereupon is perhaps better known in Bond St. than with us, but we tremble.

You speak of your own rambles, and allude to mine. It is true, as was affirmed in an offensive Paragraph in a Glasgow Paper, that I have been taking a peep at the Hebrides. My tour, which was only for a fortnight, included the Isle of Man (visited for the first time), Staffa, Iona, and a return thro' Burns' country, Renfrewshire and Airshire. The weather was mixed, but upon the whole I and my companions, Mr Robinson, an ex-Barrister, and my son John, were well repaid. About 10 days after my return I was summoned to Carlisle upon business,[3] took Mrs W. along with me, and we came home up the banks of the Eden, by Corby and Nunnery, both charming places, to Lowther, and home by Ullswater. These two Excursions united, have since produced 22 sonnets,[4] which I shall be happy to read you; the more so because I cannot muster courage to publish them, or any thing else. I seem to want a definite motive —money would be one, if I could get it, but I cannot; I find by my Publisher's acct, which I recd the other day, that the last Ed: of my Poems[5] owes us conjointly (my share being 2 thirds) nearly £200. The Ed: was 2000, of which not quite 400 had been sold last June; a fact which, contrasted with the state of my poetical reputation, is wholly inexplicable, notwithstanding the depressed state

[1] See Ls. 682 and 699 above.　　　　[2] See L. 758 above.
[3] At the Assize Courts (see L. 773 above).
[4] These sonnets formed about half of the 'Itinerary Poems of 1833', published in the *Yarrow Revisited* volume in 1835: some pieces were still to be written.
[5] The edition of 1832. Longman's accounts are preserved among the *WL MSS*.

of the book-market in England, if we do not take into consideration the injury done by the Paris Edition,[1] of which the Sale, as we have reason to believe, has been very large. At all events, those Paris publications, morally piratical, are extremely hurtful to those successful writers, whose comforts, not to say their livelihood, at all depend upon the profits of their works. I am truly happy that you are independent of West I[ndian] changes and revolutions.[2] The Stamps and Taxes, as you are aware, are about to be consolidated, as the Boards already have been: the result not improbably will be either the abolition of the office of Distributor of Stamps, or such accumulation of labour and responsiblility, with diminished remuneration, as would make the Place for me no longer worth holding. This I should regret principally because Willy, whose history you know, and my excellent Clerk,[3] who has served me for upwards of 20 years, would both be left suddenly without provision or employment; but we must bear, for I fear worse things are coming [to][4] us. My feelings at Lowther lately called forth the following sonnet,[5] which Mrs W. will transcribe: but first you must be told that our dear Sister is stronger and more comfortable than we ever expected to see her. She is now being driven out by Dora in our little Phaeton. Dora herself has suffered so much from deranged stomach, attended with long and wearying fits of tooth-ache, that we are determined to send her to Leamington for change of air, and to see some friends[6] there, and probably not without a view to medical advice. I ought also to have told you that since we met I had a ramble of 5 or 6 weeks in Scotland with Dora, my first object having been to see Sir W. Scott at Abbotsford before his departure for Naples, which visit caused a Poem called 'Yarrow *re*visited' to be added to the two former ones.[7]

Miss Hutchinson whom you kindly enquire after is with her Brother in Herefordshire and we are not likely to see her here for many months.

Now accept my parting assurances of affectionate regard to you and Mrs K. in which my wife, Sister, and Dora heartily join, and with best wishes from us all for the recovery of your Sister's health, believe me to remain, faithfully yours

[*signed*] Wm Wordsworth

[1] Galignani's edition of 1828.
[2] John Kenyon's wealth had been derived from West Indian investments.
[3] John Carter.   [4] *Word dropped out.*   [5] See *PW* iv. 48.
[6] Mrs. and Miss Hook (see L. 727 above). See also L. 780 below.
[7] See L. 645 above.

779. W. W. to PETER CUNNINGHAM[1]

Address: Peter Cunningham Esqre, 44 Dover Street, London.
Franked: Keswick September twenty four 1833 J. Marshall.
Postmark: 26 Sept. 1833. *Stamp*: Keswick.
MS. Cornell.
LY ii. 668.

[*In M. W.'s hand*]

[*c.* 23 Sept. 1833]

Dear Sir

It is some time since I rec^d your acceptable present of Drummond's Poems,[2] which I should have thanked you for sooner, had I not waited (as I usually do on such occasions) for a frank. Your time has not been misemployed in editing so elegant a Writer as Drummond, an Author with whom I became acquainted in my Youth; it is not more than two years since I visited his charming residence at Hawthornden,[3] with much pleasure: tho' I cannot think him utterly blameless as to the way in which he treated his friend Johnson,[4] I think his fault, such as it is, has been grossly exaggerated by certain persons, and by ably vindicating his memory on this point you have rendered a service to literature.

As your Edition, tho' copious, is still a Selection, it is possible you may have omitted something, which for some cause or other, might be worthy of preservation. I once possessed[5] an early ed: of Drummond's Poems which I should have pleasure in consulting,

---

[1] Peter Cunningham (1816–69), third son of Allan Cunningham, obtained a clerkship in the Audit Office in 1834 with the help of Sir Robert Peel. He was the author of *Handbook for London, past and present*, 2 vols., 1849, and numerous other historical and literary works.

[2] *The Poems of William Drummond of Hawthornden; with Life*, by Peter Cunningham, 1833.

[3] Near Lasswade, during the Scottish tour of 1831.

[4] i.e. Ben Jonson, who had visited Drummond towards the end of 1618. Drummond's notes of their conversations are an important source for Jonson's life. In his edition of Jonson (1816), William Gifford had criticized Drummond's procedure, and now Peter Cunningham came to his defence.

[5] W. W. possessed, when an undergraduate, a copy of *The most Elegant and Elabourate Poems of that great Court Wit Mr William Drummond, whose labours both in verse and prose, being heretofore so precious to Prince Henry and to King Charles, shall live and flourish to all ages, while there are men to read them, or Art and Judgment to approve them*, 1659. The book can only have been mislaid, as de Selincourt notes, for it was in his library after his death (*R.M. Cat.*, no. 519).

in order to give you my opinion whether you might have erred in this particular—but the book cannot at present be found.

I remain Sir, Your
obliged S^t.
[*signed*] W Wordsworth

If you are as I conjecture the Son of my friend Mr Allan C. pray give my respects to your Father and Mother.

780. W. W. to C. W.

MS. WL. Hitherto unpublished.

[*In M. W.'s hand*]

Wednesday 25th [Sept. 1833]

My dear Brother,

Col. Lowther being here for a couple of days I take the opportunity of a frank from him to thank you for your last letter, and to let you know how we are going on. And first for our Sister, tho' by no means so strong as she was last autumn at this time, she is in a most happy state of health compared to that which she fell into soon after you left us last winter. She can walk a little without support, and has a good appetite, and tho' subject to fits of pain has upon the whole so much comfort that we cannot be sufficiently thankful to God for her restoration. Mary and myself are both in good health except that my eyes have been, and still are, in a very bad state—so that I can neither read nor write. Dora also has not been so well as we could wish—her stomach being obviously much deranged—and it is consequently our anxious wish that she should go, before the autumn is much further advanced, to some friends she has at Leamington[1] in Warwickshire both for change of air etc.— Should this journey take place it is not impossible but that you may see her and her Aunt Sarah, who has been some time at Brinsop Court, at Cambridge, before Dora's return, should it be convenient for you to receive them. This I say knowing that it would give Miss H. much pleasure to pay her respects to you and your Sons, there, and to see the novelties of Cambridge.

During the summer we have had Isabella and her Babe with us for six weeks. Isa: tho' not strong was well and the child a nice thriving little creature. While she was here John and I made a

---

[1] Mrs. and Miss Hook, whom the Wordsworths had come to know the previous autumn. See L. 727 above.

fortnight's tour into Scotland, principally with a view to Staffa and Iona—the weather was mixed, but upon the whole our Tour was satisfactory. My friend Mr H. C. Robinson the ex-Barrister was of the Party. Soon after my return, I was called to Carlisle at the Assizes, when Lord Lonsdale prosecuted his Libellers.[1] I took Mary with me to see her Son, and we returned up the banks of the Eden by Corby and Nunnery which she had never seen before. We stopped two nights at Lowther on our return and three at Hall-steads. During the Spring Mary and Dora were absent three weeks —their object being to see Mr John Hutchinson, then in a languish-ing state, and who I am sorry to say died 3 weeks ago.[2] It was however a happy release for himself, as he had much bodily suffering. And moreover had undergone severe trials of various kinds of distress during the latter part of his life. Mr. H. Hutchin-son his Brother who attended him in his last moments, is now with us on his way to the Isle of Man—in one Town of which (Douglas) the Cholera has been raging—it is now happily abated.

I now come to thank you for the particular account your letter gave of Sockbridge John.[3] It tends altogether to confirm the opinion we all entertained of him—he seems very well disposed; but is certainly without a literary turn—so that I see no reason for hoping that either you or I could be of much use in pushing him into practice in the South, which might have been the case, had he been at all likely to be prominent in that way. The Medical Profession like every other is much overstocked, and it will be difficult to make it repay the expense of education, and of courting practice, in a re-spectable way. I trust however that his residence with you has been beneficial in awakening in him a livelier sense of the necessity of reading. Let me now mention his affairs. First I have procured an Agent in the place of the late one—Mr Slee[4]—who manages rents and is quite to my Satisfaction, but he found the principal Farmer considerably in arrears, and he still remains so, which is much to be regretted, as out of £1800 in mortage, the payment of £180 by next Candlemas is required. This Sum I will contrive to advance, but John for current expenses is in want of money which he has not funds to supply, only upon having the book inspected I find that the

---

[1] See L. 773 above. [2] See L. 778 above.
[3] C. W. had written at length on 15 July about the health of R. W.'s son: . . . I think you would decidedly say he is considerably improved in his ap-pearance; and he seems very affectionate and amiable. He is still however (one hardly knows whether to say so or not), rather too little *altered* by his Town life: rather *too much like* what he was!' (*WL MSS.*)
[4] Isaac Slee, the land agent (see *MY* ii. 383).

£25 you kindly promised him annually was due last April.—And, £25 having been paid before, I hope it may be convenient to you to have that sum paid into his hands.

I might as well say a word or two about my own concerns. Your old acquaintance Mr Thornton[1]—late Chairman of the board of Stamps, and now *deputy* Chairman of the consolidated Board of Stamps and Taxes—is at present staying at Grasmere with his family. He tells me that it is intended to make great alterations, and as the *Boards* of Stamps and Taxes have been consolidated, to unite also, as far as is practicable, the Collection of these several branches of the revenue.—How far the new arrangement may affect the Distributorships of Stamps, or whether they may not be abolished altogether like the Receiver Generalships is uncertain. Mr Thornton however seems to think upon the whole they cannot easily be dispensed with. Should they however be treated as the R[r] Gen[sps] considerably more than one half of my Income would be taken away, and I do not think I could continue to live at R.M[t]. We should therefore go abroad. Such a diminusion I should little regret, but what would become of poor W[m] whose dependant situation obviously *now* causes him to be in very low Spirits. Then there is M[r] Carter my clerk. . . .

⌈*cetera desunt*⌉

781. W. W. to EDWARD QUILLINAN[2]

Address: Miss Quillinan, Chez Mad[e] V[ve] le Leu, Haute Ville, au dessus de la Porte de Calais-sur-le-rempart, Boulogne sur Mer.
Postmark: (1) 10 Oct. 1833 (2) 12 Oct. 1833.
Stamp: (1) Kendal Penny Post (2) Boulogne-sur-Mer (3) Calais.
MS. WL. Hitherto unpublished.

⌈*In Dora W.'s hand*⌉

⌈*c*. 9 Oct. 1833⌉

Thro' M[r] Dyce I have received a dedicatory Epistle to M[r] Southey and myself from Sir E.B.[3] it is written in verse and with the

[1] John Thornton (1783–1861), successively Commissioner of the Boards of Audit, Stamps, and Inland Revenue. He succeeded his uncle Henry Thornton (1760–1815), the Clapham Evangelical and philanthropist, as treasurer of the Church Missionary Society and the Bible Society. His wife Eliza, daughter of Edward Parry and niece of Lord Bexley, was the author of several novels.
[2] Written over a long letter from Dora W. to E. Q. and Rotha Quillinan, and following the words '*I hold the pen for Father.*'
[3] Sir Egerton Brydges had dedicated his *Lake of Geneva*, 2 vols., 1832, to W. W. and Southey. See also L. 792 below.

usual force and spirit of the author. As the state of my eyes utterly disables me from both reading and writing and a mental exertion is forbidden me by my medical attendants I hope Sir E. will accept my thanks for this honor thro' the channel of the first letter which you may write. I shall take it kindly if you further say that I am happy he continues to be able to employ his mind so vigorously. About the respective merits of the cause of Pedro and Miguel[1] I know little but the duplicity and hypocrisy of our Government in this affair disgust me with the very name of Englishman. We must not think of purchasing more Port wine till the price falls.

[*unsigned*]

782. W. W. to FELICIA DOROTHEA HEMANS

MS. Cornell.
London Mercury, vi (1922), 396. *LY* ii. 669.

[*In M. W.'s hand*]

[early Oct. 1833]

Dear Mrs Hemans,

So much was I pleased with both the Brothers Grave[2] that I should have been very happy to serve either of them in the way you point out—but at present I cannot learn that any of the few Situations desired, is actually open—moreover, there is a prior claim upon me should an occasion occur where I can be useful. It must also be borne in mind that a Cure or Curacy worthy of Mr G.'s talents and attainments, is not easily found in this district they being so very few. I am aware that this is not the way in which a sincere Pastor looks, or ought to look upon his duties, still one would be sorry to see a Man like your friend buried among the lonely

---

[1] Don Pedro (1798–1834), Emperor of Brazil, had abdicated and returned to Portugal (1832) with the support of English volunteers to contest his brother Miguel's usurpation of the Crown and recover it for his daughter Maria da Glória (1819–53). Don Pedro occupied Oporto, where he was blockaded for nearly a year, and in July 1833 his troops entered Lisbon. The following year the absolutists were finally defeated, and Miguel surrendered and went into exile. He died in 1866.

[2] i.e. R. P. Graves and his brother (see L. 776 above). Mrs. Hemans had written on 12 Sept. (*WL MSS.*) to ask if a curacy could be found for Graves in the Lake District. 'As far as prospects in the . . . Church of Ireland can be called *good* at the present crisis, *his* may certainly be considered so . . . —but his mind is thoroughly unwordly in its views, his tastes and principles are *English* in the best sense of that word . . .'

parts of our mountains. It is nevertheless true, that Parishes are sometimes open, where one would be truly glad to see such a man officiating. For example both Keswick and Grasmere[1] have been recently supplied with Curates, both Irishmen: Hawkshead also has been lately supplied, and *this* we could have procured for him last winter, had he been ready to step into it at a fortnight's warning. Coniston also, I have reason to believe is about to be vacant— these particulars are mentioned merely to shew you that I take interest in the affair, both on your friend's account and your own. And I will conclude with saying, should it be in my power to forward his views, I will take care to do so, only as I said before I do not think that a young man ought to be in a place where he will have very little to do—which would not happen however in any of the places I have mentioned.

Mr G. will bear in mind that the district of the Lakes lies in the dioceses of Carlisle and Chester,—principally in Chester,[2] and if he has any influence with either of those Bishops, he would be as likely to attain his end thro' them, as thro' any other channel.

I am happy to say that this family are all very well—only that my own eyes have become much worse since Mr G. left us—which compels me to employ an amanuensis—therefore you must excuse this note merely replying to the principal point in y[r] letter and believe me to be, dear Mrs Hemans, with the united best regards from us all to yourself and your Son

faithfully yours
[*signed*] W Wordsworth

[1] Sir Richard le Fleming, rector of Grasmere, a pluralist, was inhibited from exercizing his office because of his habit of drunkenness, and his extensive parochial responsibilities in Grasmere, Ambleside, and Windermere were carried out by curates. Some local curates, like John Fleming at Bowness, John Dawes in Ambleside, and Owen Lloyd in Langdale, were conscientious; but there were others, like the Sewells at Troutbeck (see L. 431 above), who were far from satisfactory.

[2] John Bird Sumner had been Bishop of Chester since 1828. See L. 426 above.

783. W. W. to FELICIA DOROTHEA HEMANS

Address: Mrs Hemans, 20 Dawson Street, Dublin.
Franked: Penrith October Twenty three 1833 H. C. Lowther.
Postmark: 23 Oct. 1833. *Stamp*: Penrith.
MS. Harvard University Library.
LY ii. 670.

[*In M. W.'s hand*]

Oct 23, 1833

My dear Mrs Hemans

This note is full as much for Mr Graves[1] as for yourself. First let me say that my pre-engagement to a friend no longer exists, so that I shall be able to avail myself of the first opportunity of recommending Mr G. to a vacancy that may occur—be assured this gives me much pleasure; and now let me express my great mortification, in having omitted, as I think I did, to acknowledge the receipt of the very elegant Sonnet which your young friend did me the honour to address to me. The omission was unpardonable, if Mr G. will not consider the deplorable state of my eyes and the interest with which I entered into the affair of the Curacy—as a sufficient apology. Let me beg you to thank Mr G. for his interesting Letter[2]—the tone and spirit of which have much strengthened my desire to see him for some time settled in this neighbourhood. He will excuse a letter directly to himself as I am still unable to read or write, and shall I fear for some time be so.

As my Amanuensis is unavoidably much engaged I must conclude, with the united regards of this family to yourself your Son and the two Mr Graves and believe me to remain my d^r Mrs H to be very faithfully yours

[*signed*] Wm Wordsworth

Excuse this single note sheet—having to enclose to my franking friend, I am obliged to consider weight

[1] R. P. Graves.
[2] Of 12 Oct., inquiring about a curacy in the Lake District. See Ls. 776 and 782 above.

784. W. W. to ROBERT JONES

Address: The Revd Robt Jones, Plas yn Llan, near Ruthin, N.W.
Stamp: Kendal Penny Post.
MS. National Library of Wales.
Herbert G. Wright, 'Two Letters from Wordsworth to Robert Jones', RES
xiii (1937), 39–45. LY ii. 671.

[*In M. W.'s hand*]

Rydal Mount Oc^tr 29 [18]33

My dear Jones

Your letter rec^d this morning was very acceptable, and the more
so as it gave so favorable an account of your own health and the
re-establishment of your Brothers—tho' with the drawback on the
part of your two Sisters—to whom pray present our best good
wishes. I should not have replied to your letter quite so soon, but
on account of a paragraph which is going the round of the Newspapers respecting the State of my Sight—which in all probability
may fall in your way, and therefore I wish you to know, that the
account was not much exaggerated—but thank God! the apprehended blindness of the one eye that was so severely affected, has
passed away; and I am now in as fair a way of perfect recovery as
any one has a right to expect, who has been subject to such frequent
attacks as I have. My safety for the future, next to God's goodness,
must depend upon extreme care, both as to diet and exposure, and
above all in not fatiguing my mind by intellectual labor, after the
eyes become at all disordered—the severity of the last relapse was
occasioned, I believe, by want of this precaution: when unable to
read or write, one is naturally put upon thinking, and in my case
upon Composition, which always more or less disturbs the digestion,
and is accordingly injurious, even when it does not over stimulate
the brain. This attack commenced the very day I last wrote
to you.

Your present of Books you mention I have not received—if they
have come to Mr Hodskin's hands, there will be no difficulty in
their reaching me—as we can communicate with Liverpool free of
expence thro' several channels. I will cause enquiry to be made of
Mr H. immediately.

You alluded to a Welsh and En: Dictionary[1]—those I presume

---

[1] W. O. Pughe, *Abridgment of the Welsh and English Dictionary* (see
R.M. Cat., no. 412). William Owen Pughe (1759–1835) spent twenty years
(1783–1803) compiling his Welsh dictionary. The shorter version appeared in
1806, not 1826, as stated in *R.M. Cat.*

are in the Parcel—they will be truly acceptable, as I often wish to consult a book of that kind.

My Sister has been doing surprizingly well for many months, till within these three days past, when she had a bilious attack, which has reduced her a good deal, and is most unfortunate as we have now the winter to face. These last seven weeks have been very melancholy ones, as we have lost to less than 7 or 8 intimate acquaintances or friends and relatives, of all ages from 23 to 70 inclusive—the last taken was a very old friend a Mr Cookson, a manufacturer in Kendal, who having been unfortunate in business, had retired for economy's sake, to the Isle of Man, where he was living with his wife and there he died of Cholera—Two months ago we lost Mrs W's eldest Brother[1] after a painful illness. A sad case was that of my young friend Hallam[2] who was cut off at the age of 23—he was travelling with his father, the Author of the Middle Ages, and when sitting by him in a public room of a Hotel in Vienna, his father turned towards him and thought he had dropped asleep—but going up to him soon after, found he was dead. He was a young Man of genius, great acquirements and high promise. Another of our young friends of Peter House Cambridge named Lionel Fraser[3] died the other day at the age of 26—having been married and settled upon a Curacy in Shropshire—he has left a Widow and one Child. During my short summer excursion, I saw my lamented friend Mr Cookson at the Isle [of][4] Man, where his situation and character put into my head a little memorial of him which D. will transcribe, making one of a series of Sonnets, suggested during my ramble. Heartily do I concur with you in the wish that we may meet again, before *we* go hence and be no more seen. Our friendship has been most constant—never having suffered a moment's interruption, and being now of nearly $\frac{1}{2}$ a century's standing a serious thought and deserving our gratitude

[1] John Hutchinson, see L. 778 above.
[2] Arthur Henry Hallam (1811–33), the friend of Tennyson, had been at Trinity College, Cambridge, from 1828 to 1832, where he was one of a group of admirers of W. W., which included Richard Monckton Milnes (see L. 714 above) and Richard Chenevix Trench. W. W. had got to know him—along with the other Cambridge 'Apostles'—during his stay at Trinity towards the end of 1830 (see Frances M. Brookfield, *The Cambridge 'Apostles'*, 1906, p. 134). Hallam's *Remains* appeared in 1834, with a Memoir by his father Henry Hallam (1777–1859), until recently a Commissioner in the Stamp Office, and author of *A View of the State of Europe in the Middle Ages*, 1818, and *Constitutional History of England*, 1827. W. W. had met him in London in 1823 (see pt. i, L. 97).
[3] The Revd. George Lionel Fraser (1807–33), vicar of Kinlet, Salop.
[4] *Word dropped out.*

in more views than one. God bless you, with united love from Wife, Daughter and Sister ever faithfully yours,

[*signed*] W Wordsworth

For this letter requiring haste, I cannot procure a frank.

[*There follows Rushen Abbey, near Ballasalla, Isle of Man, as in PW iv. 34. except that in ll. 8–9 read 'such sparks of holy fire |As once were cherished here', and in l. 11 for 'albeit' read 'and know that'.*]

785. W. W. to FRANCIS MEREWETHER

Address: The Revd F. Merewether, Rectory, Coleorton, Ashby de la Zouch.
Stamp: Kendal Penny Post.
MS. Cornell. Hitherto unpublished.

[*In M. W.'s hand*]

Rydal Mount Octr 29 [1833]

My dear Sir,

It was very kind of you to turn your thoughts to us on the day of the interment of your Mother, whose death we had previously noticed with much regret in the Newspaper; the thanks due for your gratifying letter would have been deferred till the receipt of the Article upon Coleorton; but on account of a paragraph which is going the round of the Newspapers, relating to the State of my sight. This I thought would be almost sure to fall in your way, and that of our Friends at the Hall—and therefore I wish you to know, that the account was not much exaggerated—but thank God the apprehended blindness of the *one* eye that was so severely affected has passed away, and I am now in as fair a way of perfect recovery as any one has a right to expect, who has been subject to such frequent attacks as I have. My safety for the future, next to God's Goodness, must depend upon extreme care both as to diet and exposure—and above all in not fatiguing my Mind by intellectual labour, when the eyes become at all disordered—the great severity of the last relapse was occasioned, I believe, by want of this precaution. When unable to read or write, one is naturally put upon thinking, and in my case, upon Composition—which always more or less with me disturbs the digestion—and is accordingly injurious, even when it does not overstimulate the brain. Pray mention with my kindest regards to Sir G. and Lady B. as much of these particulars as you think proper.

We were glad to hear the account you give of your family, and wish much for the Sight of your letter to John—which we shall receive tomorrow (when our Whitehaven Monthly parcel comes round—to the Stamp Off. by which we generally receive despatches).

Coleorton well deserves that an account should be given of it in that excellent Mag:[1] and I am glad that it has fallen into your hands to describe a Place with which you have been so long intimately connected. Your fourfold division of the Population is very judicious, and I am persuaded that your notice of Coleorton will prove generally interesting. To me it is perfectly horrifying to read the Notices which I find scattered over the Newspapers and Reviews, of publications in malignant hostility to the Church—there is in particular one by a Quaker named Howitt[2] of Nottingham which shocks me above measure, and the more so as proceeding from a Man to whom I consider myself as under particular obligations—inasmuch as it was his house which so hospitably received my Wife when she was unable to proceed, on her last journey from Cambridge[3]—and there every possible attention was paid to her and my daughter by him and his excellent family for 3 weeks. But this class of enemies is not the most formidable the Church has to contend with—they are the rash and inconsiderate Reformers which she contains in her own bosom. One of the most conspicuous and foolish of whom is Lord Henley.[4]

As to the Archdeacon Bailey's[5] proposal, it would [give][6] me much pleasure to have the Eccles: Sonnets printed in that way, but I do not think they would have any chance of selling much, as a book of devotion in verse to accompany Keble's Xt^n Year, or any other work of that kind. All I have to say is, that if any Number of Clergymen or others would engage to indemnify the Publisher my consent would be given to Archdeacon B's proposal. This is mentioned because at their first publication in a separate form, those

---

[1] Merewether's article on Coleorton has not been traced.
[2] William Howitt published this year *A Popular History of Priestcraft, in All Ages and Nations*. It had reached its eighth edition by 1846.
[3] See L. 608 above.
[4] Robert Henley Eden, 2nd Baron Henley (1789–1841), M.P. for Fowey (1826–30), and Master in Chancery (1826–40). He wrote on ecclesiastical reform, and published in 1834 *A Plan for a New Arrangment and Increase in Number of the Dioceses of England and Wales*.
[5] Probably not Benjamin Bailey (see L. 638 above), but the other Archdeacon Bayley (see L. 518 above).
[6] *MS. torn.*

Sketches were I believe a loss to me at whose risk they were published. I have lately added 3 other Sonnets[1]—two upon the Vaudois and one upon the Service the Monks did to humanity, in relaxing and breaking the bonds of feudal Vassalage. If the proposal should take effect, I would strenuously recommend that the passage at the beginning of the [ ][2] Book of the Ex^n should be premised and perhaps some 2 or 3 other passage[s] from the same Work might be advantageously added, as notes. As I probably shall have occasion to write to you again shortly—you will excuse my taking leave of you abruptly. My Sister who has been wonderfully well, for the last 4 months, I am sorry to say, is at present suffering from a bilious attack—which we fear will throw her back—and at the approach of winter this is peculiarly unfortunate. The rest of us are well and join in love to you and y^{rs}.

sincerely y^{rs}
W Wordsworth[3]

[M. W. writes]

We hope you may be able to give us a good report of dear Mrs M. after her return from her afflicting sojourn in Essex—God bless her and you all! *M. W.*

[W. W. continues]

The acc^t of poor Mr Prickett[4] grieved us much but I am inclined to think his inconsiderate expences were an *effect* of his malady, tho' no doubt they would be an aggravating *cause.* Pray say to Sir G. and Lady B. that I bear steadily in mind my promise either to go to C. expressly to visit them and you or to take Coleorton going

---

[1] See *PW* iii. 363, 367. W. W.'s more favourable estimate of monastic institutions was also reflected in his *Stanzas* on St. Bees (*PW* iv. 25). The sonnets were composed several months earlier, in the spring of 1833, as is clear from Dora W.'s letter of 17 May to E. Q.: 'Father has written several 100 lines this spring but only "tiresome small Poems" as Mother calls them who is vexed she cannot get him set down to his long work. *I* dont believe the "Recluse" will ever be finished. He has written two or three sweet Poems, a few lines in one of them will please you especially, as shewing very happily the poetry of *Romanism* and making us wish that some of your Rites had been retained by our Church' (*WL MSS.*). This last remark fits the poem on St. Bees much more than the sonnets, and suggests that it may have been written, in part or completely, two months *before* W. W. set out on his recent tour, perhaps under the influence of Richard Parkinson's poem on a similar theme (see L. 729 above).

[2] Blank in MS. W. W. presumably has in mind the passage in praise of the Church of England at the beginning of Book vi of *The Excursion.*

[3] Not signed by W. W.

[4] John W.'s successor as curate of Whitwick (see L. 482 above).

or returning, on my first visit to London *W. W.* Would Lady B. be so good as favor us with a letter about the Children of whom we are anxious to hear. I dare not yet write myself to any one.

786. W. W. to THOMAS FORBES KELSALL[1]

Address: Thos Forbes Kelsall Esqre, Fareham, Hampshire.
Postmark: 31 Oct. 1833. *Stamp*: Kendal Penny Post.
MS. untraced.
The Browning Box, or The Life and Works of Thomas Lovell Beddoes as re-flected in Letters by his Friends, ed. H. W. Donner, 1935, p. lxiv. *LY* ii. 673

[*c.* 30 Oct. 1833]
Dear Sir,

As I am recovering from a severe inflammation in my eyes you will excuse my employing an Amanuensis, in reply to your letter.— Agreeable to your request the Poem will be sent, not without a wish that you may not be disappointed in the perusal. The circumstances under which Yarrow was *re*visited by me, viz. in company with Sir W. Scott not more than two or three days before his departure from Abbotsford, forced my thoughts into a more Personal channel than would otherwise have happened, and this perhaps notwith-standing the illustrious character of the Individual and his poetical connection with the scene, may have interfered with the romantic idealization which would naturally have pervaded a Poem upon such a subject.

And now having cordially acceded to your request, let me frankly say—that the Poem[2] would have been withheld had it not been for

---

[1] Thomas Forbes Kelsall (d. 1872), a solicitor at Fareham: he was the devoted friend of Thomas Lovell Beddoes (1803–49), whom he first met in 1823, and after the poet's death published *Death's Jest Book* (1850) and his *Poems* with a memoir. Shortly before his own death, he passed Beddoes's MSS. to Robert Browning. He was a great admirer of W. W.: 'Even in his old age he used to quote by heart long passages from *The Excursion*, and in 1833 he had the audacity to address Wordsworth, although personally unknown to him, with a request for a copy of *Yarrow Revisited*, then still unpublished. It is a tribute to the noble personality of Kelsall and a proof of the straightforward tenor of his letter that instead of ignoring the request Wordsworth sent him a copy of the poem together with a letter explaining the singular favour it implied.' (*The Browning Box*, p. lxiii.) See also next letter.
[2] According to Donner, the MS. poem is entitled 'Yarrow Revisited Sept. 1833'. At the end of the poem is the following remark: 'The line "for *pleasant* Baiaes" etc., will require alteration; as it alludes more to what it was in Horace's

the assurance you give me, as high as can be given—viz. the honour of an English Gentleman, that you will not suffer a copy to be taken, and will confine the perusal to two or three of your particular friends. The interest which you express in respect to my writings prompts me to name to you, that the reason why I withhold such minor pieces as I have written, is not what some have chosen to say—an over-weening conceit of their being above the taste of my countrymen: it is no such thing—but a humble sense of their not being of sufficient importance for a separate Publication; and a strong ground of apprehension that either my Publisher or myself might be a loser, by giving them to the world. My 4 or 5 last *separate* publications in verse, were a losing concern to the Trade; and I am not ashamed of saying that I cannot afford to give my Time, my Health and my Money, without something of a prudential reserve. Even the Sale of my collected works, tho' regular, is but trifling—this perhaps will surprize you—and, the state of my reputation considered, is altogether inexplicable, except on the supposition of the interference of the Paris Ed: of which I know the sale has been great—but too much of this into which I have been led from a wish to rid myself of a charge of being ungracious or unjust to those Persons, who like yourself, acknowledge that they have been both gratified and instructed by my endeavours. Is it worth while to add after the confiding spirit in which I have replied to your letter,—coming from a Stranger, that the thought crossed me, before I had finished the perusal of your's that it would be an act of worldly caution not to comply with your request.—Not more than ten days ago I rec^d from a Stranger a letter which was undoubtedly what is called a *hoax*, written with an intention, foolish enough heaven knows, of making me stare, and a third Person ridiculous—It would be paying y^r letter a poor compliment to suggest that it had anything of that character, but you are aware that encomiastic letters addressed to Public Men from entire Strangers are open to a like suspicion.

I am Sir respectfully yours
W Wordsworth

time than to what it now is.' *For pleasant Baiaes* was in the final edition altered to *For mild Sorrento's*, l. 53. Other variations in the MS. are:

l. 51:	For parched Vesuvio's ashy mount
final edn.:	For warm Vesuvio's vine-clad slopes;
l. 70:	Where'er thy path invite thee
final edn.:	Wherever they invite thee· (See *PW* iii. 262.)

Address: H. C. Robinson, 2 Plowden Buildings, London.
Postmark: 15 Nov. 1833. *Stamp*: Kendal Penny Post.
Endorsed: Nov[r] 1833, Wordsworth (books received) Politics and Opinion of the Tories.
MS. Dr. Williams's Library.
K (—). *Morley, i. 250.*

[*In M. W.'s hand*]

[*c. 14 Nov. 1833*]

My dear Friend

Your valuable Present[1] is arrived, valuable for its own sake, and still more for the most friendly and affectionate terms in which the gift is recorded by your own pen. The book furthermore will be of great use to us, who have not access to many original authorities. We have placed it upon the third shelf from the bottom, in the first compartment of the bookcase (nearest the door) in the drawing room—where the 16 books look substantially handsome. Southey's books have been forwarded. If I had had the use of my eyes I would have taken the liberty to skim them, before I had parted with them.

Now let me take you to task about a small matter. How came you to say, as you tell me you did, that the return of the Tories to Place would be the best thing that could happen for my eyes? I not only have never uttered a wish to that effect, but have over and over again spoken to the contrary—my opinion is, that the People are bent upon the destruction of their ancient Institutions, and that nothing since, I will not say the *passing*, but since the broaching of the Reform Bill could, or can prevent it. I would bend my endeavours to strengthen to the utmost the rational portion of the Tory Party, but from no other hope than this, that the march toward destruction may be less rapid by their interposing something of a check—and the destruction of the Monarchy thereby attended with less injury to social order. They are more blind than bats or moles who cannot see that it is a change or rather an overthrow of social order, as dependent upon the present distribution of property which is the object of the Radicals—they care nothing what may be the form of Gov[t] but as the changes may lead to that. As to France and your *juste milieu* it is not worth talking about—(and I M. W. *will not* write another word on this subject)

---

[1] This set of Chalmers' *Biographical Dictionary*, 16 vols., 1812–17 is now in the *WL*.

My eye has had another relapse, tho nothing like so bad as the former, but I recover from it more slowly. My dear Sister is rallying tho' she has only risen from her bed, to sit up, once. Did we tell you that Mr Hamilton is to be married to Lady Farquhar ere long.[1]

I forgot which the three sonnets were that you say have pleased your friends?

A fortnight ago I recᵈ a letter from an unknow[n] Person who signs himself Thoˢ Forbes Kelsall,[2] dated Fareham Hants—whose attention had been attracted by a notice, in Lockart's Memoir of Sir W. Scott,[3] of my M.S. Poem of Yarrow *re*visited—professing himself to have been an early admirer of my works, and having derived great benefit from them—and understanding that this Poem was not likely to soon see the light, he with many apologies, for the liberty, requested that I would favor him with a copy—adding that upon the honor of an english Gentleman he would confine the perusal to one or two of his particular friends. As the request seemed a bold and somewhat unusual one—our first determination was not to comply with it—but good nature got the better, and the Poem was sent with a letter, a fortnight ago—and no acknowledgement has been recᵈ. What do you think of this? we begin to suspect that the Poem has been got under false pretences, and that it may appear in Frazer's Mag.: or some other as respectable Publication. I much regret I did not keep a copy of my accompan[ying] letter; which, tho' it hinted at the possiblity of a ho[ax?][4] was frank and confiding—in a spirit natural to my character—If you happen to have any acquaintance in that part of the Country, pray enquire if such a Person lives there, and who he is.

We were delighted to have so good an account of the Lambs—Give our kindest love when you see them, and tell L. that his Works are our delight, as is evidenced better than by words—by April weather of smiles and tears whenever we read them. Mr Kenyon's book[5] has pleased me exceedingly, and surprized me still more. I never suspected him of being a *sinner in verse*-writing. The work does him great credit, less as a whole, than from the spirit of particular parts. Christians, however, will justly think that Tolerance is carried too far, by a philosophy that places all creeds so much upon the same footing. God bless you, say *we* all.—do not

[1] See L. 673 above. [2] See previous letter.
[3] Probably an early obituary notice of Scott is referred to.
[4] *MS. torn.*
[5] *A rhymed Plea for Tolerance*, 1833 (2nd edn., 1839), a poem in heroic couplets 'on the duty of tempering religious zeal with charity', and a satire on false religionism.

fail let us hear from you *frequently* and if you can tell us how we may reply under cover, so that you may not be charged for letters so trifling as ours. farewell most affly

Yrs

[*signed*] W Wordsworth—

788. W. W. to SIR ROBERT INGLIS

Address: Sir R H Inglis M.P., Clapham, London.
Postmark: (1) 23 Nov. 1833 (2) 25 Nov. 1833. *Stamp*: Kendal Penny Post.
Endorsed: Wm Wordsworth 23 Nov. 1833.
MS. Cornell.
LY ii. 675.

[*In M. W.'s hand*]

[*c.* 22 Nov. 1833]

My dear Sir

My daughter having rec^d a note from Miss Thornton franked by you, I take the liberty of enclosing the reply, and a letter to her Father from myself, hoping that without inconvenience you can forward them.—As the Frank will also contain a 3^d note, I do not scruple to ask you to send it to the Twopenny!

When we had the pleasure to have Mr and Mrs Thornton[1] and their family as our neighbours, neither myself nor my family were able to profit by that opportunity in any degree as we could have wished; on acc^t of a distressing complaint with which my eyes have been afflicted. You will be pleased to hear that they are now very much better, and if it pleases God that I should escape a relapse— there is good reason for believing I may soon enjoy the liberty of using them. At present I think it prudent to employ Mrs W. as my Amanuensis.

Believe me to be my dear Sir, with kind regards to Lady Inglis in which Mrs W. begs to join, ever faithfully yours

[*signed*] Wm Wordsworth

See L. 780 above.

789. M. W. to H. C. R.

Address: H. C. Robinson Esqre, Plowdens Buildings, Temple.
Endorsed: 23^d Novr 1833, Mrs Wordsworth.
MS. Dr. Williams's Library.
K (—). Morley, i. 253.

Rydal Mount
Novr 23^d. [1833]

My dear Friend

Having an opportunity to enclose this wee note, I wish to prevent your taking any trouble to make out whether Thos Forbes Kelsall Esq, was a true man or a Counterfiet[1]—we having received a satisfactory and gentlemanly letter from him, which had been written immediately upon his receiving W^m's communication—but had been delayed 3 weeks waiting for a frank.

I have the pleasure to add that our Invalids are going on hopefully—Still however the most minute caution is required to guard against injury to the eyes which are left in a delicate state.

If it should fall in your way to pick up *for me, dog cheap* the Quarto Ed of the Lay of the Last Minstrel, and of Rokeby[2]—I should be well pleased—as I do not think that these should *not* be found in a Poet's house—we have copies of Sir W's other larger Poems.

We have already found your valuable present most useful—and now that the Hall is our sitting room we take a walk to look at them upon their shelves very often.

Let us hear from you, and believe me to be sincerely and affectionately yours

M. Wordsworth

790. W. W. to JOHN MARSHALL

Address: John Marshall Esqre, Hallsteads, Penrith.
Stamp: Kendal Penny Post.
MS. Stephen Marshall MSS., Record Office, Preston.
Chester L. Shaver, 'Three Unpublished Wordsworth Letters', *NQ ccxii* (*Jan. 1967*), 14–18.

[*In M. W.'s hand*]

[late Nov. 1833]

My dear Sir,

First let me congratulate you on the marriage which has lately taken place in your family and which be assured was attended with

---

[1] See L. 786 above.   [2] First published in 1805 and 1812 respectively.

the best good wishes of us all. What I saw of Mr Elliott[1] I liked much, and I hear him highly spoken of from all quarters, so that the prospect for happiness in this union seems very favorable. Mr Thornton[2] left Grasmere some time since and has no doubt reached his home, but I do not know his address further than that he lives at Clapham. I communicate with him thro' the Stamp Office.

Mr Watson[3] is now in the Country; it is true that being very young he has not yet acquired a taste for the management of his Estates, besides his professional engagements will not allow him to do much in that way; as he is about to embark with a detachment of his Regt. for Corfu—he called here a few days ago and promised to call again before his departure; when, or before I will communicate to him the substance of your letter. One remark I may make at present, that tho' it is true the proposed new road would go principally thro' his Land, yet his Estate lies so high, and it is of so poor a quality of Soil, that the advantage of a new and better road would be by no means correspondent to the extent of the Property.

A few weeks ago I had a call from Wilson Innkeeper of Patterdale with a view to treat for the Broad How Estate—[4] he said he expected me to ask a £1000 for it, but was not prepared to give what I asked, £1200—I supposed at the time that he was applying as *an Agent*; but since find that it was with the intention of building for himself. In valuing the wood, I have always regarded it more as ornamental than as stuff for the Carpenter, and its connexion with the Common-right, tho' under present management adding nothing to the rent, cannot fairly be overlooked. Indeed in the hands of any one possessed of the other Properties, or likely to become so, this point I think really important—and I always have had a wish on that account, that it should pass into the hands of one who might derive this benefit from it, and I need not say that it he were one of Your family, it would be the most agreeable to me.[5] At the same

---

[1] The Revd. Henry Venn Elliott had married Julia Anne, John Marshall's sixth daughter, on 31 Oct. (see pt. i, L. 70).

[2] John Thornton (see L. 780 above).

[3] Richard Luther Watson of Calgarth (see L. 667 above).

[4] The estate in Patterdale at the foot of Place Fell which W. W. had acquired in 1806. See *MY* i. 20, 67, 435.

[5] John Marshall's eldest son William had owned the neighbouring Patterdale Hall estate since 1824. John Marshall replied on 28 Nov. from Headingley: 'I am desirous that we should understand one another respecting your Patterdale property. I think you purchased it some years before we went to Watermillock which was in 1810, when landed property was worth a third part more than it is now in consequence merely of the depreciation of the currency. I have had a valuation made of it by my steward, who says that £20 is a fair rent for it. The general rate at which land is at present sold is 27 years purchase, which

time having made for so many years a pecuniary sacrifice for the sake of taste, I must seek for some return.

My sister sate up yesterday for a few hours for the first time for the last 17 days—and is rallying. We all regretted much to hear of Miss Catherine Pollards[1] indisposition, and Mrs. Marshall's consequent anxiety. As to my own eyes, especially one of them, they continue in a very delicate state, tho' I hope if I have no further relapse, they may yet do well.

I will be much obliged to you if you will send to Mr. Garnett[2] for me your McCullocks book on the Highlands.[3]

All here unite with me in affec: remembrances to yourself Mrs. M. and family, including the Ladies at Old Church[4]

and believe me ever to remain very truly
yours
[*signed*] W Wordsworth

Did I send to you the Proposals for publishing by Sub: a British Biography from the earliest times by a Gent of the County of Durham?[5] It promises to be a Work of careful research and was recommended to my notice by Mr. Southey—I have parted with the Paper and have forgotten the name of the Author but it strikes me that it would be worth your while to subscribe to it as the author cannot proceed to Press without support of that kind.

amounts to £540 to which add £104 the value of the wood, and the whole value is £644, independent of what it will bring for the beauty of the situation. I believe that an inclosure of the common cannot be made without an act of parliament because the Patterdale people have rights upon it. I really wish to decline the purchase if Mr Wilson or any other person will give £1,000 for it, but if you should not succeed in realising your expectations, and continue your wish to dispose of it I will take it at £1,000.' (*WL MSS.*)

[1] Jane Marshall's sister.
[2] Thomas Garnett, postmaster at Penrith.
[3] John MacCulloch, M.D., *The Highlands and Western Isles of Scotland.* . . . *Founded on a Series of Annual Journeys between* . . . *1811 and 1821.* . . . *In Six Letters to Sir Walter Scott, Bart.*, 4 vols., 1824.
[4] The house on the Hallsteads estate where Mrs. Marshall's sisters occasionally resided.
[5] This project is unidentified.

791. W. W. to H. C. R.

Address: H. C. Robinson Esqre, Plowden's Buildings, Temple.
Postmark: 5 Dec. 1833.
Endorsed: 1st Decr 1833, Wordsworth Autograph.
MS. Dr. Williams's Library.
Morley, i. 254.

[*In M. W.'s hand*]

Rydal Mount
Decr 1st 1833

My dear Friend,

My missing Vol: of Modern Drama about which I troubled you has been found so think no more of seeking to replace it.

My Sister is doing very well again—and my eyes are also strengthening—but the remembrance of their last relapse about a month ago, makes me so afraid of exposure that I do not get anything like my usual exercise out of doors—the weather having been so very blustering—nor have I thought it prudent to attempt either to read or write—or indulge myself in composition.

This note being written in haste merely to save you trouble with regard to the book—I conclude with a hundred good wishes *from us all* your sincere and affec friend

[*signed*] Wm Wordsworth

792. W. W. to ALEXANDER DYCE

Address: The Revd Alexander Dyce, Gray's Inn.
Postmark: 9 Dec. 1833.
MS. Victoria and Albert Museum.
Mem. Grosart. K. LY ii. 677.

[*In M. W.'s hand*]

Rydal Mount, Decr 4th, 33.

My dear Sir,

Your elegant volume of Sonnets,[1] which you did me the honour to dedicate to me, was rec^d a few months after the date of the accompanying letter, and the Copy for Mr Southey was forwarded immediately, as you may have learned long ago by a letter from himself. Supposing you might not have returned from Scotland, I deferred offering my thanks for this mark of your attention; and

---

[1] *Specimens of English Sonnets*, 1833. See also L. 754 above.

about the time when I should otherwise probably have written, I was seized with an inflammation in my eyes, from the *effects* of which I am not yet so far recovered as to make it prudent for me to use them in writing or reading.

The selection of Sonnets appears to me to be very judicious. If I were inclined to make an exception it would be in the single case of the Sonnet of Coleridge upon Schiller,[1] which is too much of a rant for my taste. The one by him upon Linley's music[2] is much superior in execution; indeed, as a strain of feeling, and for unity of effect, it is very happily done. I was glad to see Mr Southey's Sonnet to Winter. A Lyrical Poem of my own, upon the disasters of the French army in Russia,[3] has so striking a resemblance to it, in contemplating winter under two aspects, that, in justice to Mr S., who preceded me, I ought to have acknowledged it in a note, and I shall do so upon some future occasion.

How do you come on with Skelton?[4] And is there any prospect of a future edition of your Specimens of British Poetesses? If I could get at the original works of the elder Poetesses, such as the Duchess of Newcastle, Mrs Behn, Orinda,[5] etc., I should be happy to assist you with my judgment in such a Publication, which, I think, might be made still more interesting than this first Ed: especially if more matter were crowded into a Page. The two volumes of Extracts of Poems by Eminent Ladies, Helen Maria Williams's Works, Mrs Smith's Sonnets, and Lady Winchelsea's Poems, form the scanty materials which I possess for assisting such a Publication. It is a remarkable thing that the two best Ballads, perhaps, of modern times, viz. Auld Robin Grey,[6] and the Lament for the Defeat of the Scots at Floddenfield,[7] are both from the Pens of Females. I shall

---

[1] *To the Author of 'The Robbers'* (1794).

[2] *Lines to W. Linley, Esq. while he sang a song to Purcell's music* (written 1797, published 1800). William Linley (1771–1835), writer and composer, was Sheridan's brother-in-law. S. T. C. submitted *Osorio* through him for production in Drury Lane, but it was rejected.

[3] See *The French Army in Russia* (*PW* iii. 140), ll. 1–6.

[4] In his reply of 24 Feb. 1834 Dyce wrote: 'My Skelton goes on slowly . . . and I begin to doubt if, at the present time when the general reader cares for nothing except a novel in three volumes, I shall be able to find any bookseller bold enough to undertake the publication of such a work.' (*Dyce MSS., Victoria and Albert Museum.*)

[5] Mrs. Katherine Fowler Philips (1631–64), letter writer and poet. *Poems By the most deservedly admired Mrs. Katherine Philips, The Matchless Orinda, to which is added Monsieur Corneille's Tragedies Pompey and Horace, with several other Translations out of French*, appeared in 1667.

[6] See L. 521 above.

[7] That beginning 'I've heard them lilting at our ewe-milking', by Jane Elliot (1727–1805), first published in David Herd's *Ancient and Modern Scottish Songs*.

be glad to hear that your health is improved, and your spirits good, so that the world may continue to be benefited by your judicious and tasteful labours.

Pray let me hear from you at your leisure; and believe me, dear Sir,

Very faithfully yours,
[*signed*] W. Wordsworth

How could I defer to a P.S. thanking you for the long and spirited Poem which you were so good as to transcribe from Sir E. Brydges' letter[1]—it was duly forwarded to Mr Southey, who like myself could not but feel honored by such notice from so able and interesting an Author. It is a pity that Mr Hartley Coleridge's Sonnets[2] had not been published before your collection was made—as there are several well worthy of a place in it. Last midsummer I made a fortnight's tour in the Isle of Man, Staffa, Iona, etc., which produced between 30 and 40 sonnets, some of which, I think, would please you.

Could not you contrive to take the Lakes in your way, sometimes to or from Scotland? I need not say how glad I should be to see you for a few days.

What a pity that Mr Heber's[3] wonderful Collection of Books is about to be dispersed.

---

[1] In his letter of 5 July (*WL MSS.*), Dyce had enclosed 'Dedication to the Lake of Geneva, a Poem in Seven Books, with notes historical and biographical, To William Wordsworth Esqre and Robert Southey Esqre LL.D.', dated 30 Sept. 1831. The Dedication was republished in *Human Fate, and An Address to the Poets Wordsworth and Southey*: *Poems*, 1846. To W. W.'s acknowledgment of the poem Dyce replied: 'I communicated to Sir Egerton Brydges your favourable opinion of his verses, being well aware of the satisfaction it would afford him. Your praise, and Mr Southey's, he seems to lay by as a sort of cordial, to which he has recourse, when any ill-natured reviewer talks slightingly of his productions . . .'

[2] Many of Hartley Coleridge's best sonnets were included in his *Poems*, published by F. E. Bingley, Leeds, 1833 (see L. 795 below). 'It was [Dyce replied] unfortunate that the Sonnets of Hartley Coleridge were unknown to me, till the Collection was printed. I was well acquainted with him at Oxford; and have always regretted that circumstances should have withdrawn him from a place, for which he was far better fitted than for the bustle of the world; besides, from all I have heard, I cannot but think that he received hard treatment from the Dons of Oriel . . .'

[3] Richard Heber had died on 11 Oct.

Address: Basil Montagu Esqre, Lincolns Inn [*readdressed to*] 56 Chancery Lane.
Postmark: 9 Dec. 1833. *Stamp*: Islington.
MS. Cornell.
LY ii. 676.

[*In M. W.'s hand*]

Decr 4th [1833]

Dear Montagu

I have been at a loss whether to write to you or wait for the Parcel which your Fragment of a letter announces—I say fragment for the 1st Sheet or Sheets are wanting.

It gives me pleasure to learn that you are disposed to resist the rash innovations which are taking place on all sides of us. Heaven grant that the efforts of those who think like you, may be sufficient to stem the torrent that threatens to sweep away every thing before it. It is *principles* of Govn^t and Society that ought mainly to be looked at: if a just Knowledge of these could be diffused and supported, the motives and characters of Individuals, however eminent for talent, would become of little consequence—an obvious remark which I make with special reference to the Person about whom you ask my opinion. Having never had but a very slight acquaintance with him I have had no opportunity of forming an estimate, beyond what is open to every one, of the inner workings of his mind—and therefore to give my opinion would be a mere waste of words. His ambition must be obvious to every one.

I shall here stop and wait a few days for the arrival of your parcel.—Having an opportunity to forward this free of postage I do so without waiting longer for the parcel—as there[1] might possibly have been something in the former part of your letter, which did not reach me, that required an answer.

Believe me very faithfully
Yours
[*signed*] Wm Wordsworth

The Papers told a dismal story about the state of my eyes—which were truly bad enough, but which thank God are now better—but I do not think it yet prudent to use them for reading or writing— God bless you——

[1] *Written* their.

794. W. W. to WILLIAM PEARSON

MS. untraced.
Pearson. LY ii. 676.

Rydal Mount,
Dec. 4th [1833]

My dear Sir,

Many thanks for your kind inquiries. Since I last saw you the state of my eyes, especially one, has caused me much privation, uneasiness and distress; but thank God, I am in a fair way of recovering the ordinary use of them; though I cannot but feel some degree of alarm for the future, as the vessels have been much weakened by repeated inflammations during the last twenty-five years.

The weather is so extremely stormy at present, that one can scarcely be so selfish as to invite friends from a distance, besides I have reason to look for the visit of a friend from London in a day or two, and next week we expect some of the Southey family—but as early in the week after as would suit you, (the weather being favourable) we should be glad to see you; and pray put your nightcap in your pocket, as I should really be sorry that you should have to go home at night. We have also a stall for your mule, or pony; and be so good, if you can spare the Corn-law Poet's book,[1] as to bring it along with you.

Miss Wordsworth's health is tolerable for her. I am glad the 'Excursion' improves upon acquaintance, and remain

Very faithfully yours,
W. Wordsworth

---

[1] *Corn-Law Rhymes*, 1831, by Ebenezer Elliott (1781–1849), the Yorkshire activist and reformer. Southey called his verses 'some of the ablest and most inflammatory poems that ever were published' (Warter, iv. 329), and W. W. expressed a similar opinion (see *HCR* ii. 485).

795. W. W. to EDWARD MOXON

Address: Mr Moxon, Bookseller, Dover St, London.
Postmark: 9 Dec. 1833. *Stamp*: Islington.
MS. Henry E. Huntington Library.
K (—). *LY ii.* 680.

[In M. W.'s hand]

[c. 8 Dec. 1833]

My dear Sir,

Having an opportunity to send a note to London free Postage, I wish to enquire after Mrs Moxon and yourself, and to let you know that we are all doing well, in which account I include my Sister; tho' she had, after making progress all the Summer, a rather severe relapse about six weeks ago.

You would see a notice, which might well have been spared, about my eyes—in the Newspapers, and it is true that since the 12th of Aug. they have been suffering from more inflammation in the first instance, which has left a disability to bear exposure and fatigue. Some want of care in these points occasioned two relapses, which have annoyed me so much. Had the weather been more favorable I believe that before this time I could have been capable of using them as much as I have been able to do for the last 15 or 20 years.

Some time ago, I rec'd from you the Maid of Elvar[1] by A. Cunningham—if you happen to see him let him know that we have lately read it aloud in my family, and that we were all exceedingly pleased with it. The beauties are innumerable, and it is much to be praised both for the general Spirit of the narrative and a faithful description of rural Scenes and manners. Its faults are, an over luxuriance of style and something of a sameness, and occasional impossibility in the incidents.

I have also to acknowledge Mr Kenyon's Plea for Tolerance.[2] It is ably done and full of animation, but I shall write to the Author myself ere long.

We indulge a persuasion in this house that Mr Rogers will not forget us when his beautiful book[3] which I see announced, makes its appearance. We are all impatience to see it, which he will be happy to hear the present state of my eyes will allow me to do with little or no inconvenience.

---

[1] Allan Cunningham's romance *The Maid of Elvar, A Poem, in Twelve Parts*, was published by Moxon in 1832.

[2] See L. 787 above.   [3] The new edition of his *Poems*. See L. 773 above.

During the earlier part of last summer I made a fortnight's Tour in the Isle of Man and the Hebrides which produced from 30 to 40 Sonnets some of which will, I think, be read with pleasure. These are bad times for publishing Poetry, in short nothing but low price—and utilitarian works seem to go down, with the exception of a few expensively illustrated works. Those of Mr R have the advantage of being managed under the direction of his own very fine Taste.

Give our affectionate regards to the Lambs, whom we should be very glad to hear from and pray tell them how we are going on, adding that H. Coleridge, in whom we know they are much interested, has returned from Leeds[1] to Grasmere, where on the whole he seems to conduct himself creditably—but alas! we have only seen him once here, which is owing to his habitual want of resolution. He flies off occasionally to *Pot house* wanderings, and these [ecce]ntricities[2] he is probably so far ashamed of as to make him shy in coming to us lest we should reproach him *inwardly*, for he knows very well that we should not teize him with censorial comments upon a custom which has become a sort of second nature to him.

Remember me kindly to young Mr Cunningham,[3] who favoured me with a letter and believe me with kindest regards to Mrs M. and yourself, in which all my family unite, to remain faithfully yours

[*signed*] Wm Wordsworth

Pray send for me to Whitaker's and Co. (to be sent by Hudson and Nicholson's Parcel to Kendal) 2 Copies of the Selections from my Poems, neatly bound in calf, and enclose your little bill for these matters.

---

[1] Hartley Coleridge had returned to Grasmere this summer after spending rather more than a year at Leeds with the publisher F. E. Bingley, who brought out his *Poems* and the *Biographia Borealis; or Lives of Distinguished Northerns* this year. The arrangement came to an end with Bingley's bankruptcy, and Hartley Coleridge was glad enough to return to his familiar lodgings at Mrs. Fleming's. See *Letters of Hartley Coleridge* (ed. Griggs), pp. 138 ff.

[2] *MS. torn.*

[3] Peter Cunningham (see L. 779 above).

796. W. W. to SAMUEL CROSTHWAITE[1]

Address: Mr Crosthwaite, 22 S. James Place Park, Liverpool.
MS. Miss Mary Crosthwaite. Hitherto unpublished.

Rydal Mount Dec. 12. 1833

Dear Sir,

The portrait gives us all great pleasure. Not only is it much liked in my own family but our acquaintance greatly approve of it. I have only to remark that I think it would be improved by a higher varnish, which I think would also tend to preserve it; and I would wish you to provide and bring with you when you come into this neighbourhood as good varnish as you can procure. You must also at the same time endeavour to improve the clouds which are not well managed, but the whole composition of the picture is most agreeable.

Your letter has been sent to Bowness, probably the bad weather has prevented the father from fetching his child, but it shall be taken care of. Mr Bolton has been unwell, and when he returns to Liverpool may not be strong enough to sit to you for his portrait, which I have earnestly pressed him to do, as agreed upon by you and me. We very much approve of the frame to my sister's portrait; I do not think it a dear one. I shall contrive that the bill for it shall be discharged by Mr Bolton.

May I trouble you to call for me at Mr Hodgkin's[2] 93 Bold St., and enquire for a parcel of books forwarded to his care for me from Wales, and will thank you to pay any carriage that may be upon it, and take it to Mr Bolton's house whence it may be forwarded by the first package they may have to send to Storrs. My eyes are

---

[1] Samuel Crosthwaite (1791–1868), artist, was born in Cockermouth, and worked as a weaver while he taught himself to paint. He studied briefly in London, but practised entirely in the north-west, chiefly around Kendal. W. W. is reputed to have sat to him four times. The portrait he had completed this autumn cannot be traced, and is only known from Dora W.'s description of it in a letter of 10 Sept. 1833 to Rotha Quillinan: 'The artist came to Rydal to claim the fulfilment of a promise which my father good-naturedly made some years ago to sit to him, and really he has succeeded in making a very respectable likeness of your God Father. It is about the size of Boxall's, only more of him, down to the knees I think, and much to Anne's delight Nep's head [Dora W.'s dog] appears in one corner—a striking likeness.' During the same visit, Crosthwaite painted the only portrait of D. W. that is known to have survived: 'Aunt's which is the same size was begun for charity—but as the work proceeded our charity turned into gratitude to the little man for putting us into possession of a thing so valuable' (*WL MSS.*). See Blanchard, *Portraits of Wordsworth*, pp. 79–80, 160.

[2] The agent mentioned in L. 784 above.

much better than they have been ever since I sate to you, but I do
not yet venture to use them. My sister is much as when you saw
her tho' she was very poorly for a fortnight. She along with Mʳˢ
Wordsworth and my daughter beg to be remembered to you, and
with my best wishes for your success, I remain very sincerely
yours

W. Wordsworth

797. W. W. to FELICIA DOROTHEA HEMANS

MS. untraced.
London Mercury, vi (1922), 397 (—).

Dec. 27ᵗʰ 1833.

My dear Mrs Hemans,—

Archⁿ Wrangham is in error as to part of his statement. The
present incumbent of Ambleside[1] is indeed old, but so far from being
infirm, that there is not one man . . . of half his age to be found
among a hundred with his share of bodily strength and activity. His
teeth however are gone which makes him inaudible and very inefficient in the reading-desk and pulpit—and I am persuaded that a
successor in Ambleside, who in point of doctrine, manners and
character might prove unobjectionable would be in a high degree
acceptable to all his Parishioners. It is my intention to call upon
him, to sound him upon the subject of Mr Graves' views,[2] and if I
had not the opportunity of enclosing this letter for a frank, I would
have deferred writing till I had seen Mr Dawes. I have already
named the subject to an Inhabitant of Ambleside, who is willing to
subscribe £10 towards the salary of a Curate—there is only one
other person in the Chapelry, who I think is in the least likely to be
as liberal—but others I am persuaded would do something—and
probably Mr D. himself a trifle. From him much could not be
expected as his income from the Chapel is only at present between
£50 and £60, as he told me himself some time ago. So that Mr G.
would have a very small allowance to look to, and if he be not
already ordained, and is in want of a title there would be a great
obstacle to his being placed at A:, as Mr D. has an almost insuper-
able objection to have any dealings with his Diocesan that he can

---

[1] The Revd. John Dawes, formerly the schoolmaster. Ambleside was at this
period divided by the Stock Ghyll into parishes: the area below the Ghyll was
in the parish of Windermere, the area above was in Grasmere parish, for
which St. Anne's Church (rebuilt 1812) was the chapel of ease.
[2] His wish to obtain a curacy in the Lake District.

avoid, and the sanction of the Bp[1] would be necessary in case a title were wanted—besides he could not feel himself at liberty to ordain but to a sufficient Stipend.

There are two or three particulars that I should wish to know from Mr G. at his earliest convenience—the one is, what is the amount of Stipend he would be content with, and next (which is a matter of importance and far more delicacy, before I could stir farther in the business) I should like to know from himself what his notions are of that Party in the Church who are somewhat vulgarly known by the name of Saints or Evangelicals. The present Bp. of C. has been the means of bringing into this neighbourhood several ministers, and is known to countenance others, who partly from the doctrine they preach and still more from the injudicious zeal with which they prosecute their views—are exceedingly obnoxious to the leading and most respectable People in A., and to Mr D.[2] not less than to others. Indeed the proceedings of these men have been very irregular, to my knowledge—and I learn from their hearers that their tenets, as to the main point of faith and works are such as I, without pretending to be a great Divine, should deem unscriptural. Will Mr G. as frankly as he well can, write to me on these subjects[3] . . . Observe one thing that the Bp. of C. must not interfere at the present stage of the affair and the less he has to do with it, the more likely will it be to prove satisfactory to the Incumbent. . . .

[cetera desunt]

798. W. W. to JOHN KENYON

MS. Harvard University Library. Hitherto unpublished.

[In M. W.'s hand]

Rydal Mount Dec[r] 31st [1833]

My dear Sir

In your kind letter rec[d] thro' Mr Southey a few days ago, you say 'Still *you* leave me in doubt whether I have pleased or pained

---

[1] The Bishop of Chester, John Bird Sumner.   [2] Mr. Dawes.

[3] Graves wrote on 4 Jan. 1834 expressing his aversion to party spirit in the Church, and including a long account of his views on faith and works: 'I feel disposed to think that the building up of the Christian character, being an education for eternity, is the adequate employment of a whole life.' (*WL MSS.*)

you' Allow me to ask you, how you could possibly have any doubt about the matter? Such Spiritted verses as yours[1] could not fail to please me, come from whom they might. I have in fact two copies of your Poem (one of which by the bye I mean to transfer to John) that which reached me first was sent me many months ago from Moxon's without intimation or hint who was the Author. Mrs W. read it to me—and we were both much pleased, both with its general Spirit and feeling—and with the vigor and freshness which often appears in the Style. Some time after Mr Quillinan told us by letter, that it was from your pen: this I scarcely believed, as I had not the least suspicion, tho' knowing well your love of Poetry, and your love of ease also, that you had ever taken the trouble to become a Practitioner. Lastly came your own avowed Copy, the receipt of which I should have immediately acknowledged but I put off doing so from an anxious wish to have the Poem read over again, less for selecting passages for praise—these would have been too numerous, than to ascertain whether I had not too lightly taken up a notion that your View of Religion was such as to make it doubtful whether there was much ground for preference of one mode of Faith over another. Had the state of my eyes allowed me to read without injury to them, this point might have soon been settled—but the only Person in the house that I can with satisfaction employ to read for me is my wife—and there are so many calls upon her time—and my own engagements with neighbours who kindly come to see me in the evenings, that I have been obliged to defer the pleasure of re-perusing your work—not without a daily hope that I shall be able to use my own eyes for the purpose—and this is the whole and sole reason, why I have not acknowledged your kindness earlier. Therefore talk no more of blotting my name out of the future Editions. (To shew you how *Great wits jump*, I will transcribe a few lines from a little M.S. poem of my own, written about 18 months ago which you may be sure was called to my mind when I read your excellent line 'And incense breathe at once thro sense and Soul'—and what immediately follows.

> Mount from the earth aspire, aspire,
> So pleads the Town's Cathedral quire
> In strains that from their solemn height
> Sink to attain a loftier flight
> While incense from the Altar breathes
> Rich fragrance in embodied wreaths,

[1] John Kenyon's *Rhymed Plea for Tolerance*. See L. 787 above.

Or flung from swinging Censor, shrouds
The taper lights, and curls in clouds
Around angelic forms, the still
Creation of the Painter's skill
That on the service wait, concealed
One moment and the next revealed
etc etc[1]—

I will bear in mind your suggestion about Landor's Ode,[2] addressed to Southey.)

We are all deeply concerned to hear of your Sister's declining health and that you do not hope for her recovery. Our own Invalid, since I wrote to you has been rallying slowly, and is now in her better way—tho' we very rarely allow her to come down stairs—she is so subject to injury from change of temperature and excitement. The paragraph in the Newspapers about my eyes vexed me much—they have not for some time been inflamed, both are irritable—and one left too weak by the late severe inflammation for use in reading or writing.

Probably you will have heard that the Archbishop of Canterbury has presented M[r] Southey's intended Son-in-Law to a living in Sussex[3]—and the marriage is about to take place.

Pray give our affectionate regards to Mrs K. together with good wishes to her Sister—and believe me ever to remain your faithful and sincere friend

[*signed*] W[m] Wordsworth

799. W. W. to EDWARD MOXON

MS. Henry E. Huntington Library.
LY ii. 684.

[*In M. W.'s hand*]

Rydal Mount
Dec[r] 31st—33.

My dear Sir,
The Bearer of this (to London at least, but I hope he will be able to present it himself) is my neighbour Mr Hamilton, Author of

[1] *Devotional Incitements*, published 1835, ll. 26–37 (*PW* ii. 313).
[2] See L. 814 below.
[3] West Tarring. John Wood Warter married Edith Southey on 15 Jan. 1834. They had spent a few days at Rydal Mount earlier this month.

Cyril Thornton, Men and Manners in America etc. Thinking it would be agreeable to you to hear something viva voce about me and mine, I have requested him, tho' his stay in Town will be short, to call upon you. He tells me also he shall be happy to charge himself with any thing that you might have to communicate or to send. My nephew Chris: Wordsworth tells me that his fellow-traveller in Greece, Mr Milnes,[1] designed for me his 'Memorials in Greece' of which, as he says, you are the Publisher—it might be sent by Mr H. if not already forwarded thro' some other channel.

Remember *us all* affectionately to the Lambs when you see them. A letter from C. would be a great treat in this house. The other day I met with a few pleasing lines addressed by him to the veteran Stoddart[2] the artist upon his illustrations of Rogers' Poems. The *Book* we have not seen but I learn from my son W^m this morning, that it is very much admired at Carlisle where he lives, not less, but even more so, than the Italy. Pray do not forget to present all the good wishes of the season from this House to Mr Rogers and his Sister when you see either of them.

I have written this day, by the same channel, to Mr Kenyon. I do not mention my eyes further than by saying that they are doing well, but from the severe inflammation one of them has undergone, I feel it necessary to spare them.

With our united good wishes to Mrs Moxon and yourself

> I remain my dear Sir,
> Very faithfully yours
> [*signed*] W Wordsworth

Pray send a neatly bound copy of the Selections[3] and an acc^t of what I am indebted to you.

---

[1] For Richard Monckton Milnes, see L. 714 above.
[2] *To T. Stothard, Esq., on his Illustrations of the Poems of Mr Rogers.* The lines first appeared in the *Athenæum* of 21 Dec. (see Lamb's *Works*, ed. Lucas, v. 75, 321; and *Lamb*, iii. 394–5). Stothard was then 78 years of age.
[3] Hine's *Selections* from W. W.

800. W. W. to ABRAHAM HAYWARD[1]

MS. untraced.
K (—). *LY i. 343.*

[? 1833–4]

I am not sure that I understand one expression in the passage your obliging note refers to, viz., that society will hereafter tolerate no such thing as literature, considered merely as a creation of art. If this be meant to say that any writer will be disappointed who expects a place in the affections of posterity for works which have nothing but their manner to recommend them, it is too obviously true to require being insisted upon. But still such things are not without their value, as they may exemplify with liveliness (heightened by the contrast between the skill and perfection of the manner, and the worthlessness of the matter as matter merely) rules of art and workmanship, which must be applied to imaginative literature, however high the subject, if it is to be permanently efficient. . . .

801. D. W. to C. W.[2]

Address: Rev. Dr Wordsworth, Joshua Watsons Esq, Park Street, Westminster
[*In hand of C. W. jnr.*]
Postmark: 6 Jan. 1834. *Stamp*: Kendal Penny Post.
MS. Cornell. Hitherto unpublished.

[Rydal Mount]
[2 Jan. 1834]

Chris assures me that a few words from my own hand will be welcome therefore in very few let me try to tell you how the house overflowed with joy when he appeared among us. I had but one

---

[1] See L. 761 above. This letter cannot be dated with any certainty. De Selincourt assigned it to 1828, but it seems more likely to belong somewhat later, since it appears to echo Hayward's thinking in the Preface to his translation of *Faust* about the beauties commonly thought peculiar to poetry (a discussion which owes something to W. W.'s Preface to *Lyrical Ballads*). Hayward visited W. W. in the summer of 1835 (*RMVB*).

[2] Written at the end of a letter from C. W. jnr. to C. W., giving the latest news from Rydal Mount. 'My Uncle's eyes are . . . much better, indeed they would be quite well, if he did not write verses: but this he *will* do; and therefore it is extremely difficult to prevent him from ruining his eyesight: he talks much of a visit to Italy, to lay in a store of images, poetical and others, against the blindness he predicts for himself.'

676

regret that you, my dear Brother, were not by his side. If this *could* have been I should have been doubly thankful—but let us hope that we may yet again meet in this world—that another year may bring more settled times and allow you more of peaceful leisure. I think Chris's looks are improved. He is always chearful and seems to have nothing to complain of except occasional head-aches. The first day I thought him looking 10 years older than when we last parted; and no wonder after the severe exercise of Body and mind which he has gone through. I trust we shall send him back to you with shallower wrinkles in his cheeks than I first perceived there. He has told you how we all are so I need only add that we wish you a happy and tranquil year

God bless you—Believe me ever your affecte Sister

D Wordsworth

802. D. W. to W. W. JNR.

Address: Mr Wordsworth, Stamp Office, Carlisle.
Stamp: Kendal Penny Post.
MS. WL.
LY ii. 685.

Thursday 2nd Jany, 1834

My dearest William,

Your Cousin Chris. arrived last Sunday—to our great surprize, and, as you may guess, joy. He is anxious to see you, and we should all much regret it if business will not allow of your coming for a few days while he is here. I do not think his stay *can* be prolonged beyond Friday, Saturday or Sunday (17th, 18th, 19th) therefore I cannot help writing to you, though one of my short dull letters would not otherwise be worth the postage. It would be grievous should I wait for a parcel till too late.

Do not let the low state of your purse prevent your coming—I will admit of no excuse or reason except that of business—as to the money I will help you out with all you may want, and take it without scruple as I have a little Fund of my own which enables me with great satisfaction to myself to give pleasure to the rich, or comfort to the poor.

John wrote that he would be with us last Monday or Tuesday; but we did not expect him on the former day as Isabella and the Babe were going to spend the time of his absence at Workington, and we thought John would stay there all night—Then came the tempest of Tuesday—and this is Thursday and he is not arrived!—We are much puzzled for a reason for their not writing if he actually should not come at all this week, which seems probable, as it will cut his parson's week very short—for most likely he can only have his pulpit filled on one Sunday. This morning brought a letter from Bertha to tell Dora that E's[1] marriage is fixed for Wednesday the 15th. Perhaps you have already heard that the Archbp. of C. gives him a Living in Sussex, and of course they will speed away to their future home as soon as the ceremony is over—What a melancholy house Greta Hall will be when she is gone—and soon to be followed by Cuthbert who is to be prepared for College by Mr Warter. Dear Wm—the Collectorship[2] is not, I believe, yet disposed of and what should hinder your own application for it through Mr Curwen or any other Friend? If your own conscience and feelings allow you to accept any thing from the party there can be no reason why you should not apply. There is no need for you to take any part in politics, and indeed did you feel yourself obliged to do so I think you could not ask any favour from them. As to your Father's asking Mr Curwen or any one else among the Whig supporters it must, if you *think* for a moment, be plain to you that he *could* not do it. Mr Thornton[3] holds place on the terms I have held out to you— takes no part in opinions and does Government Duty. Poor Betty[4] will I doubt not receive pleasure from your Xmas remembrancer— Though she will never more set foot on the house floor, your thought for her will draw a tear of grateful joy from her languid eyes. Than[k ? God][5] for me that I begin this year m[uch] better than the last—I only fear [   ] the cold—God bless you dear William and with wishes for many happy years for you and all whom you love believe me ever your affec^te Aunt

D. Wordsworth

Dora goes in a day or two to Keswick.

---

[1] Edith Southey's marriage to John Wood Warter.
[2] Perhaps the Collectorship of Customs and Excise at Workington, a sub-department of Whitehaven—but nothing can be discovered about this possible opening for W. W. jnr.
[3] For John Thornton, see L. 780 above.
[4] The ageing servant mentioned in the next letter.
[5] *MS. torn.*

803. D. W. to JULIA MYERS[1]

Address: Miss Myers, Mrs Boyce's, Langford Place, Abbey Road, St John's Wood. [*In Dora W.'s hand*]
Postmark: (1) 3 Jan. 1834 (2) 4 Jan. 1834.
MS. The late Mrs. Jane Myers.
LY iii. 1383.

[2 Jan. 1834]

A wee bit of news from this far countree will be worth two-pence, therefore dear Julia I gladly seize the opportunity of a Friend's departure for London to send you my heart-felt thanks for your kind remembrance of me and my solitary sick room at this season of merriment and good chear. The oysters arrived in the best condition possible—indeed I thought I had never eaten any that were so good. You will be glad to hear that Elizabeth Cookson enjoyed your gift no less than myself—but dear Julia when are we to see you in your own proper person? Surely you will not spend another summer in London?—but I must hasten to tell you the little news I have—good and bad—for I have already written one short letter and am tired even when I begin with you. You will forgive my brevity—knowing that the will is good, though the power tottering and crazy—yet I am wonderfully well compared with last year at this time.—All the Robinsons[2] are well and thriving—and the Norths[3] and Newtons.[4] Mr and Mrs Carr[5] in great spirits. He has an ear trumpet which makes his visits to the feeble-voiced doubly chearing. Both greatly enjoyed their continental Tour. Mrs Dowling is surprizingly well; and Miss Eliza has not a complaint to trouble her Friends with, though it is rather hard she will have to be much confined during the holidays, as poor Miss Jane is very unwell; she is, however, one of those persons who do not spread much alarm being so subject to oppressive and tedious illnesses. E. Cookson is as well as could possibly be hoped, considering her late sad affliction. Her widowed mother is still in the Isle of Man, and will remain there a prisoner till the storms abate; never was there such a season by land and by sea. Edith S.[6] and Bertha and Mr Warter left us on the 17th in a post-chaise after spending a few days here, to the great satisfaction of all parties.

[1] Daughter of D. W.'s cousin John Myers (see pt. i, L. 2).
[2] i.e. the family of Capt. Charles Robinson of Ambleside.
[3] The Ambleside family who had lived in Rydal Mount before the Wordsworths.
[4] Another prominent Ambleside family.
[5] Thomas Carr the surgeon, and his wife, formerly Ann Dowling.
[6] Edith Southey.

The morning was stormy and we would gladly have detained them another day; but they were resolute, fearing their mother would be uneasy if they did not arrive at the appointed time. Alas! when they got to Dunmail Rays they bitterly repented, for Chaise and horses were blown to the edge of a precipice and the 3 had hard work to get out and trust to feet and hands for 4 miles till they reached Matthew Jobson's,—crawling and clinging to walls and stones. Edith's arm was much bruised—and they lost a muff, combs—and other articles. They were most thankful at finding themselves alive at their own home, and the next day no worse for their fears and sufferings. On Christmas Eve Dora had a letter from Edith telling her that Warter was to be presented to a Living in Sussex by the Archbishop of Canterbury and the marriage *must* be very soon.[1] D. had fixed to go to her Friend on Thursday but Christopher Words-worth[2] unexpectedly arrived last Sunday and we are expecting John from Moresby, so she must put off her journey yet a few days. Cuthbert will soon follow the new-married pair, as Mr Warter has undertaken the charge of Cuthbert's education till fitted for one of the Universities. What a dull house Greta Hall will be for a while after the two are gone. We all liked Mr Warter much. Mrs Luff is in London with Lady Farquhar (but perhaps you have seen her)— and Lady F. is soon to be married to Mr Hamilton.[3] We are all well pleased, thinking the parties most suitably joined together.—Poor old Betty[4] is very ill, and I fear we shall soon lose her—indeed I ought not to say *I fear*, for her sufferings are great and there is no prospect of recovery.—Dear Julia excuse me for an abrupt conclu-sion. Accept a thousand good wishes from myself and all in this house, and believe me ever your affec^te D Wordsworth.

[1] It took place on 15 Jan. See L. 798 above.
[2] i.e. C. W. jnr.
[3] Capt. Thomas Hamilton.
[4] The old servant at Rydal Mount.

804. W. W. to ALLAN CUNNINGHAM

Address: A. Cunningham Esqre, F. L. Chauntrys Esq, Lower Belgrave Place.
Postmark: 17 Jan. 1834. *Stamp*: Oxford St.
MS. Mr. W. Hugh Peal.
K (—). *LT ii. 693* (—).

[*In M. W.'s hand*]

[*c. 13 Jan. 1834*]

My dear Sir,

Perhaps you may not bear in mind that several years ago a wish was expressed by me[1] to have 3 Plaster Casts of my Bust sent to near Relatives of mine; 2 of them to nephews who are fellows of Trinity Col: Cambridge, and reside there, and the third for my Daughter-in-law who lives at Moresby, near Whitehaven Cumberland. You were so kind as to say, that, out of consideration for whom they were intended, the expence sh^d be made as easy to me as possible. One of my nephews is now in my house,[2] and reminds me so urgently of that promise that I feel obliged to fulfil it. I therefore do not scruple to recall the conversation to your recollection—not doubting but it will be as agreeable to yourself as to me to have my wishes so fulfilled.

Mr Moxon, from whom I heard yesterday tells me that you were gratified by my commendation of your Maid of Elvar[3]—it was read to me when I was unable to make use of my own eyes in that way. The little audience of my family were as much pleased as myself— and indeed I can sincerely say that the Poem is full of Spirit and poetic movement. We have also read the Vol: with pleasure, of your Lives of the Painters,[4] containing that of my lamented friend Sir G. Beaumont. I wish I had seen the MS. before the book was printed, as I could have corrected some errors in matter of fact, and supplied some deficiencies. If this life should be re-printed shortly, I will with pleasure do this for you. I have also a copy of verses inspired by his memory[5] that, if not too long—for I think they amount to between 50 and 60 lines—I would place at y^r disposal for the same purpose.

I was gratified by learning from his handsome ed^n of Drummond which y^r Son[6] sent me, that he had taken a turn for Letters. Pray

---

[1] See L. 601 above.
[2] C. W. jnr., who left for Cambridge the next day, probably taking this letter with him.
[3] See L. 795 above. [4] The sixth and last volume, published in 1833.
[5] See *Elegiac Musings* (*PW* iv. 270) and L. 582 above.
[6] Peter Cunningham (see L. 779 above).

remember me kindly to him and to Mrs Cunningham, and also
to Mr and Mrs Chauntry.

I remain my d^r Sir
faithfully your obliged Friend
[*signed*] Wm Wordsworth

The Bust to Moresby may be sent by Sea directed to the Rev^d
J Wordsworth
Moresby
near Whitehaven.

The other to the Rev^d Cr. Wordsworth
Trinity Col:
Cambridge.

805. D. W. to LADY BEAUMONT

MS. Pierpont Morgan Library.
K (—). *LY ii. 686.*

Monday, Jan^{ry} 13th, [1834]

My dear Lady Beaumont,

I will not tire you with explanations of the causes of my long
silence, and still less would I burthen you with excuse and apology;
but in justice to Rydal Mount I must take upon myself the blame of
the long silence kept up by the whole household, for it belongs to
me alone; but so far from its being a proof that I was indifferent to
the kindness expressed in your letter, it was the fulness of my
gratitude which impelled me to assure my Sister that I would
myself write when she offered, as she has too often been obliged to
do, to write for me. I did, however, then think (as I have double
reasons now for thinking) that you would be no gainer by my
choice; yet it was not an unpleasing fancy to me to believe that the
pleasure of seeing my handwriting (as a proof of increased strength,
and better health) might more than compensate for your loss.

You may believe that during the long time passed since you so
kindly wrote to me, there have been many days in which, as an invalid, I have not been able to use my pen; but latterly I have delayed writing in hopes I should be able to tell you that my Niece
was really soon to have the satisfaction of meeting with you at
Leamington. Nothing, however, could be fixed till after Miss
Southey's marriage; an event which, as to time, remained all

uncertain till the Archbishop, your venerable Father, in his goodness, thought fit to present Mr Warter, the intended husband, to a Living[1] which will enable them to live in all the comfort they could wish for. The Pair are to be married on Wednesday, and Dora is gone to Keswick to act as Bridesmaid to this, the last of her unmarried Friends of an age agreeing with her own. Of course Dora is happy in anticipation of her Friend's happiness; but she so dreads the loss of her, and knows so well what a chasm will be left in her Parents' house, that she would have gone off with a sad heart under any circumstances; but at present the weight is twofold. To spend a few 'last days' with Edith Southey she was obliged abruptly to part from her eldest Brother and her cousin Christopher, who had both come unlooked-for to see us, and the former is already gone, and the cousin must depart to-morrow, to prepare for a commencement of College duties as Greek Lecturer[2] of *Undergraduates* (I add the last words to explain, not knowing exactly the title of his office). Mr and Mrs Merewether (Christ^r W. has not the happiness of being personally acquainted with *you*) will be sorry to hear that we think he has drawn too largely upon his strength during a nine months' residence in Greece, and long pedestrian Travels in Switzerland. He is thin and pale, and his lively spirits are often oppressed by the Scholar's malady, headaches, attended, as I think by something of bilious disorder. He is, however, so much better than, as it seems, he was some weeks ago, that I hope nothing is wanted but a little more time for perfect restoration.

Wednesday, January 15th.

I began my letter upon too large a scale, by which, my dear Lady Beaumont, you are no gainer, for in this case, as in most others, the longer the letter the more tiresome or dull. This, however, I trust you will kindly excuse, and this is not my reason for making this complaint against myself. It is, that I happened to be a little unwell, and therefore I was obliged to put aside my paper and have been unable to go on from various causes until this day, the very day of the wedding. My Brother and Sister are preparing to go down the Rydal Mount Hill to the turnpike road, where they will pace backward and forward to shake hands with and give their Blessing to the Bride and Bridegroom on their way southward.

[1] West Tarring, Sussex.
[2] C. W. jnr. was about to take up his appointment as Classical Lecturer at Trinity.

Though the air is as mild as in the Month of May, and the sun, after many days of gloom and darkness, shines sweetly upon them, and though there is every cause for thankfulness and hope, I fear neither sunshine nor genial breezes will dispel the sadness of Greta Hall; yet Mr Southey himself, who will perhaps most constantly and most deeply feel the loss, will, I am sure, make such efforts to hide or to stifle his feelings that the saddest heart among them cannot but be cheared. Mr Warter is much beloved by the whole Family into which he has entered, and *we* have formed a very favorable opinion of him. He and Miss Southey, and her Sister and Brother,[1] spent a few days with us as soon as my Brother's eyes would allow him to enjoy *any* company. For a very long time his Wife and Daughter were in constant watchful attendance,—either reading to or writing for him,—and I was beginning to hope that Dora might summon the resolution to go to Leamington after the marriage, but this she now declares she *cannot* do, she should be so very wretched at a distance from her Father, till his eyesight is more strengthened and secure; so we must now look forward to the time when the Two may venture on their travels together, which I hope, whenever it is, may take them within reach of you. My Sister cannot make a Third, as, Miss Hutchinson not being at Rydal,[2] she could not leave me. I somewhat boldly did once hope that *I* might next spring be able to visit Cambridge and Coleorton, but I now feel that home is likely to be the place for me—and no hardship! for my prison (if we may so call it) is one of the prettiest and most chearful in England, including what is to be seen from the windows; and I have no bodily oppression but from weakness, with occasional fits of uneasy pain that is not violent.

I was grateful to you for all your communications, domestic and parish, for as long as I live I must retain affectionate and tender recollections of Whitwick and Coleorton, and shall be thankful if the day ever comes when I again set foot in the Hall and the two parsonage-houses; and need I add that it would delight me to see your little Boys playing on the lawn? How distinctly do I recollect the nursery, and you, with your Baby on your knee, and the delighted (*grandmother*, I began to write and let it stand), looking on! Great and melancholy the changes since that day,—and your own Families have been severely tried,—yet happy are you in having such a comforter and such support at the head of them. I do not speak of public anxieties and public cares, the subject is too weighty and perplexing for my poor mind; and I hope that the Archbishop's

---

[1] Bertha and Cuthbert Southey.   [2] S. H. was still at Brinsop.

lessons are not so thrown away upon me as that I am not enabled
to trust with calmness that God's good providence will order all
things for the best.

It is time that I should lay down the pen, for again I am getting
into my old fault—seeking brevity, and never finding it. You must
forgive me, for it is in confidence of your friendship that I go on.
My Brother promises to add a few words, therefore I conclude with
begging you to present my respectful and affectionate regards to
Sir George, with sincerest wishes that the next year may be a
happy one—not like the last, a year of much sorrow and care!

Pray remember me affectionately, and with best wishes, to the
Merewethers, and believe me ever, my dear Lady Beaumont,
your affectionate and much obliged friend

Dorothy Wordsworth.

You will excuse my irregular handwriting, and my many blots
and erasures, especially when told that I always write with the
paper outspread on my knee.

Thursday morning. Mr Merewether will be interested in knowing
that my Nephew John was summoned from us by the Death of his
Wife's valuable uncle Mr Stanley,[1] Rector of Workington, a great
loss to the whole Family, and it has been a heavy affliction to
John and his wife. Mrs J. W. Warter left us marriage tokens at the
foot of the Hill, but was so much affected as to be unable to speak
to the person who took them in charge. We have not heard that
you are actually gone to Leamington, but I conclude you are there;
yet the winter has been warm enough even for Coleorton. I hope
you are stronger.

[1] The Revd. Edward Stanley (see L. 562 above) had died at Workington
on 5 Jan. The living was immediately offered to John W. for three years until
his brother-in-law Henry Curwen was ready to be presented to it. 'Workington
is considered the best living in the two counties,' Dora W. explained to E. Q.
on 20 Feb., 'and John is looked upon by the world as "a lucky fellow"—but we
who see behind the scenes know he will be a much richer and a *thousand* times
happier man when he quits this "*fat Rectory*" for his pretty little quiet vicarage
at Brigham.' C. W. was also advising W. W. at this time to apply to Lord
Liverpool (see L. 592 above) for a chaplaincy for his son. As he wrote on 2
Jan., '. . . You are so high in his favour that I should think, if you were to apply
to him direct, in your own person, he would have pleasure in complying with
your request.' (*WL MSS.*) But if the approach was made, it was unsuccessful.

806. W. W. to EDWARD MOXON

Address: Mr Moxon, Bookseller, Dover Street.
Postmark: 17 Jan. [18]34. *Stamp*: Oxford St.
MS. Henry E. Huntington Library.
K (—). LY ii. 692.

[*In M. W.'s hand*]

[January 14th, 1834]¹

My dear Sir,
    The valuable Parcel is arrived; we are charmed with the design
and execution of the illustrations, and with the taste of the whole
work² which and its companion the Italy will shine as Brother
Stars, tho' not twin-born, in the hemisphere of Literature for
many centuries. I have read also some part of Mr Milnes's Book, the
Dedication³ of which is for its length one [of]⁴ the most admirable
Specimens of that class of composition to be found in the whole
compass of English Literature. Of the Poems also I can say, tho' I
have yet read but a few of them, that they add another to the proofs
that much poetical Genius is stirring among the youth of this
Country. In the work of Alan Cunningham⁵ to which you refer he
has trifled with his own good name in Authorship. He is a man of
distinguished talents, both as a Poet and a Biographer and ought to
be more careful than he has been in the work you criticize, were it
only for considerations of pecuniary gain. I do not know who could
take the liberty to tell him this, but I am sure it would be a friendly
act.
    Many thanks for the truly friendly invitation which Mrs M.
and you have sent us: it would delight me to renew my acquaintance
with her, a desire which I feel still more strongly, both since she
became y^r Wife, and since I read Mr Lamb's discriminating verses⁶

---

    ¹ Date added in another hand, probably by reference to Edith Southey's
wedding on the 15th. C. W. jnr. may have taken this letter with him when he
left Rydal Mount for Cambridge.
    ² The new edition of Samuel Rogers's *Poems*. See next letter.
    ³ Richard Monckton Milnes, *Memorials of a Tour in some Parts of Greece*,
1834 (see L. 714 above), was dedicated to Henry Hallam in memory of his son
Arthur, 'whom I loved with the truth of early friendship . . . we, the contemporaries of your dear son . . . are deprived, not only of a beloved friend, of a
delightful companion, but of a most wise and influential counsellor in all the
serious concerns of existence, of an incomparable critic in all our literary efforts,
and of the example of one who was as much before us in everything else, as
he is now in the way of life'.
    ⁴ *Word dropped out.*   ⁵ *Written* Alingham.
    ⁶ *To a Friend on his Marriage* (*Works*, ed. Lucas, v. 75) appeared in the
Athenæum of 7 Dec. 1833. See also *Lamb*, iii. 386–7.

which I had not seen till the copy of the Athenaeum you kindly sent, reached me. C. Lamb's verses are always delightful, as is every thing he writes, for he both feels and thinks. Will he excuse me for observing that the couplet,

like a signet signed
By a strong hand seemed burnt

appears to me incorrect in the expression, as a signet [is][1] a seal and not the impress of a seal; we do not burn by a seal, but by a branding iron.

It grieved us all to the heart to hear of dear Miss Lamb's illness. Miss Southey is to be married to-morrow. Our daughter is with her, or she would have sent her thanks for the plates you have been so good as to add to the little collection she formerly received from you. But I may say that she is very sensible of your kindness.

I feel so many difficulties in the way of publishing the Poems you allude to, as I do of profitting by y^r hospitable invitation, that I know not what to say upon either subject more than that it would please me and mine *much* to meet your wishes in both cases.

My eyes continue to improve, but I cannot say that they can yet stand all seasons and all Works. My Sister continues better, and we all unite in sincere regards and best wishes to you and y^r wife.

I remain my d^r Sir
sincerely y^r friend
[*signed*] Wm Wordsworth

807. W. W. to SAMUEL ROGERS

MS. Sharpe Collection, University College, London.
Rogers. K (—). LY ii. 691.

[*In M. W.'s hand*]

Jan 14th [1834]

My dear Friend,

Yesterday I received your most valuable present of 3 copies of y^r beautiful Book,[2] which I assure you will be nowhere more prized than in this house. My Sister was affected even to the shedding of tears by this token of your remembrance. When a Person has been shut up for upwards of 12 months in a sick room it is

---

[1] *Word dropped out.*   [2] *Poems*, 1834. See L. 773 above.

a touching thing to receive proofs, from time to time, of not being forgotten. Dora is at Keswick to attend as Bridesmaid upon Miss Southey, who loses her family name to-morrow. Your book has been forwarded, and we hope it will be rec^d at Greta Hall to-day.

Of the execution of the Plates, as compared with the former Vol, and the merit of the designs, we have not yet had time to judge. But I cannot forbear adding that as several of the Poems are among my oldest and dearest acquaintance in the Literature of our day, such an elegant Ed: of them, with their illustrations, must to me be peculiarly acceptable. As Mr Moxon does not mention your health, I hope it is good, and your Sister's also, who, we are happy to hear, has drawn nearer to you. Pray remember us all most kindly to her, and accept yourself our united thanks and best wishes.

I remain, my dear R.

faithfully yours
[*signed*] Wm Wordsworth

We were grieved to notice the death of the veteran Sotheby.[1] Not less than 14 of our Relatives, friends, or valued acquaintance have been removed by death within the last 3 or 4 months.

808. W. W. to LADY BEAUMONT

MS. Pierpont Morgan Library.
K (—). *LY ii. 690.*

[15 Jan. 1834 *or soon after*][2]

My dear Lady Beaumont,

You will excuse my employing Mrs W's pen to express my regret that the health, neither of Sir Geo nor yourself, is fitted to bear the climate of Coleorton during the winter season. Sincerely do I wish the air of Leamington may agree better with you. My dear Sister was timid and scrupulous about sending so long a letter [   ][3] particulars. but in her confinement and the [   ] [she d]welt upon the events of the day and the hour as [   ] upon her, in her now comparatively narrow sphere of earthly hopes and interests.

Believe me, d^r Lady B, my wish is very strong to see your rising family, and especially if I could have that pleasure in my old

---

[1] William Sotheby, the poet and translator (see *EY*, p. 455 and pt. i, L. 278) had died on 30 Dec. 1833.

[2] As de Selincourt points out, this undated letter must have been written to accompany D. W.'s letter of 13–15 Jan., or shortly afterwards.

[3] The MS. has been partly cut away, doubtless for the sake of the signature on the reverse.

haunts at Coleorton. Our thoughts in this house turn very much upon the impending fate of the Ch: and also, as is natural, they are directed often to y^r Father,[1] whose high office had never more anxious duties attached to it since the overthrow of the Ch: in Charles I^st's time.

Were you ever told that my Son is building a parsonage house upon a small Living, to which he was lately presented by the Earl of Lonsdale? The situation is beautiful, commanding the windings of the Derwent both above and below the site of the House; the mountain Skiddaw terminating the view one way, at a distance of 6 miles—and the ruins of Cockermouth Castle appearing nearly in the centre of the same view. In consequence of some discouraging thoughts—expressed by my Son when he had entered upon this undertaking, I addressed to him the following Sonnet,[2] which you may perhaps read with some interest at the present crisis.

Pray accept Mrs Wordsworth's affectionate remembrance (and in her own name, let her add her apologies for such an ill-penned note) to yourself and Sir Geo, and at the rectory[3] [? please make] our united regards, and believe me, my d^r Lady B. to be, [faithfully yours,

Wm Wordsworth][4]

809. W. W. to ROBERT PERCEVAL GRAVES

Address: R. P. Graves Esqre, Trinity Col., Dublin.
Postmark: 1 Feb. 1834. *Stamp*: Kendal Penny Post.
Endorsed: W. Wordsworth Jan^ry 30/34.
MS. Lilly Library, Indiana University.
London Mercury, vi (1922), 398. LY ii. 694.

[*In M. W.'s hand*]

Rydal Mount Jan. 30th [1834]

My dear Sir,

My first words must thank you for your admirable letter,[5] which is in every point satisfactory; my next, to express my belief

---

[1] Dr. William Howley, the Archbishop of Canterbury.
[2] At the bottom of the sheet is the sonnet 'Pastor and Patriot!', as in *PW* iv. 24, but in l. 9 read: To Him who dwells in Heaven will be the smoke. Dora W., writing to E. Q. in February, sent him the sonnet 'addressed to John whose spirit failed him somewhat on finding he should be obliged to lay out so much money on his parsonage which might be taken from him any day by the reformed Parliament . . .' (*WL MSS.*).   [3] i.e. the Merewethers.
[4] Signature cut away from MS., but possibly *after* Knight had seen the letter.
[5] Of 4 Jan., explaining his religious position. See L. 797 above.

that you will have imputed my silence to any thing rather than remissness. I have made several fruitless attempts at an interview with Mr Dawes. He promised some time ago to call upon me, but he has not kept his engagement—yesterday I went again to his house, but did not find him at home, so that I have resolved to defer writing to you no longer. I do not know whether it was before or since my last letter, that I accidentally met him in the road, when he told me 'that if you were not in orders, there was an end of the business, as he would not give any one a title'. This objection I should have considered insurmountable, but that he has since offered to give a title to the son of a friend of his, as I know from a gentleman who was present when he made the offer. During that short accidental conversation Mr D. said to me that as long as his health was as good as at present he did not think it right that he should receive any portion of income from the Chapelry without doing its duties. This feeling I met with observing that as there was much to do, an assistant Curate might be desirable and with that view I was disposed to recommend you. He concluded by saying that you had best come over in summer and then perhaps the matter might be arranged. So that tho' I cannot reckon the affair promising in its present state it is not altogether hopeless. But far the most discouraging thing about it is Mr D's unsteadiness of mind. Tho' a Person of wonderful strength for his years, and in many respects a very amiable and excellent Man, he has been, during his whole life remarkable for extreme irritability of nerve; in fact some of his nearest relatives have been insane—and this restless temperament has produced in Mr D. contradictions and changes of purpose which have both disappointed and harassed his neighbours and friends upon many occasions. It is no doubt the cause of his not having called upon me, as he promised to do. I assure you, I attach so much importance to your being employed as a Minister of the Gospel at Ambleside, and feel confident that by the good you do there, you would entitle yourself to the gratitude of the Parish, that I will exert myself to the utmost to effect what we both desire. This is all that I can say at present—but you shall hear from me as soon as anything decisive or important occurs—in the meanwhile believe me very faithfully

Yours
[*signed*] Wm Wordsworth

Pray give my kind regards to Mrs Hemans and your Brother.

810. W. W. to GEORGE CRABBE[1]

MS. *Yale University Library*.
George Crabbe, *The Life and Poems of the Rev. George Crabbe*, 8 vols., 1834 (—).
LY iii. 1376.

[In M. W.'s hand]

[Feb. 1834][2]

Dear Sir,

My communication with Mess[rs] Longman is so unfrequent that your letter sent thro' them, and dated Nov[r] 11th only reached me last night. This delay I regret very much, as my silence may have been attributed to inattention on my part, and you may have consequently repented of having made an application that I assure you I consider as an honor. The Prospectus informs me that the first Vol. of the Work was to appear the beginning of Feb[ry]—and therefore is probably out already; but neither you nor I have, on this account, cause to regret that your letter was so long detained, as my opportunities of seeing your excellent Father were rare, and I never was in correspondence with him. Some 3 or 4 times I have met him at Mr Hoare's on Hampstead heath—and once or twice at Mr Rogers's but upon none of these occasions was I fortunate enough to have any private or particular conversation with him. I first became acquainted with Mr Crabbe's Works in the same way, and about the same time, as did Sir Walter Scott,[3] as appears from his letter in the prospectus; and the extracts made such an impression upon me, that *I* can also repeat them. The two lines

'Far the happiest they
The moping idiot and the madman gay'[4]

---

[1] George Crabbe jnr. (1785–1857), biographer of his father, graduated at Trinity College, Cambridge, in 1807. In 1834 he was presented by Lord Lyndhurst to the livings of Bredfield and Petistree, Suffolk.

[2] So dated by George Crabbe, who quotes part of this letter in the *Life and Poems*, ii. 83.

[3] In a letter dated 21 Oct. 1809, Scott had told Crabbe that, more than twenty years before, he had met with copious extracts from *The Village* and *The Library* in a volume of Dodsley's *Annual Register*, and that he had 'committed them most faithfully to my memory, where your verses must have felt themselves very strangely lodged in company with ghost stories, border riding-ballads, scraps of old plays, and all the miscellaneous stuff which a strong appetite for reading . . . had assembled in the head of a lad of eighteen'. (See *Life and Poems*, i. 191: the letter is not included in Grierson's edn. of *The Letters of Sir Walter Scott*.)

[4] *The Village*, i. 238–9.

691

struck my youthful feelings particularly—tho' facts, as far as they
had then come under my knowledge, did not support the description; inasmuch as idiots and lunatics—among the humbler Classes
of society—were not to be found in Workhouses—in the parts of
the North where I was brought up,—but were mostly at large, and
too often the butt of thoughtless Children. Any testimony from me
to the merit of your revered Father's works would I feel be super-
fluous, if not impertinent. They will last, from their combined
merits as Poetry and Truth full as long as any thing that has been
expressed in Verse since they first made their appearance.

I remain dear Sir
respectfully your's
[*signed*] Wm Wordsworth

P.S.

In the year 1828, upon the application of Miss Hoare y^r Father
was so obliging as to write in my daughter's Album the following
verses, accompanied with a note in his own hand writing, which
shall also be transcribed

> 'Beside the Summer Sea I stand
> Where the slow Billows swelling shine
> How beautiful this pearly Sand,
> Be this delicious quiet mine:
> Beneath this Cliff my Sheltered Seat,
> To watch the entangled Weeds ashore
> To hear the dimpling Waters beat
> And dream as I have dreamt before.[1]

Geo Crabbe'

'Mr Crabbe having ceased, long since, to compose Verses, is
compelled to have Recourse to some written at so early a period,
that it was not without full proof, he was convinced they were justly
imputed to him. Having no other he reluctantly troubles Miss W.
with these.'[2]

And I may add that she prizes them highly, as I, her Father do,
they being evidence of that quietness of Spirit, and gentleness of
feeling which marked his manners and conversation, as far [as][3]
we had opportunities of intercourse with him.

---

[1] Stanza xiii of *The World of Dreams* (*Life and Poems*, iv. 116). The published text differs considerably from the version given here.

[2] See also F. V. Morley, *Dora Wordsworth, Her Book*, 1924, pp. 68–9.

[3] *Word dropped out.*

811. W. W. to ROBERT PERCEVAL GRAVES

Address: Robt P. Graves Esqre, Trinity Coll, Dublin.
Postmark: 13 Mar. 1834. *Stamp*: Kendal Penny Post.
MS. Cornell.
London Mercury, vi (1922), 399 (—).

[*In M. W.'s hand*]

Rydal Mount Mar: 11th [1834]

My dear Sir,

I began a letter to you nearly a week ago, before the receipt of your last, which I found here on my return from Carlisle, where I had been detained several days upon business. The purport of *that* letter was to tell you that I had at last effected an interview with Mr Dawes, who, from the peculiarity of temper which I formerly named to you,[1] had failed in his engagement to call here, and rather shyed me. Mr D. said that he had just rec^d a letter from his Diocessan representing to him, that if he was in want of a Curate he, (the Bp:) had two *Irishmen*, that was Mr D's way of putting it, who would be glad to undertake the office, and what was more, that the Parties would serve at a very low rate. To which Mr D. replied, that as long as he retained the good health with which it had pleased God to bless him, he should do the Duty himself; and added, that he should deem it morally wrong to draw a pecuniary advantage from the Church and be an Idler, while he was capable of Work. So said he, 'there is an end of your application on the part of your friend, who I conjecture is one of the Parties alluded to by the Bishop.' At this point I let the conversation drop, but in a few minutes I came round to it, and said Mr D. your Cure is somewhat extensive and a populous district, and a Gentleman who might have no wish to supercede you, might possibly be useful as an Assistant-Curate, and you yourself still continue to be as active in the discharge of your Pastoral duties as would justify to your Conscience the acceptance from the Church of the greatest part, if not the whole of the small Sum (perhaps £60 P^er An^m) which you draw from the Benefice—So interested am I, I continued, in this matter that I am loth to consider this answer as final, and leaving no opening for the future—to which Mr D. replied—as long as I shall be in my present mind you must not encourage the expectation of your friend's wish and your own, being fulfilled. So you see my dear Sir, that you have got an answer to your proposal of coming over at the end of this Month.—So soon after such

---

[1] See L. 809 above.

a definite reply to the Bp: Mr D. could not in common decency enter into any negotiation with you—or hold out any hope. Nevertheless I do not wholly despair, and cannot but cherish the thought, that if you were to come over in the course of the Summer Vacation, and shew yourself to Mr D. our object might possibly be gained. The great obstacle is after all—his unsteadiness of mind. One particular you must allow me to add—Several Gentlemen friends of Mr D. tho' not residing with in his Cure had complained to him of the interference of the Bp. in thrusting, as they said, Natives of Ireland into the Benefices or Curacies of these Parts, by which the Yeomanry and smaller Gentry, were discouraged from educating their Sons for the Church, as they used to do—seeing now that as far as the B'p's influence extended, they were not likely to be patronized. I mention this in justice to your feelings, tho' I do not think it would be any impediment in your way—being assured your personal qualifications would set it aside—if in any quarter *here*, it existed.

I sincerely congratulate you upon the success of your Brother— to whom make my kind regards and say to him what pleasure his success at Col has given me.

Thanks Mrs Hemans for her elegant Translation of the fine Sonnet from Felicaea,[1] and if you see her, express my regret that her health should still continue unimproved. In the Sonnet— 'That those might fear thee more', would be better both for Grammar and sound That *they* might etc., tell her this from me trifling as the remark is.

I have been a little mortified lately by not having it in my power to introduce you to a Curacy, which my Son has had at his disposal—but unluckily he had committed himself—2 Years ago.[2] Besides the situation might not have suited you, as, tho' in some respects a very pleasant one, it is 30 miles from this Place—and only on the skirts of the Lake Country. Viz. at Brigham, upon the banks of the River Derwent, within two miles of the Town of Cockermouth—a distance very favorable for excursions among the Lakes and Mountains, but too far off them, for a daily walk.

---

[1] Vicenzo da Filicaia (1642–1707), best known for a series of sonnets in which he laments the condition of Italy. Mrs. Hemans's version of 'Italia, Italia! O tu, cui diè la sorte' was published in her *Poetical Remains*, 1836, p. 167. H. C. R. presented W. W. with a copy of Filicaia's poems soon after this (see Morley, i. 262 and *R.M. Cat.*, no. 531).

[2] Presumably the curacy at Brigham, held by Mr. Bray (see L. 737 above), while John W. was arranging his move from Moresby, and before he had a permanent place of residence in his new living.

I cannot conclude without a declaration that you attach to my favorable opinion of your letter and to the sentiments which I have expressed during this correspondence, an importance far beyond which I feel they are intitled to. This letter would have been sent, but for the loss of time, to London to be franked. Ever faithfully my dear Sir

Y^r sincere Friend [*signed*] Wm Wordsworth

Pray remember me kindly both to Mr Hamilton[1] and to Mr Archer.[2] The account you give of Mr H. gratified me highly. I would write to him—but I dare not yet use my own pen—pray tell him so.

812. W. W. to JOHN GARDNER

MS. untraced.
K (—).

March 12 [probably 1834]

. . . My mother died of pulmonary consumption at the age of twenty-seven.[3] She left five children, one of whom was drowned at sea. Three are still alive, the youngest[4] in his sixtieth year . . .

[*cetera desunt*]

[1] William Rowan Hamilton.
[2] See L. 747 above.
[3] As Knight notes, the age of W. W.'s mother (Ann Cookson) at her death, as given here, is incorrect. She was born at Penrith in Jan. 1747, married at the age of 19 in Feb. 1766, and died in Mar. 1778, being then 31 years of age, and predeceasing her husband by nearly six years (see *EY*, p. 1). In the *Autobiographical Memoranda*, dictated by the poet at Rydal Mount in Nov. 1847, he wrote: '. . . my mother, in the year 1778, died of a decline, brought on by a cold, the consequence of being put, at a friend's house in London, into what used to be called "a best bedroom". My father never recovered his usual cheerfulness of mind after this loss, and died when I was in my fourteenth year, a schoolboy, just returned from Hawkshead . . .' (*Mem.* i. 8).
[4] C. W., b. 9 June, 1774.

813. W. W. to AUGUST WILHELM VON SCHLEGEL[1]

MS. *Sächsische Landesbibliothek, Dresden.*
'*Une Lettre Inédite de Wordsworth à A. W. Schlegel*', *Revue Germanique*,
v (*1909*), 468.

[*In Dora W.'s hand*]

Rydal Mount
Kendal
2nd April 1834.

Dear Sir,

You will perhaps not have forgotten an Englishman by name Wordsworth who along with his friend Mr Coleridge had a few years ago the honor of making your acquaintance at Mr Aders's of Godesberg and of visiting you at your own house in Bonne. Upon the strength of this acquaintance, slight as, to my regret, it is, I have ventured to introduce to you Dr James Vose[2] a young English Physician, who is travelling upon the Continent for the purpose of completing his medical education: he will make such a stay at the most distinguished medical Schools as will enable him to add to the knowledge to be acquired in his own country. If, in furtherance to this object, you could introduce him to any distinguished Professors at Bonne I should deem it a great favor to myself which I should be most happy to repay by attention to any of your friends whom the beautiful features of that part of England in which I live may induce to pass this way.

I have the honor to be
with great respect
Your obliged Servant
[*signed*] Wm Wordsworth

---

[1] August Wilhelm von Schlegel (1767–1845), the distinguished scholar and critic, whom W. W. had met during his tour of the Rhineland with S. T. C. in 1828 (see pt. i, L. 346). He had been a Professor at Bonn since 1818.

[2] Son of Dr. James Vose of Liverpool. See next letter.

Address: H. C. Robinson Esqre, 2 Plowdens Buildings, Temple, London.
Postmark: 7 Apr. 1834. *Stamp*: Kendal Penny Post.
Endorsed: April 3^d 1834, Wordsworth, Landor Ode on Wordsworth and
    Southey.
MS. Dr. Williams's Library.
K (—). *Morley, i. 258.*

[*In M. W.'s hand*]

Rydal Mount Ap^r 3^d. [1834]

My dear Friend

Having often wondered what was become of you, we were all glad that, wishing to know something about us put you upon writing.—As you infer the mild air tho' the gift of a stormy winter, has proved singularly beneficial to my Sister's health, who has suffered much less pain than heretofore, has several favorable symptoms, but does not gather strength as might be expected, indeed she will not allow that she is any stronger at all—but in this we all think that she deceives herself.

My eyes tho' they have not been in an active state of inflammation for many months, are still alarmingly susceptible to changes in the weather, and the late sharp east winds have troubled them.

During a stay of upwards of a fortnight with my Son in Moresby —from which Mrs W. and I have just returned—(together with Willy, who joined us there, and who by the bye is quite well)—I had much enjoyment in seeing him and his wife so happy, and in making a more intimate acquaintance with my grandaughter. She has just entered the dramatic age—and is within a day or two of walking; a lively Creature as ever was seen, which strikes one the more in contrast with the manners of her Parents—and her Nurse, all still and quiet as trees, whose branches *may* have been light and flexible, but are now less so than one of my dispositions could wish. One calm and beautiful day John and I took a long and most delightful walk, following from Whitehaven, along the top of the Cliffs the indentings of the Coast, as far as the Monastry of St. Bees.[1] Our last summer's acquaintance the Isle of Man was full in sight—so were the Scotch Hills,—and when we came to a point of the Headlands which shewed the Bay of St. Bees, the whole line of the Cumberland coast, to its extreme Southern point, with Black Comb and Scafell presiding over the view—the effect was magnificent.

---

[1] i.e. the 'clerical institution', now presided over by Dr. Ainger (see L. 753 above).

A day or two since I had a letter from Dr Vose,[1] who formerly practised medicine with much distinction at Liverpool. He has retired from his profession, but, fortunately for me, was residing last autumn in Ambleside—and kindly undertook, as a friend—the care of my diseased eyes. I deem myself greatly indebted to him, and am glad of an occasion to prove my gratitude by endeavouring upon his application, to furnish his Son Dr James Vose, who is about to travel on the Continent, with such few letters of introduction as I can command. His main object is, to complete his medical education by adding to such knowledge as may be acquired in England, what the most celebrated Foreign Schools of medicine supply   and with this view his Father requested me to furnish him with some letters of introduction to Men of letters and science. Unluckily I have little or no acquaintance in that line, I ventured however to send him a note for Prof: Schlegel[2] at Bonn—and one to Mr Landor —and also a sort of circular for any of my rambling friends, with whom he might meet. I also took the liberty of giving him your address, telling him I should write to you—not without a hope that y^r long and wide acquaintance with the Continent might enable you to render him more substantial service. No doubt he will call upon you in a few days, and if you can serve him, I shall deem it a great favor to myself. I ought to add, that I have never seen the Young Person—but his Father is so amiable and excellent a Man, that I am sure he would not ask a favor of this kind, unless he knew that his Son were worthy of it.

You are quite at liberty to send my Sonnets to Landor if you think it worth while—but his antipathies are strong; and I know he has a particular dislike to the *Sonnet*.

The Ode addressed to me,[3] I never heard of till you named it, nor could I obtain a sight either of it, or the one to Southey till yesterday. They have both been read to me—but owing to a press of business, and much company on my return home only *once*. Mr Southey seemed to be more happily treated than myself—My Sister was particularly pleased with the last Stan: but one in the address to him. Dora tells me, for as yet I have been able to form no opinion myself, that *I* am complimented upon my *wisdom* and upon my *workmanship*—what more I say could a Poet desire—for no Man can be wise who writes verses to any extent without some degree of

---

[1] Dr. James Vose.   [2] See previous letter.
[3] See Landor's *Complete Works* (ed. Welby and Wheeler), xv. 143. The Ode was published in the *Athenaeum* for 1 Feb. 1834. The lines *To Robert Southey*, which W. W. goes on to mention, were published in the *Athenaeum* on 4 Jan. (*Complete Works*, xv. 141). See Morley, i. 255, 261–2.

inspiration. The daughter however is not satisfied—and as the old Ballad says 'I like her the better there*fore*'.

In much that you say about the Dissenters, I concur. But not in your opinion 'that the sooner any purposed change takes place the better chance there is that that change may have a conservative character'. Surely that maxim must be qualified by a consideration of *what* is to be changed and to what extent change is desireable. For myself I would oppose tooth and nail the petition from Cam: in behalf of the Diss[rs][1] because it is hypocritical—and if granted will inevitably lead to a demand for Degrees, which will give Votes— open to them the emoluments and offices of the University and make them a part of the governing Body. An event which for innumerable reasons—and not the least for its tendency to over- throw the Est. Ch. I earnestly deprecate. There is a fallacy in one of yr suppositions,—you think Diss[rs] if admitted upon equal terms with Churchmen—w[d] go over to the Ch: in numbers—now it is the very exclusion which induces them to go over. Mrs Barbauld, an acute observer tells as you know that she never knew a family of Dis[rs] who kept a Carriage thro' 3 generations, and continued such. Why was this? because having got so high in the World's ladder they wished to be higher. And the ready way was to step over their consciences, if they had any religious scruples left. Take away the exclusions and dissent and Carriages will go very com- fortably together for many generations if a church should survive to dissent from.

Ever affly yours
[*signed*] Wm Wordsworth

My Sister Sarah H. is now at Playford[2] busily employed by Mr C. She will shortly be at Hendon[3] and in a few weeks return to Rydal.

[1] At a meeting in Cambridge on 13 Mar., chaired by Adam Sedgwick (see pt. i, L. 382), it was decided that a Petition should be presented to Parliament for the exemption of all degrees (except those in Divinity) from religious tests. It was signed by sixty-three members of the Senate, and was presented in the Lords by Earl Grey on 21 Mar. and to the Commons by the Secretary to the Treasury, Thomas Spring Rice, M.P. for the town of Cambridge, on the 24th. See also L. 818 below.

[2] S. H. had left Brinsop on 11 Feb., and after visits to Mrs. Hook at Lea- mington, to the Arnolds at Rugby (where she was much impressed with the arrangement of the School), and to C. W. jnr. at Cambridge, she arrived at Playford early in March where she remained for some weeks acting as am- anuensis to Thomas Clarkson, who was nearly blind with cataract. See *SH*, pp. 400 ff.

[3] Around the end of April S. H. moved on to stay with Mrs. Gee, who was now keeping a school in Hendon, and met many old friends again (including Lamb and Coleridge), before returning to Rydal Mount towards the end of June.

815. D. W. to ANNE POLLARD[1]

Address: Mrs Pollard, at Mr Oddy's Lodgings, Harrowgate, Yorkshire.
Stamp: Kendal Penny Post.
MS. WL.
K (—). *LY ii. 695.*

Begun Saturday 12th April, ended Thursday. [1834]

My dear Friend,

I ought long ago to have thanked *you* for your kind and welcome letter; but ought *now* to be writing to *Mrs Marshall*; and indeed if I knew exactly where a letter would find her you would not perhaps have had this, even yet; but as you, no doubt, are in constant correspondence with her, I flatter myself that, as you will report to her that you have had good tidings from me, it will answer the same purpose as if, by chance, I had rightly directed to her. She intended visiting Julia at Easter and is probably still with her; and, if all parties be in good health, it would not be easy for us to find a happier mother than our dear Jane, during this first visit to her Daughter and excellent Son-in-law.[2] Of his *merits* I always hear whenever his name is mentioned; and I cannot but believe that the Pair are far more than *contented* with each other, they having entire sympathy in matters of most importance in this world. It must be a never-failing delight to Julia to witness the good done by her Husband, both as a preacher, and comforter and assistant to the sick and afflicted; while in these latter named duties her good sense and charitable and amiable disposition will enable her to be a most effectual helper. I will not say I envy my Friend the happiness she enjoys in her numerous and flourishing Family; but often do I think how large a portion of good has been dealt out to her, and I join in that feeling of gratitude to God which we well know is habitual to her noble mind. Never surely was there a Mother who had had so little sorrow in the bringing up of eleven Children,[3] notwithstanding the affliction of poor Ellen's life-long sickness; for in that sorrow the alleviations are many and powerful, and of these the foremost is the heavenly disposition and temper of the sufferer— her piety, resignation, and even chearfulness when not bowed down by pain—and surely the most active life of virtue and usefulness could

---

[1] Mrs. Marshall's eldest sister, *Miss* Pollard.
[2] The Revd. Henry Venn Elliott (see L. 790 above).
[3] Jane Marshall had had twelve children, but her second daughter Catherine (b. 1800) died in infancy.

not have afforded so precious an example to her Brothers and Sisters. Everyone must have been bettered by intercourse with Ellen.

But I go on prosing, unconscious that these sentiments must be so familiar to your own mind that the task of reading them is at least useless—you will, however, forgive me; for a solitary bed-chamber does not furnish a variety of incidents—solitary I call it; but my Friends are very kind and sit with me as much and as often as leisure will allow, except when the apprehension of fatiguing me keeps them away. I sometimes of late have chid myself for impatience; for the sun shines so bright and the birds sing so sweetly that I have almost a painful longing to go out of doors, and am half tempted to break my bonds and sally forth into the garden; but I must be contented to wait till the wind changes its quarters; and before that happens rain will surely come, which may still keep me confined, for damp is almost as dangerous a foe as the East wind. There has been little change with me since I last wrote, yet as I have had no bilious attack and no violent attack of *pain* (though seldom entirely free from gentle visitations) I *must* be actually much better; but the change is so very slow that I am forced to check myself and think of the past when I (perhaps some-what peevishly) have exclaimed 'I gather no strength'.

I laid down my pen half an hour ago to receive a visit from a Sister of our old Friend, Peggy Taylor,[1] whom you will remember at Mrs Threlkeld's. I am glad to be enabled to tell you that she is now, after much affliction and anxiety, in good health and spirits. Mr Lewthwaite, her Husband, about a year ago had an alarming illness, but is now perfectly recovered. Mr Briggs[2] of Halifax was, I find, an invaluable Friend to the Lewthwaites when in distress; but the bitterest part of it no friendship could heal, for it proceeded from the unfeeling misconduct of a Son. Speaking of Halifax I must say that I have nothing to tell you; for it is long since I heard from E. Ferguson, and the correspondence with our aged Friend[3] is for ever snapped off. No doubt, all things continue as when he wrote, in a state of melancholy decay, yet comforted by peaceful resigna-tion. I always rely upon hearing from Edward whenever any important change either for the better or the worse happens among the three Beings[4] to him the most interesting upon earth, but I am anxious for all fresh particulars, and my next letter shall be to

---

[1] For Margaret Taylor, see *EY*, p. 31.
[2] A Halifax friend whom D. W. had seen again during her stay with Mrs. Rawson in the summer of 1829.   [3] Mrs. Elizabeth Rawson.
[4] i.e. his surviving sisters Martha and Anne, and his aunt Mrs. Rawson.

Edward and indeed I ought sooner to have written, to tell him about myself and Rydal Mount. My dear Brother's eyes are comparatively well, though very weakly; and at present he is unluckily confined by a trifling malady, a sore upon the great Toe. I trust Dora is better than she has lately been, for her cough and shortness of breath have yielded to Mr Carr's prescriptions; but she still looks wretchedly and is very thin, and has no appetite for any kind of food, while from some kinds the stomach instantly revolts.

Thursday. Strange to say it! this poor scrawl has been the work of four days, and it is *five* since I began with it. The truth is, that a small matter stops me, and if a visitor, or two or three in succession, come in, my time and strength do not serve to fill up the rest of the day with other labour. Yesterday with a thankful heart I revisited the garden and green-terrace in my little carriage. I cannot express the joy I felt, and though much fatigued I did not suffer in any other way. No one but an invalid, after long confinement, can imagine the pleasure of being surrounded again by sunshine and fresh air, budding trees, flowers and birds. I looked about for young Lambs but discovered not one. Do not think, however, my dear Friend that my confinement has been irksome to me. Quite the contrary, for within this little square I have a collection of treasures and on the outside of my window I have had a garden of ever-blooming flowers, and you know what a beautiful prospect. Never have my flower-pots been seen unadorned with flowers in addition to the bright berries of winter, the holly etc. I have plenty of good old Books[1] and most of the news are supplied by Friends or neighbours, and I cannot help adding (for my heart prompts me to it and you will forgive) I cannot help adding that within the last two years I have had a source of enjoyme[nt] that but for your and your dear Sisters' delicate kindness my consci[ence][2] would not hav[e] allowed me. I have had the power of doing many [a] charitable deed, that I should otherwise have felt it my duty not to ind[ulge] in, besides exercising a liberality towards those who on me bestow willing and affectionate service. As to personal comforts I need not say that I never want any thing that I can desire or wish for.

I give you now the same promise I have already given to Mrs Marshall, never again to mention to you the good you have done,

[1] D. W.'s MS. Journals (*WL MSS.*) which she had now resumed, give some idea of the range of her reading lately. It included the *Spectator*, Horsley's *Sermons*, a life of Sir Christopher Wren, an article on liturgical reform in the *Quarterly*, and works by Charles Lamb, Mrs. S. C. Hall, and William Howitt.
[2] *MS. torn.*

and are doing, so let me be assured by your sending no reply to what I have said, that you take it kindly as the overflowing of a grateful mind.

The month of April gets on rapidly and you are to return to Old Church[1] in May, when I shall be anxious to hear of your being seated in your accustomed quiet Hold, in perfect resignation to your loss[2] and chearful enjoyment of the many blessings around you. I hope that before summer days are much shortened both you and Ellen[3] will find your way to Rydal Mount. You must by no means venture over Kirkstone; but coming round by Keswick only adds a few miles to the journey, of which we should think nothing, if there were not a shorter way. It is longer than usual since I heard from Mrs Marshall, and I am beginning to crave tidings concerning *her* and the Many who are bound to her in love and duty, yet I have had no right to expect a letter, for I have not written to her since her last reached me. This is again a mild and lovely day, and I must prepare for my Baby Ride in the garden. Pray excuse bad penmanship, a wretched pen, and this shabby sheet of paper. The worst part of the business is, that I fear you will find my writing not always legible and at best difficult. I hope, however, that two pair of eyes will make out the whole, and you have leisure enough not to grudge the requisite time. My Brother, Sister and Dora send their united regards and best wishes. Believe me ever, my dear Friend yours most affectionately

D. Wordsworth

I hope you have comfortable accounts of your Friend Mrs Whitaker[4] and her Family.

---

[1] The house on the Hallsteads estate.
[2] Probably the death of her younger sister **Harriot**.
[3] Miss Pollard's younger sister.
[4] Probably the widow of the Revd. Thomas Whitaker (see *EY*, p. 146), the antiquary.

816. W. W. to SIR WILLIAM MAYNARD GOMM[1]

MS. untraced.
Mem. Grosart. K. LT ii. 699.

Rydal Mount, April 16, 1834.

My dear Sir,

Your verses, for which I sincerely thank you, are an additional proof of the truth which forced from me, many years ago, the exclamation—Oh! many are the poets that are sown—By Nature.[2] The rest of that paragraph also has some bearing upon your position in the poetical world. The thoughts and images through both the poems, and the feelings also, are eminently such as become their several subjects; but it would be insincerity were I to omit adding that there is here and there a want of that skill in *workmanship*, which I believe nothing but continued practice in the art can bestow. I have used the word *art*, from a conviction, which I am called upon almost daily to express, that poetry is infinitely more of an art than the world is disposed to believe. Nor is this any dishonour to it; both for the reason that the poetic faculty is not rarely bestowed, and for this cause, also, that men would not be disposed to ascribe so much to inspiration, if they did not feel how near and dear to them poetry is.

With sincere regards and best wishes to yourself and Lady Gomm

Believe me to be very sincerely yours,

W. Wordsworth

[1] Sir William Maynard Gomm (1784–1875), Field Marshal. He served in the Peninsula under Wellington and was with Moore at Corunna, distinguished himself at Salamanca (1812), and fought at Waterloo. His *Letters and Journals*, covering his campaigns from 1799 to 1815, were published in 1881. He travelled widely and wrote much verse, and became intimate with W. W. in the 1830s while he was stationed in England. In 1839 he was appointed to Jamaica, in 1842 he was Governor of Mauritius, and in 1850 Commander-in-Chief in India. Together with Lady Gomm he called on W. W. in Oct. 1833, and again in Apr. 1834 (*RMVB*), shortly before this letter was written. He continued to send W. W. his poems, and on 24 Feb. 1835 wrote to acknowledge the efficacy of *The Excursion* in curing his early despondency: 'Some years have passed . . . since I first made acquaintance with your Writings.—It was when I was other than I am to-day:—in a season when I bore about a bleeding heart: stricken with the heaviest calamity that can befall our nature.—It was my good angel, I believe, that prompted me to open your Volumes, and breathed in me a presentiment that in them I might find my balm.' (*WL MSS.*)

[2] *The Excursion*, i. 77.

817. W. W. to FELICIA DOROTHEA HEMANS

Address: Mrs Hemans, 20 Dawson Street, Dublin.
Stamp: Kendal Penny Post.
Endorsed: W. Wordsworth to Mʳˢ H: Apˡ 1834.
MS. Harvard University Library.
Mem. (—). *K* (—). *LY ii. 700.*

[*In M. W.'s hand*]

[*c.* 30 Apr. 1834]

My dear Mrs Hemans

My first duty is to thank you for your National Lyrics[1] and the accompanying Letter—the little Volume for my daughter-in-law was delivered by myself, as I happened to be upon a visit to her and her husband, when your Parcel arrived. Mrs Harrison's[2] was sent to her, and she begs you to accept her thanks for its own sake, and as a token of your remembrance. How did it happen that all this was not written some time ago? You will be sorry to hear the reason. My eyes tho' not actually inflamed, are in that state that I am prohibited from reading and writing, by my medical attendants; and in consequence, there are upon my Table, three Volumes besides yours that I have recᵈ from their Authors some time ago— and are as yet unacknowledged—as I do not like to write on these occasions without saying something more than that the Books have been received.

With respect to your own last work I was not precisely in the same difficulty, as many of the Pieces had fallen in my way before they were collected; and had given me more or less pleasure—as all your productions do. Nevertheless I deferred my acknowledgements with a hope that open air with fine weather, might soon so far strengthen my eyes, as to enable me to report of the whole as a Volume, but the sharp east winds which I am sorry to hear have inflicted you with the influenza, have been against me, and the pleasure is yet to come of perusing your Pieces in succession. I can only say that whenever I have peeped into the volume—I have been well recompensed. This morning I glanced my eye over the Pilgrim Song to the evening Star with great pleasure.

And now my dʳ Friend to a subject which I feel to be of much delicacy—You have submitted what you had intended as a

---

[1] *National Lyrics and Songs for Music*, 1834.
[2] Mrs. Benson Harrison.

Dedication[1] for your Poems to me. I need scarcely say that as a *private letter* such expressions from such a quarter, could not have been rec^d by me but with pleasure of *no ordinary kind*, unchecked by any consideration but the fear that my writings were overrated by you, and my character thought better of than it deserved. But I must say that a *public* testimony in so high a strain of admiration is what I cannot but shrink from—be this modesty true or false, it is in me—you must bear with it, and make allowance for it. And therefore as you have submitted the whole to my judgement, I am emboldened to express a wish that you would instead of this Dedication in which your warm and kind heart has overpowered you, simply inscribe them to me, with such expression of respect or gratitude as would come within the limits of the rule which after what has been said above, will naturally suggest itself. Of

---

[1] The proposed Dedication to *Scenes and Hymns of Life* (see L. 776 above) to which W. W. objected, ran as follows:

My dear Sir,

I earnestly wish that the little volume here inscribed to you, in token of affectionate veneration, were pervaded by more numerous traces of those strengthening and elevating influences which breathe from all your poetry —'a power to virtue friendly'. I wish, too, that such a token could more adequately convey my deep sense of gratitude for moral and intellectual benefit long derived from the study of that poetry—for the perpetual fountains of 'serious faith and inward glee' which I have never failed to discover amidst its pure and lofty regions—for the fresh green places of refuge which it has offered me in many an hour when

> The fretful stir
> Unprofitable, and the fever of the world
> Have hung upon the beatings of my heart;

and when I have found in your thoughts and images such relief as the vision of your 'sylvan Wye' may, at similar times, have afforded to yourself.

May I be permitted, on the present occasion, to record my unfading re-collections of enjoyment from your society—of delight in having heard from your own lips, and amidst your own lovely mountain-land, many of those compositions, the remembrance of which will ever spread over its hills and waters a softer colouring of spiritual beauty? Let me also express to you, as to a dear and most honoured friend, my fervent wishes for your long enjoyment of a widely-extended influence, which cannot but be blessed—of a domestic life, encircling you with yet nearer and deeper sources of happiness; and of those eternal hopes, on whose foundation you have built, as a Christian poet, the noble structure of your works.

I rely upon your kindness, my dear Sir, for an indulgent reception of my offering, however lowly, since you will feel assured of the sincerity with which it is presented by your ever grateful and affectionate Felicia Hemans. (*Memoir of the Life and Writings of Mrs Hemans, By Her Sister*, 1844, pp. 270-2).

The published dedication ran: To William Wordsworth, Esq., In token o deep respect for his character, and fervent gratitude for moral and intellectual benefit derived from reverential communion with the spirit of his Poetry, this Volume is affectionately inscribed by Felicia Hemans.

course if the sheet has been struck off, I must hope that my shoulders may become a little more Atlantean than I now feel them to be.

My Sister is not quite so well. She, Mrs W. and Dora all unite with me in best wishes and kindest remembrances to yourself and yours; and believe me d^r Mrs Hemans

to remain faithfully yours
[*signed*] Wm Wordsworth

Pray thank Mr Graves for his last letter, and say that I am very anxious to find an opening by which his wishes might be gratified— but with respect to Mr Dawes[1] he has lately given such additional proofs of his temper, tho' not on this subject, so discouraging that I cannot look forward with pleasure to any arrangement with him—We see Mr Archer[2] frequently who speaks of you and y^r Poetry with much interest. Your message has been delivered to Mr Hamilton.[3] I regret that there is not time for sending this letter to London to be franked.

818. W. W. to ADAM SEDGWICK

MS. untraced.
J. W. Clark and T. M. Hughes, Life and Letters of the Revd. Adam Sedgwick,
  2 vols., 1890, i. 427.

Rydal Mount
May 14th, 1834
My dear Sir,

I am much indebted to you for a Copy of your discourse on the Studies of the University;[4] and which has been read to me twice. It is written with your usual animation, and I hope will in the course of time prove of beneficial effect, if the Universities are to continue to exist; which from some late proceedings in your own, I am disposed to doubt.

[1] See L. 811 above.
[2] Now returned from Dublin to Grasmere.
[3] Capt. Thomas Hamilton.
[4] Professor Adam Sedgwick had been called upon to preach the sermon at the Annual Commemoration of Benefactors in Trinity College Chapel on 17 Dec. 1832, and had chosen for his theme the scope and purpose of university education. His remarks caused such a stir that he published them in expanded form in Nov. 1833, and the *Discourse on the Studies of the University* went through four editions in two years.

In every part of your Discourse I was interested, but was most nearly touched by your observations on Paley's *Moral Philosophy*,[1] which, tho' like all his works a Book of unrivalled merit in certain points, is deplorably wanting in essentials: In fact there is no such thing as Morals as a Science, or even as Philosophy, if Paley's system be right. You and I, I remember, talked upon the subject when I had last the pleasure of seeing you—so that I need not say more than that I heartily concur with you in what your Discourse contains upon it.

Thank you for the drubbing you have given that odious Slanderer, Beverley.[2] I was sorry to learn from those letters that you had had so severe an accident.[3] You have the best wishes of all this family for your entire and speedy recovery.

Should I be silent upon the part you have taken as the Public Leader of the 62 or 63 Petitioners,[4] I should not be treating you with sincerity, or in the spirit of that friendship which exists between us. This is not the place for me to discuss the subject, and tho' I feel that my opinion, as an opinion merely, may not be entitled to much respect, as your personal friend I cannot hold back

[1] *The Principles of Moral and Political Philosophy* by William Paley (1743–1805), Archdeacon of Carlisle, appeared in 1785. It was based on the lectures he had given as Fellow of Christ's College, and was at once adopted as a textbook in the University, retaining its importance in the curriculum throughout W. W.'s Cambridge years (see Ben Ross Schneider, *Wordsworth's Cambridge Education*, 1957). In the third part of his discourse Sedgwick criticized Locke and the 'utilitarian' theory of morals as expounded by Paley, thereby anticipating Whewell's *Elements of Morality* (1845), a work dedicated to W. W. W. W.'s objections to Paley's system had been set out perhaps as early as 1798, in the so-called 'Essay on Morals' (*Prose Works*, i. 103–4), which may in fact be a fragment of a letter to some unknown correspondent, as the familiar style of writing suggests.

[2] Robert Mackenzie Beverley (1796–1868), a graduate of Trinity, had become a convert to the cause of Dissent and published two pamphlets in 1831 on the corrupt state of the Church of England, advocating disestablishment and the confiscation of Church property. Two years later he turned his attention to the Universities and brought out *A Letter to his Royal Highness the Duke of Gloucester, Chancellor, on the present corrupt state of the University of Cambridge.* Between Jan. and June 1834 Sedgwick published four letters attacking Beverley's pretensions and misrepresentations, in the *Leeds Mercury*, which had published extracts from Beverley's pamphlet. (See *Four Letters to the Editors of the Leeds Mercury in reply to R. M. Beverley, Esq.*, Cambridge, 1836.)

[3] See L. 814 above. The Petition was quickly succeeded by a contrary Declaration in favour of the retention of religious tests, and thus the controversy spread to all senior members of the University. On 17 Apr. a private member's bill was introduced into Parliament to abolish all tests: it passed the Commons, but was rejected by the Lords, and tests were not finally swept away until thirty-seven years later. See D. A. Winstanley, *Early Victorian Cambridge*, 1940, pp. 89–94; *Romilly's Cambridge Diary, 1832–42* (ed. Bury), pp. 52, 54.

the declaration of my conviction that the Petitioners are misguided men,—that part of them, at least, who have signed this Petition with a hope, that by so doing, they are contributing to the Support of the Institutions of the Country, the Church included.[1]

Farewell! God bless you, and be assured that whatever course you pursue either in public or private life, there is no likelihood that I shall ever have occasion to doubt that *you* act from pure and conscientious motives. At the same time allow me to say, that I have no dread of being accused of presumption by you, for not having bowed to the scientific names[2] which stand so conspicuous upon this ill-omened Instrument.

Ever faithfully yours,
Wm Wordsworth

819. W. W. to WILLIAM WHEWELL

Address: The Rev^d. Professor Whewell, Trinity Coll.
MS. Trinity College, Cambridge. Hitherto unpublished.

[*In M. W.'s hand*]

Rydal Mount May 14th. [1834]

Dear Mr Whewell,

I have been a *long time* in your debt for the present of your valuable Bridgewater Treatise[3]—and *a few weeks also*, for an excellent Discourse by Mr Birks[4] in your Chapel. Two or three words I must say upon the latter in expression of my admiration of it, and of the delight which I felt in the proof that such Strains of thinking are not unknown among your young Students. The first reflects great honor upon the course of Studies pursued in your University. As to your own Treatise I have been prevented from writing to you, first by successive inflammations in my eyes, which cut me off from reading—and latterly, and up to this hour, by a weakness consequent upon the remedies. Having only Females

---

[1] Sedgwick argued that the tests, far from strengthening the University—or religion—actually weakened it. They inhibited the development of Science, and by implying that the University was merely a school for the Church Establishment, they prepared the way for a drastic cut in her endowments.

[2] W. W.'s friend G. B. Airy, the mathematician, was among the Petitioners.

[3] W. W. had received the work almost a year before this (see L. 769 above).

[4] The Revd. Thomas Rawson Birks (1810–83). a talented preacher, was Fellow and Tutor of Trinity, 1834–6; later vicar of Holy Trinity, Cambridge (1866–77), and Knightsbridge Professor of Moral Philosophy.

about me, you will not be surprized when I frankly tell you that I am not as well acquainted with your Book as I hope to be. What I have seen of it adds to the admiration which I have always felt of the power and versatility of your talents. Again let me thank you, for what I value very much.

The other evening the Spirit of John Bunyan brushed by me, with a sort of 'mysterious dream waving at his wings', which was 'laid upon my eyelids'—not quite so softly touched as Milton felt his to be, when he put on the character of a Penseroso. To drop this figure I had a vision that presented to me your neighbour Old Cam, raised by such a flood as I witnessed on his banks once when I was at Cambridge in the month of May. Furthermore the waters were lifted out of their bed, by a sort of earthquake and, taking their course right across Clare Hall Lawn, made an attack upon the base of King's Coll Chapel. Out came the Provost, Fellows and Students, and to my great astonishment, fell to work most manfully for the destruction of the buttresses: in the meanwhile a crowd gathered, some of whom assisted in the labour. I myself went up and asked what they were about, and why? Some of the most active said we dislike these old fashioned deformities, the building would look much better without them, and instead of being of use they encumber and weaken it. Others cried out, 'down with them! we are pulling them down, that the flood may have free way.' I continued to look on, and sure enough they got rid of all the buttresses, but the roof and the walls of the Chapel fell in, and they who had been so busy were crushed in the ruins. Now dreams, as we learn from high authority, are from Jove; this vision of mine may perhaps be from the same quarter—if so, the day will come when you (one of the 62 Petitioners[1] if I have not been misinformed) will excuse me for having troubled you with the report of it.

> Ever faithfully and thankfully yours
> [*signed*] Wm Wordsworth

My Sister tells me (and I hope she is not mistaken) that your name was *not* among the sixty two.

---

[1] See L. 814 above and previous letter. Whewell had supported the radical John Lubbock in the Cambridge election of 1832 (see L. 730 above), and W. W. would naturally assume that he would sympathize with the aims of the Petitioners.

820. W. W. to C. W. JNR.

MS. British Library and WL transcript.[1]
K (—). *LY ii. 703* (—).

[*In M. W.'s hand*]

May 15th 1834.

My dear Chris,

You will wonder what is become of us, and I am afraid you will think me very unworthy the trouble you took in writing to us and sending your pamphlet.[2] A thousand little things have occurred to prevent my calling upon your Aunt, who is ever ready to write for me, and not the least weighty ones the utter hopelessness in respect to the question that you have so ably handled. Since the night when the Reform bill was first introduced, I have been convinced that the Institutions of the Country cannot be preserved from speedy destruction. That fatal measure has given such a preponderancy to the anti Ch: of E. interest, that She must fall. It is a mere question *of time.* A great majority of the present Parliament, I believe, are in their mind favorable to the preservation of the Ch: but among these many are ignorant how that is to be done. Add to the portion of those who with good intentions are in the dark, the number who will be driven or tempted to vote against their consciences by the clamour of their sectarian and infidel constituents under the Reform bill, and you will have a daily augmenting power even in this Par^{nt} which will be more and more hostile to the Ch: every week and every day. You will see from the course which my letter thus far has taken that I regard the Prayer of the Petitioners to whom you are opposed as formidable, still more from the effect which, if granted, it will ultimately have upon the Ch: and through that medium upon the Monarchy and upon social order, than for its immediate tendency to introduce discord in the universities, and all those deplorable effects which you have so feelingly painted as preparatory to their destruction.

I am not yet able to use my eyes for reading or writing, but your pamphlet has been twice read to me. No part of it was to me objectionable, except something of an air of Shew—not perhaps

---

[1] The MS. is incomplete, and the last paragraph and conclusion is supplied from a copy by Susan Wordsworth.
[2] *On the admission of Dissenters to graduate in the University of Cambridge. A Letter to ... Viscount Althorp,* dated 12 Apr. 1834, and containing C. W. jnr.'s answer to the proposals of the sixty-three Petitioners (see L. 814 above).

intended, with which it opens. Poor Lord A.[1] You seem to let out that you have not a very high opinion, either as a Man or a Minister.

As Mr Spedding[2] will tell you in what plight we are, I will confine myself to mentioning that y^r Aunt D. has had rather a bad attack lately, attended with weakness and pain, from which she is rallying, and Dora a fit of the Influenza—and after that a cold and of course she is reduced and looks thin . . .

God bless you my dear Nephew. Give our love to your Father. We were delighted with John's letter.

Affectionately yours
Wm Wordsworth

821. W. W. to MRS. JAMES HOOK[3]

Address: Mrs Hook, Clarendon Square, *Leamington*, Warwickshire. [*In M. W.'s hand*]
Stamp: Kendal Penny Post.
MS. Mrs. Ann Coatalen. Hitherto unpublished.

Rydal Mount
17th May 1834

Dear Mrs Hook

Though the state of my eyes does not allow me to read or write more than a few minutes at a time, I cannot forbear replying to your very kind Letter; which in that part of it, that relates to Lady Charlotte Bury's[4] obliging offer of presenting me a Volume, on many accounts so interesting, requires an immediate answer. Assure her Ladyship that I shall be proud of receiving her Book which if forwarded without delay to [*M. W.'s hand*: the care of Mr Moxon Books^r: Dover St] will shortly reach me through the hands of Miss Hutchinson.[5]

---

[1] Lord Althorp, the Chancellor of the Exchequer, was now increasingly vexed by the burden of public life, and on succeeding his father as the 3rd Earl Spencer later this year, he retired from active politics altogether. C. W. jnr.'s pamphlet opened as follows: 'The University of Cambridge having contributed a share, however humble, to your Lordship's education, may seem not unreasonably to have some claims on your peculiar solicitude and regard.'

[2] John Spedding had called at Rydal Mount in April and May (*RMVB*).

[3] For Mrs. Hook, see L. 727 above.

[4] Lady Charlotte Bury (1775–1861), youngest daughter of the 5th Duke of Argyll. The reference is perhaps not to one of her numerous novels but to *The Three Great Sanctuaries of Tuscany, Vallombrosa, Camaldoli, Laverna: A Poem, with historical and legendary notices. Illustrated . . . by the late Reverend Edward Bury*, 1833.

[5] S. H. was staying with Mrs. Gee at Hendon, and was frequently in London.

The strong desire which you express, to visit this Country again, with a view to a more permanent Residence in it, gives us all much pleasure. It is now in extreme Beauty; but alas! the foliage is hurrying on far too fast towards the uniform green of summer. The three views from the little Rock in Mr Hamilton's garden are now in perfection; I say *three* including as one of them the Peep at the Church tower through and between the Veil of the budding trees. Rydal Mount also is charming from all its walls and terraces. But you are in the Country and Nature is every where so rich in beauty and hope and joy at this season, that one Spot has little right to arrogate superiority over another.—We had the other day a Report that shocked us much, viz that Dr Arnold was dead. How can such distressing Accounts get into circulation, probably without the cause of even the least Indisposition in the subject of them.

The Magazine you speak of is edited by Mr Rose,[1] a particular friend of Dr Wordsworth's and I may say with pride and gratitude, of myself. He is a man of strong feelings, and from that cause or some oversight, Articles ha[ve] occasionally found their way in to the work which are not quite in the spirit of that true Christian Charity for which, to those who best know him, the Editor is so much endeared.—I must now quit my pen and with regret. As you do not mention Georgiana[2] I presume she is well. Give my love to her and believe me my dear Mrs Hook

faithfully your obliged Friend
Wm Wordsworth

822. W. W. to SARA COLERIDGE

MS. Miriam Lutcher Stark Library, University of Texas. Hitherto unpublished.

[*In Dora W.'s hand*]   [early summer 1834][3]

I hold the pen for Father

My very dear Sara,

Thirteen years ago before I stood Godfather for Rotha[4] I told her father when he asked me to take that office upon me that I was

---

[1] Hugh James Rose edited the *British Magazine*, and had now enlisted among his contributors Keble, Newman, Hurrell Froude, and others associated with the Tractarian Movement in Oxford, including Mrs. Hook's son, W. F. Hook (see L. 726 above).   [2] Mrs. Hook's daughter.

[3] This letter was written shortly before the birth of Sara Coleridge's twins, Berkeley and Florence, who died in early infancy in July 1834.

[4] Rotha Quillinan, b. 1821.

too old to allow of a hope of my being of service to the child: his answer was that as she grew up and became acquainted with my works and heard her friends speak of their author she would derive from that relation to him greater benefit than could reasonably be expected from any other Sponsor who might offer to stand for her, or he could select from among his friends. To this partial view I deferred and I have since undertaken the same office for other children being influenced chiefly by the same persuasions and if you will accept of me for your expected little one from like considerations I have only to say that it would give me great pleasure to connect myself with your family by that tie.

Your letter to Dora moved me much. With a thousand tender wishes for your perfect recovery and Kindest regards to your husband

I remain my dear Sara your affec^te and faithful friend—

[*signed*] Wm Wordsworth

823. W. W. to JOHN ABRAHAM HERAUD[1]

Postmark: 1834.
MS. untraced.
Saleroom Catalogue.

[*In M. W.'s hand*]

10 June [1834]

. . . The fact is, I am under medical restriction not to read. . . .
Once or twice have I put a friend upon reading y^r Book to me—but I felt that mode of proceeding was utterly unjust to it—You are a *thinking* writer, and I said 'I must not go on with this till I can have my eyes upon the page' and this I would beg you would take as an expression of real admiration—No man can read your works without feeling their power, ...

[*cetera desunt*]

---

[1] John Abraham Heraud (see L. 581 above) published *The Judgment of the Flood* this year.

Address: H. C. Robinson Esqre, Plowden Buildings, Temple.
Postmark: 13 June 1834.
Endorsed: 16th June 1834, Mrs Wordsworth, Latter end by W.
MS. Dr. Williams's Library.
K (—). *Morley, i. 263.*

[*In M. W.'s hand*]

Rydal Mount
June 10th [1834]

My dear Friend

Many thanks for your very agreeable letter—*very* agreeable it was for it contained much good news and nothing else,[1] which rarely happens. We congratulate you sincerely upon your Brothers convalescence;[2] and rejoice to hear of Mr Clarkson's recovery of sight—For ourselves, we ought not to complain, tho' Dora's digestion is a good deal deranged and my Sister does not gain strength—she is God be thanked much freer from pain—and for her is looking well. We expect Miss Hutchinson at the end of the week.[3] From my using Mary's pen you will see that I deem it prudent not to use my eyes much—indeed orders have been given me that I am not to do so—but since the sharp east winds disappeared they have been quite free from inflammation.

Your intended expedition to the United States was news to us—and partly in contradiction of what was said above, it was not altogether good new[s]. We are rather too old to think without some pain of our friends being separated so far from us. You yourself are no longer young—and casualties as we advance are not easily recovered from. Indeed the more I look into this scheme the less I relish it—There are not many things in America which can be called sights. Niagara it is true, is a first rate one—but not worth crossing the Atlantic for—and as to American Manners and Society—we have it in so many books, that it seems as well to be contented with what may be collected from them while at ease upon ones own Sofa—or under the shade of an English Oak, in this sweet summer weather—At all events, whether you go or not—come to us. Which you may do with little cost of time or trouble—

---

[1] But, as Morley notes, H. C. R. had written on 4 June: 'Of Coleridge I hear but a very poor account—Indeed, it is not expected by the Gilmans that he can recover.'

[2] He had had a carbuncle on the neck.

[3] S. H. actually arrived in the company of 'Keswick John' one week later, on Saturday, 21st.

as you will no doubt embark at Liverpool if you do not give up your scheme.

Poole is quite welcome to my Sonnet[1]—and if you chuse to add the Lowther Ch. and State one[2]—you have my free consent.

How could I proceed so far without thanking you for the choice presents which we are to receive thro' Miss H's hands—You are much too good to us—but with truth we can affirm that your generosity is not wasted—the Biography[3] is daily consulted by us—and of the greatest use—both for new information—and removing uncertainties about Old things. We are afraid you have not met with a Blackstone[4] to your mind—W^m often recurs to this subject, from a sincere wish I believe to read the book—I will therefore in the meanwhile send him mine, tho' it is somewhat cumbersome, being an Oxford Quarto in 4 Vols from the Clarendon Press.[5]

The Gentleman who was going abroad did not I believe pass thro London.

Thanks for all that you say about the Dissenters. An Appeal to the English Dissenters—in a letter to Wm Howitt by a Lay Dissenter—(London, Longman and Co) has been sent me by the Author.[6] it is well worth your reading. The style is somewhat verbose, but the philosophy is sound and the spirit truly Christian— If you like it, as I am confident you will, pray recommend it among your friends. We are always glad to hear of the Lambs—and pray give our love to them—and remember me to Moxon and his Wife, if you ever look in upon them.

Ever sincerely and affly
with best wishes from all.

your's
[*unsigned*][7]

This is a season of resignations, and on thursday I go to Kendal to put off my dignity of Chapel-Warden and Overseer.[8]—

---

[1] John Kenyon had applied to H. C. R. on behalf of Thomas Poole of Nether Stowey for a copy of *Steamboats, Viaducts, and Railways* (*PW* iv. 47).

[2] *Lowther* (*PW* iv. 48).

[3] Chalmers' *Biographical Dictionary* (see L. 787 above).

[4] *Commentaries on the Laws of England*, 4 vols., 1765–9, by Sir William Blackstone (1723–80), the famous judge.

[5] See *R.M. Cat.*, no. 10.

[6] This pamphlet is unidentified.

[7] The postscript is in W. W.'s hand, so presumably he intended to sign the letter.

[8] Of Rydal Chapel.

825. W. W. to HENRY TAYLOR

Address: H. Taylor Esqre.
MS. Bodleian Library.
K (—). *LY ii. 704.*

[*In M. W.'s hand*]

Rydal Mount, June 10th [1834].

My dear Sir,

I have just rec^d your two volumes,[1] and send my thanks before I have read them; not from the fear that I might not be able to report favorably of their impression upon my mind, but from apprehension that some time may elapse before the State of my eyes will allow me to read them. My eyes, I am glad to say, are not actually inflamed, nor have they been for some time, but I am under medical restrictions as to the use of them. On my table are no less than 6 books, lately received from the kindness of different authors, that I have not acknowledged, having deferred doing so from a hope that I might without injury peruse them—and I have really been so harrassed in mind, by this procrastination that I am determined your case shall not be added to them. When we meet again we will talk over your dramatic labours.

You are young, and therefore will naturally have more hope of public affairs than I can have: *principles*, which after all are the only things worth contending about, are sacrificed every day, in a manner which I have foreseen since the passing of the Reform Bill, and indeed long before, but does not on that account the less disturb me. The predominance in Parliament given to the dissenting interest, and to Towns which have grown up recently without a possibility of their being trained in habits of attachment either to the Constitution in Ch: and State, or to what remained of the feudal frame of Society in this Country, will inevitably bring on a political and social Revolution. What may be suffered by the existing generation no man can foresee, but the loss of liberty for a time will be the inevitable consequence. Despotism will be established, and the whole battle will be to be fought over by subsequent generations.

I remain very faithfully your much obliged

[*signed*] Wm Wordsworth

---

[1] Henry Taylor's drama *Philip van Artevelde* was published in two volumes in June 1834.

826. W. W. to EDWARD QUILLINAN

Address: Ed^d Quillinan Esqre.
Endorsed: Rydal, 1834. Mr Wordsworth on the death of poor Barrett.
MS. WL.
LY ii. 705.

[In M. W.'s hand]

Rydal Mount, June 11th [1834]
(for W. W., M. W. holds the pen)

Dear Mr Quillinan

Having an opportunity to send a letter to Town, I cannot let it pass without condoling with you upon the death of poor Barrett.[1] Whether on his own account his decease is to be regretted we are ignorant—one cannot however but feel sorrow that a Man who made so many sacrifices for others should be taken out of this selfish world. Upon one thing his surviving friends—his *true* ones I mean, may congratulate themselves, viz. that by his removal from Earth a temptation is removed from them who abused his goodness to the dishonor of their names and in disregard of some of the nearest charities of life. Requiescat in pace—he was in many respects a more deplorable wreck than the unhappiest of those near whom, as you tell us, he lies buried. After the warnings you have had I hope you will be able to defeat every attempt of the Plunderers, and to establish justice and reason among concerns, with which for a long time they have had little to do.

You are silent on the cause which made you think of going to Portugal[2]—You must remain in England as a duty to your

---

[1] Capt. Brydges Barrett, E. Q.'s brother-in-law, had died at Boulogne at the beginning of the month, and the Brydges family, including E. Q. himself, were plunged into renewed financial difficulties. 'Poor fellow! if ever there was a victim, Barrett was one', E. Q. wrote to W. W. on 4 June, complaining about the family neglect of Barrett in his last illness, and describing his last resting-place among the victims of the shipwrecked *Amphitrite*. 'The present owner of the Lee Estates is Mr John Brydges, who has been many years a lunatic: if his relations get hold of him and become *guardians also of his property*, I imagine it will not be much benefitted by their management. I have (already!) had reason . . . to be convinced that those of the family who have no legal claim on Lee or anything belonging to it are inclined for a *rush at the plunder*. We shall see.' (*WL MSS.*) For John Brydges, see pt. i, L. 70.

[2] E. Q. sailed for Oporto at the end of August and did not return to England until Dec. 1835. On the eve of his departure he wrote to S. H., 'I do not think the Brydges have a chance of any power to do us injury. They are *too* well-known.' But the character of Sir Egerton himself was an imponderable element in the situation. 'Strange man!—He is wild upon you one day and as civil as possible the next. All the time he is duped by his own sons, and by none else unless by himself; for his self-delusion is marvellous.' (*WL MSS.*)

Children and those who have a common interest in the remains of what will probably be their inheritance. I should like to hear some good news of Lee itself; it is a place in which I feel much interest and should be glad to learn that it were occupied by some family that could enjoy and take care of it.

Miss H.[1] whom we had expected to be now with us, but whom we are not to see till Saturday next—as she announces in a letter rec[d] this morning, will bring us news of your Children, whom she is about to see—we shall be glad to hear of their looks and every thing relating to them—we are vexed that the Aunt takes Mima for the holidays, and could not find room for my Godchild Rotha— if however she does not feel it a slight, there is no harm in Sisters being separated for a short time, they learn to value each other the more—*thinking* about friends especially before the character is formed, often does as much good as being with them.

Poor Mrs Fletcher (Miss Jewsbury that was[2]) has found a grave in India—from the first we had a fore-feeling that it would be so. She was a bright Spirit, and her sparkling, of which she had at times too much, was settling gradually into a steady light. Her journal is to her friends very interesting, and I cannot but think that if she had survived, we should have had from her pen some account of Indian appearances and doings with which the public would have been both amused and instructed. She died of Cholera, but the particulars of her death have not reached her friends.

Dora told you that I had been much pleased with the second part of Mischief;[3] it is written with great spirit and a variety of talent which does the Author no small credit. I cannot guess why this performance has not made more impression than I am aware it has done, but the political agitations of the times leave no leisure for any thing but 1d Mags and 5/- books with cuts which may be looked at but are seldom read. (William has done and I (M. W.) might have gone on but the last bell rings for Chapel and I must take up his last words) Ever aff[ly] yours

[*signed*] Wm Wordsworth

PS. If you have no objection to Rotha running wild at Rydal for a couple of months, if you or we could meet with an opportunity to send her down we should like to see her here though we cannot

[1] S. H.

[2] She had died at Poona on 4 Oct. 1833. See Gillett, p. lxiv. W. W. paid tribute to her in a note appended to *Liberty* (*PW* iv. 157).

[3] E. Q.'s satirical poem. See L. 622 above.

receive her for 6 weeks, as our Nephews[1] will be here at their vacation, and other summer visitors—But you must understand what I mean by 'running wild'—it is going without tuition. Dora's health and thoughts are too much deranged and occupied to allow of her making the least exertion in this way and indeed she is unequal to it but on this condition I mean that it is to be a perfect holiday, it will give us all great pleasure to see the Child, and we hope that you will consent, and we will be upon the lookout for some proper escort for her, and some opportunity before the end of autumn may occur for her to get safely back to school. W. W.

827. W. W. to C. W.

MS. WL transcript. Hitherto unpublished.

Rydal Mount
June 11. 1834.

My dear Brother,

... I thank you for sending the Cam. Paper regularly, but still I am anxious for private, and more information. There was, entre nous, in Mr T's[2] face and deportment an expression which often made me think of the snake in the grass: and what has happened proves that those suspicions were not unwarrantable. Holding his opinions surely his friends must regret that he did not resign his office before he published them—it is fair however to add that I have not seen his pamphlet, and I have spoken only in consequence of what I learn, or infer from the newspapers and Mr Whewell's ob-

---

[1] Tom and George Hutchinson from Sedbergh.

[2] Connop Thirlwall (1797–1875), Fellow of Trinity College, Cambridge, author of *A History of Greece*, 8 vols., 1835–47, and Bishop of St. David's from 1840. Dr. Thomas Turton, Regius Professor of Divinity, had recently published his *Thoughts on the Admission of Persons, without regard to their Religious Opinions, to certain degrees in the Universities of England*, in which he argued that if dissenters from the Established Church were allowed to proceed to degrees, the religious instruction given in the Universities as a whole would become progressively more and more unorthodox; and he was answered by Thirlwall, then Assistant Tutor of Trinity, in May with *A Letter to the Rev. Thomas Turton, D.D.* Thirlwall argued that the Colleges were not theological seminaries, and that the divinity lectures given in them were not designed to inculcate all the beliefs of the Established Church; and he went on to attack the rule of compulsory chapel attendance, which he regarded as inimical to true religion. C. W., as Master of Trinity, forced him to resign his College office (see *Letters, Literary and Theological, of Connop Thirlwall*, 1881, pp. 118–20), but incurred much unpopularity because of his high-handed approach to the controversy. See Winstanley, *Early Victorian Cambridge*, pp. 73–8.

servations upon it.[1] Mr W. has kindly sent me his little pamphlet,[2] among many parts of which that pleased, none did more so than what I had read before in the Cam: Chron^cle, his strong expression of attachment to the Ch. of England in which I heartily go along with him—and pray let him be told so by Chr: if he has not left Cambridge whither I would have addressed a letter of thanks to himself had I been sure it would have found him there. . . .

> With our united best love believe [me] to be
> ever your affectionate Brother
> Wm Wordsworth

828. W. W. to ALLAN CUNNINGHAM

Address: Allan Cunningham Esqre, 27 Low Belgrave Place, Pimlico.
Endorsed: With Mr Quillinan's Compliments.
MS. Harvard University Library.
K. LY ii. 707.

[*In M. W.'s hand*]

Rydal Mount June 14th [1834]

My dear Sir,

I have just heard from my Son, who now lives at Workington,[3] that the Bust[4] you kindly forwarded to him has been received; and as I learned some little time ago that those intended for my two Nephews at Cambridge have also reached their destination— I now write with pleasure to thank you for your obliging attention to my request, and have to beg that you will let me know the amount of my debt to you—so that I may give directions for its being discharged.

It is a long time since I was in London nor can I foresee when I am likely to be there again; which I regret principally on account

---

[1] William Whewell, who deplored both Thirlwall's pamphlet and the Master's arbitrary proceeding, published *Remarks on some parts of Mr Thirlwall's Letter on the admission of Dissenters to academic degrees*, in which he defended compulsory chapel. See also Mrs. Stair Douglas, *The Life and Selections from the Correspondence of William Whewell, D.D. . . .*, 1881, pp. 163 ff.

[2] In his letter of 4 June, Whewell spoke of his confidence in the younger generation at Cambridge to undo the mischief of 'our unhappy utilitarian morality and despairing politics', and 'the present ignoble and hopeless tone of speculation with which all the gravest interests of men are treated' (*WL MSS.*).

[3] As rector (see L. 805 above).

[4] The copy of Chantrey's bust of W. W. (see L. 804 above).

of my losing, in consequence, an opportunity of keeping up my acquaintance with works of art, ancient and modern—and of seeing my friends, who reside there, without occasionally coming into this Country. One of the last times, if not the last, I had the pleasure of seeing you was at dinner at Sir R^t Inglis's[1]—Mr Sotheby[2] was of the Party. He was an old Man, and is no more—Scarcely a Month passes without taking away some of my literary friends. Mr Chantrey and yourself I hope continue to enjoy good health— Pray make my kind regards to him, and to Mrs Chantrey, and also to Mrs Cunningham—not forgetting to present my remembrances to your Son, who I am glad to see from his elegant and judicious selection from Drummond,[3] which he kindly sent me, has a turn for literature.

Last summer I visited Staffa, Iona, and part of the Western Highlands, and returned through your Town of Dumfries, having for the first time passed through Burns's Country, both in Renfrewshire and Ayrshire (if I am correct). It gave me much pleasure to see Kilmarnock, Mauchlin, Mossgeil farm, the Air,[4] which we crossed where he winds his way most romantickly thro' rocks and woods—and to have a sight of Irwin and Lugar, which naebody sung till he named them in immortal verse. The Banks of the Nith I *had* seen before, and was glad to renew my acquaintance with them, for Burns's sake; and let me add, without flattery, for yours. By the bye, what a sorry piece of sculpture is Burns's monument in Dumfries church y^d—monstrous in conception and clumsy in the execution. It is a disgrace to the Memory of the Poet. In my native county of Cumberland I saw a piece of art which made me ample amends—it is at Wetheral Church, upon the banks of the Eden—a monument to the Memory of the first Mrs Howard of Corby[5]—You no doubt have either seen or heard of it—I first saw it many years ago in the Studio of Nollekens, in London. How a man of such a physiognomy and figure could execute a work with so much feeling and grace, I am at a loss to

---

[1] During W. W.'s visit to London early in 1831.
[2] For William Sotheby, see L. 807 above.
[3] See L. 779 above.   [4] i.e. the river Ayr.
[5] Maria (d. 1789), daughter of Andrew, Lord Archer of Umberslade, first wife of Henry Howard of Corby (see *MY* ii. 610), who died in childbirth at the age of twenty-three. The monument by Joseph Nollekens, R.A. (see also L. 428 above), which Fuseli claimed was superior to anything by Canova, is the subject of a sonnet among the 'Itinerary Poems of 1833' (see *PW* iv. 45, 409). In the I. F. note W. W. mentions the 'strange and grotesque figure' of the sculptor, 'that interfered with one's admiration of his works', when he visited Nollekens's studio.

conceive! Believe me, with kind regards from my Wife and all
my family who know you,

Very faithfully, your obliged friend,
[*signed*] Wm Wordsworth

829. W. W. to DAVID LAING

MS. Edinburgh University Library.
The Wordsworth–Laing Letters (—).

[*In M. W.'s hand*]

Rydal Mt.
July 5th. [1834]

My dear Sir,
    The Valuable Present which I have just received from you of
Dunbar's Poetical Works,[1] reminds me of 2 Vols of yours which
have been much too long in my possession; and I now avail myself
of a private opportunity to return them with thanks.
    It gives me pleasure that you have brought out your Ed: of
Dunbar, a Poet well worthy of the care and attention you have
bestowed upon them, and I look forward with the hope of being
gratified by the perusal of the Work, as soon as my eyes have been
strengthened so as to be able to bear consecutively reading without
injury. In the mean while let me thank you for this obliging mark
of your attention.
    My Sister, tho' much better than last year, is still confined to her
room; [she] joins me in best remembrances to yourself, Mother
and Sister—and also to your Brother, if he has not forgotten us.
My daughter, who is pretty well, unites in the same [?][2]
    During my last summ[er] tour in Scotland which was very
short, Staffa being my object, I did not visit Edinburgh—had I
done so, tho' only for an hour or two, I should have made a point
of calling upon you.

I remain d^r Sir
faithfully your obliged
[*signed*] Wm Wordsworth

---

[1] The first collected edition of *The Poems of William Dunbar*, edited with a
memoir of the poet by David Laing, 2 vols., 1834.
[2] *MS. torn.*

830. W. W. to EDWARD MOXON

MS. Henry E. Huntington Library.
K (—). *LY ii. 708.*

[*In M. W.'s hand*]

Rydal Mount
July 17th [1834]

My dear Sir,

Reluctant as I am, I have at last given way—and am about to send a vol of Poems to the Press.[1] Wishing to connect your name and mine by publication, I mentioned to Longman's that it would be pleasant to me to offer the publn to you, especially as we had had some conversation together on the subject—but I left it to their decision—as I felt myself bound to do, from very long connection with them—and from their answer I transcribe.

'It would be very detrimental to the Sale of your books to have part of them published by another House'—'We think you have done right to abandon the Illustrations—to have them executed as those in Rogers' Works would be so very expensive, that we should doubt their ever answering'

He then adds that the sale of the last Ed: has been good.

Hoping that you and Mrs Moxon are well—and with best regards in which my family joins, I remain my dr Sir

very sincerely yours
[*signed*] W Wordsworth

---

[1] *Yarrow Revisited, and Other Poems* 1835. Writing to Mrs. Hemans on 6 Aug., R. P. Graves, who was again visiting Grasmere, described the proposed new publication: 'A vol. of new poems will soon be given to the world by Wordsworth, but not I believe containing (certainly not, he told me, if he can make up the book without) any of the Recluse or the Introductory Poem on the growth of an Individual mind. He has promised to read to us what he himself considers the best poem of the set "an Ode to Sound".' (*WL MSS.*)

831. DORA W. and D. W. to H. C. R.

Address: H: C: Robinson Esqre, Plowden's Buildings, Temple.
Postmark: 25 July 1834. *Stamp*: Strand.
Endorsed: 24 July 1834, The Misses Wordsworths.
MS. Dr. Williams's Library.
K (—). *Morley, i. 265.*

[*Dora W. writes*]

[*c.* 24 July 1834]

My dear Mr Robinson,

I can no longer allow your kind and beautiful present[1] to remain unacknowledged; my thanks would have been sent ere this had I not been prevented troubling you with a letter from a hope that my Father or Aunt might be writing to you in which case my thanks might have been conveyed to you in a manner more agreeable to yourself and more satisfactory to me for I feel I cannot half express the pleasure which this delightful gift of yours has afforded me. My Father and I look over the prints again and again till we really fancy ourselves floating on that grand River and thank you, both with our hearts and our tongues for putting us in the way of making that pleasant trip so easily.

You will be glad to hear that my Aunt Miss Wordsworth continues tolerably well—certainly stronger on the whole than when you were with us last year. My Father too has had no return of inflammation in his eyes—yet they are but of little service to him either for reading or writing which at this time he feels a more than usual inconvenience as he has at last yielded to our oft-repeated entreaties and is about to send his short M.S. Poems to press which when collected we expect will with a little *stuffing* make a Vol: about the size of those of the last Edition which Ed: Longman tells us has sold better than any former one—The Title of the new Vol. is to be 'Yarrow Revis[i]ted with other Poems'— so you will soon have all your favorite new Scotch sonnets without the trouble of transcribing.

We are well pleased to have dear Aunt Sarah at home again and she is looking so well after her travels—my brother William is with us—and *young* Mary Monkhouse.[2] I was going to write *little* but that would be absurd she is so very tall for her years. Her

---

[1] As Morley notes, H. C. R. had sent Dora W. a copy of Tombleson's *Views of the Rhine*, 1832, on 3 June.
[2] Daughter of M. W.'s cousin Thomas Monkhouse (d. 1825), and his wife Jane Horrocks, who had just died of typhus at Clifton.

Preston relatives[1] with whom she is passing her holydays have kindly spared her to us for a week—she is very pretty but so like her Mother that it is quite startling—I have in vain watched for a look or a motion which might recall her dear Father—Of course you know that her Mother Mrs Dick[2] is dead she was carried off suddenly by Typhus fever a few days before Aunt Sarah left London.

The Arnolds are all come to Fox How[3]—and delighted with their Westmoreland home as well they may; the D^r gave us a sermon yesterday which I dare say would have been more to your taste than it was to ours—good as it was in parts and all of it tersely and beautifully expressed.

Cyril and *Maria*[4] are as happy and happier than the day is long— they frequently inquire after you as do the Hardens whenever they see us but we have lost them from our immediate neighbourhood they have left Brathey and taken a house near Hawkshead. Mrs Luff's house[5] is at present empty and she on a visit to the Askews,[6] we hope to have it occupied next month by some excellent friends of ours from Hampstead—Mrs and Miss Hoare—

I ought to apologise for troubling you with such a long gossiping letter but I will not make bad worse by so doing—

With very affec^{te} remembrances from all in this house believe me ever my dear Mr Robinson

Yours very sincerely and much obliged
Dora Wordsworth.

I think I will try to persuade Aunt to add a few lines as a reward for your patience in *wading* thro' the above but perhaps I ought not to tell her of my impertinence in writing to you at all

[*D. W. writes*]

My dear Friend,

I comply, not for the reason assigned by Dora, for I can say nothing so well as she has said her Say; but because I want to assure

---

[1] The Horrocks family. Samuel Horrocks jnr. and John Monkhouse of Stow had been appointed guardians of the child (see *SH*, pp. 420, 423–4) but she was going to live at Brinsop with Thomas and Mary Hutchinson.

[2] Thomas Monkhouse's widow, who had married again in 1827.

[3] Their new house was now built.

[4] i.e. the author of *Cyril Thornton*, Thomas Hamilton, and his second wife Maria, Lady Farquhar, whom he had married on 15 Feb. They went to live at Elleray, Professor Wilson's house on Windermere.

[5] Fox Ghyll. The visit of Mrs. and Miss Hoare is recorded in *RMVB*.

[6] The family of the Revd. Henry Askew, rector of Greystoke (see L. 463 above).

you of my affectionate regards, and I may say, *daily* remembrances. It would be a great delight to me if you would come again, and drag me on the green Terrace—for alas! my legs are but of little use except in helping me to steer an enfeebled Body from one part of the room to the other. The longest walk I have attempted has been once round the Gravel Front of the House

London John[1] is coming to us from Keswick for a short time before his return to Mr Gardiner. He is an amiable youth, and we think him much improved—I congratulate you on your good Brother's recovery of health, and on dear Mr Clarkson's recovery of eye-sight. Miss Hutchinson is grown almost as much younger during her absence, as I *older* in the course of the last 3 years.

Are not you glad about the Poems? God bless you!

Ever your affecte
D W S^r.

832. W. W. to HENRY NELSON COLERIDGE

Address: H. N. Coleridge Esqre. 7 Downshire Place, Downshire Hill, Hampstead, London.
Postmark: 31 July 1834. *Stamp*: Kendal.
MS. British Library.
K (—). *LT ii.* 709 (—).

July 29, [1834]

My dear Sir,

Though the account which Miss Hutchinson had given of the State of our Friend's health had prepared us for the sad Tidings of your Letter the announcement of his dissolution[2] was not the less a great shock to my self and all this family. We are much obliged to you for entering so far into the particulars of our ever-to-be-lamented Friend's Decease, and we sincerely congratulate you and his dear Daughter upon the calmness of mind and the firm faith in his Redeemer which supported him through his painful bodily

---

[1] R. W.'s son.
[2] S. T. Coleridge died on 25 July at the Gillmans' house at Highgate, where he had been living since Apr. 1816. S. H. had visited him in May and June and had been shocked by the deterioration in his condition (see *SH*, pp. 414, 421). For a full account of Coleridge's last hours, see *Memoir and Letters of Sara Coleridge*, ed. her Daughter, 2 vols., 1873, i. 109 ff.; and Griggs, vi. 991–3.

and mental trials, and which we hope and trust have enrolled his Spirit among those of the blessed.—

Your letter was received on Sunday Morning, and would have been answered by return of Post, but I wished to see poor Hartley first, thinking it would be comfortable to yourself and his Sister to learn from a third Person how he appeared to bear his loss. Mrs Wordsworth called on him yesterday morning, he promised to go over to Rydal, but did not appear till after Post-time. He was calm, but much dejected; expressed strongly his regret that he had not seen his Father before his departure from this world, and also seemed to lament that he had been so little with him during the course of their lives.[1] Mrs Wordsworth advised him to go over to Keswick, and there provide himself with fit mourning under the guidance of Miss Crosthwaite,[2] Ambleside being a bad place for procuring any kind of clothes. I mention this that you may name it to his Mother.—

I cannot give way to the expression of my feelings upon this mournful occasion; I have not strength of mind to do so—The last year has thinned off so many of my Friends, young and old, and brought with it so much anxiety, private and public, that it would be no kindness to you were I to yield to the solemn and sad thoughts and remembrances which press upon me. It is nearly 40 years since I first became acquainted with him whom we have just lost; and though with the exception of six weeks when we were on the continent together,[3] along with my Daughter, I have seen little of him for the last 20 years, his mind has been habitually present with me, with an accompanying feeling that he was still in the flesh. That frail tie is broken and I, and most of those who are nearest and dearest to me must prepare and endeavour to follow him.[4] Give my affectionate love to Sara, and remember me tenderly to Mrs Coleridge; in these requests Mrs Wordsworth, my poor Sister,

---

[1] See his letters to his brother Derwent and his mother, *Letters of Hartley Coleridge* (ed. Griggs), pp. 162–7. His note to R. P. Graves, declining an invitation, is quoted by Graves in his letter to Mrs. Hemans on 12 Aug.: 'Since I last saw you I have received intelligence that my revered Father is no more. He departed this life at half past six on Friday morning last. He had suffered much but died calmly testifying the depth and sincerity of his faith in Christ. Of course I am in no state of mind for society and you will excuse me from waiting on you . . . Little thought I while rattling on so wildly that my parent was even then a corpse—I trust—a blessed Spirit.' (*WL transcript.*)

[2] The Keswick draper.

[3] In 1828.

[4] For a further tribute to Coleridge's genius by W. W., see R. P. Graves's letter to Mrs. Hemans of 12 Aug. (*WL transcript*), quoted by C. W. jnr. in *Mem.* ii. 288 ff.

Miss H—, and Dora unite, and also in very kind regards to yourself; and believe me, my dear sir,

Gratefully yours,
W. Wordsworth

Pray remember us kindly to Mr and Mrs Gillman when you see
them. We shall be happy to hear from you again at your leisure.

833. W. W. to UNKNOWN CORRESPONDENT

MS. Cornell. Hitherto unpublished.

[*In M. W.'s hand*]

Rydal Mount
July 31 —34

My dear Sir

There is no need to forward you a letter of introduction to Dr
Arnold—He is gone from this place on a visit to the Archbp: of
Dublin,[1] at Barmouth—but will return to his residence here by the
end of this week—where he will remain about 3 weeks—and then
return to Rugby. I shall communicate to him the wish and intentions expressed in your letter, and prepare him either for a letter
from you, or for receiving you here or at Rugby as may best
suit you.

I remain my d^r Sir
faithfully yours
[*signed*] Wm Wordsworth

834. W. W. to JOHN BOLTON

Address: John Bolton Esqre, Storrs, Bowness.
MS. Mrs. Greenwood. Hitherto unpublished.

Rydal Mount
Monday evening [4 Aug. 1834]

My dear Sir,

I regret much that from the state of my foot which has troubled
me for so long I must deny myself the pleasure of accompanying

---

[1] Richard Whateley, D.D. (1787–1863), Fellow of Oriel College, Oxford
(1811–22), and associate of Arnold and the group of liberal churchmen at
Oriel known as the 'Noetics': Principal of St. Alban Hall (1825–31), Professor
of Political Economy (1829–31), and Archbishop of Dublin from 1831:
author of *Logic* (1826), *Rhetoric* (1828), and *Errors of Romanism* (1830).

you to Lowther. It is Mr Carr's wish that the little tumour which
annoys me should be cut off, and till that is done I cannot bring
myself to quit home.

Pray make my kindest regards and respects to Mrs Bolton and
Mrs Stannyforth[1] if with you, and believe me dear Sir

very faithfully yours
Wm Wordsworth

835. W. W. to LORD LONSDALE

MS. Lonsdale MSS. Hitherto unpublished.

Rydal Mount
Tuesday morning
August 5th 1834

My Lord,

Many thanks for your Lordship's obliging Letter. It has mortified
me not a little that I have been unable to pay my respects at Lowther
before this time; and what is worse, I cannot foresee when I shall
be at liberty. Yesterday, my Surgeon, Mr Carr of Ambleside,
and Dr Vose,[2] a Physician formerly in great practice at Liverpool,
consulted about the little tumor or nodule which has for some time
been forming on one of my Toes, in consequence probably of an
awkward accident; and it was determined, though much against
Mr Carr's wish, that, as no enlargement or change had taken place
in it for the last week, that another week or ten days should be
tried to see what Nature would do with it; and if it did not diminish,
it must then be cut out. In the meanwhile I must wait as patiently
as I can, thankful that it occasions not the least pain, being almost
insensible; but it is recommended to me to abstain from walking
much during the interval.

Pray, my Lord excuse this long story—and be assured that as
soon as I am at Liberty, it will give me the utmost pleasure to
visit you and my excellent friends at Lowther.

I am glad that Lord Lowther is coming down, and trust I shall
have the pleasure of seeing him. What a discouraging state is this
poor Country in! The government becoming more and more radical

---

[1] Mrs. Bolton's sister. See L. 455 above.
[2] See L. 814 above.

with every change in the Persons that compose it![1] The House of Lords is the only barrier between us and universal confusion.—

Mr Bolton was too much oppressed by the hot weather to venture from home on Friday—he is declining visibly. It is said that Mr Branker[2] has sold his house at Clappersgate—I wish it may be so, for he is a nuisance in the neighbourhood. Allan Bank, Mr Crump's property, has also been sold to a Mr Dawson, who has been some time resident in Grasmere. I do not exactly know his political principles, but I rather think they are conservative. Mr Redmain,[3] who bought Brathay, is about to build a Church and endow it—he is said to be of a strong religious bias, and closely connected with the Wilsons of Casterton.[4]

My Son has come over to see us from Workington, his wife having just presented him with a Son.[5]

Mrs Wordsworth and my Sister, who is rather in her better way, and my Son and Daughter, unite with me in respectful remembrances to your Lordship and Lady Lonsdale, and believe me ever

faithfully your much obliged
W Wordsworth

836. W. W. to WILLIAM FELL[6]

Address: Mr Fell, Ambleside. [*delivered by hand*]
MS. Cornell. Hitherto unpublished.

Monday Morn: [11 Aug. 1834]

My dear Sir,

Mr Rogers[7] my friend is here, he has got a lameness in one of his feet since he left London; and does not know whether it is gout

---

[1] The Whig government of Lord Grey had been progressively weakened this summer, first by the resignation of Sir James Graham (see *MY* ii. 536), Stanley, and others over the Irish Church question, and later by the opposition of Lord Althorp (see L. 820 above) to an Irish coercion bill. Grey resigned, and was succeeded on 17 July by Lord Melbourne (1779–1848), Home Secretary in the previous administration.

[2] James Branker of Croft Lodge.

[3] For Giles Redmayne, see L. 758 above.

[4] See *MY* ii. 292, 419.

[5] Henry Curwen Wordsworth (1834–65), W. W.'s first grandson.

[6] The Ambleside surgeon.

[7] Samuel Rogers had written from London that he was setting out on 6 Aug. and expected to arrive at Rydal on Monday the 11th or Tuesday the 12th (*WL MSS.*). He remained in the Lakes until about 6 Sept., twice visiting Lowther and Hallsteads with W. W. (see *SH*, p. 427; Warter, iv. 381; and

or a sprain. Pray come over in the course of the afternoon, and bring bandages and a strengthening plaister. Mr R. *now* assured me that it is a sprain—

Yours most faithfully
W. Wordsworth

837. W. W. to EDWARD MOXON

Address: Mr Moxon, Dover Street. By favor of Mr Wordsworth[1]
MS. Henry E. Huntington Library.
LY ii. 710.

[12 Aug. 1834]

My dear Sir,

Your last very friendly and judicious letter would have received an immediate answer, but I deferred writing till I should have occasion to communicate with Mr Longman etc. Be assured that I shall be most happy and proud to have your name on the title page of my new volume,[2] and that I shall state my feeling upon this point in such a way that my old Publisher, I have no doubt, will readily comply with my proposal.—I am of your opinion that the sale of my Works would be promoted, by being published monthly as you propose, and if I live to see another Edition it shall be done.—

Yesterday arrived, to the great joy of this House, our excellent Friend Mr Rogers, but also he made his appearance lame, having had an attack of the Gout in his foot. He talks of returning to London almost instantly in consequence, but we anxiously hope that the symptoms will abate, and allow him to stay. This moment has brought me a note from him (he is at Low Wood) in which he tells me he will leave almost immediately—he seems now assured that it is only a spasm.—

Rogers, ii. 96), and then went on to Scotland. R. P. Graves met him at Rydal Mount soon after he arrived, and described his appearance in a letter of 16 Aug. to Mrs. Hemans: 'He is an infirm large and pale-headed man of 70. He is very pleasant they tell me in conversation. Aristocratic society and the book-trade were the only and uninteresting topics I heard him upon. I observed he was particularly elegant and terse.' (*WL transcript.*)

[1] The address is in M. W.'s hand. This last phrase was added by Dora W., and de Selincourt assumed that she meant to write 'By favour of Mr. Rogers'. But Samuel Rogers did not return to London from this tour until November, and it is much more likely that the letter was carried down to London by 'Keswick John', on his return to Mr. Gardner's (see *SH*, p. 427).

[2] *Yarrow Revisited, and Other Poems*, published jointly by Longman and Co. and Edward Moxon.

Pray do you know Mr Heraud, author of the judgment of the flood etc.[1] He has sent me a beautiful Copy of his Poem the receipt of which I have acknowledged telling him that the state of my eyes did not allow me to read it. This is true. My eyes are not indeed at present inflamed, but reading makes them so irritable that I am obliged to leave off almost as soon as I begin. Mr H. not satisfied with this acknowledgment has written most urgently for a criticism from me upon his work, and this distressed me greatly, for I cannot read his work without injury, nor have I yet been able to read Mr Taylor's[2]—for if I become interested in what I read, I am tempted on till I feel the bad effect. Pray assure Mr Heraud, if you know him, that I much admire what I have been able to peruse of his work, and think very highly of his genius.—

ever most faithfully yours
W Wordsworth

I sent you this to London having a Frank handy, but pray don't pay the Postage of your letters to me. I must congratulate you on your success as a Publisher of which our common friend Mr R. gives me most favorable accounts.

W W.

838. W. W. to HENRY WILKINSON[3]

MS. WL.
SH, p. 425.

[*In S. H.'s hand*]

[*c.* 15 Aug. 1834]

My d^r Sir,

I sit down to trouble you with a few lines about my Nephew T.H.[4] He is in very low spirits respecting his prospects at Col: finding in himself notwithstanding his best and firmest resolutions an inability to stick to close reading, and consequently he fears

---

[1] *The Judgment of the Flood*, 1834, by J. A. Heraud (see L. 823 above).
[2] *Philip van Artevelde* (see L. 825 above).
[3] The Revd. Henry Wilkinson (see *MY* ii. 565) had been headmaster of Sedbergh since 1819. W. W.'s letter is quoted by S. H. in the course of a letter to Mrs. Hutchinson, which is probably to be dated 17 Aug. 1834.
[4] W. W.'s nephew Thomas Hutchinson jnr., a pupil at Sedbergh, and now about to enter St. John's College, Cambridge.

that he will scarcely succeed in procuring a degree. Now as no other line of Life is open to him, I do anxiously wish that during the short time he remains with you, you would be so kind as to give him all the encouragement you can. I am well aware of the difficulty of the case. He is a youth of a very nice conscience and of good and excellent dispositions, but deplorably wanting in intellectual propensities and appetites. The only knowledge which he seems capable of acquiring from Books is of a kind destitute of *vital* energy: it is kept together mechanically in his mind without any organic connection; it is against the grain, and as far as it is retained, is retained without pleasure and desire for more. This is a melancholy and appears to me a rare case, for he is not a dunce, nor a stupid Boy incapable of comprehending a thing when plainly stated to him, but he seems almost totally without voluntary activity of mind in literature. But to recur to my wish. Such encouragement as you can give him pray do. So good are his principles and so moderate his desires, that I am persuaded that he would be both happy and useful as a Minister of the Gospel in a small country Parish, and as I said before, unfortunately no other line of Life is at present open to him—

[*cetera desunt*]

839. W. W. to ALFRED BEESLEY[1]

Address: Alfred Beesley Esq, Salutation Inn.
MS. British Library. Hitherto unpublished.

Rydal Mount
Tuesday morn. [26 Aug. 1834][2]
Mr Wordsworth has a small party of Friends this evening and it would give him great pleasure to see Mr Beesley.

---

[1] Alfred Beesley (1800–47), author of a volume of poems, '*Japheth; Contemplation: and other pieces*, 1834 (*R.M. Cat.*, no. 460), and *The History of Banbury*, 1841.
[2] Date established from R. P. Graves's letter to Mrs. Hemans of 27 Aug. 1834 (*WL transcript*), in which he describes the party at Rydal Mount on the 26th. The guests included Capt. Thomas Hamilton and his wife, Mr. Archer, the Godwins, Hartley Coleridge, and Owen Lloyd.

840. W. W. to JOHN MARSHALL

MS. Cornell.
LY ii. 664.

Lowther C——
Sunday Morning—[31 Aug. 1834]

My dear Sir,

Mr Rogers and I will come to Halsteads on Thursday, if it should suit you and Mrs Marshall—I shall be on my way homewards——

ever faithfully yours
Wᵐ Wordsworth

841. W. W. to JOHN MARSHALL¹

Address: John Marshall Esqʳᵉ MP, Dovenby Hall, Cockermouth. [*readdressed to*] Hallsteads, Penrith.
Stamp: Kendal Penny Post.
MS. Miriam Lutcher Stark Library, University of Texas. Hitherto unpublished.

[? early Sept. 1834]

My dear Sir,

You were kind enough yesterday to ask if I wanted Franks. It did not then strike me that I had occasion for one, but you will oblige me by forwarding the enclosed as directed. I hope you found your Family and all at Dovenby well.

I remain dʳ Sir faithfully
yours
W. Wordsworth

842. W. W. to FELICIA DOROTHEA HEMANS

MS. untraced.
Mem. Grosart. K. LY ii. 714.

Rydal Mount, Sept., 1834.

My dear Mrs Hemans,

I avail myself gladly of the opportunity of Mr Graves's return² to acknowledge the honour you have done me in prefixing my

---

¹ Probably John Marshall jnr., who married Mary Dykes of Dovenby in Nov. 1828. This letter was written some time after that (and probably after the birth of his sons in 1832–3), and before his retirement from Parliament and illness in 1835.   ² To Dublin from Grasmere.

name to your volume[1] of beautiful poems, and to thank you for the copy you have sent me with your own autograph. Where there is so much to admire, it is difficult to select; and therefore I shall content myself with naming only two or three pieces. And, first, let me particularise the piece that stands second in the volume, *Flowers and Music in a Room of Sickness*. This was especially touching to me, on my poor sister's account, who has long been an invalid, confined almost to her chamber. The feelings are sweetly touched throughout this poem, and the imagery very beautiful; above all, in the passage where you describe the colour of the petals of the wild rose. This morning I have read the stanzas upon *Elysium* with great pleasure. You have admirably expanded the thought of Chateaubriand.[2] If we had not been disappointed in our expected pleasure of seeing you here, I should have been tempted to speak of many other passages and poems with which I have been delighted.

Your health, I hope, is by this time re-established. Your son Charles looks uncommonly well, and we have had the pleasure of seeing him and his friends several times; but as you are aware, we are much engaged with visitors at this season of the year, so as not always to be able to follow our inclinations as to whom we would wish to see. I cannot conclude without thanking you for your sonnet upon a place so dear to me as Grasmere;[3] it is worthy of the subject. With kindest remembrances, in which unite Mrs Wordsworth, my sister, and Dora,

I remain, dear Mrs Hemans,
Your much obliged friend,
Wm Wordsworth

843. D. W. to ELIZABETH HUTCHINSON[4]

MS. WL.
LY ii. 712.

Tuesday—about the 14th Sept. [? 1834]

My dear Godchild

This is not one of my vigorous days, therefore you must take it kindly though I send you a short, unentertaining, and ill-penned letter. For the last mentioned failure my excuse is, that I lie upon

[1] *Scenes and Hymns of Life* (see L. 817 above).
[2] The poem is prefaced by a quotation from *Le Génie du Christianisme*, 1802, by François René, Vicomte de Chateaubriand (1768–1848).
[3] *A Remembrance of Grasmere*, in 'Records of the Spring of 1834', published in *Poetical Remains of the late Mrs Hemans*, 1836, p. 39.
[4] Daughter of Thomas and Mary Hutchinson, now 14 years of age.

my back in bed and with uplifted knees form a desk for my paper. Do not suppose, however, that I spend all my time in bed—It is only that I rise late and go to bed before sunset, because it tires, and in other respects disagrees with me to sit up more than from 4 to 6 hours in the day.

I hope you will find the green gown useful: but wish I had also been able to send you some *book* to help you to adorn the mind, while the Body is gaily dressed in its 'gown of green'. My dear Elizabeth, I hope your good Father and Mother will consent to allow you to visit your Friends at Rydal very soon—*I* say the sooner the better—but am afraid we must not look for you till George's[1] return at Christmas—and indeed it would be unreasonable to expect you to leave home before the end of the holidays, when so large a troop of your companions will be assembled there; but we all (your Uncle and Aunt W. Aunt Sarah, Dora and myself) join in the wish and the request that your Parents will spare you to us when George returns. Probably Cousin Dora will not be at home during the first part of your visit, and you will in that case, be a lively companion and useful help to us, the old, and for myself I must add the *infirm*.

I trust you may gather much improvement among us with your own pains-taking; but cannot promise you any regular instruction, and indeed if Dora should be at home (which I trust she will *not* be) when you arrive, she has not health or strength sufficient for a Teacher. You may however, learn much, indirectly, while contributing both to my amusement and instruction by reading to me, which will be to me of great use and comfort. I can promise to do nothing more for you in the way of instruction than drawing out your comments and remarks and making my own: and further; it will be a pleasure to me to point out whatever may appear to me amiss in your manner of reading. It would fatigue me to instruct you in French—and indeed perhaps you *need* little instruction except in the pronunciation—and *that* I could not give: but a French-master has been fixed for some time at Ambleside, and we hope, and even expect, that he will *stay*, as he has a number of scholars, and there will be no difficulty in having him here to attend on you, if we cannot get you introduced into some friend's house where he may have other pupils.

I feel as if I had much to say both to you and Mary,[2] and to your dear Mother: but as I took too much exercise yesterday (tempted

---

[1] Ebba's elder brother George, now a pupil at Sedbergh.
[2] Ebba's elder sister.

by the fine weather) I must spare myself and conclude with this one assurance that I have it much at heart to have some intercourse with you, my dear God-daughter before I quit this world—Do not suppose however, that I have any feelings which make me expect the speedy approach of death. Far from it—I suffer comparatively little, and have a full enjoyment of all the blessings with which I am surrounded: but life is uncertain even with the strongest—and still more so with the old and feeble, therefore I hope the time for your coming (if all be well at home) may be fixed for next January —I send you a God-mother's Blessing, with sincerest wishes that you may not waste the happy days of Youth. Make the most of them. They will never return, and if you do not profit by present advantages you will bitterly repent when it is too late, but however happy you may be in the enjoyment of youth, health and strength never, my good child, forget that our *home* is not here and prepare yourself for what will come, sooner or later to every one of us. —Give my love to all the Inmates of Brinsop-Court—not forgetting the unseen little Sarah[1]—I have had many anxious thoughts concerning your Uncle Monkhouse:[2] and it is with a thankful heart that I congratulate him on the hopes of a complete restoration of his eyesight. Pray give my affectionate regards to him with earnest wishes that all may end as it has begun.

Again God bless you! Believe me
ever your faithful and affectionate Friend,
Dorothy Wordsworth.

Remember dear Elizabeth, that my penmanship affords no example for you. How I wish I could ever again climb the Credenhill hill with all of you—young and old!—or visit that old Tree on the top of the Hill opposite to dear Brinsop! Tell Mary I hope she will not fail to send me a sketch of your little Church—and mark Aunt M.'s[3] grave.

[1] The youngest of the family.
[2] John Monkhouse of Stow.
[3] Miss Elizabeth Monkhouse, who had died at Brinsop in 1828. See also *SH*, p. 422.

844. W. W. to JOSEPH HENRY GREEN[1]

Address: Joseph Henry Green Esqre, 46 Lincoln's Inn Fields.
Postmark: 18 Sept. 1834. *Stamp*: Gt Portman St.
MS. Pierpont Morgan Library. Hitherto unpublished.

[*In M. W.'s hand*]

[mid-Sept. 1834]

My dear Sir,

Accept my thanks for the copy of our lamented Friend's Will,[2] and for the letter which accompanied it—the Parcel only reached me a few days ago.

The few letters which we have in this house from Mr Coleridge shall be carefully looked over; and if there be any, likely to prove of general interest and not of a domestic character, the originals or extracts shall be sent to you—as also any marginal notes. Among my own books I know but one (Dr Donne's Sermons) with notes from our friend's pen—I have put the Book into his Son Hartley's hand, and he will transcribe them—and they shall be forwarded to you together with a few pages of Memoranda—from a common-place book—and any other M.S. that may be found.[3]

The Friends of the late Mr Watson[4] (*we* suppose) have, for want of due consideration, sent to the Carlisle Patriot certain Papers connected with Mr Coleridge's memory, and they are in the course of publication. I have desired my Son to forward the Paper to Mr Gillman, who will probably shew it to you. There is one letter

---

[1] Coleridge's literary executor. See L. 653 above.

[2] For Coleridge's will, see Griggs, vi. 998–1002. Coleridge wrote in it of the 'debt of gratitude and reverential affection' felt by his children towards Southey and W. W.

[3] The papers were sent to Green the following January (see *SH*, p. 439), for the use of Henry Nelson Coleridge. Sara Coleridge wrote to Thomas Poole on 5 Sept.: 'I am sorry to say that Henry does not possess and sees no means of possessing materials for a regular History of my father's Life—if he did it would be scarcely possible to represent the tenor of many parts of it as we might think justly, yet so as neither to assail the feelings nor touch the memory of some among his contemporaries. Our age has been called one of personality—more if not coarser than was ever indulged in before—yet an almost captious delicacy is felt in these times by many and affected by others. However I hope that Henry will preserve any facts of my Father's History the truth of which he may be able to ascertain and which may otherwise perish or be misunderstood—how far and in what shape they should be recorded may be an after consideration.' (*British Library MSS.*)

[4] John Watson (1799–1827), had acted as an assistant to James Gillman and as amanuensis to S. T. C. (see Griggs, v. 181). His letter to Watson of 24 June 1827 (Griggs, vi. 693), and some other papers were published in the *Carlisle Patriot* on 6 Sept. 1834 in a contribution signed Philo.

undoubtedly genuine, but Hartley, to whom the Paper was shewn, tells me that the Poems and scraps of verses are not his Father's, tho' ascribed to him, but *his own* compositions. I hope he has by this time written to the Editor of the Paper, to set him right.

To a matter of much more importance I take leave (tho' it is probably unnecessary) to direct your attention—viz, to an Article upon our Friend that appeared in the last No: of Tait's Mag: written by Mr de Quincey.[1] This notice is, in most points, relating to Mr C's personal *Character*, highly offensive, and utterly unworthy of a Person holding the rank of a Gentleman in english society. It is not to be doubted that the Writer was honoured by Mr C's confidence, whose company he industriously sought, following him into different parts of England: and how he has abused that confidence, and in certain particulars perverted the communications made to him, is but too apparent from this obnoxious publication. The Article in question is one of a promised series; and upon this account more particularly, and as holding our Friend's memory dear, I venture to submit, whether or no it would be adviseable for you, in the capacity of Executor, to address to Mr de Q., or to the Ed: of the Mag: a letter of caution, or remonstrance, as in your judgement may seem most likely to put a check upon communications so injurious, unfeeling, and untrue. Much indeed of this notice is false in its statements, and unjustifiable in its inferences to that degree, that I should have been sure the Writer was not in intimate connection of friendship with Mr C, had I not personal knowledge, and proofs from Mr C's own letters, to the contrary. In justice to Mr de Q., who was an Inmate during the space of 7 Months in my own house,[2] I must say that I did not observe any traces of *malevolent* feeling towards *Mr* C., and that the Writer extols his intellectual powers as much as the most ardent of his Admirers, if discreet and judicious, would do.

You will, my dear Sir, consider this letter strictly confidential, and believe me to be with high respect, faithfully yours,

[*signed*] Wm Wordsworth

[1] De Quincey contributed four articles to *Tait's Magazine* in Sept., Oct., and Nov. 1834, and Jan. 1835, under the title of 'Samuel Taylor Coleridge: By the English Opium-Eater'. See *Works* (ed. Masson), ii. 138 ff. S. H. called the articles 'infamous'. Julius Hare published an answer to De Quincey's allegations in the *British Magazine*, vii (1835), 15–27.

[2] At Allan Bank in 1808–9.

845. W. W. to M. S. MILTON[1]

Address: M. S. Milton Esqre, Brigham.
MS. Lilly Library, Indiana University. Hitherto unpublished.

[In M. W.'s hand]

Rectory, Workington.
[late Sept. 1834]

Sir,

Had I known thro' what channel to make my acknowledgements I should have thanked you earlier for your two Poems, which you were so kind to send me. You may perhaps have heard that I am much troubled with inflammation in my eyes, and will be sorry to hear that consequently I am enabled to read very little; but from what I have seen of your works, I have no scruple to say that the Poems are written with great animation and spirit.

I have also been a good deal from home lately, this has interfered also, but I promise myself on my return to Rydal much gratification from the perusal of your two works. I need scarcely add that should you be in the neighbourhood of Ambleside I should be glad if you would favor me with a call at Rydal Mount.

I am Sir
respectfully yours
[*signed*] Wm Wordsworth

846. W. W. to BASIL MONTAGU

Address: Basil Montagu Esqre, Lincolns Inn, London.
Postmark: 2 Oct. 1834.
MS. Harvard University Library.
LY ii. 716.

[In M. W.'s hand]

Rectory, Workington
Sepr. 30th [1834]

My dear Montagu,

Your parcel for which you will accept my cordial thanks reached Rydal just before I set off for this place, so that I have not had time

---

[1] Author of *The Ocean Bride: A Tale of the Sea*, 1834 (*R.M. Cat.*, no. 612), and *Songs of the Prophesies*, 1835.

to read a word of your Life of Bacon,[1] from which I promise myself much pleasure, knowing with what industry it has been executed. This last edition of the Selections,[2] which you have kindly sent me, enables me to place the former one, your present also, in the hands of my younger Son, who is at present settled as my Agent at Carlisle, where he has a good deal of leisure for reading; and I trust will profit by so valuable a book.

My journey to Leamington, of which I spoke to you in my last, has been deferred from week to week on account of the deranged state of my daughter's health—I still hope that she may have courage to move after my return to Rydal at the end of this week.

Since I came here where I am on a visit to my Son who is pro tempore Incumbent of this place, (the patronage of which is in his Father-in-Law, Mr Curwen) I have learnt that there is at home a letter for me, from our old and excellent friend Wrangham[3]— written in a hand scarcely legible—from which I infer he must have suffered from a paralytic attack—of which I had heard a vague report. This grieves me much—he is a very kind-hearted Man; and tho' fonder of new Acquaintance than many are—that propensity never seemed to me to weaken his attachment to his old friends.

The weather here is delightful—and I am this moment returned from bathing in the [sea] which I have done for several days past— between 7 and 8 in the morning, with a hope principally of strengthning my eyes—against the winter—which in consequence of repeated inflammations during the last 30 years are become so weak as to make reading and writing, unless for a very little at a time, injurious to them.

Farewell believe me ever affl[ly] yours

[*signed*] Wm Wordsworth

---

[1] The sixteenth and last volume of Montagu's edition of Bacon.

[2] *Selections from the Works of Taylor, Hooker, Hall, and Lord Bacon. With an analysis of the Advancement of Learning*, 1805: 3rd edn., 1829.

[3] Francis Wrangham, Archdeacon of the East Riding since 1828. See also letter of 2 Feb. 1835 (in next volume).

847. W. W. to AMBROSE POYNTER[1]

MS. Mr Arthur Houghton Jnr. Hitherto unpublished.

[*In M. W.'s hand*]

Workington Octr 2^d 1834

Sir,

I have much pleasure in sending you the enclosed note of introduction as requested by my friend Mr Courtenay[2]—and both on
his account and your own, I heartily wish your application may be
successful—

I am Sir Y^{rs} truly

[*signed*] Wm Wordsworth

848. D. W. to EDWARD MOXON

MS. Henry E. Huntington Library.
LY ii. 717.

Rydal Mount, October 2nd 1834

My dear Sir,

In the absence of my Brother (on a visit to his Son at Workington) I have ventured to offer to furnish Mr Godwin, a neighbour
of ours, with an introduction to you. He is much respected in our
Family; but that is not the cause of this introduction. He is the
Bearer of a manuscript volume of Poems by his Wife,[3] who is very
anxious to entrust her work to your inspection and, if you approve
and do not think the speculation would be altogether unprofitable,
Mrs Godwin would be happy and thankful if you would undertake
to be her publisher. I cannot give either advice or opinion, not
knowing whether my Friend's writings are likely at all to hit the
taste of the publick—only this I *can* say that her style, language,
and versification *appear to me* very much superior to those of most
of the popular female writers of the present day. I may add also
that my Brother thinks highly of Mrs Godwin's powers and attainments. Further I will say, for the satisfaction of my own friendly
feelings, that Mrs G. is a very amiable woman, and that both the
Husband and Wife are excellent and agreeable neighbours to the
Inhabitants of Rydal Mount.

---

[1] (1796–1886), architect: pupil of John Nash, designer of churches, country
houses, and public buildings, and a foundation member of the R.I.B.A. (1834).

[2] Philip Courtenay, W. W.'s financial adviser.

[3] For Mrs. Catherine Grace Godwin, see L. 423 above.

You will, I am sure, be glad to hear that my health and strength improve, though slowly. My Brother's eyes are better, yet unfit for much service.

Though I have not the pleasure of a personal acquaintance with Mrs Moxon, I feel as if she were not unknown to me,[1] and will therefore beg you to offer to her my kind regards.

I am, dear Sir,
Yours faithfully
D. Wordsworth Sen[r]

P.S. Pray do not let any thing I have said through friendly regard to Mrs Godwin have the least influence on your determination respecting the publication of her poems or, in the smallest degree, influence your prudential arrangements or views.

849. D. W. to CATHERINE CLARKSON

MS. untraced.
K (—). *LY ii. 719.*

Begun Monday, 18th Oct. [? 1834][2]

My dear Friend,

. . . If autumnal cold and dampness had not come on, I think I should now be able to walk far enough to have a look at the prospect from the old terrace, but cold is my horror, so I must not execute this large scheme till we have spring breezes and sunshine. Whenever the weather allows it I continue to go out daily either in the family phaeton, which is dragged by one of the steadiest and best of horses, guided by a very skilful driver (my dear niece), or the man-servant who takes me round and round the garden and upon the lower new-made green terrace in a Bath chair. . . .

[cetera desunt]

---

[1] She was Lamb's adopted daughter, Emma Isola.
[2] Monday was the 20th Oct. But the letter seems to belong to this year, and probably D. W. was muddled about the date.

850. W. W. to EDWARD MOXON

Address: Ed: Moxon Esqre, Dover St, London.
Postmark: 1 Nov. 1834. *Stamp*: Kendal Penny Post.
MS. Harvard University Library. Hitherto unpublished.

[In M. W.'s hand]

Octr 30th [1834]

My dear Sir,

I lose no time in replying to your letter, and should be perfectly ashamed of your having so little profit from the Selections[1] were it not that you know probably how insignificant have been my own gains from the press—for considerably more than half my life I have been from time to time a Publisher, tho' mostly in a small way— and the Sum of my gains has not probably done much more than equal $\frac{1}{2}$ the wages of a day-labourer in that time. As to a new Ed: of the Selections I quite approve of your proposition, and trust that Mr Hine will be considerate enough to give way to our joint opinion without regret or displeasure. As there are a few pieces in the Vol which is in the Press that would possibly suit your purpose—the 'Selections' should not be printed off entirely till you have an opportunity of exercising your judgement upon that point; for my own part, I am quite unable to give advice upon the Subject—about 2 thirds of the New Vol[2] must by this time be struck off—but it would be disagreeable to me to put any part of it into circulation, however limited, till the whole is off my hands, which would have been nearly so by this time, but for interruption in the sending off the franks, under which the Proof Sheets have passed.

I hope Mr Taylor[3] will defer any Review which he may be inclined to make of my Poems till this Vol. is out—as, tho' a great majority of the Pieces are upon similar Subjects to, and in the same strain with, those in the former Volumes, there is yet some variety, which would not escape the notice of the discerning Critic.

You have not sent, my dear Sir, my Private account—but beg that it may be forwarded to me when next I have the pleasure of hearing from you—as I cannot bear to be so long in your debt.

---

[1] Joseph Hine's *Selections from the Poems of William Wordsworth*, 1831, was about to go into a second edition.

[2] *Yarrow Revisited, and Other Poems.*

[3] Henry Taylor's review of 'Wordsworth's Poetical Works' appeared in the *Quarterly Review*, lii (Nov. 1834), 317–58. It was reprinted in his *Works*, 5 vols., 1877–8, v. 1–52.

You will naturally be anxious about my eyes. They are very much better than at this time last year, and for all purposes of pleasure in my Walks etc. I have little to lament. But I suffer much from Candle light, and hot rooms—and they are of little or no Service to me in reading or writing. Upon this I need not dwell, when I tell you that I have not been able yet to read more than 30 or 40 pages, of either Mr Heraud's last Poem,[1] or Mr Taylor's dramatic romance.[2] Judge then what privations I am subject to— but no one can say that upon the whole I do not bear them chearfully. My general health thank God is most excellent, and my muscular strength for walking, I think, even greater than it was three or four years ago. But it is time to release you and my Amanuensis, and I must take this to the post before dinner.

When my Vol comes out I hope Mrs Moxon will accept a Copy from myself and I will contrive to send her my Autograph to insert in it. You are, no doubt, aware that your Name will be with Longman's on the Title Page. How comes it that we have not heard from my most excellent Friend Rogers since we parted? If Lamb could find time to write to us also, we should be thankful. For my Sister's languishing state, and my daughter's recently deranged health causing us much anxiety and depression of Mind— we cannot but wish to hear occasionally from Old Friends.

Believe me with best regards from all here to yourself and Mrs M, ever faithfully yrs

[*signed*] Wm Wordsworth

If we had had time Mrs W. should have transcribed for you a little piece[3] which I composed yesterday—and which I think is exactly suited for the Selections.

---

[1] *The Judgment of the Flood.*
[2] *Philip van Artevelde.*
[3] Probably one of the *Evening Voluntaries*. See *PW* iv. 4–8.

851. W. W., M. W., and D. W. to H. C. R.

Address: H. C. Robinson Esqre, 2 Plowden's Buildings, Temple, London.
Postmark: 24 Nov. 1834. *Stamp*: Kendal Penny Post.
Endorsed: Decr 3. 1834, Wordsworth politics, Invitation, L Life Insurance.
    N.B. The name only by the poet—M^rs W—Dorothy etc the rest of the letter.
MS. Dr. Williams's Library.
K (—). *Morley, i. 268.*

[*In M. W.'s hand*]   Rydal Mount
                                                    Nov 21st [1834]
My dear Friend

Before I advert to business, I will tell you how we are—My Sister does not gain strength, and had about a month ago a backcast, from which she is in a good measure recovered—So upon the whole she cannot be said to be worse than when you saw her.

My daughter suffered so much from want of appetite and indigestion, and pains in her neck and shoulder—that we were much depressed and not a little alarmed about her. Our Medical Attendant, having no doubt that an inflammation on the spine exists, has put her under a course of treatment—bleeding, blistering, and an almost perpetual recumbent posture: She is now at full length upon the Sofa in the room where this is written—and is becoming a great student, particularly in novels—at present she is better engaged reading La Borde's account of Spain,[1] and I am in hopes that by and bye she will attack Herodotus and Thucydidees. Miss Hutchinson has been seven weeks with Mr Southey's family, she is in excellent health—the Accounts of Mrs Southey,[2] now at York in the Retreat in consequence of depression of Spirits, and alienation of mind are upon the whole rather encouraging. Mrs W. is well and so am I—except that my eyes are of little or no use to me, for either reading or writing. They are however thank God, but little subject at present, to inflammation and answer all other purposes of seeing—except looking at strong and dazzling lights—very well. I dare not expose them however to keen winds—

The publication of my little volume has been retarded by the printing being put into the most careless hands, acting under the

---

[1] *A View of Spain*, 5 vols., 1809, by Count Alexandre Louis Joseph de Laborde (1773–1842).

[2] Mrs. Southey had, without any warning, suffered a mental breakdown at the end of Sept. and spent several months in an asylum at York. (See *SH*, pp. 430–1 and Southey, vi. 243 ff.) She became well enough to return home, but never fully recovered her sanity.

most inattentive minds, with which I was ever concerned—The delay is lucky, as neither Othello, Mackbeth nor the Paradise Lost, if now first produced, would be attended to—

The Dissolution of the Melbourne Ministry[1] was by me received rather with fear than pleasure. You have known from the first my opinion of the reform bill—to speak of it in the mildest terms, it was an unwise measure carried by unworthy means: the composition of the present Ho: of C. shews, what will ever be the case where Democracy is predominant, that the people prefer their flatterers to their friends—and they will go on shewing more or less of that preference, till the Govᵗ by King Lords and Commons and the ancient Constitution of England in Ch and State are destroyd. Not being able to escape from this conviction I ought not to have used the word fear as above—for my mind is calmly made up to the worst: it is simply, in my estimation, a question of time. So no more about it, but let us be as chearful as we can and each act guided by the best lights he can procure.

Now for business. Law Shares are so unreasonably high, as Mʳ Courtenay thinks, that for this cause and others which he names, he advises me to sell.[2] As I have entire confidence in his sagacity and judgement in money matters, I mean to act upon his opinion; and should be much obliged, as you have probably more leisure than he has, if you would transact this business for me—I have told Mʳ C. that I would beg you call upon him at the Temple—and perhaps it might save him some trouble, if you would receive from him information respecting Governᵗ annuities, and transmit it to me, as I really feel anxious to save him any trouble I can. In addition to the proceeds of the Law Shares I wish to place £400 at his disposal as I told him, to be invested as he may think proper.

Your account of Germany,[3] for which I thank you is satisfactory—

[1] On 15 Nov. Lord Melbourne (see also L. 835 above) was summarily and unaccountably dismissed by the King, and Sir Robert Peel was asked to form an administration. Parliament was dissolved on 29 Dec., and Peel fought an election on the new Toryism of the *Tamworth Manifesto*. But his success was short-lived: on 8 Apr. 1835 he was forced to resign, and Lord Melbourne returned as Prime Minister.

[2] These were the shares which W. W. had purchased in the name of H. C. R.'s barrister friend Pattison. See *HCR* i. 451 and L. 745 above.

[3] H. C. R. had just returned from a stay of several months in Germany, and wrote on 18 Nov.: '. . . The political state of the country is on the whole better than I feared—The German radicals are very low and very weak: The Prussian government is, if a despotism, which may be disputed, unquestionably a wise government And the high character of the administration, together with the practical mildness of the greater part of the thirty and odd other governments, have greatly improved the public mind in Germany.' (Morley, i. 269.)

be assured of the kind regards of us all—and believe me to be my dear friend

ever faithfully yours
[*signed*] Wm Wordsworth

[*M. W. writes*]

Cannot you my dear Sir come down and pass your Christmas with us—you have never seen, nor can you guess, how beautiful our mountains are in the Winter—and how much you would chear our fire side—and Dora in her confinement, not to speak of Miss W., I will not say—Pray come and let us hear of your adventures—

aff^{ly}
Yours M. W.

[*D. W. adds*]

Dear Mr Robinson do come to us at Christmas—I cannot say how glad I should be to see you.

Alas, poor Mary and Charles Lamb!

ever your affec^{te} Friend
D Wordsworth

[*Receipt on back*]

£117·10 received for Mrs Wordsworth of Mr Robinson as the price of 5 Law Life shares at £23·10 each being the price fixed upon by me as their mutual friend

P. Courtenay

Decr 3. 1834

852. W. W. to SIR GEORGE BEAUMONT

Address: Sir G. H. W. Beaumont Bart, Coleorton Hall, Ashby de la Zouche.
  [*In M. W.'s hand*]
Stamp: Kendal Penny Post.
MS. Pierpont Morgan Library.
LY ii. 719.

27th Nov^{br} [? 1834][1] Rydal Mount, Kendal

Dear Sir George,

The Letter with which I now trouble you will not seem to require an apology, when I have mentioned the circumstance which occasions it.—

---

[1] So dated by *K* and de Selincourt; but it seems very unlikely that W. W. had failed to learn of the death of Sir George's wife (daughter of Dr. Howley) on

In the private sitting-room of my deceased Friend Lady Beaumont a small picture was hung, painted by Sir George, which he presented to me, and which at Lady Beaumont's request I gave up to her for her Lifetime. The subject is a scene in Switzerland, and on the back of it will be found a memorandum in Lady Beaumont's handwriting, certifying, if I am not mistaken, to whom it belongs. Sir George in his kindness intended to paint for me a Companion to this little Piece, as characteristic of Italy as this is of Switzerland, but the intention was not fulfilled. Having mentioned these particulars, I need scarcely add that I should be obliged by your forwarding this memorial of Sir George's friendship for me to Rydal at your convenience.

My Sister is much better in health, though still obliged to manage herself as an Invalid. She and Mrs W. unite with me in kind remembrances to yourself and Lady Beaumont, and believe me, dear Sir George, faithfully yours,

Wm Wordsworth

853. W. W. to JOHN MURRAY

MS. Cornell. Hitherto unpublished.

[*In M. W.'s hand*]

Novr 28th [1834]

Dear Sirs

If you can accommodate me with a Copy of Crabbe's Works[1] at Trade price, I will thank you to forward one, addressed to me to Whittaker's and Co—to be sent in their *first* monthly parcel to the Booksellers Kendal. I wish to make a present of it—and hope you will not object to supply me for this purpose in the way you did for myself.[2]

very sincerely y^{rs}
[*signed*] W Wordsworth

15 Feb. 1834, and the letter should probably be dated several years earlier, perhaps to 1831.

[1] *The Life and Works of the Rev. George Crabbe*, 8 vols., 1834. See L. 810 above.

[2] Murray seems to have presented W. W. with a set of the work when it appeared. The volumes were in his library when he died (see *R.M. Cat.*, no. 510).

854. D. W. to SARA HUTCHINSON JNR.[1]

Address: Miss Sara Hutchinson, Brinsop Court, near Hereford.
MS. WL. Hitherto unpublished.

[? mid–Dec. 1834]

My dear little Sara,

Though you do not know me I am a sincere Friend of yours, and though unseen I love you because I am told you are a good Girl.

I am well acquainted with your Brothers and Sisters, and they will tell you who I am; and can remember the pleasant weeks I had with them at Brinsop before you were born. No doubt you know that Elizabeth has two Godmothers in Westmorland, an old one and a young one. I am the old Godmother. Poor Miss Cookson,[2] the young God-mother, is, like me, confined to her Bed-room by sickness; and I fear it will be a long time before either of us can visit our God-daughter; but I hope *I* may hereafter become strong enough to travel again to Brinsop when I shall rejoice to see your dear mother again, and all of you.

I send you a work-bag because I hear you are a workwoman; and I think this smart Bag will be useful when you sit at work with your mother, when she has company, and when you have some nice little delicate piece of work to put into it;—and I send you this letter because I hope you can read it, and am sure can answer it, and will send me the Brinsop news in return. You must tell me all about your Cousin Mary Monkhouse,[3] and about the garden and the Doves and all other matters, and do not forget your Friends, the Miss Stevens's of Credenhill—and George Monkhouse[4]—and Christy and Sally;[5] for I know them all.

I was very unlucky in employing my nephew Charles to get the Books for Elizabeth, and am grieved she has not received the two latter volumes. I desired him to send the parcel to Hereford by some Oxford Scholar; but he has not managed well and the parcel is still in his Rooms at Christ-Church. Tell Elizabeth that I think one of her Hereford Friends is likely to go to Oxford, and perhaps she may request him to call on Mr Charles Wordsworth at Christ-Church College and ask him for a parcel from his Aunt for Miss Hutchinson of Brinsop.

---

[1] Youngest daughter of Thomas and Mary Hutchinson.
[2] Elizabeth Cookson, daughter of the late Thomas Cookson.
[3] See L. 831 above.
[4] A cousin.
[5] Probably servants at Brinsop.

I wish I had now had a trifle to send to my God-daughter, but I have nothing—so she must accept my good-will, which is accompanied with a hearty blessing.

How delighted you will all be to see Thomas and Mary![1] I must not tire you with sending a long letter, and will therefore conclude with love to your Mother, George, Elizabeth, and Mary Monkhouse.

Do not forget that Elizabeth has a God-mother at Rydal Mount, who loves you much, and will always be glad to hear that you are a good Girl. I wish you all, young and old, a merry Christmas and a happy new year, and am your affectionate Friend

D. Wordsworth

855. W. W. to ROBERT SOUTHEY

Endorsed: This letter, written to me by Mr Wordsworth, is mentioned in the Life of Cowper, Vol 1. p. 259. Robert Southey. Keswick. May 17. 1836.
MS. Berg Collection, New York Public Library. Hitherto unpublished.

[late 1834 *or* early 1835][2]
My dear S,

I have just stumbled upon the following in George Dyer's Supplement to his His: of Cambridge.[3] You may not have chanced to see it.

'We recollect a circumstance mentioned by a person of a poetical Genius of St John's, Mr Brian Bury Collins,[4] who, when at College used to visit Mr Newton,[5] of Olney, at whose house the ingenious and amiable Cowper then resided; it was, that in some of his most melancholy moments, he used to write lines affectingly

---

[1] Sara's elder brother (now at St. John's College, Cambridge) and her elder sister.

[2] Southey began work on his edition of Cowper in the spring of 1834. The first volume, which contained the *Life*, appeared the following summer. Hence the dating of this letter.

[3] For George Dyer and his *History of the University and Colleges of Cambridge*, see pt. i, L. 56.

[4] The Revd. Bryan Bury Collins (1754–1807), an evangelical clergyman, was at first refused orders in the Church because of his 'field preaching' in support of the Wesleys. He became a popular preacher in Yorkshire and London in Wesley's and Lady Huntingdon's chapels.

[5] The Revd. John Newton (1725–1807), Cowper's friend: curate of Olney, Bucks., where Cowper went to live in 1767, and joint author with him of the *Olney Hymns*, 1779.

descriptive of his own unhappy state. We record two sweet lines here, not recollecting that they are any where introduced, and conceiving [them]¹ to be more descriptive of the cirumstances of Mr Cowper's situation, than any with which we have met in his writings.

> Caesus Amor meus est, et nostro crimine: cujus,
> Ah! cujus posthinc potero latitare sub alis?

> My Love is slain, and by my crime is slain.
> Ah! now beneath whose wings shall I repose!

[unsigned]

855a. W. W. to JOHN MARSHALL [? JNR.]²

Address: John Marshall Esqre M.P., Post Office, Belfast, Ireland. [*In M. W.'s hand*]
Stamp: Kendal Penny Post.
MS. WL. Hitherto unpublished.

[1830 *or* 1832–4]

. . . Tell Mr F. Edgeworth³ that Mr J. M.'s⁴ adventures and fatigues there were much other than⁵ those we had gone through in climbing to the Summit of Carran Thouel. I wish he had been there to hear how a pair of Eagles, barked or yelped or chattered or screamed or whistled for the note was a compound of all these, while we were working our way about sunset, among the rocks below their nest. They first soared towards the setting sun and were lost in a red cloud, then they returned and spread their wings to the full width above our heads between the summit of the basalt barrier and the rack of the spray which was driving from the sea.

Previously at 7 we were able to regain the top of the cliff by a passage called the path (a strange thing for a path) of the black lake.

¹ *Word dropped out.*
² This fragment recalls W. W.'s visit to the Giant's Causeway during the Irish tour which he made in 1829 in the company of John Marshall of Hallsteads and his son James. It was addressed either to John Marshall himself, fairly soon after W. W.'s return home, and before Marshall retired from Parliament in 1830; or perhaps more likely, to his son John Marshall jnr., some time after he was elected an M.P., in 1832. In that case, the letter probably belongs to the period of the composition of *Eagles* (see L. 645 above), which refers to W. W.'s experiences at the Giant's Causeway.
³ For Francis Beaufort Edgeworth, see Ls. 412 and 466 above.
⁴ The reference is clearly to James Marshall: John Marshall had not joined in the expedition to the Giant's Causeway, as he had seen it already (see L. 470 above). ⁵ *Written to.*

The stars welcomed us to the point of safety, and we reached Bally-castle in an hour and a half. Then there was Dunluce C.[1] the evening while the evening before, while the wind was blowing a Hurricane and the Atlantic breaking his strength upon the black foundations of the Rock . . .

[*cetera desunt*]

[1] Dunluce Castle.

ADDENDUM

580a. D. W. to EDWARD ARCHER[1]

Address: Edward Archer Esqre, Red Lion Inn, Grasmere. [*delivered by hand*]
MS. Alan G. Hill. Hitherto unpublished.

Rydal Mount
Monday morning [16 Nov. 1830]

My dear Sir,

Miss Hutchinson and I were very sorry we were so unlucky as to be out of the way last Monday when you called at Rydal Mount. It was our only fine day since my Brother and Sister left us, and tempted us (as it had, no doubt, encouraged you) to take a pretty long walk.

I know you will be glad to hear that our Friends have had a prosperous journey as far as Leicestershire (where they now are), and that my Brother and his steed performed greatly to the satisfaction of all parties. Before the end of the present week we hope to hear of as happy a termination at Cambridge, where they purpose to remain at least a month.

We should be glad to hear from yourself that you have been well, and have not passed through this dreary season of stormy rain uncomfortably, or unprofitably. I mean to say that when there is a day fine enough to entice you out of doors to as great a distance as Rydal Mount, we hope you will call,—but I must warn you that we shall be absent the whole of tomorrow; therefore, whatever the weather may be, I advise you not to direct your steps hither; but at almost any other time you will have a great chance of at least finding *me* at home.—

Excuse haste, and believe me
dear Sir
yours respectfully
D. Wordsworth

---

[1] Edward Archer, a newcomer to Grasmere from Dublin (see *RMVB*, 1830), whose name occurs frequently in W. W.'s MS. Library Book at Harvard University from 1830 onwards. He seems to have had some prospects as a man of letters (see L. 747 above), but there is no record of his having published anything.

APPENDIX

First draft of W. W.'s letter to C. J. Blomfield, 3 Mar. 1829

A<small>T</small> the sight of a 2nd Letter from me you may be alarmed least I should become a troublesome Correspondent. I assure your Lordship I have no such intention, and beg at the outset you would not tax your civility with a reply to this. I am too well aware of the vast importance of your cares and duties, especially at this juncture to look or wish for it.

In noticing the Catholic question I confined myself to stating my belief that a vast majority of the nation were against further concession. The part which Ministers are about to take, and the numerous sudden conversions among the powerful aristocracy have no doubt been a cause why many have declined adding their names to petitions against further concession, some through deference to authority and mere interest, through surrender of their own judgement to those whom they have been wont to look up to. [?] The body of the State is of the same mind, being hereditarily averse to the Roman Catholic Church as Idolatrous, as persecuting, as evasive and unbindable. The reflecting part of this vast body admit that a deference to authority, and surrender or suspension of private judgement to a certain extent is indispensable for the existence of any Church—but they feel that Roman C—— stands upon the utter renuntiation of that faculty, and they are convinced in their hearts that as long as such is the root the [?shade] of the Branches must be deadly and the fruit poisonous, and [?consequently] such being the foundation the Superstructure cannot be a temple of the true God. As one of the Laity partaking [of] this Conviction, and sharing with your Lordship and so large a portion of our Fellow Countrymen the opinion that the removal of these political disabilities would not weaken that Church, as many able men believe, but would strengthen it, I cannot refrain from expressing to your Lordship the anxiety which I feel concerning the course the Bench of Bishops may take at this crisis.

Appendix

I presume, it is admitted by all that it is of the utmost importance that they should stand well in the opinion of the people and especially of that portion who are themselves of the Church which they superseded. Now should any considerable proportion of them vote in favour of the R.C. claims, it cannot be doubted that a great shock [?would be] given to that confidence which has hitherto been reposed on them by those who are averse to the measure. I do not mean merely that they would be liable to the charge of being activated by a time-serving Spirit, nor that the people would feel themselves in the condition of soldiers, who being called to fight a Battle, found themselves headed by officers, who suddenly declined leading them or because they were disputing and doubting about the justice of the war. This would be bad enough but we must go farther. The people or at least the great majority of them [   ] or would say, is Popery really the vain and fond thing we have been led to believe it to be, [?as] the Creed, and the [   ], as the Articles of our Church, its Homilies, our Preachers, and our most eminent Divines have taught. This feeling, either from the conduct of the Bishops, or from any other cause, should be more general. . . .

[rest of MS. largely illegible]

INDEX

Index

Ballasalla (I.O.M.), 624, 630, 631.
Ballycastle (Co. Antrim), 754.
Ballymena (Co. Antrim), 152.
Ballyshannon (Co. Donegal), 147, 148, 149.
Bampfylde, John Codrington, 603 and n.
Bangor, 115; Cathedral, 115.
Bankes, William John, M.P., 373 and n.
Bantry, Lord, *see* White, Richard.
Barbauld, Mrs. Anna Letitia, her poems, 260 and n.; a Dissenting poetess, 260 and n.; 699.
Barber, Samuel (of Gell's Cottage), 171, 172, 206, 256, 321, 325; death of, 507–8 and n., 512.
Barham, John Foster, M.P., 473 and n., 474, 476, 478, 570.
Barker, Edmund Henry, *Letters to*: 66, 94; *Parriana*, 66, 94; pamphlets on authorship of Junius, 94; Classical Dictionary, 94.
— Mrs. Elizabeth (W. W.'s cousin), 484 and n.
— Mary (of Boulogne), later Mrs. Slade-Smith, 180 and n., 337, 343, 362 and n.
Barlow, Mrs. John, 178 and n., 218, 223, 256.
Barnesmore Gap (Co. Donegal), 149.
Barrett, Col. Thomas Brydges, 180, 199, 203, 205, 207, 212, 249–50, 450, 539; death of, 718 and n.
Baudouins, the, 255 n.
Bayley, Revd. Henry Vincent, 228 and n., 653 and n.
Beattie, James, *The Minstrel*, 58.
Beaumont, Sir George, 7th Bart., his anecdote of Boswell, 207 and n.; annuity to W. W., 267 and n.; his Michelangelo bas-relief, 276 and n.; his painting of Switzerland, 750; 3, 92, 353, 641, 681.
— Lady (wife of 7th Bart.), death and funeral, 92–3; her grotto, 341; 240, 750.
— Sir George, 8th Bart., *Letters to*: 92, 233, 328, 553, 749; annuity to W. W., 267 and n.; 93, 337, 341, 345, 348, 357, 392, 405, 433, 509, 531, 653, 654.

— Lady (wife of 8th Bart.), *Letters to*: 357, 404, 508, 682, 688; 92, 167, 233, 328, 337, 341, 345, 348, 392, 433, 531, 553, 653, 654.
— George Howland (later 9th Bart.), 329 and n., 509.
— Thomas Wentworth (of Bretton Hall), 484 and n.
— William (W. W.'s godson), 405 and n., 406, 508, 553.
Becker, Karl Ferdinand, M.D., 7 and n.
Beckett, Sir John, Bart., M.P., 473 and n.
Beesley, Alfred, *Letter to*: 734.
Beethom, John Law, 560 and n.
Behn, Mrs. Aphra, 236 and n., 664.
Belfast, 143, 147, 151, 155.
Bell, Dr. Andrew, 334, 387, 389; his bequest, 390 and n., 391; 392 and n., 394, 402; death of, 505 and n.
— Charles (of Whitehaven), 529 and n.
— Jonathan (of the Red Lion), 208–9, 212.
— John, his text of Collins's *Ode*, 2.
Belleek (Co. Fermanagh), 148.
Bellisle (Lough Erne), 148.
— (Windermere), 283, 298 and n., 314.
Belmore, Lord, *see* Lowry-Corry, Somerset.
Benn, Joseph (land agent), 458 and n.
Bentinck, Lady Frederick, *Letter to*: 448; 105, 122, 163, 275; epitaph for her husband, 309; 330, 331, 403, 413, 451, 496, 530.
— George Augustus Cavendish, 404 and n., 450.
Bettys y Coed (Denbigh), 114.
Beverley, Robert Mackenzie, 708 and n.
Bible Society, 76.
Bijou, The, 62 and n.
Bingen, 13, 141.
Birks, Revd. Thomas Rawson, 709 and n.
Birmingham, representation, 500.
Bishop's Court (I.O.M.), 631 and n.
Black Combe, 697.
Black List, the, 457 and n., 458.
Blackstone, Sir William, *Commen-*

Index

Index

Index

Charles I, 530, 628, 689.

Charles X, 316, 319, 322, 367, 499.

Chateaubriand, François René, Vicomte de, 736 and n.

Chatsworth (Derbys.), 339–40, 353.

Chatterton, Thomas, 3; 'Rowley poems', 100, 318.

Chaucer, 234, 426, 464, 482.

Cheltenham, 387, 389, 390, 392.

Chorley (Lancs.), 114, 120.

Christian VIII (of Denmark), 516 and n.

Christian, John (Deemster of I.O.M.), 276 and n., 305, 631.

— Mrs., 631 and n.

— Margaret (daughter), 631.

— William ('Black William'), 277 and n.

Clarkson, Catherine, Letters to: 158, 244, 333, 427, 744; 36, 72, 73, 193, 243, 461, 587.

— Thomas, eye trouble, 160–1, 715, 727; 111, 193, 243, 461, 587, 630.

— Tom (C. C.'s son), 111 and n., 248, 337.

— Mrs. Mary (C. C.'s niece), 111, 243, 248.

Clonmel (Co. Tipperary), 119.

Clyde (river), falls of, 447, 453.

Cobbett, William, 610.

Coblenz, 311, 313.

Cockermouth, 498, 531, 578, 640; representation, 500, 562; Castle, 689, 694.

Colburn, Henry (bookseller), 404.

Cole, John Willoughby, 2nd Earl of Enniskillen, 147 and n.

Coleorton, 92, 233, 240, 335, 337; changes in garden, 341; 342, 346, 347, 352, 353, 392, 405, 406, 508, 509, 531, 653, 654, 684, 685, 688–9.

Coleraine (Co. Derry), 136, 150, 151, 155.

Coleridge, Derwent, Letters to: 152, 575, 576; 127, 131, 211, 243, 247, 286, 335, 344.

— Mrs. (née Pridham), 344.

— Derwent Moultrie ('Dervy'), 153.

— Hartley, proposes to publish poems, 11; his irregularities, 99, 153 and n., 206, 233, 248, 336–7, 344, 362, 669; in new lodgings, 208–9, 212, 221; dines at Rydal Mount, 209, 220; writing articles, 210, 243, 362; financial affairs, 369; Poems, 665 and n.; returns from Leeds to Grasmere, 669 and n.; 151, 163, 212, 222, 257, 318, 728 and n., 739–40.

— Henry Nelson, Letters to: 317, 727; Introductions to the Study of the Greek Classic Poets, 318 and n.; 115, 138, 153, 156, 171, 211, 336, 342, 369, 539.

— Herbert, 336, 342.

— Col. James, at Rydal Mount, 317 and n., 321.

— Samuel Taylor, Continental tour (1828) with W. W. and Dora W., 11, itinerary, 12–13, 728; visited by Willy W., 84; On the Constitution of The Church and State, 222 and n., 243, 257; The Friend, 326; at Cambridge, 613 and n.; To the Author of 'The Robbers', 664 and n.; death of, 727–8; his Will, 739 and n.; 131, 156, 179, 242, 248, 306, 310, 336, 363, 364–5, 369, 455, 587, 590, 696.

— Mrs., Letters to: 208, 342, 368; 10, 69, 115, 131, 152–3, 243, 247, 248, 286, 335–6, 728.

— Sara, Letters to: 186, 362, 713; at Rydal Mount, 69, 86, 153; wedding, 111, 127 and n., 130; birth of Herbert, 336 and n.; 10, 89, 114, 115, 138, 171, 211, 222, 243, 247, 248, 251, 286, 342, 369, 587, 727, 728.

— William Hart, Bishop of Barbados, 363 and n.

Collins, Revd. Bryan Bury, 752 and n.

— William, Ode on the Popular Superstitions of the Highlands of Scotland, 2, 157, 158; Ode to Evening, 236; 3.

Cologne, 13, 313.

Columbian Bonds, 192, 609.

Coniston, 127, 648; Water, 295.

Constantinople, 187.

Conway Bridge, 114; river falls, 114.

Index

Davies, Sneyd, *To the Hon. and Rev. F.C.*, 292 and n.

Davy, Sir Humphry, 68 and n.; death of, 310 and n.; 415, 546, 548, 549.

Dawes, Revd. John, 136, 138, 671–2, 690, 693–4, 707.

Dawson, Captain (of Moresby), 349.

— Mr. (of Allan Bank), 626, 731.

Day, John, 132 and n., 300, 301.

— Mrs., 132 and n., 300.

Dee (river), aqueduct over, 114.

Denbigh, 12, 547.

Denman, Sir Thomas, M.P., 380 and n.

De Quincey, Thomas, article on Rhetoric, 17; buys Nab estate, 63; writes tales, 206; the Opium Eater, 256; articles on S. T. C. in *Tait's Magazine*, 740 and n.; 85, 89.

— — Mrs., 206.

Derby, Charlotte, 7th Countess of, 278 and n.

Derby, 335, 339, 341.

Derwent, river (Cumb.), 6, 525, 548, 640, 689, 694.

— — (Derbys.), 339.

Derwentwater, Lord, sale of Keswick estates, 494, 502 and n., 503, 527 and n.

de Vere, Sir Aubrey, 2nd Bart., 138 and n.

— — Aubrey (son), 581 and n.; his madrigal, 581, 585, 590.

— — Ellen (daughter), 440 and n.

Dewhurst, Henry William, *The Natural History of the Order Cetacea*, 608 and n.; 621.

Dick, Mrs. (*née* Horrocks), 725 n., 726.

Dickinson, William (surgeon), 601 and n.

Digby, Kenelm Henry, *Orlandus*, 47 and n., 48; *The Broad Stone of Honour*, 354 and n.

Dinant, 360.

Dissenters, 38, 87, 260, 308, 475, 479, 699, 716.

Dixon, Miss, 271 and n.

— James (W. W.'s gardener), 128, 159, 175, 177, 178–9, 224, 346, 350, 569, 602.

Dobson, Lancelot (of Patterdale), 163 and n.

Dockray, Benjamin, *Letter to*: 605; *Egeria*, 605 and n.

Doddridge, Philip, epigram on family arms, 180 and n.

Dollond, George (optician), 543 and n.

Donaghadee (Co. Down), 155.

Donegal, 147, 149.

Donne, John, *Sermons*, 257, 739; 'Death, be not proud' recommended, 604 and n.

Doonas, falls of (Co. Clare), 141.

Douglas, George, 137 and n., 250, 285, 286.

— Harriet, *Letter to*: 283; 250, 557 and n.

— Margaret, 250 and n., 285, 286.

— William, 137 and n., 250, 285.

— Mrs., 250 and n., 286.

Douglas (I.O.M.), 344, 624, 632; cholera at, 645.

Dove Cottage, 415 and n.

Dowling, Elizabeth, 385 and n., 679.

— Jane, 679.

— Mary, funeral, 212, 219.

— Mrs., 679.

Drummond, Sir Adam (of Megginch), 109 and n.

— Revd. Robert, *Letter to*: 108; his preferment, 87 and n.; 92, 93, 94.

— William (of Hawthornden), 549 and n., 643.

Dryden, John, 234, 598; *Mac Flecknoe* referred to, 598.

Dublin, Trinity College, 117, 121; St. Patrick's Cathedral, 117, 118; Dunsink Observatory, 117, 121; 96, 101, 104, 105, 109, 110, 115, 116, 117, 120, 122, 125, 126, 155, 456.

Duddon (river), 6, 82, 84, 214, 219, 221.

Dugdale, Sir William, visitation of the North (1666), 485 and n.

Dunally Castle, 441.

Dunbar, William, 723.

Dunluce Castle (Co. Antrim), 151, 754.

Dunran (Co. Wicklow), 119, 125.

Dusseldorf, 296, 313.

Index

Dyce, Alexander, *Letters to*: 2, 156, 234, 259, 291, 292, 373, 413, 544, 579, 598, 603, 663; Bell's text of Collins's *Ode on the Popular Superstitions of the Highlands of Scotland*, 2; edition of George Peele, 156 and n.; edition of Collins, 157 and n.; *Specimens of British Poetesses*, 157 and n., 233, 234, 236–9, 259–60, 664; edition of Webster, 233 and n., 234, 250; *Dramatic Works and Poems of James Shirley*, 579 and n., 598; *Specimens of English Sonnets*, dedication to W. W., 603 and n., 663–4; 646.

Dyer, George, *History of the University and Colleges of Cambridge*, 752 and n.
— John, 3 and n.; *Grongar Hill*, 238; his paintings, 3.

Ebrington, Lord, M.P., motion on reform, 527 and n.
Eden, Robert Henley, 2nd Baron Henley, 653 and n.
Eden (river), 635, 645, 722.
Edgeworth, Emmeline (Mrs. King), 142 and n.
— Mrs. Frances (*née* Beaufort), 110 and n., 142.
— Francis Beaufort, *Letter to*: 186; his poems, 30 and n.; 97, 142, 183, 185, 287, 440, 753.
— Honora (later Lady Beaumont), 142 and n.
— Lovell, 110, 142 and n., 143, 440.
— Maria (novelist), 110 and n., 142 and n., 143.
Edgeworthstown (Co. Longford), 136, 142, 143.
Edinburgh, 329, 331, 335, 421, 428, 431, 447, 453, 456, 580, 632, 723.
Edinburgh Review, 200, 275.
Edmunds, the Misses (of Ambleside), 172 and n.
Egerton, Francis, 1st Earl of Ellesmere, 118 and n., 122, 182.
— Lady Francis, 118 and n.
Ellenborough, Lord, *see* Law, Edward.
Ellice, Edward, M.P., 371 and n.
Elliot, Jane, Lament for the defeat of the Scots at Floddenfield, 664 and n.

— Mr. (former tenant of Ivy Cottage), 178.
— Mrs., 128 and n., 178, 246.
Elliott, Ebenezer, *Corn-Law Rhymes*, 667 and n.
— Revd. Henry Venn, 661 and n., 700.
Ellis, Thomas (Master in Chancery), 117 and n., 120, 122, 138.
Elphin (Co. Roscommon), 143.
England, Church of, 37–9, 64–5, 515; reform of, 561, 569; 711, 721.
Englishman's Magazine, 410 and n., 451 and n.
Enniscorthy (Co. Wexford), 119; prices at, 120.
Enniskillen, Lord, *see* Cole, John Willoughby.
Enniskillen (Co. Fermanagh), 143, 148, 155.

Fair Head (Co. Antrim), 145, 147, 151, 440.
Fairfax, Charles Gregory Piggott, 423 and n.
— Mrs., 423 and n.
Fairfield, 548.
Farquhar, Sir Robert Townsend, 1st Bart., death of, 219 and n.
— Lady, 248, 249, 566; remarriage, 658, 680, 726 and n.
Fascally, 119, 121, 126, 167.
Favell, Redman (of Normanton), 485.
Fell, William (surgeon), *Letter to*: 731; 160–1, 208, 212, 266, 267, 508.
Fenwick, Isabella, 495 and n.
Ferguson, Anne, 130 and n., 132.
— Edward, 132 and n., 565, 701.
— Elizabeth (niece of Edward), 132 and n., 301.
— Georgina (niece of Edward), 132 and n., 300.
— Martha, 132 and n.
— General Sir Ronald Craufurd, M.P., 380 and n.
— Sarah (niece of Edward), 132 and n., 301.
Ferns (Co. Wexford), 123.
Field, Barron, *Letters to*: 5, 31; goes to Gibraltar, 31.

Index

Index

Index

Index

Index

Southey, Robert (*cont*.):
414, 424, 439, 456, 457, 482, 489, 492, 495, 514, 516, 528, 538, 543, 544, 546, 581, 613, 621, 633, 640, 646, 657, 662, 663, 665, 672, 684, 698, 747.
— Mrs., 211, 247, 286; her mental breakdown, 747 and n.
Spain, religion in, 40; 4.
Spectator, The, 31, 414.
Spedding, Edward, death of, 563 and n.
— John, *Letters to*: 562, 586, 593; 563 n., 712 and n.
— Thomas Story, marriage, 594 and n.
Spence, Robert, *Letter to*: 179.
Spenser, Edmund, 43 n., 58, 234; *Faerie Queene* quoted, 640 and n.
Spring Rice, Thomas, M.P. (later 1st Baron Monteagle), 138 and n.
— — Mary, *Letter to*: 585; 584 and n., 590.
Staffa, 79, 82, 170, 447, 470, 630, 635, 639, 641, 645, 665, 722, 723.
Stamford School, 576.
Standard, The, 514 and n., 522.
Stanger, Mrs. Joshua (*née* Calvert), 512.
Staniforth, Samuel, 112.
— Mrs., 112, 730.
Stanley, Revd. Edward, 314 and n.; death of, 685 and n.
— Edward (of Ponsonby), 539.
— Miss (of Ayrshire), 323 and n.
Stephen, James (later Sir James), 379 and n.
Stirling, 428, 447.
Stockton-on-Tees, 522.
Stoddart, Sir John, *Letter to*: 415.
Storrs Hall, 111, 169, 271, 321, 507.
Stothard, Thomas, R.A., 675 and n.
Strabane (Co. Tyrone), 147, 149.
Stuart-Wortley-Mackenzie, James Archibald, 1st Baron Wharncliffe, 522 and n.
Sudbury Pocket Book, 607 and n.
Suir (river), 119, 123, 138, 155, 167.
Sumner, Charles Richard, Bishop of Winchester, 76 and n.
— John Bird, Bishop of Chester,

65 and n.; his Charge at White-haven, 112 and n.; 648, 672, 693, 694.
Swarkeston Bridge (Derbys.), 341.
Swift, Jonathan, *Gulliver's Travels* referred to, 44; 260.
Switzerland, 242, 332, 683.
Sydenham, Thomas, 511 and n.
Sykes, Godfrey (solicitor of the Stamp Office), death of, 16.

Tabley, Lord de, *see* Leicester, Sir George.
Tait's Magazine, 740 and n.
Talfourd, Thomas Noon, 190.
Tatham, Revd. Arthur, 575 and n.
— Edward (attorney), 479 and n., 591.
Taylor, George, 495 and n.
— Henry (later Sir Henry), *Letters to*: 375, 378, 443, 495, 717; *Philip van Artevelde*, 717 and n., 733, 746; review of W. W., 745 and n.; at Rydal Mount, 421 and n.
Temple, Capt. John, 133 and n., 134.
— Mrs. (*née* Jane Dorothea Marshall), 133 and n., 134, 176, 300.
Tennyson, Alfred, 354 and n.
— Charles, 354 and n.
Thirlwall, Connop (later Bishop of St. David's), 720 and n.; *A Letter to the Rev. Thomas Turton*, 720 and n.
Thomas, William, 77 and n., 78.
Thompson, Miss (of Lowther), 105 and n.
Thomson, James, *The Seasons*, 3; *The Castle of Indolence*, 3; *Liberty*, 3; his plays, 3 and n.; 58, 157.
Thornton, John (Commissioner of Stamps), 646 and n., 659, 661, 678.
— Mrs., 659.
— Miss, 659.
Thorp, Revd. Thomas, 368 and n.
Thucydides, 747.
Tickell, Thomas, 260 and n., 414.
Tideswell (Derbys.), 338, 339.
Tillbrooke, Revd. Samuel, 251, 256, 417, 427, 429 and n., 591.
— Mrs., 429 and n.
Tiraboschi, Girolamo, *Storia della Letteratura Italiana*, 495 and n.

780

Index

294, 305, 336, 355, 357, 392, 411, 433, 461, 626, 628, 695, 713.

— Christopher (C. W.'s son), *Letters to*: 107, 112, 168, 201, 213, 228, 278, 367, 382, 625, 711; awarded Craven Scholarship, 35, 53; distinctions at Cambridge, 201 and n., 213, 215, 228, 243, 261–2; Fellow of Trinity, 336; College lecturer, 683; in Isle of Man, 105, 107; in Italy, 462; in Greece, 548, 551 and n., 683; at Rydal Mount, 124, 676–7, 680; his pamphlet on the admission of Dissenters to Cambridge, 711; 169, 170, 253, 263, 272, 374, 392, 675, 721.

— Dorothy (W. W.'s sister), *Letters to*: 104, 145, 163, 337, 373.

Family and friends: on her nephews' successes, 35, 228; on Henry and Sara Coleridge, 128, 131; on the garden at Rydal Mount, 129; on the garden at Fox Ghyll, 129; on the alterations at Rydal Mount, 128; on Miss Jewsbury's gift of goldfish, 129–30, 196; on Miss Jewsbury's verses, 130; on Mrs. Rawson and the Fergusons, 132; on Miss Trevenen, 152–3, 335–6; on Mrs. S. T. C., 152–3; on Hartley Coleridge, 153, 208–12, 248; on H. C. R., 161–2; on John W., 171, 193, 263; on James Dixon, 175, 178–9; on Ellen Marshall's sufferings, 177; on W. W.'s health, 191, 195; on Joanna Hutchinson, 191–2; on Dora W., 192; on M. W., 196, 242, 246; on Anne their servant, 219; on W. W., 229, 242, 246; on C. W.'s career, 231; on S. T. C., 243; on Southey, 243; invites C. W. to Rydal Mount, 251–2, 270–1; on John W.'s engagement, 298; on Miss Curwen, 298–9; on John Marshall's resignation from Parliament, 299–300; description of John W.'s wedding, 333–4; gives advice to Ebba H. on penmanship and

grammar, 302; on Willy W.'s prospects, 348; on Julia Marshall's verses, 349; on Rotha Q., 386; on W. W.'s attitude to Reform, 392; on Robert Jones, 429; on Jane Marshall, 700; invites Ebba H. to Rydal Mount, 737; writes to her goddaughter Sara H., 751–2.

Health: illness at Whitwick, 60 ff., 69, 71–3, 74–7, 102, 245–6, 305, 394, 509, 531, 550; ill at Halifax, 131; invalid at Rydal Mount, 158–9, 162, 164, 168, 171–2, 176, 192, 194, 196, 202, 203, 214, 218, 234, 241, 245–6, 275, 279, 290, 306; return of complaint, 483, 504; slow recovery, 505, 509, 513, 516; relapse, 520 ff., 525, 531, 535, 543, 547, 550, 551; recovering, 557, 561, 564, 568; relapse, 575, 583–4, 586, 588, 591, 594 and n.; recovering, 600 and n., 609, 611, 613, 620–1, 624–5, 633, 635, 638, 642, 644, 651, 662, 674, 687, 697, 701, 712, 723, 725, 727, 747; on the terrace in her wheelchair, 611, 624–5, 635, 638, 702, 744.

Interests: on *The Recluse*, 169, 191; on the manufacturing poor, 172; on Milman's *History of the Jews*, 217; on a new edition of W. W.'s poems, 229, 243; on social distress, 242; on the new terraces at Rydal Mount, 258 and n.; on Rogers's *Italy*, 330; on political disturbances, 350; checks Hine's *Selections*, 389; on Dr. Bell's bequest, 391; on Wilkin's portrait of W. W., 428; on the cholera, 460, 461; on the Reform Bill, 460; suggests itinerary in Isle of Man, 624 and n.

Visits and journeys: at Whitwick, 8, 11, 12, 60, 71, 80; leaves Whitwick, 76; at Cambridge, 34 and n., 54, 72; proposed tour of North Wales with W. W., 12, 26, 56, 60, cancelled, 77, 102, 106; at Halifax, 93, 100, 112, 128, 201, 248; at Saltmarsh, 113 and n.; at Staveley, 128; plans for the

Index